ARMY HISTORICAL SERIES

MOSCOW TO STALINGRAD:
DECISION IN THE EAST

by

Earl F. Ziemke
and
Magna E. Bauer

MILITARY HERITAGE PRESS
New York

This edition published by Military Heritage Press,
a division of Marboro Books Corporation.
1988 Military Heritage Press

ISBN 0-88029-294-6

Printed in the United States of America
M 9 8 7 6 5 4 3 2

ARMY HISTORICAL SERIES

David F. Trask, General Editor

Advisory Committee

(As of 1 July 1985)

U.S. Army Center of Military History

Brig. Gen. William A. Stofft, Chief of Military History

iii

Foreword

Moscow to Stalingrad: Decision in the East is the second to be completed in a projected three-volume history of the German-Soviet conflict in World War II. The first, *Stalingrad to Berlin: The German Defeat in the East,* covered the Soviet Army's liberation of its own territory and its drive across central and southeastern Europe. In the present volume, the German and Soviet forces initially confront each other on the approaches to Moscow, Leningrad, and Rostov in the late-1941 battles that produced the first major German setbacks of the war and gave the Soviet troops their first tastes of success. Later, the pendulum swings to the Germans' side, and their armies race across the Ukraine and into the Caucasus during the summer of 1942. In the course of a year, the Soviet Command goes from offensive to defensive and, finally, at Stalingrad, decisively to the offensive—meanwhile, frequently in desperate circumstances, building the strength and proficiency that will enable it to mount the relentless thrusts of the succeeding years.

In tracing the shifting Soviet and German fortunes, the author has had full access to the German military records, most of which fell into American and British hands. He has also made extensive use of the Soviet war histories, memoirs, and periodical literature. The result is both a panorama of battles, among them some of the greatest in the history of warfare, and an inquiry into the forces in war that shape and test the military power of nations.

WILLIAM A. STOFFT
Brigadier General, USA
Chief of Military History

Washington D.C.
1 September 1985

v

The Authors

Earl F. Ziemke is a graduate of the University of Wisconsin, where he received M.A. and Ph.D. degrees in history. In World War II he served with the U.S. Marine Corps in the Pacific Theater. In 1951, he joined the staff of the Bureau of Applied Social Research, Columbia University. From 1955 to 1967 he was a historian and supervisory historian with the Office of the Chief of Military History (now the Center of Military History), and since 1967 he has been a research professor of history at the University of Georgia.

Dr. Ziemke is the author of *The German Northern Theater of Operations, 1940–1945; Stalingrad to Berlin: The German Defeat in the East;* and *The U.S. Army in the Occupation of Germany, 1944–1946.* He is a contributor to *Command Decisions; A Concise History of World War II; Soviet Partisans in World War II; New Dimensions in Military History; U.S. Occupation in Europe After World War II; Strategic Military Deception;* and *Americans as Proconsuls: United States Military Government in Germany and Japan.*

Magna E. Bauer was a member of the staff of the U.S. Army Center of Military History from 1947 until her retirement in 1970. Educated in Italy, Germany, and the United States, Mrs. Bauer was proficient in German, Italian, French, and English. During her tenure with the center, she did research studies and translations for several volumes in the center's World War II series. These included: Forrest C. Pogue, *The Supreme Command;* Hugh M. Cole, *The Ardennes: Battle of the Bulge;* Albert N. Garland and Howard McGaw Smyth, *Sicily and the Surrender of Italy;* and Charles B. MacDonald, *The Last Offensive.* Mrs. Bauer also taught Italian and German at the U.S. Department of Agriculture Graduate School from 1943 to 1980. Mrs. Bauer died in December 1981.

Preface

During 1942, the Axis advance reached its high tide on all fronts and began to ebb. Nowhere was this more true than on the Eastern Front in the Soviet Union. After receiving a disastrous setback on the approaches to Moscow in the winter of 1941–1942, the German armies recovered sufficiently to embark on a sweeping summer offensive that carried them to the Volga River at Stalingrad and deep into the Caucasus Mountains. The Soviet armies suffered severe defeats in the spring and summer of 1942 but recovered to stop the German advances in October and encircle and begin the destruction of the German Sixth Army at Stalingrad in November and December. This volume describes the course of events from the Soviet December 1941 counteroffensive at Moscow to the Stalingrad offensive in late 1942 with particular attention to the interval from January through October 1942, which has been regarded as a hiatus between the two major battles but which in actuality constituted the period in which the German fortunes slid into irreversible decline and the Soviet forces acquired the means and capabilities that eventually brought them victory. These were the months of decision in the East.

In the nearly two decades since *Stalingrad to Berlin: The German Defeat in the East* was published, much new information has become available. When *Stalingrad to Berlin* was written, the cloak of secrecy had barely been raised on the Soviet side of the war. Since then, Soviet war histories, memoirs, and articles have come in a flood; consequently, the author has treated the Soviet aspect of the war somewhat differently in *Moscow to Stalingrad* than in *Stalingrad to Berlin*. Where contradictions or discrepancies occur, the present volume can be assumed to be the more nearly correct. It would, in fact, have been easily possible to have written *Moscow to Stalingrad* predominantly from Soviet sources. The author elected not to do so for two reasons: the active impetus in the operations was German during most of the period and the German military records constitute a reasonably complete and reliable body of direct evidence while political doctrine and policy color and limit the Soviet depiction of the war. The Soviet war history has, moreover, undergone two general revisions, and there could still be others to come.

The reader may find a few explanatory remarks helpful. The order in which the volumes are appearing has necessitated a fairly comprehensive introduction. Military ranks above that of colonel are given in the Russian and the German forms because translation or conversion into U.S. equivalents would have engendered inconsistencies. Appendix A provides a table of equivalent ranks—and demonstrates the problem. To keep them readily distinguishable from one another, German unit names are set in roman and Soviet in italic type. Diacritical marks to indicate hard and soft signs have been omitted in the transliterations from the Russian, which otherwise follow the U.S. Board on Geographic Names system. The maps are based on the 1:1,000,000 German Army High Command *Lage Ost* (Situation East) maps corrected, with respect to Soviet deployments, from the Soviet official histories.

The author is indebted to Professor Gerhard L. Weinberg, Dr. William J. Spahr, and Professor Bruce W. Menning, who took time from other pursuits to read and comment on the manuscript and who contributed insights from their extensive knowledge of German and Russian history. He is likewise grateful to his former colleagues at the Center of Military History, Dr. Maurice Matloff, Mr. George W. Garand, Mr. Charles V. P. von Luttichau, and Col. William F. Strobridge, for their advice on the manuscript and for their help and counsel over the years.

Members of the Editorial and Graphic Arts Branches in the Center of Military History carried the main burden of converting the manuscript into a book. Mrs. Sara J. Heynen was the substantive editor. Mr. Lenwood Y. Brown was the copy editor, and Mrs. Joycelyn M. Canery assisted in the copyediting. Mr. Roger D. Clinton and Mr. Arthur S. Hardyman prepared the maps and photographs, and Sp 6c. Marshall Williams designed and executed the cover for the paperback edition. The author hopes that his work may prove worthy of their efforts.

Possible errors and omissions can only be attributed to the author's failure to profit from the assistance available to him.

Athens, Georgia   EARL F. ZIEMKE
1 September 1985

Contents

Maps

Maps

Illustrations

MOSCOW TO STALINGRAD:
DECISION IN THE EAST

CHAPTER I

"The World Will Hold Its Breath"

At first light on 22 June 1941 German troops stormed into the Soviet Union. Operation BARBAROSSA had begun. The invasion achieved a total strategic surprise. The German offensive was well across the border before Moscow issued the first order to counterattack.[1] By then, several hours after sunrise, the Germans had taken every bridge on all the border rivers from the Baltic to the eastern tip of the Carpathians. Soviet troops were being captured in their barracks. At daylight the *Luftwaffe* had struck the airfields in western Russia destroying the Soviet planes on the ground, and German bombers had attacked the cities on a line from Murmansk to Odessa and Sevastopol. By afternoon, the Germans had broken Soviet frontier defenses, and panzer columns were gathering speed as they knifed into stunned and disorganized Soviet forces.

Adolf Hitler had said, "The world will hold its breath and fall silent when BARBAROSSA is mounted."[2] The world did not fall completely silent. British Prime Minister Winston S. Churchill proposed a military alliance to the So-

viet Union on the day of the invasion, and President Franklin D. Roosevelt offered U.S. lend-lease aid two days later. But the world did hold its breath. In Washington, the War Department War Plans Division expected a Soviet defeat in one to three months.[3] Sir Stafford Cripps, the British ambassador in Moscow, predicted a German victory in three to four weeks, while the British Joint Intelligence Committee gave the Russians "a few months at the outside."[4] Indeed, BARBAROSSA appeared to be, as Hitler claimed, the greatest military operation of all time, capable of defeating the Soviet Union in a single summer's campaign.

The Deployments

German and Allied Forces

Hitler was the *Fuehrer* ("leader") and chancellor of Germany and supreme commander of the German armed forces. The latter role had emerged in 1938 when Hitler had combined what had been the president's constitutional powers (under the Weimar Constitution) as commander in chief of the armed forces with the minister of war's direct command responsibility. The Armed Forces High Command

---

[1] Institut Marksizma-Leninizma, *Istoriya Velikoy Otechestvennoy Voyny Sovetskogo Soyuza, 1941–1945* (Moscow: Voyennoye Izdatelstvo, 1961), vol. II, pp. 11, 17 (hereafter cited as *IVOVSS* in footnotes and *History of the Great Patriotic War* in text).

[2] Max Domarus, ed., *Hitler, Reden und Proklamationen, 1932–1945* (Munich: Sueddeutscher Verlag, 1965), vol. II, p. 1664.

[3] Robert E. Sherwood, *Roosevelt and Hopkins* (New York: Harper, 1950), p. 303.

[4] J. M. A. Gwyer, *Grand Strategy* (London: Her Majesty's Stationery Office, 1964), vol. III, pt. I, p. 90.

(*Oberkommando der Wehrmacht,* OKW),
under the Chief, OKW, Generalfeldmarschall Wilhelm Keitel, had assumed
the minister of war's former administrative roles, and the OKW Operations Staff did Hitler's military
operational planning. General der Artillerie Alfred Jodl, the chief of the
OKW Operations Staff, was Hitler's
personal chief of staff. The service
commands—the Army High Com-
mand (*Oberkommando des Heeres,* OKH),
the Air Force High Command (*Oberkommando der Luftwaffe,* OKL), and the
Navy High Command (*Oberkommando der Kriegsmarine,* OKM)—executed operations on the basis of strategic directives from Hitler issued
through the OKW Operations Staff.
The service commanders in chief—
Generalfeldmarschall Walter von
Brauchitsch (army), Reichsmarschall
Hermann Goering (air force), and
Grossadmiral Erich Raeder (navy) reported directly to Hitler and also received verbal instructions from him.

The campaign in the Soviet Union
brought a split in the German command structure. Hitler limited the
OKH's sphere of responsibility to the
Eastern Front and gave the OKW control in the Western Theater, the Balkans, North Africa, and Scandinavia
(including Finland). The OKH thereby
lost control of army elements in the
other theaters but did not achieve full
independence in the East since Hitler
continued to issue his strategic directives through the OKW Operations
Staff.

When BARBAROSSA began, the military and political decisionmakers in
Germany moved from Berlin to the
forests of East Prussia. Berlin, with its
centers of military communications,

could have served as well, but Hitler
chose to build an elaborate special
headquarters, the *Wolfsschanze* ("Wolf's
Lair"), in the Goerlitz Forest east of
Rastenburg. A field headquarters apparently had two advantages that to
Hitler made it worth the inconvenience
and expense: it placed him symbolically at the head of the troops and
physically at the top and the center of
the command hierarchy.

Situated astride the Rastenburg-An-
gerburg railroad, the *Wolfsschanze* consisted of painstakingly camouflaged,
mostly concrete buildings and bunkers
sealed off from the outside by rings of
steel fences, palisades, and earthworks.
Hitler lived and worked with his intimate military and political advisers in
one compound; another, a short distance away, housed a detachment of the
OKW Operations Staff and a communications center. About a dozen
miles away and also on the railroad,
which was closed to general traffic, the
OKH maintained a compound in the
Mauerwald just outside Angerburg.
Elaborate as they were, the *Wolfsschanze*
and the Mauerwald compound could
only accommodate fractions of the
OKW and OKH staffs; the rest stayed
in and around Berlin and kept in contact with the *Wolfsschanze* by air and
courier train.[5]

The German allies were Italy,
Rumania, Hungary, and Slovakia. Bulgaria was an ally but did not declare
war on the Soviet Union. Finland did
declare war on the Soviet Union on 26

---

[5]Percy Ernst Schramm, gen. ed., *Kriegstagebuch des
Oberkommandos der Wehrmacht* (Frankfurt: Bernard &
Graefe, 1961–1965), vol. IV, pp. 1752–53 (hereafter
cited as *OKW, KTB*). See also R. Raiber, "FHQ 'Wolfs-
schanze,'" *After the Battle,* no. 19 (London: Battle of
Britain Prints, Ltd., 1977).

THE GERMAN FIELD ARTILLERY MOVES OUT

June but as a "cobelligerent," not as an ally. Maintaining that it was useless to base operations on forces that could not be "counted on with certainty," Hitler had kept the allied commands, except those of Rumania and Finland, out of the planning. He had allowed the Rumanians and Finns to be brought in during the final stages because German forces would have to deploy on those countries' territory—and, in the case of the Finns, because their army's performance against the Soviet Union in the Winter War of 1939–1940 had favorably impressed him.[6]

The senior German field commands

were to be three army group headquarters, each responsible for operations in one of the main sectors: Army Group North, led by Generalfeldmarschall Wilhelm von Leeb, was to attack out of East Prussia, through the Baltic States toward Leningrad; Army Group Center, under Generalfeldmarschall Fedor von Bock, assembled on the frontier east of Warsaw for a thrust via Minsk and Smolensk toward Moscow; and Army Group South, Generalfeldmarschall Gerd von Rundstedt commanding, was responsible for the sector between the Pripyat Marshes and the Black Sea and was to drive toward Kiev and the line of the Dnepr River. Seven armies and four panzer groups were assigned to the army groups: Sixteenth, Eighteenth, and Fourth Panzer to North; Fourth, Ninth, Second Panzer,

---

[6]Franz Halder, *Kriegstagebuch* (Stuttgart: W. Kohlhammer, 1964), vol. II, p. 319 (hereafter cited as *Halder Diary*).

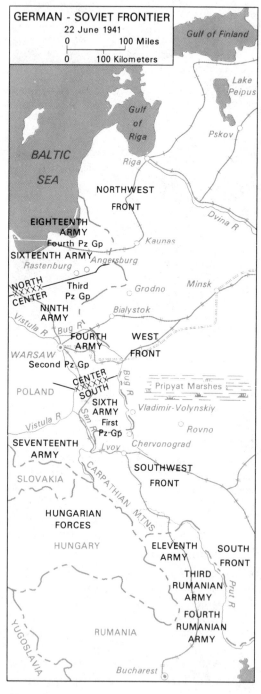

MAP 1

and Third Panzer to Center; and Sixth, Eleventh, Seventeenth, and First Panzer to South. The panzer groups were in fact full-fledged armored armies, but owing to conservatism among some of the senior generals, they were not yet designated as such. *(Map 1.)*

The OKL attached an air force *(Luftflotte)* to each of the army groups: First Air Force to Army Group North, Second to Army Group Center, and Fourth to Army Group South. The air forces were operationally independent, and their relationship with the army groups was confined to cooperation and coordination. During the first five months of 1941, the *Luftwaffe* had been almost totally committed against Great Britain and would have to continue its attacks on a reduced scale during BAR-BAROSSA. Because a sudden drop in the number of flights over Britain could have given BARBAROSSA away, the *Luftwaffe* also could not shift its planes east until the last minute. Moreover, the Balkans campaign (April 1941) and the invasion of Crete (May 1941) had required unanticipated expenditures of effort. Because of these complications, particularly the strain that fighting on two widely separated fronts would impose on his resources and organization, Goering had talked against attacking the Soviet Union.[7]

The navy also was heavily engaged against Great Britain, and Raeder, like Goering, would have preferred not to become engaged elsewhere. The navy's missions were to take control of the Baltic Sea and to conduct limited operations in the Arctic Ocean and the

[7]British Air Ministry Pamphlet 248, *The Rise and Fall of the German Air Force* (London: His Majesty's Stationery Office, 1948), pp. 162–66.

Black Sea. But Raeder did not believe the navy could carry out any of them until after German air and ground action had eliminated most of the Soviet ships and bases.[8]

The Finnish Army operated independently under its own Commander in Chief, Marshal Carl Mannerheim. The main direction of its attack was to be to the southeast on both sides of Lake Ladoga to increase the pressure on the Soviet forces defending Leningrad and thereby facilitate Army Group North's advance. An Army of Norway expeditionary force of two German and one Finnish corps, under OKW control, was to advance out of northern Finland toward Murmansk and the Murmansk (Kirov) Railroad. The primary assignment of the Army of Norway and its air support command, Fifth Air Force, was the defense of Norway. The Rumanian Third and Fourth Armies, attached to Army Group South, had the very limited initial mission of assisting in the conquest of Bessarabia.

The OKH assigned 3,050,000 men and 148 divisions, including 19 panzer and 15 motorized divisions, or 75 percent of the existing German Army field strength to BARBAROSSA.[9] The Army of Norway deployed another 4 German divisions, 67,000 troops, in northern Finland. The Finnish Army added 500,000 men in 14 divisions and 3 brigades. Rumania's contribution of about 150,000 men consisted of 14 divi-sions and 3 brigades, all under-strength. The BARBAROSSA force initially had 3,350 tanks, 7,184 artillery pieces, 600,000 motor vehicles, and 625,000 horses. The number of German ground troops actually committed up to the first week of July apparently was 2.5 million. The OKL provided 2,770 aircraft, 65 percent of its total first-line strength of 4,300.[10]

Soviet Forces

Josef Stalin, the general secretary of the Soviet Communist Party, had become head of the Soviet government on 6 May 1941 when he made himself chairman of the Council of People's Commissars. Although he undoubtedly could have done so, he had not, as of 22 June 1941, assumed a clear statutory relationship to the armed forces, which were subordinated to several bodies. Nominally the highest of these was the Defense Committee of the Council of People's Commissars. Marshal Sovetskogo Soyuza Kliment Voroshilov was the chairman, and Stalin, Vyacheslav M. Molotov (the deputy chairman of the Council of People's Commissars) and the people's commissars of defense and the navy were members. The Defense Committee supervised and coordinated all the state agencies engaged in building up the armed forces. The People's Commissariat of Defense, under Marshal Sovetskogo Soyuza Semen Timoshenko, and the People's Commissariat of the Navy, under Admiral N. G. Kuznetsov, were the top military agen-

---

[8]*Die Seekriegsleitung und die Vorgeschichte des Feldzuges gegen Russland,* H22/439 file.

[9]Panzer divisions had about 17,000 men and 125 tanks; motorized divisions, 14,000 men and 50 tanks. The infantry in both was truck mounted. Infantry divisions had 15,000 men and used horse-drawn equipment in part.

[10]Department of the Army, Pamphlet 20–261a, *The German Campaign in Russia—Planning and Operations, 1940–1942* (Washington, D.C.: GPO, 1955), pp. 38–41; *OKW, KTB,* vol. I, p. 1213; British Air Ministry Pamphlet 248, p. 165.

cies. Within the Defense Commissariat, the Main Military Council was the decision-making body. Timoshenko was the chairman, and Stalin, Molotov, and eight deputy defense commissars (of which the Chief of the General Staff, General Armii Georgi Zhukov, was one) were members. Zhukov was the council's secretary, and the General Staff drafted plans for it and acted as its channel to the lower commands. Additionally, the people's commissar of defense exercised command of the army through the General Staff and his deputy commissars. The navy had a separate command structure and its own main council.[11] The war plans anticipated that in the event of a general war, an all-powerful war cabinet similar to one (the Defense Council, later Council of Labor and Defense) V. I. Lenin had headed from 1918 to 1920 and a general headquarters modeled after the imperial *Stavka* ("staff") of World War I would be created, but neither of these existed on 22 June 1941.[12]

The highest-level army field commands prior to the outbreak of the war were the military districts. In peacetime, they conducted training, supervised garrisons and cadres, and provided the machinery for mobilization. Those districts on the frontiers

were set up to be converted into *front* (that is, army group) headquarters in the event of war. As of early 1941, there were sixteen military districts and one *front*, the *Far Eastern*.[13] The military districts on the western frontier were the *Leningrad, Baltic Special, Western Special, Kiev Special,* and *Odessa* districts. On 22 June 1941, the five became *fronts. Leningrad,* with three armies and General Leytenant M. M. Popov in command, became *North Front* with responsibility for the Baltic coast and operations against Finland. *Baltic Special,* also with three armies and under General Polkovnik F. I. Kuznetsov, became *Northwest Front* and took over the defense on the East Prussian border. *Western Special* and *Kiev Special* became *West Front* (four armies under General Armii D. G. Pavlov) and *Southwest Front* (four armies under General Polkovnik M. P. Kirponos) and divided the vital zone from East Prussia to the Carpathians between them at the Pripyat River. The fifth, *Odessa,* which originally had just one army, became *South Front* several days later, after General Armii F. V. Tyulenev took command with what had been the Headquarters, *Moscow Military District,* and built a second army from *Southwest Front* divisions. The *South-Southwest* boundary was at Lipkan on the upper Bug River.[14]

[11]M. V. Zakharov, ed., *50 let vooruzhennykh sil SSSR* (Moscow: Voyennoye Izdatelstvo, 1968), pp. 199, 234; Institut Marksizma-Leninizma, *Velikaya Otechestvennaya Voyna Sovetskogo Soyuza, 1941–1945 (Kratkaya Istoriya)* (Moscow: Voyennoye Izdatelstvo, 1970), p. 62 (hereafter cited as *VOV (Kratkaya Istoriya)* in footnotes and *Short History* in text. See also John Erickson, *The Soviet High Command* (New York: St. Martin's Press, 1962), p. 478.

[12]I. Kh. Bagramyan, *Istoriya voyn i voyennogo iskusstva* (Moscow: Voyennoye Izdatelstvo, 1970), pp. 67, 102.

[13]S. A. Tyushkevich, et al., *Sovetskiye vooruzhennye sily* (Moscow: Voyennoye Izdatelstvo, 1978), p. 233. (To help the reader distinguish between opposing forces, all Soviet military organizations appear in italics throughout this volume.)

[14]P. A. Zhilin, ed., *Velikaya Otechestvennaya Voyna, Kratkiy nauchnopopularnyy ocherk* (Moscow: Izdatelstvo Politicheskoy Literatury, 1970), p. 74 (hereafter cited as *VOV* in footnotes and *Popular Scientific Sketch* in text); Institut Voyennoy Istorii Ministerstva Oborony SSSR, *Istoriya Vtoroy Mirovoy Voyny, 1939–1945* (Moscow: Voyennoye Izdatelstvo, 1973–1982), vol. IV, p. 38 (hereafter cited as *IVMV* in footnotes and *History of the Second World War* in text).

MARSHAL S. K. TIMOSHENKO

GENERAL G. K. ZHUKOV

Soviet command at all levels was complicated by political surveillance and control embodied in the commissar system. As it had been developed in the civil war and reinstituted in 1937 following a period in which politically reliable commanders had been allowed to act as their own commissars, the system required all orders to be reviewed and countersigned by a commissar. So-called unity of command excluding the commissars from military decision making had been installed in August 1940, after the war with Finland, but the structure of the commissar system had remained in place.[15] In the regimental and higher staffs the former commissars had stayed on as deputy commanders for

political affairs and "members of the military councils," which consisted of themselves, the commanders, and the chiefs of staff.[16] On 16 July 1941, the *Politburo* reinstalled commissars in the military staffs and restored their authority to review and revoke commanders' decisions; it also installed *politruks* ("political leadership officers") at the lower echelons, down to the platoons. The Chief of the Army's Main Political Administration, L. Z. Mekhlis, henceforth saw to it that every commander had a political officer at his elbow watching his every move and schooled to see sabotage or treason in war's ordinary mischances.[17]

An organization that had no command functions but power at all levels

[15]*IVMV*, vol. III, p. 418.

[16]*IVOVSS*, vol. I, p. 463.
[17]*IVMV*, vol. IV, p. 55.

was the secret political police of the People's Commissariat of Internal Affairs (*Narodnyy Komissariat Vnutrennikh Del*, NKVD). It had vast and elastic authority over state security and, through its special duty (*Osobyi Otdel*, O.O.) sections in the armed forces, maintained surveillance of officers and men. It also had troops of its own that were often formed into blocking detachments and used to prevent or stop retreats by passing summary judgment on anyone, officer or private, culpable under NKVD directives. The NKVD and the Main Political Administration provided Stalin with a constant stream of information, outside military channels, about officers' actions and behavior.

In June 1941, the Soviet forces, the army in particular, were in a state of flux. In part it involved modernization and expansion, which had been going on throughout the 1930s and at an accelerated rate after war broke out in September 1939. Most immediately, the changes were an effort to act upon the lessons learned in the war with Finland. Mannerheim, the Finnish Army's commander in chief, had compared the Soviet performance in that war to that of a badly conducted orchestra in which the players could not keep time.[18] The trouble had not been primarily with manpower or equipment. Despite Soviet deficiencies in the latter, the Finnish Army had been so much smaller and more lightly armed that equipment should not have been a significant factor. Inexperience had counted heavily at all levels but most particularly in the upper ranks. Purges in the mid-1930s had carried away

many senior officers who had been hurriedly replaced by men advanced from posts far down the line.[19] Beyond that, the Finnish War had exposed deep-seated rigidity, lack of initiative, and failure to grant and to assume responsibility. Since these failings stemmed directly from the autocracy Stalin had imposed to maintain his own position and that of the Communist Party, they were extraordinarily difficult to correct.

Efforts during 1940 to correct these shortcomings had met with mixed results. In the spring, the Commissariat of Defense and the army issued revised field regulations and training manuals condemning formula-ridden, oversimplified training. Commissariat of Defense Order 120 of 16 May 1940 had called for combat-oriented training during the summer and had emphasized military discipline and tradition. Also in May, general officer and admiral ranks, which had been abolished since the revolution, had been instituted to enhance commanders' authority and self-esteem. Unity of command was, of course, the major effort to boost their authority. Still, by year's end, improvement "had only begun." After a conference of top army commanders in December 1941, the

---

[18]Carl Mannerheim, *Erinnerungen* (Zurich: Atlantis Verlag, 1952), p. 374.

[19]The military purge had begun in the summer of 1937 with the arrest and execution of Marshal Sovetskogo Soyuza M. H. Tukhachevskiy and continued thereafter through 1938. In it the Soviet Army lost all of its military district commanders, all of its corps commanders, "nearly all" of its division and brigade commanders, and half of its regimental commanders. The purge reduced the then existing officer strength in all ranks by one fifth. The navy and air force were hit equally hard. Institut Marksizma-Leninizma, *Velikaya Otechestvennaya Voyna Sovetskogo Soyuza, 1941–1945 (Kratkaya Istoriya)* (Moscow: Voyennoye Izdatelstvo, 1965), p. 39. The information cited does not appear in the 1970 edition of *VOV (Kratkaya Istoriya)*.

Defense Commissariat issued Order 30, "On the Tasks of Combat and Political Training for 1941," specifying aspects of troop and command training in which deficiencies persisted.[20]

The effort to modernize equipment was also just beginning to take effect in June 1941, although, in strictly numerical terms, the Soviet forces may actually have been the best equipped in the world at that time. By 1937, 15,000 tanks had been produced, and the output thereafter had been over 3,000 per year. Stalin may well not have exaggerated when he told Harry L. Hopkins, the U.S. lend-lease negotiator, in July 1941, that the Soviet Union had 24,000 tanks when the war broke out. Military aircraft production from 1 January 1939 to June 1941 totaled 17,745 airplanes, and the army had 67,335 artillery pieces and mortars (larger than 50-mm.) in June 1941.[21] But many of the tanks and aircraft were obsolete, and most were below standard for the time.

Two new tank types, the T–34 and KV (Kliment Voroshilov), were far superior to any the Germans had, even on the drawing boards. The Soviet T–34 medium tank at twenty-eight tons outweighed by three tons the heaviest German tank, the Panzer IV, and had a top speed of thirty-two mph against the Panzer IV's twenty-four mph. The Panzer IV's short-barreled 75-mm. gun was no match, either in range or velocity, for the T–34's longer-barreled 76-mm. gun. The KV, twenty tons heavier than the T–34 but powered with the same twelve-cylinder diesel engine, was slower (with a top speed of twenty mph) but more heavily armored, and it also carried a 76-mm. gun. Despite their greater weights, wide treads on the T–34 and KV gave them as much as 25 percent lower ground pressures per square inch than the German tanks and yielded better traction on mud or snow. Moreover, their welded, sloping hull and turret armor made them impervious to all but the heaviest German antitank weapons. The Russians began producing both in 1940 but had managed to build only 639 KVs and 1,225 T–34s before June 1941.[22]

A third new Soviet tank type was the light (6.5 tons) T–60. It was a two-man vehicle, mounting a 20-mm. cannon and a 7.62-mm. machine gun and carrying a maximum 30-mm. of armor. Roughly comparable to the German Panzer II, on which it may, in part, have been modeled, the T–60 was much inferior to the Panzer III or IV. Its outstanding virtue was that its chassis and gasoline engine could be built quickly in ordinary automobile plants using standard automotive components. In 1940, the Russians had built 2,421 T–60s as against 256 KVs and 117 T–34s.[23]

Having assumed from experience in

[20]IVOVSS, vol. I, pp. 463–69. See also John Erickson, The Road to Stalingrad (London: Weidenfeld and Nicholson, 1975), pp. 50–54 and A. I. Eremenko, Pomni voyny (Donetsk: Donbass, 1971), pp. 128–30.

[21]Zakharov, 50 let, pp. 202, 236; Bagramyan, Istoriya voyn, p. 96; Sherwood, Roosevelt and Hopkins, p. 303; VOV (Kratkaya Istoriya), p. 42.

[22]S. P. Ivanov, Nachalnyy period voyny (Moscow: Voyennoye Izdatelstvo, 1974), p. 200; IVMV, vol. III, p. 420. See also B. Perrett, Fighting Vehicles of the Red Army (London: Ian Allen, 1969), pp. 32–36, 49–52.

[23]Tyushkevich, Vooruzhennye sily, p. 273; G. A. Deborin and B. S. Telpukhovskiy, Itogi i uroki velikoy otechestvennoy voyny (Moscow: Izdatelstvo "Mysl," 1975), p. 260.

the Spanish civil war as other armies also did that tanks would chiefly perform infantry support, the Soviet Army had disbanded several mechanized and tank corps organized in the early 1930s and did not reform large armored units until after the fall of France. In late 1940, it activated eight mechanized corps, each with 36,000 troops and an allotment of 1,031 tanks. In February and March 1941, it began setting up another twenty. Apparently, few of the mechanized corps were fully equipped by June 1941.[24]

Although the great majority of the Soviet aircraft were not equal to the high performance types the Germans had introduced into the war in 1939, Soviet designers had developed some newer models, particularly the MIG–3, YAK–1, and LAGG fighters and the IL–2 (*Shturmovik*). The *Shturmovik*, publicized early in the war as a competitor with the German *Stuka* (JU–87) dive-bomber, was primarily a ground attack plane and dive-bomber, slow but well armored and difficult to shoot down. The three fighters had the features of the advanced western types, but only the MIG–3, at 370 mph plus, could match the speed of the standard German fighter (the ME–109). By June 1941, Soviet air units had received 2,739 planes of these types.

The Soviet preparations had concentrated on weapons but neglected the supplementary equipment needed to make them effective. The artillery, for instance, used ordinary farm tractors as prime movers, and the motorized divisions had less than half their planned allotments of trucks. The army was weak in all kinds of motor vehicles except tanks and would remain so until the flow of American-built trucks and cars through lend-lease took effect. Railroad transportation also was deficient. Railroad investment during the 1930s had mostly favored industrial development projects and had slighted the existing network. The expansion into Poland, the Baltic States, and Bessarabia in 1939 and 1940 had made the frontier military districts dependent on several different railroad systems, whose variations in gauge and other problems, often necessitated transloading from one railline to another at the old border.[25]

Still another weakness was signal communications. Moscow had contact with the military districts by telephone, telegraph, and radio but mainly by telephone, apparently over the lines of the civilian system. Communications in the field were uncertain. The radio networks were thin. The masses of booty the Germans took in 1941 contained only 150 radio sets. Zhukov's and other high ranking commanders' memoirs confirm that they spent much time out of touch with subordinate headquarters. Even the newest tanks did not carry radios. In the air forces, only the squadron commanders' planes had radios, of which, because of their poor quality, the *History of the Great Patriotic War* states, "flight personnel made little use while in the air."[26]

On 22 June 1941, according to most Soviet accounts, the western military districts had 2.9 million men in 170

[24]I. E. Krupchenko, et al., *Sovetskiye tankovye voyska* (Moscow: Voyennoye Izdatelstvo, 1973), pp. 12–14; Tyushkevich, *Vooruzhennye sily*, p. 240.

[25]*IVOVSS*, vol. I, pp. 417–19, 453, 476.
[26]*Ibid.*, p. 454.

divisions and 2 brigades; none of the divisions were at full strength.[27] This figure includes rifle (infantry) and cavalry divisions and, apparently, also tank and motorized divisions, although the Soviet accounts are not clear on the latter.[28] As of early July, the number of divisions increased to 212, of which 90 were at full strength. The western military districts also had 7 of the newly formed mechanized corps, and 13 more were being set up there.[29] The Soviet accounts vary on the types and numbers of tanks the mechanized corps had. Two give a total of 1,800 heavy and medium tanks—1,475 of them KVs and T–34s—plus "a significant number" of older, lighter models.[30] One gives the figure 5,500 for the heavy and medium tanks and does not mention others.[31] The western military districts' allotment of artillery pieces and mortars is given as 34,695, a specific enough number but one that lumps together two not exactly comparable weapons; and the air units are said to have had 1,540 planes of the new types and "significant numbers" of older models.[32]

German Strategy

On the last day of July 1940, when Hitler announced his decision to invade the Soviet Union to a small group of his generals, he described his grand strategic design as follows: "England's hope is Russia and America. If Russia is lost, America will be also, because the loss of Russia will result in an enormous rise of Japan in East Asia. If Russia is smashed, then England's last hope is extinguished. Then Germany will be the master of Europe and the Balkans."[33] Therefore, he concluded, the Soviet Union had to be "finished off in one go" and "the sooner the better."[34]

To Hitler and his military advisers, the strategic concerns associated with a war in the Soviet Union appeared to be mostly geographical. One was the climate, which was markedly continental, with short, hot summers and long, extremely cold winters and an astonishing uniformity from north to south, considering the country's great expanse. Hitler observed at the group's first conference that it would be "hazardous" to winter in the Soviet Union, and, therefore, it would be better to delay the invasion until the next spring.[35] Finishing off the Soviet Union then in "one go" would mean a single summer's campaign of no more than five months. Its beginning and end would also have to be adjusted to the *rasputitsy* ("times without roads") brought on by the spring thaw and the fall rains, which at both times turned the Soviet roads into impassable quagmires for periods of several weeks.

[27]VOV, p. 51; VOV (Kratkaya Istoriya), p. 54; Ivanov, Nachalnyy period, p. 208; IVMV, vol. IV, p. 25, gives 2,680,000 men.
[28]Krupchenko, Tankovye voyska, p. 21, indicates that the Russians formed 21 tank and 7 motorized divisions and were forming 39 tank and 13 motorized divisions in the western military districts. The authorized strength of rifle divisions was set at 14,483 men in April 1941, down from a previous 18,000. A rifle division consisted of 3 infantry and 2 artillery regiments. IVMV, vol. III, p. 118; Tyushkevich, Vooruzhennye sily, p. 236.
[29]IVMV, vol. IV, p. 60; Krupchenko, Tankovye voyska, p. 21.
[30]Ivanov, Nachalnyy period, p. 215; VOV, p. 51.
[31]Krupchenko, Tankovye voyska, p. 14; Ivanov, Nachalnyy period, p. 215.
[32]Ivanov, Nachalnyy period, p. 214; VOV, p. 51.
[33]Halder Diary, vol. II, p. 49.
[34]Ibid.
[35]Ibid.

The big strategic question was the one that had also confronted earlier invaders: how to accomplish a military victory in the vastness of the Russian space? Apart from the Pripyat Marshes and several of the large rivers, the terrain did not offer notable impediments to the movement of modern military forces. But maintaining troop concentrations and supplying armies in the depths of this country presented staggering, potentially crippling, difficulties. The entire Soviet Union had only 51,000 miles of railroad, all of a different gauge than those in Germany and eastern Europe. Of 850,000 miles of road, 700,000 were hardly more than cart tracks; 150,000 miles were allegedly all-weather roads, but only 40,000 miles of those were hard surfaced.[36]

Hitler and the OKH agreed that the first objective in the campaign would have to be to cripple the Soviet resistance close to the frontier. In December, however, when they were drafting the strategic directive, their thinking diverged on how to accomplish the second objective, the final Soviet defeat. Brauchitsch and the General Staff proposed to aim the main thrust toward the Moscow area. The roads were best in that direction, and the General Staff believed the Soviet Command could be induced to commit its last strength there, to defend the capital, which was also the center of a vital industrial complex and the hub of the country's road and railroad networks. Hitler, however, did not believe the war could be decided on the Moscow axis. Directive 21, "for Opera-

tion BARBAROSSA," which Hitler signed on 18 December 1940, circumvented the issue by providing for simultaneous thrusts toward Leningrad, Moscow, and Kiev; a modified main effort toward Moscow; and a possible halt and diversion of forces from the Moscow thrust to aid the advance toward Leningrad. For the moment, the differences in opinion on strategy did not really interfere with the operation planning. The objectives were to trap the "mass" of the Soviet Army in sweeping envelopments close to the frontier, to annihilate it, and thereafter to occupy the Soviet territory east to the line of Arkhangelsk and the Volga River. The initial main effort would be in the center toward Moscow, and staff studies showed that the Soviet Union could be defeated in eight weeks, ten at most.[37]

To compel the Soviet forces to stand and fight appeared to be the chief requirement, and if they did that, they would be defeated. The Soviet Army, Hitler maintained, alluding to the military purge, "was leaderless." It had, he added, recently been given opportunities to "learn some correct lessons in the conduct of war" presumably by the German early campaigns and the war with Finland but whether it was exploiting them was "more than questionable," and, in any event, no substantive change could be accomplished by the spring of 1941. The Soviet armor, he believed, was no match even for the 24-ton German Panzer III, mounting a 50-mm. gun, and the rest of the Soviet weaponry, "except for a

---

[36]Georges Jorre, *The Soviet Union* (London: Longmans, 1961), pp. 183–84, 192.

[37]*Der Fuehrer und Oberste Befehlshaber der Wehrmacht, OKW, WFSt. Abt. L (I) Nr. 33408/40, Weisung Nr. 21, Fall Barbarossa, 18.12.40*, German High Level Directives, CMH files; DA Pamphlet 20–261a, pp. 17–25.

few modern field batteries," was "copied old material."[38]

Under these circumstances, although Hitler did not entirely overlook other strategic problems, he did regard them as irrelevant to the kind of war being planned. One such problem was manpower potential. Greater Germany had a population of 89 million; the Soviet Union had 193 million people.[39] But the Soviet people, in Hitler's opinion, were "inferior."[40] Also, Hitler had not yet shifted the German economy to a wartime footing. The early blitzkrieg campaigns had been so successful and so relatively cheap that he had kept the economy on a quasi-peacetime basis. War production in 1941 was at the 1940 level, which itself had been lower than the original economic mobilization plans had specified. In the meantime, however, the Soviet Union had more than caught up with Germany in budgeting for war production. From 1935 through 1938, the Soviet Union had invested the equivalent of $4.7 billion in armaments, and Germany $8.6. The 1939 figures had been $3.3 (Soviet) and $3.4 (German). In 1940, they had risen to $5.0 (Soviet) and $6.0 (German), and in 1941, $8.5 (Soviet) and $6.0 (German).[41]

But Hitler had no time for doubts. He made just one comparison: "In the Spring [of 1941], we will be at a discernable high in leadership, material, and troops, and the Russians will be at an unmistakable low."[42] On 11 June 1941, he issued Directive 32, "Preparations for the Period After BARBAROSSA," in which he anticipated leaving sixty divisions on security duty in the Soviet Union and having the rest of the forces redeployed for other missions by the late fall.[43]

Soviet Preparedness

Strategic Planning

For the Soviet Union, the French surrender in June 1940 made war with Germany a real and distinctly unwelcome contingency. Suddenly, the government and the armed forces, having just begun to digest the lessons of the war with Finland, found themselves alone on the Continent with a hugely expanded Germany that had accomplished in less than six weeks what it had been unable to do in the four years of World War I. Nikita Khrushchev, who by his own account was with Stalin when the news of the French capitulation came in, has described Stalin's cursing the British and French for having failed to resist and the gloom in the Soviet government at being isolated and facing "the most pressing and deadly threat in all history. . . ."[44]

In July 1940, the Soviet Army General Staff turned to what from then until the following June would be its priority concern: devising a strategy to meet a German attack. Marshal Sovetskogo Soyuza Boris Shaposhnikov, who

---

[38]*Halder Diary,* vol. II, p. 214.

[39]Nikolai Voznesenskiy, *The Economy of the USSR During World War II* (Washington, D.C.: Public Affairs Press, 1948), p. 8.

[40]*Halder Diary,* vol. II, p. 214.

[41]Deutsches Institut fuer Wirtschaftsforschung, *Die deutsche Industrie im Kriege, 1939–1945* (Berlin: Dunkker & Humblodt, 1954), pp. 23, 27, 34, 87.

[42]*Halder Diary,* vol. II, p. 214.

[43]*OKW, WFSt, Abt. L (I Op.) Nr. 4488641, Weisung Nr. 32, 11.6.42,* German High Level Directives, CMH files.

[44]Nikita Khrushchev, *Khrushchev Remembers* (Boston: Little, Brown, 1970), p. 134.

was then chief of the General Staff, assumed that Germany would have Finland, Hungary, Rumania, and Italy as allies, and, although he was "not excluding" the possibility of a two-front war involving Japan, he took the most pressing threat to be the one on the west.[45] Even though Japan had been an active enemy of the Soviet Union for the previous several years, Shaposhnikov concluded that Germany was obviously the stronger, was closer to the Soviet vital centers, and was thought to be the one most likely to attack first. He and his subordinates then undertook to devise a response to the problem as he had broadly defined it.[46]

In September 1940, General Armii Kiril Meretskov, who had taken Shaposhnikov's place as chief of the General Staff in August, presented the results of the General Staff's work during the summer to Stalin and the *Politburo* as a plan for strategic deployment on the western frontier. At the meeting, by Stalin's decision, two fundamental premises became fixed elements in Soviet preinvasion strategy. One of these concerned the direction of the German main effort; the other concerned the nature of the Soviet response to an attack. The Soviet literature offers two versions of how those decisions were reached.

As Marshal A. M. Vasilevskiy, who was then the deputy operations chief, relates it, the General Staff view held that the probable main lines of the German attack would lie north of the lower San River; hence, in the center, toward Moscow, and on the north

flank. Therefore, the General Staff proposed to deploy its strongest forces in the same area, specifically, between the Pripyat Marshes and the Baltic coast. However, according to Vasilevskiy, Stalin insisted the German main effort would be in the south, to capture the "rich resources and agricultural land of the Ukraine," and ordered the deployment reversed.[47] Zhukov, who commanded the *Kiev Special Military District,* adds that Stalin was convinced the Germans would have to try to seize the Ukraine first and "it never occurred to anybody to question the correctness of his opinion."[48] The *History of the Second World War,* citing Vasilevskiy and Zhukov, gives a similar account without mentioning Stalin.[49] The three imply that the General Staff's purpose was to bring the Soviet main effort to bear in the direction of the probable strongest German attack.

A study on the initial period of the war done under General Armii S. P. Ivanov, who was at the time of the writing commandant of the Voroshilov Academy of the General Staff, sets the mislocation of the Soviet main effort in a different context. Ivanov says the General Staff had concluded that the German main effort would be directed southeast, to take the Ukraine, the Donets Basin, and, eventually, the Caucasus oil fields. It "did not exclude the possibility," however, that the main effort might be north of the Pripyat Marshes toward the "Smolensk Gate" and Moscow.[50] The General Staff's concern in setting the location of the

[45]A. M. Vasilevskiy, *Delo vsey zhizni* (Moscow: Izdatelstvo Politicheskoy Literatury, 1976), p. 101; Ivanov, *Nachalnyy period,* pp. 202–03.
[46]*IVMV,* vol. III, p. 434.

[47]Vasilevskiy, *Delo,* pp. 101, 106–07.
[48]G. K. Zhukov, *The Memoirs of Marshal Zhukov* (New York: Delacorte Press, 1971), p. 211.
[49]*IVMV,* vol. III, p. 434.
[50]Ivanov, *Nachalnyy period,* p. 203.

Soviet main effort, the Ivanov study adds, was to mount the strongest possible blow with the aims of "repulsing aggression and carrying the war to the enemy's territory." Therefore, the General Staff proposed to deploy the Soviet main forces between the Pripyat Marshes and the Baltic coast, that is, in the center and on the north flank. At the meeting in September, the Ivanov study states, Stalin "expressed thoughts" on the enemy's main effort being in the south, and thereafter the General Staff reworked its plan to situate the Soviet main forces in the south as well.[51]

From the Ivanov study, which in point of time at least, supersedes Vasilevskiy's and Zhukov's writings on this period, it appears that Stalin and the General Staff were independently agreed on the location of the German main effort, and were both wrong. They apparently also overestimated the Soviet ability to respond offensively to a German attack. Without reading too much into Ivanov, it can be assumed then that the real difference of opinion was on the premises that would govern the choice of location for the Soviet main effort. The General Staff was looking for the shortest lines on which to carry the war to German territory. On the other hand, Stalin seems to have concluded that carrying the war to the enemy's territory along the line of the main enemy advance better satisfied his own theoretical requirement to "organize the decisive blow in the direction in which it may produce maximum results."[52]

During the last week of December 1940 and the first week of January 1941, the Defense Commissariat held a conference of senior officers in Moscow. The *History of the Great Patriotic War* and the *History of the Second World War* depict it as having been an extended symposium in which the generals exchanged views and had an opportunity to absorb the latest in Soviet military thought. Accounts in the memoirs of some of those who attended indicate it was also a war readiness review that disclosed deficiencies in the generals' ability to conduct large-scale operations and in armament, equipment, and training.[53]

After the conference closed, the military district commanders and their chiefs of staff stayed on to participate in a war game, which was played from 8 to 11 January and was based on the strategic plan the General Staff had developed in the past summer and had just finished revising in December.[54] The game, Zhukov states, "abounded in dramatic situations for the red (Soviet) side" that "proved to be in many ways similar to what really happened after June 22, 1941. . . ."[55] In brief, the Soviet side lost. When the chief of the General Staff, Meretskov, failed to explain this development satisfactorily, Stalin relieved him and appointed Zhukov (who had led the play on the "blue" [enemy] side) as his replacement.[56]

[51]*Ibid.*, p. 204.
[52]J. V. Stalin, *Sochineniya* (Moscow: Izdatelstvo Politicheskoy Literatury, 1947), vol. V, p. 163; *IVOVSS*, vol. I, p. 437.

[53]*IVOVSS*, vol. I, p. 433; *IVMV*, vol. III, pp. 409–10. See A. I. Eremenko, *V nachale voyny* (Moscow: Izdatelstvo "Nauka," 1964, pp. 36–48; K. A. Meretskov, *Serving the People* (Moscow: Progress Publishers, 1971), pp. 125–26; Zhukov, *Memoirs*, pp. 183–84.
[54]See Vasilevskiy, *Delo*, p. 106.
[55]Zhukov, *Memoirs*, p. 185.
[56]*Ibid.*, p. 187; Meretskov, *Serving the People*, pp. 126–27.

Manifestly displeased with the outcome of the war game, Stalin critiqued it in the Kremlin on 13 January. In the last of his several memoirs, the late Marshal Sovetskogo Soyuza A. I. Eremenko, who took part in the war game as a newly appointed military district commander, and who also attended the critique, has given the most explicit account to date of Stalin's comments.[57] According to Eremenko, Stalin criticized the Commissariat of Defense and the General Staff for not having given the "military districts problems they will have to solve in actual war." He also reminded those present of the "complications" that had arisen in finding competent commanders and staffs for the Finnish War, and he laid down specific requirements: to prepare for a two-front war, to expand and rearm the forces, to create reserves, to "learn how to conduct" a war of fast movement and maneuver, and to "work out" the organizational "questions" evolving from the other requirements. Most significantly, Eremenko remembered Stalin's having said, "War is approaching fast and now is not distant. . . . We must gain a year and a half to two years' time to complete the rearmament plan."[58] For Stalin, time had become a most precious strategic resource.

Operational Planning

The Soviet war literature offers two views of the state and nature of the nation's operational plans prior to the invasion: one asserts that such plans as did exist were tentative and not designed to do more than provide a limited capability to meet an attack; the other maintains that the plans were comprehensive and were believed to be adequate not merely to meet aggression but to repel it and to initiate operations to defeat it. The first view derives primarily from the early post-Stalin version of the war given in the *History of the Great Patriotic War* but is retained in the *History of the Second World War*. The second appears in Vasilevskiy's and Zhukov's memoirs, and the Ivanov study on the initial period of the war presents it in detail.

The *History of the Great Patriotic War* mentions two plans drafted in early 1941, a mobilization plan (MP–41) and a "covering plan for the state frontier" (Plan 9). It describes the mobilization plan as having been geared to a schedule that extended through the second half of 1941 and into early 1942 and the covering plan as no more than one to distribute approximately two-thirds of the troops stationed in the western military districts more or less uniformly along the border, their mission in the event of war being to hold the border and to "cover" the mobilization and assembly of the main forces. The *History of the Great Patriotic War* does not mention the strategic plan the General Staff worked on in the summer and fall of 1940 and concludes that it is only "possible to speak of a plan of general operations" because the mobilization and covering plans "were infused with one idea," which was "to repel the enemy's aggression at the line of the state frontier and subsequently deal him a

[57]Eremenko also dealt with the critique in his first memoir, written in the early 1960s. There he gave the impression that Stalin's remarks were haphazard and superficial. Comparison of the two versions shows that the variances between them lie less in the reporting than in the author's emphasis and interpretation. See Eremenko, *V nachale*, pp. 34–37. See also Erickson, *Road to Stalingrad*, p. 54.

[58]Eremenko, *Pomni voyny*, pp. 129–30.

crushing defeat."[59] The *History of the Second World War* gives some specifics of the mobilization and covering plans, alludes to the 1940 decision on the location of the main effort (but not to the associated strategic plan), and addresses the additional problem of border fortifications; but it also leaves the impression that fully developed operational plans did not exist.[60]

On the other hand, Vasilevskiy speaks in his memoirs of an "operational plan to repel aggression" that was developed in the General Staff and conveyed to the commanding generals, chiefs of staff, and chiefs of operations of the frontier military districts in conferences held in Moscow between February and April 1941.[61] Zhukov mentions "operational-mobilization plans regarding preparations for repulsing possible aggression."[62]

The Ivanov study on the initial period of the war describes two plans: an "operational plan" and a "special plan for the defense of the state frontier." The operational plan, which the General Staff completed in late 1940, was concerned with how "answering blows" would be delivered "after the strategic deployment of the main forces of the Red Army." The special plan, completed in early 1941 and the basis on which the frontier military districts "worked out their concrete war plans," dealt with "covering" and "active defense" in the first stage of hostilities, before the main forces had been mobilized and deployed.[63]

The special plan, as described in the Ivanov study, embraced what is referred to in the *History of the Great Patriotic War* as the covering plan but, in its active defense aspect, also included much more: "active air operations" to deliver blows against the enemy's concentrations and to achieve air superiority; concentration of the mechanized corps, antitank artillery brigades, and aviation to "liquidate" break-ins; and, if so directed by the General Headquarters, delivery of blows that would "smash" the enemy on the borders and carry the war to his territory. The military districts' initial mission would be to cover the concentration of the main forces, but that would be done in a three-echelon offensive deployment (infantry, armor, and reserves) from which the three could be merged to form a "first strategic echelon." Combined, the three original echelons could begin to carry out the operational plan by dealing the enemy an "answering blow" and "possibly," by carrying the war to enemy territory before the main forces were assembled. In that event, a "second strategic echelon" would form behind the first to support it and to further develop the answering blow "in accordance with the general strategic idea."[64] The initial three-echelon deployment conformed to the best Soviet offensive doctrine of the time so much so, in fact, that it has been cited occasionally as evidence of a Soviet intention to attack Germany.[65] Vasilevskiy has said:

. . . if our military units and formations had been mobilized at the proper time,

[59]*IVOVSS*, vol. I, pp. 172–74, 179.
[60]*IVMV*, vol. III, pp. 234–39. See also Erickson, *Road to Stalingrad*, pp. 80–81.
[61]Vasilevskiy, *Delo*, p. 113.
[62]Zhukov, *Memoirs*, p. 211.
[63]Ivanov, *Nachalnyy period*, pp. 204–05.

[64]*Ibid.*, pp. 205–06.
[65]See *IVOVSS*, vol. I, p. 443. See also Reinhard Gehlen, *The Service* (New York: World Publishing, 1972), p. 26.

had been deployed as specified in their plans for border war, and had, in accordance with those, organized close coordination between artillery, armor, and aviation, it could be asserted that the enemy would have been dealt such losses already on the first day of the war that he could not have advanced further into our country.[66]

War Readiness

In March 1941, rumors of war were circulating among the foreign diplomats in Moscow, and U.S. Under Secretary of State Sumner Welles told the Soviet ambassador in Washington that the State Department had information, which it regarded as "authentic," of a plan for a German attack on the Soviet Union "in the not distant future."[67] By then, no doubt, information about the planned attack as authentic as Welles' was available to the Soviet government from its own sources.[68] The *History of the Great Patriotic War* states:

In the existing situation it was necessary to be extremely careful to avoid provocations . . . while at the same time taking all possible measures to bring the Soviet Armed Forces to full readiness for war. But because J. V. Stalin made serious errors in evaluating the politico-military situation as it developed prior to the outbreak of the Great Patriotic War, such a dual policy did not exist.[69]

In Vasilevskiy's opinion, Stalin could not decide what to do.[70] The *History of the Second World War* maintains that " . . .

the military leadership of the Soviet Union [which included Stalin] knew a collision with Germany to be unavoidable," but "preparations to resist aggression were accompanied by a necessity not to give Germany a direct excuse to unleash a war."[71]

Stalin's effort to gain time failed. His most astute move, the signing of a neutrality treaty with Japan on 13 April 1941, valuable as it might be in the longer run, at best made only a negligible change in his position with regard to Germany. The treaty had no effect as a deterrent, and Hitler ignored its more likely intent as a gesture of Soviet willingness to collaborate. The treaty gave Stalin a none too dependable confirmation of what he already believed, namely, that Germany and Japan would not attack at the same time, and it created a remote possibility that Japan, freed to turn toward likely conflict with the United States, might draw Germany, its partner in the Tripartite Pact, in and away from the Soviet Union.[72]

Stalin's play for time, however, was not nearly as detrimental to Soviet preparedness as some accounts make it appear. He gave the armed forces as much support as they believed they needed. The covering plan called for 170 divisions and 2 brigades, and as of June 1941, those were deployed: 56 divisions and 2 brigades in the first

[66]Vasilevskiy, *Delo*, p. 117.

[67]U.S. Department of State, *Foreign Relations of the United States, 1941* (Washington, D.C.: GPO, 1958), vol. I, pp. 133, 712–14; Erickson, *Road to Stalingrad*, pp. 73–75.

[68]See *IVOVSS*, vol. I, p. 403.

[69]*Ibid.*, p. 404.

[70]Vasilevskiy, *Delo*, p. 116.

[71]*IVMV*, vol. III, p. 439.

[72]See also *IVOVSS*, vol. I, pp. 399–401; Erickson, *Road to Stalingrad*, p. 76; Raymond James Sontag and James Stuart Beddie, eds., *Nazi-Soviet Relations, 1939–1941* (Washington, D.C.: GPO, 1948), pp. 212, 220; Gerhard Weinberg, *Germany and the Soviet Union, 1939–1941* (Leiden: E. J. Brill, 1954), pp. 159–63; U.S. Department of State, *Documents on German Foreign Policy, 1918–1945*, Series D (Washington, D.C.: GPO, 1960), vol. XI, p. 204.

echelon, 52 divisions in the second, and 62 divisions in the third echelon. On 13 May, the General Staff ordered 28 divisions and 4 army headquarters from the Urals, the Caucasus, and the Far East transferred to the western frontier and began organizing an army at Mogilev on the Dnepr River behind the *Western Special Military District.* (The second strategic echelon was to form along the line of the Dnepr and Dvina rivers.) A call-up of nearly 800,000 reservists in late May brought the total of men under arms to about 5 million, and early graduations from the officers' schools provided officers for the increase. In May, also, instructions went out to the *Ural, North Caucasus, Volga,* and *Kharkov Military Districts* to have elements of their forces ready to move to the Dnepr-Dvina line.[73]

These actions, of course, achieved far less than full war readiness. Aside from the gaps in personnel and equipment of the divisions and mechanized corps, the frontier military districts' dispositions were loose.[74] The first covering echelon had seven divisions less than were planned; the third, seven divisions more. The first echelon was mostly in barracks up to 30 miles away from the border. The second echelon's divisions were 30 to 60 miles from the border, and those of the third echelon, as much as 180 miles back. In addition, nonmechanized units were going to have to depend for mobility on being able to draw some quarter million motor vehicles and forty thousand tractors from civilian use. Bringing up the reinforcements from the interior and integrating them into the plans would take time. Moreover, the border to be defended was the 1940 one, almost none of which had been under Soviet control before September 1939 and some only since the spring and summer of 1940. Fortifications along the old border, the so-called Stalin Line built in the 1930s, had been abandoned and in part dismantled. A new line had been under construction since November 1939, and 2,500 reinforced concrete emplacements had been built, but only 1,000 of those had artillery; the rest had only machine guns.[75]

On the other hand, the shortcomings in the defensive deployment do not seem to have weighed very heavily in the Soviet strategic thinking of the time. The *History of the Second World War* says, "As a practical matter, the military leadership left a strategic defensive out of consideration. Defensive operations in the initial period of the war were regarded as significant only for parts of the strategic front and for the assignments of the covering armies."[76] The Soviet planning apparently also did not take the possibility of a surprise attack into account. Zhukov tells why:

The Peoples Commissariat of Defense and the General Staff believed that war between such big countries as Germany and Russia would follow the existing scheme: the main forces engage in battle after several days of frontier fighting. As regards the concentration and deployment deadlines, it was assumed that conditions for the two countries were the same.[77]

---

[73]*IVMV,* vol. III, pp. 338–41, 440; *VOV (Kratkaya Istoriya),* p. 53; Ivanov, *Nachalnyy period,* p. 213; Deborin and Telpukhovskiy, *Itogi i uroki,* p. 74.

[74]See p. 23.

[75]*IVMV,* vol. III, pp. 435, 439, 441; *VOV (Kratkaya Istoriya),* p. 54. See also Erickson, *Road to Stalingrad,* pp. 70, 71 and Zhukov, *Memoirs,* pp. 211–14.

[76]*IVMV,* vol. III, p. 415.

[77]Zhukov, *Memoirs,* p. 215.

In short, the military leadership anticipated a lag between the outbreak of war, declared or undeclared, and the actual beginning of operations. Zhukov mentions "several days." Vasilevskiy says the plans from the summer of 1940 until BARBAROSSA assumed ten to fifteen days.[78] Ivanov gives "not less than two weeks," and Marshal V. D. Sokolovskiy, in his work on Soviet strategy, specifies fifteen to twenty days.[79] This was the period, Sokolovskiy indicates, in which mobilization was to be completed and the covering plan would be in effect.[80] Moreover, and perhaps more significantly, Soviet theory assumed that, after the hiatus, the hostilities would fall into a predictable pattern, and the war would "inevitably take on a character of extended attrition, with battles being decided primarily by the ability of the rear to provide the front with more material and human resources over a prolonged period of time than were available to the enemy."[81]

On the Eve of Invasion

Since Stalin's death, some Soviet accounts of the war, particularly those written during the Khrushchev period, have maintained that up to the last minute Stalin refused to respond to the signs of an impending invasion. The most often cited evidence is a TASS news agency release printed in *Pravda* on 14 June 1941. It quoted "responsible circles in Moscow" as condemning the "absurd rumors of war between Germany and the Soviet Union" and dismissed the rumors as propaganda "concocted by forces hostile to Germany and the Soviet Union." The "circles" declared that Germany and the Soviet Union were abiding strictly by the terms of the nonaggression pact.[82] Zhukov has added that on the same day, 14 June, he and Timoshenko asked to put the troops in the frontier military districts on alert, but Stalin refused, saying, "That means war. Do you understand that or not?"[83] The *History of the Great Patriotic War* attributes "a negative influence on the military readiness of the Soviet Armed Forces and on the alertness of command and political personnel" to the TASS dispatch.[84] One account infers that the dispatch sustained a peacetime atmosphere among the troops of the frontier districts when the Germans were about to overrun the country.[85]

On the other hand, Vasilevskiy states that the dispatch "at first" aroused surprise in the General Staff, "as it did also among the Soviet people," but "thereafter no new instructions were issued, which made clear that it was not directed to the Armed Forces or to the public." "At the end of the same day," Vasilevskiy continues, "the Deputy Chief of the General Staff, General N. F. Vatutin, explained that the objective of the TASS communique was to test the true intentions of the Hitlerites and did not otherwise require our attention."[86] The *History of the Second World War* maintains, as Vasilevskiy does, that

[78]Vasilevskiy, *Delo*, p. 101.
[79]Ivanov, *Nachalnyy period*, p. 206; V. D. Sokolovskiy, *Soviet Military Strategy* (Englewood Cliffs, N.J.: Prentice Hall, 1963), p. 232.
[80]Sokolovskiy, *Strategy*, p. 232.
[81]Ivanov, *Nachalnyy period*, p. 203.

[82]*IVMV*, vol. III, p. 440.
[83]Zhukov, *Memoirs*, p. 230.
[84]*IVOVSS*, vol. II, p. 10.
[85]S. P. Platonov, ed., *Vtoraya Mirovaya Voyna* (Moscow: Voyennoye Izdatelstvo, 1958), p. 1979.
[86]Vasilevskiy, *Delo*, p. 119.

the dispatch was a probe for a German reaction and says that the Soviet government quickly took the subsequent German silence as a sign that war was about to break out. Therefore, the *History* adds, the Commissariat of Defense, between 14 and 19 June, ordered the frontier military districts to set up command posts from which they could exercise their appointed wartime functions as army group commands and to camouflage airfields, military units, and "important military objectives."[87]

If Stalin and the military leadership were convinced war was impending, they also had a very good idea of exactly when to expect it. Richard Sorge, a Soviet master spy in Tokyo, who was a German newspaperman with extremely well-informed contacts, gave them that information. On 15 June he sent a radiogram that read, "War will begin on 22 June. . . ." and another that stated, "Attack will proceed on a broad front commencing 22 June."[88]

In any event, Stalin knew by mid-June that "to escape war, even in the very near future, was impossible" and permitted the final preparations to begin. The rule, however, was "to do what was necessary to strengthen the defenses . . . but not do anything in the frontier zone that could provoke the fascists or hasten their attack on us."[89] The Defense Commissariat ordered the frontier military districts to shift their divisions closer to the border and into the positions designated for them in the special plan for defending the state frontier. The movements began on 15 June, but, on the 22d, "only certain" of the divisions were in position.[90] On the 21st, the *Politburo* acted to create a single command for the armies being brought from the interior military districts to the line of the Dnepr and Dvina. On the night of the 21st, a war alert directive went out from Moscow. It ordered all units to combat readiness and those close to the border to man the fortifications and firing points in secret during the night. Troops on the border were not to respond to any German provocations or to take any other action without special orders.[91] The directive did not reach all the field commands in the hours left before the German attack, and the state of readiness otherwise was far from complete. Nevertheless, there was, in general, no conflict with "the concept of initial operations projected by the Commissariat of Defense and the General Staff, which assumed that the aggressor would first undertake to invade our territory with partial forces and instigate border battles under the cover of which both sides would complete their mobilizations and mass their forces."[92]

First word of the German attack, reports of airfields and cities being bombed, reached the Commissariat of Defense at about 0400 on 22 June.[93] Four hours later, after consulting with Stalin, Timoshenko issued a second directive. It ordered the ground forces to "attack and annihilate all enemy forces"

[87]*IVMV*, vol. III, p. 441.
[88]Deborin and Telpukhovskiy, *Itogi i uroki*, pp. 102–03.
[89]Ivanov, *Nachalnyy period*, p. 212.

[90]*Ibid.*
[91]Deborin and Telpukhovskiy, *Itogi i uroki*, p. 75; Zhukov, *Memoirs*, p. 232; *IVOVSS*, vol. II, p. 11; *IVMV*, vol. IV, p. 28.
[92]Ivanov, *Nachalnyy period*, p. 213.
[93]Vasilevskiy, *Delo*, p. 119.

that had violated the frontier and the air units to strike sixty to ninety miles inside German territory and to bomb Koenigsberg and Memel.[94]

In Moscow, apparently, most of the day of the 22d was consumed trying to get information about what was happening from the *fronts*, which, in turn, were trying to do the same with their subordinate commands. By evening, "regardless of incomplete reports . . . the situation required an immediate decision to organize further resistance against the enemy."[95] At 2115, Ti-

moshenko dispatched a third directive: *Northwest* and *West Fronts* were to mount converging thrusts by infantry and armor from Kaunas and Grodno to Suwalki, and *Southwest Front* was to do the same toward Lublin to cut off the Germans on the sixty-mile stretch of frontier between Vladimir-Volynskiy and Krystynopol.[96] Therewith, the frontier forces were ordered to "the offensive in the main directions for the purposes of destroying the enemy's assault groupings and carrying the war to his territory."[97]

---

[94]*IVOVSS*, vol. II, p. 18. See also Zhukov, *Memoirs*, p. 236.

[95]*IVMV*, vol. IV, p. 37.

[96]*Ibid.*, p. 38.

[97]Ivanov, *Nachalnyy period*, p. 260.

CHAPTER II

The Blitzkrieg

Barbarossa

Several hours before the third Soviet directive went out on the night of 22 June, Generaloberst Franz Halder, Chief of the German General Staff, had enough information to conclude that the Soviet forces had been tactically unprepared and "must now take our attack in the deployment in which they stand."[1] Halder's Soviet counterpart, General Zhukov, who arrived at General Kirponos' Headquarters, *Southwest Front*, that night on the first of what would become a long series of similar coordinating missions, held much the same opinion, believing that neither a counterattack nor any other concerted move ought to be attempted until a clear picture of what was happening at the front was formed.[2] Yet Zhukov would not have concurred in Halder's further assumption that the Soviet leadership "perhaps cannot react operatively at all." He found the *Southwest Front* staff confident and capable. That as much could be said for the other two *fronts*, however, was doubtful. *West* and *Northwest Fronts* had become increasingly confused on the first day, and their commanders Generals Pavlov and Kuznetsov, who were trying to rally their forces, had been out of contact with their own headquarters most of the time.[3]

On 23 June, the Main Military Council, reduced from eleven to seven members, became the *Stavka* ("general headquarters") of the High Command. Six deputy defense commissars dropped out, and two new members, Marshal Voroshilov, the chairman of the Defense Committee, and Admiral Kuznetsov, people's commissar of the navy, were added. Marshal Timoshenko continued as chairman, and Stalin, Molotov, people's commissar for foreign affairs, and Zhukov remained as members, as did Marshal Sovetskogo Soyuza Semen Budenny, who was first deputy people's commissar of defense. Kuznetsov's presence made the *Stavka* an armed forces headquarters but did not resolve the ambiguity as to where the supreme authority really lay.[4] As Zhukov later put it, there were two commanders in chief, Timoshenko *de jure* and Stalin *de facto*, since, "Timoshenko could not make any fundamental decisions without Stalin anyway."[5] This was, in fact, the long-established Soviet practice, and it ought not to have impaired the actual conduct of the war—and perhaps did not. However, in February 1956, Khrushchev, as general secretary of the

---

[1]*Halder Diary*, vol. III, p. 5.
[2]Zhukov, *Memoirs*, p. 239.

[3]*Ibid.*; IVOVSS, vol. II, p. 29.
[4]Zakharov, *50 let*, p. 256.
[5]Zhukov, *Memoirs*, p. 238.

THE GERMAN ADVANCE
22 June - 12 November 1941
- - - - - German positions, 21 Jun
ooooooo Approximate front, 10 Jul
———— Approximate front, 12 Nov

0 ———————— 200 Miles
0 ———————— 200 Kilometers

GULF OF FINLAND
LENINGRAD
LENINGRAD FRONT
Schluesselburg
Tikhvin
BALTIC SEA
Tallinn
EIGHTEENTH ARMY
NORTH FRONT
Luga
Chudovo
Staraya
Russa
NORTHWEST FRONT
Yaroslavl
EIGHTEENTH ARMY
Pskov
FOURTH PANZER GROUP
SIXTEENTH ARMY
NORTHWEST FRONT
KALININ FRONT
Kalinin
Volga R.
MOSCOW
Riga
Dvina R.
SIXTEENTH ARMY
NINTH ARMY
THIRD PANZER GROUP
FOURTH PANZER GROUP
WEST FRONT
Vitebsk
Vyazma
Mozhaysk
WEST FRONT
ARMY GROUP
Koenigsberg
Kaunas
THIRD PANZER GROUP
Yartsevo
FOURTH ARMY
Oka R.
Ryazan
NORTH
NINTH ARMY
Orsha
Smolensk
Kaluga
Tula
POLAND
Grodno
Minsk
Mogilev
RESERVE FRONT
SECOND PANZER ARMY
Mtsensk
ARMY
SECOND ARMY
SECOND PANZER GROUP
Bryansk
Orel
GROUP
Bialystok
FOURTH ARMY
CENTRAL FRONT
SECOND ARMY
BRYANSK FRONT
WARSAW
CENTER
Pripyat
Marshes
Konotop
Don R.
XXXXX
SIXTH ARMY
SOUTHWEST
Romny
Lublin
Rovno
FIRST PANZER GROUP
Kiev
Lokhvista
SIXTH ARMY
SOUTHWEST FRONT
Vistula R.
Lvov
FRONT
Dnepr R.
Kharkov
SOUTH FRONT
ARMY
SLOVAKIA
SEVENTEENTH ARMY
SEVENTEENTH ARMY
Kremenchug
GROUP
CARPATHIAN MOUNTAINS
Southern Bug R.
Uman
Pervomaysk
FIRST PANZER ARMY
Stalino
HUNGARY
ELEVENTH ARMY
SOUTH FRONT
Rostov
SOUTH
Taganrog
Melitopol
RUMANIA
Odessa
Perkop
ELEVENTH ARMY
Kerch
BUCHAREST
BLACK
Sevastopol
SEA

MAP 2

CAPTURED SOVIET TROOPS MARCH PAST A PEASANT VILLAGE

Communist Party, told the Twentieth Party Congress, ". . . for a long time Stalin actually did not direct military operations and ceased to do anything whatever."[6] Soviet accounts written since then generally have had little to say about Stalin's role in the war between 22 June and 3 July 1941. Zhukov maintained that Stalin recovered quickly from a spell of depression on the morning of 22 June, but Zhukov was away from Moscow until the 26th and reported seeing Stalin only twice in the week after he returned.[7]

The Battles of the Frontiers

Except at *Southwest Front,* where six

mechanized and three rifle corps kept pressure on Army Group South to the end of the month, the principal effect of the order to counterattack was to pin Soviet units in exceedingly dangerous positions.[8] Against *West* and *Northwest Fronts,* the German Second, Third, and Fourth Panzer Groups rolled ahead. By 29 June, on the direct route to Moscow, Second and Third Panzer Groups and Fourth and Ninth Armies had closed two large encirclements around the *fronts,* east of Bialystok and east of Minsk, that would yield over three hundred thousand prisoners. In four more days, Third Panzer Group, under Generaloberst Herman Hoth, had a spearhead on the upper Dvina

---

[6]*Congressional Record,* 84th Cong., 2d sess., June 4, 1956, p. 9395.

[7]Zhukov, *Memoirs,* pp. 253–61.

[8]*IVMV,* vol. IV, p. 42.

River west of Vitebsk, and Second Pan-
zer Group, under Generaloberst Heinz
Guderian, had one approaching the
Dnepr near Mogilev. Army Group
North by then had cleared the line of
the Dvina upstream from Riga to the
army group boundary and had deep
bridgeheads north of the river. Army
Group South, still under pressure from
Southwest Front, had passed Rovno and
Lvov. Neither of the latter two had
executed encirclements like those of
Bialystok and Minsk but all had cov-
ered impressive distances: Army
Group Center, up to 285 miles; Army
Group North, 180 miles; Army Group
South, 120 miles.[9] In the meantime,
Finland had declared war on the Soviet
Union (on 25 June), and Army of Nor-
way had begun advances out of north-
ern Finland toward Murmansk and
Kandalaksha. *(Map 2.)*

Looking at the progress as of 3 July,
Halder concluded that "on the whole,
one can say already now that the mission of smashing the mass of the Soviet
Army forward of the Dvina and Dnepr
has been carried out. It is very likely
not saying too much when I observe
that the campaign against the Soviet
Union has been won in less than fourteen days."[10] Halder predicted that
beyond the Dvina and the Dnepr, the
job would be less to destroy the enemy's
forces than to take his means of production, and "thus to prevent him from
creating new armed forces out of his
powerful industrial base and his inexhaustible manpower reserves."[11]

The Soviet leadership, although
aware that its situation was desperate,
did not see itself as being as helpless as
Halder thought. Once it was clear to all
of its members that not only the third
directive of 22 June but the whole
previous concept of carrying the war to
the enemy's territory was a mistake—
and it was clear by the fourth day of
the invasion—the newly formed *Stavka*
set about developing an "active strategic defense." The objectives would be
to stop the enemy along the whole
front, to hold him and wear him down
while the strategic reserves were being
assembled, and then to shift to a "decisive strategic counteroffensive." To
accomplish the first two of these aims,
the Soviet Command would deploy the
second strategic echelon, provided for
in the state defense plan, behind the
first strategic echelon, already in action. The main effort was to be in the
center where four reserve armies
(thirty-seven divisions) would be
moved up to the Dnepr-Dvina line behind *West Front. Northwest Front* was to
use its reserves to build a line between
Pskov and Orlov, 160 miles south of
Leningrad, and *Southwest Front*, together with the right flank of *South
Front*, was to occupy and hold the "old"
Stalin Line fortifications on the
pre-1939 border.[12] The Soviet manpower that Halder was concerned
about was coming into play. An order
of the Presidium of the Supreme
Soviet, issued on 22 June, had called
up all reservists aged twenty-three to
thirty-seven and by 1 July, 5.3 million
had been mobilized.[13]

[9]*OKW, KTB*, vol. I, p. 1217; Kurt von Tippelskirch,
Geschichte des Zweiten Weltkrieges (Bonn: Athenaeum-
Verlag, 1956), pp. 181–88; Albert Seaton, *The Russo-
German War, 1941–1945* (New York: Praeger, 1971),
pp. 98–106, 116–225.
[10]*Halder Diary*, vol. III, p. 8.
[11]*Ibid.*, p. 39.

[12]Ivanov, *Nachalnyy period*, p. 273; *IVMV*, vol. IV, p.
44.
[13]*VOV*, pp. 106, 110; *IVMV*, vol. IV, p. 53.

In Moscow, on 30 June, Stalin created the State Defense Committee, the *GKO (Gosudarstvennyi Komitet Oborony),* which superseded the Defense Committee of the Council of People's Commissars and became the war cabinet that had been envisioned in the prewar plans. Stalin was the chairman; Molotov the deputy chairman; and the other members were Voroshilov and G. M. Malenkov, who was the party personnel chief and Stalin's right-hand man. The *GKO* was the highest wartime organ of the Soviet government, and its decrees had the force of law. Its authority encompassed both the military and civilian spheres, and the *Stavka* was subordinate to it, but the *GKO* concerned itself mainly with directing the nonmilitary aspects of the war effort.[14]

On the twelfth day of the war, 3 July, Stalin, who had made no prior public statement, addressed the nation by radio. He was obviously under strain. His voice was dull and slow. He sounded tired, and he could be heard pausing to drink water as he talked.[15] Addressing the people as "brothers and sisters" and "friends," he told them for the first time, after two and a half weeks in which government communiques had depicted the fighting as being confined to the border, that Soviet territory had been lost and that the Germans were advancing.[16] Reiterating instructions given to all party offices four days earlier, he called for evacuation and a scorched earth policy in threatened areas and partisan warfare in enemy-occupied territory. He asked the *kolkhoz* ("collective farm") peasants to drive their livestock eastward ahead of the Germans and the workers to follow their fellows in Moscow and Leningrad by organizing *opolcheniye* ("home guards") "in every town threatened with invasion." The speech emphasized the national rather than ideological character of the war and referred to Great Britain and the United States as "trustworthy partners" in a common struggle for "independent and democratic freedom."[17]

To Smolensk

As the battles of the frontiers ended in the first week of July, both sides' attention became fixed on three places, Leningrad, Moscow, and Kiev, and most particularly on Moscow. Flanking the Vitebsk Gate, a fifty-mile-wide gap between them, the upper Dvina and Dnepr rivers afforded the most defensible line west of the Soviet capital. Timoshenko had taken command of *West Front,* including the four reserve armies on the Dnepr River line, on 2

---

[14]Four members were added "a short while later": the Chief of the State Planning Commission, N. A. Voznesenskiy; and *Politburo* members N. A. Bulganin, L. M. Kaganovich, and I. A. Mikoyan. Institut Istorii SSSR, *Istoriya SSSR* (Moscow: Izdatelstvo "Nauka," 1973), vol. X, p. 30.

[15]Adam B. Ulam, *Stalin* (New York: Viking, 1973), p. 541.

[16]Alexander Werth, *Russia at War: 1941–1945* (New York: Dutton, 1964), pp. 162–65.

[17]*IVOVSS,* vol. II, p. 57. British Prime Minister Winston S. Churchill had pledged assistance to the Soviet Union on the day of the invasion, and President Franklin D. Roosevelt had opened the way for U.S. aid on 23 and 24 June. See Gwyer, *Grand Strategy,* vol. III, p. 89; Robert H. Jones, *The Roads to Russia: United States Lend-Lease to the Soviet Union* (Norman, Okla.: University of Oklahoma Press, 1969), pp. 35–37; Richard M. Leighton and Robert W. Coakley, *Global Logistics and Strategy, 1940–1943* (Washington, D.C.: GPO, 1955), p. 97.

July.[18] By then, Army Group Center had regrouped for the crossing. Generalfeldmarschall Guenther von Kluge's Headquarters, Fourth Army, renamed Fourth Panzer Army, had taken over Second and Third Panzer Groups, and an army headquarters from the reserve, Second Army, had assumed control of Kluge's infantry, which was then engaged with Ninth Army in mopping up the Minsk pocket. The panzer groups jumped off on 10 July, Hoth's Third Panzer Group north of the Vitebsk Gate and Guderian's Second Panzer Group south of it. In six days, one of Guderian's corps covered eighty miles and took Smolensk. Third Panzer Group went even farther, and Hoth had a spearhead at Yartsevo, thirty miles northeast of Smolensk, on 16 July. In between the corps' and groups' advances, an elongated pocket was forming around the Soviet *Sixteenth* and *Twentieth Armies*.[19]

In the meantime, on 10 July as the battle for the Dnepr River line was beginning, Stalin had emerged as the supreme commander of the Soviet armed forces. The *Stavka* of the High Command then became the *Stavka* of the Supreme Command with Stalin as chairman and the most experienced Soviet staff officer, Marshal Shaposhnikov, was added to the membership. (On 19 July, Stalin assumed the post of people's commissar of defense, and on 8 August he entered the military hierarchy with the title supreme high commander, whereupon the *Stavka* became the *Stavka* of the Supreme High Command.) Although directives and orders were issued in the names of *GKO* and the *Stavka* throughout the war, neither had any authority independent of Stalin. After he became supreme high commander, meetings of the whole *Stavka* apparently were infrequent, and Stalin used the members as personal advisers and assistants and the General Staff as his planning and executive agency. *Stavka* representation in the field, either by its members or by others acting under its authority, became an established feature of Soviet command technique. Zhukov, for instance, was almost always away from Moscow, either as a *Stavka* representative or in a major field command.[20]

Also on 10 July, the *GKO* authorized theater commands for the main "strategic directions" *(napravleniy):* the *Northwestern Theater,* under Voroshilov; the *Western Theater,* under Timoshenko; and the *Southwestern Theater,* under Budenny.[21] The theater commands corresponded roughly to the German army groups, but their roles appear to have been less clearly defined, and the *fronts* continued as the main operational commands.

In mid-July, the *Stavka* set up a reserve *front* of four armies behind *Northwest* and *West Fronts* on the Staraya Russa-Bryansk line and another of three armies flanking Mozhaysk, sixty miles west of Moscow. Not yet ready to regard the battle for the Dnepr-Dvina

[18]*IVMV,* vol. IV, p. 46. Pavlov had been recalled to Moscow at the end of June together with his chief of staff and deputy for political affairs. All three were court-martialed and shot. The commander of *Northwest Front,* Kuznetsov, and his chief of staff and deputy for political affairs also were relieved—but with less severe consequences. See Khrushchev, *Khrushchev Remembers,* p. 132 and Eremenko, *V nachale,* pp. 36–48.

[19]Tippelskirch, *Geschichte,* p. 191; *IVOVSS,* vol. II, p. 66; Seaton, *Russo-German War,* pp. 124–27.

[20]Zakharov, *50 let,* p. 267.

[21]*IVMV,* vol. IV, p. 53.

SS-Men Cross the Beresina River Alongside a Wrecked Bridge

line as lost, the *Stavka* diverted twenty divisions from the reserve armies for counterattacks from the north and the south against the prongs of the German pincers.[22] Mobilization was providing men to fill new units, but not enough officers qualified to staff and to command higher headquarters; consequently, the *Stavka* disbanded the corps headquarters on 15 July, leaving the armies in direct command of their divisions.

In part by design and in part out of necessity, the Soviet Army reorganized in July to a basis of smaller tactical units. Most rifle divisions were already 30 percent below authorized strengths, at between nine and ten thousand men,

and they were short 50 percent of their artillery, the equivalent of one regiment per division. Infantry brigades of forty-four hundred to six thousand men were a faster and cheaper means of bringing manpower to bear, and the army formed 159 of these between late July and the end of the year. During this period, motorized corps were broken down into tank divisions, brigades, and independent battalions, apparently because the field commands believed the armor would be more useful in direct infantry support than in large mobile formations. The authorized strength of a tank division (7 of which were formed in 1941) was 217 tanks; a brigade (76 formed in 1941), 93 tanks; and an independent battalion (100 formed in 1941), 29 tanks. The actual

---

[22]*IVOVSS*, vol, II, p. 69.

strengths of these tank units varied widely. The *8th Tank Brigade,* for instance, when activated in September 1941, had what it then considered a full complement: 61 tanks, 22 of them T–34s; 7 KVs; and 32 light tanks.[23]

Although the intensity of fighting increased through the second half of July, and Timoshenko launched several determined counterattacks, the battle for Smolensk and the Dnepr-Dvina line was lost. In the fourth week of the month, the panzer armies closed the pocket east of Smolensk. By then, Generaloberst Adolf Strauss' Ninth Army and Second Army, under Generaloberst Maximilian von Weichs, had broadened the bulge east of the rivers, and the *Stavka* had had to divide the frontage, giving the southern arc to a newly created Headquarters, *Central Front,* under Kuznetsov. On the 30th, Zhukov, whom Shaposhnikov had replaced the day before as chief of the General Staff, took over the reserve *fronts* behind *Northwest* and *West Fronts* and on the Mozhaysk line as the *Reserve Front.* The Germans liquidated the Smolensk pocket on 5 August and counted over three hundred thousand prisoners and three thousand captured or destroyed tanks. Soviet accounts maintain that *Sixteenth* and *Twentieth Armies* escaped practically intact.[24]

The North and South Flanks

During the month of the battle for the Dnepr-Dvina line and Smolensk, Army Groups North and South covered as much and more ground as Army Group Center, though less spectacularly. For Army Group North in the first week of August, Generaloberst Erich Hoepner had the point of Fourth Panzer Group approaching Luga, seventy miles south of Leningrad. On his right, Generaloberst Ernst Busch's Sixteenth Army was keeping contact with Army Group Center on the Dvina, and on his left, Eighteenth Army, under Generaloberst Georg von Kuechler, was clearing Estonia, the northernmost of the three Baltic States. A Finnish offensive begun on 10 July was tying down *North Front* forces, under General Popov, east of Lake Ladoga.[25]

Army Group South broke through the Stalin Line on the pre-1939 Soviet border at the end of the second week in July, and Generalfeldmarschall Walter von Reichenau's Sixth Army got to within ten miles of Kiev on the 11th. Thereafter Sixth Army advanced slowly on its left against stubborn resistance from Soviet *Fifth Army* under General Mayor M. I. Potapov and stretched its right flank to cover Generaloberst Ewald von Kleist's First Panzer Group as the latter drove south and southeast into the Dnepr bend. In the first week of August, Kleist and Generaloberst Carl-Heinrich von Stuelpnagel, commander of Seventeenth Army, maneuvered parts of two Soviet armies into a pocket between Uman and Pervomaysk and took over a hundred thousand prisoners. At Pervo-

[23]*IVMV,* vol. IV, p. 61; Ivanov, *Nachalnyy period,* p. 277; Tyushkevich, *Vooruzhennye sily,* pp. 281, 284; Krupchenko, *Tankovye voyska,* p. 33; M. V. Zakharov, ed., *Proval gitlerovskogo nastupleniya na Moskvu* (Moscow: Izdatelstvo "Nauka," 1966), p. 165.

[24]Seaton, *Russo-German War,* p. 130; Tippelskirch, *Geschichte,* p. 191. For the Soviet position on the two armies in the pocket, which varies somewhat among the sources but generally holds that they withdrew in good order, see *IVOVSS,* vol. II, p. 72; *IVMV,* vol. IV, p. 75; *VOV (Kratkaya Istoriya),* p. 76; and K. K. Rokossovskiy, *A Soldier's Duty* (Moscow: Progress Publishers, 1970), p. 39.

[25]Tippelskirch, *Geschichte,* pp. 192–94; *IVMV,* vol. IV, pp. 64–66.

maysk, Kleist's armor was in position to strike behind *South Front,* which, on the west, faced the Rumanian Third and Fourth Armies as adjuncts of the German Eleventh Army under Generaloberst Franz Ritter von Schobert. To avoid being trapped between the Germans and the Black Sea, General Tyulenev, commander of *South Front,* with the *Stavka's,* that is Stalin's, approval, began a retreat toward the Dnepr, leaving behind an independent force to cover Odessa.[26]

A Change in Plans

Meanwhile, the issue of the main effort side-stepped in the original BARBAROSSA plans, had raised a command crisis at the *Fuehrer* Headquarters. In two directives (numbers 33 and 34 of 19 and 30 July, respectively) and supplements to them, Hitler had given Leningrad and the Ukraine priority over Moscow as strategic objectives. He had also ordered Army Group Center to divert forces, particularly armor, to the north and the south on a scale that would practically halt the advance in the center after the fighting ended at Smolensk. The objective given in Directive 33 was "to prevent the escape of large enemy forces into the depths of the Russian territory and to annihilate them." In the final supplement, Hitler had added another: "to take possession of the Donets [Basin] and Kharkov industrial areas."[27]

The generals in the OKH, in the field, and even in the OKW, were dismayed at being told to turn to what they regarded as subsidiary objectives when it seemed the Soviet Command was clearly determined to make its decisive stand on the approaches to Moscow. During a month's debate, Hitler refused to change his mind except to settle for a weaker effort in the north, and on 21 August, he sent down orders that would dispatch Second Army and Second Panzer Group south into the Ukraine and divert a panzer corps and air support elements from Field Marshal Bock's Army Group Center to Army Group North.[28] Guderian, whom Halder and Bock thought Hitler might listen to as a tank expert, failed to get the orders changed in a last-minute interview on 23 August.[29]

The advances of Army Groups Center and South in July had, by early August wrapped their lines halfway around the Soviet forces standing at Kiev and along the Dnepr north and south of the city, creating a potential trap for almost the whole *Southwest Front.* Hitler, no doubt, had entrapment in mind, and Zhukov certainly also did. The danger was obvious, but Stalin could not bring himself to sacrifice Kiev, and after Zhukov proposed doing that, Stalin removed him as chief of the General Staff. On 4 August, Stalin ordered *Southwest* and *South Fronts* to hold the Kiev area and the line of the lower Dnepr. In midmonth, the *Stavka* set up the *Bryansk Front,* two armies under General Eremenko, between *Central Front* and *West Front.* Stalin's instructions

---

[26]Seaton, *Russo-German War,* pp. 136–40; *IVOVSS,* vol. II, pp. 98–103. See also K. S. Moskalenko, *Na yugo-zapadnom napravlenii* (Moscow: Izdatelstvo "Nauka," 1969), pp. 46–55.

[27]*Der Fuehrer und Oberste Befehlshaber der Wehrmacht, OKW, WFSt, Abt. L (I Op.) Nr. 44 1230/41, Weisung Nr. 33, 19.7.41; Nr. 44 1298/41, Weisung Nr. 34, 30.7.41; Nr. 44 1376, Ergaenzung der Weisung 34, 12.8.41,* German High Level Directives, CMH files.

[28]DA Pamphlet 20–261a, pp. 50–70.

[29]Heinz Guderian, *Panzer Leader* (New York: Dutton, 1952), pp. 198–200.

to Eremenko were to prevent the armor of Guderian's Second Panzer Group from breaking through toward Moscow. On the 19th, Shaposhnikov told Zhukov that he and Stalin now agreed with Zhukov's prediction of an attack to come south, off Army Group Center's flank. The *Stavka* passed the same information, which apparently was based on intelligence, to Budenny at Headquarters, *Southwestern Theater,* and to *Southwest* and *South Fronts* and simultaneously reiterated its previous orders to hold Kiev and the line of the lower Dnepr.[30]

Second Army and Second Panzer Group started south against the relatively weak forces of *Central Front* on 25 August. To make matters worse for it, Headquarters, *Central Front,* was just then, as the result of another *Stavka* decision, at the point of being deactivated and was turning its sector over to *Bryansk Front.* To check *Bryansk Front,* which might have endangered his flank and rear, Guderian left behind most of Second Panzer Group's infantry and a panzer corps. These units became Fourth Army under Kluge's headquarters, which had relinquished its panzer army designation. Guderian's course took him on an almost straight line toward Romny, 120 miles east of Kiev. When Guderian's point passed Konotop on 10 September, narrowing the open end of the bulge to less than 150 miles, Kleist's First Panzer Group struck north from a bridgehead at Kremenchug on the Dnepr. From then on, most of the Soviet troops in the bulge had farther to go to escape than the panzer groups did to close the encircle-

ment, and on the 11th, Budenny asked to withdraw *Southwest Front* from Kiev and the Dnepr upstream from Kremenchug. Stalin refused and sent Timoshenko to replace him. On the 16th, the German points met at Lokhvitsa, 25 miles south of Romny, and the Germans wiped out the pocket in another week, counting 665,000 prisoners. The *Short History* gives *Southwest Front's* strength as 677,085 men at the beginning of the battle and 150,541 at its end.[31]

Taifun

The Main Effort in the Center

Describing the advances in the north, toward Leningrad, and in the south, east of Kiev, as being about to create "the basis" on which Army Group Center could "seek a decision" against *West Front,* Hitler, on 6 September, issued Directive 35 for what became Operation TAIFUN ("typhoon"). Under the directive, the main effort would revert to Army Group Center at the end of the month, and by then it would have its detached panzer and air units returned along with reinforcements in armor from the other two army groups and the OKH reserves. Thereafter, Army Groups North and South would continue their operations with reduced strength. Army Group North would make contact with the Finns on the Isthmus of Karelia east of Leningrad and push across the Volkhov River to meet them

---

[30]Zhukov, *Memoirs,* pp. 289, 296; Eremenko, *Pomni Voyny,* p. 143; *VOV (Kratkaya Istoriya),* p. 90.

[31]Guderian, *Panzer Leader,* pp. 202–25; Tippelskirch, *Geschichte,* pp. 199–201; *IVOVSS,* vol. II, pp. 103–11; *IVMV,* vol. IV, p. 85; *VOV (Kratkaya Istoriya),* p. 91.

CREW OF 88-MM. GUN SEARCHES FOR TARGETS ON THE APPROACH TO KIEV

also east of Lake Ladoga.[32] Army Group South would continue east to take Kharkov and Melitopol and dispatch Eleventh Army south into the Crimea.[33]

In the last week of September, Army Group Center recalled Second and Third Panzer Groups and acquired Headquarters, Fourth Panzer Group, from Army Group North together with panzer corps from Army Groups North and South. By then, Army Group North had taken Schluessel-

burg on the Neva River at Lake Ladoga, thereby cutting Leningrad's contact by land with the Soviet interior, and Finnish forces had lines across the Isthmus of Karelia north of the city and on the Svir River east of Lake Ladoga. Army Group South had spearheads approaching Kharkov and closing up to Melitopol. Army Group Center held the line it had occupied east of Smolensk in August.

On the Soviet side, the commands for the northwestern and western theaters, whose functions the General Staff and the *Stavka* had assumed, had gone out of existence in August and September, leaving only Timoshenko's *Southwestern Theater*. In the far North, between Lake Onega and the Barents Sea, *Karelian Front*, under General Leytenant V. A. Frolov, was managing,

---

[32]Hitler had already ordered Army Group North to invest Leningrad but not enter it or accept a surrender if one were ordered. The city was to be left to starve. *OKW, WFSt, Abt. L(I Op.) Nr. 00 2119/41, Vortragsnotiz Leningrad, 21.9.41,* OKW/1938 file.

[33]*Der Fuehrer und Oberste Befehlshaber der Wehrmacht, OKW, WFSt, Abt. L(I Op.) Nr. 44 1492/41, 6.9.41,* German High Level Directives, CMH files.

WOMEN FIRE FIGHTERS KEEP LOOKOUT OVER THE ROOFTOPS OF LENINGRAD

aided by the approaching winter, to hold the Germans and Finns away from Murmansk and the Murmansk Railroad. Against Army Group North, *Leningrad Front,* with Zhukov in command after 10 September, defended Leningrad, and *Northwest Front,* under General Leytenant P. A. Kurochkin, held the line from Lake Ladoga south to Ostashkov. On the south flank, Timoshenko took personal command of *Southwest Front* on 26 September and, with it, *South Front,* and *Fifty-first Independent Army* on the Crimea, was responsible for the defense south of the level of Kursk. Against Army Group Center were ranged the *West Front,* under General Polkovnik Ivan Konev; Eremenko's *Bryansk Front;* and the *Reserve Front,* where Budenny had re-

placed Zhukov. The long pause in the center had given the *Stavka* time to rebuild the defense. The three *fronts* had a combined total of at least 1,250,000 men.[34] Army Group Center had more men, 1,929,000 but those included a large auxiliary contingent. The army group's combat effective strength of seventy-eight divisions would hardly have given it more than numerical equality.[35]

The March to Victory?

The quiet west of Moscow ended on 2 October. In bright fall sunshine, Army Group Center's tanks roared

[34]*IVMV,* vol. IV, pp. 93, 110–19.
[35]Klaus Reinhardt, *Die Wende vor Moskau* (Stuttgart: Deutsche Verlags-Anstalt, 1972), p. 57.

eastward once more. Konev and Eremenko had *West Front* and *Bryansk Front,* respectively, concentrated west of Vyazma, on the direct route to Moscow, and west of Bryansk.[36] Bock's armor, Third Panzer Group on the north, Fourth Panzer Group in the center, and Second Panzer Group on the south, went around the outer flanks and between the two Soviet groupings. Within a week they had encircled six Soviet armies west of Vyazma and were forcing almost the entire *Bryansk Front,* three armies, into pockets southwest and northeast of Bryansk. Halder described the performance as "downright classical."[37] The German final count of prisoners from the Vyazma pocket was 663,000 and from those near Bryansk about one hundred thousand.[38] But the results of the operations in the extensive forests around Bryansk were not quite "classical." The fighting tied down parts of Second Army and Second Panzer Group until late in the third week of the month, and many of Eremenko's troops eventually either made their way out to Soviet territory or hid in the deep woods where the Germans would later have to contend with them again as partisans.[39]

Zhukov, hurriedly recalled from Leningrad where he had succeeded in stabilizing the front, took over the combined *West* and *Reserve Fronts* on 10 October. His assignment was to man the Mozhaysk line with survivors from the Vyazma pocket, recent conscripts, and a sprinkling of seasoned troops

rushed from other sectors and Siberia. The Mozhaysk line, however, began to crumble on the 14th when Third Panzer Group took Kalinin. On the 17th, the *Stavka* set up *Kalinin Front* under Konev to take over Zhukov's right flank and to narrow his responsibility to only the direct western and southwestern approaches to Moscow. Around the capital, civilians, mostly women, were building three semicircular defense lines, and in the city, workers' militia battalions were preparing to man the lines.[40] While the most intensive Soviet effort was directed toward Moscow's defense, the main German thrusts were aimed past it. On the north, in the second week of October, Third Panzer Group had headed toward Yaroslavl, and Second Panzer Group had been coming from the southwest on a line taking it via Orel and Mtsensk (which it reached on 12 October) toward Tula, Ryazan, and Gorkiy. On 12 October, Hitler had given the same order for Moscow he had given for Leningrad: German troops were to surround the city and to starve it out of existence. No German soldier was to set foot in Moscow until hunger and disease had done their work.[41] *(Map 3.)*

The crisis came in the second and third weeks of October 1941. Loss of Kalinin, on the 14th, set off panic and looting in Moscow and gave rise to symptoms of disintegration among the troops. On the 19th, the State Defense Committee put Moscow under a state of siege. At the front, Zhukov says with astringent understatement, "A rigid order was established. . . . Stern mea-

[36]*IVMV,* vol. IV, p. 94.

[37]*Halder Diary,* vol. III, p. 268.

[38]Tippelskirch, *Geschichte,* p. 206; Guderian, *Panzer Leader,* p. 238.

[39]Reinhardt, *Moskau,* pp. 63–67.

[40]*IVOVSS,* vol. II, pp. 240–47; *IVMV,* vol. IV, pp. 97–100.

[41]*OKW, KTB,* vol. I, p. 1070.

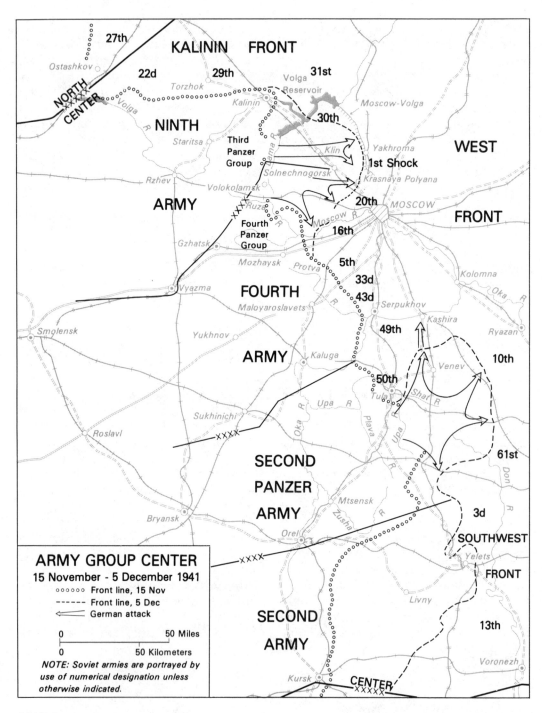

KALININ FRONT

27th
22d
29th
31st
30th

Ostashkov
Torzhok
Volga Reservoir
Moscow-Volga

NORTH
CENTER

Volga
Staritsa
Kalinin
Klin
Yakhroma

WEST

NINTH

Third
Panzer
Group
1st Shock

Rzhev
Volokolamsk
Solnechnogorsk
Krasnaya Polyana

ARMY

Ruza
Moscow R.
20th
MOSCOW

FRONT

Fourth
Panzer
Group
16th

Gzhatsk
Moscow

Mozhaysk
Protva
5th

Kolomna

FOURTH
33d
43d

Oka R.

Smolensk
Maloyaroslavets
Serpukhov
Kashira
Ryazan

Vyazma
Yukhnov
49th

ARMY
Kaluga
Venev
10th

Sukhinichi
50th
Tula
Shat R.

Roslavl
Upa R.
Plava R.
Upa

61st

SECOND
Don R.

PANZER
Mtsensk

ARMY
3d

Bryansk
Orel
SOUTHWEST

Yelets

FRONT

ARMY GROUP CENTER
13th

15 November - 5 December 1941

○○○○○○ Front line, 15 Nov

- - - - - Front line, 5 Dec
Livny

⇐ German attack

SECOND

0	50 Miles
0	50 Kilometers

ARMY

NOTE: Soviet armies are portrayed by
use of numerical designation unless
otherwise indicated.

Kursk
CENTER
Voronezh

Zusha R.

MAP 3

sures were introduced to prevent breaches of discipline."[42] The diplomatic corps and most of the government offices were evacuated to Kuibyshev. Hitler's address on 3 October opening the "Winter Relief" program had already sounded like a victory speech, and on the 9th, Dr. Otto Dietrich, secretary of state in the Propaganda Ministry and chief press spokesman, had told the Berlin foreign press corps that the campaign in the East was "decided."[43] On the 10th, the OKW had called off Army of Norway operations out of northern Finland because it believed the war was about over on the main front.[44] Much of the world, the British and United States governments especially, wanted to believe otherwise, but to do so, except as a desperate act of faith, hardly seemed reasonable. The U.S. military attache in Moscow had reported on 10 October that it seemed "the end of Russian resistance is not far away."[45] The British government had suspected the end might be near in September, before TAIFUN began, when Stalin had called urgently on the British and the Americans for a second front on the Continent and, failing that, had asked for twenty-five to thirty British divisions to fight in Russia.[46]

Bad as the Soviet situation looked, it was, for the moment, actually worse than either the Germans or the Western Allies imagined. Four months of war and territorial losses had reduced Soviet productive capacity by 63 percent in coal, 68 percent in iron, 58 percent in steel, and 60 percent in aluminum. In October, after having risen during the summer, Soviet war production also dropped drastically, probably by 60 percent or more.[47] During October the Moscow and Donets industrial complexes had to shut down and to begin evacuating. (The decline continued into November and December, during which months the Moscow and Donets basins did not deliver "a single ton" of coal, the output of rolled ferrous metals fell to a third of that of June 1941, and ball bearing output was down by 95 percent.)[48] W. Averell Harriman, U.S. lend-lease expediter, who had been in Moscow at the end of September, had accepted a shopping list from Stalin for a billion dollars in lend-lease supplies, but their delivery would take months.

On 18 October, Fourth Panzer Group, having pushed past Mozhaysk and Kaluga, began turning to skirt Moscow on the north and to open the way for Fourth Army's infantry to execute the encirclement. Fourth Army, anticipating a similar assist on its right from Second Panzer Group, had issued the orders for the encirclement on the 16th and had set the line of the Moscow belt railroad as the closest approach to the city.[49] At the speeds they had attained in the early days of the month, the tanks of Hoepner's Fourth Panzer Group would have been less than two days' from Moscow when they passed Mozhaysk, but they were not moving as fast as they had before.

[42]Zhukov, *Memoirs*, p. 331.

[43]Domarus, *Hitler*, vol. II, pp. 1758–67.

[44]*AOK Norwegen, Befehlsstelle Finnland, Ia Kriegstagebuch, 3.6.41–13.1.42*, 10 Oct 41, AOK 20 35198/1 file.

[45]Sherwood, *Roosevelt and Hopkins*, p. 395.

[46]Gwyer, *Grand Strategy*, vol. III, pt. I, pp. 197–201.

[47]Platonov, *Vtoraya Mirovaya Voyna*, p. 243; *IVOVSS*, vol. II, pp. 158–60.

[48]Voznesenskiy, *Economy of the USSR*, p. 23.

[49]First and Second Panzer Groups were elevated to full army status on 5 October.

Mud and Frustration

The Germans were having their first encounter with the *rasputitsa*. The first snow fell on the night of 6 October. From then on, alternating rain and snow and the pounding of tanks and trucks turned the roads into ever deeper quagmires of mud. By the end of the third week in the month, Fourth Panzer Group's and Second Panzer Army's (Second Panzer Group elevated to army status, 5 October 1941) spearhead divisions had become stretched out over twenty-five to thirty miles, and the infantry was sometimes outdistancing the tanks. Third Panzer Group contemplated dismounting the tank crews and going ahead on foot and with *panje* wagons, the Russian peasants' one-horse carts. Meanwhile, dismayingly strong counterattacks on Third Panzer Group at Kalinin and on Second Panzer Army along the Zusha River at Mtsensk had demonstrated that even though aerial reconnaissance reports showed Moscow being evacuated, the Russians would not give up the city without a fight.[50]

Because of the weather, the Russians, for almost the first time in the war, were able to meet their enemy on nearly equal terms. The Germans, moving slowly and confined to the roads, could be confronted head-on and forced to fight for every mile. The Soviet T–34 tanks, which had been too few to influence the fast-moving encirclement battles, came into their own. Having wider tracks than the German tanks made them more buoyant in the mud. Their heavy armament and ar-

mor allowed one or two T–34s in a roadblock to stop an advance until the Germans could bring up either 88-mm. antiaircraft guns or 10-cm. field guns, the only reasonably mobile artillery pieces capable of cracking the T–34's armor. Both weapons, though, especially the 88s, were heavy and bulky, hence vulnerable, and aggravatingly difficult to move over rutted, potholed roads.

At the end of October, Army Group Center was practically at a standstill on a line from Kalinin to the Oka River west of Tula, its center thirty-five miles from Moscow. Army Group North had, in the meantime, given up on closing the siege line around Leningrad west of Lake Ladoga in September, after the Finns— whose Commander in Chief, Marshal Mannerheim, had scruples about further involving his troops in operations against Leningrad because he had pledged in 1918 not to use the border on the Isthmus of Karelia to attack the city—declined to push any farther south. Being left then holding an uncomfortable six-mile-wide "bottleneck" east of Schluesselburg, Field Marshal Leeb, commander of Army Group North, on Hitler's orders, had begun a thrust east on 14 October aimed from Chudovo northeast past Tikhvin to the Finnish line on the lower Svir River. This drive also had slowed, and at the end of the month, the *rasputitsa* stopped it short of Tikhvin. In the last week of October Army Group South managed to take Kharkov and Stalino and to break through the Perekop Isthmus into the Crimea before the *rasputitsa* also stopped it.[51]

---

[50]Guderian, *Panzer Leader*, pp. 233–44; DA Pamphlet 20–261a, pp. 79–81.

[51]See Earl F. Ziemke, *The German Northern Theater of Operations, 1940–45* (Washington, D.C.: GPO, 1959), pp. 200–02; Tippelskirch, *Geschichte*, pp. 202–06.

MOVING SUPPLIES IN THE RAINY SEASON

As seen from the Soviet side, the German frustration, welcome as it was, did not lessen the mortal threats hanging over the country. If Army Group North reached Tikhvin, it would cut the one railline to the south shore of Lake Ladoga and thereby further isolate Leningrad. At Stalino, Army Group South almost had control of the industry and coal mines of the Donets Basin. The panzer units northeast and south of Moscow were poised to devastate the industrial heart of central Russia and to leave the Soviet forces from the Arctic to the Caucasus hanging at the ends of a disconnected railroad system.

Early on the morning of 7 November, the twenty-fourth anniversary of the Communist Revolution, Stalin reviewed an impromptu parade for the occasion from his accustomed stand atop the Lenin mausoleum. In his address to the troops, most of whom would go directly from Red Square to the front, he called on them to emulate the old Russian national heroes—Alexander Nevskiy who had defeated the Teutonic Knights in the thirteenth century; Dimitry Donskoi who had defeated the Tatars a century later; and Alexander Suvorov and Mikhail Kutuzov who had served the tsars against the French Revolution and Napoleon. In a speech to the Moscow Communist Party organization the night before, he had adopted a similar Russian nationalist tone. He had also told the party leaders about the recent billion-dollar-lend-lease agreement—while blaming the defeats so far on the absence of a second front in the West.

In both days' speeches he predicted
Hitler's ultimate defeat but did not
comment on the probable outcome of
the current campaign. Before the party
audience, he repeatedly spoke of the
coalition with Britain and the United
States as the guarantee of ultimate victory.[52]

As Stalin looked out over Red
Square on the 7th, where light snow
and freezing cold signaled the end of
the *rasputitsa*, the future must have
appeared dark to him. Within days, the
soldiers marching before him could be
trapped in a pocket with Moscow at its
center. He himself could become a ref-
ugee, not only driven out of Moscow,
the world capital of communism, but
into the eastern fringe of European
Russia. Evidently, he regarded these
possibilities as grimly potential realities. The *Stavka* had started forming
nine reserve armies on a line from
Vytegra on the southeastern tip of
Lake Onega to the Rybinsk Reservoir
and from there east and south along
the Volga River.[53] If the *Stavka* contemplated having to defend that line,
the future must have appeared dark
indeed. When it was reached, the
Leningrad and Moscow industrial regions would have been occupied, and
the Soviet Union could be eliminated
as a military power. Stalin had almost
said as much the previous summer in

telling Hopkins, the U.S. lend-lease negotiator, that a German advance of 150
miles—to the east of Leningrad,
Moscow, and Kiev—would destroy 75
percent of existing Soviet industrial capacity.[54]

Toward the end of the first week in
November, the front was beginning to
stir again, on the flanks, though not yet
in the center. Army Group North, after
having been almost ready to fall back to
the Volkhov River the week before,
raised enough momentum in the mud
and against constantly stiffening Soviet
resistance to take Tikhvin on the 8th.
Leeb observed that "[Leningrad] is
now also cut off from contact across
Lake Ladoga."[55] In the south, Eleventh
Army, under General der Infanterie
Fritz-Erich von Manstein, who had
taken command in September after
Schobert died in an airplane accident,
cleared the Crimea by 8 November
except for the Kerch Peninsula in the
east and the Sevastopol fortress on the
west.[56] At Army Group Center, Bock
had issued an order on 30 October for
TAIFUN to resume, and he was waiting
impatiently for the weather and
ground conditions to improve.[57]

In the second week of November, as
the weather began to clear and the
ground to freeze, the armor could
move again. The OKH and the field
commands contemplated a troublesome question raised by the time

[52]*IVOVSS*, vol. II, pp. 252–54; Werth, *Russia at War*, pp. 244–49.

[53]*VOV (Kratkaya Istoriya)*, p. 124; *IVOVSS*, vol. II, p. 257. The *VOV (Kratkaya Istoriya)* and *IVMV* (vol. IV, p. 280) state that ten reserve armies were being formed and imply that *First Shock* and *Twentieth Armies* were among them. *IVOVSS* gives the number as nine, not including *First Shock* and *Twentieth Armies*, and lists them as *Tenth*, *Twenty-sixth*, and *Fifty-seventh Armies* (formed in later October) and *Twenty-eighth*, *Thirty-ninth*, *Fifty-eighth*, *Fifty-ninth*, *Sixtieth*, and *Sixty-first* (formed in the first half of November).

[54]Sherwood, *Roosevelt and Hopkins*, p. 338.

[55]Wilhelm Ritter von Leeb, *Tagebuchaufzeichnungen und Lagebeurteilungen aus zwei Weltkriegen* (Stuttgart: Deutsche Verlags-Anstalt, 1976), pp. 381–89.

[56]DA Pamphlet 20–261a, p. 81. See also Erich von Manstein, *Lost Victories* (Chicago: Henry Regnery, 1958), pp. 205, 220–22.

[57]*H. Gr. Mitte, Ia Nr. 2250/41, Befehl fuer die Fortsetzung der Operationen*, 30.10.41, Pz. AOK 4 22457/14 file.

lost in the *rasputitsa:* where to stop for the winter? The invasion plans and preparations had not included continuing active operations into the winter, but all levels of command had assumed the campaign would be successfully completed in 1941. On 7 November, Hitler conceded to Field Marshal Brauchitsch, commander in chief of the army, that the German Army could not reach such vital objectives in the Soviet Union as Murmansk, the Volga River, and the Caucasus oil fields during 1941.[58] Speaking in Munich the next day, the anniversary of the 1923 Beer Hall Putsch, Hitler called *blitzkrieg* an "idiotic word" and declared himself ready to carry the war into 1942 and beyond—to the "last battalion," if necessary.[59] The dream of a single-season victory had vanished, and winter winds were beginning to blow through the Russian forests and across the steppes. Halder had told Colonel Adolf Heusinger, his chief of operations, on 5 November, that the Germans needed some basis on which to close out the current campaign.[60]

What such a basis could be appeared different to each of the principals involved. Leeb had exhausted his reserves getting to Tikhvin, could not go forward, was not inclined to go backward, and described Army Group North as existing "from hand to mouth."[61] Bock had severe doubts about how much further he could go but, recalling the fateful consequences of the German decision to stop on the Marne in September 1914, he did not want to miss whatever chance of taking

Moscow still existed. He could not, for the moment, imagine anything worse than having to sit out the winter just thirty-five miles from Moscow with the Russians in unimpaired control of the city and the half-dozen railroads running into it from the north, south, and east.[62] Field Marshal Rundstedt, commander of Army Group South, called on the OKH to let him stop the army group where it was to conserve its remaining strength after the long summer's march and to give him time to rebuild for the next spring. Halder saw the possibilities as falling into two categories: one he called an *Erhaltungsgedanken* in which conservation of strength was the determinant; the other a *Wirkungsgedanken* in which exploitation of the existing strength to achieve the maximum effect in the time remaining would be the determinant. The two he maintained, would have to be weighed and balanced against each other and the results converted into guidance for the field commands.[63]

On 7 November, Halder sent each army group and army chief of staff a copy of an eleven-page top secret document and a map with notice to "the Gentlemen Chiefs of Staff" that both options would be the subject of a General Staff conference to be held in about a week at Orsha. The map (of European Russia) had two north-south lines drawn on it. One was designated "the farthest boundary still to be attempted"; the other "the minimum

[58]*Halder Diary,* vol. III, p. 283.
[59]Domarus, *Hitler,* vol. II, pp. 1776, 1778.
[60]*Halder Diary,* vol. III, p. 281.
[61]Leeb, *Tagebuchaufzeichnungen,* p. 391.

[62]See Alfred W. Turney, *Disaster at Moscow* (Albuquerque: University of New Mexico Press, 1970), pp. 130–33 and *Halder Diary,* vol. III, p. 287.
[63]*H. Gr. Sued, Ia Nr. 2090/41, an den Chef des Generalstabes der 1. Pz. Armee 4.11.41,* Pz. AOK 1 58682 file; *Halder Diary,* vol. III, pp. 281, 285.

boundary." The "farthest boundary" ran from Vologda on the north via Gorkiy and Stalingrad to Maykop. It would cut central Russia off from railroad contact with the northern ports, Murmansk and Arkhangelsk, and with the Caucasus, and it would bring in hand the entire Moscow industrial complex, the upper and middle Volga, and the Maykop oil fields. Whether this action would end the war was doubtful, but it would, as Halder saw it, bring German forces into an alignment they could maintain indefinitely, "in case the highest leadership should decide against resuming the attack in the East later." The "minimum boundary" terminated in the north on the middle Svir River, 30 miles east of Lake Ladoga, and on the south at Rostov, at the mouth of the Don River; in the center, it passed 160 miles east of Moscow. It would provide a secure tie-in with the Finnish Army on the Svir, bring Moscow and the cluster of industrial cities to the northeast between Rybinsk and Yaroslavl under control, cut all the railroads running toward Moscow from the east, and position Army Group South for later advances to Stalingrad and the Caucasus. But it would still be an interim, not a final boundary, and another offensive would be needed to bring in Vologda, Gorkiy, Stalingrad, and the oil at Maykop and Baku.[64]

Halder and his branch chiefs for operations, organization, intelligence, and supply arrived at Orsha, in the Army Group Center zone on the night of 12 November aboard a special train.

The General Staff conference began the next morning at 1000 and ran through the day and into the night. Halder's own thinking, in which he said Hitler had concurred, inclined strongly toward the *Wirkungsgedanken*.[65] He had given the chiefs his position in the paper he sent with the map. The objective, before closing out the current offensive, he had stated, should at least be to get favorable starting positions for 1942 while "minimizing" the danger of the troops' being caught unprepared by the winter. In fact, he had added, it would be worthwhile "to take some risks" before the onset of winter to get to the "farthest boundary" or at least the "minimum boundary."[66]

At the Orsha meeting, Halder argued that carrying the offensive at least to the minimum boundary was necessary as well as advantageous. The "fundamental idea" of the campaign, he said, had been to defeat the Soviet Union in 1941. This was no longer "one hundred percent attainable" for various reasons, among them "natural forces," but primarily because of the enemy's "astonishing" military and material strength. Even though the Soviet Union was weakened "by at least fifty percent," its remaining potential was so great that it could not yet be dismissed as a military threat and simply "kept under observation" as had been intended. Consequently, the East would remain an active theater of war into the next year, and that raised problems. For one, he explained, the OKH had been aware from the first that the forces assembled for BARBAROSSA could

---

[64]*Lebenswichtige russ. Rue-industrien u. Verkehrslinien sowie anzustrebende Operationsziele, Karte 1,* AOK 18 35945/1 file. See also Earl F. Ziemke, "Franz Halder at Orsha," *Military Affairs,* 39(1975), 173–76.

[65]See *Halder Diary,* vol. III, p. 283.
[66]*Der Chef des Generalstabes des Heeres, Op. Abt., Ia Nr. 1630/41, 7.11.41,* AOK 18 35945/1 file.

not be sustained beyond the end of 1941, which meant that personnel losses thus far could not be replaced in the coming year, and cutbacks in motor vehicle allotments would reduce mobility. The Soviet Union, on the other hand, still had enough men and industry to rebuild its forces by the summer of 1942 if it could survive until then. Consequently, the German Army would still have to "strive to" inflict enough damage on the enemy before the end of 1941 "so that the troops will not have to pay in blood next year for what is neglected now."[67]

The chiefs of staff, for their part, reminded Halder of some things he already knew very well. German casualties stood, as of 1 November, at 686,000 men—20 percent of the 3.4 million, including replacements, committed since June, the equivalent of one regiment in every division. Of half-a-million motor vehicles on the Eastern Front, a third were worn out or damaged beyond repair; only a third were fully serviceable. Panzer divisions were down to 35 percent of their original tank strengths. The OKH itself rated the 136 divisions on the Eastern Front as equivalent to no more than 83 full-strength divisions. All of these conditions could only get worse if operations continued—and one other, namely, that of logistics, would get much worse. Every mile the armies moved eastward put an added strain on the railroads. Winter clothing for the troops was already having to be left in storage because it could not be brought forward without cutting off other supplies. German equipment could not

run on the Soviet railroads until the tracks were relaid to the standard gauge; and in the entire territory occupied thus far only 500 Soviet locomotives and 21,000 cars had been captured, barely a tenth of what was needed.[68]

The chiefs' estimates of what might still be accomplished were equally bleak. Generalmajor Kurt Brennecke, Leeb's chief of staff, told Halder that Leeb's command, Army Group North, had no divisions for a drive east and could acquire these only by first eliminating the Soviet *Eighth Army,* which it had confined in a pocket west of Leningrad. Brennecke noted that Halder did not mention Vologda again. Bock's chief, Generalmajor Hans von Greiffenberg, was cold to a suggestion from Halder that Army Group Center not resume the advance toward Moscow for two weeks or so to let strength accumulate for a deeper thrust. Generalmajor George von Sodenstern, the Army Group South chief of staff, pointed out that Rundstedt believed an advance to Maykop, if it were undertaken after the long march already made, would remove his only large armored unit, First Panzer Army, from action for most of the next year.[69]

After dinner on the evening of the 13th, Halder gave his conception of the meeting's results. He had concluded, he said, that the extensive operations he had proposed on 7 November and in the morning session could no longer

---

[67]*H. Gr. Nord, Der Chef des Generalstabes, Ia Nr. 769/41, 21.11.41,* AOK 18 35945/1 file.

[68]*Ibid.; Halder Diary,* vol. III, p. 286; *OKW, KTB,* vol. IV, pp. 1074–75.

[69]*H. Gr. Nord, Der Chef des Generalstabes, Ia Nr. 769/41, 21.11.41,* AOK 18 35945/1 file. See *Halder Diary,* p. 287. H. Gr. Sued, Der Chef des Generalstabes, Ia Nr. 2123/41, Vortragsnotiz, AOK 6 181117 file.

be considered. Nevertheless, he believed that the army groups would still have to get as much as possible from their troops until about mid-December. Army Group South would have to push ahead, though "apparently" not as far as Stalingrad. Army Group Center would not gain "substantial" ground beyond Moscow, but it would still, at least, have to "achieve a stronger pressure" on the city. Army Group North would be expected to resume its drive at Tikhvin, close in on Leningrad, and assist the Finnish Army east of Lake Ladoga. Vologda, Gorkiy, Stalingrad, and Maykop would have to be left for the next summer, when "the Russians [would] have a plus in strength and we a minus."[70] On the other hand, Guderian's chief of staff, Lt. Col. Kurt von Liebenstein, alluding to the 1940 campaign, had already reminded Halder that the war was not being fought in France and the month was not May.[71]

---

[70]*H. Gr. Sued, Der Chef des Generalstabes, Ia Nr. 2123/41, Vortragsnotiz,* AOK 6 181117 file; *H. Gr. Nord, Der Chef des Generalstabes, Ia Nr. 769/41, 21.11.41,* AOK 18 35945/1 file.

[71]Guderian, *Panzer Leader,* p. 247.

CHAPTER III

To Moscow

On the Defensive in the Heartland

The Soviet literature describes the strategic situation at the time of the November lull in somewhat contradictory terms. The official accounts maintain that Soviet resistance brought the Germans to a stop west of Moscow and dismiss the effect of the weather as a German excuse for failure, perpetuated by "falsifiers of history."[1] On the other hand, they indicate that the effect of the Soviet success was temporary, and the initiative remained entirely the Germans'. The picture, then, is one in which the Soviet armies fought the enemy to a total standstill and gained a brief respite. As the *Popular Scientific Sketch* gives it, the enemy needed two weeks to prepare his next moves, and the pause allowed the Soviet Command to reinforce the front and consolidate the Moscow defenses.[2]

The Soviet Condition

For the Soviet Command, as for the German, the crucial strategic consideration in early November, aside from the approach of winter, which was as welcome on the Soviet side as it was unwelcome on the German, was the relative state of the two forces. The manpower and material that had kept the Soviet Union in the war thus far, despite enormous losses, were sufficient to sustain another round of operations.[3] As of 1 December the Soviet armies in the field would have 4.2 million men, a slight numerical superiority in armor over the Germans, approximate equality with them in aircraft, and a small inferiority in artillery and mortars.[4]

The Germans substantially underestimated the Soviet strength. Estimates given to the chiefs of staff on 13

---

[1]*VOV (Kratkaya Istoriya)*, p. 122; *IVOVSS*, vol. II, p. 250; *IVMV*, vol. IV, pp. 98–101.

[2]See Zhukov, *Memoirs*, p. 337; *VOV*, p. 99.

[3]The Soviet literature provides virtually no information on Soviet losses and, except in the instance of the Kiev battle, dismisses the German counts as vastly exaggerated. However, if, as a scattering of figures indicates, 461 divisions were committed to the campaign between June and December (170 divisions were in the frontier military districts on 22 June 1941, and 291 divisions were committed from the *Stavka* reserves between 22 June and 1 December) and only 279 of these divisions were in the field in early December, then the divisions lost alone could have totaled 182, or 39 percent. Since not all of the divisions and other units employed in the campaign were either in place on 22 June or deployed from *Stavka* reserves thereafter, this number would have to be regarded as the minimum possible loss. The military districts, *fronts,* and armies undoubtedly mobilized a number of other divisions and units during this period. Additionally, peoples' militia divisions and so-called independent regiments and battalions, numbering about two million men, were recruited in the threatened areas. What became of them is impossible to determine. See V. Zemskov, *"Nekotoriye voprosy sozdaniya i ispolzovaniya strategicheskikh rezervov,"* M. Kazakov, *"Sozdaniya i ispolzovaniye strategicheskikh rezervov,"* and V. Golubovich, *"Sozdaniya strategicheskikh rezervov,"* *Voyenno-istoricheskiy zhurnal,* 3(1971), 12–16; 12(1972), 45–49; 41(1977), 10–13, respectively.

[4]*VOV (Kratkaya Istoriya)*, p. 129.

KV Tank Headed for the Front Rumbles Through Pushkin Square, Moscow

November at the Orsha Conference put the totals of Soviet larger units at 160 divisions and 40 brigades and rated their combat effectiveness at below 50 percent because more than half of those units' troops and officers were believed to be untrained.[5] The actual numbers as of 1 December, according to the Soviet sources, would be 279 divisions and 93 brigades. In part, these units, particularly those from the reserves, lacked training and experience. Interspersed among them, however, was a growing core of seasoned divisions. The individual principally, though indirectly, responsible for this increase in readiness was the Soviet

agent, Richard Sorge. He had apparently supplied enough information on Japanese plans to let the Soviet Command begin shifting some forces west even before 22 June.[6] Through Sorge, Stalin had undoubtedly then known about a Japanese decision of 30 June to uphold its neutrality treaty of April 1941 with the Soviet Union and to risk war with the United States.[7] By the fall, Stalin had either become convinced of Sorge's reliability or desperate enough (or both) to redeploy more troops from the east to the west. Some had appeared at the front in October, more in

[5]H. Gr. Nord, Der Chef des Generalstabes, Ia Nr. 769/41, Niederschrift ueber die Besprechung beim Chef des Gen-StdH am 13.11.41, AOK 18 35945/1 file.

[6]Golubovich, "Sozdaniya strategicheskikh," p. 17; VOV (Kratkaya Istoriya), p. 69; VOV, vol. I.

[7]Institut fuer Zeitgeschichte, Deutsche Geschichte seit dem ersten Weltkrieg (Stuttgart: W. Kohlhammer, 1973), vol. II, p. 115.

November. The *Stavka* had held most troops back from the front to stiffen the reserve armies being formed. By 1 December it had transferred 70 divisions from the Soviet Far East and had brought another 27 divisions out of Central Asia and the Transcaucasus. Together these units constituted at least 30 percent of the total strategic reserves committed during the 1941 campaign.[8]

Departing from previous practice, Stalin did not commit his main reserves when the German advance resumed. The reserve armies were still being formed, and it is possible that Stalin had not yet decided to undertake an all-out stand at Moscow. Nevertheless, in Stalin's view, the defense of the Moscow area would remain the paramount strategic requirement. (So far during the campaign—June through November—Stalin had committed 150 divisions, 51 percent of the *Stavka*'s total divisional reserves, in the *West Front* zone.) In late October, *West Front*, under General Zhukov, had received 11 rifle divisions, 16 tank brigades, and 40 artillery regiments from the reserve and from other *fronts*. Then in the first half of November, it acquired 100,000 troops, 300 tanks, and 2,000 artillery pieces. Meanwhile, workers from Moscow and surrounding cities had been recruited to form 12 militia divisions and 4 line rifle divisions. On 10 November Zhukov took over *Fiftieth Army* from *Bryansk Front*, which was being deactivated, and a week later he acquired *Thirtieth Army* from *Kalinin Front*. These extensions of his flanks

gave him control from just south of Kalinin to Tula.[9]

In mid-November, before the weather changed and the lull ended, the *Stavka* had incorporated almost all of its forces into the defense of Moscow. *West Front* was to hold the direct approaches and to counter anticipated strong-armored thrusts west of Klin and at Tula. *Kalinin Front*, commanded by General Konev, and *Southwest Front*, under Marshal Timoshenko, were to pin down Army Group Center's outer flanks and thus prevent its commander, Field Marshal Bock, from shifting more weight toward Moscow. *South Front*, commanded by General Polkovnik Ya. T. Cherevichenko, and *Leningrad Front*, under General Leytenant M. S. Khozin, had orders to ready offensives near Rostov and at Tikhvin, respectively, to draw enemy reserves away from the center.[10]

The German November Offensive

In the second week of November, Army Group Center retained the same general deployment it had had at the beginning of the lull. Ninth Army, under General Strauss, held the line from the North-Center boundary, west of Ostashkov, to Kalinin. Third Panzer Group, under Generaloberst Hans Reinhardt, who had replaced General Hoth in October, stood on the Lama River, thirty miles west of Klin, with Fourth Panzer Group, under General Hoepner, on its right in a sector north of the Smolensk-Moscow highway. Un-

---

[8] Zemskov, *"Nekotoriye voprosy sozdaniya i ispolzovaniya strategicheskikh rezervov,"* p. 14. See also p. 42.

[9] Kazakov, *"Sozdaniya i ispolzovaniya strategicheskikh rezervov,"* p. 48; *VOV,* p. 99; *IVMV,* vol. IV, p. 104; A. Sinitsyn, *"Iz istorii sozdaniya dobrovolcheskikh chastey i soyedineniy Sovetskoy Armii,"* *Voyenno-istoricheskiy Zhurnal,* 1(1973), 11–15.

[10] *VOV (Kratkaya Istoriya),* p. 124.

der Field Marshal Kluge, Fourth Army's left flank straddled the highway and its right tied in with Second Panzer Army, under General Guderian, on the Oka River. Second Panzer Army's main weight of armor was concentrated in a salient projecting eastward south of Tula. Second Army, commanded by General Weichs, covered the south flank east of Orel and Kursk. Against these, *Kalinin Front, West Front,* and the right flank of *Southwest Front* had twelve armies.

In spite of his doubts about how much farther he could go, Bock had tried to retain his option for a deep thrust past Moscow. He had drawn his armor inward toward Moscow somewhat but still had it arching well around and to the east of the city. He aimed Third Panzer Group south of the Volga Reservoir toward the Moscow-Volga Canal; Fourth Panzer Group, via Klin, toward the canal; and Second Panzer Army, past Tula, to Kashira and Ryazan. Those lines of advance would bring Third and Fourth Panzer Groups out on the Moscow-Volga Canal to strike toward Rybinsk and Yaroslavl, give Second Panzer Army a choice of going north from Kashira toward Moscow or east across the Oka River toward Gorkiy, and leave the close-in encirclement of the city to Fourth Army alone.[11] As the time grew shorter, however, Bock's doubts increased, and he told Halder, chief of the General Staff, and the army commanders that he did not expect the army group to have enough troops, supplies, or tanks to get beyond the Moscow-Volga Canal on the north and the Moscow River on the south. But he let the armies' original orders stand, thereby, as Third Panzer Group put it, making their missions "unclear."[12]

On 14 November, Zhukov intervened—reluctantly—in what so far had been considered by both sides to be an exclusively German initiative. *Forty-ninth Army*—reinforced with a cavalry corps (2 cavalry divisions of 3,000 men each), a rifle division, a tank division, and 2 tank brigades, hit the Fourth Army right flank east of Serpukhov.[13] At the last minute, because Zhukov expected the renewed German offensive any day, Stalin had insisted on "counterblows," which Zhukov believed could accomplish nothing other than to complicate the defense.[14]

During the morning on the 15th, one infantry corps of Ninth Army, which was only supernumerary in the offensive, jumped off south of Kalinin and experienced what Halder noted as "something new in this war": Soviet *Thirtieth Army* gave way without a fight.[15] Although Third and Fourth Panzer Groups had less luck when they joined in a day later, the Soviet forces against them fared badly. A "counterblow" by *Sixteenth Army's* right flank, reinforced with a tank division and five cavalry divisions, ran head on into Fourth Panzer Group's attack east of Volokolamsk and collapsed.[16] On the 18th, Second Panzer Army began its drive south of Tula, and one of its corps

[11] *H. Gr. Mitte, Ia Nr. 2250/41, Befehl fuer die Fortsetzung der Operationen, 30.10.41, Pz. AOK 4 22547/14 file.*

[12] *Pz. AOK 3, Ia Nr. 520/42, Gefechtsbericht Russland 1941–42, 29.4.42, Pz. AOK 3 21818/2 file; Halder Diary,* vol. III, p. 287.

[13] *IVOVSS,* vol. II, p. 256.

[14] Zhukov, *Memoirs,* p. 338.

[15] *Halder Diary,* vol. III, p. 290.

[16] Rokossovskiy, *Soldier's Duty,* p. 70; *IVOVSS,* vol. II, p. 256.

covered nearly twenty-five miles during the day; the following day, Stalin
asked Zhukov, "Are you sure we will be
able to hold Moscow? It hurts me to ask
you that. Answer me truthfully as a
communist." Zhukov replied that
Moscow would be held "by all means"
but said he would need at least another
two armies and two hundred more
tanks.[17] Stalin agreed to provide the
two armies, but not the tanks, and said
the armies would not be ready until the
end of the month, which left the situation around Moscow unlikely to improve anytime soon unless relief came
from the operations about to begin
elsewhere.

West and north of Rostov, Timoshenko had doubled *South Front*'s
strength in the first half of the month
by deploying two fresh armies, *Thirty-
seventh Army* and *Fifty-sixth Independent
Army*. On the 17th, *Thirty-seventh Army*
together with elements of *Ninth* and
Eighteenth Armies hit the shoulder of
General Kleist's First Panzer Army fifty
miles north of Rostov. Timoshenko had
thought to fulfill the *Stavka*'s requirement for a diversion and to block the
gateway to the Caucasus, but the first
days' results were discouraging: XIV
Panzer Corps stood fast on the north
while III Panzer Corps broke away to
the southeast toward Rostov.[18]

The outlook for an effective diversion at Tikhvin appeared even dimmer.
There, General Meretskov took command of the shattered *Fourth Independent Army* on 7 November, just as
Tikhvin was being lost. Twelve days
later, responding to "urgent demands"
from the *Stavka,* he went over to the

offensive at Tikhvin with the one infantry division and two tank battalions of
reinforcements he had received so far.
These forces were actually enough, in
view of Army Group North's straitened
circumstances, to alter the balance in
the Soviet favor, but they were not
likely to produce swift or devastating
effects.[19]

Bock's armor had made good progress in the first three days of the
offensive. The ground was frozen hard
and dusted with light, dry snow. The
Germans had painted their tanks,
trucks, and guns white to blend with
the landscape. Shortening days, low-
hanging clouds, and snow flurries restricted air support, and temperatures
ten to twenty degrees below freezing
were new to troops so far accustomed
to campaigning in warmer seasons. On
the other hand, armor could move
across country as if it were on paved
roads. The fall mud and the summer's
dust and mosquitoes were gone. The
scenery was also improved. The Belorussian forests and swamps had given
way to the Moscow upland dotted with
prosperous-looking villages clean under the new-fallen snow.

This, the Germans were uneasily
aware, was not the real Russian winter.
Fighting then would be altogether different. Third Panzer Group had already told the OKH that while infantry
could be made mobile in the coldest
weather and the deepest snow, tanks
and trucks did not respond like men
and could not be ordered to master
difficulties they were not built to meet.
But meteorological statistics from as
far back as the nineteenth century gave

[17]Guderian, *Panzer Leader,* p. 251; Zakharov, *Proval,* p. 39.
[18]*IVOVSS,* vol. II, p. 222; *IVMV,* vol. IV, pp. 120–21.

[19]Meretskov, *Serving the People,* pp. 157–70; *IVMV,* vol. IV, p. 113; Leeb, *Tagebuchaufzeichnungen,* pp. 392–94.

PANZER III TANK AND INFANTRY ADVANCE OVER RUTTED BUT FROZEN ROAD

no reason to expect heavy snow and extreme low temperatures before mid-December.[20]

For the moment the weather was the least of the troubles that faced Army Group Center on the 18th. In three days of fighting, Fourth Army just barely had repulsed the Serpukhov "counterblow." When a second counterblow, in which some Siberian troops well fitted out for winter fighting, came at the same spot on the 18th, Kluge talked about pulling back ten to fifteen miles to cover on the Protva River. Since some of his regiments were reduced to four of five hundred men and

commanded by first lieutenants, his right flank, he said, was unlikely to be able to complete the southern sweep of the Moscow encirclement.

Bock and Halder exchanged opinions late on the 18th on "what prospects the whole operation still had." They concluded that both sides were close to the end of their strengths, and the victory would go to the one who had the most will.[21] Two days later, determined to be the one to commit his last regiment, Bock, using his special train as a command post, moved out to the army group left flank behind Third and Fourth Panzer Groups. From there, he revised the plan again, ordering Fourth Panzer Group to bear east, south of Klin, and to add weight on

[20]Pz. AOK 3, Ia Nr. 520/42, Gefechtsbericht Russland 1941–42, 29.4.42, Pz. AOK 3 21818/2 file; Pz. AOK 3, Ic/AO, Klimatische Verhaeltnisse an der oberen Wolga im Winter, 27.10.41, Pz. AOK 3 20839/5 file.

[21]Halder Diary, vol. III, p. 294.

Fourth Army's left flank. He told Third Panzer Group to take Klin and dip southeast along the road and the Klin-Moscow railroad toward Solnechnogorsk. But when Third Panzer Group took Klin on the 23d, Bock changed his mind again. Fourth Panzer Group's left flank units were already in Solnechnogorsk, and Bock responded to a proposal from Reinhardt to turn his Third Panzer Group southeast toward Moscow anyway with an order to cover Fourth Panzer Group's flank but also to push due east "as far as possible."[22]

After the 23d, as Third Panzer Group headed east away from Klin, the blitzkrieg worked surprisingly well. The Russians retreated steadily and, for once, did not set fire to their villages as they left, which the group's intelligence officers took to mean either that they were becoming demoralized or, though that seemed much less likely, that they expected to return.[23] The lead division, 7th Panzer, picked up a deserter, an NKVD lieutenant, who said the Russians were evacuating the area west of the Moscow-Volga Canal and were readying fresh troops off the panzer group's open flank on the north for an attack toward Klin. Talk among the Soviet officers, he said, was that "Klin will be a *klin* [in Russian, a wedge] against the Germans." The interrogation report did not find its way to panzer group headquarters until the second week of December.[24]

On 27 November, 7th Panzer Division reached the Moscow-Volga Canal. The next morning, assuming its mission would still be to push east, Third Panzer Group took a bridgehead on the east bank of the canal at Yakhroma. During the day, Fourth Panzer Group's spearhead, 2d Panzer Division, came almost to a standstill twenty miles to the south, west of Krasnaya Polyana, and twelve miles north of Moscow. Echeloned in a fifteen-mile line on the 2d Panzer Division right, General Hoepner, commander of Fourth Panzer Group, had 11th Panzer Division, 5th Panzer Division, 10th Panzer Division, and the SS "Das Reich" Division all aimed toward Moscow but barely moving as they crunched head-on into the minefields and fiercely defended earthworks ringing the city. Kluge's Fourth Army left flank was inching ahead, but not enough to keep Hoepner's forces from having to stretch to maintain contact. Second Panzer Army had driven in a large bulge south of Tula, but Soviet *Fiftieth Army* held on grimly around the city, and a raid by one of Second Panzer Army's divisions north to Kashira was drawing a swarm of Soviet cavalry and tanks down on the 17th Panzer Division. On the night of the 28th, Bock, while changing the plan again, at least symbolically, committed his "last regiment." Giving Third Panzer Group the Lehrbrigade 900 (actually one battalion), the only reserve he had, he ordered Reinhardt to forget about the Yakhroma bridgehead, turn south along the west bank of the canal, and join Hoepner's push toward Moscow.[25]

Meanwhile, during the past week, Army Group South had undergone

[22]*Pz. AOK 3, Gefechtsbericht Russland 1941–42*, Pz. AOK 3 21818/2 file.

[23]*Pz. AOK 3, Ic/AO, Taetigkeitsbericht Nr. 3, 23.11.41*, Pz. AOK 3 16911/32 file.

[24]*Pz. Gr. 3, Ic, Mitteilungen, 26.12.41*, Pz. AOK 4 16911/36 file.

[25]*Pz. AOK 3, Ia Nr. 520/42, Gefechtsbericht Russland 1941–42*, Pz. AOK 3 21818/2 file.

some decidedly unpleasant experiences at Rostov. The SS division "Leibstandarte Adolf Hitler" had taken the city on the 21st. This was a notable but dangerous feat. In and around Rostov, III Panzer Corps came under attack from the south across the frozen Don River and from the north over the open steppe, and on its left, elements of three Soviet armies battered away at XIV Panzer Corps. Kleist, the First Panzer Army commander, had begun to realize several days earlier that this onslaught was more than he had anticipated, and on 22 November, he ordered III Panzer Corps to evacuate Rostov and to go behind the Mius River.[26] He had to cancel this order a day later, however, after Field Marshal Rundstedt, commander of Army Group South, told him that he personally approved of the evacuation, but Field Marshal Brauchitsch, commander in chief of the army, had demanded that the city be held because giving it up would have military and "far reaching political consequences."[27] The timing was indeed inopportune since Hitler was preparing to stage a publicity spectacle for the renewal of the 1936 Anti-Comintern Pact, the cornerstone of the Rome-Berlin-Tokyo Axis.

With Rostov lost, Leningrad isolated, and Moscow in imminent danger, the Soviet strategic position looked worse than ever. But Stalin apparently believed as strongly as Bock and Hitler did that the contest was one of willpower, and on 22 November, the *Stavka* told Timoshenko that the loss of

Rostov did not abrogate the counterattack against First Panzer Army. A directive issued two days later gave Cherevichenko's *South Front* the mission of destroying First Panzer Army and retaking the Taganrog-Rostov area. However, Cherevichenko, apparently aware by then that he could not outfight the whole panzer army, chose a smaller but more promising approach and in three days shifted the weight of his forces from the north front to the line at Rostov.[28]

Tension, no doubt already enormous for the Russians, was also gripping the Germans in late November. Brauchitsch, not yet recovered from a heart attack earlier in the month, became more and more querulous, impatient for successes to smooth his interviews with Hitler. Bock developed the "Russian disease," diarrhea. Rundstedt lapsed into haughty silence, letting his Chief of Staff, General Sodenstern, talk to the OKH. Hitler circulated between the *Wolfsschanze* and Berlin on business of state that had some ominous undertones. On 21 November, he was in Berlin for the funeral of Generaloberst Ernst Udet, the *Luftwaffe*'s chief of aircraft development, whose death, actually a suicide, was being attributed to an airplane accident. On the 25th, Hitler was back in Berlin to sign the Anti-Comintern Pact and to welcome two new and reluctant members, Finland and Denmark. He spent the next two days in ceremonies and festivities associated with the signing, and on the 28th, he attended another funeral, that of Germany's top air ace, Colonel Werner Moelders, who had been killed in an airplane crash.

[26]*Pz. AOK 1, Ia Nr. 5108/41, Pz. Armeebefehl Nr. 31, 22.11.41*, Pz. AOK 1 19194/5 file.
[27]*H. Gr. Sued, Ia Nr. 3463/41, an OB der 1. Pz. Armee, 23.11.41*, Pz. AOK 1 19194/5 file.
[28]*IVMV*, vol. IV, pp. 120–21; *IVOVSS*, vol. II, p. 223.

Hitler devoted the rest of the day to talks with visiting diplomats.

The Turnabout

Retreat from Rostov

At his return to the *Wolfsschanze,* early on 29 November, Hitler found awaiting him the rarest kind of news thus far in the war: German troops were retreating. By the 28th, Cherevichenko had brought up twenty-one Soviet divisions against III Panzer Corps at Rostov. The corps commander, General der Kavallerie Eberhard von Mackensen, had reported several weeks earlier, before the last advance began, that his two divisions, the "Leibstandarte" and the 13th Panzer, were worn out, short on everything from socks to antifreeze, and down to a half to two-thirds their normal strengths. During the day on the 28th, as he expected to have to do, Kleist ordered Mackensen to give up Rostov.[29] When Hitler arrived at the *Wolfsschanze,* III Panzer Corps had evacuated Rostov, and the advantage in position and numbers was still heavily on the Soviet side.

On the morning of the 30th, as he had tried to do a week earlier, Kleist ordered his whole right flank, including III Panzer Corps, to go behind the Mius River forty-five miles west of Rostov.[30] Tactically Kleist was making the right move. He had nothing to gain militarily from a prolonged stand in the open, and the short but relatively straight Mius offered a good winter line. On the other hand, a forty-five-mile German retreat in a strategically important sector at this stage was bound to have the psychological effect of a Soviet victory. Nobody could be more sensitive to such an implication than Hitler. In an afternoon interview with Brauchitsch on the 30th, Hitler, using "accusations and invective," browbeat Brauchitsch into trying to get Rundstedt to delay executing Kleist's order. When Rundstedt refused and offered his resignation, Hitler dismissed him early the next day and named Field Marshal Reichenau to succeed him at Army Group South. After insisting through the day that he could hold a line somewhere east of the river, Reichenau finally had to give in at dark and let the withdrawal to the Mius be completed that night.[31] *(Map 4.)*

Before daylight on the morning of 2 December, Hitler left East Prussia by air for Kleist's headquarters in Mariupol on the Black Sea. He stopped at Poltava later in the morning to pick up Reichenau and change from his comfortable but vulnerable four-engine "Condor" transport to a faster and better defended Heinkel 111 bomber. The weather was unusually cold for December in the Ukraine, and from Mariupol east a five-mile-wide, foot-thick band of ice already fringed the Gulf of Taganrog. At Mariupol, Hitler and Reichenau, as Kleist obliquely put it, "visited" with Kleist and the commanding general of the "Leibstandarte," SS Obergruppenfuehrer Josef Dietrich. The visit was far from routine, if only because Hitler seldom traveled so near to the front as an army headquarters. It was also not pleasant for the partici-

---

[29]*III AK, Stichwort-Beurteilung der Lage, 29.10.41,* Pz. AOK 1 58682 file; *Pz. AOK 1, Ia Nr. 5119/41, Pz. Armeebefehl Nr. 38, 28.11.41,* Pz. AOK 1 19194/5 file.

[30]*Pz. AOK 1, Pz. Armeebefehl Nr. 40, 30.11.41,* Pz. AOK 1 19194/5 file.

---

[31]*Halder Diary,* pp. 317–22.

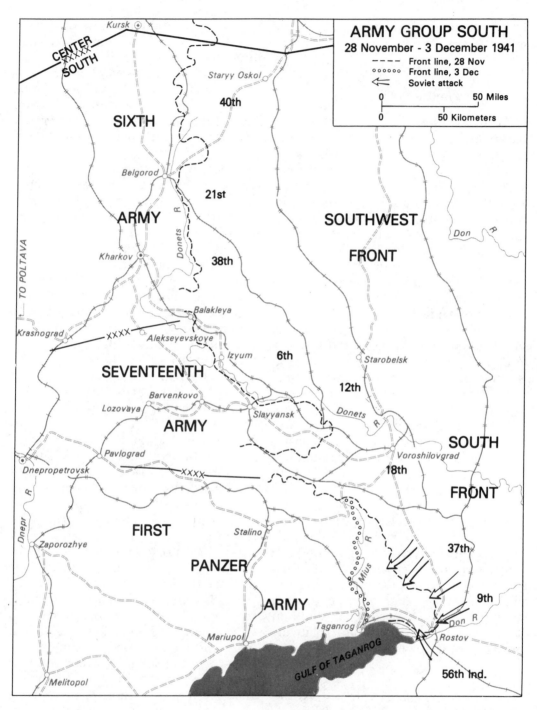

MAP 4

pants and was generally pointless since there was nothing more to be decided. Hitler apparently wanted an assurance from Dietrich, one of his oldest party cronies and former bodyguard, that Rostov could not have been held and assurances from all three generals that the Mius line would be. After receiving those, Hitler switched to talk about restarting the offensive in the new year, promising Kleist everything from tanks and self-propelled assault guns to parachute troops and fresh divisions.[32]

At the *Wolfsschanze,* when he returned early on 4 December, after an overnight stop in Poltava caused by bad flying weather, Hitler found a prediction of another Rostov awaiting him. Field Marshal Leeb, commander of Army Group North, believed the Russians were beginning to see a chance not only to retake Tikhvin but to liberate Leningrad, which would constitute a substantial political and military success for them. A German push north out of the Tikhvin salient toward Lake Ladoga had been stopped on 1 December at Volkhov, thirty-five miles south of the lake. *(Map 5.)* If the Russians retook Tikhvin and opened the railroad to Volkhov, they could readily sluice the reinforcements they were bringing up northwest for an attack on the Leningrad bottleneck. (German air reconnaissance had reported twenty-nine trains headed west on the Vologda-Tikhvin line on 2 December.) What concerned Leeb most was less his own situation than that of Army Group Center. As he saw it, if a strong threat to Moscow could not be maintained, the enemy would surely be able to release enough

reserves to go after Tikhvin and Leningrad.[33]

"Something Does Not Add Up"

Although it was not exactly the brightest of days for Army Group Center, 27 November was one of acute crisis in the Soviet Moscow defense. North of the capital, the advances of Third Panzer and Fourth Panzer Groups past Klin and Solnechnogorsk had opened a twenty-seven-mile-wide gap between Dimitrov, on the Moscow-Volga Canal, and Krasnaya Polyana, twelve miles north of Moscow. General Mayor D. D. Lelyushenko, who had taken command of *Thirtieth Army* on 18 November, had brought the army back under control but had not done so in time to prevent its being pushed into a corner in the angle of the Volga River and the Moscow-Volga Canal. There, for the moment, *Thirtieth Army* could do nothing to block German progress to the east and south.[34] *Sixteenth Army,* under General Leytenant Konstantin Rokossovskiy, had, since the front had broken open between Klin and Solnechnogorsk, been having to stretch its flank east to cover Moscow and to take the whole shock of the enemy's sweep toward the city. The 17th Panzer Division's thrust toward Kashira was beginning to form a deep pocket around Tula and was putting a Second Panzer Army spearhead within sixty-five miles of Moscow on the south.

Thirtieth Army's debacle had paid one dividend. It had given the *Stavka* early

[32]*Pz. AOK 1, Ia Nr. 1294/41, an die Herren Kommandierenden Generale, 3.12.41,* Pz. AOK 1 19194/6 file.

[33]*H. Gr. Nord, Ia Kriegstagebuch,* 1–3 Dec 41, H. Gr. Nord 75128/4 file; Leeb, *Tagebuchaufzeichnungen,* pp. 401–03.

[34]D. D. Lelyushenko, *Moskva-Stalingrad-Berlin-Praga* (Moscow: Izdatelstvo "Nauka," 1970), p. 73.

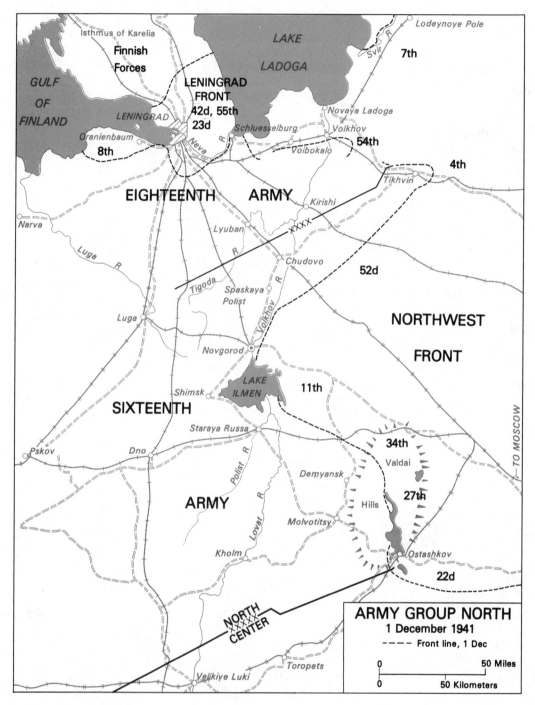

Isthmus of Karelia
Finnish
Forces
LAKE
LADOGA
Lodeynoye Pole
Svir R
7th
GULF
OF
FINLAND
LENINGRAD
FRONT
42d, 55th
23d
Novaya Ladoga
LENINGRAD
Schluesselburg
Volkhov
54th
Oranienbaum
8th
Neva R
Voibokalo
Tikhvin
4th
Narva
EIGHTEENTH   ARMY
Kirishi
Lyuban
XXXX
Luga R
Chudovo
52d
Tigoda R
Spaskaya
Polist
Volkhov R
NORTHWEST
Luga
FRONT
Novgorod
LAKE
ILMEN
11th
Shimsk
SIXTEENTH
Staraya Russa
34th
Pskov
Dno
Valdai
Polist R
Demyansk
27th
ARMY
Hills
Lovat R
Molvotitsy
Kholm
Ostashkov
22d
NORTH
XXXXX
CENTER
Velikiye Luki
Toropets

TO MOSCOW

ARMY GROUP NORTH
1 December 1941
- - - - Front line, 1 Dec

0   50 Miles
0   50 Kilometers

MAP 5

SOVIET GUNNERS MAN A MACHINE GUN WEST OF MOSCOW

warning of the trouble to come, and so when the crisis arrived, means were being assembled to meet it. Unlike Bock, Stalin was apparently not prepared to venture his last regiment in the battle for Moscow, but he also had enough resources to stay in the fight for one more round. In late November, he gave *West Front* 9 rifle divisions, 2 cavalry divisions, 8 rifle brigades, 6 tank brigades, and 10 independent tank battalions.[35] Of those, 3 rifle divi-

sions went to *Thirtieth Army;* a rifle division, the 2 cavalry divisions formed into the *I Guards Cavalry Corps* under General Mayor P. A. Belov, and a portion of the armor went to the Kashira area; and the rest went to *Sixteenth, Fifth,* and *Fiftieth Armies* and the *front* reserve.[36]

Additionally, as the Germans were passing Klin, Stalin and the *Stavka* had begun setting up two reserve armies to cover the gap that would be developing farther east. On 23 November, General Kuznetsov took command of one of these, *First Shock Army,* on the line of the Moscow-Volga Canal south of Dimitrov. The shock armies were con-

[35] Marshal V. D. Sokolovskiy puts the strengths of tank brigades at that time at 1 battalion of fourteen medium tanks, 1 battalion of light tanks, and 1 motorized rifle battalion. He places the independent tank battalions at 11 T–34s and 3 KVs. Figures for individual tank brigades given in Krupchenko, *Tankovye voyska,* pp. 38–44, indicate strengths of thirty to sixty tanks. See V. D. Sokolovskiy, *"Die sowjetische Kriegskunst in der Schlacht vor Moskau,"* Wehr-Wissenschaftliche Rundschau, 1(1963), pt. 2, 87.

[36] V. N. Yevstigneyev, ed., *Velikaya bitva pod Moskvoy* (Moscow: Voyennoye Izdatelstvo, 1961), p. 178; Zhukov, *Memoirs,* p. 340.

ceived of as being particularly heavy in armor, motorization, artillery, and automatic weapons, but *First Shock* (and the others of this category created during the winter of 1941–1942) was not so well equipped. When Kuznetsov arrived in Dimitrov on the 23d, his command consisted of a rifle brigade. By the end of the month he had 1 rifle division, 9 rifle brigades, 10 separate battalions, a regiment of artillery, and a contingent of rocket launchers. About 70 percent of the troops were over thirty years old.[37]

The second of the two new reserve armies, *Twentieth Army*, was built in what, by 27 November, had become the most critical spot on the entire front, the sector between the right flank of *Sixteenth Army* and the Moscow-Volga Canal. This area included the much-fought-over village of Krasnaya Polyana. Because of the subsequent behavior of its commander, General Leytenant Andrei Vlasov, the Soviet histories are reticent in dealing with *Twentieth Army's* role at Moscow.[38] In late 1941, however, Vlasov was regarded in the Soviet Army as one of the most brilliant younger Soviet generals. He had commanded the *Thirty-seventh Army*, which had been destroyed in the Kiev pocket, but he and some of his staff had escaped. Like Kuznetsov, Vlasov initially had just odds and ends: he said later, a Siberian brigade, some ten thousand criminal prisoners, and fifteen tanks.[39] No doubt, *Twentieth Army*, which was also in position to take over some of *Sixteenth Army's* right flank elements, was quickly brought up to a strength at least equal to that of *First Shock.*

In the last week of November, the *Stavka* also began bringing five of the newly formed reserve armies forward from the line of the Volga River. Three—*Twenty-fourth, Twenty-sixth,* and *Sixtieth Armies*—were stationed east of Moscow, and one, *Sixty-first Army,* behind *Southwest Front's* right flank. The other, *Tenth Army,* was deployed west of the Oka River, downstream from Kashira in position to block Second Panzer Army thrusts toward Kolomna and Ryazan.[40]

Tenth Army, under General Leytenant F. I. Golikov, was very likely typical of the ten reserve armies. Its main forces were seven reserve rifle divisions recruited in the Moscow region. It had approximately one hundred thousand troops. After receiving its marching orders on 24 November, *Tenth Army* had to negotiate the more than three hundred miles from its original station at Syzran on the Volga by rail and on foot, since it had almost no motor vehicles.[41]

During the day on 29 November, Third and Fourth Panzer Groups made contact with elements of *First Shock* and *Twentieth Armies* at Yakhroma and west of Krasnaya Polyana. Late in the day, after Zhukov had assured him that the Germans would not commit any new large forces in the near future, Stalin turned over *First Shock, Twentieth,* and *Tenth Armies* to Zhukov's control for a counterattack.[42] During the day, also,

[37]Zakharov, *Proval,* p. 278.
[38]See p. 259.
[39]Sven Steenberg, *Vlasov* (New York: Alfred A. Knopf, 1970), pp. 16–19.

[40]*IVOVSS,* vol. II, p. 271; *IVMV,* vol. IV, p. 280. See p. 42.
[41]Zakharov, *Proval,* pp. 256–58. See also F. I. Golikov, "*Rezervnaya armiya gotovitsiya k zashchite stolitsy,*" *Voyenno-istoricheskiy zhurnal,* 5(1966), 65–76.
[42]Zhukov, *Memoirs,* p. 348.

Third Panzer Group made its turn south, and Fourth Panzer Group registered a small gain. Talking to Halder, Bock said he was afraid that if the attack from the north did not succeed the battle would soon degenerate into a "soulless frontal confrontation" similar to the World War I Battle of Verdun.[43]

On the night of the 30th, while his one colleague, Leeb, worried about what might happen at Leningrad once the pressure was off Moscow and the other, Rundstedt, was a few hours away from dismissal over the Rostov affair, Bock, musing about his own situation, concluded that "something does not add up." During the day, while the panzer groups were again reporting very small gains, Colonel Adolf Heusinger, the operations branch chief in the OKH, had been on the telephone to Bock talking as if encircling Moscow were only a preliminary to thrusts toward Voronezh and Yaroslavl. When Bock later called Brauchitsch to tell him that Army Group Center did not have enough strength to encircle at Moscow much less to do anything more, he had to ask several times whether Brauchitsch was still listening. Early the next morning, wondering whether Brauchitsch had listened, Bock repeated by teletype what he had said the day before, adding that the belief in an impending Soviet collapse had been proved "a phantasy."[44] His troops, he said, were exhausted, and the offensive had therewith lost "all sense and purpose." The army group, he concluded, was shortly going to be at a standstill "before the gates of Moscow," and it was time to decide what to do then.

At the Gates

In the morning on 30 November, Zhukov submitted to the *Stavka* a *West Front* plan for a counteroffensive north and south of Moscow. The idea, of course, was not new. As Zhukov has put it, "The counter-offensive had been prepared all through the defense actions. . . ."[45] The continuing Soviet strategy, since June, had been "let the enemy wear himself down, bring him to a stop, and create the conditions for a subsequent shift to the counterattack."[46] Counteroffensives had been launched on the frontiers in June and on the Dnepr–Dvina line in July, and the *Stavka* and the General Staff had considered others throughout the campaign, most recently, when the Germans had been stopped on the Moscow approaches in early November.[47]

However, neither the plan Zhukov sent in on the 30th—in response to earlier instructions from the General Staff—nor the circumstances under which the plan was expected to be executed actually conformed to previous thinking, which had envisioned a counteroffensive against an enemy who had been stopped. The plan was conceived as a near-to-last move in a battle that was likely to turn against the Russians. Zhukov says he told Stalin on the night of the 29th that the Germans were "bled white" and gives the essence of the plan as having been to strike past Klin and Solnechnogorsk sixty miles to Teryaeva Sloboda and Volokolamsk in

[43]*Halder Diary*, vol. III, p. 316.

[44]Generalfeldmarschall Fedor von Bock, *Kriegstagebuch, Osten I*, 30 Nov 41, CMH files MS # P–210 (hereafter cited as *Bock Diary, Osten I*).

[45]Zhukov, *Memoirs*, p. 347.

[46]Sokolovskiy, *"Die sowjetische Kriegskunst,"* p. 76.

[47]Vasilevskiy, *Delo*, p. 161.

the north and up to the same distance past Stalinogorsk to the Upa River in the south.[48] On the other hand, General Vasilevskiy, acting chief of the General Staff, in briefing the *Kalinin Front* commander, Konev, who would have two of his armies included in the counterattack, said: "We can only halt the German attack toward Moscow and thereby . . . lay the groundwork for beginning to inflict a serious defeat on the enemy by active operations with a decisive aim. If we do not do that in the next few days, it will be too late."[49] The order for the counterattack Kuznetsov, the *First Shock Army* commander, received on the morning of 2 December was to have the Zakharov group attack toward Dednevo and Fedorovka and "in the longer run" strike toward Klin.[50] Dednevo and Fedorovka were villages directly opposite the army's left flank, and the Zakharov group, parts of three divisions and a tank brigade under General Mayor F. D. Zakharov, had been the rear guard at Klin and were pinned down west of the Moscow-Volga Canal by Third Panzer Group's spearhead.[51]

Zhukov's chief of staff at the time, General Leytenant V. D. Sokolovskiy, wrote later, "The main objective of our counterattack was to break up the enemy's attack conclusively and give him no opportunity to regroup and dig in close to our capital."[52] Zhukov also qualifies his statement of the objectives by saying the "initial task" was to be "removing the immediate threat to

Moscow," and "we would need more forces to assign further-going and more categorical missions."[53] However, Stalin, who had been willing during the summer to commit reserve armies into counterattacks as fast as they could be formed, was being remarkably parsimonious in dealing them out for this counterattack. The reserve armies stationed east of Moscow were earmarked to be used "in the defense, if necessary, or, if they were not required, in developing a counteroffensive." But the decisions as to how and when the armies would be committed were reserved to the *Stavka,* which meant to Stalin, and he had not yet made up his mind.[54]

In the first two days of December, it looked as though Bock might have been too pessimistic, and the Soviet counterattack might very well come too late. To the Germans' surprise as much as the Russians', Fourth Army's 258th Infantry Division broke through the Soviet line south of the Moscow-Smolensk highway on the 1st. Northeast of Tula, the next day, Second Panzer Army began a hook to the west which, if it succeeded in pinching off the city, could have brought the Fourth Army right flank into motion. Bock at Army Group Center had reverted to fighting what he assumed to be the battle of the last regiments, vacillating between desperate hope and gloomy apprehension. Early on the 2d, he told Kluge, Reinhardt, and Hoepner that the enemy was close to breaking. Talking to Halder later in the day, however, he said that owing to declining strength, cold, and stiffening resistance, "doubts

[48]Zhukov, *Memoirs,* p. 348.
[49]Vasilevskiy, *Delo,* p. 164. See also *VOV,* p. 110.
[50]Zakharov, *Proval,* p. 283.
[51]*Ibid.,* pp. 278–81; Yevstigneyev, *Velikaya bitva,* pp. 144–47.
[52]Sokolovskiy, *"Die sowjetische Kriegskunst,"* p. 92.

[53]Zhukov, *Memoirs,* p. 348.
[54]*VOV,* p. 110.

of success are beginning to take definite form."[55]

On the 3d, despite even more reasons for doubts, Bock's determination increased slightly. In the morning, when Kluge proposed giving up Fourth Army's attack because it would not get through to Moscow, Bock opted to wait two or three days to see what effect Third Panzer Group could have. By late afternoon, 258th Infantry Division was fighting its way westward out of an encirclement; Fourth Panzer Group had reported its offensive strength "in the main exhausted"; and Third Panzer Group was embroiled with *First Shock Army* at Yakhroma. Second Panzer Army was still advancing northeast of Tula but through a blizzard that was piling up snow all along the army group front. Bock told General Jodl, Hitler's operations chief in the OKW, that although his troop strength was almost at an end, he would stay on the attack. The reason he was holding on "with tooth and claw," Bock added, was because keeping the initiative was preferable to going over to the defensive with weakened forces in exposed positions.[56]

During the previous two weeks the weather had been getting colder, with temperatures ranging between 0° F. and 20° F. On the morning of 4 December, after heavy snowfalls the day before, the temperature stood at −4° F. In his diary, Bock observed in passing that it was "icy cold." During that day, Fourth Army went over to the defensive, its front quiet. Fourth Panzer Group repelled several tank-led Soviet counterattacks southwest of Krasnaya Polyana but declared itself unable to advance until Third Panzer Group came fully abreast. Third Panzer Group, meanwhile, while trying to bring three panzer divisions to bear southwest of Yakhroma, was getting pressure on its front northwest of Yakhroma from Soviet reinforcements, some of which Reinhardt, its commander, believed were Siberian troops. And Second Panzer Army was regrouping to try again to pinch off Tula. Again Bock had decided to stay on the offensive. Mildly disturbed by a reported half-dozen new enemy divisions in the front northwest of Moscow, all well provided with tanks and rocket launchers, he concluded that they were probably not new strength but units shifted from nearby quiet sectors. A counteroffensive, he stated in his last report of the day to the OKH, was unlikely: the enemy did not have enough forces.[57]

Stalin, the *Popular Scientific Sketch* says, kept in close communications with Zhukov in the first days of December, calling him several times a day to inquire about the progress of the fighting. "In the complicated situation . . . , it was very important to time the shift from the defense to the counteroffensive correctly. The most favorable moment for the shift to the counteroffensive presented itself when the enemy was forced to stop his attack but could not yet go on the defensive because his troops were not yet properly re-

[55]*H. Gr. Mitte, Ia Kriegstagebuch, Dezember 1941,* 1 and 2 Dec 41, H. Gr. Mitte 26974/6 file; *Bock Diary, Osten I,* 1 and 2 Dec 41; Guderian, *Panzer Leader,* p. 257.

[56]*H. Gr. Mitte, Ia Kriegstagebuch, Dezember 1941,* 3 Dec 41, H. Gr. Mitte 26974/6 file; *Bock Diary, Osten I,* 3 Dec 41.

[57]*H. Gr. Mitte, Ia Kriegstagebuch, Dezember 1941,* 4 Dec 41, H. Gr. Mitte 26974/6 file; *Bock Diary, Osten I,* 4 Dec 41.

CREW OF GERMAN S.F.H. 18, 150-MM. HOWITZER, BUNDLED-UP AGAINST THE COLD

grouped, no reserves had been created, and the defense lines were not prepared."[58] While most Soviet accounts do not specify a day, according to Sokolovskiy, the decision was made to shift to the counterattack on 4 December. On that day, he says, the *West Front* troops had brought the enemy near Moscow to a standstill, and it then became "urgently necessary" to go over to the counteroffensive "without any pause." Vasilevskiy says the *Stavka* set the date for the counterattack as 5 and 6 December.[59]

Vasilevskiy went to the *Kalinin Front* headquarters on the night of the 4th to deliver the directive from the General Staff to start the counteroffensive— and, possibly, to make certain it began on the 5th. Konev, claiming he had neither the tanks nor the infantry to attack, had opposed a counterattack when Vasilevskiy had talked to him about it three days earlier.[60] *Kalinin Front*'s mission was to hit the German Ninth Army front southeast of Kalinin with the *Twenty-ninth* and *Thirty-first Armies* and to bear south and west "in the general direction of Minkulino-Gorodishche," twenty-five miles east of Klin.[61] Vasilevskiy indicates that he told Konev on 1 December to have *Kalinin Front* ready to start "in two or three days."[62] Timoshenko, at *Southwest Front,*

[58]*VOV*, p. 111.
[59]Sokolovskiy, *"Die sowjetische Kriegskunst,"* p. 92; Vasilevskiy, *Delo*, pp. 164–65.

[60]Vasilevskiy, *Delo*, pp. 164–65.
[61]Yevstigneyev, *Velikaya bitva*, p. 177.
[62]Vasilevskiy, *Delo*, p. 163.

received orders on 4 December to strike against German Second Army on the 6th with the *Third* and *Thirteenth Armies* and to aim for Yefremov and past Yelets toward Livny.[63] Yefremov was just behind the front on the Second Army north flank, and Yelets, in the center, was then still in Soviet hands.

Vasilevskiy's account indicates that the *Stavka's* orders to begin the counteroffensive on 5 and 6 December applied to *West Front* as well as *Kalinin* and *Southwest Fronts.*[64] However, Zhukov describes his telephone conversation with Stalin late on 4 December in which they talked about air and armor reinforcements for *West Front* and which Stalin closed by reminding Zhukov to "remember" that *Kalinin Front* would be going over to the counteroffensive on the 5th, and *Southwest Front* would follow on the 6th.[65]

During the night of 4 December, the temperature dropped to −25° F. One German regiment on a night march had over three hundred frostbite casualties, and several of its wounded men froze to death. The next morning, tanks would not start; machine guns and artillery would not fire because their lubricants and the oil in their recoil mechanisms had congealed; and all the armies reported numerous frostbite cases. In the paralyzing morning cold, the Soviet *Twenty-ninth Army* attacked across the ice-covered Volga west of Kalinin and broke into the Ninth Army line about a mile before being stopped.[66] Reinhardt and Hoep-

ner both reported more fresh Soviet troops on their fronts and their own offensive capabilities evaporating. Reinhardt's Third Panzer Group tried to push a wedge south between the left flank of Hoepner's Fourth Panzer Group at Krasnaya Polyana and the Moscow-Volga Canal, but his automatic weapons did not work; the cold quickly drained the troops' energy; and the attack had barely begun before it had to be called back. In the morning, Guderian thought Second Panzer Army could still take Tula, but by evening his confidence had faded, and he proposed a gradual withdrawal from the whole bulge east of Tula to the Don and Shat rivers. His tanks, he complained, were breaking down in the cold, while Soviet tanks kept running.[67]

Zhukov's order to begin the counteroffensive on 6 December went to *West Front's* armies on the 5th.[68] The Germans later believed that the drastic temperature drop on the night of the 4th had much to do with Zhukov's timing. Early in 1942, too late to be of use, German intelligence circulated to the commands in the East a partial transcript of statements Timoshenko and Zhukov allegedly had made at a Moscow conference in late November urging a counteroffensive at Moscow. The information was described as having come from a very good source. Timoshenko, whose *Southwest Front* forces were at the time of the conference building toward victory at Ros-

---

[63] Yevstigneyev, *Velikaya bitva*, p. 177.

[64] Vasilevskiy, *Delo*, p. 166.

[65] Zhukov, *Memoirs*, p. 349.

[66] Yevstigneyev, *Velikaya bitva*, p. 183; *IVOVSS*, vol. II, p. 277.

[67] *Pz. Gr. 4, Ia, Lagebeurteilung, 5.12.41*, AOK 4 13763/7 file; *Pz. Gr. 3, Ie Morgenmeldung, 6.12.41*, Pz. AOK 3 16911/30 file; *H. Gr. Mitte, Ia Kriegstagebuch, Dezember 1941*, 5 Dec 41, H. Gr. Mitte 26974/6 file; Guderian, *Panzer Leader*, pp. 258–59.

[68] Zakharov, *Proval*, p. 284.

tov, recommended giving priority to Zhukov's *West Front,* stating:

The great danger for the German Command is that the first big change in the weather will knock out all of their motorized equipment. We must hold out as long as in any way possible but immediately go over to the attack when the first few days of cold have broken the back of the German forces. This backbone consists of the tanks and motorized artillery that will become useless when the temperature hits 20° [F.] below zero.

Zhukov supposedly added that he proposed to let the "start and the course of the offensive be determined by the weather" and expected its success to be in proportion to the "freezing off" of the German equipment.[69]

The Soviet accounts, however, totally ignore the possibility of the weather's having had any part in the timing of the counteroffensive. They respond to German and other contentions that it worked to the Soviet advantage by pointing out that both sides had to cope with cold and snow and that temperatures in December 1941 were not actually as low (−25° to −50° F.) as was claimed. One Soviet work asserting these two points does give the December mean temperature as recorded by Soviet weather stations around Moscow as −28.6° C. (−19.3° F.)— which was, after all, quite cold.[70] The relationship between the weather and the counteroffensive appears coincidental up to 4 December. After then, however, the probability of its having influenced the timing of *West Front*'s operations increases.

As of 5 December, Second Panzer

Army and Third and Fourth Panzer Groups were at a standstill, enforced by the cold, regardless of whether Soviet resistance could have achieved the same effect. For the counteroffensive, *West Front* was to aim "blows" toward Klin, Solnechnogorsk, and Istra to "smash" the enemy on the right flank, and to deliver "blows in the flanks and rear of the Guderian group [Second Panzer Army]" to Uzlovaya and Bogoroditsk "to smash the enemy on the left flank."[71] The final order Kuznetsov's *First Shock Army* received on 5 December instructed it again to clear the Dednevo-Fedorovka area and "in the longer run" to advance in "the direction of Klin."[72]

Soviet postwar accounts treat the strengths of both sides' forces on the eve of the counterattack as a matter of outstanding historical significance. They emphasize that, as of 5 December, German forces outnumbered Soviet in the Moscow sector. However, the figures they employ vary and in the aggregate do not substantiate the existence of an actual Soviet numerical inferiority. The latest, hence presumably most authoritative figures, those given in the *History of the Second World War,* are 1,708,000 German and 1,100,000 Soviet troops on the approaches to Moscow.[73] The numbers used in earlier Soviet works were 800,000 or "more than 800,000" German and between 719,000 and 760,000 Soviet troops.[74] The German strength as it appears in the *History of the Second*

---

[69]*Pz. AOK 3, Gefechtsbericht Russland, 1941–42,* Pz. AOK 3 21818/2 file.

[70]Deborin and Telpukhovskiy, *Itogi i uroki,* p. 129.

[71]*IVMV,* vol. IV, p. 281; Yevstigneyev, *Velikaya bitva,* p. 177.

[72]Zakharov, *Proval,* p. 284.

[73]*IVMV,* vol. IV, p. 283.

[74]*VOV (Kratkaya Istoriya),* p. 130; *VOV,* p. 110; Zakharov, *50 let,* p. 295.

World War comprises all personnel assigned to Army Group Center including air force troops.[75] The Soviet strength is that of the forces assigned to the counterattack.[76] The strengths given in the other works are said to be those of the divisions and brigades in Army Group Center and those of the Soviet *fronts*, in other words, the combat strengths for the two sides.[77] None of the Soviet strengths given include the eight armies still in the *Stavka* reserve, a total of about eight hundred thousand men.

It is clear that, even without the reserve armies, the Soviet forces opposing Army Group Center were relatively stronger on 5 December than they had been in October when Operation TAIFUN began. While Army Group Center had not been able to replace its losses in troops and equipment, the Soviet armies in the Moscow sector had acquired a third more rifle divisions, five times more cavalry divisions, twice as many artillery regiments, and two-and-a-half times as many tank brigades by 5 December than they had had on 2 October.[78]

Along the front around Moscow at daybreak on 6 December, the temperature dropped as low as −38° F. During the night, Bock at Army Group

Center had approved Guderian's proposed withdrawal of Second Panzer Army, and he had told Reinhardt and Hoepner to "adjust" their plans for Third and Fourth Panzer Groups to pullbacks from Yakhroma and Krasnaya Polyana to a line covering Klin. He had also called General der Panzertruppen Rudolf Schmidt at Second Army, which had been drifting slowly eastward toward Yelets for the past several days, and had told him he had better come to a stop; otherwise, his army would soon find itself standing farther east than any of the others.[79]

The Soviet armies, entering the first day of the full counteroffensive, gave variously executed solo performances. *Thirty-first Army* joined in with the stalled *Twenty-ninth Army* at *Kalinin Front* but failed to get across the Volga south of Kalinin. *Thirtieth Army* made the day's best—and, for the Germans, most dangerous—showing by breaking into the Third Panzer Group deep flank northeast of Klin to a depth of eight miles. *First Shock* and *Twentieth Armies* hit Third and Fourth Panzer Groups from Yakhroma to west of Krasnaya Polyana, but only *Twentieth Army* made a gain, a small one, on the southern edge of Krasnaya Polyana. *Tenth Army*, most of which was still on the march from Syzran, began its attack on Mikhaylov, on the eastern rim of the Tula bulge, with one rifle division and two motorized infantry regiments.[80] During the day Second Army took Yelets while *Southwest Front's*

---

[75]Army Group Center's total complement, which included a very large rear echelon that the army group was having to maintain to support its operations and to control and to administer the Soviet territory it occupied, was about 1.7 million men. Reinhardt, *Moskau*, pp. 57, 315.

[76]*IVMV*, vol. IV, p. 283.

[77]The 800,000 troops appear to be about the maximum Army Group Center could have had in the first week of December considering that its seventy-eight divisions then had 207,000 unreplaced losses. Zakharov, *50 let*, p. 295; Reinhardt, *Moskau*, p. 57.

[78]Yevstigneyev, *Velikaya bitva*, p. 178.

[79]*H. Gr. Mitte, Ia Kriegstagebuch, Dezember 1941*, 6 Dec 41, H. Gr. Mitte 26974/6 file.

[80]*VOV*, pp. 112–13; Zakharov, *Proval*, pp. 135, 260; *IVOVSS*, vol. II, p. 280.

Thirteenth Army was shifting to the offensive there.[81]

Before noon on the 6th, Reinhardt told Bock that Third Panzer Group would have to start pulling away on the south during the night to provide some armor to put against *Thirtieth Army.* That meant Fourth Panzer Group, Third Panzer's neighbor on the south, also would have to start back soon. The Soviet pressure subsided everywhere that afternoon, and Kluge talked to Bock about keeping the pace of the withdrawals slow to evacuate all the equipment and supplies.[82] Nevertheless, in the bitter night that followed, the battle turned. From Tikhvin, to Moscow, to the Mius River, the BARBAROSSA campaign had run its course.

---

[81]*H. Gr. Mitte, Ia Kriegstagebuch, Dezember 1941,* 6 Dec 41, H. Gr. Mitte 26974/6 file.

[82]*Ibid.,* 6 Dec 41.

CHAPTER IV

The Counteroffensive: First Phase

Hitler on the Defensive

Hitler and General Halder, chief of the German General Staff, talked about a directive for the winter campaign at *Fuehrer* Headquarters on the afternoon of 6 December. Neither of them had, until recently, anticipated having to devote much thought to the subject. Before the October rains had set in, they had expected German troops to be home by Christmas except for those infantry divisions left behind to watch over the remains of the Soviet Army. Since early November, recognizing by then that victory was not so close, the Germans had been trying to wring profit from what was left of the 1941 campaign and to delay decisions on when, where, or whether to stop for the winter.

The setback at Rostov and ominous reports from Army Groups Center and North had apparently at last moved Halder to send Hitler a statement on German strength, which was down 25 percent, and to ask for a decision. Hitler made the decision on the afternoon of the 6th. Numbers, he said, meant nothing. The Russians had lost at least ten times as many men as he had. Supposing they had three times as many to start with, that still meant they were worse off. Single German divisions might be holding fifteen-mile fronts (as Halder apparently claimed),

but that was more an indication of the enemy's weakness than their own. Army Group North should hold Tikhvin and be ready to advance to make contact with the Finns when it received tank and troop reinforcements. Army Group Center should remember that "the Russians never gave up anything of their own accord and neither should we." The weather permitting and with some reinforcements, Army Group South ought to be able to retake Rostov, possibly also the entire Donets Basin.[1]

Hitler, as he must have known, had not made a decision but had evaded one. He did so again the next day. Having received a request during the night of the 6th to approve Third and Fourth Panzer Groups' and Second Panzer Army's withdrawals then in progress, he agreed on the morning of the 7th to let Third and Fourth Panzer Groups straighten their lines but said nothing about Second Panzer Army or the Army Group Center situation in general. In schoolmasterly tones, he pointed out to the OKH that since the pressure on Moscow was released, the Russians could be expected to try to relieve Leningrad. Since Army Group North would need all of its strength to keep its hold on Leningrad, it could not attack past Tikhvin and ought to be

---

[1]*Halder Diary*, vol. III, pp. 328–30.

permitted to shorten its front there somewhat but not enough to put the east-west road and railroad through Tikhvin out of German artillery range.[2]

Black Days

Sunday, 7 December, dawned clear and cold at the front. Early morning *Luftwaffe* reconnaissance flights brought back reports of continuing heavy rail traffic toward Moscow and toward Tikhvin. At ground level, plumes of blowing snow restricted visibility, and roads drifted shut. During the night, the roads running east and southeast from Klin had filled with Third Panzer Group rear echelon trucks and wagons all heading west. How far west nobody knew. The front had begun to pull back from the Moscow-Volga Canal. *First Shock Army* was following hesitantly behind the panzer group which because of the weather had already abandoned fifteen tanks, three heavy howitzers, a half-dozen antiaircraft guns, and dozens of trucks and passenger cars—more material than would ordinarily be lost in a week's heavy fighting. Troops could not tow the guns out of their emplacements. The motors of some vehicles would not start; the grease on bearings and in transmissions in others froze while they were running. The 1st Panzer Division, which had been headed toward Krasnaya Polyana, had turned around during the night with orders to block the Soviet thrust toward Klin. In the morning, it was extended over forty miles, bucking snowdrifts on jammed roads, with its tanks low on fuel.[3] *(Map 6.)*

West Front's strongest army, *Sixteenth*, under General Rokossovskiy, joined the counteroffensive on the 7th along its front west of Krasnaya Polyana. But the most dangerous threat continued to come from *Thirtieth Army*, which had deepened its thrust toward Klin during the night.[4] Army Group Center put out a call for reinforcements to Third Panzer Group's neighbors, "even for the last bicyclist."[5] *Twenty-ninth* and *Thirty-first Armies* hammered at Ninth Army west and southeast of Kalinin but as yet had nothing to show for it. *First Shock* and *Twentieth Armies*, joined by *Sixteenth Army*, kept Third and Fourth Panzer Groups under frontal pressure without acquiring an outright tactical advantage anywhere. *Tenth Army* occupied Mikhaylov after a skirmish with the German rear guard.[6] At Fourth and Second Armies the front was quiet.

Although the counteroffensive was forming slowly, tension was increasing on the German side of the 700-mile front from Tikhvin to the Army Group Center right flank east of Kursk. The army group was being subjected to a prolonged shock as successive Soviet units entered the fighting and broke radio silence. German radio monitors picked up signals from two dozen more enemy brigades and divisions on the army group front on 7 December than had been there on 15 November.

[2]*OKH, GenStdH, Op. Abt. Nr. 32034/41, an OKW, WFSt, 6.12.41* and *OKH, GenStdH, Op. Abt. Nr. 41957/41, OKW an Ob.d.H., 7.12.41*, H. Gr. Mitte 26974/6 file.

[3]*Pz. Gr. 3, Ic Abendmeldung, 7.12.42*, Pz. AOK 3 16911/36 file.

[4]Yevstigneyev, *Velikaya bitva*, pp. 188–90.

[5]*H. Gr. Mitte, Ia Kriegstagebuch, Dezember 1941*, 7 Dec 41, H. Gr. Mitte 26974/6 file.

[6]Zakharov, *Proval*, p. 262.

HALF-TRACK ATTEMPTS TO HAUL A 150-MM. HOWITZER

The army group intelligence had believed, as had Field Marshal Bock, the army group commander, that the Russians could not introduce significant new forces and were compelled to strip the front in some places to supply the battle elsewhere. Field Marshal Leeb had seen the consequences he feared for his command, Army Group North, as inevitable after Fourth Army's advance on Moscow collapsed on 4 December. And these consequences were soon felt. General Meretskov had regrouped *Fourth Independent Army* and had assimilated enough reinforcements by 5 December to bear in on Tikhvin from three sides.[7]

At Tikhvin, on the 7th, in a blizzard that also spread over the Moscow region in the afternoon, the Army Group North spearhead was almost encircled. The Russians had brought in twenty-seven trainloads of troops in the past three days, and the Germans were outnumbered two to one. Hitler had promised about a hundred tanks and twenty-two thousand troops in a week or two, but for the present, all Leeb had in Tikhvin were some half-frozen infantry and five tanks, four of which were not operable because of the cold. In the afternoon, Leeb gave the order to evacuate the town.[8]

On the 8th, when the Russians

---

[7]*H. Gr. Mitte, Ia Nr. 2799/41, an Pz. Gr. 4, 7.12.41,* Pz. AOK 4 22457/14 file; Leeb, *Tagebuchaufzeichnungen,* p. 404; Meretskov, *Serving the People,* p. 171.

[8]*H. Gr. Nord, Ia Kriegstagebuch, 1.12.-31.12.41,* 7 Dec 41, H. Gr. Nord 75128/4 file.

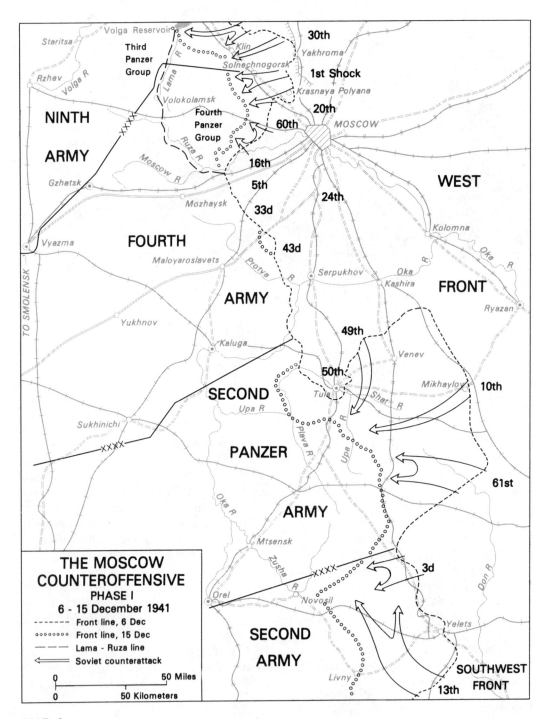

Staritsa

Volga Reservoir

Third
Panzer
Group

Klin

30th

Yakhroma

Rzhev

Volga R

Solnechnogorsk

1st Shock

Volokolamsk

Krasnaya Polyana

NINTH

Lama R

Fourth
Panzer
Group

20th

60th

MOSCOW

ARMY

Ruza R

16th

Moscow R

5th

WEST

Gzhatsk

Mozhaysk

24th

Kolomna

33d

Oka R

FOURTH

43d

Ryazan

Maloyaroslavets

Protva R

Serpukhov

FRONT

Vyazma

Oka R

Kashira

TO SMOLENSK

Yukhnov

ARMY

49th

Kaluga

Venev

SECOND

50th

Mikhaylov

10th

Upa R

Tula

Shat R

Sukhinichi

Pilava R

Upa R

XXXX

PANZER

61st

Oka R

ARMY

Mtsensk

Zusha R

XXXX

3d

Don R

THE MOSCOW
COUNTEROFFENSIVE
PHASE I
6 - 15 December 1941

Orel

Novosil

Yelets

- - - - - Front line, 6 Dec
∘∘∘∘∘∘ Front line, 15 Dec
– – – Lama - Ruza line
⟵ Soviet counterattack

SECOND

Livny

SOUTHWEST
FRONT

ARMY

13th

0   50 Miles
0   50 Kilometers

MAP 6

passed westward across the Klin-Ka-linin railline and bore down to within two or three miles of the Klin road junction that was crowded with miles-long columns of Third Panzer Group vehicles, Bock began trying to scrape reserves out of the front. All he could get for Third Panzer Group was a single infantry battalion. OKH told him not to expect replacement bat-talions before mid-January because the railroads could not handle them until then. When he asked Halder for trained divisions not replacements, Halder replied that OKH did not have any. Such divisions would have to come from the Western Theater that was under the OKW. Desperate to do something, Bock put Third Panzer Group under Fourth Panzer Group that was itself under Fourth Army. Third Panzer Group saw this action as an abdication of the army group's re-sponsibility for the panzer group; Bock said he thought it would make General Hoepner, Fourth Panzer Group com-mander, and Field Marshal Kluge, Fourth Army's commander, more in-clined to help Third Panzer.[9] Ninth Army, Third Panzer Group's neighbor on the north, was having more than enough trouble of its own as *Thirty-first* and *Twenty-ninth Armies* pressed their attack on Kalinin. How much help Fourth Panzer Group or Fourth Army would be or could be was problemat-ical. The faster General Reinhardt ex-tricated Third Panzer from the trap east of Klin the sooner Hoepner's ar-mor would have to embark on the same kind of westward trek, and once the two panzer groups were out, Kluge's

front would be exposed. He would then have to decide whether to risk being overwhelmed where he was or to take Fourth Army out of its relatively well-built line into the snow and cold. Reinhardt, with the Russians before him, was in a hurry. Hoepner did not want to be rushed. Kluge would have preferred not to have to make a decision.

Bock did not know it yet on the 8th, but he was about to have greater trou-ble on his south flank. General Guderian's Second Panzer Army had started the complicated job of reducing the bulge east of Tula, which in just two days cost Second Panzer Army many vehicles and guns that had to be aban-doned. One corps alone had 1,500 frostbite cases, 350 requiring amputa-tions. Supplies were not getting to the panzer army's railhead at Orel because, as was happening all up and down the front, only the insulated Soviet-built locomotives could hold steam in the below-zero cold. The army group had promised to fly in diesel oil and gas-oline on the 8th but had to divert the airplanes to Third Panzer Group. Moreover, at Mikhaylov, *Tenth Army* was throwing trainloads of troops into the front as fast as they arrived. German air reconnaissance on the 8th reported fifty trains headed in each direction between Ryazan and Mikhaylov. Over the telephone, on the 8th and again on the 9th, the usually ebullient Guderian told Bock that a serious crisis in con-fidence had broken out among the troops and the NCOs. He refused to say against whom and declined Bock's suggestion to report in person to Hitler but asked, as Bock said, "for the hun-dredth time" whether the OKH and the OKW were being given a clear

[9]*Ibid.*, 8 Dec 41.

picture of what was happening at the front.[10]

Second Army, Second Panzer Army's neighbor on the south, held a front of 180 miles, which was longer than that held by any other army in the east. It had seven divisions with twenty-five miles of front for each, nearly two miles for every company. On the offensive, its mission had been to fill in between Second Panzer Army and Sixth Army, which had been easy as long as Soviet attention was fastened on Moscow and the Soviet Command had no time to worry about open space and a scattering of small provincial towns like Yelets, Livny, and Novosil. On the defensive, though, Second Army with its one division per twenty-five miles of front became all that was standing before Kursk, its chief (and only) railhead, and Orel, Second Panzer Army's chief (and only) railhead. On 7 December, Second Army stopped after taking Yelets, the last town of any consequence within fifty miles. The army's commander, General Rudolf Schmidt, proposed in the next several days to devastate a ten-mile strip parallel to his entire line and then pull back behind that ready-made no-man's-land to settle in for the winter.

The next day, even more suddenly than it had dropped, the temperature rose to above freezing along the whole Army Group Center front. At the Second Army center south of Yelets, in snow and rain that froze when it hit the stone-cold ground, half-a-dozen Soviet tanks created a hole between the 45th and 95th Infantry Divisions, and a So-

viet cavalry division galloped through. The two German divisions' self-propelled assault guns could barely negotiate the ice, and by the next morning after heavy fresh snow had fallen and blown into drifts during the night, they could not move at all, which was almost immaterial since both divisions had by then also run out of motor fuel. In another day, two more cavalry divisions and a rifle division had opened the gap to sixteen miles and had driven a fifty-mile-deep wedge northwest toward Novosil and Orel. The 95th Division had lost half its strength. The 45th had lost more. Nobody knew how much. Both were out of motor fuel and short on ammunition and rations. Air supply was promised, but the airplanes could not fly in the snow and rain. Schmidt told Bock that Second Army was about to be cut in two and driven back on Kursk and Orel leaving an 85-mile gap in between.[11]

On 8 December, Hitler issued what purported to be a directive for the winter campaign. Because the cold weather had come early, he announced, all "larger offensive operations" were to cease—which they already had done. But there would be no withdrawals except to prepared positions. Ignoring the events then taking place at the front, he ordered the OKH to start recalling the panzer and motorized divisions to Germany for refitting.[12]

"The Worst Crisis in Two World Wars"

Ineffectiveness was something the

[10]H. Gr. Mitte, Ia Kriegstagebuch, Dezember 1941, 8 and 9 Dec 41, H. Gr. Mitte 26974/6 file; Bock Diary, Osten I, 9 Dec 41. See also Guderian, Panzer Leader, pp. 260–61.

[11]AOK 2, Ia Kriegstagebuch Russland, Teil II, 8–12 Dec 41, AOK 2 16690/2 file.
[12]OKW, WFSt, Abt. L (I Op.) Nr. 442090/41, Weisung Nr. 39, 8.12.41, German High Level Directives, CMH files.

German commands had not so far experienced. They had perfected the art of directing military operations. Breakthroughs like those at Klin and Yelets were nuisances that they were supposed to liquidate without fuss. The first two or three days would reveal the measure of an enemy's effort, and by then the German divisions on the scene would either be back in control, or the corps, army, and army group staffs would have begun dispensing reinforcements, artillery, tanks, and air support. Somewhere the enemy might prevail no matter what, but he would have to possess more of the military art than the Russians did. The gentlemen of the General Staff would ordinarily have thrashed out the problems that had arisen at Klin and Yelets in the evenings over cognac and cigars and would have directed these retreats by telephone and teletype the next morning. Meanwhile the commanding generals, if necessary, would have gone out to have a look for themselves and to pass out encouragement or reprimands, whichever seemed likely to do the most good. After all, everybody knew what he had to do. Corps and army staffs could take some battalions here, a regiment there, a scattering of companies someplace else, and a division or two, if necessary, and then get the troops on the march to where they were needed without stirring from their desks. An army group would have reserves or could make some by taking divisions out of the line. Usually a division or two was on the railroad going somewhere up or down the front. Withdrawals like those Third Panzer Group and Second Panzer Army had started were still novel for both troops and staffs, but the operations ("Ia") officers and chiefs of staff knew how to move anything from a division to a whole army five or ten miles in a night, and the troops were seasoned enough to leave the enemy small satisfaction no matter what direction they were going.

All of this the German Army could do—but not in December 1941. The 1st Panzer Division should have blocked the Russian drive to Klin, but how could it when it could not get to the Russians? Third Panzer Group's and Second Panzer Army's withdrawals were, considering the complications, minor masterpieces of military art. But everywhere the troops pulled back they left equipment standing. Guns, tanks, and trucks that would not soon be replaced would make each successive move more difficult and more dangerous and would in the meantime silently encourage the enemy. Soviet attacks were still mostly extemporaneous. Yet worse would come when the Russians became certain of their advantage, which they could easily deduce from the abandoned equipment. All the German armies needed fresh troops, but Bock had none to give. To create reserves out of what he had was hopeless; no army commander was going to relinquish even a battalion when he might need it desperately himself very soon.

On the morning of the 9th, resuming a telephone conference begun the night before, Bock told Halder that Army Group Center had to have reinforcements because it could not stand off a determined attack anywhere on its whole front. He said he was already converting every kind of specialist except tank drivers into infantry. Halder speculated that the Russians were using

A GERMAN COLUMN STALLED IN THE SNOW

cadres and untrained troops that they really wanted to save for the coming spring, and so things could be expected to become quieter "by the middle or the end of the month." From there on the exchange trailed off into futility. Bock responded, "By then the army group will be *kaputt* [smashed]." Halder replied, "The German soldier does not go *kaputt!*" Bock said he did not want to "whine and complain," but he wanted reserves. Halder replied that the army group would "certainly get whatever small reserves [could] be scraped together."[13]

After that Bock instructed the army commands to plan to take the entire army group back sixty to ninety miles to the Rzhev-Gzhatsk-Orel-Kursk line. But he did not believe that would help either because it would take weeks to prepare the new line and to start back before then would be "an excursion into nowhere." Furthermore, the equipment losses sustained in the small withdrawals undertaken so far would be multiplied by the hundreds. At best, the potential relief would probably be negligible. As Kluge pointed out, the Russians could be hammering at the new line within three days. To Kluge, Bock confessed, "I am at the point of sending the *Fuehrer* a personal telegram telling him I am confronted with decisions here that go far beyond the military." What those might be he did not say. A general retreat, possibly of

[13]*H. Gr. Mitte, Ia Kriegstagebuch, Dezember 1941,* 8 and 9 Dec 41, H. Gr. Mitte 26974/6 file.

Napoleonic proportions, appears the most likely.[14] On the 10th, an OKH promise of two or three fresh divisions gave Bock a slim excuse for deferring the talk of retreat. However, these divisions would not start leaving the Western Theater until the 16th and could not be expected on the Eastern Front for at least a month.

Although he would scarcely have imagined it, Bock's situation could have been much worse. Soviet tactical performance in the first four days of the counteroffensive had been disappointing. A *West Front* directive issued on 9 December read:

Some of our units are pushing the enemy back frontally instead of going around him and encircling him. Instead of breaking through the enemy's fortifications, they stand before them and complain about problems and heavy losses. These negative modes of operations give the enemy the chance to redeploy to new lines, regroup, and organize resistance anew.[15]

Zhukov ordered the *West Front* armies to set up mobile groups with tanks, cavalry, and infantry armed with automatic weapons to strike behind the enemy, particularly against his motor fuel dumps and artillery positions.

On the 10th, the Russians cut the road out of Klin, Third Panzer Group's single route to the west. Third Panzer Group described the scene on the road east of Klin:

. . . discipline is breaking down. More and more soldiers are heading west on foot without weapons, leading a calf on a rope or pulling a sled loaded with potatoes. The road is under constant air attack. Those killed by the bombs are no longer being buried. All the hangers-on (corps troops,

Luftwaffe, supply trains) are pouring to the rear in full flight. Without rations, freezing, irrationally they are pushing back. Vehicle crews that do not want to wait out the traffic jams in the open are drifting off the roads and into the villages. Ice, inclines, and bridges create horrendous blockages. Traffic control is working day and night and barely maintaining some movement. The panzer group has reached its most dismal hour.[16]

Guderian characterized his Second Panzer Army as a scattered assemblage of armed baggage trains slowly wending their way to the rear. Second Army could not mount a counterattack against the fast-moving but vulnerable Soviet cavalry because it had no motor fuel and its troops were exhausted. In another dubious command shuffle, Bock put Second Army under Guderian. He admitted that Guderian's recent emotional outbursts raised a question as to his fitness to command two armies, but he said, "At least he has energy."[17]

For Bock everything was going wrong. Ice and snow were tearing down the telephone lines in all directions. He had transferred a security division of overage and limited service troops from railroad guard duty to Second Army where they were unlikely to be of much use, and the Soviet partisans had blown up a bridge on the army group's main line. At Vyazma, two trains crashed head on and blocked the track. A train of tank cars carrying motor fuel reached Fourth Panzer Group empty. On the 12th, during an interval when the telephones were working, Halder heard some of

---

[14]*Ibid.*, 10 Dec 41.
[15]*VOV*, p. 114.

[16]*Pz. AOK 3, Gefechtsbericht Russland 1941–42*, Pz. AOK 3 21818/2 file.
[17]*H. Gr. Mitte, Ia Kriegstagebuch, Dezember 1941*, 12 Dec 41, H. Gr. Mitte 26974/6 file.

the army group's troubles and, changing his opinion of two days before, pronounced the situation "the worst crisis in the two world wars."[18]

Hitler, meanwhile, had spent three days in Berlin on an errand he found as handy at the moment as it would be problematical in its longer range implications. Recently he had been less well informed than Stalin about the plans of his ally Japan, and the attack on Pearl Harbor on 7 December had surprised him about as much as it had most of the world. Hitler would probably have welcomed more a Japanese attack on the Soviet Union, but he had known since midsummer that the Japanese would not commit themselves against the Soviets in East Asia except to reap what they could from a German victory. Also, he would have viewed a continuing Japanese threat to the United States in the Pacific as more useful than an outright war since his policy thus far had been to keep the United States out of the conflict. On the other hand, Pearl Harbor came when he needed something to turn attention from the Eastern Front and when he had convinced himself that the United States was going to be an annoying but not decisive opponent in or out of the war. On the 11th, in a speech before the *Reichstag,* he declared war on the United States.

Brauchitsch at the Front

Desperate, the army commanders, especially Guderian and Kluge, clamored for Field Marshal Brauchitsch to come to the front and see their plight for himself. They did not believe that the top leadership was getting accurate

information about their situation. Bock denied any fault on his part for the poor communications but more than half agreed with them otherwise. What substantive help they could have expected from Brauchitsch is difficult to discern. In the best times, his authority had not been commensurate with his post as commander in chief, army. Since October, he had been an ambulatory cardiac patient. Lately, Hitler had ignored him and used him, as Halder put it, "as little more than a letter carrier."[19] Brauchitsch had already decided to resign and was preoccupied mostly with how to do so since he felt obligated to Hitler for his appointment and, apparently, for more personal favors.[20]

On 10 December, Brauchitsch had tried to keep himself aloof from Army Group Center's troubles by sending telegrams to Bock and each army commander telling them that he and Hitler were "aware of the difficult situation on the front in the battle with the enemy and with nature."[21] When this effort to reassure them failed, Brauchitsch appeared shortly after 1200 on the 13th at Bock's headquarters in Smolensk. By then Bock and the army commanders had agreed that they had to take the army group back to the Rzhev-Gzhatsk-Orel-Kursk line. Kluge, who had objected to the withdrawal when the army group had proposed it three days before, now said he had changed his mind. His troops, he warned, especially Third and Fourth Panzer

---

[18]*Ibid.*

[19]*Halder Diary,* vol. III, p. 332.

[20]See Harold C. Deutsch, *Hitler and His Generals* (Minneapolis: University of Minnesota Press, 1974), pp. 220–30.

[21]*H. Gr. Mitte, Ia Kriegstagebuch, Dezember 1941,* 10 Dec 41, H. Gr. Mitte 26974/6 file.

GERMAN MORTAR SQUAD ON THE MARCH

Groups, would be destroyed in another eight or ten days the way things were going, and it was necessary, therefore, to sacrifice the equipment to save the men. General Adolf Strauss, who also had believed earlier that he could hold his position, said Ninth Army would have to give up Kalinin, the northern cornerpost of the army group front. In his first conversation with Brauchitsch, Bock said the question was whether the army group should stand and fight and risk "being smashed to pieces" or withdraw and take substantial losses in material.[22]

Early on the 14th, Brauchitsch went to Roslavl to confer with Kluge and Guderian, and Generalmajor Rudolf

Schmundt, Hitler's chief adjutant, arrived in Smolensk. Although Schmundt held a relatively low rank, he was a member of Hitler's inner circle, which Brauchitsch was not. Most likely Hitler sent Schmundt to show the *Fuehrer*'s concern and to protect his interests in any decisions Brauchitsch might make. Brauchitsch returned to Smolensk late that afternoon. He had learned that Guderian's front west of Tula was also beginning to tear, and he agreed that the army group would have to pull back to Bock's proposed line. For an hour or so it looked as if they had at last achieved a consensus. Schmundt called General Jodl at the OKW Operations Staff to get a quick decision from Hitler who answered with a prompt but apparently qualified

---

[22]*Ibid.*, 13 Dec 41.

"no." Hitler said Ninth Army and Third Panzer Group could draw west from Kalinin and Klin enough to "straighten" their lines. Second Panzer Army could do the same around Tula. Otherwise, he forbade "giving up any place or taking any evasive action" until "something" was done to ready a line in the rear. Neither Brauchitsch nor Bock talked to Jodl, who had relayed Hitler's decision. Both assumed "some" preparation would satisfy Hitler, and Bock ordered the armies to get ready to go back and to prepare the Rzhev-Gzhatsk-Orel-Kursk line "to the extent possible."[23]

A Time for Decisions

The morning of the 15th saw Brauchitsch on his way back to East Prussia as another cold wave numbed the Eastern Front. During the night the temperature had dropped to $-33°$ F. at Tikhvin. In the morning, Leeb telephoned Hitler, something his colleague Bock had thus far avoided, and he told the *Fuehrer* that the time had come to give up the idea of holding close to Tikhvin. To Hitler's familiar protest that giving up their last handhold at Tikhvin would expose the Leningrad bottleneck, Leeb replied that the troops had to have some shelter and rest; therefore, they had to take them forty-five miles west to the Volkhov River line. When Hitler failed to give a clear decision either way, Leeb assumed the choice was his and, at 1200, issued the order to start for the Volkhov. Seven hours later Field Marshal Keitel, chief of the OKW, called and asked Leeb to stop because Hitler could still

not decide. Leeb thereupon chose to visit the *Fuehrer* Headquarters.[24]

At Army Group Center that day, Ninth Army was ready to evacuate Kalinin, having set demolition charges throughout the city and particularly on the Volga River Bridge. Third and Fourth Panzer Groups were retreating in $-15°$ F. weather and snow that Hoepner predicted would cost Fourth Panzer Group most of its artillery. Bock urged him to "consider every step back a hundred times." Guderian had a ten-mile-wide gap in Second Panzer Army's front west of Tula, and Schmidt reported that Second Army could only hold forward of the Orel-Kursk railroad if the enemy made bad mistakes, which he showed no signs of doing. At noon on the 15th, the OKH operations branch chief, Colonel Heusinger, telephoned advance notice of a *Fuehrer* order he said would follow. Under it, he said, Ninth Army and Third and Fourth Panzer Groups could withdraw thirty to forty miles to Staritsa and the line of the Lama and Ruza rivers. The army group, Heusinger added, would also be free to withdraw "gradually" to the Rzhev-Gzhatsk-Orel-Kursk line.[25]

The Fuehrer Takes Command

Hitler's "Yes" and "No"

The 16th was a day of decisions at *Fuehrer* Headquarters. Hitler had returned there the night before after he had prolonged his stay in Berlin for some minor diplomatic affairs. His absence from the *Wolfsschanze*, however,

[23]*Ibid.*, 14 Dec 41.

[24]*H. Gr. Nord, Ia Kriegstagebuch, 1.12.-31.12.41*, 15 Dec 41, H. Gr. Nord 75128/4 file.
[25]*AOK 2, Ia Kriegstagebuch Russland, Teil II*, 15 Dec 41, AOK 2 16690/2 file; *H. Gr. Mitte, Ia Kriegstagebuch, Dezember 1941*, 15 Dec 41, H. Gr. Mitte 26974/6 file.

did not mean he was out of touch with what was going on at the front. Everything he needed or wanted to know was available to him by telephone or through the army's communications center at Zossen, twenty miles south of Berlin. But he was out of personal contact with the military chiefs, which may have suited him since he tended to vacillate near lethargy while making crucial decisions. On the 14th, he had given Bock and Brauchitsch a "no" that sounded like a "yes." On the 15th, he had been unable to decide about Tikhvin after more than seven hours but had apparently agreed to a far more extensive withdrawal for Army Group Center. A day later, though, this thinking too would change.

In a morning interview with Leeb on the 16th, Hitler, barely protesting, agreed to let Army Group North give up the Tikhvin salient. With Brauchitsch present, he blamed the current predicament on bad advice from the OKH. He had always known, he declared, that Army Group North was too weak. If the OKH had given Third Panzer Group to Army Group North in August as he had wanted it to, Leningrad would have been completely surrounded, contact would have been made with the Finns, and there would be no problem.[26]

Having made his decision on Tikhvin, Hitler considered the questions pertaining to Army Group Center. At 1200, Halder telephoned Hitler's decisions to Bock. Army Group Center, he said, would receive an order allowing Ninth Army and Third and Fourth Panzer Groups to complete their withdrawals, "if no other choice

existed." The other armies would close the gaps in their lines and stand fast. Halder had not attended the morning's meeting and was transmitting what he had heard from Jodl. The order, as Hitler was having those in the OKW Operations Branch write it, was much stronger than Halder knew. They were making a strategic decision equal to any thus far in the war, and the OKH was out of the picture, primarily because Brauchitsch had ceased to function even as a "letter carrier." After the morning conference, Schmundt told Bock's chief of staff, General Greiffenberg, that Hitler had "sidetracked" Brauchitsch as far as the discussions of the current situation were concerned. For now Schmundt said he would be the army group's point of contact at *Fuehrer* Headquarters because Hitler "was taking everything into his own hands."

When Bock asked later whether Brauchitsch had reported how close the army group was to being "smashed to pieces," Schmundt said he had not. Implying that Hitler had not been told how serious Bock's situation was, Schmundt added that Hitler had said he "could not send everything out into the winter just because Army Group Center had a few gaps in its front." Still unwilling to talk to Hitler in person, Bock recapitulated his troubles to Schmundt and asked him to relay them to Hitler. Lamely he added that it was really impossible to tell which was more dangerous, to hold or to retreat. Either way the army group was likely to be destroyed. At midnight, Hitler called Bock. Schmundt had reported their earlier conversation, Hitler said, and there was only one correct decision, "not to go a step back, to close the gaps

[26]*H. Gr. Nord, Ia Kriegstagebuch, Dezember 1941,* 15 Dec 41, H. Gr. Nord 75128/4 file.

and hold." He assured Bock that infantry reinforcements and air transport were in a state of readiness, and he was supervising their deployment himself. When Bock, trying to turn the talk to what might happen before the reinforcements came, remarked that the front "could rip open any hour," Hitler cut him off with a curt, "I will have to take that chance into the bargain," and hung up.[27]

If Hitler prided himself on one thing above all, it was his ability to handle a crisis. He liked to describe himself as beset by crises throughout his life, many of which he mastered against seemingly hopeless odds. On that score, in fact, he did not have to boast; his record spoke for him. He had not only mastered crises; he had profited from them. Some he had even contrived. The one on the Eastern Front in December 1941 was a crisis he did not want, but when he knew he could not evade it, he did what he had done with all of the others. He set out to resolve it on the terms most satisfactory to himself, terms of power, his power which, whatever qualms he might have begun to have about the future, he judged would be more than enough to bring him through that winter in Russia. What the army could not do in its own fashion it would have to do in his. He could not control the weather or the Russians, but he could manipulate the German Army.

"Fanatical Resistance"

How he would do that began to emerge on the morning of the 18th when the order announced two days

before came over the teletype to Army Group Center. It read:

The Fuehrer has ordered: Larger evasive movements cannot be made. They will lead to a total loss of heavy weapons and equipment. Commanding generals, commanders, and officers are to intervene in person to compel the troops to fanatical resistance in their positions without regard to enemy broken through [sic] on the flanks or in the rear. This is the only way to gain the time necessary to bring up the reinforcements from Germany and the West that I have ordered. Only if reserves have moved into rearward positions can thought be given to withdrawing to those positions.[28]

Within the army group the reaction ranged from resignation to outrage. Kluge predicted that no matter what the orders the army group could not hold the line. Reinhardt and Hoepner doubted that they could bring the Third and Fourth Panzer Groups' divisions to even a temporary stop on the Lama-Ruza line. Bock passed the order on without protest and told Hoepner to "hold your fist in the backs of these people." Guderian asked for an airplane to take him to Hitler. Over the telephone he told the army group chief of staff:

The situation is more serious than one could imagine. If something does not happen soon, things will occur that the German armed forces have never before experienced. I will take these orders and file them. I will not pass them on even under threat of court-martial. I want at least to give my career a respectable ending.[29]

[27]H. Gr. Mitte, Ia Kriegstagebuch, Dezember 1941, 16 Dec 41, H. Gr. Mitte 26974/6 file.

[28]Der Fuehrer und Oberste Befehlshaber der Wehrmacht, WFSt, Abt. L. (I Op.) Nr. 442182, 16.12.41, OKW 2018 file; OKH, GenStdH, Op. Abt. Nr. 3170/41, an H. Gr. Mitte, 18.12.41, H. Gr. Mitte 65005/7 file.
[29]H. Gr. Mitte, Ia Kriegstagebuch, Dezember 1941, 17–19 Dec 41, H. Gr. Mitte 26974/6 file.

With the order to stand fast, Hitler took all command initiative out of the generals' hands. Later some would say it was probably the best that could have been done under the circumstances, but that was later. At the moment, Hitler had mercilessly saddled an entire army group with a suicide mission. Ruthless compulsion now replaced leadership and transformed Army Group Center into a mere agent for Hitler's will.

What the order would accomplish on the snowfields of Russia remained a question. It did abolish the last pretense of army autonomy within the Nazi state with remarkable ease. Talking to Schmundt on the 16th and aware then that he was about to be given an order that would very likely put him in the position of presiding over his army group's destruction, Bock had remarked about his own shaky health, which he said was "hanging by a thread," and had added that Hitler might need "fresh strength" in the army group command. He did not mean, Bock hastened to assure Schmundt, to imply any kind of a threat but was merely stating fact. Whatever his intent had been, he was not prepared for the response he received the next day when Brauchitsch called and told him Hitler wanted him to submit a request for leave. This now struck Bock as "somewhat sudden," and from then on he became more concerned with learning whether "the Fuehrer has a reproach to raise against me on any ground" than with the fate of the army group. On the 19th, having promptly received leave until his health was "fully restored," he turned over command to Kluge and parted from his staff with a limp assertion that the "end of the dirt period" was in sight.[30]

Brauchitsch Resigns

In the meantime, after having been cut out of the decisions on the 16th, Brauchitsch had finally submitted his own resignation. Hitler accepted it on the 19th and immediately dispatched the following proclamation:

Soldiers of the Army and the Waffen SS! Our struggle for national liberation is approaching its climax! Decisions of world importance are about to be made! The Army bears the primary responsibility for battle! I have therefore as of this day myself taken command of the Army! As a soldier who fought in many World War battles I am closely tied to you in the will to victory.[31]

Brauchitsch's going was no great surprise, and he, no doubt to Hitler's satisfaction, made it as banal and pointless an event as a commander in chief's departure at the height of battle could possibly be.

Hitler's taking command of the army, on the other hand, had the effect of an administrative earthquake. In the tangle of agencies with overlapping functions Hitler used to run the war—in particular OKW, OKH, SS, the Munitions Ministry, and the Transport Ministry—a commander in chief, army, even one as weak as Brauchitsch, at least gave the army an identity. Without its own commander in chief, the army lay open to dismemberment; the offices which assumed its functions were clusters of power cut adrift. One such was the Office of the Chief of Army Armament and the Replacement Army

---

[30]*Ibid.*, 16 Dec 41; *Bock Diary, Osten I*, pp. 300–04.
[31]*H. Gr. Mitte, Ia Kriegstagebuch, Dezember 1941*, 19 Dec 41, H. Gr. Mitte 26974/6 file.

under Generaloberst Friedrich Fromm and another was the Office of the Chief of Army Personnel under Generalmajor Bodwin Keitel. Controlling army procurement and production and commanding all army troops inside Germany, Fromm had enough power at his disposal to control the German state. Keitel, younger brother to Wilhelm Keitel, the chief, OKW, kept the officer personnel files and could influence promotions and appointments in all ranks. Fromm and Keitel were directly subordinate to the commander in chief, army. Hitler, however, had no time for what he called "ministerial" functions and put both their offices, nominally at least, under Keitel, the chief, OKW. The OKW, having failed to establish itself as a true joint command over the three services, had for several years been acting as a kind of second army command, superior in its closer relationship to Hitler but unable to reach past the commander in chief, army, directly into army concerns. How much capital the OKW could make out of the army personnel office and the replacement training was perhaps a question, but in armament production, the OKW and the OKH were hard-bitten rivals.

For the heart of OKH, the Army General Staff, the position was even more critical. Jodl's Armed Forces Operations Staff, aside from counseling Hitler on strategy, was already the general staff for all theaters except the East. When Hitler named himself commander in chief, army, if either OKW or OKH did not become superfluous, certainly either the Armed Forces Operations Staff or the Army General Staff did. Hitler, who seldom objected to having two agencies doing one job as

long as he controlled both, told Halder on the afternoon of the 19th to carry on activities in OKH as usual; but within hours word had leaked from *Fuehrer* Headquarters that Jodl soon would replace Halder as chief of the Army General Staff, and General Manstein would move from Eleventh Army to replace Jodl. According to the rumor, the changes would occur as soon as Manstein finished his operations in the Crimea, which were then expected to last only a few more weeks.[32] Manstein stood well with Hitler, who had profited from his strategic ideas particularly in the 1940 campaign in the West, and not well at all with the General Staff who had long viewed him as too importunate for Halder's post. Jodl and Manstein could have spelled the end for the OKH as it had existed under Brauchitsch and Halder.

If Hitler had deprived the field commands of their initiative, he had done even more to OKH. In the prevailing atmosphere of change charged with apprehension and ambition, he could do exactly as he pleased. No one was going to oppose him. On the 20th, he gave Halder orders on how he wanted the war in the East conducted. A "fanatical will to fight" would have to be instilled in the troops by "all, even the most severe, means." Soldiers had no "contracts" restricting them to specific duties. Those in support positions, such as bakers, could defend their own positions, and all troops would have to learn to "tolerate breakthroughs." Rifle pits were to be dug by blasting holes in

---

[32]*Der Chef der Heeresruestung und Befehlshaber des Ersatzheeres, Der Chef des Stabes, Tagebuch,* 19 Dec 41, CMH X–124 file.

GERMANS SURRENDER TO A SOVIET SOLDIER

the ground or by blowing them in with artillery fire. The Germans could take winter clothing from Soviet civilians; the army was solely obligated to take care of its own troops. And, he demanded, "Every man must defend himself where he is."[33] Halder transmitted a summary of these orders to the army groups as an "elucidation" of the standfast order.[34]

Guderian at the Fuehrer Headquarters

On the morning of the 20th, also, Guderian set out for the *Fuehrer* Headquarters by airplane—without stopping at the army group headquarters

as protocol would ordinarily have required. While Guderian's Second Panzer Army was in flight, Kluge was occupied with telegrams from his other army commanders. Fourth Army reported:

Enemy attacking in the army's deep flank, aiming toward Kaluga. Army has no more forces at its disposal. Combat strength sinking. Holding present positions not possible in the long run.[35]

From Hoepner at Fourth Panzer Group Kluge had heard that:

The Commanding Generals of XXXXVI and V Corps have reported they cannot hold. Heavy losses of trucks and weapons in recent days. They had to be destroyed

---

[33]*Halder Diary,* vol. III, pp. 356–60.
[34]*OKH, GenStdH, Op. Abt. Nr. 32081/41, an H. Gr. Mitte, 21.12.41,* H. Gr. Mitte 65005/7 file.

[35]*H. Gr. Mitte, Ia, an OKH, GenStdH, Op. Abt., 20.12.41,* H. Gr. Mitte 65005/7 file.

for lack of gasoline. Weapons now 25–30 percent of requirements. Only course to give orders to hold to the last man. The troops will then be gone and there will be a hole in the front.[36]

And from Strauss at Ninth Army:

Present battle area wooded and has poor visibility. If it has to hold there the army is likely to be broken through and smashed.[37]

To Halder at OKH with whom he was in telephone contact throughout the day, Kluge presented various proposals for withdrawals. All of them Halder rejected, citing Hitler's diverse strictures against giving up positions.

After nightfall, Kluge was back on the telephone to Halder telling him that Guderian's courage had waned, and he did not intend to hold his line. On checking Second Panzer Army's reports and dispositions, Kluge said, he had discovered that Guderian had moved one regiment from each of the army's divisions back forty miles to the Oka River, which could only mean he was going to retreat. Guderian had by then arrived at the *Fuehrer* Headquarters and was with Hitler when Halder phoned in the information from Kluge. In a stormy interview, which Keitel, chief of the OKW, witnessed in dismay, Hitler accused Guderian of having concocted "an insane scheme."[38] Afterward, Halder called Kluge and told him that Hitler had "straightened out" Guderian and given

him a direct order to hold his front exactly where it stood.[39]

Having exposed Guderian's plan, Kluge returned to his own proposals for withdrawals. The trouble with what Guderian wanted to do, he said, was that it would have been a "full-blown retreat," not a step-by-step withdrawal. Halder, who did not want to have to discuss either alternative with Hitler, tried the next morning to influence Kluge, through General Brennecke, his chief of staff, to hold at all positions for another two weeks. He predicted the crisis would pass by then, and he said the army group would be sorry if it pulled back too soon.[40]

Finally, on the morning of the 22d, Bock, who had made the trip by stages in a sedan, arrived at the *Fuehrer* Headquarters. He was much relieved by the friendly way Hitler received him that afternoon, and they proceeded to talk about Army Group Center in general terms. Bock apparently was satisfied when Hitler assured him that he knew how serious the army group's situation was. After Hitler also assured him that he could report back when he was recovered, Bock took his leave. Stopping only long enough to ask Schmundt again whether there were any "reproaches" against him, he resumed his winter's drive, this time toward Berlin.[41]

As commander in chief, army, Hitler was no more moved by the troubles of any one group than he ever had been. He hated to lose ground, but human

[36]*Pz. AOK 4, (Hoepner) an H. Gr. Mitte, 18.12.41,* H. Gr. Mitte 65005/7 file.
[37]*AOK 9, Ia Nr. 4517/41, an H. Gr. Mitte, 19.12.41,* H. Gr. Mitte 65005/7 file.
[38]*General Halder's Daily Notes,* vol. I, 20 Dec 41, EAP 21–g–16/4/0 file.

[39]*H. Gr. Mitte, Ia Kriegstagebuch, Dezember 1941,* 20 Dec 41, H. Gr. Mitte 26974/6 file. See also Guderian, *Panzer Leader,* pp. 264–68.
[40]*H. Gr. Mitte, Ia Kriegstagebuch, Dezember 1941,* 21 Dec 41, H. Gr. Mitte 26974/6 file.
[41]*Bock Diary, Osten I,* p. 304.

misery did not touch him. In one of the late-night monologues he delivered to his secretaries and selected guests, he observed:

Luckily nothing lasts forever—and that is a consoling thought. Even in raging winter, one knows that spring will follow. And if, at this moment, men are being turned into blocks of ice, that won't prevent the April sun from shining and restoring life to these desolate places.[42]

In fact, his thoughts shifted readily away from human suffering to other concerns. He worried about a loss of prestige at Leningrad and discussed with Halder the possibility of using poison gas to end the resistance in the city fast.[43]

On the 23d, Hitler called Fromm in from Berlin to report on manpower and armaments. (Fromm appreciated this call as a significant triumph over his recently designated chief, Keitel, who had tried to make himself the channel for such reports.) Hitler talked to Fromm for hours about rebuilding the army for a 1942 offensive and about a "tractor of the future," which would use far less raw material than would trucks. He said Dr. Ferdinand Porsche, the Volkswagen designer, would have a prototype ready "in a few days." As far as the Eastern Front was concerned, he expected to be "over the hump" in ten days to two weeks. He said "there had been a hole near Tula," but elsewhere, the front would hold.[44]

After the first few days, the generals found having Hitler in direct command, if ominous, also somewhat stimulating. For a long time none of them had known what went on between Brauchitsch and Hitler, if anything; and in recent weeks, Brauchitsch had virtually not communicated with Hitler or his own subordinates. From 19 December on, Halder and two or three of his branch chiefs saw Hitler every day. True, he lectured to them more than he consulted them, but they were at the center and no longer getting their instructions second or third hand through Keitel, Jodl, or Schmundt. Fromm was even encouraged. He wrote to his military district commanders, "The Fuehrer's taking command is an honor for the Army. The Army's work will become easier, not more difficult."[45] After his conference with Hitler on the 23d, he believed that either the OKH or the OKW would "disappear," but he had enough confidence in the OKH's prospect for survival to instruct his staff to "march with all energy" in the cause of the OKH.[46] Kluge was commanding an army group in desperate peril, but he was, at last, holding a command commensurate with his field marshal's rank. When Bock arrived in Berlin, however, he learned—with anguish—that he was not the commanding general, Army Group Center, on leave, but had been put along with Rundstedt, ex-commanding general, Army Group South, in the command reserve pool.[47]

---

[42]*Hitler's Secret Conversations* (New York: Farrar, Strause & Young, 1953), p. 140.

[43]*General Halder's Daily Notes*, vol. I, 23 Dec 41, EAP 21–g–16/4/0 file.

[44]*Der Chef der Heeresruestung und Befehlshaber des Ersatzheeres, Der Chef des Stabes, Tagebuch*, 23 Dec 41, CMH X–124 file.

[45]*Ibid.*, 22 Dec 41.

[46]*Ibid.*, 23 Dec 41.

[47]*Bock Diary, Osten I*, p. 306.

CHAPTER V

The Counteroffensive: Second Phase

Roles Reversed

The Soviet Initiative

The first phase of the counteroffensive ended on 16 December with the German spearheads, which had been aimed at Moscow, eliminated and the majority of the original Soviet objectives taken. *Twentieth Army* had entered Solnechnogorsk on the 12th, and *Tenth Army* was in Stalinogorsk the next day. A mobile group set up by *Thirtieth Army* took Klin on the 15th, and *Thirty-first Army* troops marched into Kalinin on the 16th. The armies had advanced over thirty miles on the north flank and better than fifty miles on the south. No new armies had been deployed during the first phase; however, the number of troops committed had probably grown substantially during the ten-day period. General Lelyushenko, at *Thirtieth Army,* had been awaiting the arrival of the larger part of a half-dozen Siberian and Urals divisions when the counteroffensive began.[1]

General Zhukov had issued an initial second phase directive to his right flank armies on 13 December. In it, he ordered them to advance to "an average distance of 130 to 160 kilometers [78 to 96 miles] west and northwest of Moscow."[2] Zhukov believed that the ob-

jective for the rest of the winter should be to drive the entire Army Group Center back 150 miles to the line east of Smolensk from which it had launched TAIFUN in early October. To do so, he estimated, would require resupply and replacements for the armies already in action and four fresh armies from the *Stavka* reserves. Zhukov's thought was to keep the advance essentially frontal while using mobile groups, which were being formed in all the armies (typically out of a cavalry division, a tank brigade, and a rifle brigade), to strike at targets of opportunity ahead of the main forces.[3]

Stalin and the *Stavka,* however, were beginning to think in less conservative terms. They allowed *West Front* to go into the second phase as Zhukov proposed but without the four armies as reinforcements. Zhukov made this change, bringing his center, which consisted of *Fifth, Thirty-third, Forty-third,* and *Forty-ninth Armies,* into the counteroffensive on 18 December. Elements of *Fifth Army,* including a mobile group under General Mayor L. M. Dovator, had been in action since the 11th, and *Forty-ninth Army's* left flank had been engaged together with *Fiftieth Army* in the Tula sector since the 14th. *Thirty-third* and *Forty-third Armies* took a week to move out of their starting positions.[4] *(Map 7.)*

---

[1]*IVMV,* vol. IV, p. 289; *VOV,* p. 115; Yevstigneyev, *Velikaya bitva,* p. 184; Lelyushenko, *Moskva,* p. 90.

[2]Lelyushenko, *Moskva,* p. 110.

[3]Zhukov, *Memoirs,* p. 351. See *VOV,* p. 115.

[4]*IVOVSS,* vol. II, pp. 286–88; *IVMV,* vol. IV, pp. 289–91; *VOV,* p. 118.

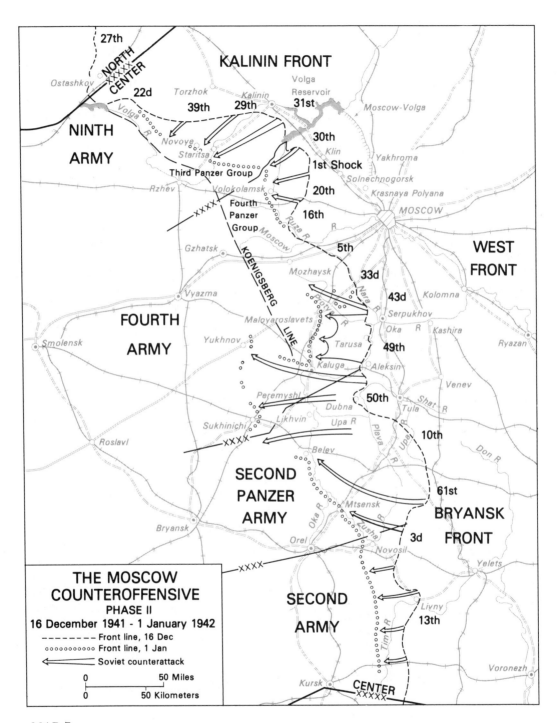

27th

NORTH
XXXX
CENTER

Ostashkov

KALININ FRONT

Volga
Reservoir

Moscow-Volga

22d

Torzhok

39th

Volga R.

29th

Kalinin

31st

NINTH

ARMY

Novoye

30th

Klin

Yakhroma

Staritsa

Third Panzer Group

1st Shock

Solnechnogorsk

Rzhev

Volokolamsk

Fourth
Panzer
Group

20th

16th

Krasnaya Polyana

Ruza R.

MOSCOW

Gzhatsk

Moscow R.

5th

WEST

Vyazma

KOENGSBERG

Mozhaysk

33d

Nara R.

43d

Kolomna

FRONT

FOURTH

ARMY

Smolensk

LINE

Maloyaroslavets

Protva R.

Serpukhov

Oka R.

Kashira

Ryazan

Yukhnov

Tarusa

49th

Aleksin

Venev

Kaluga

Peremyshl

Dubna

50th

Shat R.

Tula

Likhvin

Upa R.

Plava R.

10th

Don R.

Sukhinichi

Roslavl

XXXX

Belev

Upa R.

61st

SECOND

PANZER

ARMY

Mtsensk

Oka R.

Zusha R.

BRYANSK

Bryansk

3d

FRONT

Orel

Novosil

Yelets

XXXX

SECOND

Livny

ARMY

13th

Tim R.

Voronezh

THE MOSCOW
COUNTEROFFENSIVE
PHASE II
16 December 1941 - 1 January 1942

- - - - - - - Front line, 16 Dec
ooooooooooo Front line, 1 Jan
⟵⟵⟵⟵ Soviet counterattack

0   50 Miles

0   50 Kilometers

Kursk

CENTER
XXXX

MAP 7

The reinforcements went to the outer flanks of the offensive, which were not under Zhukov's control. *Thirtieth Army,* from *West Front,* and *Thirty-ninth Army,* from the *Stavka* reserves, went to *Kalinin Front,* and General Konev's orders as of 18 December were to employ those and his *Twenty-second, Twenty-ninth,* and *Thirty-first Armies* in a drive west and southwest behind the Army Group Center left flank to Rzhev. On the south, between 18 and 24 December, the *Stavka* reactivated the *Bryansk Front* under General Cherivichenko, giving it *Third* and *Thirteenth Armies* and *Sixty-first Army* from the reserve.[5] Cherivichenko had orders to break through Second Army and strike northwest behind the Army Group Center right flank to Mtsensk.

The *Stavka,* at that point, had nothing less in mind than to encircle Army Group Center by having *Kalinin Front* head south past Rzhev to Vyazma while *Bryansk Front* came west and northwest to Vyazma and Bryansk.[6] Ambition was high in Moscow.

"When Things Start To Go Wrong"

In mid-December, across the front on the German side, new Soviet units were still being identified in such numbers that the OKH almost did not want to hear the reports. General Halder sent an advisory letter through General Staff channels in which he said, "The large number of enemy units identified has sometimes had a paralyzing effect on our leadership. . . . The leadership must not be allowed to fall into a numbers

psychosis. Intelligence officers must be trained to be discriminating."[7] The Soviet troops, as Halder meant to imply, were in fact often short on quality. Many were boys or middle-aged men, half-trained and thrown into battle sometimes without hand weapons, often with inadequate artillery and automatic weapons support, always with a ruthless disregard for losses. In *Tenth Army,* 75 percent of the troops were in the thirty- to forty-year age bracket or older; in *First Shock Army,* 60 to 70 percent.[8] The same was probably true of the other reserve armies. But the troops were warmly dressed and their levels of supplies and equipment appeared to be rising. Moreover, in their seeming ability to endure cold, they appeared almost superhuman. The Germans marveled at the Soviet troops' ability to remain in the open at temperatures far below zero for days in succession. Some did freeze, but most survived and kept on fighting.[9] Like the Soviet troops, the Soviet T–34 tank was also proving itself in the winter. Its compressed air starter could turn its engine over in the coldest weather, and its broad tracks could carry the T–34 across ditches and hollows holding five feet of snow.

Field Marshal Bock had remarked earlier in the month, "In these situations, when some things start to go wrong everything does." By the middle of the month, the aphorism, as far as it applied to Army Group Center, had become a statement of fact. In the midst of winter and under constant enemy pressure, the armies were beset with troubles. Nor-

[5]*IVOVSS,* vol. II, pp. 283, 288–89, 294; *IVMV,* vol. IV, pp. 289, 291.

[6]*IVOVSS,* vol. II, p. 288; *IVMV,* vol. IV, p. 291. See also V. D. Sokolovskiy, ed., *Razgrom nemetsko-fashistkikh voysk pod Moskvoy* (Moscow: Voyennoye Izdatelstvo, 1964), p. 270.

[7]*OKH, GenStdH, Chef des Generalstabes Nr. 10/42, Beurteilung der Feindlage, 17.1.42,* H 3/2 file.

[8]Zakharov, *Proval,* pp. 257, 278.

[9]*Pz. AOK, Ic Taetigkeitsbericht Nr. 3, 12.8.41–30.1.42,* 16 Dec 41, Pz. AOK 3 16911/32 file.

SOVIET INFANTRY ON THE ATTACK

mally each had enough transport to move between 2,500 and 3,000 tons of supplies a day. Because of snow, cold, breakdowns, and losses, Second Panzer Army could manage no more than 360 tons a day, and the others were no better off. Winter clothing, except for items overlooked in planning months before, such as fur parkas and felt boots, was in the army depots at the railheads. So far the Germans had not yet issued a third of the clothing to the troops because they could not deliver these items to the front. Movement of ammunition, gasoline, and rations had to receive an iron priority.[10] Trucks, tanks, and other vehicles, run down after six months in the

field, could not take the strain of being driven through snow and over ice. The Germans were having to abandon some every day, and others were simply worn out or had vital parts broken by the cold. Lubricants froze in crankcases, on bearings, in artillery recoil mechanisms, even in the lightly oiled works of machine guns. Second Panzer Army had 70 tanks in running order and another 168 in repair out of 970 tanks which it had or had received since June. Third Panzer Group would, by the time it reached the Lama River, have destroyed or abandoned 289 tanks. Hitler had ordered 26 new tanks and 25 self-propelled assault guns driven from Army Group South to Second Panzer Army. On the first 60-mile lap, from Dnepropetrovsk to Krasnograd, 8 tanks and 1 assault gun

---

[10]*Pz. AOK 2, O. Qu., Beurteilung der Versorgungslage, 19.12.41, Pz. AOK 2 25034/154 file.*

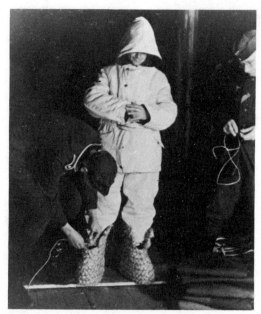

TRYING ON WINTER GEAR, WHICH WAS TOO
SLOW IN COMING

had broken down, and the rest still had 300 miles to go—carrying their own fuel because the truck column transporting the fuel was stuck in mud south of Krasnograd.[11]

Against the Soviet tanks, the armies were having to rely more and more on their field artillery, most of which was not mobile enough or powerful enough to cope with the T–34s. In the fall, the Germans had tested what they called *Rotkopf* ("redhead") ammunition, a hollow-charge artillery shell that could penetrate the Soviet armor, but Hitler had recalled the shells in November. The thought had struck him that if the Russians learned the secret, the hollow-charge would be vastly more effective

against his own lightly armored tanks. Almost daily pleading by the army group and the armies had not persuaded him to release the *Rotkopf* ammunition.

On the Flanks

Pursuit Ends on the North

The crisis on the Army Group Center left flank unexpectedly eased in the week after 15 December. Ninth Army, after giving up Kalinin, was falling back toward Staritsa with *Twenty-second, Twenty-ninth, Thirty-first,* and *Thirtieth Armies* close behind, but *Thirty-ninth Army* was slow in preparing to move, and Konev would be unable to bring it to bear until late in the month.[12] Despite earlier bleak forecasts, by Generals Reinhardt and Hoepner, Third and Fourth Panzer Groups came to a complete stop along the Lama and Ruza rivers by the 19th. After evacuating Klin and Solnechnogorsk, they had moved fast enough to break contact with the Russians and reach the rivers ahead of them. The troops then had time to settle into the villages and organize them as strongpoints, get a night or two of sleep, and eat a few hot meals. The infantry, which had served as the rear guard, saw for the first time how few tanks and how little heavy equipment had survived. Nevertheless their morale recovered—somewhat to the commands' surprise.[13]

The Russians became aware that the pursuit had ended on the 19th when Dovator, the commander of *Fifth Army's* mobile group, *II Guards Cavalry Corps,* was killed on the Ruza River trying to force a crossing with dismounted cos-

[11]*Pz. AOK 2, Panzer-Lage, 19.12.41,* Pz. AOK 2 25034/154 file; *Pz. AOK 3, Panzerkampfwagenlage, 19.1.42,* Pz. AOK 3 16911/8 file; *AOK 6, Ia Nr. 2938/41, an Pz. AOK 2, 19.12.41,* Pz. AOK 2 25034/154 file.

[12]*IVOVSS,* vol. II, p. 289.

[13]*Pz. AOK 3, Gefechtsbericht Russland 1941–42,* Pz. AOK 3 21818/2 file.

AFTER A PAUSE IT IS TIME FOR THE GERMAN TROOPS TO MOVE ON AGAIN

sack cavalry.[14] As would be true for many of his countrymen in succeeding days, Dovator's sacrifice had gone for nothing. Five Soviet armies, *Thirtieth, First Shock, Twentieth, Sixteenth,* and *Fifth* (from north to south), closed to the rivers and were stopped.

Third Panzer Group was ready to sit the winter out on the Lama, and the command believed it could if its neighbors were able to dig in solidly.[15] Fourth Panzer Group, however, was weak on its north flank west of Volokolamsk where the Moscow-Rzhev railline ran through a ten-mile gap between the rivers. There V Panzer Corps, also weak because it had been closest to Moscow and had

made the longest retreat, wavered under *First Shock Army's* attacks and by the 20th was beginning to drain strength from both panzer groups.

On the north at Ninth Army, General Strauss' situation was less acute but in the longer run more dangerous. Strauss went back slowly from Kalinin, a few miles a day, which enabled him to hold his front together but gave his troops no opportunity to break contact with the Russians, get some rest, and dig in as the two panzer groups had done. Moreover, he had no river line on which to fall back. Between Kalinin and Rzhev, Ninth Army would be moving parallel to the Volga. Staritsa, Hitler's choice as Ninth Army's stopping point, was nothing more than a spot on the map and on the ground only a small break in the wilder-

---

[14]Yevstigneyev, *Velikaya bitva*, p. 197.
[15]*Pz. AOK 3, Gefechtsbericht Russland 1941–42,* Pz. AOK 3 21818/2 file.

ness of forest and swamp flanking the Volga from Rzhev to Kalinin.

On the morning of the 21st, when his Ninth Army was about halfway between Kalinin and Staritsa, Strauss flew to Army Group Center headquarters in Smolensk, where he tried to persuade Field Marshal Kluge, its commander, to let the withdrawal continue by small stages, as it was doing, past Staritsa to the K-Line (KOENIGSBERG Line). The K-Line was the Rzhev-Gzhatsk-Orel-Kursk line that Bock had proposed and that the armies continued to talk about as the "winter line." Some work had been done to prepare the K-Line, Strauss explained, while none had been or could be done at Staritsa. Kluge, in reply, cited Hitler's "definitive" order to the army to hold when it reached Staritsa that he said he was determined to execute.[16]

As far as Kluge was concerned, Ninth Army was still in one of the best positions of any of his armies. It had a continuous front and some room to maneuver forward of Staritsa. But whether it would have either one much longer was doubtful. While Strauss was in Smolensk on the 21st, General Leytenant I. I. Maslennikov, Commanding General, *Thirty-ninth Army*, was deploying two divisions between *Twenty-second* and *Twenty-ninth Armies* in the line east of Staritsa to join the strike toward Rzhev. They were a bare beginning. Maslennikov had another six divisions echeloned to the rear, and they were being brought to full readiness at top speed.[17] When the six divisions came into play they would count for a great deal more

than Hitler's order or Kluge's determination in deciding where or when Ninth Army's retreat would end.

General Guderian Does Not Obey

While the Army Group Center left flank appeared after 15 December to have passed the first crisis, the same could hardly be said for the right flank. There Second Panzer and Second Armies, now loosely joined in the so-called Armeegruppe Guderian, were beset by five Soviet armies, by the winter, and by rigidity in the higher headquarters that denied them even the little leeway to maneuver that the left flank armies had. In his decisions culminating in the stand-fast order, Hitler had demanded that Armeegruppe Guderian close the gaps in its front west of Tula and north of Livny and hold the line Aleksin-Dubna-Livny.[18] When he issued the order on the 18th, the Second Panzer Army north flank was already several miles west of Aleksin. Dubna was in the center of the ten-mile-wide gap west of Tula, and Livny, at the southern end of a fifteen-mile gap in the Second Army center, was half surrounded.

Second Army, holding the Armeegruppe Guderian's south flank and covering both its own and Second Panzer Army's main bases, Kursk and Orel, had succeeded in screening Novosil and Livny after the Soviet breakthrough at Yelets. But to defend fifty miles of front from Livny to northeast of Novosil, which included the fifteen-mile gap north of Livny, Second Army's commander, General Schmidt, had only three divisions. The known Soviet forces opposing them were 6 rifle divi-

[16]General der Infanterie a. D. Rudolf Hofmann, MS P–114b, *Der Feldzug gegen die Sowjetunion im Mittelabschnitt der Ostfront*, vol. III, p. 135, CMH files.
[17]*IVOVSS*, vol. II, p. 289.

[18]*OKH, GenStdH, Op. Abt. Nr. 3170/41, an H. Gr. Mitte, 19.12.41,* H. Gr. Mitte 65005/7 file.

sions, 3 motorized divisions, 1 tank brigade, and 2 cavalry divisions. Two German divisions, the 45th and 134th Infantry Divisions, after being trapped in the Soviet breakthrough, were trying to battle their way west between Yelets and Livny. In a few days their fight would be finished. What the Russians did not claim the cold and snow would. The rest of the army was not much better off. From captured Soviet resupply orders, Second Army intelligence predicted that the Soviet drive to the west, toward Livny and Novosil, which had slackened on the 15th would resume in increased strength on the 18th. When the drive did not pick up again, the army was far from reassured. Air reconnaissance reported Soviet reinforcements marching west past Yelets in three columns abreast.[19]

On the morning of the 19th, Schmidt asked Army Group Center for two more divisions because the Russians were forty miles from the Kursk-Orel railroad, he said, and the divisions were needed because:

Second Army's fate hangs on holding the railroad. In the pathless, scoured land west of the railroad the troops can neither stand nor retreat because they cannot be supplied. If the railroad cannot be held then what happens to Second Army will undermine the entire Eastern Front and everything will be set to rolling in the midst of winter.[20]

That night Schmidt went to Orel to deputize for Guderian while the latter was at the *Fuehrer* Headquarters and to ask him for reinforcements from Second Panzer Army which, after the

withdrawal from the bulge east of Tula, had a front only half as long as Second Army's. But instead, Guderian told him to start work on a retreat order and to move his headquarters and supplies back to Bryansk. Guderian, "the great optimist," Schmidt said, appeared to have reached "the end of his hopes."[21]

Second Panzer Army had received Bock's permission on 5 December to withdraw east of Tula to the line of the Shat and Don rivers. Hitler neither approved nor specifically disapproved the withdrawal. Before the army reached the rivers, Guderian came to believe he could not stop there, and on the 12th, while giving him command also of Second Army, Bock authorized him to take his center and right flank another fifty miles west to the Plava River. By then he had two gaps in the front to contend with as well: the one at Yelets in Second Army's center that he was expected to help close by supplying reinforcements for Second Army and the one west of Tula that steadily widened as his left flank corps, XXXXIII Corps, holding fast to the Fourth Army flank, fell back westward and slightly northward toward Aleksin and Kaluga while XXIV Panzer Corps on the south side of the gap withdrew southwestward along the Orel-Tula road.

For his part, Guderian, by the 12th, had apparently considered it pointless to try either to close the front or to stop east of the Oka and Zusha rivers along which Second Panzer Army had built some field fortifications in October before launching the attack past Tula. Going to the Oka and the Zusha would have added approximately forty miles to the total distance of Second Panzer

[19]*AOK 2, Ia Kriegstagebuch, Teil III,* 17–19 Dec 41, Pz. AOK 2 16690/3 file.

[20]*AOK 2, Ia Nr. 690/41, an H. Gr. Mitte, 19.12.41,* H. Gr. Mitte 65005/7 file.

[21]*AOK 2, Ia Kriegstagebuch, Teil III,* 19 Dec 41, AOK 2 16690/3 file.

Army's retreat. Both rivers were included in the Rzhev-Gzhatsk-Orel-Kursk line, the winter or K-Line, that Bock proposed on 14 December; and Guderian maintained in his memoirs that Field Marshal Brauchitsch gave him permission to go to the Oka and the Zusha during their meeting in Roslavl on the 14th.[22] However, Hitler's decisions culminating in the standfast order on the 18th made it extremely uncertain whether Guderian could be allowed to continue his withdrawal even to the Plava. The uncertainty was particularly acute in the mind of Bock's successor, Kluge, who personally believed a retreat was necessary but as commanding general, Army Group Center, committed himself to executing Hitler's orders.

On the 18th, Guderian had had most of four Second Panzer Army divisions strung out along the Orel-Tula road and had headed west. Gangs of drafted civilians kept the snow shoveled off the road, but motor fuel was short, and the speed of the traffic depended less on the condition of the road than on the interval between refuelings. The front was still five to ten miles east of the Plava. During the day Hitler called Guderian directly and urged him to do something about closing the gap on his left flank west of Tula. Guderian replied that to close the gap from the south was impossible. Second Panzer Army, he said, had conducted extensive reconnaissance and had found the whole area impassible owing to poor roads and deep snow.[23]

What, if anything, Guderian would do to assist Second Army was equally doubtful even though his Second Panzer troops on the Orel-Tula road were moving southwestward toward the Second Army flank. Guderian was obligated morally to help Second Army since it was also protecting his own headquarters and main base Orel, but in his continuing argument with Schmidt over where and when to send reinforcements, Guderian insisted that Second Panzer Army was worse off than Second Army and so far had refused to send a single man.[24]

During the night on the 18th, Army Group Center had transferred XXXXIII Corps from Second Panzer to Fourth Army and thereby had converted what had been a gap in the Second Panzer Army front to one between the two armies. Henceforth there would be fewer prospects for closing the front than before. Kluge, whose replacement had not yet arrived, was still commanding Fourth Army as well as the army group, and relations between Fourth Army and Second Panzer Army and their commanding generals were anything but cordial. Second Panzer Army had been subordinated to Fourth Army in the early months of the Russian campaign, which Guderian resented, and Guderian had received more publicity and attention from Hitler, which Kluge resented. Obsessed with his own army's troubles and with his center of gravity lying to the south and the west, Guderian was not likely to exert himself for the benefit of his neighbor on the north, particularly since Fourth Army had so far had the advantage of fighting on a stable front in positions built before winter set in.

---

[22]Guderian, *Panzer Leader*, p. 262.
[23]Hofmann, MS P–114b, vol. III, p. 135.

[24]*AOK 2, Ia Kriegstagebuch, Teil III*, 17 Dec 41, Pz. AOK 2 16690/3 file.

Even after it took control of XXXXIII Corps, Fourth Army would still be unable to do anything about the gap west of Tula. During the day on the 18th, complying with the *Stavka* orders for the second phase of the counteroffensive, *Thirty-third, Forty-third,* and *Forty-ninth Armies* hit the whole length of the Fourth Army front. Fourth Army's line of trenches and dugouts on the Nara River stopped the *Thirty-third* and *Forty-third Armies,* but *Forty-ninth Army* drove XIII Corps, XXXXIII Corps' neighbor on the north, back on both sides of Tarusa while *Fiftieth Army* began working its way around and behind XXXXIII Corps' open flank.[25]

While Guderian was at the *Fuehrer* Headquarters on the 20th, and Kluge was unhappily analyzing Guderian's dispositions, General Leytenant I. V. Boldin, Commanding General, *Fiftieth Army* was unleashing nasty surprises for both German generals. After having watched the gap in the German front widen for almost two weeks to a width of almost thirty miles by the 18th, Boldin had decided to exploit it. He assembled a mobile force of a tank, a cavalry, and a rifle division under his deputy army commander, General Mayor V. S. Popov, and sent it that night around the XXXXIII Corps' open flank in a sneak attack on Kaluga, Fourth Army's railhead and supply base. At the same time he reinforced *I Guards Cavalry Corps* with a rifle division for a strike forty miles due west to Chekalin on the Oka River. By nightfall on the 20th, Popov's group was fighting south of Kaluga, and *I Guards Cavalry Corps* had covered half the distance to Chekalin. On Boldin's left, several *Tenth Army* divisions had also come through the gap and were driving toward Belev on the Oka, fifteen miles south of Chekalin.[26]

When Guderian returned to Orel on the 21st he found awaiting him, in addition to the order Hitler had already given him orally to hold his line exactly where it stood, a second order from Hitler shifting the Second Panzer-Fourth Army boundary north to make Second Panzer Army responsible for defending the Oka River to Peremyshl, twelve miles north of Chekalin. The night before Soviet tanks had broken into Kaluga, and Kluge and his chief of staff talked to Hitler and Halder by telephone several times during the day about taking Fourth Army back and about letting Second Army, which was getting into deeper trouble, give up Livny. Hitler promised "every available aircraft on the whole Eastern Front" for the defense of Kaluga; and Halder, reverting to what was becoming his standard response, opined again that it would be a mistake to give up anything because the crisis would pass in two weeks and then the army group would be sorry.[27]

The next two days were desperate ones for Fourth Army. On the 22d, in a driving snowstorm, Soviet *Forty-ninth Army* broke through the Fourth Army front at Tarusa, splitting XXXXIII Corps off from the army's main body. This action put the Russians in position to disrupt Fourth Army's center and simultaneously encircle XXXXIII Corps which already had the Popov group standing behind it at Kaluga. Kluge told Hitler that he had given orders to

[25]*IVOVSS,* vol. II, p. 292.

[26]*Ibid.,* p. 293.
[27]*H. Gr. Mitte, Ia Kriegstagebuch, Dezember 1941,* 21 Dec 41, H. Gr. Mitte 26974/6 file.

stand fast but believed that "tomorrow we could be confronted with a big decision."[28]

In the afternoon on the 23d, he told Hitler, "We must now answer the question whether we are to stand and let ourselves be killed or take the front back and sacrifice a certain amount of material but save the rest." After asking in detail about how much would be lost and how much saved, Hitler replied, "If there is no other way, I give you liberty to issue the order to withdraw." Kluge assured him he would only use the authority "if I see no other way out of the dilemma" and in any event not in less than twenty-four hours. Later Halder came on the telephone to remark that the air force had reported that the enemy which had broken through between XXXXIII and XIII Corps was "only several ski units" and "history ought not to record that Fourth Army had given an order for its left flank and center to retreat because of a few skiers." The army group chief of staff, General Greiffenberg, answered that the corps had orders to stand fast for the present, but when Halder called back an hour later, Greiffenberg told him that the corps had orders to retreat.[29]

At Chekalin on the 22d, German construction troops, the only Germans nearby, had sighted several small Soviet sled columns approaching the town. A third of a German division, approximately a regiment, was somewhere on its way to Chekalin, but could not get there through the snow in less than forty-eight to seventy-two hours. Guderian was at the front all day, at LIII Panzer Corps. One of its divisions,

296th Infantry Division, had been broken through in several places; and after he returned to Orel shortly before midnight, Guderian told Kluge that in order to follow Hitler's orders, he would have to sacrifice the division.[30] On the 23d, 296th Infantry Division fell back to the Oka River at Belev after its neighbor, the 167th Infantry Division, was almost totally destroyed. Second Panzer Army then reported that it would have to take its entire front behind the Oka and Zusha rivers within the next two or three days. The army group pointed out that the 296th's withdrawal that day had not had Hitler's approval, and that one to the Oka and Zusha could not be made "under any circumstances" unless he agreed.[31]

In the morning on the 24th, Kluge told Halder that Guderian had let 296th Infantry Division go back farther the day before than had been reported, had also taken XXXXVII Panzer Corps, his right flank corps, back without prior authorization, and had not been getting troops to the Oka River between Belev and Chekalin and to the north of them on time. Halder thereupon declared that Guderian should be court-martialed. Kluge, however, could not make up his mind. After all, he said, the snow had drifted badly on the routes to Belev and north, and Second Panzer Army had executed its withdrawals "under the compulsion of circumstances."[32] The OKH

---

[28]*Ibid.*, 22 Dec 41.

[29]*Ibid.*, 23 Dec 41.

[30]Guderian maintained in his memoirs that the purpose of his trip was to explain Hitler's orders. This explanation, however, is inconsistent with his attitude as expressed to the army group. See Guderian, *Panzer Leader*, p. 268.

[31]*H. Gr. Mitte, Ia Kriegstagebuch, Dezember 1941*, 23 Dec 41, H. Gr. Mitte 26974/6 file.

[32]*Ibid.*, 24 Dec 41.

VILLAGERS GREET THE CREW OF A SOVIET T–60 TANK

then tried sending a direct order to Guderian in Hitler's name again forbidding any withdrawals, directing him to dispatch a division to Belev, and requiring him to report his dispositions directly to the OKH before midnight that night.[33]

Whether Guderian could be made to stop or not, Second Army, which was tied in on his right flank, had to move along with it. During the afternoon of the 24th, Second Army's Schmidt told the army group that he was issuing orders to give up Novosil and Livny and to go to the winter line, and he could not wait for approval. Because of low visibility in blowing snow, he did not know where Guderian's flank was or where the Russians were, but in another day he would be unable to make any kind of orderly retreat and maybe no retreat at all from Livny, which was almost encircled.[34]

During that day and much of the night Kluge was alternately on the telephone to Guderian and Halder, warning Guderian against any further withdrawals without Hitler's explicit approval and telling Halder that Chekalin was in flames, the Russians had crossed the Oka, and the Kaluga defense was crumbling. Before midnight he called Halder once more, apologizing for "disturbing your

[33]OKH, GenStdH, Op. Abt. Nr. 32096/41, an H. Gr. Mitte, 24.12.41, H. Gr. Mitte 65005/7 file.

[34]AOK 2, Ia Kriegstagebuch, Teil III, 24 Dec 41, Pz. AOK 2 16690/3 file.

Christmas spirit which probably was not very rosy anyway," to tell him Guderian had asked to be relieved and court-martialed, and the whole Oka line from Belev to Kaluga was in danger.[35]

Christmas, Halder recorded, was "a difficult day." Schmidt reported Soviet tanks across the Tim River, which had been part of the winter line, and called for 88-mm. guns and *Rotkopf* ammunition. The guns and ammunition his troops had were useless against these tanks. Halder and his chief of operations, Colonel Heusinger, and Kluge argued with Guderian over how to defend Chekalin and Belev. Guderian had the 3d and 4th Panzer Divisions free near Orel, but he said he needed 3d Panzer Division to support Second Army. After nightfall, he reported some 4th Panzer Division troops at Belev but the roads from there north impassable except to sleds. In the meantime, Hitler had intervened with an order to put the Belev-Chekalin-Peremyshl sector under Headquarters XXIV Panzer Corps, which had commanded 3d and 4th Panzer Divisions but currently had no units of its own.

Not until later in the night did Kluge look at the day's situation reports. When he did, he discovered that Second Panzer Army had, in the past twenty-four hours, retreated almost to the Oka-Zusha line. Calling Guderian, Kluge accused him of having deliberately given orders opposite to those he had received—to which Guderian replied, "In these unusual circumstances I lead my army in a manner I can

justify to my conscience." Kluge then complained to Halder, "I have the greatest respect for General Guderian. He is a fantastic commander. But he does not obey, and I can only transmit and execute the *Fuehrer*'s orders if I can rely on my army commanders." Always the Hamlet, Kluge added, "I am basically entirely on Guderian's side; one cannot simply let himself be slaughtered, but he must obey and keep me oriented." Within the hour Hitler called to tell Kluge he would "do what is necessary with regard to Generaloberst Guderian," and in the morning an order arrived relieving Guderian of his command and transferring him to the command reserve.[36] A few hours later, as an afterthought, Hitler forbade Guderian to issue any farewell order to his troops.[37]

The Question of a Retreat

Kluge Takes Time To Think

During the night of the 25th, a cold wave swept the Eastern Front while wind and a heavy snowfall added to the drifts already left by the previous days' storms. In the morning Schmidt took command of the Armeegruppe Guderian, now Armeegruppe Schmidt, and General der Gebirgstruppe Ludwig Kuebler, just arrived from Berlin, set out from Smolensk into the snow to

[35]*H. Gr. Mitte, Ia Kriegstagebuch, 1.12.–31.12.41*, 24 Dec 41, H. Gr. Mitte 26974/6 file; *Ferngespraech G.F.M. v. Kluge-Gen. Obst. Halder*, 24 Dec 41, H. Gr. Mitte 65005/7 file.

[36]*H. Gr. Mitte, Ia Kriegstagebuch, 1.12.–31.12.41*, 25 Dec 41, H. Gr. Mitte 26974/6 file.

[37]*General Halder's Daily Notes*, Historical Division, United States Army, Europe, EAP 21–g–16/4/0, vol. 1, 26 Dec 41. On 28 December, Hitler issued instructions through the Army Personnel Office stating, "The weather and battles have worn the nerves of some of the best commanders, and they will have to be relieved. When they are relieved, they are not to issue any farewell orders to subordinate units." *H. Gr. Nord, Ia Kriegstagebuch, 1.12.–31.12.41*, 28 Dec 41, H. Gr. Nord 75128/4 file.

make his way east 120 miles to Yukhnov and take command of Fourth Army. Hitler told him by telephone before he left to make his army stand fast and not give up "a step" except under compulsion.

Up and down the front, roads were drifted shut, and on the raillines locomotives were freezing. Frostbite casualties exceeded available replacements or those scheduled to come. Schmidt was expecting an attack through the winter line toward Kursk; a deep Soviet thrust across the Oka between Belev and Kaluga was clearly in the making; Hoepner did not think Fourth Panzer Group could hold much longer west of Volokolamsk; and Strauss was expecting a heavy attack on Ninth Army's left flank west of Staritsa any day.

Kluge was near—but true to his nature not quite at—the point of forcing a decision. In a long, rambling telephone conversation he told Halder that "the time has come to consider whether it is necessary to take the entire east front of the army group back." Lateral movement, he said, had become impossible. Everything was snowed in. Reinhardt had tried to take over Fourth Army before Kuebler arrived and had not been able to get there by automobile, airplane, or sled. Roads were being drifted shut as fast as they were shoveled clear. The troops could not get anything to eat, and if they did not eat they could not fight. If the Russians made a strike at his lines of communication, he could not move troops fast enough to counter it. "The Fuehrer," he said, "must now come out of his castle in the clouds and be set with both feet on the ground." Halder repeated Hitler's standard objection to

a retreat: once it began it could probably not be stopped. And at the end Kluge admitted that he did not know what line he would want to go back to and would have to "think about it."[38]

On 27 December, noting temperatures of −15° F. in the daytime and −25° F. at night, the Army Group Center journal entry for the day opened with the following general remarks:

All movements burdened by the enormous snowdrifts. Rail transport is stalled for the same reason, and the loss of locomotives owing to freezing increases the problem. The shifting of the few available reserves is stopped by the snow. For the above reasons all time schedules are meaningless. The Russians must contend with the same difficulties, but their mobile, well-equipped cavalry, ski, and sled units (the latter used to bring rations and fodder to the cavalry and to transport infantry) give them tactical advantages that, together with larger manpower reserves, they are now trying to exploit operationally.[39]

The armies' reports were alarming. Second Army had its back to Orel and Kursk and was not certain of holding either one. The OKH promised a division from the west for Kursk, but no more than a battalion or two could arrive before the end of the month. At Second Panzer Army, elements of the 4th Panzer Division heading north along the Oka from Belev were stopped by snow and had to turn back, leaving the Oka open to Soviet *Tenth* and *Fiftieth Armies,* and they were beginning to push west another forty miles to Yukhnov and the Sukhinichi railroad junction. Fourth Army, besides its other troubles, had to deter-

[38]*H. Gr. Mitte, Kriegstagebuch, Dezember 1941,* 26 Dec 41, H. Gr. Mitte 26974/6 file.
[39]*Ibid.,* 27 Dec 41.

mine where to get troops and how to get them to Yukhnov and Sukhinichi to defend those critical points on its supply and communications lines. Hoepner's V Panzer Corps was barely surviving west of Volokolamsk, and he had to throw in a replacement battalion newly arrived by air from Germany armed with pistols and wearing laced shoes. Soviet *Thirty-ninth Army* finally got all of its divisions into action against Ninth Army during the day. Ninth Army repelled the developing thrust toward Rzhev, and at the end of the day Strauss reported, "I will resume the battle tomorrow, but if this mode of fighting is continued, the army will bleed to death."[40]

Army Group Center was disintegrating. On the 28th all the armies reported sharply declining strengths owing to combat casualties and frostbite. Schmidt said Second Army was "blind" because its aerial reconnaissance had failed completely. The *Luftwaffe* planes could not start at low temperatures, and they were not equipped to take off or land in deep snow.[41] Kuebler at Fourth Army was having to consider how to defend his own headquarters. Soviet cavalry had crossed the Sukhinichi-Kaluga railroad and were coming toward Yukhnov with nothing in between to stop them. Hoepner said his troops, particularly V Corps, could not go on beating off Soviet attacks much longer; they were exhausted after fighting for weeks in the snow and cold without relief.[42]

The most alarming reports came from Ninth Army's 6th and 26th Infantry Divisions which were defending the front northwest of Staritsa against the Soviet *Thirty-ninth Army*. The commanding general, 6th Infantry Division said:

Today I was in Novaya [*sic*] with the counterattack regiment all day. I saw the men. I can only say they are physically and psychologically finished. Today I saw men whose boots were frozen to their frozen feet. These men would rather let themselves be beaten to death than attack in this condition.[43]

The commanding general, 26th Infantry Division stated:

Infantry Regiment 78 [one of 26th Division's regiments] can no longer be considered a regiment. It has only 200 men. The Russians have cut its communications. Its radios are frozen and its machine guns are frozen; and the machine gun crews are dead alongside their weapons.[44]

Having mulled over his predicament for three days, Kluge phoned Hitler in the afternoon on the 29th. Hoping to make a partial retreat palatable to Hitler, he proposed giving up Kaluga, letting Strauss at Ninth Army go into the K-Line "gradually," and taking the whole Fourth Army front back ten to fifteen miles to shorten the line and release three divisions to defend Yukhnov and Sukhinichi. All Fourth Army then had at Yukhnov, he said, were a replacement battalion and an SS battalion, and Fourth Army's supplies depended on these two supply points. Hitler, after long hesitation and repeated questions as to how much material and supplies would be lost, agreed

[40]*Ibid.*

[41]*AOK 2, Ia Kriegstagebuch, Teil III*, 28 Dec 41, Pz. AOK 2 16690/3 file.

[42]*H. Gr. Mitte, Ia Kriegstagebuch, 1.12.–31.12.41*, 28 Dec 41, H. Gr. Mitte 26974/6 file.

[43]*H. Gr. Mitte, Ia, an OKH, GenStdH, Op. Abt., 28.12.41*, H. Gr. Mitte 65005/7 file.

[44]*Ibid.*

to let Fourth Army evacuate Kaluga, which in fact was all but lost already. He forbade any other withdrawals, and Kluge dutifully transmitted the decisions to the armies.[45]

The "Voice of Cold Reason"

Twenty-four hours later Kluge tried again to secure permission for Fourth Army to withdraw. The Russians had in the meantime smashed and broken through two of Fourth Army's divisions in the center of its front. Hitler remarked that withdrawals always "perpetuated" themselves, and once they started "one might as well head for the Dnepr [River] or the Polish border right away." It was time for "the voice of cold reason to be heard," he said. What sense was there in going from one line to another that was not any better? In World War I, he had experienced "ten-day barrages often," and the troops had held their positions even when no more than 10 percent survived. When Kluge reminded him that World War I was fought in France where the temperatures were not −15° F. or −20° F. and that Fourth Army's troops were mentally and physically exhausted, Hitler replied, "If that is so then it is the end of the German Army," and hung up. Half an hour later he called to ask whether the proposed new line was fortified. Kluge said it was not, but the Protva River offered some natural protection. In that case, Hitler responded, Fourth Army would have to stay where it was until a new line was built "which the troops can claw themselves into and really hold."[46]

Kluge had talked to Hitler in the middle of the day on the 30th, before the armies reported to him. When they did, there was more bad news. At Ninth Army, Staritsa was almost encircled, and *Thirty-ninth Army* was bearing down on Rzhev. Strauss said his army was close to collapse, and that could spell doom for the whole army group if the Russians were then to pour south deep into its flank and rear. The most Ninth Army could still do, he thought, was fight a delaying action to cover the flank while the army group fell back to escape the trap.

The next day Kluge was on the telephone repeatedly with Strauss, Kuebler, Hoepner, Reinhardt, and Halder. Of the army commanders only Reinhardt spoke against going back. His line on the Lama River was solid, and his equipment was so tightly snowed and frozen in that he did not think he could move any of it. If Third Panzer Group had to move, Reinhardt said, the troops could do so only with rifles on their shoulders. They would have to leave everything else standing. Halder's chief concern was to avoid having to take any proposals to Hitler. The *Fuehrer*, he protested, would never approve any withdrawal to a predetermined line and would certainly never order one. Finally Kluge told Halder that Strauss had already ordered VI Corps at Staritsa to fall back gradually "in three or four" days to the K-Line.

Half an hour before midnight Kluge talked to Hitler. Without telling him what he had told Halder, he asked for authority to withdraw Ninth and Fourth Armies and part of Fourth Panzer Group. Some of the exchange went as follows:

[45]*H. Gr. Mitte, Kriegstagebuch, Dezember 1941,* 29 Dec 41, H. Gr. Mitte 26974/6 file.
[46]*Ibid.,* 30 Dec 41.

Kluge: I request freedom of action. You must believe that I will do what is right. Otherwise I cannot function. We do not only want what is best for Germany we want what is best for you.

Hitler: Fine. How long can you hold the new line?

Kluge: That I cannot say.

Hitler: Enemy pressure will also force you out of the new line.

Kluge: We are under compulsion. One can turn and twist as much as he pleases; we must get out of this situation.

Hitler then said he would have to confer with his "gentlemen." An hour later he called again. He and all his "gentlemen," including particularly General Halder, he said, had come to one conclusion: no major withdrawals could be made. Too much material would be lost. When Kluge then told him that the order to VI Corps had been given, he replied coldly, "It is impossible to initiate an operative movement without the approval of the Supreme Command. The troops will have to stop right where they are."[47] Kluge thereupon sent the following teletype message to Strauss:

The Fuehrer has categorically forbidden any retrograde movement to the KOENIGSBERG Position. Only local evasive movements under direct enemy pressure will be allowed. All reserves are to be sent to the front, and [you are] ordered to hold every locality and support point.[48]

---

[47]*Ibid.*, 31 Dec 41.

[48]*H. Gr. Mitte, Ia Nr. 7/42, an AOK 9, 1.1.42,* H. Gr. Mitte 65005/7 file.

CHAPTER VI

Crisis in the Crimea

When winter broke over the Eastern Front in the first week of December 1941, Army Group South was relatively the best off of the three German army groups. It had completed the retreat from Rostov and occupied a defensible front on the Mius and Donets rivers from Taganrog to the boundary with Army Group Center forty miles east of Kursk. On the left flank, Sixth Army held Kharkov, Belgorod, and Oboyan. Seventeenth Army, in the center, and First Panzer Army, on the right along the Mius, covered the western half of the Donets Basin coal and industrial area. Eleventh Army occupied the Crimea except for the Sevastopol Fortress on the southwestern tip of the peninsula. Hitler's directive of 8 December that closed down the offensive for the winter everywhere else on the Eastern Front gave Army Group South two residual missions: to occupy the whole Donets Basin and retake Rostov, "in favorable weather," and to capture Sevastopol.[1]

In conjunction with the operations at Rostov, Tikhvin, and Moscow, the *Stavka* had decided to expand the counteroffensive to include the *Transcaucasus Front* and the *Black Sea Fleet*. On 7 December, it instructed the *Transcaucasus Front* to prepare and execute within two weeks an amphibious attack on the Kerch Peninsula. The objective was to encircle and to destroy the enemy on the peninsula by simultaneously landing troops of the *Fifty-first* and *Forty-fourth Armies* near Kerch and in the harbor at Feodosiya. The *Stavka* anticipated subsequently expanding the operation to relieve Sevastopol and to liberate the entire Crimea. The landings were put under the control of the Commanding Admiral, *Black Sea Fleet*, Vitse Admiral F. S. Oktyabrskiy, and the operations on land under General Leytenant D. T. Kozlov, the Commanding General, *Transcaucasus Front*.[2]

Sevastopol

The Fortress

Army Group South's second residual mission, to capture Sevastopol, was the only one of the two it actually pursued after 8 December. Sevastopol, which had been a fortress even under the tsarist regime, was the Soviet Union's main naval base and naval shipyard on the Black Sea. It had some fortifications dating back to the Crimean War (1854–1856) and others built more recently, in particular twelve naval gun batteries (forty-two guns in calibers from 152- to 305-mm.) in armored

---

[1]*OKW, WFSt, Abt. L (I Op.) Nr. 442090/41, Weisung Nr. 39, 8.12.41, German High Level Directives, CMH files.*

[2]*IVMV*, vol. IV, p. 295.

turrets and concrete emplacements and about two hundred antiaircraft weapons ranging from 85-mm. guns to multiple-mounted machine guns. In the last two weeks of October, ships of the *Black Sea Fleet* had brought in as much of the *Independent Maritime Army* as they could evacuate from Odessa, about thirty thousand troops. With these, plus some twenty-two thousand naval and other troops, and fire and supply support from naval vessels, the commander of the *Maritime Army*, General Leytenant I. E. Petrov, prevented General Manstein's Eleventh Army from overrunning the fortress during the pursuit in early November.[3] Manstein had an organized assault almost ready to start at the end of November, but then heavy rain set in and forced a three-week delay.[4]

As time passed, however, taking the fortress had become more difficult. By late November, Oktyabrskiy, who had also assumed command of the *Sevastopol Defense Region,* had brought to completion three defense lines on the landward side: the "Outer Perimeter," twenty-seven miles long, running from three miles north of the Kacha River to three miles east of Balaklava; the "Main Line," twenty-three miles long, from the mouth of the Kacha to Balaklava; and the "Rear Line," eighteen miles long, just forward on an antitank ditch around the fortress proper. Behind all of the lines, artillery and machine guns had been dug-in—most densely behind the antitank ditch, which actually constituted the fourth and potentially strongest

line. Oktyabrskiy had also created another eight armored batteries at the fortress by emplacing the guns and turrets off two disabled cruisers. Only the antiaircraft defense was weaker, reduced to about one hundred guns by withdrawals of batteries to protect ports on the eastern coast. Petrov had 5 rifle divisions, 1 cavalry division, 2 naval infantry brigades, and "several" independent regiments. Soviet accounts do not give a total numerical strength, but they indicate it must have been at least ten thousand above the early November number.[5]

While Oktyabrskiy was strengthening the Sevastopol defenses, Eleventh Army's position on the Crimea was becoming less secure. Although the peninsula generally did not get as cold as the mainland, it did experience sudden, drastic ups and down in temperature and frequent, violent rain or snowstorms. The likelihood of the latter, because of the effect they would have on the roads, restricted the lines of attack on Sevastopol to the north and northeast. Thére, besides the Soviet lines, the Germans faced three east-west river lines to be crossed—the Chernaya, the Kacha, and the Belbek. The Chernaya emptied into the Severnaya Bay, which shielded the heart of the fortress on the north. Bad weather of any kind, on the other hand, benefited the *Black Sea Fleet* by providing its ships, never more than half-a-day's running time from their base at Novorossiysk, with the cover from German air attack they needed to approach the coast safely anywhere between Sevastopol and Kerch. *(Map 8.)* More-

---

[3]G. I. Vaneyev, et al., *Geroicheskaya oborona Sevastopolya, 1941–1942* (Moscow: Voyennoye Izdatelstvo, 1969), pp. 50–67.

[4]Manstein, *Lost Victories,* p. 223.

[5]Vaneyev, *Geroicheskaya oborona,* pp. 109, 138–40, 144; *IVOVSS,* vol. II, pp. 304–06.

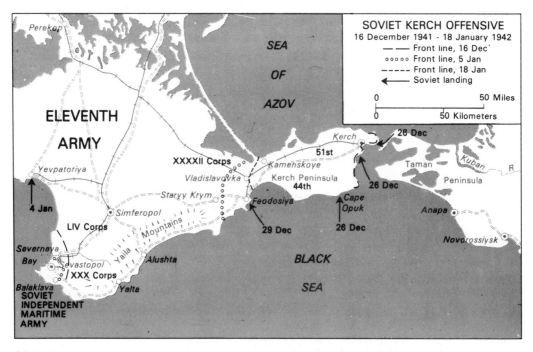

MAP 8

over, the strait between the Kerch and the Taman peninsulas, at places only two miles wide, froze over in winter and could be crossed on foot. Under these conditions, Eleventh Army's seven divisions, all at least 25 percent understrength, could not mount an attack on Sevastopol and guard the coast adequately at the same time.

The Attack

When the weather improved in the second week of December, Manstein decided to go ahead with the attack. He had orders to do so; he had a reputation as a skillful and daring tactician to defend and enhance; and he was enjoying his first army command. Besides, the whole German position on the Crimea would be precarious as long as

the Soviet Army and Navy held a foothold at Sevastopol. On the other hand, even if he could not reduce the fortress, he could weaken it decisively, possibly in a few days, by driving a wedge approximately six miles deep through the northeastern perimeter. With that, his artillery could sweep the Severnaya Bay and cut off the naval lifeline supporting the fortress. To stage the effort, however, he had to use two of his three corps headquarters and six of his seven divisions, leaving only three Rumanian brigades and Headquarters, XXXXII Corps with some corps troops and the 46th Infantry Division to cover 170 miles of coast and ports at Kerch, Feodosiya, Alushta, and Yalta.

Eleventh Army Intelligence observed steady Soviet ship traffic to and from Sevastopol which seemed to have two purposes: to evacuate machinery and naval supplies that would be lost if the fortress suddenly collapsed and to bring in reinforcements for the landward defenses. By mid-December, the Soviet resurgence along the front on the mainland and the troops pouring into the Taman Peninsula by ship and truck countered any assumption that the Russians would not stubbornly defend Sevastopol but raised forebodings of possibly even less convenient developments to come.[6]

Eleventh Army's assault at Sevastopol began on the morning of 17 December along the entire 27-mile-long Outer Perimeter, the first of the three defense lines. Inside still lay the Main Line, the Rear Line, and thickets of forts, pillboxes, and antitank obstacles. The LIV Corps, on the north, carried the main effort because it was closest to Severnaya Bay, and heavy artillery in calibers up to 300-mm. could support its attack. On the south, XXX Corps could do no more than tie down the Soviet Outer Perimeter defense since it had to bring its supplies across the rugged and virtually roadless Krymskiye Gory.

Certain that the Russians, who had partisans and agents in nearby mountains and the cities, knew how short he was on strength as well as he did, Manstein gambled on surprise—and very nearly won. Oktyabrskiy was away at Novorossiysk planning the landings the *Stavka* had ordered at Kerch and Feodosiya when the attack began on the 17th. By the end of the day, the German 22d Infantry Division was through the Outer Perimeter, and during the next two days, it pushed along the valley of the Belbek River to the Main Line. But the *Stavka* reacted fast and on the 20th—as the 22d Infantry Division was beginning to crack the Main Line—put the fortress under the *Transcaucasus Front.* The next day, Kozlov, the front's commander, sent by ship a rifle division, a naval infantry brigade, and 3,000 replacements, and the *Black Sea Fleet* brought a battleship, a cruiser, and 2 destroyers into action as artillery support. The 22d Infantry Division, having broken the Main Line, was into the Rear Line and approaching Mekenzlyevy Gory almost within sight of Severnaya Bay on 22 December, but its thrust was weakening, and by nightfall the newly arrived *345th Rifle Division* and *79th Naval Infantry Brigade,* with supporting fire from the warships, had entangled it in a desperate battle that would run on long enough for events elsewhere to take effect.[7]

Kerch and Feodosiya

Oktyabrskiy and Kozlov initially had proposed to put 42,000 troops with artillery and tanks ashore simultaneously on the peninsula at a number of beachheads spread from northeast of Kerch to Feodosiya. The landings on the northeastern and eastern coasts were to be made by *Fifty-first Army,* under General Leytenant V. H. Lvov; those on the south coast, at Feodosiya and Cape Opuk, by *Forty-fourth Army,* under General Leytenant A. N. Pervushin. As it did for Manstein, the weather raised problems for Oktyabrskiy and Kozlov, slowing the as-

[6]*AOK 11, Ic/AO, Kriegstagebuch, 22.6.41–31.3.42,* 1–15 Dec 41, AOK 11 22409/1 file.

[7]*IVOVSS,* vol. II, pp. 305–08; *IVMV,* vol. IV, p. 300; Vaneyev, *Geroicheskaya oborona,* pp. 145–63.

SOVIET NAVAL CRAFT LAYS A SMOKE SCREEN OFF SEVASTOPOL

sembly of troops and air units on the Taman Peninsula and restricting the employment of smaller naval vessels. The final objective of the landings was to destroy the Germans on the Kerch Peninsula by forcing them west against a line *Forty-fourth Army* would build across the Isthmus of Parpach north of Feodosiya.

Originally scheduled for 21 December, the landings had to be postponed after Manstein attacked Sevastopol on the 17th, and Kozlov had to send reinforcements there. To support the Sevastopol attack, men and ships had to be diverted from the landing forces, particularly from the Feodosiya force. During the delay of more than a week, the landings on the eastern end of the peninsula were set to be made sepa-

rately several days before the one at Feodosiya.[8]

German agent and Russian deserter reports had alerted Eleventh Army and 46th Infantry Division to expect landings on the Kerch Peninsula, but this knowledge was not particularly helpful since there were far more potential landing sites than the division could cover. The Russians could easily bring forces out of the ports on the Taman Peninsula and put them ashore under the cover of a single night's darkness.[9]

The Landings

In the early morning darkness on 26

---

[8]*IVMV*, vol. IV, pp. 296–97.
[9]*AOK 11, Ic/AO, Kriegstagebuch, 22.6.41–31.3.42*, 16 and 19 Dec 41, AOK 11 22409/1 file.

December and in gale-force winds, the *Azov Naval Flotilla* began putting troops ashore on the beachheads at the eastern end of the Kerch Peninsula. Having no proper landing craft, the troops had to wade to the beaches from the boats and ships that had brought them in and had to do without vehicles or artillery. Because of the weather and rough sea, some landings were made in the wrong places and others, including a strong one which was to have been made at Cape Opuk, were not made at all. Instead of requiring one or two days, nearly five were needed to get 20,000 troops to the beaches, and many heavy weapons were lost.[10]

The weather and the Russians' complicated scheme of operations that involved merging the beachheads for drives first on Kerch and then westward toward the neck of the peninsula proved advantageous to the Germans. The beachheads were peppered over forty miles of coastline, none held strongly enough to constitute a crucial threat. The Germans could seal all of them off close to the coast, and in some instances they could also cut off parties that had advanced inland from the beaches. The forces in the beachheads and the ships offshore appeared much of the time not to know what to do next. The 46th Infantry Division, on the other hand, did not have strength enough to counterattack everywhere. By the 29th, it had all but wiped out two of the smaller beachheads and was preparing to go after the others systematically.[11]

To sustain the counterattacks on the beachheads, 46th Infantry Division had brought east an infantry battalion it had originally stationed at Feodosiya on the south coast at the western end of the Isthmus of Parpach. Shortly before dark on the 28th, an engineer battalion, also going east, arrived in Feodosiya and took up quarters there for the night. Although the battalion commander merely made a casual decision to stay rather than to continue east in the dark over an unfamiliar road, the engineers became the main element in the Feodosiya garrison that night. The rest consisted of two construction companies, a battery of artillery, and an antitank gun company. The engineers bedded down one street away from the waterfront without knowing what kind of an alert was in effect.

At 0400 on the 29th, the engineers were roused by the noise of machine gun and rifle fire coming from the direction of the port. As the Germans learned later, ten naval cutters had landed parties of sailors on the harbor breakwater. If a defense had been ready, the parties might easily have been driven back to sea because at first the only reinforcement they got was brought in by the small boats shuttling back and forth to naval vessels lying outside the harbor. After about an hour, however, three destroyers, *Shaumyan, Nezamozhnik,* and *Zheleznyakov,* tied up at the breakwater and began landing troops and heavy weapons. In the next hour the cruisers *Krasniy Krim* and *Krasniy Kavkaz* also drew up to the breakwater, bringing the total number of troops put ashore by the end of the second hour to just under 5,000. By then some of the

[10]*IVOVSS*, vol. II, pp. 308–10; *IVMV*, vol. IV, p. 297.
[11]*46. Division, Kommandeur, an XXXXII A.K., 10.1.42,* AOK 11 28654/13 file.

SOVIET TROOPS LANDING ON THE KERCH PENINSULA

German coast artillery was in action and had scored a hit on the *Krasniy Kavkaz*.[12]

Before the engineers, who until then did not know that they were practically the only German troops in the city, had sorted themselves out, the Russians were holding the waterfront and probing along the streets running inland. At an impromptu council of war in the town mayor's quarters, the Eleventh Army chief of engineers, a Colonel Boehringer—who also by accident had happened to spend that night in Feodosiya—took command. At daylight, Boehringer ordered the engineer battalion and the other smaller units to assemble half-a-mile inland at the junction of the roads to Simferopol and Kerch. One of the construction companies was already there as were some truck, artillery, and antitank gun crews. For an hour or so quadruple-mounted machine guns on one of the trucks kept the Russians off the roads, but they could still fire down on the Germans from the upper stories of buildings and from rooftops. Later in the day Boehringer took the line back to a hill flanked by an antitank ditch on the western outskirts of the town. From the hill the Germans could see the two cruisers and the destroyers in the harbor and a transport docked at the breakwater. Since the Germans had pulled away to the west along the Simferopol road, the Russians had the

---

[12]*AOK 11, Ia Nr. 354/42, 24.2.42,* AOK 11 22279/19 file; *IVOVSS,* vol. II, p. 312.

Kerch road open to them, but they appeared in no hurry to push out of Feodosiya either to the east or to the west.

During the night the Rumanian 4th Cavalry Brigade arrived at the antitank ditch, and the Germans planned to counterattack the next morning. When they told the Rumanian commander, however, he insisted that he was due to be relieved and therefore could not give the order to attack because it could only be given by his replacement who had not yet arrived. At 0900 on the 30th the Germans attacked alone under the cover of a sudden heavy snowstorm driven by a strong west wind. But the attack ended almost as soon as it began when nine Soviet tanks suddenly appeared out of Feodosiya, and the Germans could not fire their antitank guns because of ice in their breech mechanisms. The Rumanians, seeing the Germans drop back, mounted and decamped into the Krymskiye Gory leaving their baggage behind on the Simferopol road. When the Russians, who had been maneuvering cautiously until then, observed the Rumanians' headlong departure, their tanks advanced and pushed the Germans back in the succeeding several hours to a hastily formed screening line around Staryy Krym, five miles west of Feodosiya.[13] By then the number of *Forty-fourth Army* troops at Feodosiya was nearing 20,000.[14]

Sponeck's Retreat

Generalleutnant Graf Hans von Sponeck, Commanding General XXXXII Corps, had his headquarters on the Kerch Peninsula about halfway between Feodosiya and Kerch. When word of the landing on the 28th at Feodosiya reached him, about an hour after the first Russians went ashore, he decided to seal off the beachhead as units under his command had done with the beachheads around Kerch. He ordered the Rumanian 4th Cavalry Brigade in from the west and dispatched the Rumanian 8th Cavalry Brigade, which he had stationed near Kerch, to seal off the beachhead from the east. At about daylight on the 29th he changed his mind after receiving a report (that later proved false) of another strong landing northeast of Feodosiya in position to cut the ten-mile-wide Isthmus of Parpach. Apparently believing the Russians were about to trap XXXXII Corps, he ordered 46th Infantry Division to do an immediate about-face and evacuate the peninsula.

Having given the order, Sponeck departed with some of his staff by car to set up a new command post at Vladislavovka seven miles north of Feodosiya. Although the trip was hardly more than twenty miles, motor trouble and air attacks kept him out of contact with his corps and with Eleventh Army until midafternoon. In the meantime, Manstein had learned of the order through routine radio channels and tried to countermand it, but XXXXII Corps radio had also closed down. By noon, 46th Division's regiments were turning and beginning to move west.[15]

[13]*Pionier-Bataillon 46, Einsatz des Pi. Bn. 46 in der Zeit vom 28.12.–30.12.42*, AOK 11 22279/19 file.
[14]*IVOVSS*, vol. II, p. 311.

[15]*Gen. Kdo. XXXXII A.K. Ia Kriegstagebuch Nr. 4*, 29 Dec 41, XXXXII A.K. 19649/1 file; *AOK 11, Ia, (Statement by Gen. Lt. Graf Sponeck)* 30.12.41, AOK 11 28654/3 file.

On the northern face of the Sevastopol perimeter strong counterattacks, apparently timed to coincide with the Feodosiya landing, forced LIV Corps to shift to the defensive on the 29th. Consequently it would not be able to take the initiative again for at least a day or two, which under the existing circumstances made the future of the Sevastopol offensive totally uncertain. From Vladislavovka at 1500, Sponeck reported that 46th Infantry Division would be a third of the way off the Kerch Peninsula at the end of the day. Manstein decided to let LIV Corps try to get its attack going again and ordered Generalleutnant Franz Matenklott, who commanded XXX Corps, to take over XXXXII Corps from Sponeck. He shifted Sponeck "for the time being" to the quiet XXX Corps front.[16] He then sent an order to the 46th Infantry Division to get into the Isthmus of Parpach as quickly as possible.[17]

By the end of the day, 46th Infantry Division had orders from XXXXII Corps and Eleventh Army to clear the Kerch Peninsula quickly. But by this stage of the campaign the infantry division was no longer mobile. In a condition report of a week earlier, the division had rated its motor vehicles as 20 percent serviceable. Those that were running were using captured Russian gasoline, which was low in octane and high in water content. Having been fed mostly hay and not overly much of that, the horses did not have the strength to pull heavy loads long distances. On the morning of the 29th, the division actually had only 250 of its 1,400 motor vehicles in working order, with most of the rest either disassembled in the shops or awaiting replacement parts.[18] The distance the division had to go, on the other hand, was not excessive, only about sixty miles. Moreover, Sponeck's order authorized destruction of immobile equipment, and he knew as well as anyone the division's condition. The division commander, Generalmajor Kurt Himer, therefore, assumed that his mission was to get his men out regardless of the cost. And during the day and through the night of the 29th Himer did this brilliantly. What could be moved was and what could not be moved was rendered useless to the enemy. The troops disengaged from the bridgeheads and were miles to the west, apparently before the Russians knew they were gone. By keeping on the move through the night they would be able to pass the Isthmus of Parpach in another day and a half.

All day and all night on the 29th the division marched through rain mixed with occasional snow in temperatures just above freezing. Two hours after daylight the snowstorm that had provided momentary assistance to the engineers' counterattack west of Feodosiya hit the division head-on. In blinding, driving sleet and snow the temperature dropped below zero. Wet uniforms and shoes froze. The watery captured gasoline plugged carburetors with ice crystals. Towed guns and vehicles skidded into ditches and could not be pulled out. Although the division was not under attack either from the

---

[16] *AOK 11, Chef des Generalstabes, Fuer K.T.B., 29.12.42*, AOK 11 22279/19 file.

[17] *AOK 11, Ia Nr. 4721/41, Armeebefehl, 29.12.41*, AOK 11 22279/19 file.

[18] *Eberth, Gen. D. Art., an den Kommandierenden General der XXXXII A.K. 23.1.42*, AOK 11 22279/19 file; *Oberstlt. Assmann, Bericht ueber den Rueckzug der 46. Division auf der Halbinsel Kertsch*, AOK 11 22279/19 file.

east or the west, Himer still believed his mission was to save the troops; and the division moved on, leaving a trail of abandoned equipment.[19]

By midmorning Manstein knew the attempt to contain the beachhead at Feodosiya had failed. He then told Sponeck, who was still nominally in command at XXXXII Corps, to have the 46th Infantry Division add speed and attack through the Isthmus of Parpach toward Feodosiya.[20] When the order reached Himer, his trucks and artillery, what was left of them, had already passed through the isthmus and were headed northwest away from Feodosiya over narrow, snow-covered roads on which they could barely advance, much less turn around. The infantry, which was just coming onto the isthmus, exhausted and freezing, Himer dutifully redirected on an oblique march to the southwest, toward Feodosiya.

Forty-fourth and Fifty-first Armies had more than forty thousand men ashore on the Kerch Peninsula by the 29th. Possession of Feodosiya and Kerch enabled them also to land several dozen tanks, over two hundred cannon and mortars, and better than three hundred motor vehicles.[21] Rain and snow helped by hindering German interference from the air but also forced Fifty-first Army to abandon a landing on the north side of the Isthmus of Parpach which, had it resulted as planned in the capture of the Ak-Monay Heights, could have turned the 46th

Infantry Division's march into more of a shambles than it already was. The weather and the Germans' misadventures, however, were not enough to compensate for the two Soviet army commands' inexperience. Forty-fourth Army bore northwest out of Feodosiya. A quick thrust to the northeast, however, could have put it astride the isthmus in hours. Instead of pursuing the 46th Infantry Division, Fifty-first Army sorted itself out at the eastern end of the peninsula. German air reconnaissance observed tanks moving into formation on the 30th, but the heads of two columns bearing west had only moved to within ten miles of Kerch by the afternoon of the 31st.[22]

After a short rest in the morning, the 46th Infantry Division began its attack northeast of Vladislavovka during the afternoon of the 31st. Without artillery support, the exhausted infantry barely made an effort. For reasons he later found very difficult to explain, Himer appeared at the front only briefly and then went off to set up a command post outside the isthmus. After dark, fearing they would yet be cut off, the division's regiment commanders continued the march through the isthmus and set up a line west of Vladislavovka facing east.[23] The division's one success of the day had been to wipe out a hundred Soviet parachute troops who had jumped into the path of one of its columns in broad daylight.

---

[19]46. Division, Kdr., an den Herrn Kommandierenden General des XXXXII A.K., 10.1.42, AOK 11 28654/13 file.

[20]AOK 11, Chef des Generalstabes, Fuer K.T.B., 30.12.41, AOK 11 22279/19 file.

[21]IVOVSS, vol. II, p. 312.

[22]AOK 11, Ia Tagesmeldung, 31.12.41, AOK 11 22279/19 file.

[23]Oberstlt. i.G. Assmann, Bericht ueber den Rueckzug der 46. Division auf der Halbinsel Kertsch, 6.1.42, AOK 11 28654/13 file; Gen. Kdo. XXXXII A.K., Ia Kriegstagebuch Nr. 4, 31 Dec 41, XXXXII A.K. 19649/1 file.

The Trap Does Not Close

Troubles on Both Sides

Manstein, meanwhile, had stopped the attack on Sevastopol four hours before the 46th Infantry Division attack began, and he had begun taking the 132d Infantry Division out of the Sevastopol perimeter. The decision to move this division, which was initially a precaution, soon appeared to have been made barely in time, if not actually too late. When all of the 46th Infantry Division was off the Kerch Peninsula, it proved incapable of anything but a limited defensive mission. It had sacrificed four-fifths of its trucks, half of its communications equipment, and nearly all of its engineer equipment, not to mention two dozen artillery pieces and sundry machine guns and mortars. Enough of its troops had vanished into the interior of the Crimea for Manstein to issue an order threatening all those who did not rejoin their units by nightfall on 2 January with execution for cowardice.[24]

For a period of at least a week, if the *Forty-fourth* and *Fifty-first Army* commands had had enterprising leadership they could have created severe problems for Eleventh Army, and some daring on their part could have endangered the whole German position on the Crimea. The Russians could very easily trap Eleventh Army on the Crimea, Manstein pointed out to Army Group South. The enemy already held three of the five ports—Sevastopol, Kerch, and Feodosiya—and the Germans were not protecting the remaining two—Yalta, on the south coast, and Yevpatoriya, north of Sevastopol. What Manstein did not know was that the Russians were for the moment having troubles enough of their own: the cold weather had blocked the port at Kerch with ice, and the roadstead at Feodosiya was littered with wrecks—the work of German *Stuka* dive-bombers—which made it almost unusable.[25]

Whatever else the events on the Crimea might lead to, they were an instantaneous and monumental embarrassment to the Germans. Sponeck of XXXXII Corps had flagrantly disregarded the standfast order, and Hitler had him recalled to Germany to face a court-martial.[26] The 46th Infantry Division had been reduced to a wreck without actually having had contact with the enemy. Manstein opened an inquiry into the division's losses of equipment and weapons and the behavior of the officers. Without waiting for the results, Field Marshal Reichenau, the commanding general of Army Group South, declared, " . . . the division has lost its honor. Until it has restored its honor [in combat] no decorations or promotions will be allowed in the division."[27] Hitler demanded to

---

[24]*AOK 11, Chef des Generalstabes, Fuer K.T.B., 31.12.41*, AOK 11 22279/19 file; *H. Gr. Sued, Ia Nr. 49/42, Vorlaeufige Meldung ueber Zustand 46. Div., 6.1.42*, H. Gr. Sued 23208/29 file; *AOK 11, Ia Nr. 6/42, an Kommandierenden General XXXXII A.K., 1.1.42*, AOK 11 22279/19 file.

[25]*O.B. der 11. Armee, Lage der 11. Armee, 4.1.42*, H. Gr. Sued 23208/29 file; *Chef der Luftflotte 4, 5.1.42*, H. Gr. Sued 23208/29 file.

[26]A court sitting under Goering sentenced Sponeck to death. The sentence was not carried out, however, until 1944 when the SS executed him. Erich von Manstein, *Verlorene Siege* (Bonn: Athenaeum Verlag, 1955), p. 245.

[27]*H. Gr. Sued, Ia Nr. 47/42, an den O.B. der 11. Armee, 1.6.42*, H. Gr. Sued 23208/29 file. The commanding general, 46th Infantry Division, Himer, died in combat before the disciplinary proceedings against him were completed.

have the "situation on the Crimea solved offensively" by smashing the Soviet concentrations at Feodosiya and on the Kerch Peninsula, and he wanted Manstein to do it without weakening the grip on Sevastopol.[28]

Manstein's Counterattack

Manstein's own first thought was to attack toward Feodosiya and Kerch as the alternative to a precarious defense on two fronts, one in the east and one in the west. Without more troops and ammunition, neither of which he was likely to get during the winter, he could not take Sevastopol, but on the defensive there he could spare two divisions and some artillery from the Sevastopol perimeter for an attempt against the less solidly dug-in Russians on the east. One division, the 132d Infantry Division, would have to go east under any circumstances to support the 46th Infantry Division and the Rumanians.

Before dark on 4 January, the lead regiment of the 132d Infantry Division reached Simferopol on the march toward Feodosiya. During the night Soviet troops landed in Yevpatoriya, thirty miles farther to the northeast, this time with the support of parachute troops and a partisan uprising in the town, and the next morning the Germans were forced to divert the regiment to Yevpatoriya. The fighting went on there for another three days accompanied by attempted Soviet landings along the fronts at Sevastopol and Feodosiya. These had been a failure from the first, however, since the German coast artillery had heard the Russian ships coming in, had sunk one of

two escort destroyers, and had driven off two large troop transports.[29]

As soon as he knew he had Yevpatoriya under control, Manstein pushed ahead with readying the attack at Feodosiya, which he set for the 11th. Every delay there was working to the Russians' advantage because the Kerch Strait had frozen over and the *Forty-fourth* and *Fifty-first Armies* were bringing troops across on the ice. But the Crimean weather in winter is fickle. On the 8th and 9th, as suddenly as it had dropped below zero a week before, the temperature rose to well above freezing, which was not helpful to the Russians but was even less so for the Germans. In the thaw the Crimean clay turned to oozing mud and left Manstein no choice but to wait for another cold spell.[30]

Once more the weather did not oblige. It stayed warm with beautiful springlike days and only an occasional touch of frost, and the mud stayed. The Russians helped most. Although *Forty-fourth Army* had at least three and more likely four divisions and some tanks ashore it did not attempt to break out of the seven- to ten-mile-deep beachhead it had established around Feodosiya at the end of December, and the *Fifty-first Army* units opposite 46th Infantry Division busied themselves with digging in on the isthmus. How long the Russians would remain passive Manstein could not know. Since air reconnaissance reported a continuing flow of reinforcements from the mainland, he had to assume it would not be very long. Therefore, when he had

[28]*H. Gr. Sued, Ia Nr. 19/42, an AOK 11, 1.1.42,* H. Gr. Sued 23208/29 file.

[29]*AOK 11, Ia Nr. 173/42, Untersuchung Jewpatorija,* 11.1.42, AOK 11 22279/19 file.
[30]*Gen. Kdo. XXX A.K., Ia Tagesmeldung,* 10.1.42, AOK 11 22279/19.

assembled the maximum force he could muster—three German divisions (46th, 132d, and 170th Infantry Divisions), the Rumanian 18th Division, and two Rumanian brigades—he let the attack begin on 15 January regardless of the mud.

Although *Forty-fourth Army* had held Feodosiya for nearly three weeks, it seemed only perfunctorily determined to defend it. The strongest resistance existed around Vladislavovka and that was apparently aimed at holding the retreat route open into the isthmus. In the first two days, mud slowed the Germans. During the next two, frost set in, and they moved faster. On the night of the 18th the *Forty-fourth* and *Fifty-first Armies* withdrew into the isthmus to a line of trenches left from fighting in the fall of 1941.

The time seemed right to Manstein to keep the pressure on and to drive through to Kerch. Army Group South contributed Panzer Detachment 60 which, with seventy-five tanks, had about one-third the strength in armor of a panzer division. In snow and sinking temperatures, the tanks worked

their way into position while the infantry regrouped for the breakthrough across the isthmus. Both were ready at nightfall on the 23d, except the Panzer Detachment 60, newly arrived from Germany, was waiting to draw sidearms and other incidentals from Eleventh Army. The schedule was set: in one night's march on the 25th the tanks would come up to the front line arriving just after dawn; the infantry by then would be cutting a path for them through the Soviet trenches. But that final march was not going to be made. Army Group South needed the tanks more elsewhere and recalled them on the 24th. Thereafter Eleventh Army had to resign itself to a winter of defense on two fronts—if no worse. Meanwhile, the Kerch Strait had frozen over solidly and *Forty-fourth* and *Fifty-first Armies* were bringing trucks and tanks as well as infantry across the ice.[31]

_____

[31]*Gen. Kdo. XXXXII A.K., Ia Kriegstagebuch Nr. 4*, 10–24 Jan 42, XXXXII A.K. 19649/1 file; *AOK 11, Ie/ AO Kriegstagebuch, 22.6.41–31.3.42*, 10–24 Jan 42, AOK 11 22409/1 file.

CHAPTER VII

Hitler and Stalin

Hitler Orders a Retreat

1 January 1942

After 2400 on New Year's Eve, Radio Berlin broadcasted the sounds of bells from German cathedrals. Few on the Eastern Front had the time to listen, and to those who did they brought little cheer. Among the latter was the Fourth Panzer Group who saw the new year in while waiting for an order to withdraw. The army group had told the staff members earlier in the night that they, along with Ninth and Fourth Armies, could expect it soon. After 2400, General Hoepner, Fourth Panzer Group's commander, attempted to do what was expected of a panzer general and spoke briefly about the past year's successes. In honesty, however, he could not avoid expressing what he and the others present most deeply felt, that at the turn of the year the forces in the east lay under "a deep shadow." The shadow deepened an hour later when he and his staff read off the pale violet print on the teletype tape that the *Fuehrer* had forbidden all withdrawals.[1]

At dawn on New Year's Day the temperature stood at −25° F., and the moisture in the air had frozen to form a cold white fog. The waist-deep snow blanketing central Russia was cut only by a thin network of roads cleared enough to take slow-moving, single-lane traffic. Soldiers and Russian civilians, men and women of all ages, shoveled, widening the lanes and opening new ones to keep the front from strangling. When and if the order to retreat came, whole armies would have to march westward along these narrow tracks that could be drifted shut again in an hour or two. On the roads, the armies calculated that infantry could cover six to eight miles a day, trucks sixteen or twenty miles. Shifting an infantry battalion a distance of twelve miles from one point on the front to another could take as much as four days. Tanks could do the same distance in two days, but as many as half could be expected to break down before they reached the destination. In the cold, machine guns jammed, and tank turrets would not turn. Truck and tank motors had to be kept running continuously. Consequently, vehicles that did not move at all burned one normal day's load of fuel every forty-eight hours.[2]

On New Year's Day, no doubt to raise their morale, the Third and Fourth Panzer Groups were elevated to army status. The commanding generals would henceforth be addressed as

---

[1] *Pz. AOK 4, Ia Kriegstagebuch, Teil III, 31.12.41*, Pz. AOK 4 22457/35 file.

[2] *Pz. AOK 4, Ia Nr. 58/42, Notizen ueber jetzige Fuehrungs-u. Kampfgrundlagen, 5.1.42*, Pz. AOK 4 22457/39 file.

CIVILIANS SHOVEL SNOW TO OPEN THE ROAD THROUGH A VILLAGE

"Oberbefehlshaber" instead of "Be-fehlshaber," but the advancement, General Reinhardt observed, came at a time when Third Panzer Army's actual strength was more nearly that of a corps than an army.

In the Nazi party newspaper, the *Voelkische Beobachter,* Hitler gave a New Year's proclamation to the German people, and he sent an order of the day to the troops through *Wehrmacht* channels. In both he talked about the past year's victories and promised more to come, and he portrayed himself as a man of peace who had war forced upon him.[3] His private mood was dominated by the previous night's exchanges with Field Marshal Kluge,

commander of Army Group Center. The generals were coming close to disputing his authority. General Strauss, commander of Ninth Army, had actually attempted to issue an order that contradicted both the word and the spirit of his instructions. The Army was being "parliamentarized."[4]

During the day, Hitler undertook to make his will finally and unmistakably clear. To Kluge and the army commanders he wrote that the Soviet leadership was using the last of its resources in men and material to exploit the "icy" winter and defeat the German forces. If the Eastern Front stood against this assault, it would assure the final victory in the summer of 1942. Therefore, the

---

[3]Domarus, *Hitler,* vol. II, pp. 1820–23.

[4]*Halder Diary,* vol. II, p. 372.

existing lines were to be held "even if they appear to those occupying them to have been outflanked." Gaps in the front were to be filled by divisions coming from Germany and the West, and columns of trucks with supplies and replacement battalions were on the way. "In the meantime," he concluded, "to hold every village, not give way a step, and fight to the last bullet and grenade is the order of the hour. Where single localities no longer can be held, the flames blazing from every hut must tell the neighboring units and the *Luftwaffe* that here courageous troops have done their duty to the last shot."[5]

When Hitler talked about new divisions to plug the gaps, he was, from his point of view, not merely trying to create an illusion. Help for Army Group Center was on the way. When it would arrive was another question. The OKH had authority to mobilize a half-a-million trained men for the Eastern Front by the end of April and had two programs, code named WALKUERE and RHEINGOLD, underway. The first would produce four divisions from troops in the Replacement Army that could possibly be ready by late January or early February. The second would draw previously deferred men from industry to make up six divisions, and those would take longer to outfit and train. WALKUERE, RHEINGOLD, and the additional men to round out the half million would cut into the German work force and would thereby mitigate one shortage, while aggravating another.[6]

The OKH did not know where it could find the weapons, particularly artillery, mortars, and machine guns, to equip the WALKUERE and RHEINGOLD divisions. Current production of these was insufficient to cover the recent losses on the Eastern Front. The OKH also had two movements going, ELEFANT and CHRISTOPHORUS, the first to provide 1,900 trucks and the second to supply 6,000 vehicles of other kinds for Army Group Center; and the *Reichspost* was assembling 500 buses to transport troops into Russia. But the vehicles were having to be collected from all over Germany and as far away as Paris and driven east, and most would probably need repairs by the time they reached Warsaw. All across Germany, under Propaganda Minister Joseph Goebbels' sponsorship, Nazi party offices were collecting furs and woolen garments, and Goebbels was about to open a drive to requisition restaurant tablecloths for use in making camouflage snow pants and jackets. The OKH, however, seeing a public relations coup for the party in the making, insisted that the fighting troops had adequate clothing and consigned the collected goods to storage until they could be issued to replacements going out later in the winter.[7]

A Thrust Past Sukhinichi

The Soviet second phase objective, to encircle the Army Group Center main force, was only becoming faintly discernible to the Germans at the beginning of 1942. The first indication, not

---

[5]*H. Gr. Mitte, Ia Nr. 11/42, Lage und Kampffuehrung im Osten, 1.1.42,* Pz. AOK 4 22457/36 file.

[6]*Der Chef der Heeresruestung und Befehlshaber des Ersatzheeres, Der Chef des Stabes, Tagebuch,* 5 Jan 42, CMH X–124 file.

[7]*OKH, GenStdH, Org. Abt. Kriegstagebuch,* 1–5, 6–9 Jan 42, H1/213 file; *Der Chef der Heeresruestung und Befehlshaber des Ersatzheeres, Der Chef des Stabes, Tagebuch,* 1 Jan 42, CMH X–124 file.

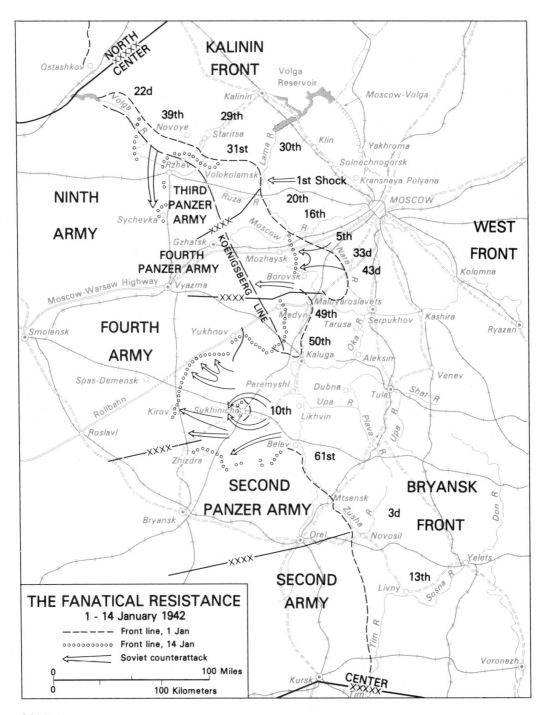

KALININ
FRONT

NORTH
XXXX
CENTER

Ostashkov

Volga Reservoir

Moscow-Volga

22d

39th   29th

Novoye   *Staritsa*

31st   30th

Kalinin

Klin   *Yakhroma*

Ruza R.   *Lama R.*

Solnechnogorsk

Volokolamsk   1st Shock →

Kransnaya Polyana

NINTH

ARMY

THIRD
PANZER
ARMY
XXXX

Rzhev

Sychevka

20th

16th

MOSCOW

WEST

FRONT

Gzhatsk

Moscow R.

FOURTH
PANZER ARMY

Mozhaysk

5th

33d

43d

Borovsk

Kolomna

Moscow-Warsaw Highway   *Vyazma*

KOENIGSBERG LINE
XXXX

Maloyaroslavets

Medyn   49th

Tarusa   *Serpukhov*   *Kashira*

Oka R.

Nara R.

FOURTH

ARMY

Yukhnov

50th

Kaluga

Aleksin

Ryazan

Venev

Smolensk

Spas-Demensk

Peremyshl

Dubna

Upa R.

Tula

Shat R.

Rollbahn

Kirov   *Sukhinichi*

10th

Likhvin

Plava R.

Upa R.

Roslavl

XXXX

Zhizdra

Belev

61st

SECOND

PANZER ARMY

Mtsensk

Zusha R.

3d

BRYANSK

Don R.

FRONT

Bryansk

XXXX

Orel   *Novosil*

Yelets

SECOND

ARMY

13th

Livny   *Sosna R.*

Tim R.

Voronezh

THE FANATICAL RESISTANCE
1 - 14 January 1942

— — — — Front line, 1 Jan

ooooooooooo Front line, 14 Jan

←——— Soviet counterattack

0 _____ 100 Miles

0 _____ 100 Kilometers

Kursk   CENTER
XXXXX
Tim R.

MAP 9

yet actually taken for what it was, had come on Christmas Day when the *Tenth* and *Fiftieth Armies'* thrusts that had been directed toward Belev and Kaluga in the gap between Fourth and Second Panzer Armies began to bear westerly and north-westerly toward Sukhinichi and Yukhnov.[8] The second, *Thirty-ninth Army's* southward drive toward Rzhev that had begun in full strength on 27 December, was still obscured four days later by wild fighting along the entire Ninth Army front. *(Map 9.)*

On Army Group Center's right flank, circumstances were changing the Soviet plan. Zhukov's left flank armies, *Tenth* and *Fiftieth,* were moving faster and in better position to pursue an envelopment from the south than was *Bryansk Front.* Of the latter's three armies, only *Sixty-first Army,* by riding on *Tenth Army's* flank, attained some momentum. *Third* and *Thirteenth Armies* were becoming "exhausted" by the end of December.[9] Consequently, Army Group Center's right flank was being left outside the southern arm of the projected encirclement, which would bring quick changes for Armeegruppe Schmidt and its two armies, Second and Second Panzer.

In late December, Second Army was straining to hold onto its "new winter line" on the Zusha and Tim rivers, some miles behind the original winter line although still thirty to thirty-five miles west of the Kursk-Orel railroad. General Schmidt gave Kluge notice on 30 December that Second Army could have to give up both Kursk and Orel and the railroad in-between. If it did, it would have to split in two parts to follow the railroads west. Doing so would open a sixty-mile-wide hole in the front, but the army could not survive in the snow-covered wilderness away from the railroads.[10] The *Bryansk Front,* however, could not accomplish a breakthrough to force Second Army into another retreat, and by the end of the first week in January all of its armies were stopped. *Bryansk Front's* part in the counteroffensive ended at the Tim and the Zusha, leaving Mtsensk, Kursk, and Orel in German hands.[11] By mid-January, the new winter line was solid, and to reduce Kluge's span of control Hitler then transferred Second Army to Army Group South. General Weichs, who had commanded the army in the summer and fall and had been on sick leave since early November, resumed his command; and Schmidt moved from Kursk to Orel to become commanding general of the Second Panzer Army.

During the first week in January, Second Panzer Army's front facing east also stabilized. But at the same time the army was acquiring a long and acutely unstable north front. The gap between Fourth Army and Second Panzer Army was fifty miles wide and had become the mouth of a great bulge ballooning westward past Sukhinichi and arching northwestward almost to Yukhnov and southwestward toward Bryansk. Second Panzer Army was having to stretch its left flank west from Belev across seventy and more miles of roadless country. Headquarters, XXIV Panzer Corps, which had been assigned—without troops—to defend

[8]*H. Gr. Mitte, Ia Kriegstagebuch, Dezember 1941,* 25 Dec 41, H. Gr. Mitte 26974/6 file.
[9]*VOV,* p. 120.

[10]*AOK 2, Ia Nr. 709/41, Ueberlegungen fuer des Zurueckgehen der 2. Armee von Kursk-Orel nach Westen, 31.12.41,* H. Gr. Mitte 65005/7 file.
[11]*IVOVSS,* vol. II, pp. 294, 295, 320; *VOV,* p. 120.

the Oka River north of Belev, was shifting eighty miles west to Bryansk, still without troops, to try to stop the Soviet drive past Sukhinichi. It acquired a second mission on 3 January when Soviet *Tenth Army* trapped 4,000 German troops in Sukhinichi. Hitler refused to let the garrison break out and demanded that the town be defended to the last man "as the Alcazar had been held during the Spanish Civil War."[12]

When Headquarters, XXIV Panzer Corps arrived in Bryansk on the 4th, it had command of a clutch of odds and ends, 2 infantry battalions, 1 engineer battalion, assorted construction troops that had been stationed in the towns around Sukhinichi, and an armored train. The latter had been involved in the fighting at Sukhinichi and had only its locomotive and one car still serviceable. An infantry division and a security division were coming into Bryansk by rail from the west, but Army Group Center had already diverted a regiment from each, and the infantry division had left its motor vehicles in Poland. At Bryansk everything going to the front had to be unloaded and reloaded from German to Soviet-gauge trains.

Meanwhile, *Tenth Army*'s cavalry, assisted by partisans and some Soviet soldiers who had hidden in the forests since the October 1941 battles, were fanning out rapidly west and south of Bryansk. On the 7th, after air reconnaissance reported two Soviet divisions headed southwest away from Sukhinichi, Schmidt, to protect the army's lifeline, the railroad through Bryansk,

stripped the Armeegruppe's front on the east of its last reserves, the 4th and 18th Panzer Divisions, and sent them to XXIV Panzer Corps. Having done that, he tried for the next several days to secure Hitler's permission to bend the east front back slightly and thus acquire some reserves. Instead, Hitler, on the 13th, ordered him to keep the east front where it was, take more troops out of it if possible, and use the troops XXIV Panzer Corps had and was getting to mount a counterattack toward Sukhinichi. Occasional airdrops of ammunition and food interspersed with messages of encouragement from Hitler were keeping the Sukhinichi garrison fighting.

A breakout from Sukhinichi had become impossible after 9 January when *Tenth Army* reached Kirov, forty miles to the west, and Zhizdra, thirty-five miles to the southwest. Having such distances to go, a relief also appeared impossible, particularly since XXIV Panzer Corps' infantry were mostly recent arrivals not hardened either to the weather or the fighting in the Soviet Union. On the 15th, XXIV Panzer Corps expected to start the attack in another four days— "at the earliest."[13] Whether XXIV Panzer Corps would be driving toward Sukhinichi in four more days or fighting to hold Bryansk was actually still open. For more than a week, the *Stavka* had been shifting troops into the gap from the stalled *Bryansk Front,* and on the 13th it had moved the Headquarters, *Sixty-first Army* more closely in on *Tenth Army*'s left.[14]

---

[12]Hofmann, MS P–114b, vol. III, p. 45.

[13]*Pz. AOK 2, Ia Kriegstagebuch, Abschnitt b,* 1–15 Jan 42, Pz. AOK 2 25034/162 file; *AOK 4, Ia Kriegstagebuch Nr. 11,* 9 Jan 42, AOK 4 17380/1 file.
[14]*IVOVSS,* vol. II, p. 326.

AN ARMY COMMANDER *(Weichs, fourth from left)* SETS OUT FOR THE FRONT

The Grand Envelopment

By comparison with the center and left flank armies, Army Group Center's right flank armies, Second and Second Panzer Armies, were, nevertheless, in a virtually ideal situation. The storm of the Soviet offensive was passing away from Second and Second Panzer Armies as it mounted assaults of greater intensity against Fourth and Fourth Panzer Armies in the center and Ninth Army and Third Panzer Army on the left. While the armies on the right faced threats, those of the center and left confronted outright destruction, both piecemeal and en masse. At the beginning of the year, each one of the four had good reason to assume that given its circumstances and the orders

it was receiving, it was on an accelerating descent into oblivion. Their peril was in fact so great and appeared so imminent that it obscured for a time the grand Soviet design to encircle and destroy them all. Consequently, the conflict assumed a dual character as the German armies, on Hitler's orders, each fought for survival of its own area while the Soviet *Kalinin* and *West Fronts* concentrated on a second objective, Vyazma.

Vyazma, a small city on the Moscow-Smolensk road and railroad, was 125 miles west of Moscow and 90 miles east of Smolensk. It was a railroad junction from which lines ran due north and south to Rzhev and Bryansk, northeast to Moscow, and southeast to Kaluga and Tula. The line to Rzhev carried all

of the supplies for Third Panzer Army and most of those for Ninth Army. The Vyazma-Moscow line and road sustained Fourth Panzer Army, and Fourth Army depended on the Vyazma-Kaluga line for its supplies. The railroad to Bryansk had provided an alternate route for Fourth Army, but lost much of its usefulness when the Russians passed to the west of Sukhinichi. At the turn of the year, *Kalinin Front's* right flank armies were 90 miles from Vyazma. *West Front's* left flank operating in the gap between Fourth and Second Panzer Armies had about 55 miles left to get there via Yukhnov. The farthest easterly extensions of Fourth and Fourth Panzer Armies' fronts were 90 miles from Vyazma. Except possibly at Kiev, the Germans themselves had not attempted an envelopment on such a scale.

The Soviet effort also differed markedly from the German in its combining of maneuver and brute force. The Germans had designed the so-called pincers movement to be accomplished with minimum effort; not so the movements of the Soviet forces. Zhukov, for one, appears to have had greater confidence in the frontal assaults that had served well enough on the approaches to Moscow than in the more elegant but also more demanding envelopment.[15] Regardless of the envelopment being attempted, his command, the *West Front,* never ceased battering the whole length of the Fourth, Fourth Panzer, and Third Panzer Armies' lines. Konev's *Kalinin Front* did the same against Ninth Army. To the German commands, riveted in place by Hitler's

orders, the weight of the Russian forces bearing in on them from the east, therefore, made the envelopment almost an academic concern.

In the toe-to-toe contest that had gone on along nearly the whole front, both sides had had a month's experience in winter warfare, and patterns had emerged. The Germans clung to the villages. The peasant cottages, verminous as they invariably were, provided shelter where no other existed. In ground frozen like rock six to eight feet deep, to dig or to build was impossible. The *izbas*, the cottages, were no small asset, and to deny their comfort to the Russians, the Germans destroyed any left standing when they retreated. Consequently, the Russians usually had to stay in the open which, although they were more accustomed to and better prepared for the winter, was only relatively less hazardous for them than for the Germans, particularly when the temperature reached $-30°$ F. or $-40°$ F. The villages the Germans held, on the other hand, were islands in a sea of snow, stationary and frequently jammed with ill-assorted troops whose presence in them was dictated by the elements rather than by any tactical purpose. The villages had the additional disadvantage of being acutely vulnerable, as the Russians were quick to appreciate, to standardized assault patterns. A single man who knew the lay of the land could direct fire from the back of a tank and smash a village from a distance with high explosives. At night, in snowstorms, or in fog, one or two tanks with infantry could drive straight into a village, blasting the buildings one by one. If the defenders came out into the open, the Soviet infantry occupied lo-

---

[15]Zhukov, *Memoirs*, p. 351ff.

GERMAN INFANTRY ENTER A VILLAGE

cal houses. If they stayed indoors, their position was equally hazardous since thatched roofs and wooden construction offered little protection against 76-mm. shells. The German 88-mm. guns and field howitzers with *Rotkopf* hollow-charge ammunition, which Hitler had released in December, could knock out Soviet T–34 tanks. A direct hit with a *Rotkopf* shell could generally be counted on to kill the whole tank crew and any infantry riding on the vehicle. But the Germans guns were not maneuverable and were vulnerable to the tanks' cannon and, at close range, to the weapons of the Soviet infantry as well. The 88s, nicknamed "elephants," had a particularly high profile. In using field artillery as anti-tank guns, the Germans had to con-

tend with a loss ratio of close to one for one and a consequent decline in their artillery strength.

The German troops, particularly the infantry and artillery, had not been accustomed in the war thus far to accepting losses equal to those of their opponents, and they had not even imagined anything like the apparent Soviet disdain for life evidenced in a seeming unconcern for casualties either from cold or from enemy fire. Soviet forces could take the villages but not usually cheaply, and their commanders always seemed willing to pay the price no matter how high it might be. The Russian "tramplers," for instance, were unarmed men whose sole function was to trample paths through the snow to German positions. By the time an attack began, the field was often littered with the bodies of these humble contributors to its success.[16]

General Hoepner Does Not Obey

At the turn of the year, Army Group Center's newest crisis was at Fourth Army where on 2 January the Soviet *Forty-third Army,* after punching at the XX Corps-LVII Panzer Corps boundary for several days, opened a ten-mile gap between Borovsk and Maloyaroslavets. Therewith, Fourth Army, having already lost contact with Second Panzer Army, was practically cut adrift. Fourth Panzer Army was hardly any better off: V Panzer Corps' hold was steadily weakening west of Volokolamsk, and as the armies on their outer flanks were driven back, Fourth Panzer and Third Panzer Armies' fronts were being left on the eastern face of a dangerous outward bulge. When Hoepner asked the army group, on the afternoon of 2 January, to review the latest standfast order in light of these conditions, he received an expression of "the Fuehrer's greatest trust in the Fourth Panzer Army and its leadership," a "categorical" refusal to permit any kind of withdrawal, and an order to transfer two infantry regiments and an artillery battalion to help XX Corps. Kluge then also gave Hoepner command of XX Corps.[17]

In placing XX Corps under Hoepner, Kluge converted what had been a gap in an army front into one between two armies. Technically the decision was absolutely correct. The corps had contact with Hoepner's Fourth Panzer Army and no longer had any with Kuebler's Fourth Army. Therefore, Hoepner could give it support, and Kuebler could not. On the other hand, as had happened west of Tula, the gap now became the concern of two commands both of which had equally serious problems elsewhere. On the 3d, Kluge ordered Hoepner to stage an attack from his side to close the gap between Barovsk and Maloyaroslavets. To do so Hoepner had to move one of his divisions out to the XX Corps right flank. That took two days, and on the morning of the 6th, when the division was in place and ready, Fourth Army reported that its flank had been pushed back during the night thus opening the gap to eighteen miles but leaving the point at which Hoepner's attack was aimed under Russian control.[18] Also during the night, three Soviet divisions had turned north behind the XX Corps flank. In the morning, Hoepner proposed bending his flank back, which Kluge, because of Hitler's orders, instantly forbade, countering with an order to begin the attack anyway. Fourth Army, he said, would help from its side—with one battalion.

For two days Hoepner's one division on the XX Corps right flank attacked south while the Soviet division pushed north behind it and XX Corps, until finally on the morning of the 8th General der Infanterie Friedrich Materna, commanding XX Corps, told Hoepner he could no longer be responsible for the corps' situation. The Russians, he said, had cut his one cleared road to the west. He could no longer get any supplies in, and if they fastened their

---

[16]*Pz. Div, Ia Bericht ueber russische und deutsche Kampfesweise, 30.1.42,* Pz. AOK 3 21818/7 file.

[17]*Pz. AOK 4, Ia Besprechungsnotizen,* 2 Jan 42, Pz. AOK 4 22457/45 file.

[18]*Pz. AOK 4, Ia, Nr. 72/42, an H. Gr. Mitte, 6.1.42,* Pz. AOK 4 22457/39 file.

hold tighter, he would never get the corps out. Hoepner then told Kluge that XX Corps would "go to the Devil" in a short time if it were not allowed to pull back. Kluge insisted the corps was "still a long way from going to the Devil," but said he would call General Halder. Two hours later, at 1200, Kluge said he had "categorically" demanded a decision on XX Corps and Halder was on his way to Hitler to get it. Hoepner was to alert the corps because the order could come at any minute. An hour and three-quarters later, after having tried several times and failed to reach Halder directly, Hoepner, on his own responsibility, issued the order for the corps to pull back.

After nightfall, having been out of touch with Hoepner's army for seven hours, Kluge, who apparently had learned of the order, called and confirmed that Hoepner had given it. Kluge then said an order to retreat was "impossible"—not because it was wrong but because it went against Hitler's orders. Kluge saw this case as being the same as the one involving Guderian, and he hastened to dissociate himself from responsibility for it by pointing out that at 1200 he had specifically used the word "prepare" and not the word "order." Kluge called again at 2330. Hitler, he told Hoepner, had disapproved the order given to XX Corps in the afternoon and had relieved Hoepner as commanding general, Fourth Panzer Army, effective immediately.[19]

Fourth Army Adrift

After XX Corps passed from Fourth Army to Fourth Panzer Army, four of Fourth Army's five remaining corps, outflanked on the north and the south, were caught in a detached loop of the front touching the Oka River west of Kaluga and reaching north thirty-five miles not quite to Maloyaroslavets, which the Soviet *Forty-third Army* had taken on 2 January. What might befall the four corps from the north depended entirely on the Russians and on Fourth Panzer Army. The northernmost corps, LVII Panzer Corps, barely had the strength to cover the flank. The same was true of XXXXIII Corps on the south. The danger was greater at the moment on the south because *Fiftieth Army*'s spearheads northwest of Sukhinichi were forty miles behind the eastern face of the loop and less than ten miles from the *Rollbahn*, the highway used by Fourth Army as its one good road.[20]

By the 5th, Fourth Army had mustered enough strength at Yukhnov to deflect the Russians from the *Rollbahn* there, but since the road ran across rather than away from the Russian line of advance, they had merely to shift their attack on the highway southward a few miles to cut it. The Fourth Army chief of staff told Hitler's adjutant, General Schmundt, "If the Russian

---

[19]*Pz. AOK 4, Ia Kriegstagebuch, Teil III*, 6–8 Jan 42, Pz. AOK 4 22457/35 file; *Pz. AOK 4, Ia, Besprechungsnotizen*, 6–8 Jan 42, Pz. AOK 4 22457/45 file. Hitler also ordered that Hoepner be expelled from the army with loss of pay, pension, and the rights to wear the uniform and decorations. The military courts,

however, upheld Hoepner's contention that he could not be deprived of those rights and benefits without a court-martial; and he continued on inactive status with rank and full pay until he was arrested and subsequently tried and executed as a member of the 20 July 1944 plot against Hitler's life.
[20]Fourth Army's *Rollbahn* (the Germans also used the term for other through roads) was the Moscow-Warsaw Highway, one of the best in the Soviet Union and one of the few all-weather roads in the occupied territory.

thrust gets through, it will be deadly."[21] All the army had on the whole western rim of the Sukhinichi bulge was the Headquarters, XXXX Panzer Corps, with parts of two divisions and several *Luftwaffe* construction battalions.

On the night of the 5th, General der Infanterie Gotthard Heinrici, the commanding general of the XXXXIII Corps, called the Fourth Army chief of staff and asked whether the army was being deliberately sacrificed and whether it was being treated the way the Soviet Command had treated its troops during the summer encirclements. His men and officers, Heinrici added, were well aware that the Russians were many miles behind them on the south, and they would have to be told what was in store for them. When the report on what Heinrici had said reached army group headquarters, which it did less than ten minutes after Heinrici stopped talking, Kluge came on the telephone to admonish the whole Fourth Army to keep its nerves under control. He would not leave his old army in the lurch, he insisted, but things had not gone that far yet. If the army stood fast, he believed a "state of balance" could be achieved.[22] If it "marched off the field," the consequences would be incalculable.

Two days later, on the afternoon of the 7th, XXXX Panzer Corps reported that with the forces it had, it could not keep the Russians off the *Rollbahn* anywhere along the fifty-mile stretch southwest of Yukhnov. Giving up on achieving a "state of balance," Kluge then tried to persuade Hitler to allow Fourth Army's east front to go back

thirty miles or so to the vicinity of Yukhnov, which would shorten the front and release troops to defend the *Rollbahn*. After a long telephone conversation late in the night, Kluge believed Hitler's "mind was no longer closed to the reasons for such a withdrawal."[23] But in the morning Hitler was full of ideas for small shifts that he insisted could solve the problem on the *Rollbahn* by themselves.

Throughout the day, Hitler engaged Kluge and Halder in a tug-of-war, refusing time after time to be pinned down to a decision while the reports from Fourth Army became progressively darker. At 1200, the Fourth Army chief of staff told Kluge that Soviet columns were behind both flanks of the four corps in the east, and the corps could no longer just withdraw; they would have to fight their way back. Kluge told him he was expecting a "big decision" from Hitler soon. Six hours later the decision had not come, and the army's chief of staff told him the time was close when Kluge would have to give the order himself, which Kluge had earlier said he would do if necessary to save Fourth Army. Finally at 2200 General Jodl, chief of the OKW Operations Staff, called Halder, and Halder called Kluge. Hitler had agreed to let Fourth Army's four corps on the east go back ten miles in stages and not the thirty miles the army and army group had proposed.[24]

"On the Razor's Edge"

In the order put out on New Year's Day, Hitler had attempted to rivet

[21]*AOK 4, Ia Kriegstagebuch Nr. 11,* 5 Jan 42, AOK 4 17380/1 file.
[22]*Ibid.*

[23]*Ibid.,* 7–8 Jan 42.
[24]*Ibid.,* 8 Jan 42; *Halder Diary,* vol. II, p. 377.

Army Group Center's left flank tight where it stood: Third Panzer Army facing east on the Lama River and Ninth Army in a 120-mile-long line running almost due west past Rzhev along the upper reaches of the Volga River to the junction with Army Group North south of Ostashkov. Rzhev was Army Group Center's northern cornerpost. Lying on the Volga at the junction of a north-south and east-west railroad, it gave the army group left flank something to hang onto in what was otherwise a wilderness of forest and swamp in all directions for many miles.

The sector north and east of Rzhev was the most threatened spot on the left flank. There, VI Corps was being battered by the Soviet *Thirty-ninth, Twenty-ninth,* and *Thirty-first Armies* and being made an example of by Hitler. On 29 December, after some airplane pilots had drawn a much more favorable picture of the situation around Staritsa than had VI Corps' reports, Hitler had dismissed the corps commander and appointed in his place for several days General der Flieger Wolfgang von Richthofen, who was also commanding general of the VIII Air Corps, Army Group Center's air support command.[25]

During the night on 1 January Hitler forbade any except "local evasive movements," and in the morning he ordered the words "KOENIGSBERG Position" abolished because they represented a "dangerous myth." Twenty-four hours later, he commanded Ninth Army—VI Corps and its neighbor on the left,

XXIII Corps, in particular—not to retreat a "single step" for any reason.[26]

Having been told that Hitler was highly annoyed by his attempt to order a retreat and having also been promised 300 JU–52 transports to fly in reinforcements for Ninth Army, General Strauss passed on Hitler's order to VI and XXIII Corps with his own emphatic endorsement. Privately, he and his staff believed Ninth Army was "on the razor's edge" and that it could not stand where it was more than a few days. Generalleutnant Eccard von Gablenz, commanding general of the XXVII Corps that held an exposed sector between VI Corps and the Third Panzer Army left flank, was even less confident. Fearful that VI Corps would collapse no matter what orders it was given and that his own corps would follow, Gablenz repeatedly asked Strauss on the 2d to disregard Hitler's order. The troops, he insisted, knew their position was hopeless, and he "could not put a policeman behind every soldier."[27] After his corps and VI Corps lost more ground during the day, and Strauss ordered him again to hold, Gablenz sent a radio message that read, "I cannot carry the responsibility for my command any longer and therefore ask to be relieved of my post." Strauss ordered him to relinquish his command immediately and to proceed by air to the army group headquarters in Smolensk at daylight the next morning.[28]

Before nightfall on the 2d, a gap had

[25]*H. Gr. Mitte, Ia Kriegstagebuch, Dezember 1941,* 29 Dec 41, H. Gr. Mitte 26974/6 file.

[26]*AOK 9, Kriegstagebuch, 1.1–31.3.42,* 1–2 Jan 42, AOK 9 21520/1 file.
[27]*Pz. AOK 3, Ia Kriegstagebuch Nr. 2,* 2 Jan 42, Pz. AOK 3 16911/1 file.
[28]*Frhr. von Gablenz, an den Herrn O.B. der 9. Armee,* 2.1.42, AOK 9 21520/14 file.

opened northwest of Rzhev between XXIII Corps and VI Corps, but when it did not widen the next day, the Ninth Army staff took heart. In −40° F. weather and snow the troops were fighting well; Richthofen's fighters and dive-bombers were flying; and a battalion of reinforcements arrived in Rzhev by air during the day. The army also congratulated itself on having overcome the worst of the deficiencies it had experienced during the winter warfare. Frostbite casualties were still high, but the troops were outfitted with furs and felt boots requisitioned from the Russian civilians, and they had devised ways of keeping their machine guns and other automatic weapons working in low temperatures.

When *Thirty-ninth Army* widened the breach northwest of Rzhev to several miles on the 4th, Strauss thought he could close it by attacks from the east and the west. He had a reserve of sorts, the SS Cavalry Brigade, stationed behind XXIII Corps on security duty. The SS Cavalry Brigade was noteworthy on two counts: it was one of only two active cavalry units in the *Wehrmacht,* and it was commanded by Brigadefuehrer ("Brigadier General") Otto Hermann Fegelein, who was married to Hitler's mistress' sister. As a regiment and later a brigade, it had been in the Eastern Front since early in the campaign as an anachronistic showpiece for the SS. Its commander was an impassioned horseman with minimal military qualifications. To it, Strauss assigned the mission of attacking from the west while VI Corps created an infantry assault group to make the effort from the east.

So flimsy a German effort could hardly have been expected to succeed

without more cooperation from the enemy than the Soviet commands were likely to give. Three Soviet armies were bearing in on Rzhev, and air reconnaissance had for several days been reporting a new Soviet buildup on the XXIII Corps left flank south of Ostashkov. Early in the day on the 5th, *Thirty-ninth Army* opened the gap northwest of Rzhev to eight miles and began "pouring" troops through to the south. Strauss could not have the SS Cavalry Brigade into position for another day, and the mood at the army group and in the OKH was close to being hysterical. Kluge ordered Strauss to "tell every commander that Rzhev must be held." Halder pronounced Rzhev to be "the most decisive spot on the Eastern Front" and added, "There must be a man who can put things to rights there, if not the division commander then some colonel and if not he then a major who has the necessary energy and determination."[29]

Concurrently, Strauss and Reinhardt fell to arguing over a division sector. On the 3d, to let Hoepner's Fourth Panzer Army concentrate on the Borovsk-Maloyaroslavets breakthrough, Hitler and Kluge had transferred Third Panzer Army from Kluge's command and V Panzer Corps from Hoepner's to Strauss' Ninth Army command. To Reinhardt's huge annoyance, Strauss had refused to give him command of V Panzer Corps because General der Infanterie Richard Ruoff, the corps' commanding general, was somewhat Reinhardt's senior. (The seniority question was resolved ten days later when Ruoff replaced Hoepner at Fourth Panzer Army, and V Panzer

---

[29]*AOK 9, Notizen der Abt. Ia,* 5 Jan 42, AOK 9 21520/14 file.

Corps then passed to Third Panzer Army.) Partly out of pique but also partly with reason, Reinhardt then claimed that his Third Panzer Army, sandwiched between two Ninth Army corps, was going to be robbed of strength through both flanks, and he refused an order from Strauss to take over a division sector from XXVII Corps on Third Panzer Army's left flank. Kluge finally broke into the quarrel, threatened Reinhardt with a court-martial if he did not obey orders, and for good measure extended the threat to all commanding generals under Ninth Army.[30]

The SS Cavalry Brigade and VI Corps attacked at Rzhev on the 7th and were forced to a stop by the afternoon of the 8th. The next day two Soviet divisions rolled over the thin line south of Ostashkov opening a gap on the army group boundary, and the gap west of Rzhev widened by several miles because the SS Cavalry Brigade ran out of ammunition and had to pull back. Four Soviet divisions were ranging south parallel to the Vyazma-Rzhev railroad with nothing between them and it. Strauss told Kluge and the OKH, "The Fourth Army, Fourth Panzer Army, Third Panzer Army and Ninth Army are double-enveloped. The absolutely last possibility to prevent their destruction is to take them into the Gzhatsk-Volga Position [the KOENIGSBERG Line that Hitler had declared nonexistent] which may free enough strength to eliminate the northern arm of the envelopment west of Rzhev." Strauss added, "It is the last minute."[31] Kluge

agreed but would not give an order unless Hitler approved it.[32] Halder and Kluge talked to Hitler, but Hitler insisted on seeing Kluge in person first.

"A Sigh of Relief"

During the night on the 9th, a blizzard blew down on Army Group Center and for twenty-four hours all but stopped the war. Kluge's airplane could not get off the ground the next morning for his flight to *Fuehrer* Headquarters, and nothing changed at the front during the day because even the Russians could not move. From Smolensk east, trains on the railroads and trucks on the roads were buried in snowdrifts. When Kluge finally arrived at the *Fuehrer* Headquarters on the 11th, he found Hitler, who apparently had drawn encouragement from the temporary paralysis caused by the weather, eager to talk about anything but a withdrawal—snowshoe battalions, the method of getting more men into a train, and the coming spring and summer campaigns. And Hitler insisted that as far as withdrawal was concerned, "every day, every hour" it could be put off was a gain, and if the front could be made to stand, "all the acclaim" would fall to Kluge.[33]

Kluge arrived back in Smolensk on the afternoon of the 12th. A few hours later, following a procedure he had recently established to eliminate any misunderstandings, Hitler reinforced his previous day's remarks via teletype to Army Group Center under the superscription, "The Fuehrer and Supreme

[30]*Ibid.; Pz. AOK 3, Ia Kriegstagebuch Nr. 2,* 5 Jan 42, Pz. AOK 3 16911/1 file.
[31]*AOK 9, Ia Nr. 62/42,* 9.1.42, Pz. AOK 3 16911/8 file.
[32]*AOK 9, Notizen der Abt. Ia,* 9 Jan 42, AOK 9 21520/14 file.
[33]*General Halder's Daily Notes,* vol. I, 11 Jan 42, EAP 21–g–16/4/0.

Commander of the *Wehrmacht* has ordered." "Every day of continued stubborn resistance," the message read, "is decisive. It provides the possibility of bringing reinforcements into action to buttress the front. Therefore the break-ins must be eliminated." As if there were no other causes for concern than the wide-open gaps west of Rzhev and between Fourth Panzer and Fourth Armies, the message went on to order that German forces close them. Fourth Panzer Army would be allowed to take its front back about ten miles on the condition that in doing so it released enough units to restore contact with Fourth Army. Ninth Army would have to strip the rest of its front to get troops to counterattack and close the gap at Rzhev.[34]

Hitler's effort to uphold the stand-fast doctrine was now hopelessly at odds with reality. The order to Fourth Panzer Army only permitted it to complete the movement Hoepner had started four days earlier. During those days the troops had been fighting in the open in below-zero weather and snow, unable to go forward and forbidden to go backward. They were discouraged, confused, and exhausted. Surprise had been lost. The Russians knew what was afoot and would be on the army's heels all the way. Ninth Army did not merely have one gap to contend with as Hitler pretended. XXIII Corps had breakthroughs on both its flanks, and Ninth Army did not know for certain what was happening to this corps because all the telephone and telegraph lines were out. On the Third Panzer Army right flank, V

Corps was crumbling as Soviet armor and infantry chewed through its front, village by village. Reinhardt at Third Panzer Army was running out of ammunition, rations, and motor fuel, and he threatened, because of this and V Corps' trouble, to give the order to retreat himself.[35] Snow stalled traffic on the railroad north of Vyazma, and the Russian railroad men who operated the trains had disappeared.

On the 12th, as they had for several days, Soviet airplanes bombed Sychevka on the railroad halfway between Vyazma and Rzhev. During the intervals when bombers were not overhead and at night, Strauss and his staff at the Ninth Army headquarters in Sychevka could hear the noise of battle coming from the northwest. After nightfall on the 12th, it grew louder and more distinct every hour.[36]

In the early morning hours of the 13th the *Fuehrer* order, dutifully forwarded by Army Group Center, reached the armies. Its tenor was already known to them, and the dismay it occasioned was overshadowed within hours by the events of the day. In the morning, the Soviet *I Guards Cavalry Corps* pressing north toward Vyazma crossed the *Rollbahn* on Fourth Army's right flank. By nightfall the army was having to evacuate Medyn, its anchor on the left and Fourth Panzer Army's intended target for its attempt to close the gap. During the afternoon, Strauss and the Ninth Army staff could see as well as hear the battle then being fought in the Sychevka railroad yards. One last supply train for Ninth and

---

[34]*H. Gr. Mitte, Ia Nr. 0455/42, an AOK 9, 13.1.42,* AOK 9 21520/11 file.

[35]*Pz. AOK 3, Ia Kriegstagebuch Nr. 2,* 12 Jan 42, Pz. AOK 3 16911/1 file.

[36]*AOK 9, Ia Kriegstagebuch, 1.1.–31.3.42,* 12 Jan 42, AOK 9 21520/1 file.

Third Panzer Armies, however, did escape north toward Rzhev. When the next one would get through nobody could tell. Strauss sent part of his staff south to Vyazma before 1200 but stayed in Sychevka with his chief of staff until late in the afternoon to keep contact with V Panzer Corps and XXIII Corps, both of which reported themselves near collapse.[37]

The OKH wrote up two "solutions" to the Vyazma-Rzhev problem for Hitler. The one, to have Army Group Center stand fast as it had been doing, could still produce about a division and a half in ten days or so for another try at closing the Rzhev gap. But if it failed in this effort, the Russians would also get Vyazma. The other, to order the retreat to the KOENIGSBERG Line, would give Fourth Army and Fourth Panzer Army a chance to eliminate the gap between them and yield three divisions for a counterattack at Rzhev.[38]

Kluge struggled through the day on the 13th, trying to convince the army commands in Army Group Center that the latest Hitler order was workable and relaying his mounting troubles to the OKH in a succession of desperate telephone calls. For the next two days he did the same, making himself the instrument for imposing the *Fuehrer's* will on the armies while trying to extract small concessions from Hitler. On the afternoon of the 14th, he talked at length to Hitler about the necessity for holding Rzhev as the army group's northern bastion to prevent a lateral collapse of the front. Hitler said he wanted to wait another day. Later, after

the day's situation conference, Halder observed that Hitler knew a retreat was necessary but simply could not bring himself to make the decision.[39] What came finally, transmitted by Halder twenty-four hours later, was a grudging "agreement in principle" to a general retreat to the KOENIGSBERG Line.[40] As the Third Panzer Army war diary put it, "A sigh of relief swept the whole front."[41] Hitler's own feeling found its way into the confirming order issued the next day, in which he wrote, "This is the first time in this war that I have issued an order for a major withdrawal."[42] It was undoubtedly for him the most difficult order he had yet given.

Stalin Projects a General Offensive

The Look of the New Year

The war had taken on a new aspect for the Soviet Union by 1 January 1942. From the Arctic Ocean to the Black Sea the Russians had stopped the enemy. At Rostov, at Tikhvin, above all, at Moscow, the Germans had been driven back. In the dead cold of winter, the enemy was not likely to advance again soon. Japan had turned away into the Pacific. Turkey, an old opponent and doubtful neutral, would not move, nor would the Finnish Army, experienced though it was in winter warfare and standing on the doorstep of Leningrad. Life had returned to Moscow in December as government

---

[37]*AOK 4, Ia Kriegstagebuch Nr. 11*, 13 Jan 42, AOK 4 17380/1 file; *AOK 9, Ia Kriegstagebuch, 1.1.–31.3.42*, 13 Jan 42, AOK 9 21520/1 file.
[38]*Halder Diary*, vol. III, p. 383.

[39]*Ibid.*, p. 385.
[40]*AOK 4, Ia Kriegstagebuch Nr. 11*, 14 Jan 42, AOK 4 17380/1 file.
[41]*Pz. AOK 3, Ia Kriegstagebuch Nr. 2*, 15 Jan 42, Pz. AOK 3 16911/1 file.
[42]*H. Gr. Mitte, Ia Nr. 423/42, an AOK 9*, 16.1.42, AOK 9 21520/1 file.

agencies reopened, and the German retreat from Tikhvin had vastly improved Leningrad's chances for survival. Stalin could receive British Foreign Secretary Anthony Eden in December and not only talk about a second front in western Europe, which he had been doing since summer, but begin to lay down his terms for the postwar settlement, which, to Eden's dismay, included Soviet retention of the Baltic States, Bessarabia, and territory taken from Poland and Finland before 1941 and certain territorial changes in Germany. For the last five days of the old year, the Soviet Information Bureau claimed the capture of 60 German tanks, 11 armored cars, 287 artillery pieces, 461 machine guns, 2,211 rifles, a trainload of ammunition, and a trainload of clothing.[43]

In its New Year's Day editorial, the government newspaper, *Pravda,* predicted victory in 1942. *Pravda* said that Soviet forces had reached the turning point of the war, and with their own "inexhaustible reserves" as well as tanks and aircraft from Britain and America, they would accomplish the "complete defeat of Hitlerite Germany" during the year. The editorial also pointed out, as would all future Soviet writing on the war during Stalin's lifetime, that Stalin had correctly observed the true basis for a successful strategy, namely, the "permanent operating factors," which were stability, morale, and quantity and quality of manpower and equipment. These, according to the newspaper, far outweighed the "temporary factors," such as surprise, on which the Germans had relied.[44]

The counteroffensives brought to an end the evacuation of industries, made it possible to concentrate on developing the war economy, and in places, such as the Moscow region and the Donets Basin, made it possible to resume production in areas that had been evacuated. Weapons and ammunition production thereby increased during the first quarter of 1942. On the other hand, these successes of the new year retrieved very little of what had been lost. Moscow's gross industrial output in January 1942 was two-thirds less than it had been in June 1941. The Moscow Basin coalfield east of Tula, which before the war had yielded 35,000 tons of coal a day, in January 1942 yielded less than 600 tons a day. An equally drastic decline occurred in the Donets Basin. In comparison with the first six months of 1941, electricity output from January to June 1942 would be down by nearly half, coal by nearly two-thirds, and pig iron and steel by close to three-quarters.[45]

At Leningrad, in the dead of winter, one of the war's bitterest tragedies had begun. Two million civilians—men, women, and children—and the troops of two armies were trapped between the Finnish front, ten miles to the north, and the German front, somewhat closer on the south. New Year's Day was the 123d day of this siege. Trucks had begun to travel across the

[43]Winston S. Churchill, *The Grand Alliance* (Boston: Houghton Mifflin, 1950), pp. 328–32; Embassy of the USSR, Washington, D.C., *Information Bulletin No. 1,* 3 Jan 42.

[44]*Pravda,* January 1, 1942. See also G. F. Aleksandrov, et al., *Iosif Vissarionovich Stalin, Kratkaya biografiya,* 2d ed. (Moscow: Izdatelstvo Politicheskoy Literatury, 1949), p. 195.

[45]*IVMV,* vol. IV, p. 326; Voznesenskiy, *Economy of the USSR,* pp. 30–32; Tyushkevich, *Vooruzhennye sily,* p. 269.

BEFORE A SIGN READING, "DEFEND MOSCOW! FOR YOURSELVES AND FOR THE WHOLE SOVIET PEOPLE," *Women Work on Artillery Shells*

ice on Lake Ladoga on 22 November, but in the first weeks it was a perilous trip. A two-ton truck could not carry more than two or three hundred pounds added weight, and many broke through the ice. Moreover, as long as the Germans held the railroad through Tikhvin, all the supplies going across the lake had to make a long, round-about, overland trip by truck from the interior.

The December victory at Tikhvin had saved Leningrad, but it came too late to prevent a winter of misery, starvation, and death. The railroad through Tikhvin was single-track, much of which, along with several bridges, had been destroyed during the fighting. When the first train passed through to Volkhov and Voibo-kalo Station on 1 January, its benefit was mostly psychological. The freight still had to be hauled thirty miles to the lake shore by truck over a snow-covered, makeshift road and then across the ice, and the traffic control was not organized. The city's food stocks, including such marginal substances as oil cake, bran, and flour mill dust, had been exhausted in mid-December, and the population thereafter subsisted on the supplies that came across the lake each day. The daily minimum freight requirement was 1,000 tons of provisions, not including gasoline, ammunition, and other military supplies. A good day's haul in December after the railroad was opened was 700 to 800 tons, never 1,000, and it always included one-third or more inedible supplies. At the turn of the year, the civilians particularly were not just going hungry; they were starving and dying in rapidly growing numbers; and a third of the work force was too weak to work.[46]

The Soviet Union had gained a reprieve, not a release, from destruction. The enemy had clearly underestimated the Soviet capacity to absorb punishment and to keep on fighting, and he had compounded his error by drifting into a winter campaign for which he was totally unprepared. He was trapped in a raw struggle with the elements that drained his strength and neutralized his advantages in military skill and experience. For the first time in the war, the initiative, the precious ability to make an opponent fight on one's own terms, had slipped from his grasp. To the Soviet Union it was a gift beyond price. It could not be refused, but it did not come free. It exacted a mortgage on the future: next year's armies with next year's equipment were marching into the winter's snow, and winter, though powerful, was a temporary ally. In four months the snow would melt and the ground would thaw. Then a balance would be cast. How it would read would depend on how the intervening four months had been used. That was the Soviet strategic problem.

Stalin's Strategy

On 11 December 1941, the *Stavka* instructed Marshal Timoshenko, as *Southwestern Theater* commanding gen-

eral, to plan a winter operation by *Southwest* and *South Fronts* that would smash the Army Group South right flank and restore the entire Donets Basin to Soviet control. On the following day, in Moscow, Stalin and Marshal Shaposhnikov, chief of the General Staff, instructed General Meretskov and General Leytenant M. S. Khozin, the commanding general of *Leningrad Front,* also to prepare a winter offensive on the north flank. Meretskov was appointed to command a newly created *Volkhov Front,* which, with *Fourth, Fifty-second, Fifty-ninth,* and *Second Shock Armies,* would occupy a line from Kirishi on the Volkhov River thirty-five miles south of Lake Ladoga to Lake Ilmen. Meretskov and Khozin were to employ their forces to destroy the Germans besieging Leningrad and to liberate the city.[47]

During the night of 5 January 1942, the *Politburo* met with members of the *Stavka* to consider a projected general offensive. It was to consist of a continuing and expanded drive in the center and offensives to liberate Leningrad, the Donets Basin, and the Crimea. Two of the offensives, in the center and on the Crimea, were already in progress; and the *Stavka* scheduled the other two to begin in two days (on the north flank) and within two weeks (on the south flank).[48] Stalin, who, as always, presided, said, "The Germans are in confusion as a result of their setback at Moscow. They are

---

[46]Dimitri Pavlov, *Leningrad 1941* (Chicago: University of Chicago Press, 1965), pp. 136–51; Harrison E. Salisbury, *The 900 Days* (New York: Harper & Row, 1969), pp. 412–15; *IVOVSS,* vol. II, p. 334.

[47]A. A. Grechko, *Gody voyny* (Moscow: Voyennoye Izdatelstvo, 1976), p. 85; K. A. Meretskov, "Na volkhovskikh rubezhakh," *Voyenno-istoricheskiy Zhurnal,* 1 (1965), 54f.

[48]Meretskov, "Na volkhovskikh rubezhakh," p. 184; I. Kh. Bagramyan, *Tak shli my k pobede* (Moscow: Voyennoye Izdatelstov, 1977), p. 10.

badly prepared for winter. Now is the best moment to go over to the general offensive."[49] General Zhukov spoke against the general offensive, arguing that the entire effort should concentrate in the center where the Germans were off-balance and should not divert to the flanks where they were solidly dug-in. Nikolai Voznesenskiy, a member of the State Defense Committee and the chief of war production, added that there would not be enough weapons and ammunition to sustain offensives on all fronts. Finally, Stalin observed, "We must pound the Germans to pieces as soon as possible so they won't be able to mount an offensive in the spring"; and when no one else asked to speak, he adjourned the meeting. Afterward, Shaposhnikov told Zhukov he should not have argued because "the supreme commander had that question settled." When Zhukov asked why then had his opinion been sought, Shaposhnikov replied, "That, my dear fellow, I do not know."[50]

Soviet postwar assessments of the idea of the general offensive vary. Zhukov regards it as a mistake brought on by the optimism that the success at Moscow had generated in Stalin's mind.[51] At the Twentieth Party Congress, Zhukov cited the general offensive as evidence of Stalin's obsession with "ceaseless frontal attacks and the capture of localities one after the other."[52] One account treats it as an accident that occurred in late December 1941 when the Moscow counteroffensive "transformed itself" into a

general offensive.[53] The *History of the Great Patriotic War* states:

The Soviet Supreme High Command calculated that the defeat which had been inflicted on the German-Fascist troops in the course of the counteroffensive had created the necessary prerequisites for the Red Army's fulfillment of this task. The Soviet Command's certainty of success was based on the high morale of the Soviet people and the Red Army, on the uninterruptedly growing possibilities of the Soviet economy, and on the steady rise of the strength and military mastery of the Soviet troops.[54]

The *History of the Second World War* hedges its comment as follows:

The Soviet leadership's certainty of success in the general offensive was based on the high morale of the troops, on the enhanced possibilities of the Soviet war economy, and on the increased numbers and military skill of the troops. As subsequent events demonstrated, however, to support simultaneous offensives by all the *fronts* fully, larger reserves and more armament were required than the Soviet Union possessed at this time.[55]

The *Popular Scientific Sketch* says that "the planning of such grandiose missions" did not conform "to the capabilities of the Soviet Army and Navy at that time."[56]

Soviet sources attribute the flaw in the concept of the general offensive to the absence of a significant Soviet numerical advantage. By the Soviet count, the troop strengths (4.2 million men, Soviet, and 3.9 million, German and Allied) were almost equal. The Ger-

[49]Zhukov, *Memoirs*, p. 352; *IVMV*, vol. IV, p. 306.
[50]Zhukov, *Memoirs*, pp. 352–53.
[51]*Ibid.*, p. 352.
[52]*Congressional Record*, 4 Jun 56, p. 9395.

[53]P. A. Zhilin, ed., *Vazneyshye operatsiy Velikoy Otechest-vennoy Voyny* (Moscow: Voyennoye Izdatelstvo, 1956), p. 142.
[54]*IVOVSS*, vol. II, p. 317.
[55]*IVMV*, vol. IV, p. 306.
[56]*VOV*, p. 122.

mans are said to have had an advantage in mortars and artillery pieces (35,000 to 27,000) while the Soviet forces had an advantage in tanks (1,784 to 1,500) and in reserves (14 divisions and 7 brigades to 8 divisions and 6 brigades). According to the *History of the Second World War,* the Russians were counting mostly on an increase in their strength and a decline in the Germans' as the offensive progressed. These figures, however, do not reflect the whole Soviet status, particularly concerning reserves. At the beginning of the 1941–1942 winter campaign, which includes the Moscow counteroffensive (and perhaps also the efforts at Rostov and Tikhvin), the *Stavka* had total reserves of 123 divisions, 31 brigades, and 16 independent regiments. During the campaign it created or rebuilt 128 divisions, 158 brigades, and 209 independent regiments. Of the total of 665 units (251 divisions, 189 brigades, and 225 independent regiments), the *Stavka* committed only 181 (99 divisions, 82 brigades, and no independent regiments) during the winter campaign.[57]

The Missions

The general offensive would set in motion nine of the ten Soviet *fronts,* that is, all of those between the Gulf of Finland and the Sea of Azov. The one not included was *Karelian Front,* which was holding the line from Lake Onega north to the Barents Sea. Four massive encirclements were to be accomplished initially: one southeast of Leningrad on a north-south span of 150 miles, one

west of Moscow spanning over 200 miles, and one reaching west 120 miles from the Donets River near Izyum to Dnepropetrovsk and thence south, about again as far, to the vicinity of Melitopol. Liberation of the Crimea, already begun, constituted the fourth mission.

The main force for the offensive in the north around Leningrad was the *Volkhov Front.* It had two new armies, *Fifty-ninth,* which was brought forward from the *Stavka* reserve, and *Second Shock,* which was the *Twenty-sixth Army* renamed and shifted from the reserve in the Moscow area. Meretskov's other two armies, *Fourth* and *Fifty-second,* had been engaged at Tikhvin and stayed in action there until late December against the Germans retreating to the Volkhov River. *Leningrad Front* would be able to take to the offensive only with one army, *Fifty-fourth,* which was on the east face of the bottleneck, between Lake Ladoga and Kirishi.

The tactical plan, and apparently almost all other segments of the general offensive were worked out by the General Staff under Stalin's supervision and given to the *fronts* for execution. Meretskov's assignment was to cross the Volkhov with *Second Shock* and *Fifty-second* and, after they had broken through the German front, to send *Second Shock Army* on a wide sweep north toward Leningrad while *Fifty-second Army* pushed south to Novgorod and then turned west to Luga. *Fifty-fourth Army* was to bear in toward Leningrad south of Lake Ladoga.[58]

The most unusual role in the general

---

[57]*IVMV,* vol. IV, p. 305; Golubovich, *"Sozdaniya strategicheskikh,"* p. 17.

[58]Meretskov, *Serving the People,* p. 180; *IVMV,* vol. IV, p. 314; Meretskov, *"Na volkhovskikh rubezhakh,"* p. 55.

offensive went to General Kurochkin's *Northwest Front*. Prior to the offensive, Kurochkin had three armies, *Eleventh*, *Twenty-seventh*, and *Thirty-fourth*. During the past fall their function had been to tie together the Leningrad-Tikhvin and Moscow sectors of the front by holding a line across the almost roadless stretch of swamp and forest from the southeastern tip of Lake Ilmen to Ostashkov. For the general offensive, Kurochkin was given the newly activated *Third Shock Army*, and his *Twenty-seventh Army* was rebuilt with units from the reserves and renamed *Fourth Shock Army*, and his *front* was given three missions. On the north, *Eleventh Army* was to drive west along the south shore of Lake Ilmen and past Staraya Russa to Dno, then turn north and join *Fifty-second Army*'s advance on Luga. On the south, *Third* and *Fourth Shock Armies* were to break through near Ostashkov and make two, long, parallel thrusts to the west and south, *Third Shock* going via Kholm to Velikiye Luki and *Fourth Shock* past Toropets and Velizh to Rudnya. At Rudnya, *Fourth Shock Army* would have Army Group Center half-encircled and would stand about thirty-five miles northwest of Bock's headquarters in Smolensk. Between the two thrusts would be left what remained of the German Sixteenth Army's main force, which *Thirty-fourth Army* was to "pin down" at its center around Demyansk.[59]

The "western direction," that is, west of Moscow and opposite Army Group Center, was the designated area of the main effort in the general offensive.

What the *Stavka* proposed was to execute two envelopments, an outer one aimed at Smolensk and an inner one that would close at Vyazma. The inner envelopment would be accomplished by the operations *Kalinin Front* and *West Front* already had under way, the former going via Rzhev and Sychevka to Vyazma and the latter, from Kaluga past Yukhnov to Vyazma. In addition to those, the *Stavka* projected a vertical envelopment to be carried out by the *IV Airborne Corps*, which would be landed southwest of Vyazma in position to cut the Smolensk-Vyazma railroad.[60] The outer envelopment would trap whatever was left of the Ninth, Third Panzer, Fourth Panzer, and Fourth Armies and would push the front at least another seventy-five miles away from Moscow, if not all the way to the Dnepr-Dvina line.

While *Fourth Shock Army* could be expected to provide the northern sweep of an outer envelopment, what was to be done on the south was, apparently, much less certain. The *History of the Great Patriotic War* states that originally *Bryansk Front* was to carry out "the deep envelopment of the enemy . . . which was operating before Moscow" by reaching a line from Bryansk to Sevsk and sending a force to Sumy. That would have turned *Bryansk Front* to the southwest, behind Second Panzer and Second Armies, rather than the northwest, but, according to the *History*, "more moderate tasks had to be assigned" to the *front* because the *Stavka* could not supply it with the reinforcements it would have required. Therefore, *Bryansk Front* was ordered to collaborate with the two right flank ar-

[59]V. Zhelanov, "*Iz opyta pervoy operatsii na okruzheniye*," *Voyenno-istoricheskiy Zhurnal*, 12(1964), 20–22; *IVOVSS*, vol. II, p. 321; *IVMV*, vol. IV, p. 314.

[60]*IVMV*, vol. IV, p. 307.

mies of *Southwest Front, Fortieth* and *Twenty-first Armies,* to capture Orel and Kursk.[61] The *History of the Second World War* gives *Bryansk Front's* mission as having been to cover *West Front* on the south by active operations toward Orel and Bryansk.[62] Moskalenko says *Bryansk Front,* together with *Fortieth Army,* was to advance to Bryansk, Orel, Sevsk, and Sumy and, thereafter, "depending on conditions, operate toward Smolensk and westward."[63] What appears to have happened is that *Bryansk Front,* like *Northwest Front,* was given missions in two directions, one toward Smolensk and the other toward Orel, Sevsk, and Sumy, and not given the assured strength to complete either one. *Bryansk Front's* being under the *Southwestern Theater,* however, added a complication for Timoshenko who also had a second mission in another direction.

The *History of the Great Patriotic War* gives the original objectives on the south flank, for the *Southwestern Theater* forces, as having been to retake the Donets Basin and advance to the line of the Dnepr River. These plans, it says, also had to be "moderated" and, consequently, were changed to an assignment to *Southwest Front,* under General Leytenant F. Ya. Kostenko, to take Kharkov and one to *South Front,* under General Leytenant R. Ya. Malinovskiy, to advance from the Donets near Izyum to Dnepropetrovsk and Zaporozhye on the Dnepr.[64] Bagramyan, Grechko, and Moskalenko, however, describe more extensive long-term mis-

sions. Bagramyan says *South Front* was to have encircled First Panzer Army, and parts of Seventeenth Army, in the Donets Basin by driving to the Sea of Azov and cutting off their retreat routes to the west. Moskalenko says the advance was to have gone south past Zaporozhye to Melitopol and that the plans included a late winter push to the lower Dnepr and a spring campaign across the river to take Nikopol, Krivoy Rog, and Nikolayev.[65] Grechko states the intent as having been "to improve the operational-strategic position of our forces in the entire *Southwestern Theater,* to force the enemy to give up the Crimea and the territory east of the lower Dnepr River, and to make it possible for our troops to cross the Dnepr and to carry their later operations in the directions of Kiev and Odessa."[66]

Transcaucasus Front, having been charged with liberating the entire Crimea in December, submitted a plan on 2 January. In it, Kozlov projected thrusts from the vicinity of Feodosiya to Perekop and Simferopol and landings at Alushta, Yalta, Yevpatoriya, and Perekop. The *Independent Maritime Army* had orders to attack to the northeast out of the north face of the Sevastopol perimeter.[67]

In sum, the *Stavka,* indeed, planned a general offensive. It appears to have been designed specifically not to leave a single German army untouched. Its execution would also involve practically all of the Soviet *front* and army commands, most of which had little or no experience in conducting offensives.

---

[61]*IVOVSS,* vol. II, p. 339.

[62]*IVMV,* vol. IV, p. 307.

[63]Moskalenko, *Na yugo-zapadnom napravelenii,* p. 134.

[64]*IVOVSS,* vol. II, pp. 339–40. See also *IVMV,* vol. IV, p. 387.

[65]Bagramyan, *Tak shli my k pobede,* p. 8; Moskalenko, *Na yugo-zapadnom napravlenii,* p. 134.

[66]Grechko, *Gody voyny,* p. 86.

[67]*IVOVSS,* vol. II, pp. 343–44; *IVMV,* vol. IV, p. 390; Vaneyev, *Geroicheskaya oborona,* p. 204.

On 10 January, the *Stavka* sent all *fronts* and armies a directive on the principles of offensive operations. In part, it read:

It is necessary that our forces learn how to break through the enemy's defense line, learn how to break through the full depth of the enemy's defenses and open routes of advance for our infantry, our tanks, and our cavalry. The Germans do not have a single defense line; they have and can quickly build two and three lines. If our forces do not learn quickly and thoroughly how to break enemy defense lines our forward advance will be impossible.

What is necessary to guarantee breaking through the enemy defense lines in their full depth?

To do that two conditions are necessary above all: first, it is necessary for our armies, fronts, and divisions . . . to adopt the practice of concentrating in a single direction, and, second, it is necessary to convert the so-called artillery preparation into an artillery offensive.

An offensive will have the best effect if we concentrate the larger part of our forces against those of the enemy on one sector of the front. To do that it is necessary for each army to undertake to break through the enemy defenses, to set up a shock group of three to four divisions, and to concentrate the attack on a specific part of the front.[68]

This was good advice but, on its face, somewhat elementary for senior commands embarking on a major offensive. Actually, however, for most of the commands that received it, it was far from being redundant. Vasilevskiy says the General Staff regarded the instructions, which were Stalin's idea, as "extremely important," although in some respects "insufficient."[69] The *History of the Great Patriotic War* states that the guidance was based on the experience of the 1941 counteroffensives and was intended to correct "serious operational and tactical deficiencies in troop operations."[70] Grechko says that "owing to lack of strength and of experience in directing offensive operations, our commands did not always mass strength and effort at the point of breakthrough and, consequently, did not fulfill their assignments. Many commanders attempted to organize simultaneous attacks in several directions. This dispersed the strength and effort along the front and did not produce the required superiority over the enemy in the direction of the main blow."[71] In the general offensive, then, the commands were going to be expected to apply a body of operational doctrine many of them had not yet mastered.

---

[68]Grechko, *Gody voyny,* pp. 91–92.

[69]Vasilevskiy, *Delo,* p. 169.
[70]*IVOVSS,* vol. II, p. 318.
[71]Grechko, *Gody voyny,* p. 91.

CHAPTER VIII

The General Offensive

On the North Flank

The Army Group North Front

Army Group North finished the retreat from Tikhvin on the day after Christmas. On the situation maps its front appeared as a rough right angle with the transverse on the north running east and west and the vertical on the east and oriented north and south. Eighteenth Army held the front on the north. West of Schluesselburg on Lake Ladoga at the head of the Neva River the front had not changed since September; an arc around Leningrad touched the Gulf of Finland 3 miles south of the city; and a second around Oranienbaum terminated on the coast 50 miles west of Leningrad. East of Schluesselburg the so-called bottleneck, which had almost been eliminated during the drive to Tikhvin, had reappeared in the retreat. From a 10-mile-wide hold on Lake Ladoga the front dropped off abruptly south for 10 miles and then veered southeastward to the Volkhov River and the junction with Sixteenth Army on the river near Kirishi. *(Map 10.)* Under his Headquarters, Eighteenth Army, General Kuechler had seventeen divisions. Sixteenth Army's 200-mile-long front facing due east tied in on the Volkhov south of Kirishi and followed the river to Lake Ilmen. Taking up again south of the lake, it bulged eastward to the Valdai Hills east of Demyansk and then followed a chain of lakes south to the army group boundary near Ostashkov. The Sixteenth Army commander, General Busch, had eleven divisions, five north of Lake Ilmen and six south of it.

For Army Group North on the defensive, Lake Ilmen was a far more significant reference point than the boundary between the two armies. The 25-mile-wide lake divided the army group's front on the east almost exactly in two. Novgorod, at the lake's northern tip and just barely inside the German line, controlled lateral roads and railroads running north all the way to the bottleneck. Tactically the front north of the lake covered the rear of the line around Leningrad and the Oranienbaum pocket. It did that at a distance of 10 miles at the bottleneck and 60 miles midway on the Volkhov River. At the south end of the lake, Staraya Russa, 10 miles behind the front, straddled the sole railroad and the main road servicing the south flank. From the lake to the army group boundary and beyond and from the front in the Valdai Hills west for 130 miles stretched an expanse of tangled rivers, swamps, and forest in which the most important points were the road junctions at Demyansk, Kholm, and Toropets, each 50 or more miles distant from one another and from Staraya Russa.

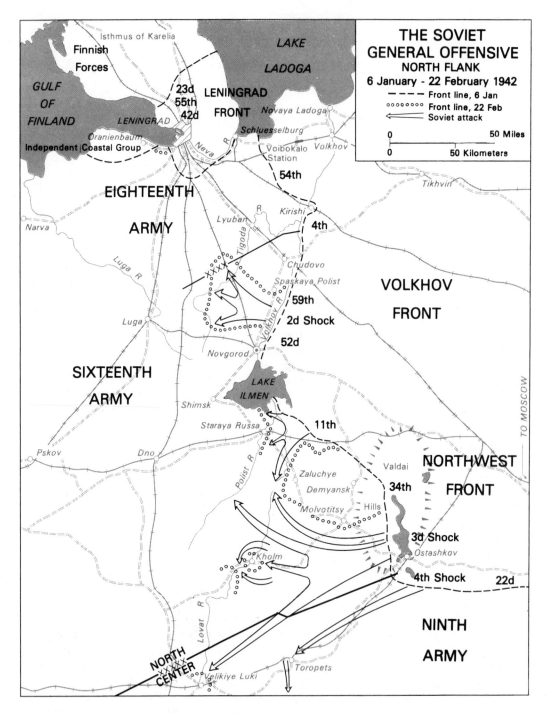

THE SOVIET
GENERAL OFFENSIVE
NORTH FLANK
6 January - 22 February 1942
- - - - Front line, 6 Jan
ooooooooo Front line, 22 Feb
⟵ Soviet attack

0   50 Miles
0   50 Kilometers

Isthmus of Karelia

LAKE LADOGA

Finnish Forces

GULF OF FINLAND

23d
55th
42d

LENINGRAD FRONT

LENINGRAD

Novaya Ladoga

Oranienbaum

Schluesselburg

Independent Coastal Group

Neva R.

Voibokalo Station

Volkhov

54th

EIGHTEENTH ARMY

Narva

Luga R.

Lyuban

Tigoda R.

Kirishi

Tikhvin

4th

Chudovo

Spaskaya Polist

VOLKHOV FRONT

Volkhov R.

59th

2d Shock

Luga

52d

Novgorod

SIXTEENTH ARMY

LAKE ILMEN

Shimsk

Staraya Russa

11th

Pskov

Dno

Polist R.

Zaluchye

Valdai

NORTHWEST FRONT

Demyansk

34th

Molvotitsy

Hills

3d Shock

Kholm

Ostashkov

4th Shock

22d

Lovat R.

NINTH ARMY

NORTH CENTER

Velikiye Luki

Toropets

TO MOSCOW

MAP 10

Meretskov's First Attempt on the Volkhov

After the new year, in paralyzing cold, Soviet bids to squeeze a last advantage out of the drive from Tikhvin by probing across the Volkhov River declined and then stopped completely on 4 January. Field Marshal Leeb, Army Group North commander, reported a quiet day on the 4th along his whole front, the first such in many weeks, but he hardly expected the respite to last long. For several days the army group's monitors had been picking up radio traffic new to them— from *Second Shock Army*. The only real question, as Leeb saw it, was whether the Russians would try again on the Volkhov or regroup to the north and attempt to take the shorter route to Leningrad across the bottleneck: they would certainly do one or the other.[1]

On the Soviet side, of course, the decision had already been made on a larger scale than Leeb suspected, and the *Stavka* had sent L. Z. Mekhlis, the army's chief commissar, to *Volkhov Front* to make certain that General Meretskov got an early start. Meretskov had, by 6 January, deployed *Fifty-ninth* and *Fourth Armies* on the Volkhov between the Leningrad-Moscow railroad and Kirishi and *Second Shock* and *Fifty-second Armies* south of the railroad. *Second Shock Army*, under General Leytenant N. K. Klykov, was to break through across the Volkhov and advance northwest toward Lyuban with *Fifty-ninth* and *Fourth Armies* giving it support on the right and *Fifty-second Army* widening the breach on its left and taking Novgorod. *Fifty-fourth Army*, which belonged to *Leningrad Front*, and the right flank elements of *Fourth Army*, starting from the area around Kirishi, were to surround and wipe out the Germans in the bottleneck.[2]

On the whole north flank, that is, including *Northwest* and *Leningrad Fronts*, the Russians had comfortable numerical superiorities: 1.5:1 in troops, 1.6:1 in artillery and mortars, and 1.3:1 in aircraft. *Volkhov Front* had received new troops and supplies, but in the first week of January, Meretskov did not yet have enough of either to start an offensive. *Fifty-ninth Army*, with apparently at least eight rifle and two cavalry divisions, was his strongest. Many of *Second Shock Army*'s units, on the other hand, had not yet arrived, and, according to Meretskov, its one rifle division and seven rifle brigades gave it only the strength of an infantry corps. The armies' reserves of rations and fodder were small, and they had only about a quarter of their required ammunition stocks. In these respects, *Second Shock* and *Fifty-ninth Armies* were the worst off because supplies were distributed from the rear separately to each individual army, not through the *front*, and these armies were just establishing their lines.[3]

Nevertheless, on the 7th, the front north of Lake Ilmen came to life, and the offensive started—in a somewhat loose order. *Fourth* and *Fifty-second Armies* led off, and *Fifty-ninth* and *Second Shock Armies* joined in at intervals during the next several days.[4] For five days, the Germans stood off flurries of at-

[1] *H. Gr. Nord, Ia Kriegstagebuch, 1.–18.1.42*, 1–4 Jan 42, H. Gr. Nord 75128/5 file; Leeb, *Tagebuchaufzeichnungen*, pp. 428–29.

[2] Meretskov, *Serving the People*, pp. 180–86.
[3] *IVOVSS*, vol. II, p. 333; Meretskov, *Serving the People*, pp. 185, 187. See also *IVMV*, vol. IV, map 10.
[4] *IVMV*, vol. IV, p. 315.

SOVIET 152-MM. GUN-HOWITZER FIRING NORTH OF LAKE ILMEN

tacks conducted without much determination or, as far as they could tell, purpose. The danger was that one or another of the Soviet armies would strike a weak spot, of which there were several. On the morning of the 13th, that happened when *Second Shock Army,* making its first real effort, brought down a heavy artillery barrage and then hit the boundary of the 126th and 215th Infantry Divisions south of the railroad. Boundaries were always difficult to defend, and this one was more difficult because the 126th Infantry Division was a recent arrival to the Eastern Front. In a day, a gap four miles wide opened between the two divisions. *Second Shock Army* had almost executed the first stage of its assignment, but, during two more days of fighting, it

was unable to open the gap wider.[5] Something, much in fact, was going wrong on the Soviet side. On the 15th, *Fourth Army* and *Fifty-second Army* stopped and went over to the defensive. The *History of the Great Patriotic War* says, "There were serious defects in the organization of the offensive, such as the dispersion of the forces in many directions. . . ."[6] On the 16th, Meretskov stopped to regroup.

South of Lake Ilmen

As the Germans watched *Volkhov Front* get off to a ragged start, they began to believe the actual Soviet main

---

[5]*H. Gr. Nord, Ia Kriegstagebuch, 1.–18.1.42,* 13–16 Jan 42, H. Gr. Nord 75128/5 file.
[6]*IVOVSS,* vol. II, p. 335.

effort was going to be south of Lake Ilmen, where General Kurochkin's *Northwest Front* also began the offensive on 7 January. Late in the day on the 7th, Sixteenth Army outposts on the south shore of the lake saw Soviet motor convoys and ski troops with sleds coming southwest across the lake. In the wilderness south of the lake, in fact over most of the distance to the army group boundary, Sixteenth Army had only established a line of strongpoints, not a solid front. By daylight the next day, two Soviet divisions were across the lake and beginning to push south ten miles behind the front. On the 9th, while Sixteenth Army scraped together a few battalions to screen Staraya Russa, Russians on skis and pulling sleds moved south along the frozen course of the Lovat River to the Staraya Russa–Demyansk road.

Eleventh Army was beginning to carry out its share in the counteroffensive, and Leeb and Busch saw at once that the army could be dangerous. Staraya Russa, close behind the front, was the railhead and main supply base for all of Sixteenth Army's line south of Lake Ilmen and an *Eleventh Army* thrust past Staraya Russa to Dno, eighty miles to the west, could cripple the German lateral railroad and road communications all the way north to Leningrad.[7]

West of Ostashkov, on Sixteenth Army's extreme right flank, *Third* and *Fourth Shock Armies* went over to the offensive on the 9th. Their attack hit two regiments of the 123d Infantry Division which were holding a thirty-mile-long line of widely spaced strongpoints running north from the army group boundary. Many of the strong-points were so far apart that the first Soviet waves simply marched west between them. In three days all of the strongpoints were wiped out and a thirty-mile-wide gap had been created.

The breakthrough on the south raised the immediate prospect of an encirclement that seemed to be the only worthwhile purpose the Soviet initiative could serve.[8] Kurochkin had, in fact, "amended" his instructions from the *Stavka* and ordered *Thirty-fourth Army* to become "more active toward the west" and *Eleventh Army* and *Third Shock Army* to dispatch forces off their flanks to block the line of the Lovat River against a German retreat.[9] Sixteenth Army was managing to cover Staraya Russa by bringing in police and security troops from the rear area, but there were no reserves to be had for the south flank. On the afternoon of the 12th, Leeb ordered Busch to have II Corps, his southernmost corps and the one standing farthest east, to get ready to pull back. Then he called Hitler and proposed to begin taking the whole front south of Lake Ilmen back gradually to the Lovat. Hitler replied that he had to consider the effect on the whole front and told Leeb to come to the *Fuehrer* Headquarters the next morning when they would "discuss the matter in its full context."[10]

The "discussion" was brief and one-sided. Hitler ordered Leeb to hold the line south of Lake Ilmen where it was and to scavenge enough strength out of the existing front to counterattack and close the gap on the south. A withdrawal he said would expose the

---

[7]Leeb, *Tagebuchaufzeichnungen*, p. 431.

[8]See *ibid.*
[9]Zhelanov, *"Iz opyta,"* p. 23.
[10]*H. Gr. Nord, Ia Kriegstagebuch, 1.–18.1.42*, 12 Jan 42, H. Gr. Nord 75128/5 file.

Army Group Center flank and that would be intolerable. The order had been cleared to go out over the teletype before Leeb arrived at *Fuehrer* Headquarters, and after his departure, Field Marshal Keitel, chief of the OKW, called ahead to the Army Group North command post in Pskov to leave the message that the *Fuehrer* "would be pleased" if Leeb, on his return, would personally impress on Busch "the unconditional necessity for holding the south flank."[11] Whatever the necessity, Leeb did not believe it was possible to hold the flank, either before he talked to Hitler or after.[12]

When Leeb returned to Pskov, *Third Shock Army* was approaching the Kholm-Demyansk road. On the 15th, the Russians were fanning out across the road. Believing the whole front south of Lake Ilmen would henceforth have to be drawn in toward Staraya Russa, Leeb asked either that he be relieved or that he be allowed to order the retreat while he still had some room for maneuver. A clue to what the answer would be came through General Halder, chief of the General Staff, who called Leeb's chief of staff, General Brennecke, and told him to "put all of the powers of the General Staff in motion . . . and extirpate this mania for operating. The army group has a clear order to hold," Halder added, "and the highest command will assume all the risk."[13] On the 17th, Hitler relieved Leeb "for reasons of health" and appointed Kuechler to command the army group.

The "Brawl"

For Hitler the lines were drawn. The winter's battles on the north flank would be fought toe-to-toe wherever they occurred. Hitler had made his decision. Army Group North would stand fast.

For the time being, Hitler's instinct was better than Leeb's professional judgment. The encirclement Leeb had believed imminent did not develop—not yet. *Eleventh Army* had a foothold on the Staraya Russa–Demyansk road but no more. *Third* and *Fourth Shock Armies* were bent on executing the operation laid out for them in December, namely, to drive a wedge between Army Groups North and Center, but both were advancing in two directions at once and their "strengths were not sufficient for such assignments."[14] Like *Second Shock Army,* they were not the powerful aggregations of combined arms that their designations implied. General Eremenko, who had been wounded in October 1941 while commanding *Bryansk Front* and had taken over *Fourth Shock Army* after he returned from the hospital in December, had been short 1,000 officers and 20,000 enlisted men when the offensive began. His table of organization had provided for three tank and ten ski battalions. One of the tank battalions and five ski battalions had then not arrived. Eremenko had been relatively better off than his colleague at *Third Shock Army,* General Leytenant M. A. Purkayev, because *Fourth Shock* had the former *Twenty-seventh Army* as a basis on which to build. *Third Shock Army* was new from the ground up and could

[11]*Ibid.,* 13 Jan 42.
[12]*Halder Diary,* vol. III, p. 383.
[13]*H. Gr. Nord, Ia Kriegstagebuch, 1.–18.1.42,* 16 Jan 42, H. Gr. Nord 75128/5 file.

[14]Zhelanov, *"Iz opyta,"* p. 23.

only be made ready at the last minute by transfers of personnel from *Fourth Shock Army,* which also had to share its supplies. On the day the offensive began, both armies had been close to the edge in rations and ammunition, and the only gasoline *Fourth Shock Army* had was that which was in its vehicles' tanks.[15]

On 21 January, *Fourth Shock Army* took Toropets, and a day later *Third Shock* encircled Kholm. The distances were impressive, sixty miles to Toropets, fifty-five to Kholm, but the substantive accomplishments were less so. Both armies had run out of supplies, and a scattering of German units was still able to hold Kholm. *Fourth Shock Army* captured enough German stores at Toropets to keep on the move, but the *Stavka's* plan now required Eremenko to head due south out of the Army Group North area into the rear of Army Group Center. On 22 January, *Third* and *Fourth Shock Armies* were shifted to the control of *Kalinin Front,* which reduced Kurochkin's problems but increased those of the *front's* commander, General Konev.[16] To the Germans, although it further endangered Army Group Center, Eremenko's turn south was almost a relief. Halder remarked that it was better than if the turn had been to the north because then holding Leningrad would have become impossible.[17]

Seen from the German side, one of the most disconcerting features of the offensive against Army Group North thus far was its erratic execution. His

GENERAL A. I. EREMENKO

tactical sensibilities offended, Halder was even moved to complain that the whole war appeared to be "degenerating into a brawl." The drive by the two shock armies was "senseless," he said, because it could not in the long run accomplish anything decisive against either of the two German army groups.[18] Unable to conceive that the *Stavka* would deliberately fritter away strength in secondary attacks, Hitler, Halder, and Kuechler concluded that the main blow was yet to come and would be aimed at the Leningrad bottleneck, where a ten-mile advance could break the siege. They were wrong. The "brawl" was going to continue.

[15]Eremenko, *V nachale,* pp. 403–07.
[16]*Ibid.,* pp. 441–45; *IVOVSS,* vol. II, p. 322.
[17]*Halder Diary,* vol. III, p. 389.

[18]*Ibid.,* p. 394.

Breakthrough on the Volkhov

In the week after *Volkhov Front's* attacks had bogged down north of Lake Ilmen, Meretskov had reassessed his prospects and had regrouped to exploit a weak spot *Second Shock Army* had found on the Volkhov. The Germans had managed to screen the gap but in doing so had had to leave the Russians holding a three-by-five-mile bridgehead. On 21 January, *Second Shock Army,* flanked on the left by *Fifty-second Army* and on the right by *Fifty-ninth Army,* began battering the western face of the bridgehead. The flanking armies were drawn in close to roll up the enemy front to the south and to the north when the breakthrough was made.[19] In the meantime, the offensive had changed from a grand, five-army effort to chop up the whole front between Lake Ladoga and Lake Ilmen into essentially a single thrust by *Second Shock Army* that was still seventy miles from the siege line at Leningrad.

Second Shock Army did well in the first five days of the second attempt, getting through the front to a distance of almost twenty-five miles, but in doing so, it did not put itself within range of any significant objectives. The territory in which it was operating was the headwaters country of the Luga and Tigoda rivers, a vast, almost unsettled stretch of swamps and peat bogs, that was mostly underwater except in winter. Having a Soviet army roving behind their front was, of course, disconcerting to the Germans, but the greater immediate danger was that the flanking armies would widen the breakthrough. *Fifty-ninth Army,* particularly,

by pushing north as far as Chudovo on the Moscow-Leningrad railroad, could have opened a 25-mile gap and a clear approach along the railroad to Leningrad. But the Germans kept a tight grip on Spaskaya Polist, twenty miles south of Chudovo, and by also tying *Fifty-second Army* down limited the breach to six miles and forced *Second Shock Army* to operate in a pocket.[20]

A Mutual Frustration

Volkhov and *Northwest Fronts* were, in the Soviet postwar view, unable to exploit their numerical superiorities to the fullest because of three problems: difficult terrain, weaknesses in support, and inexperienced commands. Since the first affected both sides about equally, the latter two were the most significant. Supplies had been short in all the armies, but Meretskov experienced some improvement at *Volkhov Front* after late January when A. V. Krulev, who was the deputy defense commissar in charge of logistics, arrived to expedite the shipments. The inexperience of the commands was, according to the *History of the Great Patriotic War,* the most persistent problem. Meretskov had already removed one commanding general of *Second Shock Army* a day or two before the offensive began, and later he wrote his account of the army's operations that reads in places like a roster of failed staff officers. Eremenko, writing from the point of view of an army commander, sees his own and his subordinate staffs as confident and competent, and the *front* command as elaborately cautious on the one hand and ca-

---

[19]Meretskov, *Serving the People,* p. 195.   [20]See *ibid.*

pricious on the other.[21] The Germans became aware as the fighting went on that the commands of the lower echelons were having troubles. Army Group North's radio monitors intercepted messages from army NKVD O.O. sections to division and brigade sections calling attention to a large increase in "nonfulfillment of combat assignments" and ordering the sections to intervene "to reestablish proper order among the units."[22]

As January ended, the fighting on the north flank appeared to be settling into a state of slow motion. Snow over three feet deep covered the ground and below-zero temperatures persisted, but these were not the reasons for the slowdown. Mutual uncertainty had simply brought into being a near-deadlock. The Germans' position was precarious, and they could do nothing to change it. The Russians had the initiative, but they could not exploit it. South of Lake Ilmen, two German corps, II Corps and X Corps, were holding an eastward projecting salient around Demyansk. The Soviet *Eleventh Army* had driven a twenty-mile-deep wedge into the corps' north flank east of Staraya Russa that cut their best supply routes and made a substantial start toward enveloping the salient. On the south flank, II Corps had *Third Shock Army* standing at Kholm fifty miles to its rear and *Thirty-fourth Army* probing northward into the mostly vacant space in-between.

Having no more than a scattering of reserves, Sixteenth Army had to thin

the front on the east to screen the corps' flanks. Its commander, Busch, disgruntled at having been passed over for command of the army group and, as Leeb had been, fearful of an encirclement, wanted to strengthen the south flank against an enveloping thrust from that direction. Kuechler, irked by Busch's clinging to the idea of a potential threat on the south flank that had already cost Leeb his command, agreed with Halder that the greater danger was on the north. Halder insisted that as an old soldier he had "a certain nose for such things," and it told him the threat was not from the south but in the north, specifically at Staraya Russa which was the key to the entire German position south of Lake Ilmen.[23]

While the argument at the top ran on, the troops that II and X Corps were able to free were just barely enough, as long as the enemy moved slowly, to keep the Russians from swinging in behind the corps. On the Volkhov the situation was similar. Eighteenth Army, which had taken over the area of the breakthrough, was confident it could deal with *Second Shock Army* after it closed the gap in the front, but all the troops it could spare were having to be used just to keep the gap from widening.[24]

Toward the end of the first week in February, Army Group North for several days could report "nothing particularly wrong."[25] The Soviet offensive seemed to be decaying into a succession of uncoordinated attacks, some locally dangerous, but none likely to alter the

[21]*IVOVSS*, vol. II, p. 338; Meretskov, *Serving the People*, pp. 196, 199–205. See Eremenko, *V nachale*, pp. 405–20.

[22]*H. Gr. Nord, Ia Kriegstagebuch, 18.1–12.2.42*, 8 Feb 42, H. Gr. Nord 75128/6 file.

[23]*Ibid.*, 27 Jan 42.

[24]*Ibid.*, 28 Jan 42.

[25]*Ibid.*, 8 Feb 42.

situation drastically. For the moment Army Group North was almost less concerned about the Russians than about how its railroads were running. The problem was not a new one although the snow and cold had made it worse. It could be traced all the way back to the planning for BARBAROSSA that had left the operating of the railroads in the occupied areas as well as in Germany under civilian control. Working on the Eastern Front was the least popular of the railroad men's assignments, and there the Army Group North zone was apparently the most undesirable. The army group believed its raillines were being run by the culls of the whole system. Halder suggested arresting a few and turning them over to the *Gestapo* as an object lesson for the others.[26]

In Leningrad, time and the weather appeared to be working for the Germans. Prisoner-of-war and deserter interrogations indicated that Leningrad was in catastrophic condition owing to hunger and to cold. Hitler urged the army group several times to consider taking advantage of the relative quiet on the front and to push in closer toward Leningrad, but Kuechler refused because he could not spare enough troops to take the city, and any line closer than the one Eighteenth Army then held would be underwater when the spring thaw began. The approaching thaw, which could come in five or six weeks, also gave rise to speculation that the Soviet winter offensive might be nearing its end. Halder thought the Russians would not attempt anything big so late in the season.[27]

In the midst of what almost appeared to be an impending calm, Sixteenth Army identified two new Soviet units, *I* and *II Guards Rifle Corps,* on 6 February. The two corps were deployed back to back in the wedge *Eleventh Army* had driven in east of Staraya Russa. From this position, the corps could split the German front in several directions, but for the moment their actions did not disclose any particular purpose, and they could themselves be trapped by an attack across the base of the wedge. General Brennecke, the Army Group North chief of staff, saw the deployment of the two Russian corps as the beginning of a final attempt to cut off II and X Corps around Demyansk. Halder, on the other hand, was puzzled as to what the Russians might do. The Soviet commanders were so browbeaten, he believed, that they would try almost anything just to have a tactical success to show. Rather than to wait and see what they would do, Sixteenth Army decided to strike east behind the two Soviet corps with the 5th Light Division. The division although fresh from Germany was forced to attack directly off the trains that brought it in, and half of it was still scattered along the railroad as far back as Riga. The result of the attack was almost instantaneous failure, and the few parties that had advanced had to be brought back under the cover of darkness on the night of the 10th.[28]

The Germans' uncertainty had been more than matched by complications on the Soviet side of the front. In the third week of January, Kurochkin had proposed concentrating first on encircling and then destroying II and X

---

[26]*Ibid.*
[27]*Ibid.*, 9–10 Feb 42.

[28]*Ibid.*, 10 Feb 42.

Corps west of the Lovat, but the *Stavka* had not been willing to delay the projected advance past Staraya Russa toward Dno and Luga. By then it had also begun thinking about turning *Third Shock Army* northwest after it reached Kholm for a deep thrust to Pskov. Late in the month the *Stavka* had given Kurochkin the *I* and *II Guards Rifle Corps* and the *First Shock Army* with orders to do both the thrust to the west and the encirclement. *First Shock Army,* which had been shipped north from the front west of Moscow without a rest, was to spearhead the attack past Staraya Russa. The two rifle corps were to be used against II and X Corps, and the area to be encircled was much enlarged. *Third Shock Army,* in the meantime transferred to *Kalinin Front,* would act as the southern arm, and *II Guards Rifle Corps* would close the ring from the north by a long drive west of the Lovat to Kholm where it would join *Third Shock Army* and subsequently take part in the advance to Pskov. Although it would be starting deep in Kurochkin's territory, *II Guards Rifle Corps* was subordinated to *Kalinin Front.*[29]

North of Lake Ilmen, in the second week of February, time was getting short. Leningrad was starving, and another four to six weeks could bring the mud and floods of the spring thaw. *Volkhov Front* had widened the gap enough at least to put *Second Shock Army's* supply line out of enemy rifle and machine gun range, but the Germans held tight at Spaskaya Polist on the crucial north shoulder. Under fierce pressure from the *Stavka* to accomplish something toward relieving Leningrad, Meretskov tried to get *Sec-*

ond Shock Army aimed toward Lyuban, which would put it about halfway to Leningrad. *Second Shock Army,* however, persisted in pushing due west where the German resistance was lighter. Neither the presence at the *front* headquarters of Marshal Voroshilov as a representative of the *Stavka* nor the relief of *Second Shock Army's* chief of staff and its operations officer was enough to get the army headed in the right direction.[30]

Encirclement at Demyansk

Lyuban and Staraya Russa were going to stay in German hands for a long time, the latter long enough to become a legend on the Eastern Front. The winter, and Hitler, however, were going to give the Soviet forces their first opportunity in the war to execute a major encirclement. It was one that, once Hitler had tied the II and X Corps down around Demyansk, the Russians could hardly have helped achieving. The pocket had begun forming in the first days of the offensive, and from then on it was almost a collaborative work between the Soviet commands and Hitler.

As *Eleventh* and *Thirty-fourth Armies* turned in behind Demyansk in January, II and X Corps, which had been forbidden to maneuver, wrapped their lines around to the west. On the south, II Corps held Molvotitsy as a cornerpost. The 290th Infantry Division established a northern cornerpost fifteen miles due east of Staraya Russa. By retaining the 5th Light Division at Staraya Russa, Sixteenth Army kept alive a hope that it could strike across the

---

[29] Zhelanov, *"Iz opyta,"* pp. 26–28.

[30] Meretskov, *Serving the People,* pp. 196–98.

gap to the 290th Infantry Division and turn the tables on the enemy, but the chances of doing that dwindled after *I* and *II Guards Rifle Corps* and *First Shock Army* put in their appearances. One of the first effects of the Soviet reinforcement was to compress the 290th Infantry Division's front into a narrow, fingerlike projection off the main line of the Demyansk pocket, which was pushed away to the south.

I and *II Guards Rifle Corps* had the job of completing the encirclement, and they had instructions on how to do it directly from Stalin, who told their commanders, General Mayor A. S. Gryaznov and General Mayor A. I. Lizyukov, "Move in strong groupings, and do not stretch out. If you become extended, you cannot move fast. Maintain your groupings, and do not divide regiments and battalions. Do not lose contact with advance detachments."[31] The instructions were good, but, "as a practical matter," the "exceedingly long distances" the corps had to cover made them "unfulfillable."[32]

Since the Germans could not prevent it and did not propose to attempt to escape from it, completing the encirclement became almost a technicality. The *II Guards Rifle Corps* cut the last German overland supply line on 9 February, and thereafter II Corps, under Generalleutnant Graf Walter von Brockdorff-Ahlefeldt, became responsible for the six divisions in the pocket, since Headquarters, X Corps, was located outside, at Staraya Russa. A supply airlift began three days later, and Brockdorff reported on the 16th that he had 95,000 men in the pocket and

needed at least 200 tons of supplies a day to survive. He was then getting 80 to 90 tons a day.[33]

The *II Guards Rifle Corps* completed an outer ring on 15 February when it made contact with elements of *Third Shock Army* northeast of Kholm.[34] In fact, the outer ring had little more than token significance, since there were no Germans within miles of it over most of its length. A much more dismaying event for the Germans came on the 18th, when the 290th Infantry Division had to withdraw into the main line of the pocket. Until then the OKH and the army group had been able to talk about launching the 5th Light Division east "in a few days."[35] Losing the northern cornerpost was also more important to the Germans than the closing of the inner ring, which they were not aware of when it happened. Soviet accounts give two dates. The *History of the Great Patriotic War* gives 20 February, at Zaluchye, just outside the pocket and due east of Demyansk.[36] Zhelanov says the inner encirclement "advanced slowly" and was not completed until 25 February, when *I Guards Rifle Corps* made contact at Zaluchye with a *Third Shock Army* rifle brigade coming from the south.[37]

On 22 February, Hitler designated the Demyansk pocket a "fortress." The next such fortress would be Stalingrad, and after it there would be many more, but in the winter of 1942 the term was new. It implied permanence. A *Kessel*

---

[31]Zhelanov, "*Iz opyta*," p. 29.
[32]*Ibid.*

[33]*AOK 16, Ia Kriegstagebuch Band II*, 9 Feb 42, AOK 16 23468/3 file; *H. Gr. Nord, Ia Kriegstagebuch, 18.1.–12.2.42*, 16 Feb 42, H. Gr. Nord 75128/6 file.
[34]Zhelanov, "*Iz opyta*," p. 29.
[35]*H. Gr. Nord, Ia Kriegstagebuch, 13.2.–12.3.42*, 13–18 Feb 42, H. Gr. Nord 75128/7 file.
[36]*IVOVSS*, vol. II, p. 337.
[37]Zhelanov, "*Iz opyta*," p. 30.

("encircled pocket") was an accident of war. A fortress was a deliberate creation and, in Hitler's conception, a purposeful tactical device. On the 18th he had already talked about staging a thrust from Demyansk south to close the eighty-mile-wide gap to Army Group Center. By the 22d he and the OKH were mulling over several plans for restoring contact with the fortress. And the war was giving them time: a sudden quiet was falling over the whole Eastern Front, which was remarkable by itself because 23 February was the Day of the Red Army and attacks to commemorate it had been expected. Around Demyansk the perimeter of the pocket stabilized. The gap between it and the main front at Staraya Russa was twenty miles and somewhat less farther south on the Polist River.

On the South Flank

Bock Goes to Poltava

On the morning of 16 January, Field Marshal Bock, his intestinal ailment abated, was getting ready to follow his doctors' advice and take several weeks' rest in the Austrian mountains when an officer telephoned from the army personnel office to ask whether Bock would be willing to take immediate command of Army Group South. The army group commander, Field Marshal Reichenau, the caller explained, had suffered a stroke and was not expected to live. The next day, Bock was aboard a dirty, unheated sleeping car on a train to East Prussia that was late. He stopped on the morning of the 18th at the OKH command post in Angerburg, where he learned that Reichenau had died, and then went on to a late breakfast with Hitler in the *Wolfsschanze*

compound. At the table Bock complained about the decrepit state of the railroads. Hitler agreed but added that he had recently put all the systems under the railroad minister and with that seemed to imply that he had done what was needed.

Afterward, General Schmundt, Hitler's chief adjutant, told Bock that the current topic of concern at *Fuehrer* Headquarters was the exodus of the generals, not the condition of the railroads. First there had been Field Marshals Runstedt and Brauchitsch, Schmundt said, then Generals Guderian and Hoepner, and in the last few days, Strauss, Leeb, and Reichenau had followed. It was causing talk in Germany and abroad. To counteract the talk, Schmundt disclosed, Hitler had sent Brauchitsch, who had recently undergone a heart operation, a warm telegram, which was being released to the news services. Rundstedt was being asked to represent the *Fuehrer* at Reichenau's funeral, and, Schmundt added as an aside that Hitler wanted to have some pictures taken with Bock before he departed to Army Group South.

Bock's main qualification at the moment appeared to be his publicity value. His mission, as Hitler explained it, hardly seemed to justify his recall. The Army Group South front, Hitler said, was "secure"; a little "cleaning up" needed to be done. But all he really expected Army Group South to do was sit tight through the winter.[38]

When he alighted at the Poltava airfield on the morning of the 19th, Bock found General Hoth there to meet him. Hoth, who had commanded

[38]*Bock Diary, Osten II,* 16–18 Jan 42.

Third Panzer Group in the summer of 1941, was currently commanding Seventeenth Army, and for the past several days, had been acting commander of Army Group South. Hoth's presence was a modest courtesy. In better times and a better season—the temperature was several degrees below zero—a field marshal could have expected more. On the quiet, secure front to which Bock had been told he was going, he could have expected a more ceremonious welcome even in such weather, but the front was no longer quiet, and it was far from secure. On the ride to Poltava, Hoth told Bock that the Russians had broken through at Izyum the day before and were streaming westward practically unimpeded. The army group, Bock also then learned, had no reserves. A Rumanian division and two German divisions were coming in, but the railroads in Russia were infinitely worse than what Bock had experienced in Germany, and moving the divisions would take weeks.[39]

The Izyum Bulge

Izyum was an insignificant town on the Donets River. The lay of the front and the objectives of the general offensive had temporarily made it a focal point of Soviet strategy. It was closer than any other locality on the front to the main southern crossings of the Dnepr River, Dnepropetrovsk and Zaporozhye. It was the key, as well, to the southern approaches to Kharkov and a good springboard for a thrust into the rear of Seventeenth and First Panzer Armies. *(Map 11.)*

In accordance with the *Stavka* plan,

Marshal Timoshenko, commander of *Southwestern Theater,* on 18 January, launched two related but separate thrusts across the Donets in the Izyum area. In one, to be conducted by *Southwest Front, Sixth Army* and *VI Cavalry Corps* would strike northwest to meet a thrust coming west off *Thirty-eighth Army's* right flank and would envelop Kharkov. In the other, *South Front's Fifty-seventh Army* would advance west to Dnepropetrovsk and Zaporozhye and then south in the direction of Melitopol. Timoshenko held *Ninth Army* as his *Southwestern Theater* reserve and stationed *I* and *V Cavalry Corps* behind *Fifty-seventh Army* as General Malinovskiy's *South Front* reserves. Malinovskiy and Timoshenko expected General Leytenant D. I. Ryabyshev, the *Fifty-seventh Army* commander, to reach Bolshoy Tokmak, just north of Melitopol, in twenty-two to twenty-four days.[40]

The offensive on the south flank was simplified somewhat by the early elimination of the other parts of the general offensive originally scheduled in the *Southwestern Theater.* Its prospects of succeeding, however, were probably also reduced. *Bryansk Front* and the right flank armies of *Southwest Front* had begun their attacks toward Orel and Kursk in the first week of January, had not made worthwhile gains, and were winding down to a stop by the middle of the month. General Manstein's counterattack on the Crimea turned the tables there after 15 January. The *Crimean Front (Transcaucasus Front* renamed) was created at the end of the

---

[39]*Ibid.,* 19 Jan 42.

[40]Grechko, *Gody voyny,* pp. 86–92; Bagramyan, *Tak shli my k pobede,* pp. 20–22.

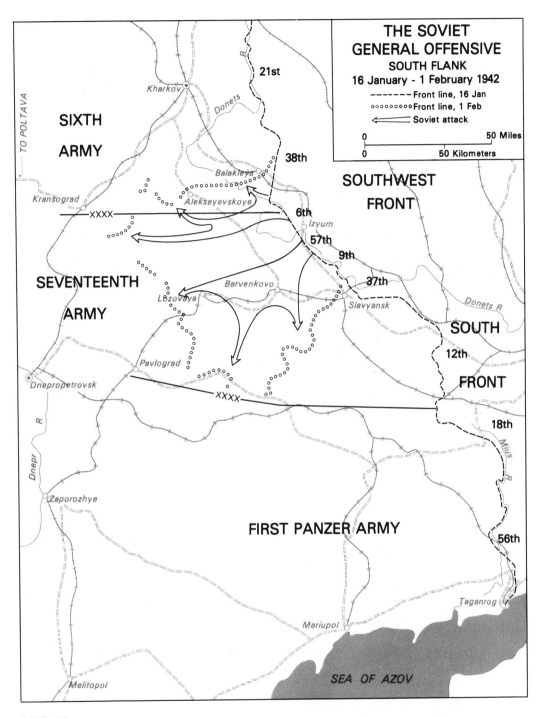

MAP 11

month and given orders to resume the offensive, but it would not be ready until the last of February.[41]

Seventeenth Army's left flank covered Izyum and the loop of the Donets and tied in with Sixth Army at Balakleya twenty-five miles to the northwest. On the morning of the 18th, the Soviet *Fifty-seventh* and *Sixth Armies* opened the attack on a sixty-mile front flanking Izyum on both sides from Slavyansk to Balakleya. Although the ground in the Ukraine was more open than that of the northern forest zone, the weather and their shortage of troops had forced the Germans to resort to a strongpoint line there as well. Bypassing some of the strongpoints and overrunning others, the Russians had penetrated the front in a number of places before nightfall, and Seventeenth Army was beginning to evacuate hospitals and supply dumps close to the line. Before 1200 the next day the army had committed its last reserves, and by afternoon, one Soviet spearhead supported by a brigade of tanks was heading toward Barvenkovo, twenty miles southwest of Izyum on the army's main supply line, the railroad from Dnepropetrovsk to Slavyansk. Seventeenth Army was being pushed away to the east into a pocket on the river that could become a trap for both it and First Panzer Army if the Soviet drive carried through to the Dnepr crossings.[42]

By the 22d, Seventeenth Army's entire flank north of Slavyansk was torn away, and *Southwest Front* units were turning behind Sixth Army. General

der Panzertruppen Friedrich Paulus, who had taken command of Sixth Army just one week before, had to commit all of his reserves around Alekseyevskoye, forty-five miles northwest of Izyum, to cover the southern approach to Kharkov. In two more days the offensive secured an unanticipated dividend: during the night of the 24th, Bock decided to bring Panzer Detachment 60 north out of the Crimea that meant the end of Manstein's attempt to retake the Kerch Peninsula.[43]

Between 22 and 24 January, Malinovskiy committed the *I* and *V Cavalry Corps* on the left flank of *Fifty-seventh Army* west of Slavyansk.[44] By the end of the day on the 25th, after one week on the offensive, the Russians had chewed a 3,600-square-mile chunk out of the German front and had covered better than half the distance from Izyum to Dnepropetrovsk. The next morning Hoth proposed that Seventeenth Army's mission henceforth be to cover Dnepropetrovsk. Late in the day he told Bock that there were only two possibilities left: either a "desperate" attack to the west across the line of the Soviet advance toward Dnepropetrovsk or "quick" action to organize countermeasures with resources from elsewhere.[45] Especially after he heard that one or two of the corps commanders were talking about sacrificing their equipment to save the troops, Bock believed that Hoth was on the verge of turning the whole army around and

[41]*IVOVSS*, vol. II, p. 340, 344.

[42]*AOK 17, Fuehrungsabteilung, Kriegstagebuch Nr. 2*, 18–21 Jan 42, AOK 17 14499/85 file.

[43]*AOK 6, Fuehrungsabteilung, Kriegstagebuch Nr. 10*, 22 Jan 42, AOK 6 17244 file; *Bock Diary, Osten II*, 22 Jan 42.

[44]Grechko, *Gody voyny*, p. 99.

[45]*AOK 17, Fuehrungsabteilung, Kriegstagebuch Nr. 2*, 26 Jan 42, AOK 17 16719/1 file.

heading west. Alarmed at this prospect, Bock the next morning ordered Hoth to hold the army where it stood under all circumstances until reserves could be brought up. Bock also had the feeling that Hoth and his staff were "overtired from the strain of the last days" and decided to put Seventeenth Army under General Kleist, the "enterprising" commander of First Panzer Army. Creating such ad hoc commands had been a favorite, and not uniformly successful, device of Bock's while he commanded Army Group Center. He believed it would spur Kleist to give more and faster help to his neighbor, Seventeenth Army, and Hoth, less a prima donna than many German army commanders, agreed.[46]

Early in its second week, the battle in the Izyum bulge was also reaching a climax for the Soviet commands—and producing some disappointments for them. The sharpest of these was their failure to expand the opening in the front. The Germans held tight to Slavyansk and Balakleya, which kept their lines north and south of those places firmly anchored and stable. Channeled into a fifty-mile-wide corridor, the Soviet armies tended to lose momentum—and confidence. *Sixth Army* hesitated to make the turn north toward Kharkov while its neighbor on the right, *Thirty-eighth Army*, was stuck at Balakleya. *Thirty-seventh Army*, which was to have pinched off Slavyansk and to have accompanied *Fifty-seventh Army* on its push south, did not do that, and *Fifty-seventh Army* and the two cavalry corps, as they bore south, entered a region heavily dotted with towns

which the Germans could exploit as strongpoints.

Consequently, as the *History of the Great Patriotic War* puts it, the *Stavka* "refined" the missions of *Southwest* and *South Fronts*. On 26 January, Timoshenko committed *Ninth Army* alongside *Fifty-seventh Army*, and between then and the end of the month the *Stavka* gave *Southwest Front* 315 tanks, 4 rifle divisions, and 4 rifle brigades. *Fifty-seventh* and *Ninth Armies* and the cavalry corps were to head south to "coax" Seventeenth Army out of its line on the east and into battle in the open and to reach the coast between Mariupol and Melitopol. *Sixth Army*, apparently putting its thrust toward Kharkov in abeyance, was to drive west toward the Dnepr.[47]

In refining the missions, the *Stavka* and the *Southwestern Theater* seemed in actuality to have converted the offensive into a clutch of tank-supported, deep cavalry raids. Seventeenth Army captured Soviet orders of 25 January assigning the thrusts to the west and south to the three cavalry corps. The *VI Cavalry Corps*, still attached to *Sixth Army*, was to drive west via Lozovaya toward the Dnepr, and *I* and *V Cavalry Corps* were to push south ahead of *Fifty-seventh* and *Ninth Armies*.[48] Against these, Kleist was moving in from the south the "von Mackensen" Group— 14th Panzer Division, 100th Light Division, and Panzer Detachment 60 under General von Mackensen—and from the west XI Corps, which at first had only remnants of two divisions but was

---

[46]*Bock Diary, Osten II*, 26–28 Jan 42.

[47]*IVOVSS*, vol. II, pp. 339–42; Grechko, *Gody voyny*, pp. 106–12; Bagramyan, *Tak shli my k pobede*, pp. 33–42.
[48]*OKH, GenStdH, FHQ, Wesentliche Merkmale der Feindlage am 27.1.42*, H 3/197 file.

SLED-MOUNTED GERMAN ANTITANK GUN

getting an infantry division and several regiments via Dnepropetrovsk. General von Mackensen, who was commanding general, III Panzer Corps, brought his staff with him from its sector on the First Panzer Army right flank. Paulus, at Sixth Army, had already set up two groups of mixed regiments (the Groups "Dostler" and "Friedrich") to cover the north face of the bulge.

For three days, in snowstorms that closed the roads to everything but tanks and horse-drawn sleds, Kleist's units maneuvered into position to meet the more mobile Soviet cavalry and tanks. On the 31st, the advance elements of Panzer Detachment 60 and 14th Panzer Division came up against the *I* and *V Cavalry Corps'* spearheads

forty miles south of Barvenkovo, and the Soviet cavalry, having outdistanced their own tanks, faltered and turned back.

Observing that the Soviet forces "are split into three groups and have given way under localized counterattacks," Bock then ordered the "von Mackensen" Group, XI Corps, and the "Dostler" and "Friedrich" Groups to attack from the south, west, and north "with the aim of destroying the enemy."[49] After a week and a half of fighting in zero-degree weather, high winds, and drifting snow, the "von Mackensen" Group pushed north to within ten miles of Barvenkovo by 11

---

[49]*H. Gr. Sued, Ia Nr. 210/42, an AOK 6, Armeegruppe von Kleist, 31.1.42*, H. Gr. Sued 23208/30 file.

February. The XI Corps and the "Dost-ler" and "Friedrich" Groups did not succeed in driving the Russians back more than a few miles, but, together with Seventeenth Army and the "von Mackensen" Group, they had drawn a reasonably tight line around the bulge by the 11th, one that would stand up during the weeks before the thaw set in as a deterrent to repeated Soviet attempts to break away to the west and south.

In the Center

The retreat to the KOENIGSBERG Line, according to Hitler's order of 15 January, was to be made "in small steps" and accomplished "in a form worthy of the German Army." The gap at Ninth Army west of Rzhev was to be closed as was the one between Fourth and Fourth Panzer Armies west of Maloyaroslavets, and Yukhnov was to be held "under all circumstances." The troops to carry out these missions were to be acquired by thinning the front as it came back.[50] To ensure execution as Hitler had specified, Field Marshal Kluge, Army Group Center commander, told Third and Fourth Panzer Armies, both of which had thirty to forty miles yet to go, that the withdrawal would not begin until he gave the order, and when it did begin, he would control the movements day by day.[51] For Fourth Army he made an exception, allowing it to begin "as of now."[52] (Map 12.)

[50]H. Gr. Mitte, Ia Nr. 423/42, an AOK 9, 16 Jan 42, AOK 9 21520/11 file.
[51]Pz. AOK 3, Ia Kriegstagebuch Nr. 2, 16 Jan 42, Pz. AOK 3 16911/1 file.
[52]H. Gr. Mitte, Ia Nr. 426/42, Zusaetze der H. Gr. zur Fuehrerweisung vom 15.1.42, 16.1.42, AOK 9 21520/11 file.

Fourth Army Fights To Survive

Fourth Army was an island, the remains of four corps jammed into a 25-by-20-mile space east of Yukhnov with a fifth corps struggling to hold open 40 miles of the *Rollbahn* west of Yukhnov. The gap between Fourth Army and its neighbor on the north, Fourth Panzer Army, was 15 miles wide at the mouth and ballooned westward behind both armies to an unknown extent. The light *Storch* reconnaissance planes that occasionally flew over parts of the area brought back conflicting reports, their pilots being understandably reluctant to linger over a hostile, frozen wilderness where being downed meant certain death. After having been cut on the 13th, the *Rollbahn* was open again on the 15th, but the situation maps showed the front almost on the road, and in places on the ground the Russians were only an easy rifle shot of 400 yards away. Kluge's permission for Fourth Army to go back brought no sense of relief. The army chief of staff told the OKH that the army was fighting for its "naked existence" and all decisions were too late. General Heinrici, XXXXIII Corps commander and the senior officer at the front (army headquarters was at Spas-Demensk, 60 miles southwest of Yukhnov), said the troops' confidence in their leadership was collapsing. Orders to hold at all cost had been read to them only a day before, and now they were being told to pick up and move.[53]

To save itself, Fourth Army would have to keep the *Rollbahn* open and, in coming west, stretch its front north to

[53]AOK 4, Ia Kriegstagebuch Nr. 11, 15 and 16 Jan 42, AOK 4 17380/1 file.

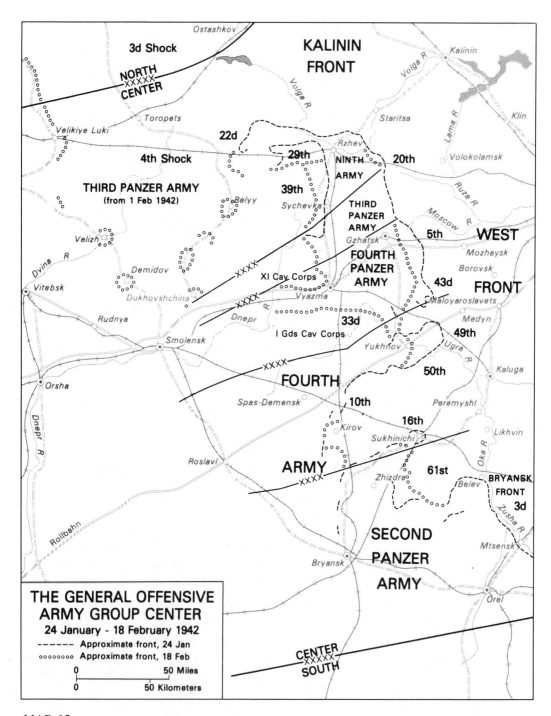

THE GENERAL OFFENSIVE
ARMY GROUP CENTER
24 January - 18 February 1942
- - - - - Approximate front, 24 Jan
ooooooooo Approximate front, 18 Feb

0   50 Miles
0   50 Kilometers

MAP 12

meet Fourth Panzer Army and close the gap. Doing so meant shifting almost the whole army obliquely to the northwest a distance of some fifteen miles. That maneuver became vastly more complicated on the 18th when a Soviet force drove toward the *Rollbahn* from the north and another unit of Russian cavalry coming from the south cut the road in two places. The noose was closing. Soviet divisions were in front of and behind the army. Shuttle flights of twenty to twenty-five planes were delivering troops and supplies every night deep at the rear of the army. In the vast forested triangle between Vyazma, Spas-Demensk, and Yukhnov, partisan detachments were conscripting men from farms and executing village elders who had worked for the Germans.

On the morning of 19 January, General Kuebler went to the *Fuehrer* Headquarters to report himself sick and to give up command of Fourth Army. Kuebler, who was not one of the better known generals, departed quietly on the 21st, and Heinrici took command of the army, also quietly. Nevertheless, the day brought a change of mood to the army. Heinrici, as commanding general, XXXXIII Corps, had been a prophet of catastrophe but had never yet failed to bring his corps out of the tightest spot. The staffs and troops obviously hoped he could do the same for the whole army. And the army did seem at once to get a new start, if a coincidental one. On the 21st, the temperature was −40° F. all day, and the fighting stopped. The next day, in weather −10° F., LVII Corps took the Russians by surprise and reduced the gap to Fourth Panzer Army to about five miles. After XXXX Corps also

cleared the *Rollbahn* and kept it open for twenty-four hours, Heinrici told Kluge the situation was "beginning to turn"; although the gap on the north was not closed yet, "something" was beginning to happen.[54]

In knee-deep snow and temperatures ranging as low as −40° F., both sides had to prepare and time every move precisely. Frostbite and exhaustion could claim as many casualties as the enemy's fire. Soviet soldiers frequently fell dead of exhaustion minutes after being captured. No one knew how often the same thing happened to the troops in battle.

Heinrici opened another attack to the north on the morning of the 25th with "enough artillery to cover the whole gap," but a fresh Soviet division had moved in, and the temperature was down to −40° F. again. One regiment advanced three miles, saw no sign of XX Corps, which was to have pushed south off Fourth Panzer Army's flank, and fell back. Heinrici then proposed shifting the line of attack west to the Yukhnov-Gzhatsk road, but Kluge thought that also might fail because the Soviet forces behind Fourth Army "may be stronger than we suspect."[55]

Kluge was, in fact, slightly prescient. Within the next few days, Soviet strength behind Fourth Army would be greatly increased. On the nights of the 26th and 27th, *I Guards Cavalry Corps,* under General Belov, a mustachioed veteran cavalryman, crossed the *Rollbahn* and headed north. The cavalry corps, 5 cavalry divisions, 2 rifle divisions, and artillery detachments,

---

[54]*Ibid.,* 21–22 Jan 42.
[55]*Ibid.,* 25–26 Jan 42.

was *Tenth Army*'s mobile group. Belov was looking to gather up partisan detachments as he went and to make contact with *IV Airborne Corps,* which was landing southwest of Vyazma. He and General Mayor A. F. Levashev, the airborne commander, were to coordinate their operations with Headquarters, *Thirty-third Army,* under General Leytenant M. G. Yefremov, which was setting up inside the gap between Fourth and Fourth Panzer Armies. Belov also had orders to link up with *XI Cavalry Corps,* which was bearing in on Vyazma from the northwest.[56] Fourth Army's position would have been even worse had the Soviet commands not been directing their efforts primarily toward Vyazma.

Contact at Sukhinichi

In the midst of its own flight for survival, Fourth Army received and recorded occasional radio reports from Sukhinichi. It could do nothing else for its 4,000 troops isolated there. When the weather permitted, the *Luftwaffe* dropped in enough supplies to enable Generalmajor Werner von Gilsa, the commander of the garrison in Sukhinichi, to withstand a siege that was being conducted more than a bit lamely. But time was on the Soviet side. It hardly appeared possible that four battalions could survive long in the dead of winter or that Second Panzer Army could muster enough strength on its stretch of the Sukhinichi perimeter to stage a relief. On 16 January, however, as XXIV Panzer Corps was being assembled around Zhizdra to attempt to relieve Sukhinichi, one battalion of the 18th

Panzer Division—the only one there at the time—made a sudden easy jump to the northeast. When it learned that the battalion had only met rear elements of Soviet divisions standing north of Zhizdra, the corps ordered 18th Panzer Division and the 208th Infantry Division to push ahead toward Sukhinichi. By the 19th, the day the attack had originally been scheduled to begin, they were nearly halfway there, but the Russians were hanging on their heels and closing in behind them. Expecting not to have the momentum to reach Sukhinichi, XXIV Panzer Corps told the garrison there to get ready to break out, but the army group also picked up the radioed message, and Kluge sharply warned Gilsa that Hitler had not lifted the order to hold the town. When the garrison passed to the control of Second Panzer Army on the 20th, General Schmidt took the opportunity to ask Hitler whether the order was still in force and received the reply that it most definitely was. After another day, in −40° F. weather and against at least one fresh Soviet division, the *Stavka* had rushed in from the Moscow area, XXIV Panzer Corps could no longer sustain thrusts by both of its divisions, and 18th Panzer Division had to attempt to go the last ten miles alone. On the afternoon of the 24th, with just two battalions still in motion, 18th Panzer Division made the contact.[57]

To the K-Line

Determined to retreat to the K-Line (KOENIGSBERG Line) in as "worthy" a manner as Hitler desired, Kluge held

[56]See P. Belov, "*Pyatimesyachnaya borba v tylu vraga,*" *Voyenno-istoricheskiy Zhurnal* 8(1962), 55–60.

[57]*Pz. AOK 2, Ia Kriegstagebuch 27.12.41–31.3.42,* 15–24 Jan 42, Pz. AOK 2 25034/162 file.

GERMAN SENTRY ON THE RUZA RIVER LINE

Third and Fourth Panzer Armies back for three days. He waited until after 1200 on the 18th before giving their commanders, Generals Reinhardt and Ruoff, permission to start the withdrawal, and then he stipulated that it was to be done in four stages of five to eight miles with a day's pause at each phase line. The main forces were to move at night, the rear guards in the daytime, with the final line to be reached on the morning of the 24th by the main forces and "if possible" not before the morning of the 25th by the rear guards.[58] Again, as they had on their march to the Lama and Ruza rivers in December, the armies would have to fight their way back without breaking contact with the enemy and in the open in below-zero weather.

The first night and day of the withdrawal showed that what was a tactical masterpiece on paper was working out as a near disaster. The Soviet infantry followed their every step, and it had tanks, T–34s, and some of the 52-ton KVs. Field howitzers with *Rotkopf* hollow-charge ammunition and 88-mm. guns could handle the tanks, but they had to stay on the roads, and without protection they were not only vulnerable to direct hits, as were the tanks, but to near and sometimes not so near misses. Among the infantry, many of whom were replacements or men combed out of the rear echelons, the sight or sound of tanks was often

---

[58]*Pz. AOK 4, Ia, Fernspruch von H. Gr. Mitte, 13.30 Uhr, 18.1.42, Pz. AOK 4 22457/36 file.*

enough to raise a panic. But the tanks were not the troops' most pervasive enemy; the cold was. The earth, a foot soldier's first and last refuge, became a menace. Frozen hard as iron, it drew heat from a man's body faster than the air did. The soldier who remained upright still did not have as good a chance of surviving as one who did not, but most had seen too many others never rise again to believe it. The cold destroyed the will to survive. Officers frequently had to drive their troops with pistols and clubs. The soldiers did not become cowards; they became apathetic, indifferent to what was going on around them and to their own fate. Growing losses in men and equipment and the expressed concern of the army commanders that the troops would be too few and too exhausted to hold the final line when they reached it persuaded Kluge at last to let the retreat be completed on the night of the 22d, two days earlier than he had originally ordered.[59]

Unknown to them, the two panzer armies, as they drew into the K-Line, were the possible recipients of a tactical "gift" from Stalin and the *Stavka*. The weakest point on the Lama-Ruza line had been the wedge driven in at V Panzer Corps west of Volokolamsk. Pushed farther west past Gzhatsk, it could have cut Ninth and Third Panzer Armies adrift and left Fourth Panzer standing with both flanks exposed. On 19 January, however, General Zhukov received orders to take *First Shock Army* out of the Volokolamsk sector and transfer it to the *Stavka* reserve. Two days later,

Headquarters, *Sixteenth Army* also was pulled out.[60] According to Zhukov, losing *First Shock Army* in particular weakened his offensive at exactly the crucial moment. The *History of the Great Patriotic War* concurs that the two shifts "brought about undesirable circumstances."[61]

On the other hand, the "gift" to the Germans may not have amounted to all that much. *First Shock Army* was in poor shape when it reappeared in action south of Lake Ilmen late in the month, and General Rokossovskiy, who commanded *Sixteenth Army,* states in his memoirs that his army had virtually evaporated by the time the headquarters was taken out.[62] The wear and tear on the Soviet units was certainly no less than that on the German. They had been on the offensive without a pause for nearly a month and a half, and the Third and Fourth Panzer Armies had put up a murderous defense on the Lama-Ruza line.

Model Closes the Rzhev Gap

Two days before Hitler gave his consent, Kluge had established the release of enough strength to close the gap in the Ninth Army front as the first objective of the withdrawal to the K-Line. On the 14th, he had earmarked Headquarters, XXXVI Panzer Corps and SS Division "Das Reich" from Fourth Panzer Army and a reinforced infantry regiment from Third Panzer Army for transfer to Strauss' Ninth Army as soon as the movement to the K-Line began. Word of Hitler's approval the next day spread "great relief" in the Ninth Army staff, relief that turned to "em-

---

[59]6. *Panzer Division, Ia, Bericht ueber Russische und Deutsche Kampfweise, 30.1.42,* Pz. AOK 3 21818/7 file; *Pz. AOK 3, Ia Kriegstagebuch Nr. 2,* 22 Jan 42, Pz. AOK 3 16911/1 file.

[60]Zhukov, *Memoirs,* p. 355; *IVOVSS,* vol. II, p. 325.
[61]*IVOVSS,* vol. II, p. 325.
[62]Rokossovskiy, *Soldier's Duty,* p. 95.

bitterment" two hours later when the army learned Kluge had given XXIII Corps permission to fall back about ten miles but ordered it not to shorten its front that then stretched about forty miles from the west side of the Rzhev gap into the wilderness east of Toropets. Strauss, as Kluge no doubt knew, wanted to shorten the XXIII Corps front on the west and use the troops in the attack into the gap. Kluge apparently suspected, probably not mistakenly, that Strauss was also attempting to give the corps a better chance to save itself in case the attack failed. That was part of the cause for embitterment, but only part. Kluge's order to XXIII Corps also constituted *hineinbefehlen* ("issuing orders over the head of the responsible command"), something even Hitler, much as he liked to interfere in the workings at the lower levels, did not permit himself. Kluge's act could only be interpreted in two ways: as grossly bad form—which Kluge was too much a stickler for punctilio to commit—or as a deliberate expression of no confidence. When Kluge refused to change the order, Strauss asked to be put on sick leave.[63] The reply from Army Group Center stated, "Since Generaloberst Strauss has asked to be relieved of his post, . . . General Model will assume command of Ninth Army without delay."[64] General der Panzertruppen Walter Model had been the commanding general, XXXXI Panzer Corps, Third Panzer Army, until the afternoon of 14 January when he had been summoned to

the army group headquarters "to receive a new assignment."[65]

In appearance the picture of a pre-World War I Prussian officer even to the monocle that he wore on all occasions and in demeanor outrageously self-assured, Model also had a solid reputation as an energetic commander and brilliant tactician. After a fast trip to the *Fuehrer* Headquarters to receive his charge from Hitler, Model arrived at Ninth Army headquarters in Vyazma on the 18th, stopped long enough to issue a characteristic order of the day expressing his "unshakable confidence and determination to withstand this crisis shoulder to shoulder with my troops," and headed north to Rzhev to take personal charge of the attack preparations.[66]

The breach west of Rzhev was two weeks old, and three large Soviet formations, *Thirty-ninth Army, Twenty-ninth Army,* and the *XI Cavalry Corps,* had already passed through. *Thirty-ninth Army* was engaged at Sychevka, *XI Cavalry Corps* was aiming for Vyazma, and *Twenty-ninth Army* was inside the gap, southwest of Rzhev.[67] Fortunately for the Germans, the Soviet commands were, as the Ninth Army staff observed, "almost lamentably slow" in exploiting the breakthrough.[68] They appeared to be having supply troubles and heavy casualties from the cold and to be short on initiative and experience at all levels. Although the Russians were within four to six miles of the

[63]*AOK 9, Fuehrungsabteilung Kriegstagebuch, 1.1.– 31.3.42,* 13–15 Jan 42, AOK 9 21520/1 file.
[64]*Anruf Oberst Lauche, H. Gr., 16.1.42,* AOK 9 21520/11 file.

[65]*Pz. AOK 3, Ia Kriegstagebuch Nr. 2,* 14 Jan 42, Pz. AOK 3 16911/1 file.
[66]*AOK 9, Fuehrungsabteilung Kriegstagebuch, 1.1.– 31.3.42,* 18 Jan 42, AOK 9 21520/1 file.
[67]*IVOVSS,* vol. II, p. 322.
[68]*AOK 9, Fuehrungsabteilung Kriegstagebuch, 1.1.– 31.3.42,* 18 Jan 42, AOK 9 21520/1 file.

GERMAN MACHINE GUNNERS DIG IN WEST OF SYCHEVKA

Vyazma-Rzhev railroad over the whole stretch from Sychevka to Rzhev, they did less to stop traffic on the line than the snow and cold did. At Sychevka, 1st Panzer Division, brought in from Third Panzer Army, acquired enough elbowroom in two days to raise the possibility of a subsidiary thrust northwest to XXIII Corps. At 1030 on the 21st the temperature was −42° F. The VI Corps, which was to begin the attack west from Rzhev the next day, asked for a 24-hour postponement because of the weather and because the unit from which it expected the most, the SS Division "Das Reich," still had parts scattered all the way back into the Fourth Panzer Army area. The army staff was disposed to take the request "under serious consideration," but Model decided to hold to the schedule

and later in the day also turned down a proposal to reduce the objectives. At the start the next morning he was in Rzhev until full daylight and from then on hedgehopped along the front in a light plane, landing at command posts and looking for "hot spots" where he made it a point to appear in person to lend encouragement "in word and deed."[69]

Taking the enemy by surprise, the attack got off to a fast start in clear weather with well-directed air support and with some tanks, and more self-propelled assault guns, whose crews managed to keep their machines running in spite of the cold. The short winter's day ended before the XXIII

[69]*Ibid.*, 21–22 Jan 42.

Corps and VI Corps spearheads pushing along the Volga River were in sight of each other, but in the morning a company of the 189th Self-propelled Assault Gun Battalion shot its way across the remaining several miles to make the contact shortly after 1200, and Ninth Army had a continuous front again.[70] Konev countered, however, by ordering General Eremenko to speed up *Fourth Shock Army*'s drive south from Toropets.[71]

In the K-Line

The closing of the Rzhev gap was the brightest event thus far in Army Group Center's dismal winter, and it would bring Model a promotion to *Generaloberst* and an oak-leaf cluster to his Knight's Cross of the Iron Cross. But it was for the moment also the only assured accomplishment of the retreat to the K-Line. Off the Ninth Army left flank, where no front existed at all over a hundred-mile stretch on either side of the Army Group Center-Army Group North boundary, *Fourth Shock Army* was pushing south from Toropets toward Velizh sixty miles north of Smolensk. Closer in on the Ninth Army flank, *Twenty-second Army* was bearing toward Belyy behind XXIII Corps. Between Fourth Panzer Army and Fourth Army, Soviet units were pouring through the gap and disappearing into the wide expanse of forest south and west of Vyazma. Four of Fourth Army's five corps were squeezed into a twenty-by-twenty-mile pocket around Yukhnov. The *Rollbahn* was closed more than it was open, and when it was open, which was usually no

more than an hour or two at a time, the Russians could bring it under machine gun and mortar fire. The telephone lines were out between the army headquarters in Spas-Demensk and the pocket, and to keep the command functioning, Heinrici and his operations officer commuted by airplane to Yukhnov. West and south of Spas-Demensk the army's front was paper-thin and shot through with holes, the largest of which was the twenty-mile-wide Kirov gap on the boundary with Second Panzer Army.

Having reached Sukhinichi, Second Panzer Army was embroiled in an exposed salient and in an argument with higher headquarters over what to do next. The army wanted to evacuate the garrison and fall back. Hitler demanded that the town be held. Halder lamented that after "so great a moral success," giving up Sukhinichi, "although tactically correct," would be "a great loss." Kluge argued the army's point of view with Hitler and Hitler's point of view with the army. Finally, after being told that in accordance with earlier orders Gilsa had destroyed so much of the town that it could not be reoccupied in full strength, Hitler consented to let the garrison be evacuated but ordered the army to keep within artillery range.[72]

The Ninth Army staff, at Vyazma, was a helpless and unhappy witness to a remarkable piece of tactical incongruity. On the map, Vyazma was forty miles behind the front, yet, much closer by, Soviet forces were boxing it in from three directions. General Belov's *I Guards Cavalry Corps* was coming

---

[70]*Ibid.*, 23 Jan 42.
[71]*IVOVSS*, vol. II, p. 322.

[72]*Pz. AOK 2, Ia Kriegstagebuch, 27.12.41–31.3.42,* 27–29 Jan 42, Pz. AOK 2 25034/162 file.

north after having brought all of its elements across the *Rollbahn.* Parachute troops were in the woods on the south, and Yefremov's *Thirty-third Army* was massing its infantry on the east. Most dangerous of all for the moment, was *XI Cavalry Corps.*[73] Its scouts were on the Moscow-Warsaw highway fifteen miles west of Vyazma on the morning of the 26th. The guards and drivers of the truck convoys on the road were able to drive them off, but during the night a strong detachment of the *18th Cavalry Division* settled in astride the road which was the main supply and communications artery for Ninth, Third Panzer, and Fourth Panzer Armies. The railroad running parallel to the road a few miles to the south was still open, but practically no traffic was moving on it because of snow, cold, and a lack of train crews, locomotives, and cars.[74]

The Russians seemed to be everywhere, and all converging on Vyazma. They were reported to have been briefly on the railroad five miles northeast of the town. The *Luftwaffe* sighted a long column moving in from the southeast, and Fourth Army observed dozens of transport planes crossing its front and landing in the area south of Vyazma both at night and during the day.[75]

Zhukov in Command

The encirclement of Army Group Center was within an ace of being com-pleted, and the *Stavka* had almost read-ied its two final moves. *Fourth Shock Army,* on reaching Velizh and Rudnya, would be in position to cut the Moscow-Warsaw highway west of Smolensk and take control of the land bridge between the Dnepr and Dvina rivers. Belov, Levashev, and Colonel S. V. Sokolov, the commander of *XI Cavalry Corps,* had orders to make firm contact with each other and lay a solid block across the road and railroad west of Vyazma. On 1 February, the *Stavka* reactivated the Headquarters, *Western Theater,* giv-ing Zhukov control of all operations against Army Group Center.[76]

Victory may indeed have been close, but the two plays designed to achieve it had been easier to conceive than they would be to carry out. Of the *IV Air-borne Corps,* only one brigade (out of three), 2,000 men, could be delivered. Zhukov says the Russians did not have enough transport planes to carry the men.[77] Unless the *Stavka* miscalculated in the first place, the likely reason for a shortage of planes was a sudden de-mand for air supply elsewhere. Ninth Army observed that three days after the Rzhev gap was closed *Thirty-ninth Army* was having to be provisioned by airdrop.[78]

Fourth Shock Army headed south out of Toropets without cover on its flanks and running on captured supplies.[79] At first, as far as the fighting was con-cerned, the going was relatively easy in a roadless wilderness that the Germans

[73]See *IVOVSS,* vol. II, p. 323 and Belov, "*Pyatimesyachnaya borba,*" p. 59.

[74]*AOK 9, Fuehrungsabteilung Kriegstagebuch, 1.1.–31.3.42,* 26–30 Jan 42, AOK 9 21520/1 file.

[75]*AOK 4, Ia Kriegstagebuch Nr. 11,* 27 Jan 42, AOK 4 17380/1 file.

[76]See Eremenko, *V nachale,* pp. 445–53. Belov, "*Pyatimesyachnaya borba,*" p. 60; *IVOVSS,* vol. II, p. 327.

[77]Belov, "*Pyatimesyachnaya borba,*" p. 60n; Zhukov, *Memoirs,* p. 356.

[78]*AOK 9, Fuehrungsabteilung Kriegstagebuch, 1.1.–31.3.42,* 27 Jan 42, AOK 9 21520/1 file.

[79]See Eremenko, *V nachale,* pp. 449–54.

had, in fact, never thoroughly occupied; but Army Group Center was receiving reinforcements that it would rather have used farther east but which it could divert to occupy Velizh, Demidov, Dukhovshchina, and Belyy. For the effort at Velizh, the army group deployed a security division and two infantry divisions. One of the latter was the 330th Infantry Division, a WALKUERE division hastily put together from overage officers and NCOs and recent recruits in the Replacement Army, but the three divisions were enough to force Eremenko to carry out several exhausting sieges in the dead of winter in which the besieged, having shelter, had the upper hand in the constant, deadly contest with the elements. On 1 February, Headquarters, Third Panzer Army, was shifted west—by air because all roads were blocked—to take command of the sector from Velikiye Luki to Belyy and to engage *Fourth Shock Army* in a duel that would last the rest of the winter.[80]

If the Russians were going to destroy Army Group Center, Zhukov's main forces would have to do it. But they were weakened by, as he points out, the loss of *First Shock Army* and more by the closing of the Rzhev gap behind *Twenty-ninth* and *Thirty-ninth Armies*. Then on 30 January Ninth Army's XXXXVI Panzer Corps, bucking snowstorms and drifts but facing an enemy whose confidence was shaken, broke away quickly from Sychevka. In six days it covered thirty miles, making contact with XXIII Corps on 5 February and sealing *Twenty-ninth Army* in a tight pocket southeast of Rzhev.

On the south Zhukov's position was stronger. From 26 to 30 January Fourth Army's *Rollbahn* was closed completely, and the army, which had for a long time not been getting enough supplies, began rapidly to sink into starvation. On the other hand, the Russians were not altogether better off; their radio traffic indicated that some of the units behind Fourth Army were actually starving. At the end of the month, Heinrici's Fourth Army and Ruoff's Fourth Panzer Army mounted a desperate push north and south along the Yukhnov-Gzhatsk road. To get the troops, Heinrici had, after much arguing with Kluge and Hitler, taken his front back to where it barely still covered Yukhnov. On the morning of 3 February, XII Corps going north and 20th Panzer Division coming south "bridged the gap."[81] A bridge was all it was. *Thirty-third Army* stood on the west and *Forty-third Army* on the east; the two in places were no more than three or four miles apart.

In the meantime, other bridges had been opened, and convoys were moving again on the *Rollbahn*—and on the highway west of Vyazma. For the moment the most dangerous gaps were closed, and Army Group Center's vital arteries were functioning. For *Twenty-ninth*, *Thirty-ninth*, and *Thirty-third Armies* and the two cavalry corps it was beginning to look like the entrapment was becoming a trap.

On 12 February, Kluge submitted his first situation estimate in two months in which he had no imminent disasters to report. Dangers existed aplenty, but the armies were back on their feet, and

---

[80]*Pz. AOK 3, Ic, Gefechtsbericht von 1.2.–25.4.42*, Pz. AOK 3 21818/9 file.

[81]*AOK 4, Kriegstagebuch Nr. 11*, 26 Jan–3 Feb 42, AOK 4 17380/1 file.

the Soviet effort was becoming dispersed. It was not the end, but Kluge expected the next round to be fought on better terms.[82] A week later, taking

the larger view, Hitler told the army group commanders that his first objective for the winter was accomplished: the "danger of a panic in the 1812 sense" was "eliminated."[83]

[82]*H. Gr. Mitte, Ia Nr. 1160/42, Beurteilung der Feindlage vor H. Gr. Mitte, 12.2.42*, Pz. AOK 4 22457/36 file.

[83]*H. Gr. Nord, Ia Kriegstagebuch, 13.2.–12.3.42*, 18 Feb 42, H. Gr. Nord 75128/7 file.

CHAPTER IX

The Clinch

The Front, February 1942

Every day, cartographers in the Operations Branch of the OKH drew and printed on a scale of 1:1,000,000 the *Lage Ost,* a map depicting the Eastern Front as it appeared from the latest situation reports. Classified *Geheime Kommandosache, Chef-Sache* ("top secret controlled"), copies of the seven-by-five-foot map showing, in blue, the front and all German units down to the divisional level and, in red, the known Soviet units, went to Hitler and the service high commands. They were used in the situation conferences at the *Fuehrer* Headquarters, sometimes with baneful results because there was no way of making a line in a map convey the actual strength of the positions it represented.

Of those *Lage Ost* maps that survived the war, the most remarkable are those for the month of February 1942. They look like the work of an operations corporal gone mad. From the Black Sea coast north to the boundary between Army Groups South and Center, even with the deep, square-cornered chunk carved out west of Izyum, the front appears conventional enough. At Belev, 80 miles north of the South-Center boundary, however, it veers west, then south, then north nearly to Sukhinichi and then west again to a hairpin loop south of Kirov 80 miles west of Belev. *(Map 13.)* To the north of

Kirov it becomes a train of intermittent squiggles bending 50 miles north and east along the Fourth Army's *Rollbahn* to Yukhnov. Between Yukhnov and Rzhev, Ninth, Fourth Panzer, and Fourth Armies stand back to back and in places face to face in a welter of fronts going in all directions that look from a little distance like a specimen in a Rorschach test. Beyond Ninth Army's north flank, which is also its center because the army has another front facing west, a void bisected by the Army Group Center-Army Group North boundary extends north to the edge of the Demyansk pocket and west 130 miles. What passes for a Third Panzer Army front are blue circles and hooks around Velikiye Luki, Velizh, and Demidov. North of the army group boundary, Sixteenth Army is represented by a scattered tracery of curves and dashes around Kholm, the same marks covering a broader area around Demyansk, and a short tail hanging off the southern tip of Lake Ilmen. The Eighteenth Army front on the Volkhov River has only one gap, about 5 miles across, but behind it red numerals denoting Soviet units range 40 miles to the north and west. Behind all of the armies the word *Partisanen* ("partisans") appears printed in red, and red question marks indicate the probable presence of some kind of enemy forces. The maps more than

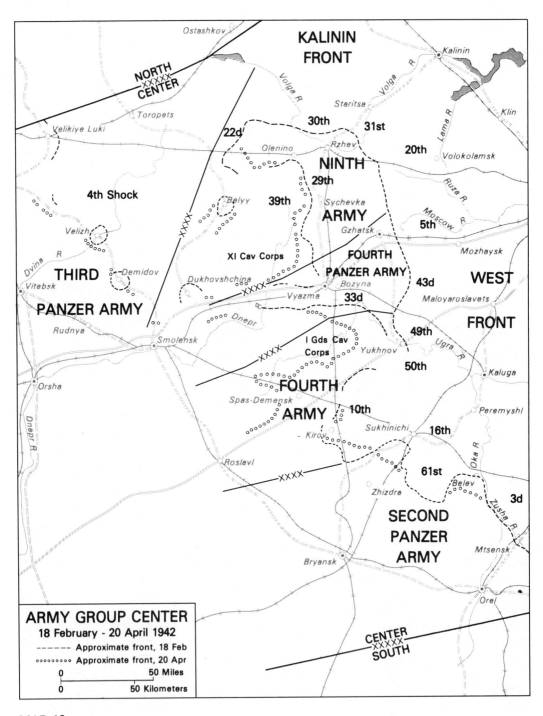

Ostashkov

KALININ
FRONT

Kalinin

NORTH
XXXX
CENTER

Volga R

Staritsa

Volga R

Klin

Toropets

Velikiye Luki

22d

30th

31st

20th

Olenino

Rzhev

Volokolamsk

Lama R

Ruza R

NINTH

4th Shock

Belyy

39th

29th

ARMY

Sychevka

Moscow

5th

Gzhatsk

Mozhaysk

Velizh

Dvina R

Demidov

XI Cav Corps

FOURTH
PANZER ARMY

43d

WEST

THIRD

Dukhovshchina

Bozyna

Vitebsk

Vyazma

33d

Maloyaroslavets

PANZER ARMY

Dnepr

49th

Ugra R

FRONT

Rudnya

Smolensk

I Gds Cav
Corps

Yukhnov

50th

Kaluga

Orsha

Dnepr R

FOURTH

Spas-Demensk

ARMY

10th

Peremyshl

Kirov

Sukhinichi

16th

Roslavl

XXXX

61st

Oka R

Belev

3d

Zhizdra

SECOND

Zusha R

Mtsensk

PANZER

Bryansk

ARMY

Orel

CENTER
XXXX
SOUTH

ARMY GROUP CENTER
18 February - 20 April 1942
- - - - - Approximate front, 18 Feb
ooooooooo Approximate front, 20 Apr
0   50 Miles
0   50 Kilometers

MAP 13

GERMANS DUG-IN: FOUR KNOCKED-OUT SOVIET TANKS IN THE DISTANCE

bear out the words of the officer who noted in Ninth Army's war diary, "This is the strangest front the army ever had."[1]

The front was also extraordinary in another way. Convoluted as it was, the Soviet forces were in a sense as dangerously snared in its coils as the Germans were. At the critical points they were still operating through gaps that were potentially subject to enemy control. A German advance of five miles or less would close the front on the Volkhov behind *Second Shock Army.* Farther south to achieve similar effects the patches would have to be bigger: ninety miles of new front between Sta-

raya Russa and Rzhev and sixty-five miles between Yukhnov and Belev. But these were distances the Germans had at other times often negotiated easily, and successes in all three places could potentially decide the war since a dozen or more Soviet armies might be trapped, and the Germans could then restore a solid front ninety miles west of Moscow. In the worst of the winter, Hitler had an eye on those possibilities. When he authorized the retreat to the KOENIGSBERG Line on 15 January, he ordered Second Panzer Army to narrow and eventually "tie off" the Sukhinichi bulge east of the Yukhnov-Sukhinichi road.[2] Two days after Ninth

[1]*AOK 9, Fuehrungsabteilung Kriegstagebuch, 1.1.–31.3.42,* 27 Jan 42, AOK 9 21520/1 file.

[2]*H. Gr. Mitte, Ia Nr. 423/42, an Pz. AOK 2, 15.1.42,* Pz. AOK 2 25035/2 file.

Army closed its front west of Rzhev, he was asking Ninth and Sixteenth Armies for estimates as to how soon they could repair the breach between them by making thrusts to Ostashkov.[3]

As Hitler was beginning to see the germ of a victory, the Soviet commands were becoming desperate for the victory that was almost in their hands. The *History of the Great Patriotic War* says a "complicated situation had formed," and this caused "serious alarm" in the *Stavka*.[4] The *History of the Second World War* says, "The situation of the Soviet troops in the western direction became decidedly worse. Weakened by extended battles, they lost their offensive capabilities."[5] As had happened to the Germans in December, suddenly the Russians had no good choice as to what to do next. To go ahead would probably be futile, and to stop might well be disastrous. Army Group Center's retreat had ended. *Twenty-ninth* and *Thirty-third Armies* were cut off. *Thirty-ninth Army,* two cavalry corps, and sundry airborne units were in trouble.

On the other hand, the Germans still appeared to be in relatively much poorer shape, and the *Stavka*'s appetite for victory was strong. On 16 February, it directed General Zhukov "to mobilize all the strength of *Kalinin* and *West Fronts* for the final destruction of Army Group Center." He was to smash the enemy in the Rzhev-Vyazma-Yukhnov area and drive west another sixty miles by 5 March to the line of Olenino, the Dnepr River, and Yelnya. The armies of his left flank were to "liquidate" the enemy in the Bolkhov-Zhizdra-Bryansk area and take Bryansk.[6]

Zhukov's implementing order was less categorical as to objectives and time but, in essence, only slightly less ambitious. He ordered *Kalinin Front* to smash the Ninth Army flank west of Rzhev; *Forty-third, Forth-ninth,* and *Fiftieth Armies* to break through at Yukhnov; and *Sixteenth* and *Sixty-first Armies* to advance toward Bryansk. Following these assaults, *Kalinin Front* and *West Front* would proceed to surround and destroy Ninth, Fourth Panzer, and Fourth Armies in the Rzhev-Vyazma area.[7]

Any fresh effort was going to demand new muscle, and both sides were at the point where every move was already an exertion. The *Stavka* again reached into its reserves. *Kalinin Front* got a guards rifle corps, 7 rifle divisions, and some air units. *West Front* was given 60,000 replacements, a guards rifle corps, 3 rifle divisions, 2 airborne brigades, and 200 tanks.[8] The reinforcements probably did not add strength commensurate with their numbers. The quality of the Soviet reserves, which had not been high in December, had declined progressively during the winter. They would also be facing an enemy whose morale was picking up simply because he had survived thus far.

Hitler had been engaged since early January with various programs for reinforcing the Eastern Front. He had directed the OKH to supply 500,000 replacements, but these were to be deferred men who would have to be recalled to active duty and given some

[3]*AOK 9, Fuehrungsabteilung Kriegstagebuch, 1.1.–31.3.42,* 7 Feb 42, AOK 9 21520/1 file.
[4]*IVOVSS,* vol. II, p. 328.
[5]*IVMV,* vol. IV, p. 311.

[6]*Ibid.*
[7]*IVOVSS,* vol. II, p. 328.
[8]*Ibid.*

training.[9] In February, Army Group Center received nearly 70,000 replacements, three and one-half times as many as in the previous month, but the number was still 40,000 short of those needed to cover the month's losses, and the army group was left with a total deficit of 227,000 men for the period since December. The armies had received new men and returnees from hospitals as replacements for about one in four of their casualties.[10]

During January and February the army group also was given nine infantry divisions. Three were WALKUERE divisions. The others came from occupation duty in France and the Low Countries, and all were untrained for winter warfare. Most had to be committed piecemeal by battalions and regiments as they arrived, and their artillery and other noninfantry components were left to make their way forward "on foot," which meant by whatever means they could devise other than on the already swamped and all but paralyzed railroads. The ELEFANT and CHRISTOPHORUS programs that were supposed to have brought in thousands of trucks and other vehicles from all over Europe had been completed, but only about 25 out of every 100 vehicles reached the front.[11] The other three-quarters had broken down and were awaiting repairs or had become snowed or frozen in on the roads back to Poland.

With the winter's end approaching,

all plans, no matter whose, were subject to a primeval force of nature, the rasputitsa. The Germans had had a taste of it in October 1941—but only a taste, as they learned from talking to the inhabitants. During the fall, heavy prolonged rain made the mud. How much depended on the amount of rainfall and on when the freeze came. The spring rasputitsa was something else: it was as inevitable as the change of seasons and varied little from year to year. During the winter the ground froze to depths of eight or nine feet locking in much of the previous fall's rain. Several feet of snow and ice accumulated on the surface. The spring thaw worked from the top downward, first turning the snow and ice to water over the still frozen ground, then creating a progressively deepening layer of watery mud above the frozen subsoil. In the generally flat and at best poorly drained terrain, the water had no place to go until the thaw broke completely through the frost. The process usually took five or six weeks and included three weeks or more in which the mud was too deep for any kind of vehicular traffic other than peasant carts. The Panje wagon's high wheels and light weight enabled it to plow through mud several feet deep while riding on the frozen stratum beneath, and its wooden construction allowed it to be used almost as a boat. Exceptionally heavy snow and low winter temperatures assured a full-blown rasputitsa for 1942 but also made its onset difficult to predict. In normal years the thaw could be depended upon to begin in about the third week of March at the latitude of Moscow, a week or two earlier in the Ukraine, and at least a week later in the north.

---

[9]AOK 9, Fuehrungsabteilung Kriegstagebuch, 1.1.–31.3.42, 21 Jan 42, AOK 9 21520/1 file.

[10]Counted in the losses were the frostbite cases and the dead, wounded, missing, and sick. AOK 4, Ia Kriegstagebuch Nr. 11, 27 Feb 42, AOK 4 18710 file.

[11]AOK 9, Fuehrungsabteilung Kriegstagebuch, 1.1.–31.3.42, 21 Jan 42, AOK 9 21520/1 file.

Army Group Center

Second Panzer Army's "Small Solution"

As Hitler had anticipated in the 15 January directive, the Sukhinichi bulge afforded the first practicable opportunity for a counterstroke. In spite of the Kirov gap and Fourth Army's troubles along the *Rollbahn* and at Yukhnov, it had a comparatively stable configuration and at least theoretically manageable distances. Second Panzer Army's unexpected success at the start of the Sukhinichi relief operation fueled Hitler's imagination, and on 21 January he tried to get General Schmidt, the army's commander, to convert the relief into a drive past Sukhinichi to the northeast and to have General Heinrici, Fourth Army commander, stage a quick thrust south out of Yukhnov. The meeting of the two forces would have closed the northern two-thirds of the bulge, eliminated the problems of the Kirov gap and the *Rollbahn,* and trapped three Soviet armies. But XXIV Panzer Corps did not have the strength to go past Sukhinichi, and Heinrici declared that Fourth Army could not begin an attack south before the second week in February, if then.

After XXIV Panzer Corps reached Sukhinichi, three potential "solutions" presented themselves. Hitler continued to want a "big" one, a push to Yukhnov, and, therefore, insisted on keeping a foothold close to Sukhinichi. Field Marshal Kluge, commander of Army Group Center, and Schmidt tried to substitute as an intermediate solution an attempt to extend the left side of XXIV Panzer Corps' line north to the Spas-Demensk–Sukhinichi road, which would reduce the bulge by about

half and close off the Kirov gap. The third solution was to close the Kirov gap. It was talked about as "small" because either of the other two would accomplish as much automatically, but it was the most feasible in terms of means available to achieve a solution. In the first two weeks of February, XXIV Panzer Corps received a succession of orders to prepare for or to cancel one or the other of the three movements, and at last the corps' chief of staff was moved to comment on the absurdity of the situation by acknowledging one transmission with the words, *"Difficile est, satiram non scribere."* ("The difficulty is not to write satire.")[12]

Because partisans who were being supplied through the gap were endangering Fourth Army's *Rollbahn,* Second Panzer Army, at Kluge's insistence, began an attack toward Kirov on 16 February. The succeeding days exposed the Germans' quandary. The drive toward Yukhnov and the "intermediate solution," attractive as they might be, could not be attempted without reinforcements that were nowhere in sight. The army was down to forty-five tanks that were operational, about a quarter of one panzer division's normal complement. At the same time, XXIV Panzer Corps, because it was having to hold the exposed salient reaching toward Sukhinichi, could not bring enough strength to bear toward Kirov, and the attack there wavered and limped, and at the end of the month, while still nominally in progress, was all but forgotten. As long as the three solutions were kept on the docket, none of them would be executed. On

---

[12] *Pz. AOK 2, Ia Kriegstagebuch, 27.12.41–31.3.42,* 21 Jan–16 Feb 42, Pz. AOK 2 25034/162 file.

the other hand, however, Second Panzer Army's situation may have been better than it knew since the Soviet advance toward Bryansk also did not materialize. The Russians' activity stepped up after the middle of the month, but as long as the Germans were standing close to Sukhinichi and pushing toward Kirov the Soviet commands were not disposed to attempt any sweeping maneuvers of their own.

At the turn of the month the *rasputitsa* was possibly no more than a few weeks away, and time was running short. In a conference at the *Fuehrer* Headquarters on 1 March, Schmidt persuaded Hitler that an attack from Sukhinichi toward Yukhnov could not start until after the *rasputitsa*. Hitler also agreed to let Schmidt prepare to move back the front projecting toward Belev since the possibility of a thrust from there toward Yukhnov had become even more remote.[13]

On the 9th, Kluge, who had avoided personal contact with Second Panzer Army since the Guderian affair in December, met with Schmidt and his corps commanders at the army headquarters in Orel.[14] In an hours-long discussion the generals concluded that the "small solution" at Kirov was the only one that could succeed and therefore the Sukhinichi and Belev salients were worthless. Kluge said he would take the matter up with Hitler. Three days later he told Schmidt that Hitler "did not attach as much value as before" to the Sukhinichi salient and

would not object to the army's pulling back from Sukhinichi and Belev as soon as adequate lines were built to the rear.[15]

In the meantime the attempt to close the Kirov gap had continued sporadically. On 20 March, Kluge told Schmidt that Kirov would "have to be cleaned up definitively" before the *rasputitsa*, which meant within the next two or three weeks at most; but on that same day he told Heinrici not to commit any Fourth Army forces to the Kirov operation until after the *Rollbahn* and the army's rear area were secure.[16] In another week the daytime temperatures were above freezing; the snow and ice were melting; the two salients were being evacuated; and the Kirov operation was still in progress mainly because no one had had as good a reason to stop it as the weather would soon provide.

Fourth and Fourth Panzer Armies

Fourth Army's and Fourth Panzer Army's prospects for the future looked somewhat brighter after they bridged the gap between them on 3 February even though the bridge was narrow, and the enemy was behind as well as in front of them. They now had a continuous front for the first time in weeks, which was a relief for them and apparently a disconcerting surprise to the Russians. Soviet radio traffic disclosed that *Thirty-third Army* and the airborne units and cavalry behind the two armies had believed their mission was to block a demoralized German retreat. They had not expected to have to deal

---

[13]*Ibid.*, 1 Mar 42.

[14]Kluge said during the meeting that he "regretted the loss of so outstanding an army commander," and he implied that the reasons for Guderian's dismissal were too sensitive a matter to be discussed (*Ibid.*, 9 Mar 42).

[15]*Ibid.*, 12 Mar 42.

[16]*Ibid.*, 20 Mar 42; *AOK 4, Ia Kriegstagebuch Nr. 11*, 20 Mar 42, AOK 4 17380/1 file.

with determined opposition, and they showed it. *Thirty-third Army* stopped and seemed at a loss about what to do next. The airborne troops, youthful but undertrained, stayed scattered and became preoccupied with their supply shortages. Some who were captured said that they were often not aware of their actual situation.[17] Encouraged, Fourth Panzer Army first shifted the 5th Panzer Division in position to set up a perimeter defense around Vyazma and then brought in the Headquarters, V Panzer Corps.

At midmonth, having temporarily acquired elements of another panzer division and two infantry divisions, V Panzer Corps was getting ready to encircle and drive inward on *Thirty-third Army* which was standing still southeast of Vyazma; but by then the *Stavka* had issued its order to renew the offensive. *Forty-third Army* thereafter tried desperately day after day to break down the German bridge between it and *Thirty-third Army. Forty-ninth* and *Fiftieth Armies* battered Fourth Army around Yukhnov and along the *Rollbahn;* and waves of transports, flying day and night—in weather the *Luftwaffe* considered too dangerous for flying—and frequently landing within sight of the Germans, delivered more airborne troops behind the front. Estimating twenty men to a plane and counting the planes, Fourth Panzer Army figured at least 3,000 troops were landed south of Vyazma in two days, 19 and 20 February.[18] Fortunately for the two German armies the Soviet units inside the front were not as aggressive as those outside. The V Panzer Corps was reduced again to defending Vyazma, but it could do that since the new Soviet arrivals appeared to have much the same uncertainty about their mission as the forces already there had.

The decision hinged on the outer front where a Soviet breakthrough anywhere could be deadly. Fourth Army was the more vulnerable: both its flanks were weak, and its center was jammed into a round-nosed bulge around Yukhnov. Beset everywhere and enmeshed in a constant battle for the *Rollbahn,* Heinrici on 18 February proposed giving up Yukhnov in favor of a shorter line behind the Ugra River ten miles to the west. Any attempt to close the Sukhinichi bulge, his chief of staff added, was going to be made farther west anyway, and the Yukhnov-Gzhatsk road, which had been the original reason for holding Yukhnov, was "a fiction."[19] However, nobody was eager to pass the idea onto a higher level. Kluge's operations officer said permission was going to be difficult to get because the Yukhnov-Gzhatsk road was shown as a major thoroughfare on the maps and would, therefore, appear valuable to Hitler.

Some days later, the OKH gingerly agreed to let Fourth Army start building a line on the Ugra, and after several more days, Kluge made an appointment for Heinrici to see Hitler. At the *Fuehrer* Headquarters on 1 March, no doubt to Heinrici's considerable astonishment, Hitler gave his approval at once, explaining that before he had been "deliberately obstinate" but now whether the army went five miles for-

[17]*Pz. AOK 4, Ia Kriegstagebuch Nr. 8,* 5 Feb 42, Pz. AOK 4 24932/17 file.
[18]*Ibid.,* 20 Feb 42.

[19]*AOK 4, Ia Kriegstagebuch Nr. 11,* 18 Feb 42, AOK 4 18710 file.

SOVIET INFANTRY FIRE ON A VILLAGE IN THE ENEMY REAR

ward or backward was no longer important to him.[20] The decision having been made, Kluge added a requirement of his own: to "rescue" a particularly old and valuable icon of the Virgin Mary from the Sloboda monastery near Yukhnov.[21] The latter done, Fourth Army evacuated Yukhnov on 3 March and went behind the Ugra on the 6th, which did not solve its problems but raised its prospects of at least surviving after the onset of the *rasputitsa*.

While Fourth Army withdrew to the Ugra—which also shortened its bridge with Fourth Panzer Army—5th Panzer

Division was mopping up part of *I Guards Cavalry Corps* in a pocket south of Vyazma. Looking to build on that success, V Panzer Corps was again beginning to lay an encirclement around the *Thirty-third Army*. The 5th Panzer Division finished its movement on the 10th in the midst of a snowstorm and started to turn to move in on *Thirty-third Army* from the west. Although snow was not a novelty by then, this late winter downfall was an event not even the local people had ever seen before. It began on the 10th and by 1200 on the 12th reached such an intensity that every kind of movement stopped. Drifts piled up in minutes and made plowing and shoveling totally useless. The 5th Panzer Division was buried in its tracks. The Fourth Panzer Army

[20]*Ibid.*, 2 Mar 42.
[21]*Ibid.*

staff could barely keep contact between its sections which were housed in separate buildings along the village street in Boznya, eight miles east of Vyazma. Drifts covered the street and the buildings to beyond the tops of the doors.[22]

The storm at last subsided enough for the digging out to begin on the 16th. Eight days later, when the roads were about cleared, the thaw set in. Under warm sunshine the snow melted. The roads became torrents of water, their surfaces broken by potholes as much as several feet deep that froze at night into sheets of slick ice. Corpses of men, animal cadavers, garbage, and human waste that had been frozen for weeks and could not have been buried in any case began to thaw thus adding to the troops' discomfort and raising the threat of an epidemic.

Since the full-blown *rasputitsa* could not be long in coming it appeared that the active phase of the winter's operations was over, especially after Army Group Center ordered 5th Panzer Division to begin assembling at Vyazma on the 24th for transfer to Ninth Army. But as melting snow and ice filled the low areas, of which there were many, with waist-deep water, the fighting flared up once more.[23]

On 20 March, the *Stavka* gave Zhukov a new directive. He was ordered to stay on the offensive for another thirty days and, in that time, drive Fourth, Fourth Panzer, and Ninth Armies back to a line about halfway between Vyazma and Smolensk. Zhukov proposed to use *Forty-third, Forty-ninth,* and *Fiftieth Armies* to

break through again from the east and to concentrate *I Guards Cavalry Corps, IV Airborne Corps,* and *Thirty-third Army* south and west of Vyazma. To General Belov, *I Guards Cavalry Corps* commander, who, having the most mobile force, was to maintain contact between the airborne troops, the partisans, and *Thirty-third Army*'s infantry, the Inspector of Cavalry, General Polkovnik O. I. Gorodovikov, sent Belov a message congratulating the *I Guards Cavalry Corps* on its accomplishments thus far.[24]

On the 28th, Army Group Center decided to leave 5th Panzer Division at Fourth Panzer Army to restore control over the road west of Vyazma, which was again threatened by the renewed Soviet offensive, and, after that, to complete the long-projected encirclement of *Thirty-third Army*. Contrary, probably, to original Soviet and German expectations, the fighting rolled on as the thaw continued into the *rasputitsa,* and with the warming nights the ground turned rapidly to mud during the second week of April. The Soviet attacks, coming as they did at places that had already been held under the extreme winter conditions that had been less favorable for a defense, added to the general misery of the season for the Germans and delayed their long overdue rest and refitting but otherwise served only to mark the definitive end of the winter campaign.

The V Panzer Corps, on the other hand, managed at the last minute to bring 5th Panzer Division to bear against *Thirty-third Army* on 10 April. During the next five days in rapidly

[22]*Ibid.,* 14 Mar 42.
[23]*Ibid.,* 16–22 Mar 42.

[24]*IVOVSS,* vol. II, p. 331; Belov, "*Pyatimesyachnaya borba,*" p. 65.

MELTING SNOW HAS TURNED ROADS INTO RIVERS

deepening mud, the army was squeezed out of existence. At the end, on the 15th, an estimated five hundred to a thousand troops, among them Yefremov, the commanding general, escaped from the pocket into the woods along the Ugra River. Several days later, the Germans saw a single plane with a fighter escort attempt a landing, possibly to pick up Yefremov, but it failed to do so.[25] When the last of his command was trapped and destroyed before it could make its way through the front to *Forty-third Army,* Yefremov committed suicide.[26]

---

[25]*Pz. AOK 4, Ia Kriegstagebuch Nr. 8,* 15 Apr 42, Pz. AOK 4 24932/17 file.

[26]Zhukov, *Memoirs,* p. 358.

Ninth Army's Bridge to Ostashkov

Of the late-winter possibilities to recoup his fortunes, the Ostashkov operation was the one that most firmly held Hitler's attention, and it could, indeed, have been the most profitable. As its code name BRUECKENSCHLAG ("bridging") suggested, its first objective was to bridge the gap between Army Groups Center and North. If Ninth Army and Sixteenth Army could do that they would entrap six, possibly seven, Soviet armies and deprive the Russians of a good third of all the territory they had reoccupied in the winter offensive. General Model, the new Ninth Army commander, was the man to attempt the 65-mile drive to Ostashkov if anyone was. Nevertheless, the army's first

GERMAN OUTPOST LINE WEST OF RZHEV

response to Hitler's 7 February request for an opinion on the operation was noncommittal: the army would be occupied for some time to come with the encircled *Twenty-ninth Army* and with the ferocious attempts *Kalinin Front* was making to reopen the Rzhev gap. On the 12th, Kluge and Model and their chiefs of staff concluded that Ninth Army's next concern after finishing with *Twenty-ninth Army* and stabilizing its north front would have to be *Thirty-ninth Army* that was "twisting and turning in the army's bowels" west of Sychevka. Then, they agreed, it would be too late to start toward Ostashkov before the *rasputitsa*. Furthermore, the railroad from Vyazma to Rzhev would have to be renailed to the standard gauge to accommodate German locomotives because the Soviet-built locomotives on the line were nearly all broken down. The time required to make this change would delay the logistical buildup.[27]

After several desperate attempts to break out, *Twenty-ninth Army* collapsed on 20 February, but by then *Kalinin Front*, under *Stavka* orders to renew the offensive, was hammering at the curve of the front around Olenino trying to get direct contact with *Thirty-ninth Army* for the drive to Vyazma. Hitler postponed a decision on the Ostashkov operation while making it clear,

[27]*AOK 9, Fuehrungsabteilung Kriegstagebuch, 1.1.–31.3.42,* 2, 7, 12 Feb 42, AOK 9 21520/1 file.

however, that preparations for it were to be carried out at the highest possible priority. Meanwhile, 6th Panzer Division had begun pushing *Thirty-ninth Army* away from the Vyazma-Sychevka section of the railroad by what it called a "snail offensive," namely, by occupying villages one by one at random along a 25-mile front wherever doing so was easiest. The 6th Panzer Division found that it could advance a mile or two a day without much effort, and *Thirty-ninth Army* appeared to be becoming progressively more nervous and uncertain. After almost daily exchanges between the army, army group, OKH, and Hitler, Kluge and Hitler gave Ninth Army a "basic order" on 1 March to encircle and destroy *Thirty-ninth Army,* but Hitler stipulated that the preparations for the Ostashkov attack had to continue and both operations were to be completed before the *rasputitsa.*[28]

Ninth Army sent orders for the attack on *Thirty-ninth Army* to the corps on the 1st, but because *Kalinin Front* redoubled its effort to smash the Olenino bulge, the orders could not begin to have any effect for another week. By then time was getting perilously short; the army group had set the 20th as the latest date before the *rasputitsa* on which active operations could continue. On the 8th the pressure on the bulge eased, but two days later the great snowstorm began. In the midst of deepening snow, Model managed to secure a flight to the *Fuehrer* Headquarters on the 11th. There the next day, while reports from the front were describing the snowfall

as "a catastrophe of nature," he promised Hitler to pursue the Ostashkov preparations "with force," which, characteristically, he did after needing another two days to get back to his army.

In spite of the snow and the rapid thaw that followed, Model had assembled 56,000 troops and 200 tanks for BRUECKENSCHLAG by the fourth week in March. In the meantime, however, the *Stavka* had issued the 20 March directive to Zhukov that included orders for *Kalinin Front.* General Konev was to cut off Olenino and take Rzhev and Belyy. He was not, in fact, going to be able to do any of those, but he had been given reinforcements in infantry and tanks, and those did make their presence felt.[29]

Finally, on the 27th, frustrated by "two imponderables, the enemy and the weather," Model had to concede that BRUECKENSCHLAG was not possible. Hitler rejected a substituted plan for a truncated version of the operation that Model and Kluge had proposed and called them to the *Fuehrer* Headquarters on the 29th. By then, as elsewhere along the front, the roads became rivers during the day and were only passable at night and for a few hours in the early morning, and BRUECKENSCHLAG had become too daring even for Hitler. He shifted the objective of the German assault to *Thirty-ninth Army,* but that could only mean prolonging the snail offensive for a week or so until the weather completely overtook it as well.[30]

[28]*Ibid.,* 21 Feb–1 Mar 42.

[29]*IVOVSS,* vol. II, p. 331.
[30]*AOK 9, Fuehrungsabteilung Kriegstagebuch, 1.4–30.6.42,* 1 Apr 42, AOK 9 28504 file.

Army Group North

The Stavka Faces the Rasputitsa

In the last week of February, the Soviet commands opposite Army Group North faced the unpleasant possibility that in a matter of weeks they might have no more to show for their winter's efforts than some thousands of square miles of forest and swamp. *Northwest* and *Kalinin Fronts* had torn the Army Group North right flank completely loose from its moorings west of Ostashkov, encircled Kholm, and trapped one German corps plus half of another around Demyansk; but the key point south of Lake Ilmen, Staraya Russa, stayed in German hands. North of the lake, *Second Shock Army* had cut deep behind Eighteenth Army's line on the Volkhov River without affecting thus far the German grip on Leningrad. The general offensive was swimming in successes on the one hand and promising little evidence of durable accomplishment on the other. *(Map 14.)*

The *Stavka's* problems, aside from the escalating pressure of time, were two: the wide dispersion of command effort inherent in the general offensive from the start and the local offensive efforts occasioned by the operating methods of the field commands. The first, if it were perceived, which is by no means certain, was past the stage at which it could be reversed. The second, apparently, could not be eliminated, but it could be mitigated, and to do that, the *Stavka* applied what had become its standard correctives, fresh orders, exhortations, and reinforcements.[31]

On 25 February, the *Stavka* put all of the units operating against the Demyansk pocket under Headquarters, *Northwest Front*. It then also gave General Kurochkin, the *front's* commander, an order to "squeeze" the pocket out of existence "in four or five day's time" and get on with the drive past Staraya Russa.[32] A week later, it gave him five artillery regiments, three mortar regiments, and air reinforcements and then followed with orders to intensify the offensive and not only "squeeze" the pocket but also "crush the enemy in the directions of the main effort."[33]

Volkhov Front, which had, by the last week in February, not yet managed to get *Second Shock Army* turned north toward Lyuban in spite of repeated admonishments to do that, was an even more difficult problem for the *Stavka*. Unless the Russians could cut the Leningrad-Lyuban-Chudovo railroad, their prospects of accomplishing anything toward the relief of Leningrad were small. After sending Marshal Voroshilov to act as its representative on the spot, the *Stavka*, on 28 February, ordered General Meretskov, commander of *Volkhov Front*, to get an attack toward Lyuban going without, as he proposed, a pause to regroup. It also ordered General Khozin, at *Leningrad Front*, to set *Fifty-fourth Army* in motion toward Lyuban from the northeast and promised strong air support for both of the thrusts.[34]

The View From Fuehrer Headquarters

In the last week of February, 3,500

---

[31]See *IVMV*, vol. IV, p. 327.

[32]Zhelanov, "*Iz opyta*," p. 30.
[33]*Ibid.*, p. 31; *IVOVSS*, vol. II, p. 337f.
[34]*IVOVSS*, vol. II, p. 335; Meretskov, *Serving the People*, p. 199.

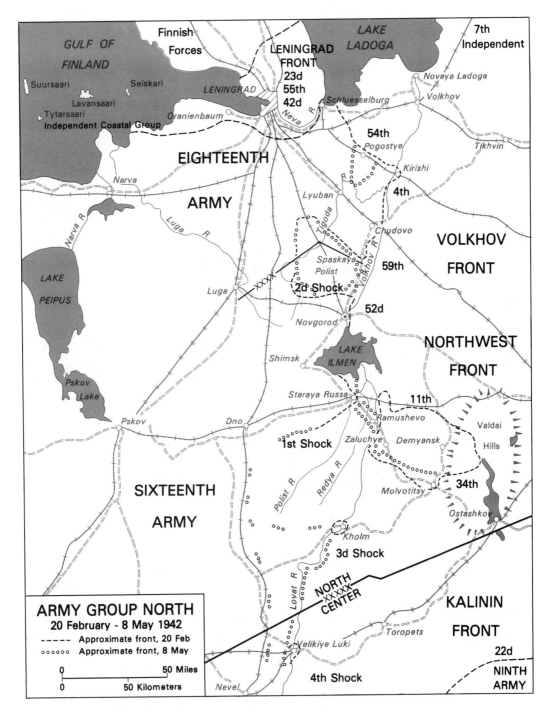

MAP 14

troops, commanded by Generalmajor Theodor Scherer were beginning their second month under siege in Kholm, and the perimeter that they held around the town had shrunk to the point at which supplying them by air became difficult and exceedingly dangerous. On 25 February, four out of ten planes flying to Kholm were shot down, bringing the *Luftwaffe*'s losses of tri-motored JU–52 transports during the airlift to fifty. After the 25th, only gliders could land and then only on a cleared strip of ice on the Lovat River. Henceforth, planes making airdrops had to come in at very low altitudes to hit the target and in doing so were exposed to ground fire from all directions.[35]

In the Demyansk pocket, II Corps needed 300 tons of supplies a day which required a full-scale, sustained airlift, the first such in aviation history. To mount the airlift the *Luftwaffe* had to divert almost all of the transports assigned to Army Group Center and half of those stationed in the Army Group South area. The slow JU–52s had to fly in groups of twenty to forty with fighter cover, and Soviet bombing of the airstrips in the pocket scrambled the flight schedules and created additional hazards for the planes and crews. Total deliveries up to 28 February were short by 1,900 tons, about one-half of the requirement.[36]

German I Corps, holding the northeastern face of the Volkhov pocket, was

shaken on 25 February when Soviet ski troops pushed north through frozen swamps along the Tigoda River to within five miles of Lyuban. The army group's intelligence had known for several days that the *327th Rifle Division* was on the march northward from near Spaskaya Polist. Also knowing how deliberately the Soviet commands generally operated, Army Group North had expected an attack, but not so soon.[37] What it had not known was that Meretskov and *Second Shock Army* were then under "categorical instructions" from the *Stavka* to get an attack going without delay.[38]

Nevertheless, when Hitler met with General Kuechler, the Army Group North commander; the commanding generals of Sixteenth and Eighteenth Armies; and the I, II, X, and XXXVIII Corps commanders at the *Fuehrer* Headquarters on 2 March, he spoke about initiatives with some confidence. Although Army Group North's situation had not improved, it had for more than two weeks balanced on the edge of disaster without going over, which in itself gave encouragement to Hitler.

On the other hand, the conference disclosed that no substantive improvement in the army group's position had yet occurred. At Kholm, half of the original garrison were dead or wounded. Replacements could be brought in by glider, and enough to make up for about half the losses were, but each of these men reduced the space available for carrying supplies and increased consumption of those supplies transported in the remaining

---

[35]*H. Gr. Nord, Ia Kriegstagebuch, 13.2.–12.3.42*, 25 Feb 42, H. Gr. Nord 75128/7 file.

[36]Hermann Plocher, *The German Air Force Versus Russia, 1942*, USAF Historical Division, USAF Historical Studies, no. 154, pp. 78–81; *H. Gr. Nord, Ia Kriegstagebuch, 13.2.–12.3.42*, 28 Feb 42, H. Gr. Nord 75128/7 file.

[37]*H. Gr. Nord, Ia Kriegstagebuch, 13.2.–12.3.42*, 25 Feb 42, H. Gr. Nord 75128/7 file.

[38]Meretskov, *Serving the People*, p. 199.

space. A relief force of half-a-dozen mixed battalions under Generalmajor Horst von Uckermann had cut through from the southwest almost to within sight of Kholm, but it was stalled in deep snow and practically encircled. General von Brockdorff, the commander of II Corps in the Demyansk pocket, told Hitler that his force depended completely on each day's supply flights. For the Scherer and Uckermann groups at Kholm and II Corps at Demyansk, the margin of survival was thin. South of Lyuban, I Corps was having an expectedly easy success. Goaded by the *Stavka*, Meretskov had hastily pushed the *80th Cavalry* and *327th Rifle Divisions* into the breach the ski troops had opened on 25 February, and I Corps had then closed the gap in its front, trapping about 6,000 Soviet troops.[39] But if *Second Shock Army* on the south and *Fifty-fourth Army* in the northeast one day made good their bids to reach Lyuban, I Corps would be locked in a pocket exactly like the one at Demyansk.

Hitler received the generals' gloomy reports with sympathetic detachment. He promised a regiment of reinforcements to get Uckermann's relief force back in motion, and he gave instructions to have an order of the day written honoring the Kholm garrison. To von Brockdorff, he made the limp observation that the hardships II Corps was having to endure resulted from having to defend the Demyansk pocket as if it were a fortress even though it was not. "On the other hand," he added, this imposed a moral obligation

on the troops outside the pocket to come to the corps' aid.

When the conference turned to its main concerns, plans to close the Volkhov River line behind *Second Shock Army* and to restore contact with II Corps, Hitler's tone changed. After General Busch, commander of Sixteenth Army, and General der Kavallerie Georg Lindemann, commander of Eighteenth Army, offered tentative proposals for counterattacks toward Demyansk and at the Volkhov gap, he set approximate starting dates for both—7 to 12 March for the Volkhov operation and 13 to 16 March for the one toward Demyansk. To compensate for shortages of ground forces, he said the *Luftwaffe* would employ aircraft as "escort artillery," using the heaviest demolition bombs it had to blast the bunker systems the Russians had built in the forests. The Demyansk operation, he indicated, would also have to be coordinated with Ninth Army's proposed thrust from the south toward Ostashkov.[40]

One item in the discussion took the generals completely by surprise. In the midst of talking about the Demyansk and Volkhov operations, Hitler had offhandedly given the army group a new mission. With spring coming, he had observed, it would be necessary to tighten the siege of Leningrad and, particularly, to keep the Soviet *Baltic Fleet* from steaming out into the Baltic after the ice had melted. To do that, Army Group North would have to provide troops to take and occupy a group of islands at the eastern end of the Gulf of Finland. The islands, Suur-

[39]*H. Gr. Nord, Ia Kriegstagebuch, 13.–31.3.42,* 1 Mar 42, H. Gr. Nord 75128/8 file.

[40]*Ibid.,* 2 Mar 42; *Halder Diary,* vol. III, p. 408.

saari, Lavansaari, Seiskari, and Tytar-saari, had Soviet garrisons on them, which presumably were small, but the Germans could not be certain of that.[41]

Raubtier

The army group and army staffs, working against time, the enemy, and a clutch of uncertainties, were given between five and ten days to get the Volkhov operation, code-named RAUBTIER ("beast of prey"), going. The thaw was beginning in the Crimea, and it would spread northward in the coming weeks. It had to be taken into account. On the other hand, air support could only be effective if it went one place at a time; therefore, Volkhov had to come before Demyansk, and a delay with the former operation could cripple the latter. Hitler's talk about taking the islands in the Gulf of Finland added a complication. That mission would also require troops and air support. No date had been set for it, and the army group regarded it as a waste of time. The OKH insisted, however, that Hitler took it most seriously because he believed he would be made a "laughing stock" if the Soviet warships steamed out into the Baltic after the ice melted.[42]

That the Russians were not going to allow the Germans to carry out their plans without opposition went without saying. In the first week of March, Politburo and State Defense Committee member G. M. Malenkov joined Voroshilov at Volkhov Front headquarters, and the Stavka sent General Vlasov, who as commander of Twentieth Army had been one of the heroes of the Moscow counteroffensive, to be Meretskov's deputy. Before the week's end, Second Shock Army was regrouping for another push toward Lyuban, and Fifty-fourth Army was hammering at Pogostye, twenty miles northeast of Lyuban.[43] At Kholm, the Russians were using tanks. One 52-tonner stopped the Uckermann relief force for a day until it could bring up an 88-mm. gun, and the Soviet T–34s were dueling with the strongpoints on the perimeter of the pocket.

Eighteenth Army was ready on the 7th to start RAUBTIER two days later if the air support Hitler had prescribed could be given by then. The "if" was substantial. The Luftwaffe was engaged at Kholm, trying to help the Uckermann force across the last few miles to the pocket at Kholm before it was overrun by Soviet tanks. At the moment, the air support was keeping the pocket in existence but was doing less to carry the Uckermann group forward. German planes could pin the Russians down when they were in the open, but they were not effective against the Soviet prepared defenses, which were concealed under the snow. On the 7th and for the next several days, Hitler could not bring himself to withdraw the air support for Kholm in part because he was afraid the pocket would collapse if he did and in part because he was casting about for a replacement for Uckermann whom a Luftwaffe liaison officer had accused of lacking confidence. By the 11th, the Luftwaffe, also, was demanding

---

[41]*H. Gr. Nord, Ia Kriegstagebuch, 13.–31.3.42*, 2 Mar 42, H. Gr. Nord 75128/8 file.

[42]*Ibid.*, 2, 4 Mar 42.

[43] Meretskov, *Serving the People*, pp. 200–02; Meretskov, *"Na volkhovskikh rubezhakh,"* p. 65.

postponements because the weather was causing icing conditions on planes that made it too dangerous for the German *Stuka* dive-bombers to carry the extra heavy bombs they were supposed to use.

Meanwhile, Soviet *Fifty-fourth Army* was beginning a drive from the northeast toward Lyuban that could cut off I Corps completely if, as one army group report put it, "RAUBTIER remained a rubber lion." Kuechler and Lindemann were ready to go ahead on the 12th, without air support, but Hitler would not agree to this action because he feared the losses would be too high. By then, the delays in RAUBTIER were beginning to cut into the time allotted for the Demyansk operation and to threaten the projected attacks on the islands in the Gulf of Finland. Internally the army group staff now regarded the latter assaults as "insane," but Hitler insisted they had to be carried out while the ice was still thick enough to be crossed. The Finns, who were to join in from their side of the gulf, had said that they would be ready to attack on the 20th. Fog and low-hanging clouds forced another postponement on the 13th, but the *Luftwaffe* reported that it expected the weather to clear by the next morning, and then its planes could start sometime between 0900 and 1200.[44] During the night, however, the temperature fell to −30° F. Anticipating having to choose between the effects of letting the troops stand in the open while waiting for the planes in such ferocious cold or letting the attack start before the planes arrived and having the

bombs possibly drop on his own men, Kuechler decided to wait another day.

The mouth of the Volkhov pocket was, as it had been since January, about six miles wide. The Novgorod-Chudovo road and railroad crossed the pocket from north to south, but there were no east-west roads. Approximately at its center, about a mile apart, the Russians had cut two 100-foot-wide lanes running east to west through the trees and underbrush. Inside the lanes, they had laid down several feet of compacted snow, enough to cover the tops of the tree stumps, and these had served as *Second Shock Army's* supply and communications lines. To distinguish between these lanes, the Germans named the northern one Erika and its southern twin Dora. At nightfall on 14 March, the cold had not abated, but the *Luftwaffe* was certain its planes could make their first strikes at daylight the next morning, and Eighteenth Army had tents and stoves ready to be moved along with the troops. Because of the cold, the risks were still extraordinarily high. In such weather, weapons, machine guns especially, jammed, and men lost the will to fight. But Kuechler decided that RAUBTIER could not be delayed again.

At 0730 the next morning, the planes arrived over the front. After the *Stukas* had hit their targets, XXXVIII Corps and I Corps troops pushed into the gap from the south and north. During the day, 263 planes flew missions for RAUBTIER, and, by dark, XXXVIII Corps had gained a half mile and I Corps slightly more than two miles. In the next two days, RAUBTIER went ahead but without gaining the distance it had on the first day. The

---

[44]*H. Gr. Nord, Ia Kriegstagebuch, 13.–31.3.42*, 5–14 Mar 42, H. Gr. Nord 75128/8 file.

planes were not living up to Hitler's expectation in their role as escort artillery: when they laid their barrages close to the line of advance some of their bombs generally fell among their own troops; when they allowed a safe margin, the Russians usually had time to recover before the Germans, who were moving through deep snow, could reach them.

The Russians, on the other hand, were defending static strongpoints, and each one that fell narrowed the mouth of the pocket somewhat. On the 18th, I Corps crossed the Erika Lane, and the following day both corps reached the Dora Lane where their spearheads made contact late in the day.[45] *Second Shock Army,* which had had trouble enough keeping the Lyuban operation going, now was going to have to fight for survival. On the 21st, Vlasov went into the pocket to take command of the army.

Brueckenschlag at Demyansk

In the meantime, Sixteenth Army's attack toward the Demyansk pocket had fallen five days behind the date originally set for its latest possible beginning. Although, owing to their experiences at Kholm and in RAUBTIER, the field commands had concluded that it was not worthwhile to sacrifice time, which was becoming precious, for the sake of air support, Hitler had insisted on keeping all available planes committed to RAUBTIER until that operation was finished and on holding the Demyansk operation in abeyance until he could shift full air support to it. At

the same time, he had also insisted that the effort at Demyansk be part of the grand design to close the Ostashkov gap that had been given the code name BRUECKENSCHLAG, the same name which had been assigned to Ninth Army's projected drive to Ostashkov. The code name again was not inappropriate because Sixteenth Army's share of this larger BRUECKENSCHLAG effort was in fact also to build a bridge—across the twenty miles between X Corps' front south of Staraya Russa and the western face of the Demyansk pocket.

The plan, as approved during the 2 March conference at *Fuehrer* Headquarters, was to have five more-or-less full-strength divisions strike east from the X Corps line to the Lovat River. When they reached the Lovat, the distance to the pocket would be somewhat under five miles, and at that point II Corps would join in with a push from its side. During the conference, Halder had concluded that Busch and the II and X Corps commanders were "not sufficiently firm personalities," and afterward he prevailed on Kuechler to shift control of BRUECKENSCHLAG away from Sixteenth Army by constituting the forces for this operation as separate combat teams with authorization to communicate directly to the army group and the OKH outside the normal channels. Command of the main force went to Generalmajor Walter von Seydlitz-Kurzbach and that of the secondary force in the pocket to Generalmajor H. Zorn, both of whom were senior division commanders.

Seydlitz, working under the eye of the OKH, exercised his troops in loose order infiltration tactics modeled on tactics the Finnish Army had used dur-

---

[45]*AOK 18, Ia Kriegstagebuch, Band II,* 14–15 Mar 42, AOK 18 19601/6 file; *AOK 18, Ia Kriegstagebuch, Band III,* 16–20 Mar 42, AOK 18 19601/7 file.

ing the Winter War of 1939–1940. To exploit these tactics, he laid the line of advance through woods and swamp south of the Staraya Russa–Demyansk road. The questions were whether the Germans could be as effective fighting in the forest as the Finns had been, whether they could beat the oncoming thaw, and how much longer the pocket could survive. The answers to the latter two became critical as soon as RAUBTIER began consuming the time allotted to BRUECKENSCHLAG.

On the 16th, Kuechler made a somewhat hazardous flight into the pocket to reassure Brockdorff, who was talking about staging a breakout. During the flights in and out, Kuechler had the opportunity to observe firsthand what would be a positive circumstance for BRUECKENSCHLAG: from an altitude of about 4,000 feet in clear weather he could see no evidence of combat between the pocket and the X Corps front. The Russians, by being set on breaking the pocket open from the north and south, at which they might well succeed, were thereby allowing the Germans to have a stable basis from which to launch BRUECKENSCHLAG.[46]

In midafternoon on the 19th, after he knew the Dora Lane was cut and the Volkhov gap was being closed, Hitler gave the order for the final deployment for BRUECKENSCHLAG. The *Luftwaffe* would shift its full force south the next morning, and Seydlitz would have one day to bring his units, which were dispersed behind the X Corps front, up to their line of departure.

When the advance began at daylight on the morning of the 21st, the objectives were a succession of diminutive villages, some with imposing names— Ivanovskoye, Noshevalovo, and Vasilievshchina, all otherwise insignificant except as reference points in the wilderness of trees and snow. The Russians responded with determination and confusion, holding fanatically to some places and giving way in others. After two days, the temperature rose above freezing. On the fourth day, several regiments reached the Redya River, halfway to the Lovat. By then, too, the three feet of snow on the ground had turned to slush, and aerial reconnaissance had reported Soviet reinforcements moving along the valleys of the Redya and Lovat from the north and the south. Two Soviet parachute brigades had landed inside the pocket not far from Demyansk and the airfield. Like the paratroops who had landed behind Army Group Center, however, once on the ground they appeared uncertain as to what to do next.

East of the Redya, Seydlitz's advance slowed almost to a stop. Ahead, all the way to the Lovat the forest was dense, unbroken by roads or settlements, and matted with underbrush. Against the Soviet troops dug-in there the German *Stukas* were useless: they could not spot the enemy positions through the trees and brush. By the 26th, a foot and a half of water covered the ice on the Redya, and if the thaw continued the entire stretch between the rivers would soon be swamp. On the 30th, Seydlitz told Kuechler that he was going to stop, regroup, and shift his line of attack north to the Staraya Russa– Demyansk road.[47]

---

[46]*H. Gr. Nord, Ia Kriegstagebuch, 13.–31.3.42*, 2–16 Mar 42, H. Gr. Nord 75128/8 file.

[47]*AOK 16, Ia Kriegstagebuch, Band III*, 21–30 Mar 42, AOK 16 23468/4 file.

At the end of the month, the *Stavka* also was engaged in planning a fresh start. It had, for two weeks, had *Politburo* member N. A. Bulganin as its representative at *Northwest Front*, but Bulganin's competence in military affairs was "small," and his presence had done more to complicate than to facilitate the *front's* conduct of operations. On 29 March, the *Stavka* gave command of all troops on the perimeter of the pocket to General Leytenant N. F. Vatutin, who had, until then, been the *front's* chief of staff, and made Kurochkin, the *front's* commander, solely responsible for the defense against Seydlitz's relief operation. At the same time, it gave Kurochkin five regiments of antitank guns and "four divisions" of light antiaircraft artillery.[48]

A Month of Mud and Crises

For both contestants, the Germans and the Russians, the final lap in the race with the *rasputitsa* was on. The stakes were high. If BRUECKENSCHLAG failed, the Germans would not be able to hold the Demyansk pocket through the spring nor would *Second Shock Army* be able to survive if its lines to the rear remained cut. The *rasputitsa* could save the German effort at Kholm and it might be all that could save I Corps from being cut off the way II Corps already was. While the *rasputitsa* was certain to have an effect, what that might be at any one place was entirely uncertain. From Kholm, for instance, where the Soviet lines were long and the roads poor at best, Scherer reported on 26 March that some of the Russians appeared to be withdrawing.

His own position, however, was getting worse. The sudden and rapid thaw had completely melted the snowbanks that had given his troops concealment; the entrenchments had become mudholes half-filled with water; and the felt boots, indispensable as protection against the cold, were useless to the troops who now spent their days submerged to the hips in mud and melted snow. One half-way determined Soviet attack with artillery and tanks, he predicted, could well be enough to finish off the pocket.[49]

Eighteenth Army's grip on the Volkhov pocket was desperate but uncertain. *Fifty-fourth Army* had pushed a wedge past Pogostye to within five miles of Lyuban on the northeast, and *Second Shock Army* had no more than seven or eight miles to go to reach Lyuban from the south, which it appeared determined to do even after the RAUBTIER operation had closed the mouth of the pocket. On 23 March, the day the thaw began, the army group chief of staff told the OKH chief of operations that it was "gradually" becoming impossible for Eighteenth Army to keep the Russians from taking Lyuban because the army did not have enough men to do it. The thaw slowed the Russians as it did the Germans, but they were clearly not going to let it stop them. By keeping tanks in position to rake the Erika Lane with fire, they had managed to prevent the Germans from actually taking possession of it and to convert the lane into a no-man's-land. On the 27th, the tanks, with infantry behind them, drove through the lane and reopened it as a supply road for

[48]Zhelanov, "*Iz opyta*," pp. 31–33.

[49]*H. Gr. Nord, Ia Kriegstagebuch, 13.–31.3.42*, 26 Mar 42, H. Gr. Nord 75128/8 file.

Second Shock Army. At the end of the month, Eighteenth Army did get one small bit of relief: Finnish troops, with some Estonian auxiliaries supplied by Eighteenth Army took the islands Suursaari, Lavansaari, and Tytarsaari, thus ending the army's worry that it would have to divert men of its own to those enterprises.

BRUECKENSCHLAG resumed on 4 April. Seydlitz had regrouped his force, and his Soviet opposition had been regrouped and reinforced. Soviet infantry were not only dug in on the ground but were firing from the tree-tops. Airplanes, mostly slow, single-engine biplanes, cruised over the German bivouac areas all night long dropping bombs from altitudes of from one to two hundred feet. On the softening ground, Soviet tanks were again showing their superiority, and the tank crews had discovered that the trees and underbrush gave them excellent protection because the *Rotkopf* hollow-charge shells frequently exploded when they struck branches. The Germans were using a new weapon, the *Panzerschreck*. It fired a rocket-propelled, hollow-charge grenade and could knock out a T–34, but Seydlitz observed that manning it required nerve "and a generous endowment of luck" because it was not effective at ranges over fifty yards.[50] The nighttime temperatures were staying above freezing, and the roads, including those the Russians had surfaced with layers of packed snow and sawdust, were thawing. Maneuvering was out of the question. The only way BRUECKENSCHLAG could succeed was by punching through to the Lovat by the most direct route.

The six-mile distance to the Lovat was an ordinary two-hour walk. It took Seydlitz's troops eight days to get within 500 yards of the river and to begin a slow turn upstream toward Ramushevo. The II Corps force under Zorn began its attack out of the pocket on the 14th. It was a gamble. Zorn was not supposed to have begun moving until Seydlitz had Ramushevo, but Seydlitz had over ten thousand casualties, and by the time he reached Ramushevo—if he did—the *rasputitsa* was certain to be in full swing.

April was a month of mud and crises. Army Group North and the OKH considered having II Corps attempt a breakout. Since Army Group Center was giving up on its share of BRUECKENSCHLAG, the Demyansk pocket was at best a doubtful tactical asset, but no one wanted to argue that point with Hitler. Kuechler did tell Hitler that with three more divisions he could wipe out the Volkhov pocket. Hitler responded that henceforth Army Groups North and Center would be on their own because all troops and material not already committed would be going into the summer offensive. Kuechler then scraped together five battalions that he could have used to pump strength into BRUECKENSCHLAG but that he had to put into the Kholm relief "because humanity and comradeship make it unthinkable to abandon the Scherer Group."[51] The *Luftwaffe* had a battalion of paratroops to land in Kholm. To drop them there, however, would necessitate diverting transports from the Demyansk airlift

---

[50]*H. G. Nord, Ia Kriegstagebuch, 1–30.4.42,* 3 Apr 42, H. Gr. Nord 75128/9 file.

[51]*Ibid.,* 12–14 Apr 42.

MACHINE-GUN NEST ON THE VOLKHOV FRONT

which would probably result in sub-stantial losses. The army group pre-dicted dourly that if the drop were attempted half the men would land among the Russians and the others would "break all the bones in their bodies" coming down among the build-ings in the town.[52]

The *Luftwaffe*, discontented with its support role, wanted to withdraw the *Stukas* from BRUECKENSCHLAG for oper-ations against the Soviet naval vessels at Leningrad to assuage Hitler's concern about the ships. To capture Hitler's in-terest and circumvent the army group's objections to this action, the *Luftwaffe* raised the project's status to that of an

air offensive under the grandiloquent code name GOETZ VON BERLICHINGEN. The first raid, on the 24th, scored hits on the battleship *October Revolution* and the cruisers *Maxim Gorkiy* and *Marty* and drew down heavily on the am-munition for Eighteenth Army's long-range artillery then employed in sup-pressing Soviet antiaircraft fire. Subse-quent raids, continuing into the first week in May with reduced artillery sup-port, met more intensive antiaircraft fire than the pilots had experienced be-fore, even in the London blitz.

In and around the Volkhov pocket a disaster was almost certainly develop-ing. The only real question was, for whom? After the Russians broke open the Erika Lane, Kuechler relieved the XXXVIII Corps commander. At the

[52]*Ibid.*, 14 Apr 42.

Fuehrer Headquarters, the feeling was that the 58th Infantry Division commander, in whose sector the mishap had occurred, should also be relieved because he was "more a professor than a soldier." While Kuechler protested in vain for two days that being "educated and well-read" did not necessarily make an officer ineffectual, the Russians also retook the Dora Lane.[53]

The benefit the Russians gained from retaking the two lanes, however, did not quite equal the pain the loss occasioned for the Germans. The XXXVIII Corps and I Corps held the corridor formed by the lanes to a width of less than two miles, and, by mid-April, the thaw and constant air and artillery bombardment had turned the lanes into cratered ribbons of mud. *Second Shock Army* was not strangled but it was choking. Eighteenth Army, for its part, reported that its continuing hold on Lyuban owed entirely to "luck and entirely unfounded optimism" both of which could be dispersed at any time by Soviet infantry "and a few tanks."[54]

All of Army Group North was indeed, as it put it to Hitler and the OKH, "living from hand to mouth and on an almost indefensible optimism."[55] On the other hand, the *rasputitsa,* at least, was nobody's ally. It was impartial. The winter had not been; it had given the Russians the initiative; but that was inexorably melting away with snow and ice. *Second Shock Army* and *Fifty-fourth Army* held low ground, swamp, and bottomland. The Germans expected the Russians to know how to deal with

the *rasputitsa* better than their own commands did, and the Soviet armies, no doubt, did know how to deal with the inevitable thaw as well as anyone.

Stalin, however, wanted more. The *Leningrad Front* commander, General Khozin, had declared that if he were given full command, he could still bring off a victory despite the *rasputitsa.* Marshal Shaposhnikov, chief of the General Staff, did not believe Khozin was capable of controlling operations by ten armies and several independent corps, but Stalin was for giving him a chance. On 23 April, the *Stavka* relieved Meretskov and abolished *Volkhov Front,* turning it over as an operational group to Headquarters, *Leningrad Front.* Khozin then was given orders to step up the offensive and break the Leningrad siege.[56] The job that had been too big for Meretskov and Khozin together was not likely to be mastered by one of them alone, and the time was poor for experimenting with ad hoc commands—the Volkov River had an open channel down its center; the Erika and Dora lanes were underwater; and *Second Shock Army's* perimeter in the pocket was starting to shrink.

On the afternoon of the 29th, Kuechler talked by telephone to Brockdorff in the Demyansk pocket. Seydlitz's and Zorn's troops standing opposite each other on the Lovat had strung a telephone line across the river. *Northwest Front* would be denied its final victory over II Corps.

At Kholm, *Third Shock Army* mustered artillery and tanks and broke into the pocket from the south on 1 May,

---

[53]*H. Gr. Nord, Ia Kriegstagebuch, 1.–31.3.42,* 29 Mar 42, H. Gr. Nord 75128/9 file.

[54]*Ibid.,* 16 Apr 42.

[55]*Ibid.*

[56]Vasilevskiy, *Delo,* p. 184f; Meretskov, *Serving the People,* p. 207.

the ninety-sixth day of the siege. The relief force under Generalmajor Werner Huehner, Uckermann's successor, was stalled a mile to the west where it stayed for three more days while the infantry probed for an opening and the *Stukas* rained bombs on the Russians. Hitler claimed that more bombs were dropped during this attack than in all of World War I. During the morning of the 5th, a predawn tank and infantry attack reached the western edge of the pocket at daylight.[57]

----

[57]*H. Gr. Nord, Ia Kriegstagebuch, 1.–31.5.42*, 1–5 May 42, H. Gr. Nord 75128/10 file.

The winter had ended. The occasional snow that continued to fall was heavy and wet. The mud on the roads was a yard or more deep, and horses sometimes drowned in the potholes. Every gully and dip was filled with water. The woods were submerged, and in them and the swamps, which during this season were actually shallow lakes, populations of vipers were coming to life. As if in competition for a doubtful honor, Sixteenth and Eighteenth Army units lavished craftsmanship and some artistry on signs asserting, "The arse of the world begins here."

CHAPTER X

The War Behind the Front

The Partisan Movement, Beginnings

Organization

The Germans assumed throughout the war in the East that the Soviet leadership had prepared intensively for a partisan campaign well before the war broke out. Partisan warfare, after all, had been important in earlier Russian wars, and Soviet literature had highlighted the activities of the Red partisans in the 1918–1920 civil war. German analyses of the partisan movement made during the war took prior preparation for granted, as is shown in the following statements from the first "Bulletin on Partisan Warfare" put out by the Eastern Branch of Army Intelligence and from a similar Air Force Intelligence series:

The use of partisans is a well known and tested means of warfare in the internal and external conflicts of the Russian people. It is, therefore, not surprising that the Soviet Government prepared for partisan warfare before the outbreak of the war through the use of the NKVD, creation of a plan of organization, recruitment of former partisans, secret courses of instruction, instructions for the responsible officers of all political organizations, and so forth.[1]

The Soviet authorities very carefully prepared for partisan warfare, even before the war, within the framework of the secret state police of the Soviet Union [NKVD].[2]

The German documents, however, do not contain any direct evidence to support their conclusions. Erickson states that Stalin stopped "experimentation and limited contingency planning connected with possible partisan operations on Soviet territory" after 1937.[3] In addition, the most comprehensive German postwar study states, "Before the war, Stalin repeatedly expressed the conviction that the Soviet Army was prepared to ward off any attack on its territory. . . . Because of this conception, preparations for popular resistance were not undertaken. . . ."[4] As Erickson indicates, the theory of "carrying the war to enemy territory" and the possible untoward effects of fostering insurgency would, very likely, have kept the Soviet government from preparing for partisan warfare beforehand.[5]

Nevertheless, when the war started, the Soviet government immediately undertook to call a partisan movement to life. On 29 June 1941, the Council of People's Commissars and the Central

---

[1]*OKH, GenStdH, FHQ, Nachrichten ueber Bandenkrieg Nr. 1, 1.5.43, H3/738.*

[2]*OKL, Ic, FLO, Einzelnachrichten des Ic Dienstes Ost der Luftwaffe, Nr. 29, 2.8.42, OKL/254.*

[3]Erickson, *Road to Stalingrad,* p. 240.

[4]Erich Hesse, *Der sowjetrussische Partisanenkrieg, 1941 bis 1944* (Goettingen: Musterschmidt, 1969), p. 41.

[5]Erickson, *Road to Stalingrad,* p. 240f.

Committee of the Communist Party ordered all party and government organs in the frontier areas to create partisan detachments and to "kindle partisan warfare all over and everywhere." "For the enemy and his accomplices," the order read, "unbearable conditions must be created in the occupied territories. They must be pursued at every step and destroyed, and their measures must be frustrated."[6] In Belorussia, where the Germans were making their deepest advances, the republic central committee, on 30 June, issued its "Directive No. 1 on the Transition of Party Organizations to Underground Work in Enemy Occupation." The directive ordered party organizations to employ partisan detachments "to combat units of the enemy armies, to kindle partisan warfare everywhere, to destroy bridges and roads and telephone and telegraph lines and set fire to supply dumps. . . ."[7]

On 18 July, the All-Union (national) Central Committee issued an order to all party committees in which it "expanded and concretized [sic]" the 29 June directive.[8] The order informed the committees that they would "receive in every town and also in every village willing support from hundreds, even thousands of our brothers and friends" and "demanded" that the committees assign "reliable, leading Party, Soviet, and Komsomol activists" to lead and spread partisan activity. It called to the committees' notice also that "there are still cases in which the leaders of the Party and Soviet organizations of the *rayons* [counties] threatened by the Fascists shamelessly leave their combat posts and retreat deep into the rear area to safe positions" and that "the Party and the Government will not hesitate to take the most severe measures in regard to those slackers and deserters."[9]

The central committee order, although it designated partisan warfare as a party function, was supplemented by army instructions on organization, objectives, and tactics.[10] These specified that the detachments were to consist of 75 to 150 men, organized into two or three companies, with the companies divided into two or three platoons. Operations, which were to take the form of "attacks on columns and concentrations of motorized infantry, on dumps and ammunition transports, on airfields, and on railroad transports," were to be conducted primarily in company and platoon strengths and "carried out, as a rule, at night or from ambush." The detachments would have to locate in areas with enough forest to provide cover, but each *rayon* ought to have at least one detachment. The instructions went on to describe methods of laying ambushes, destroying dumps and bridges, and wrecking trains and the precautions to be ob-

---

[6]*IVMV*, vol. IV, p. 52.

[7]A. A. Kuznyaev, *Podpolnye partiynye organy kompartii belorussii v gody velikoy otechestvennoy voyny* (Minsk: Izdatelstvo "Belarus," 1975), p. 6.

[8]V. Andrianov, "Rukovodstvo kommunisticheskoy partii vsenarodnoy borboy v tylu vraga," *Voyenno-istoricheskiy Zhurnal*, 10 (1977), 61.

[9]The 18 July order is often cited in Soviet publications, but its content is not given. The full text of a copy found in German records is printed in John A. Armstrong, ed., *The Soviet Partisans in World War II* (Madison: University of Wisconsin Press, 1964), pp. 653–55.

[10]The "Instruction Concerning the Organization and Activity of Partisan Detachments and Diversionist Groups" issued by *Northwest Front* on 20 July 1941 is printed in Armstrong, *Soviet Partisans*, pp. 655–62.

POSTER READS, "PARTISANS! AVENGE
WITHOUT MERCY!"

served on the march, in camp, and under pursuit.[11]

Under the instructions, a first stage in preparing for partisan warfare would be to set up "destruction battalions." These, each consisting of about two hundred men who, because of age or for other reasons, were not eligible for regular military service, were to be organized in threatened areas by the local party and NKVD offices. Their tasks initially would be to fight against enemy parachutists, arrest deserters, hunt down "counterrevolutionaries" and enemy agents, and to employ massed rifle and machine gun fire against enemy aircraft. When oc-

cupation became imminent, the "best-trained, most courageous, and most experienced fighters" were to be detailed to fight as partisans.[12]

The party involvement brought a massive apparatus to bear on the organization of the partisan movement. One line ran from the Central Committee of the All-Union Communist Party through the central committees of the republics to dozens of provincial (oblast) and hundreds of rayon party committees. At each level, a section "X" (Roman "10"), also designated "Partizanskiye Otryady" ("partisan detachments"), was responsible for creating and directing partisan units. A second line branched off below the All-Union Central Committee to the Main Administration of Political Propaganda of the Army, which also created a chain of tenth sections extending down to the fronts and armies. Alongside these, the NKVD, which had networks of offices in both the civilian and military sectors, projected itself into the partisan movement through its functions related to the destruction battalions. While the party committees were the designated command channel for the partisans, the operational and tactical directives on partisan warfare came mainly from L. Z. Mekhlis, the chief political commissar and head of the Main Administration of Political Propaganda of the Army, and the NKVD, through the destruction battalions, probably supplied the largest single block of recruits to the early partisan movement.[13]

[11]Ibid., pp. 656–61.

[12]Earl Ziemke, The Soviet Partisan Movement in 1941 (Washington, D.C.: Air Research and Development Command, 1954), p. 11.

[13]Ibid., pp. 11–13. See also OKH, GenStdH, GenQu, Abt. K-Verw., "Erfahrungen ueber Aufbau, Aufgaben, Auftreten und Bekaempfung der Partisanenabteilungen," 15 Jan 42, Wi/ID 2.217 file.

All three of the organizing agencies worked on the Soviet side of the front, setting up destruction battalions and partisan detachments ahead of the German advance. What they accomplished from place to place depended on the speed with which the front moved, how much central direction could be given under often chaotic conditions, and how such direction was interpreted and applied at the local levels. The organizers, except for some who subsequently became members of underground party committees, were, for the most part, not themselves participants in the movement; consequently, when the front passed over an area, the partisans, who were often recruited or drafted only days before from factories and collective farms, were left to learn from experience, if they could. As a result, the effort, no doubt, was more impressive on the Soviet side of the front than its effects were on the German side.

At its inception, the partisan movement was what the Germans termed *Ortsansaessig*, that is, the detachments operated out of fixed bases and over relatively short distances. In most instances, a detachment was identified with one *rayon*, which was also its primary operating area.[14] This remained a predominant characteristic of the World War II Soviet partisan movement throughout its existence.[15] Geography, more than anything else, made

it possible for fixed detachments to develop and survive. The partisan movement grew up and always was strongest east of the Dnepr-Dvina line, in eastern Belorussia and the western RSFSR (Russian Soviet Federated Socialist Republic). There an almost unbroken stretch of forest and swamp, reaching from the Pripyat Marshes to north of Lake Ilmen, afforded excellent cover, and the German troops, by preference as well as necessity, stayed close to the roads and railroads. Familiarity with the terrain and contacts with the inhabitants gave added protection.

The Shmyrev Otryad

The *Shmyrev Otryad* ("detachment"), while not typical, affords the most substantial existing example of an early partisan unit. While much of what happened to it was characteristic of the whole movement, it was not typical because it was, in all likelihood, much more active, better led, and effective than all but a very few of the original detachments. From it would evolve (in 1942) the *1st Belorussian Partisan Brigade*, one of the premier partisan units of the war. Its first commander, Mihay Filipovich Shmyrev, would be given the highest Soviet decoration, Hero of the Soviet Union, and under his *nom de guerre*, "Batya ['papa'] Mihay," would become a legendary figure in the movement. Important at the outset was that Shmyrev had some actual previous

---

[14]See Kuznyaev, *Podpolnye*, which gives the partisan units associated with the *rayons* of Belorussia. See p. 215.

[15]The Soviet accounts also describe roving and raiding types of partisan units. Outside of Karelia, however, where the partisan bases were located on the Soviet side of the front, those did not come into existence until the summer of 1942. Even then, expeditions by roving detachments, such as those of S. A.

Kovpak and A. N. Saburov, were apparently staged primarily to cultivate local partisan activity in areas in which it had hitherto been weak or nonexistent, the Ukraine, in particular. See Armstrong, *Soviet Partisans*, pp. 114–16; *IVMV*, vol. V, p. 292; and A. Bryukhanov, "Geroicheskaya borba sovetskikh partizani v gody Velikoy Otechestvennoy Voyny," *Voyenno-istoricheskiy Zhurnal*, 3(1965), 36–42.

experience in partisan warfare. In the literature of the movement, he is said to have been a partisan during the civil war.[16] Actually, his experience apparently came from fighting anti-Soviet partisans, whom the Soviet authorities called "bandits," as the Germans later referred to the Soviet partisans.[17] What makes the *Shmyrev Otryad* a useful example is that it achieved sufficient prominence to be given more than ordinary treatment in the Soviet literature, and the Germans, as well, accumulated considerable information on its operations, primarily from two captured diaries that had been kept by officers in the *otryad*.[18]

The *Shmyrev Otryad* was formed in Surazh *rayon*, thirty miles northeast of Vitebsk, in eastern Belorussia. Its first recruits were the employees of a small cardboard factory in the village of Pudoti. Tsanava states that the detachment was founded on 9 July when Shmyrev called a meeting of the workers and proposed that they form a partisan unit.[19] The two diaries indicate that the process of organization had started on 5 July when the secretary of the *rayon* party committee and the head of the *rayon* NKVD office "suggested" to Shmyrev that he start a partisan unit.[20] However, their backing stopped

with that, and they refused Shmyrev's request for weapons, possibly because they did not have any.

Shmyrev became the commander of the detachment, apparently, because he was the director of the factory, not because of his earlier experience in partisan warfare. His commissar was one R. V. Shkredo, who had been the party secretary at the factory. At the outset, the detachment consisted of twenty-three men, all employees of the factory. From 9 to 13 July, the men worked at preparing a camp in the woods, and on the night of the 13th, they acquired weapons, including a machine gun, and ammunition from retreating Soviet troops, who also told them the Germans were close. The next day, German troops entered Surazh, the *rayon* center ten miles to the southeast. From then on, the detachment was behind the enemy front and, technically at least, in action. During the day, eight Soviet Army stragglers and two local men joined the detachment. However, there was no prospect of acquiring large numbers of recruits since all the men fit for regular military service had been drafted and sent to Vitebsk during the first week of July. On 17 July, eleven men did show up from a destruction battalion that had been organized in Surazh and had broken up, and on the 18th, six local policemen joined, setting off a dispute over who should have their revolvers, they or the more senior men in the detachment.[21]

The detachment saw its first action on 25 July when Shmyrev and ten men surprised a party of German cavalry bathing in a river and claimed twenty-

[16]L. Tsanava, *Vsenarodnaya partizanskaya voyna v Belorussii protiv fashistskikh zakhvachnikov* (Minsk: Gosizdat, 1949–1951), vol. I, p. 168.

[17]See *Bolshaya Sovetskaya Entsiklopediya*, 3d ed., 1978, vol. 29, p. 446.

[18]See Earl Ziemke and Ralph Mavrogordato, *History of the First Belorussian Partisan Brigade* (Washington, D.C.: Air Research and Development Command, 1954), p. 2.

[19]Tsanava, *Vsenarodnaya partizanskaya voyna*, p. 169.

[20]*II. SS Kav. Regt.*, "Partisanen-Tagebuch Nr. 1," 5 Jul–5 Oct 41 and "*Partisanen-Tagebuch Nr. 2*," 5 Jul–17 Aug 42, Waffen SS, I. and II. SS Kav. Regts., 78037/196 file.

[21]*Ibid.*, 9–18 Jul 42.

five to thirty casualties with no harm to
themselves. The next day, for three-
and-a-half hours, twenty of the partisans watched a German column move
through Pudoti. They fired on the last
four trucks, destroying one and
damaging others.[22] After these ven-
tures, probably because no more Germans were passing through Pudoti, the
detachment, for a month, engaged in
looking for enemy collaborators and
marauding Soviet stragglers. The *Popular Scientific Sketch* credits the *Shmyrev
Otryad* with having carried out twenty-
seven raids in August and September
in which it killed 200 "fascists," destroyed fourteen enemy motor vehicles, and set eighteen tank trucks on
fire.[23] Neither the diaries nor the German records give evidence of activity
on such a scale.

In the first week of September, a
dozen Soviet Army men arrived in the
camp from the Soviet side of the front.
At the same time, the detachment received 4 heavy machine guns with
15,000 rounds of ammunition, a heavy
mortar, and a light mortar. With these,
the partisans and the soldiers attacked
Surazh on 13 September, killing several
Germans and collaborators.[24] Remarkably, the Soviet Information Bureau in Moscow issued a press release
on the attack almost as it was being
made.[25]

The German efforts to get rid of the
detachment had been sufficiently hap-

hazard to build the partisans' confidence. At first, the Germans apparently had taken them for army
stragglers who were afraid to surrender. During the first week of August, they had found a peasant who
had offered to lead them to the camp,
but the partisans had gone before they
arrived. They had tried also to spread a
rumor that Shmyrev had been shot.
Their assumption, not always incorrect, had been that the partisan rank
and file would disperse if they believed
the leaders were out of the way. In
August, also, a small German detachment had taken up quarters in Pudoti
for a time, and light aircraft had
scouted—unsuccessfully—over the
forest. The Germans made their biggest effort on 17 September, after the
Surazh raid, when 200 troops came
into Pudoti, but they only fired into the
woods and departed again the same
day.[26]

The *Shmyrev Otryad* had been one of
the most—possibly the most—active
and successful original partisan detachments in Belorussia, but the course of
its development in 1941, as far as that is
known, had not indicated a surge of
resistance to the occupation. Although
it was situated at the heart of potentially ideal territory for partisan warfare, the detachment only had contacts
with three other, much smaller and
apparently less active, bands. Out of its
own original membership, fourteen
men had deserted by the end of July.
By the last week in August, the detachment had increased to sixty-eight men,
but by then thirty-eight others had

[22]*Ibid.*, 25 Jul 42; "*Partisanen-Tagebuch Nr. 1*" and
"*Nr. 2*," 26 Jul 42, Waffen SS, I. and II. SS Kav. Regts.,
78037/196 file. See also Tsanava, *Vsenarodnaya partizanskaya voyna*, p. 169.

[23]*VOV*, p. 329.

[24]"*Partisanen-Tagebuch Nr. 1*," 31 Aug and 1, 13–14
Sep 42, Waffen SS, I. and II. SS Kav. Regts.,
78037/196 file.

[25]Tsanava, *Vsenarodnaya partizanskaya voyna*, p. 170.

[26]"*Partisanen-Tagebuch Nr. 2*," 3, 13, 20 Aug and 17
Sep 42, Waffen SS, I. and II. SS Kav. Regts.,
78037/196 file.

PARTISANS LISTEN TO A SOVIET NEWSPAPER BEING READ

deserted or been expelled for cowardice, and one had been shot. On the last day of September, the latest time for which either of the diaries gives a figure, the strength was eighty men, probably still including the twelve from the regular army.[27]

Strength in 1941

The *Short History* states, "All Soviet people mounted a monolithic resistance to the enemy forces. At the front and in the rear and in the areas occupied by the fascist oppressors, they did not spare themselves in fighting for the honor, freedom, and independence of their socialist country."[28] What this meant in terms of the strength of the partisan movement, however, is uncertain. The *Short History* gives the number of partisan units formed in 1941 as 3,500.[29] The *History of the Second World War* states that "more than two thousand" were in existence by the end of the year.[30] The *Great Soviet Encyclopedia* (third edition) gives the partisan strengths by months, but only for the period after 1 January 1942, for which it gives a figure of 90,000 men. The *History of the Second World War* gives about the same overall number and a breakdown by areas which yields fig-

---

[27] "*Partisanen-Tagebuch Nr. 1*" and "*Nr. 2*," 29 Jul–30 Sep 42, Waffen SS, I. and II. SS Kav. Regts., 78037/196 file.

[28] *VOV (Kratkaya Istoriya)*, p. 113.
[29] *Ibid.*, p. 110.
[30] *IVOVSS*, vol. IV, p. 127.

ures of 20,000 partisans behind Army Group North, 40,000 behind Center, and 35,000 behind South. However, these numbers are based on Communist party records, which even for later periods when closer control and more accurate counts were possible, give numbers up to and over twice as high as those of the Central Staff of the Partisan Movement.[31] Most likely, what party records show are numbers of partisans recruited. Since no systematic control of the movement as it functioned behind the German lines had existed in 1941, the numbers in operation would have been unknown.

The Underground

Partisan detachments required space and cover; hence, they could not function in urban areas. Their targets were the remote stretches of road and railroad, the out-of-the-way places. The enemy would ordinarily be too strong and too much on his guard in or near towns and cities. There the resistance would have to take another form.

Consequently, the directives of June and July 1941 that established the guidelines for the early partisan movement also called for an "underground" (podpolya) of "diversionist" groups. These would consist of thirty to fifty men each and would carry out their operations in smaller groups of three to five, or at most ten, men. The members of one group would usually not know those of any other, and the organization would exist only to receive and transmit instructions and carry out recruitment. Whereas the partisans

would have a combat capability, the diversionists would do their work by stealth. Otherwise, the objectives of the two were much the same: to destroy telegraph and telephone lines, railroad lines, supply dumps, and trucks and other vehicles. The diversionists would also kill individual enemy officers and spread rumors designed to create panic among the enemy.[32] The particular advantages of the diversionists would be that they could operate in places where the enemy was strong, stay close to him, and strike from within his midst.

A specialty of the diversionist groups was railroad sabotage, since the railroads were the largest still functioning industry in the occupied territory and the most vital to the Germans. Two diversionists reportedly put the entire Minsk railroad water system out of commission for nearly a month in December 1941.[33] A group operating in the railroad yards at Orsha, under one K. S. Zaslonov, is said to have derailed 100 military trains and crippled "almost" 200 locomotives in the months December 1941 through February 1942.[34] Other groups were organized in power plants, factories, and among workers in mechanical trades. In Vitebsk, fifty groups, numbering more than seven hundred persons, are said to have been recruited. The diversionist activity probably took its most unusual form in Odessa, where extensive catacombs beneath the city made partisan warfare practicable in an urban setting. The outstanding success

[31] Bolshaya Sovetskaya Entsiklopediya, 3d ed., 1978, vol. 19, p. 235; IVMV, vol. IV, p. 127. See p. 217.

[32] Armstrong, Soviet Partisans, p. 656.
[33] V. Ye. Bystrov, ed., Geroi podpolya (Moscow: Izdatelstvo Politicheskoy Literatury, 1970), p. 38f.
[34] VOV, p. 336.

attributed to diversionists in 1941 had been the destruction in one week, beginning on 19 September, of the Kiev railroad freight station, the shops of the Kiev locomotive works, and two factories.[35]

Under the early directives, control and coordination of both the partisan detachments and the diversionist groups were to be vested in another kind of underground organization, the "illegal" party committees. These, composed of several particularly trustworthy party men and established on the same territorial basis as the legal committees, would stay behind in the occupied areas and assume a leadership role.[36] Reportedly, the sections "X" each had a member assigned to them whose identity was kept secret and who would take over as party secretary during the occupation.[37] The *History of the Great Patriotic War* states that in the first months of the war, in the Ukraine alone, 23 *oblast* ("district") committees, 67 urban *rayon* committees, 564 rural *rayon* committees, and 4,316 lesser party committees, with membership totaling 26,500 people, had been formed. However, other figures indicate that in Belorussia, where partisan and underground activity had been much more widespread than in the Ukraine, particularly in the early period of the war, these illegal party committees had existed in only 2 out of 10 *oblasts* and 15 out of over 170 urban and rural *rayons* as of December 1941.[38]

German Rear Area Security

The Germans had expected the Soviet regime to resort to partisan warfare, and Hitler had even anticipated it with a degree of satisfaction. On 16 July 1941, he said, "The Russians have now ordered partisan warfare behind our front. This also has its advantages: it gives us the opportunity to . . . exterminate . . . all who oppose us."[39] Two weeks later he embodied this thought in an order to the forces on the Eastern Front stating, "The troops available for security in the conquered territories will not be sufficient if offenders are dealt with by legal means, but [will be sufficient] only if the occupation force inspires sufficient terror among the population to stamp out the will to resist."[40] In an infamous "Order Concerning Military Justice in the BARBAROSSA Area," issued before the invasion, he had already given the troops immunity from prosecution for atrocities committed during the campaign.[41] For him, partisan warfare was less a provocation than an excuse and pretext for the ruthlessness with which he proposed to conduct the war in the Soviet Union.

Although Hitler was perfectly willing to be merciless in stamping out any kind of resistance in the Soviet Union, he was actually not ready to do so in the vast areas occupied during 1941 except on a hit-or-miss basis. Anticipating a

---

[35]Bystrov, *Geroi podpolya*, pp. 73–75, 297–303; *IVMV*, vol. IV, p. 126.

[36]See Armstrong, *Soviet Partisans*, p. 654.

[37]*GFP Gr. 725*, "Partisanen Erfahrungsbericht," 22.1.42, H. Geb. 30910/37 file.

[38]*IVOVSS*, vol. VI, p. 275; Kuznyaev, *Podpolnye*, p. 243.

[39]*Reichsleiter Bormann, Aktenvermerk ueber eine Besprechung mit Reichsleiter Rosenberg, Reichsminister Lammers, Feldmarschall Keitel, und mit dem Reichsmarschall Goering*, 16.7.41, NMT 221–L/USA–544 file.

[40]*OKW, WFSt/L (1 Op.), Ergaenzung zur Weisung 33*, 23.7.41, NMT C–52/GB–485 file.

[41]*Der Fuehrer, Erlass ueber die Kriegsgerichtsbarkeit im Gebiet "Barbarossa" und ueber besondere Massnahmen der Truppe*, 13.5.41, NMT C–50 file.

quick victory, he expected to be in the mopping-up phase before rear area security could become a significant military problem. For that reason, and because he disliked giving the military what he considered to be political authority and also to save on manpower and equipment, the BARBAROSSA forces went into the Soviet Union with a strictly limited capacity for controlling the occupied territory.

The territory the army administered was restricted to the "operations zone," which was adjacent to the front and which moved with it. The operations zone could be extensive—that of Army Group Center, for instance, in December 1941 extended 150 miles west of Smolensk and nearly to Moscow, which was over 200 miles to the east—but it was always temporary and primarily a maneuver and staging area. Within the operations zone a slice, often over 100-miles deep, directly behind the front came under the control of the armies, each of which had appointed a *Korueck (Kommandant Rueckwaertiges Armeegebiet)*, the commandant of an army rear area. The remainder of the operations zone became the army group rear area. As the front moved east, the army group rear area commanders and the *Koruecks* became the military governors of broad stretches of Soviet territory.[42] The *Koruecks* and the army group rear area commanders were subordinate to their respective army and army group commanders, but they took their direction for the most part from the chief supply and administration officer *(Generalquartiermeister)* in the OKH. Before the

invasion, the OKH had set up nine security divisions, composed mostly of officers and men in the upper-age brackets and equipped with captured French and Czech weapons and vehicles. Each army group rear area command was assigned three of the security divisions.

On 1 September 1941, what was approximately the western two-thirds of the entire German operations zone had passed to two civilian *Reich* commissariats, the *Reichskommissariat Ostland* (the Baltic States and Belorussia) and the *Reichskommissariat Ukraine*. In the *Reich* commissariats, military security was in the hands of an armed forces commander who came under the OKW and, hence, functioned outside normal OKH Eastern Front command channels.

The SS, which exercised both police and military functions, also operated in the occupied territory, where it installed "higher" SS and police commanders *(Hoeherer SS-und Poliziefuehrer)* who were loosely affiliated with, but neither attached nor subordinate to, the *Reich* commissariats and the army group rear area commands. The SS and police commanders had at their disposal various kinds of police ranging from the secret state police *(Gestapo)* to the SS intelligence service *(Sicherheitsdienst, SD)* to German civil police and police auxiliaries recruited in the Baltic States.[43]

In a category by themselves were the *SS Einsatzgruppen* ("task groups"). They were neither police nor troops, although their personnel were drawn from both: their mission was mass kill-

---

[42]*AOK 4, O.Qu., Qu.2, Besondere Anordnungen fuer das Operationsgebiet, 8.6.41*, AOK 4 11193/9 file.

[43]*Befh. d. Rueckw. H. Geb. Mitte, Ia Hoeherer SS-und Polizeifuehrer, Stand vom 1.8.42*, H. Geb. 14684/2 file.

ing, pure and simple. They consisted of just four groups, designated by the letters "A" through "D," and their combined strength was barely over three thousand. But where they went, and they went nearly everywhere in the occupied territory, thousands died. The Jews were their primary target, but they also did away with communists or any others who might threaten or inconvenience the occupation.[44] The latter aspect of their operations may have significantly reduced the number of potential recruits for the underground.

In general, from the German point of view, control of the occupied territory had been adequately organized in 1941. Its main purposes were to subjugate and exploit a conquered population and to keep the front commands' lines of communications open, and those were being accomplished. Consequently, the army group rear area commanders, *Koruecks*, and SS and police commanders did not stage extensive antipartisan campaigns. During the rapid advance, their other missions were more urgent. The partisans were seen as a temporary annoyance that could be eradicated, in its turn, with minimum effort. The OKW advised, "The appropriate commanders are responsible for keeping order in their areas with the troops assigned to them. Commanders must find means for preserving order, not by demanding more security troops, but by resorting to the necessary Draconian measures."[45]

Army Group Center believed it could eliminate the partisans in its area after the front settled down for the winter by having each corps provide one motorized company to hunt down the partisans in the army areas and by detaching one division to do the same in the army group rear area.[46]

The Partisan Movement Established

Soviet Power Resurgent

The winter of 1941–1942 was bound to have been decisive for the partisan movement one way or the other. If the Germans had kept the initiative, the movement would probably have withered. If the Germans had held their own, they could also have kept the partisans in check. But when they could not do either, their latent vulnerability became outright weakness. General Leytenant Sokolovskiy, chief of staff of the *West Front*, saw the German predicament in the late summer when he remarked, "The enemy strong-points are separated by great stretches of territory. Many districts in his rear have not yet been brought under his control, and his defenses are thus subject to the blows of our partisans."[47] The Army Group Center rear area commander saw the danger in the first week of the Moscow counteroffensive and voiced his alarm on 14 December:

As the Russians have become more active on the front, partisan activity has in-

[44]See Raul Hilberg, *The Destruction of the European Jews* (Chicago: Quadrangle Books, 1961), pp. 182–90 and George H. Stein, *The Waffen SS* (Ithaca, N.Y.: Cornell University Press, 1966), p. 263.

[45]*OKW, WFSt/L (I Op.), Ergaenzung zur Weisung 33, 23.7.41,* NMT C–52/GB–485 file.

[46]*H. Gr. Mitte, Ia Richtlinien fuer Kampffuehrung im Winter und Besonderheiten des Winterkrieges in Russland, 10.11.41,* Pz. AOK 3 15415/42 file; *AOK 9, Ic/AO, O.Qu. 2, Partisanenbekaempfung, 18.8.41,* AOK 9 14008/9 file.

[47]*AOK 16, Ic, AO, Feindnachrichtenblatt Nr. 51, 15.8.41,* AOK 16 75873 file.

IMPROVISED ARMORED TRAIN ON PATROL AGAINST PARTISANS

creased. The troops left to this command are just sufficient to protect the most important installations and, to a certain extent, the railroads and highways. For active anti-partisan operations there are no longer any troops on hand. Therefore, it is expected that soon the partisans will join together into larger bands and carry out attacks on our guard posts. Their increased freedom of movement will also lead to the partisans' spreading terror among the people, who will be forced to stop supporting us and will then no longer carry out the orders of the military government authorities.[48]

The Moscow counteroffensive and the general offensive pumped new life into the partisan movement and accomplished a physical and psychologi-cal transformation so complete as to constitute virtually a whole new beginning. The *History of the Second World War* concedes as much when it states, "The winter of 1942 initiated the mass participation of Soviet patriots in partisan activity."[49] On the scene at the time, the Germans observed the phenomenon and ascribed it to influences other than patriotism. Fourth Army's *Korueck* reported:

The situation in the army rear area has undergone a fundamental change. As long as we were victorious, the area could be described as nearly pacified and almost free of partisans, and the population without exception stood on our side. Now the people are no longer as convinced as they

---

[48]*Befh. d. Rueckw. H. Geb. Mitte, Ia, Zufuehrung weiterer Sicherungskraefte, 14.12.41, H. Geb. 14684/file.*

[49]*IVMV*, vol. IV., p. 347.

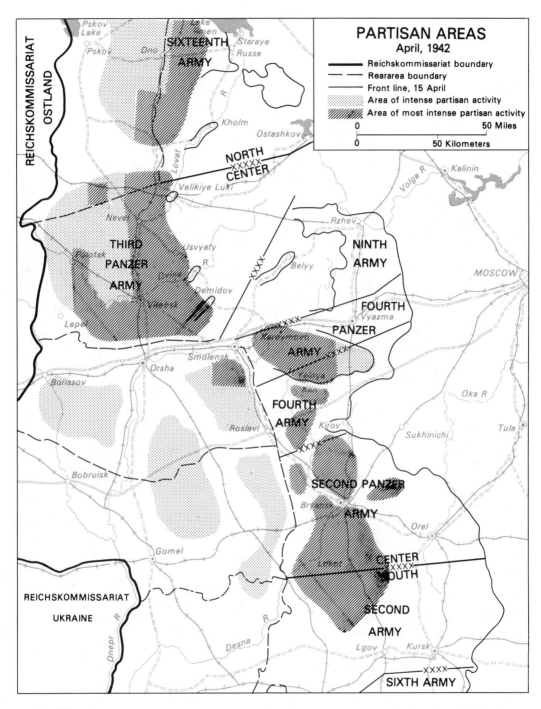

PARTISAN AREAS
April, 1942

——— Reichskommissariat boundary
– – – Reararea boundary
——— Front line, 15 April
Area of intense partisan activity
Area of most intense partisan activity

0   50 Miles
0   50 Kilometers

REICHSKOMMISSARIAT
OSTLAND

Pskov Lake
Lake Ilmen
Pskov
Staraya Russa
Dno

SIXTEENTH
ARMY

Kholm
Ostashkov

NORTH
XXXXX
CENTER

Lovat R
Velikiye Luki

Volga R
Kalinin

Rzhev

Nevel

NINTH
ARMY

MOSCOW

THIRD
PANZER
ARMY

Usvyaty
Belyy

Velizh
Demidov

FOURTH
PANZER

Vyazma

Lepel

ARMY

Smolensk
Orsha

Oka R

Borissov

FOURTH
ARMY

Roslavl
Kirov
Sukhinichi
Tula

Bobruisk

SECOND PANZER
ARMY

Bryansk
Orel

Gomel

CENTER
XXXXX
SOUTH

REICHSKOMMISSARIAT
UKRAINE

SECOND
ARMY

Dnepr R

Desna
Lgov
Kursk

XXXX
SIXTH ARMY

MAP 15

were before of our power and strength. New partisan bands have made their way into our territory; and parachutists have been sent in who assume the leadership of bands, assemble the civilians suitable for service along with the partisans who up to now had not been active, the escaped prisoners of war, and the Soviet soldiers who have been released from the military hospitals.[50]

The Fourth Army *Korueck* was in a good, though, in that winter, hardly unique, position to watch the partisan upsurge. Situated on the northern arc of the Sukhinichi bulge, with the Kirov gap on its right flank, Soviet cavalry and parachute troops behind its front, and its rear swept clean of security troops that had long ago been thrown into the front, Fourth Army was a prime target for partisan activity. What the *Korueck* believed it saw was not a mass patriotic uprising but Soviet power reaching into the occupied territory to bring the population back under its control. Through the Kirov gap, trained partisan cadres, under army and NKVD officers, were ranging deep behind the front, drafting the men to fill out their ranks. Their domain covered the entire Smolensk, Roslavl, Vyazma triangle, more than five thousand square miles.[51] (*Map 15.*)

To the south, around Bryansk, where the forest still harbored survivors of the Soviet units destroyed there during the fall, another partisan center had sprung up. From the great bulge *Third* and *Fourth Shock Armies* occupied around Toropets, partisan organizers were fanning out in all directions. Since virtually no front existed there, access was open to the deep rear areas of Army Groups North and Center and into the *Reichskommissariat Ostland* west to the Polish border. In February 1942, Field Marshal Kluge, then the commander of Army Group Center, told General Halder (chief of the General Staff):

The steady increase in the numbers of enemy troops behind our front and the concomitant growth of the partisan movement in the entire rear area are taking such a threatening turn that I am impelled to point out this danger in all seriousness.

While formerly the partisans limited themselves to disruption of communications lines and attacks on individual vehicles and small installations, now, under the leadership of resolute Soviet officers with plenty of weapons and good organization, they are attempting to bring certain districts under their control and to use those districts as bases from which to launch combat operations on a large scale. With this the initiative has passed into the hands of the enemy in many places where he already controls large areas and denies these areas to the German administration and German economic exploitation.[52]

While the German and Soviet accounts agree, in general, on what happened to the partisan movement in the winter of 1941–1942, they diverge widely as to why and how. Concerning the impetus for the partisans, the *History of the Great Patriotic War* asserts:

The victory of the Soviet troops before Moscow had an exceptional significance for the strengthening of the moral-political feeling of the Soviet people who were struggling in the enemy's rear and for the development of the partisan movement. News of the destruction of the Hitlerite armies on the approaches to the capital

---

[50]*Korueck 559, Abt. Qu., Lage im rueckwaertigen Armeegebiet, 25.2.42*, Korueck 29236/5 file.
[51]*Ibid.*

[52]*Ob. d.H. Gr. Mitte, an den Herrn Chef des Generalstabes des Heeres, 24.2.42*, Pz. AOK 3 20736/6 file.

quickly spread in the towns and villages of the occupied territory. This notable victory of the Red Army inspired the population of the occupied areas to a still more active struggle with the enemy. The Soviet people, who had suffered under the enemy yoke, strove to aid the Red Army in every way possible in order to expel the aggressors more quickly from the boundaries of our Motherland. They left their homes and went to the partisans. . . .[53]

The *History* describes the Soviet intervention as follows: "During the winter, the detachments and formations received new and qualified replacements from the rest of the nation. In the enemy's rear, via the gaps that had formed in the enemy's front and from the air, came radiomen, mine planters, and also party and *komsomol* workers who were specially trained for carrying out partisan warfare."[54]

The Partisans of Kardymovo

As was to be expected, the Germans seldom managed to penetrate the inner structure of the partisan network. One of the few instances in which they did occurred in March 1942 when the 10th Panzer Division uncovered a partisan detachment that was being organized near Smolensk. The detachment was distributed among several villages clustered around the railroad fifteen miles east of Smolensk. What was unique was that the Germans were able to capture and interrogate not only rank and file partisans but nearly all of the leaders, a total of fifty-five men and women.

The action began when a civilian in one of the villages, Molokovo, reported one of his neighbors as a partisan. The investigation led to the nearby village of Sokolovo and the arrest of a section leader, his commissar, 2 platoon leaders, 4 liaison men, and 7 partisans. Rigorous interrogations of these people over a three weeks' period turned up leads to some weapons caches, most of which had already been emptied, and to other echelons of the detachment.

One trail led to Shaduby and the arrest of another section leader, who admitted to being an NKVD man who had been sent through the lines to organize partisans but who hanged himself in his cell before more information could be extracted from him. A second trail ended at Kardymovo, which proved to have been the command center for the whole detachment, and there the 10th Panzer Division captured the commander, the commissar, and 38 partisans. The Kardymovo headquarters had consisted of a commander, a commissar, a deputy commissar, 4 liaison persons (women), 8 section leaders (each assigned a village in which he directed the partisan activity), and a number of persons who carried out special assignments.

The commander was a Major Gasparyan, a regular army officer detailed to command the partisans by the Headquarters, *West Front*. He had kept his subordinates in hand with utter ruthlessness, and those who were captured with him shook with fear even when they faced him in jail. From him the Germans learned nothing, and he was beaten to death during the interrogation. The commissar, who inspired almost as much fear as the commander, did disclose that he had come through the front several months earlier, after having been trained as a partisan

---

[53]*IVOVSS*, vol. II, p. 355.
[54]*Ibid.*, p. 349.

organizer, and that he had worked in Smolensk as a locomotive engineer before joining Gasparyan at Kardymovo.[55]

Based on interrogations of all the prisoners, among whom were twelve women, the 10th Panzer Division report concluded:

Terror was the most important motivation. Betrayal, hesitation to participate, or failure to fulfill missions were declared to be punishable by death. At the very least, a 'certain and horrible' death was promised after the return of the Soviet forces. It is important for the sovereignty of the German administration that the Russian fears his own 'Red' comrades far more than he fears the German authorities. For example, if a peasant has a cache of weapons in his house, he will not reveal it to the Germans out of fear of the vengeance of his comrades even though he is at the same time threatened with death by the Germans.[56]

The Movement Remodeled

In late July 1941, the then *Central Front* set up a school to train partisan commanders, commissars, mine and demolition specialists, and agents and radio operators. Taken over later by *West Front*, the school turned out over four thousand persons in the last four months of the year. Similar schools, apparently also under military auspices, were run in Kiev, Kharkov, Poltava, and other cities. On orders of the Central Committee of the Soviet Communist Party, three schools were established in January 1942: one to instruct party and *komsomol* members in underground and partisan activity, one to produce partisan leadership personnel, and the third to train radiomen.[57]

By March 1942, so-called operative groups were formed to work with and work under army commands, particularly in sectors where the lay of the front, or absence of it, gave ready access to the enemy rear. Headed usually by a party functionary, they were composed of party, army, and NKVD personnel who had some form of competence relative to partisan activity. Their functions were to recruit, organize, equip, and control the partisans across the front and make them, in effect, an adjunct of the army to which the operative group was attached.

Among the first and most effective of the operative groups was the one with *Fourth Shock Army* in the Toropets bulge, where the front practically had dissolved in January 1942. There a twenty-mile-wide gap on the western rim of the bulge, sometimes called the Vitebsk Corridor and other times the "Surazh Gate," spanned the whole of the Usvyaty and Surazh *rayons*, northeast of Vitebsk. Through the gap, men and horse and wagon columns kept up steady traffic in both directions, carrying in weapons and ammunition for the partisans and taking out supplies for *Fourth Shock Army*. The partisan units, the former *Shmyrev Otryad* which, as a brigade, was the most prominent of them, reportedly passed thousands of tons of grain, hay, and potatoes and several thousand head of cattle through the Soviet side. They are said also to have mobilized and delivered

---

[55]*10. Pz. Div., 7 Pz. Rgt., Pz. Werkstattkompanie, Partisanenbekaempfung, 11.3.42*, 10 Pz. Div. 23245 file.
[56]*Ibid.*

[57]*IVMV*, vol. V, p. 418f.

25,000 recruits for the Soviet Army.[58] Before the end of March 1942, the operative group with *Fourth Shock Army* had brought the strength of the partisan units in its area from 500 to almost 7,500, a fifteenfold increase.[59]

As of December 1941, apparently, few partisan detachments had had strengths of more than fifty, the prescribed minimum. By February 1942, the average for both old and new detachments had been between two and three hundred, and by April, some were over a thousand. Under the increasing army influence, those in the range of one to three thousand members were beginning to be called regiments and brigades and to adopt the organizational features of regular military units. The *1st Smolensk Partisan Division,* which operated for a time in conjunction with Belov's *I Guards Cavalry Corps,* claimed a strength of over five thousand. The operative group with *Third Shock Army,* on the northern arc of the Toropets bulge, united 7 brigades and 3 *otryads* to form the *I Kalinin Partisan Corps.* The operative group with *Fourth Shock Army* transformed what had been 14 average *otryads* into 7 brigades, 2 regiments, and 7 independent *otryads.* The shift to large units also brought into existence the partisan *kray* (a stretch of territory, sometimes a whole *rayon,* in which a brigade or several brigades held un-

challenged sway). Reportedly, 4 of those were established in Belorussia in the spring of 1942, and 4 in the Smolensk *Oblast* of the RSFSR.[60]

The shift toward the brigade and territorial forms was accomplished by combining units as well as by expanded recruitment. As a result, the independent detachments, such as the *Shmyrev Otryad,* had all but disappeared. There were advantages to consolidation both for the partisans and for the Soviet authorities: for the partisans, more security and recognition, and, on the Soviet side, more effective control and surveillance. During the shift, also, the partisan movement became tied to the army and ceased to be more than a token party activity. The regiment and brigade commanders were often still party men, but they had military advisers at their sides, and their orders came through military channels. The units were organized on the regular army model, including the O.O. sections of the NKVD to keep all personnel under political police scrutiny.

From the Soviet standpoint, the partisan movement was a weapon to be exploited with caution as well as enthusiasm. When arms were placed in the hands of the citizenry at large, there was no telling how they might ultimately be used. The winter's recruits, in the majority peasants and soldiers who had been hiding out since the last summer, were, in Soviet terms, far short of being the most reliable elements. And the peasants, who comprised the largest and least voluntary contingent of the partisan rank and file, harbored memories of the forced

---

[58]Although it appears to have been Soviet practice to do more detailed quantitative bookkeeping on the achievements of the partisans and the underground than on almost any other aspect of the war, the figures on these activities tend to vary from place to place. See A. I. Zalesskiy, *Geroicheskiy podvig millionov v tylu vraga* (Minsk: Izdatelstvo "Belarus," 1970), p. 141 and P. Vershigora, *Lyudi s chistoi sovestyu* (Moscow: Sovetskiy pisatel, 1951), p. 394.

[59]*IVMV,* vol. IV, p. 346.

[60]*IVOVSS,* vol. II, p. 351; *IVMV,* vol. V, p. 347; *Ibid.,* vol. IV, p. 353.

collectivization of the 1930s. One example, perhaps from many, of the mixed loyalties of the Soviet population that did not escape the attention of Soviet authorities occurred in the Lokot *rayon,* south of Bryansk. There, in the heart of partisan territory, an anti-Soviet Russian engineer of Polish extraction, Bronislav Kaminski, had organized a force of nearly fifteen-hundred volunteers who had fought the Soviet partisans throughout the winter under the tsarist emblem, the St. George's Cross. The Kaminski organization also grew and reached a strength of 9,000 by late spring. In the early summer, the Germans, who themselves were able to do little against the partisans in this area, turned the entire *rayon* over to Kaminski as the *Selbstverwaltungsbezirk* ("autonomous district") Lokot. The *History of the Second World War* lists the task of convincing the people to boycott such autonomous areas as being among the priority missions of the party underground.[61]

While the remodeling and expansion of the partisan movement increased Soviet control of the movement, the effort and material expended were probably not repaid in operating effectiveness. The *History of the Second World War* maintains that it was "necessary" to combine the smaller units, and the brigade was the "most appropriate" form into which they could be combined.[62] The *History of the Great Patriotic War,* on the other hand, says, ". . . it was not expedient to develop large partisan formations."[63] The big units lost mobility and tended to become preoccupied with self-defense, naturally enough, since concealment became more difficult. They were also neither heavily enough armed nor sufficiently proficient tactically to challenge the Germans in open combat, and they were too conspicuous to operate covertly against really vital targets. They could establish territorial hegemony, but usually only in areas in which German control would have been superficial anyway. P. K. Ponomarenko, who as first secretary of the Belorussian Communist Party and chief of the Central Staff of the Partisan Movement was closely associated with the partisan activity throughout the war, has said that the trend toward larger units actually played into the hands of the Germans.[64]

In Ponomarenko's view, the root of the problem had been in the absence of central direction during 1941 and early 1942, which resulted in "a variety of ill-conceived experiments and an outbreak of faulty tendencies."[65] The *History of the Great Patriotic War* and the *Short History* also mention "errors" and "incorrect . . . forms and methods" in the organization of the movement.[66] The *History of the Second World War* states, "Absence of a single directing organ frequently resulted in duplication and occasionally also led to divergences on organizational questions."[67] Committees had been appointed in the

---

[61]Edgar M. Howell, *The Soviet Partisan Movement, 1941–1944* (Washington, D.C.: GPO, 1956), p. 89; *IVMV,* vol. IV, p. 354.

[62]*IVMV,* vol. V, p. 286.

[63]*IVOVSS,* vol. II, p. 361.

[64]See P. Ponomarenko, "*Borba sovetskogo naroda v tylu vraga,*" *Voyenno-istoricheskiy Zhurnal,* 4(1965), 35.

[65]*Ibid.,* p. 35.

[66]*IVOVSS,* vol. II, p. 349; *VOV (Kratkaya Istoriya),* p. 84.

[67]*IVMV,* vol. V, p. 284.

summer of 1941 to guide and organize the partisan activity at the republic and lower levels.[68] Ponomarenko says a decision had been made in July 1941 to establish a national "commission" with him, Mekhlis, "and others" as members, but it had "stayed on paper." In November, Stalin had charged Ponomarenko with setting up a central staff that had not materialized, according to Ponomarenko, because Lavrenti Beria, the NKVD chief, had insisted he could manage the movement by himself, "without a special staff."[69]

Finally, on 30 May 1942, Beria had lost his bid for control, and the State Defense Committee had established the Central Staff of the Partisan Movement, with Ponomarenko as its chief. The State Defense Committee decision also, Ponomarenko indicates, made the central staff a command for the partisan movement, not merely an organ working under party direction. Although Ponomarenko and the chiefs of his subordinate staffs were party men, the directive setting up the central staff shifted the partisan movement closer to the military. Ponomarenko and his staff were attached to the Headquarters of the Supreme Commander, Stalin, and staffs were ordered to be created and attached to Headquarters, *Southwestern Theater*, and the *Bryansk, West Kalinin, Leningrad*, and *Karelian Fronts*.[70]

The establishment of the central staff also brought about a revision in the estimated strength of the partisan movement. The *Great Soviet Encyclopedia* gives a party figure of 125,000 persons in the movement on 30 June 1942 and a separate central staff figure of 60,000.[71] The *History of the Second World War* gives a total of 72,000 for "the spring of 1942," distributed as follows: 6,000 behind Army Group North and in Karelia, 56,000 behind Army Group Center, and 10,000 behind Army Group South.[72] While it is said that these figures are based on incomplete records, it seems apparent that the numbers given above for the end of 1941 need to be revised downward.[73] By how much, may be roughly indicated by the factor of fifteen which the *History of the Second World War* indicates applied in the area under the *Fourth Shock Army* operative group's control.

Accomplices Against the Bolshevik System?

The Soviet successes in the winter made it certain that the war would last through another summer—very likely, much longer—and the partisan movement would be a genuine challenge to the Germans' hold on the occupied territory. Certainly a German victory was not going to come easily, if at all. Concentration and economy of effort, always worthwhile, had become absolute necessities, and forces diverted to antipartisan operations would be wasted as far as progress in the war was concerned. An alternative, the only one in fact available to the Germans, was to create an indigenous counterresistance. The obstacle was Hitler's avowed determination not to allow natives of the occupied territory in the

[68] Andrianov, "*Rukovodstvo*," p. 61.
[69] Ponomarenko, "*Borba*," p. 34.
[70] *Ibid.*, p. 34f; *IVMV*, vol. V, p. 284.

[71] *Bolshaya Sovetskaya Entsiklopediya*, 3d ed., 1978, vol. 19, p. 235.
[72] *IVMV*, vol. V, p. 342.
[73] See p. 205f.

WOMAN PARTISAN HANGED FROM
LENIN STATUE IN VORONEZH

Soviet Union to serve in any military or police capacity.

During the worst of the winter, Army Group Center did, finally, get permission to experiment with some local police, who were called *Ordnungsdienst* ("order service") and not police, and to recruit a few Cossack and Ukrainian detachments from prisoner-of-war camps and form them into what were called *Hundertschaften* ("hundreds") to give them only the most nebulous military character. Both had one asset, they had men who knew the language, and the *Ordnungsdienst* men usually knew the local countryside and its people, often including the partisans.

What they did not have was a cause, and the Soviet effort had become too pervasive to be mastered by mercenaries and collaborators. Under the

strain of the winter, the German Army saw that. In evaluating the *Ordnungsdienst,* the Army Group Center rear area commander stated, "One condition for the successful organization of the *Ordnungsdienst* is that the population be kept [*sic*] friendly to the Germans by a distribution of land and by the recognition of certain national aspirations."[74]

When Field Marshal Bock took command of Army Group South from Field Marshal Reichenau, he found in Reichenau's papers the draft of a letter to Hitler proposing an alliance with the Russian people. Bock forwarded it to the OKH with his endorsement.[75] Later talking to a representative of the Ministry for the Occupied Eastern Areas, Bock urged making the Russian people "accomplices against the Bolshevik system" by giving them land and restoring religion. Only then, he contended, would the population have an interest in preventing the return of the Soviet regime.[76] Like Bock, most German observers believed that even after the winter, the peasants' longing for land of their own could still be exploited to draw them into an alliance against the Soviet regime. (The Germans had not abolished the collective farms because they found them a convenient means of economic exploitation.) For the commands in the East, such an alliance appeared to be worth the price and more. The Third Panzer Army counterintelligence chief observed, "An effective anti-partisan campaign is conceivable only if it in-

---

[74]*Befh. d. Rueckw. H. Geb. Mitte, Vorschlaege zur Vernichtung der Partisanen im Rueckw. H. Geb. und den rueckw. Armeegebieten, 1.3.42,* H. Geb. 24693/2 file.
[75]*Bock Diary, Osten II,* 24 Jan 42.
[76]*Ibid.,* 5 Mar 42.

cludes the assistance of dependable elements of the population."[77]

Hitler, however, was not to be persuaded. During the worst of the winter, he was saying, "We'll get our hands on the finest [Soviet] land. . . . We'll know how to keep the population in order. There won't be any question of our arriving there with kid gloves and dancing masters."[78] In April, he declared, "The most foolish mistake we could possibly make would be to allow the subject races to bear arms. So let's not have any native militia or police. German troops alone will bear the sole responsibility for the maintenance of law and order throughout the occupied Russian territories."[79]

---

[77]*Pz. AOK 3, Ic/AO, Abwehrnachrichtenblatt, 19.3.42,* Pz. AOK 3 20839/2 file.

[78]*Secret Conversations,* p. 265.

[79]*Ibid.,* p. 345.

CHAPTER XI

The Northern Theater

Cobelligerents and Brothers-in-Arms

The military objectives of the German-Finnish cobelligerency in 1941 were to interdict the Murmansk (Kirov) Railroad and to secure overland contact between the German and Finnish forces. For Germany, or rather for Hitler both objectives served psychological and political ends more than they did strategic necessities. The first would demonstrate to the British and Americans, as well as to the Soviet Union, the futility of outside aid or intervention. The second would confirm German hegemony in the Baltic and Scandinavian areas. Neither of those effects would have been in any doubt if operations against the Soviet main forces went as planned.

The OKH, for its part, was primarily concerned with employing the light but good Finnish Army as an adjunct to Army Group North.[1] The drive to the Murmansk Railroad, which was to be conducted by the German Army of Norway as a second assignment, indeed almost a summer exercise, Halder dismissed as a mere "expedition." To Finland, Hitler's objectives offered the opportunity to regain all of the territory ceded to the Soviet Union after the Winter War of 1939–1940; nevertheless, for Finland, also, the real decision hinged entirely on the outcome of the contest between the German and Soviet main forces.

The 1941 campaign ended without either of Hitler's objectives being attained. In the summer, the Army of Norway, under Generaloberst Nikolaus von Falkenhorst, had staged a trio of attacks out of northern Finland toward the Murmansk Railroad: one by a German corps along the Arctic coast from the vicinity of Pechenga toward Murmansk; another, 150 miles to the south, by a German corps via Salla, 30 miles north of the Arctic Circle, toward Kandalaksha on the railroad; and the third by an attached Finnish corps, south of the Arctic Circle, toward Loukhi also on the railroad. *(Map 16.)* The first had stalled completely the last week of September on the Zapadnaya Litsa River 40 miles west of Murmansk. The other two Hitler ordered stopped in the second week of October when it appeared that the drive on Moscow would end the war before either could be completed.[2] The Finnish Army had pushed southeast along the Isthmuses of Karelia and Olonets. After reaching the pre-1940 border on the Isthmus of Karelia and at the Svir River east of Lake Ladoga in the first week of September, the army had stopped, consid-

---

[1] For the preinvasion plans see Ziemke, *Northern Theater,* pp. 113–36.

[2] *Der Fuehrer und Oberste Befehlshaber der Wehrmacht, WFSt, Abt. L (I Op.), Nr. 441696/41, Weisung 37, 10.10.41,* AOK 20 19070/3 file.

NORTHERN THEATER
Winter 1942
---- Front line

0   100 Miles
0   100 Kilometers

BARENTS SEA

NORWAY
FINLAND

Rybachiy
Peninsula

Pechenga

Norway
Mtn

Murmansk

Zapadnaya

Litsa R

14th

ARMY
OF
LAPLAND

XXXVI Mtn

Kandalaksha

KARELIAN
FRONT

26th (Apr 42)

Salla

Rovaniemi

Loukhi

WHITE
SEA

Tornio

Kestenga

III Finnish

Ukhta

LAPLAND

Belomorsk

Rugozero

U.S.S.R.
FINLAND

LAKE

Svir R

Helsinki

Finnish
Forces

LADOGA

7th
Independent

LENINGRAD FRONT

GULF OF FINLAND

Leningrad

EIGHTEENTH ARMY

MAP 16

ering its contribution made, and had waited for Army Group North to complete the junction from the south.

The OKW would have preferred a combined command for the front in Finland and had expected to offer it to Marshal Mannerheim, commander in chief of the Finnish Army, but the Finns had insisted on what they called a brotherhood-in-arms that kept the commands separate except for the token attachment of Finnish III Corps to Army of Norway for the attack toward Loukhi and the German 163d Infantry Division to the Finnish Army as Mannerheim's reserve.[3] As the summer campaign drew to a close, the Finnish conception of the brotherhood-in-arms changed markedly. On 25 September, Mannerheim refused a request from the OKW to resume the advances on the Isthmus of Karelia and the Svir River stating that Finland could not afford to maintain 16 percent of its population in military service, as it had been doing, and his next task would, therefore, have to be to reorganize the army by reducing the divisions to brigades and returning the released men to civilian employment.[4] Shortly afterward he asked to have German troops take over the III Corps positions so that the corps could be returned to him for the reorganization. In mid-November, Kenraalimajuri ("Major General") H. Siilasvuo, the III Corps commander, after having agreed with Falkenhorst

[3] OKW, WFSt, Abt. L, Nr. 44594/41, Vorschlag fuer die Vorbereitung der Besprechungen ueber Beteiligung Finnlands am Unternehmen "Barbarossa," 28.4.41, OKW/1938 file; Mannerheim, Erinnerungen, p. 450.
[4] Verbindungsstab Nord, Ia Nr. 84/41, Oberbefehlshaber der finnischen Wehrmacht an Herrn Generalfeldmarschall Keitel, 25.9.41, AOK 20 20844/2 file.

that a late season breakthrough to Loukhi might succeed, suddenly cancelled the operation, saying only that he was "not in a position" to continue it.[5]

Pressures on Finland

The Finns' successes in the field raised troubles for them in other respects. In late September and early October the British and United States governments had both warned them against invading Soviet territory. On 27 October the United States had demanded that Finland cease all offensive operations, adding, " . . . should material of war sent from the United States to Soviet territory in the north by way of the Arctic Ocean be attacked on route either presumably or even allegedly from territory under Finnish control in the present state of opinion in the United States such an incident must be expected to bring about an instant crisis in relations between Finland and the United States."[6]

On the other hand, Finland was having difficulty keeping what political distance it had between itself and Germany. In October, the Germans, irked by the Finnish contacts with the West, pointedly invited Finland to join the Anti-Comintern Pact, which was due for renewal the following month. The pact was not a military alliance, but it was regarded worldwide as the cornerstone of the Rome-Berlin-Tokyo Axis. At the same time, Finland was

finding itself forced to ask Germany for 150,000 tons of grain to tide its population over the winter and for 100 to 150 locomotives and 4,000 to 8,000 railroad cars to keep its transportation system running. The Finnish railroads, which had a low hauling capacity to start with, had deteriorated rapidly after the war broke out and were on the verge of a complete collapse. Since the Army of Norway also depended on the railroads, the OKW promised some locomotives and cars, but it was less forthcoming on the request for grain. On 25 November, Finnish Foreign Minister Rolf Witting signed the Anti-Comintern Pact in Berlin under the spotlight of as much publicity as the German Foreign Ministry could arrange. Two weeks later, Britain declared war, and on 19 December, Germany agreed to supply Finland with 70,000 tons of grain before the end of February 1942 and a total of 260,000 tons before the next harvest.[7]

Command and Deployment

At the turn of the year, Falkenhorst returned to Norway, and the Army of Norway forces in Finland became Army of Lapland, under General der Gebirgstruppe Eduard Dietl. Falkenhorst, whether deservedly or not, had been tagged as a hard-luck general by the 1941 campaign, and his abrasive personality did not make him the best man to deal with the Finns when relations were delicate. Dietl,

[5]Generalkommando III A.K., N. 652/III/3.b., an Herrn Oberbefehlshaber der Armee Norwegen, 19.11.41, AOK 20 20844/2 file.

[6]William L. Langer and S. Everett Gleason, The Undeclared War, 1940–1941 (New York: Harper and Brothers, 1953), p. 831.

[7]Der Chef des Oberkommandos der Wehrmacht, WFSt, Abt. L (I Op.), Nr. 441979/41, an Se. Exzellenz Generalfeldmarschall Freiherr von Mannerheim, 21.11.41, H 22/227; Dir. Ha. Pol., Aufzeichnung, No. 226, 19.12.41, Serial 1260, U.S. Department of State, German Foreign Ministry Records.

who had commanded the attack toward Murmansk, had not been much more lucky in Finland, but he had been the hero of the 1940 campaign in Norway. He was also one of the few generals whom Hitler liked and trusted. In creating the Army of Lapland, the OKW also saw an opportunity to tie Mannerheim more closely to German interests by offering him the supreme command in Finland. Mannerheim stated in his memoirs that in the winter of 1941–1942, such an offer was made to him, and he refused it.[8] Dietl's first task, with active operations by both sides having stopped six weeks before he took command, was to regroup Army of Lapland and return the attached Finnish units to Mannerheim.

In the far north, Dietl's former command, Mountain Corps Norway, passed to Generalleutnant Ferdinand Schoerner. He had two mountain divisions and two infantry regiments, a ten-mile front on the Zapadnaya Litsa River, and a four-mile front across the neck of the Rybachiy Peninsula, which had been bypassed during the summer's advance. He stationed one division, 6th Mountain, in the river line; a regiment, the 288th Infantry, on the peninsula; and held the 2d Mountain Division and 193d Infantry Regiment in reserve at Pechenga. Schoerner was known by his troops—as he would be by the whole German Army before the war was over—as a ruthlessly determined general. Told that the Arctic winter's darkness and cold were affecting morale, he issued the order: "*Arktis*

ist nicht." ("The Arctic does not exist.")

The XXXVI Mountain Corps held a line on the Verman River forty miles east of Salla and sixty miles short of its 1941 objective, Kandalaksha. The corps was a mountain corps by courtesy only. It consisted of one infantry division, the 169th, plus one infantry and one mountain regiment. General der Infanterie Karl. F. Weisenberger had taken command of the corps in November 1941 after the drive to Kandalaksha had failed.

Finnish III Corps had two fronts: one twenty-five miles west of Loukhi held by the SS Division "Nord" and Finnish Division J, the other held by the Finnish 3d Division eight miles west of Ukhta. The two were separated by forty miles of lake and forest. The Division "Nord" was composed of two SS "death's-head" regiments that were trained as police and concentration camp guards not as combat units. Division J had been created in the summer by dividing the 3d Division. Since the SS Division "Nord" had performed erratically during the summer, it was to be returned to Germany and replaced by another SS division when one became available. One regiment departed in December, leaving the division with an actual strength of three infantry and two motorized machine gun battalions.

Mannerheim's reorganization of the Finnish Army was less thoroughgoing than he had planned. During the winter he furloughed 100,000 older men and men with essential civilian occupations, but the conversion of divisions to brigades proceeded slowly, and he finally abandoned this effort in May 1942, after he had converted two divisions. The III Corps stayed with Army

---

[8]General der Infanterie a.D. Waldemar Erfurth, Comments on Part II of Ziemke, *Northern Theater,* 6 May 1956, CMH files; Mannerheim, *Erinnerungen,* p. 472.

OUTPOST ON THE VERMAN RIVER LINE

of Lapland through the winter because Mannerheim retained an interest for a time in an operation against the Murmansk Railroad and because Army of Lapland did not have any troops with which to take over the corps' front. The German 5th and 7th Mountain Divisions, originally earmarked as reinforcements for XXXVI Mountain Corps, could have done so, but only one regiment arrived before ice closed the Finnish Baltic ports.[9]

A Thrust to Belomorsk

On 25 September, at the same time as he refused to carry farther the Finnish offensives on the Svir and the Isthmus of Karelia, Mannerheim presented a proposal to the OKW for a winter offensive to be directed against Belomorsk, the Soviet port on the White Sea at which the Murmansk Railroad branched southward toward Leningrad and southeastward via Obozerskaya toward Moscow. He thought that after Leningrad had fallen he would be able to spare eight or nine brigades for such an operation and that the German and Finnish advances toward Kandalaksha and Loukhi could be continued at the same time.[10] Hitler and the OKW took up Mannerheim's proposal immediately. It was more than welcome at *Fuehrer* Headquarters as a chance for a fresh start for the then nearly moribund operations against the Murmansk Railroad, and Hitler promptly designated the 5th and 7th Mountain Divisions as reinforcements for the thrust to Kandalaksha. He also elevated XXXVI Corps to the status of a mountain corps.

During the late fall, after the Germans and Finns had stopped everywhere else, part of the Finnish Army kept on the move through Eastern Karelia reaching Rugozero, sixty miles west of Belomorsk, in early December. Army Group North, meanwhile, had been stopped for more than two months around Leningrad and was stalled at Tikhvin. To the last of several OKW communications on the projected winter operation, Mannerheim replied on 4 December that he regarded the cutting of the Murmansk Railroad as extremely important; but, he pointed out, his proposal in September had been predicated on the

---

[9]*Ibid.*, p. 470.

[10]*Verbindungsstab Nord, Ia Nr. 84/41, Oberbefehlshaber der finnischen Wehrmacht an Herrn Generalfeldmarschall Keitel, 25.9.41,* AOK 20 20844/2 file.

assumption that Leningrad would fall and contact would be established on the Svir in a few weeks. Since then the condition of his troops had deteriorated and the war had created internal troubles for Finland. The attack on Kandalaksha, he thought, would have to begin on 1 March at the latest, and he added, somewhat bleakly, that Finnish troops would begin the drive to Belomorsk at the same time, "if the situation in any way permits."[11]

On 14 December, following a staff conference at Finnish Army Headquarters, Mannerheim and Falkenhorst met at Falkenhorst's headquarters in Rovaniemi. By then, because of the railroad situation, which he described as catastrophic, Mannerheim was taking a dim view of the Kandalaksha operation—so dim, according to Falkenhorst, that he was unwilling to risk involving Finnish troops in it. On the other hand, he maintained that the British declaration of war on Finland and the United States' entry into the war had given the Murmansk Railroad greatly increased significance, and it would have to be cut. He believed Belomorsk was the key point and proposed converging attacks from the west and southwest by combined German and Finnish forces. The OKW promptly accepted the change in the operation and offered him the 7th Mountain Division, then still expected to arrive in Finland during the winter.[12]

Before long, however, as the Soviet winter offensive developed, Mannerheim's determination flagged again.

On 20 January, General der Infanterie Waldemar Erfurth, chief of the OKW liaison staff at Finnish Army Headquarters, reported that the question of a Belomorsk operation was completely up in the air and Mannerheim would not make a positive decision unless the situation on the German front, particularly around Leningrad, improved. Erfurth could only recommend that all possible means of persuasion be brought to bear on Mannerheim. The other Finnish officers he thought were less pessimistic, but none of them had any influence.[13] In response, Field Marshal Keitel, chief of the OKW, wrote to Mannerheim, telling him that the Russians were wearing themselves out in their attacks and before spring would have exhausted their reserves. "This," he told the marshal, "can be expected also to help your intended operation in the direction of Sorokka [Belomorsk]."[14]

In the first week of February, Dietl, who was by then commanding the Army of Lapland, also discussed the Belomorsk operation with Mannerheim. During the conversation, Mannerheim avoided a direct refusal to involve his forces, repeatedly stating that things would be different if the Germans were to take Leningrad, but he left no doubt that in the existing situation he would not stage a winter offensive. Erfurth, who reported on the conference to the OKW, concluded that, in addition to his negative assessment of the war, Mannerheim was in-

---

[11] *Oberbefehlshaber der finnischen Wehrmacht an Herrn Generalfeldmarschall Keitel, 4.12.41,* H 22/227 file.

[12] *Verbindungsstab Nord, Ia, an OKH, GenStdH, Op. Abt., 15.12.41,* H 22/227 file.

[13] *Verbindungsstab Nord, Ia Nr. 13/41, nachr. OKH, Chef des GenStdH, 20.1.41,* H 22/227 file.

[14] *Der Chef des Oberkommandos der Wehrmacht, Nr. 55208/42, an den Oberbefehlshaber der finnischen Wehrmacht, 26.1.42,* H 22/227 file.

fluenced by Finnish domestic politics. He and Risto Ryti, the president of Finland, had for months promised the people that the end was in sight and only another small effort would be needed. An offensive against Belomorsk would far exceed what the Finnish government had led the population to expect. Above all, Erfurth stated, Mannerheim would not undertake such an operation if it were possible that he might suffer a setback.[15]

On 3 February, Mannerheim answered Keitel's letter, saying that, if the war did not take a favorable turn soon, he doubted whether he would be able to make troops available for a winter operation against Belomorsk, but he would not give up the idea.[16] In Erfurth's opinion, "a favorable turn" meant that Leningrad would have to be taken before Mannerheim would undertake another offensive. He needed the fall of Leningrad, Erfurth added, to make troops available and for the sake of morale at home; moreover, as inquiries from the Finnish chief of staff revealed, he recently had become worried that the German 1942 offensive would be concentrated in the Ukraine and the northern sector of the Eastern Front would be left to languish. As far as Mannerheim's keeping the Belomorsk operation in mind was concerned, Erfurth believed it was merely intended to give his letter a courteous tone and could not be taken as a commitment either for the present or the future.[17]

The Soviet Spring Offensive

Initially, the *Leningrad Military District*, which became *North Front* at the outbreak of the war, was responsible for the Finnish-Soviet frontier. It had *Twenty-third Army* between the Gulf of Finland and the north shore of Lake Ladoga, *Seventh Army* north of the lake, and *Fourteenth Army* in the Murmansk-Kandalaksha area. On 23 August 1941, *North Front* became *Leningrad Front* and soon thereafter lost direct contact with its original armies except for *Twenty-third Army*, which held the line across the Isthmus of Karelia north of Leningrad. Subsequently, *Seventh Army* became an independent army, and on 1 September, *Karelian Front* was activated, under General Leytenant V. A. Frolov, to take over the 550-mile sector from Lake Onega north to the Arctic coast west of Murmansk.[18]

Karelian Front did not figure in the Soviet general offensive, but neither was it out of the *Stavka*'s eye, particularly not in the late winter as the likelihood grew to a certainty that the Germans would be able to mount a second summer campaign. Frolov was given orders in early April 1942 to attack along the line from the Zapadnaya Litsa River to Kestenga and to drive the enemy back to the Finnish border. Winter lingers long in the northern latitudes, and the *Karelian Front* operations, therefore, took on the appearance of a postscript to the general offensive. They evolved, in fact, from the Soviet strategy for the coming spring and summer.[19]

---

[15]*Verbindungsstab Nord, Ia Nr. 20/42, an OKW, WFSt, Abt. L, 2.2.42,* H 22/227 file.

[16]*Verbindungsstab Nord, Ia Nr. 24/42, an OKH, GenStdH, Op. Abt., 3.2.41,* H 22/227 file.

[17]*Verbindungsstab Nord, Ia Nr. 25/42, an OKH, Op. Abt., 9.2.42,* H 22/227 file.

---

[18]See *IVMV,* vol. IV, maps 2 and 5.

[19]*Ibid.,* vol. V, p. 115. See pp. 238–40.

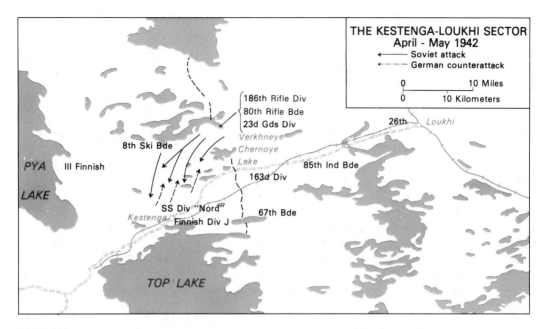

MAP 17

The Buildup

Karelian Front's deployment had remained static through the winter. Headquarters, *Fourteenth Army,* kept two divisions, two brigades, three border regiments, and two machine gun battalions standing against Mountain Corps Norway along the Zapadnaya Litsa River. Frolov kept the command on the approaches to Kandalaksha and Loukhi under his own headquarters. During the winter, he had two divisions, a border regiment, and two ski battalions on the Verman River line opposite XXXVI Mountain Corps and two divisions, two brigades, a border regiment, and three ski battalions facing Finnish III Corps.[20]

In the first two weeks of April, the picture changed suddenly—and, for Army of Lapland, disconcertingly. A guards division and two ski brigades joined the *Fourteenth Army* force on the Zapadnaya Litsa; Headquarters, *Twenty-sixth Army* moved in opposite the III Corps main force west of Kestenga, bringing with it two new divisions; and the ski battalions in the lines opposing XXXVI Mountain Corps and III Corps were raised to brigade strength. The buildup was diminutive by the standards of the main front but enormous for the Far North. It was possible for the Russians only because they had the Murmansk Railroad but impossible for the Germans and Finns to match.

On 13 April, III Corps canceled a small attack it was about to start when air reconnaissance reported over 700 cars in the Loukhi railroad yards, but

---

[20]*AOK 20, Ic Taetigkeitsbericht fuer die Zeit vom 1.4–31.12.42, 6.3.42,* AOK 20 27252/19 file.

the weather thereafter was so bad that the only new Soviet units identified were the two ski brigades in the Mountain Corps Norway sector. Considering how late the season was, the tempo of the final Soviet deployment was, in fact, somewhat sluggish, and when the third week in April had passed and nothing had happened, it looked to Dietl as if the Russians had concluded that they could not outrace the oncoming thaw.[21] He was wrong, at least to the extent of having failed to appreciate the Soviet determination to seize the initiative and to exploit the fading winter by getting in one more blow.

Double Strikes

On the morning of 23 April, *23d Guards Division* and *8th Ski Brigade* hit the thinly held III Corps left flank east of Kestenga. Frontal attacks on the center and right pinned the corps tight between Verkhneye Chernoye Lake and Top Lake. In two days the III Corps left flank cracked. By then enough was known about the extent of the Soviet buildup to make it apparent that the least to be expected was an effort to smash the corps front and drive it west of Kestenga. Dietl had in reserve one tank battalion, equipped with obsolete Panzer Is (armed with two 30-caliber machine guns), and a company of the Brandenburg Regiment (specialists for sabotage operations behind the enemy lines). These he threw in along with the entire XXXVI Mountain Corps reserve, one infantry battalion. The III Corps brought up one battalion from the Ukhta sector. German Fifth Air Force, which was under orders to concentrate on the Allied Arctic shipping and the Murmansk Railroad except in crises, began shifting its fighters and dive-bombers from Banak and Kirkenes in northern Norway to Kemi behind the III Corps front. *(Map 17.)*

On the 27th, *Fourteenth Army* hit the 6th Mountain Division line, on the Zapadnaya Litsa, on the right with *10th Guards Division* and on the left with *14th Rifle Division.* During the night, *12th Naval Brigade,* coming by sea, landed on the west shore of Zapadnaya Litsa Bay and began to push behind the German line. The landing was a complete surprise to Mountain Corps Norway, and it could have been devastating had it been made in greater strength. As it was, 6th Mountain Division had time to overcome the shock when, two days later, the worst snowstorm of the winter stopped everything for several days.[22] *(Map 18.)*

By 1 May, the Soviet spearheads were standing due north of Kestenga. Dietl then asked Mannerheim for the Finnish 12th Brigade (formerly the 6th Division) to reinforce III Corps. Mannerheim, unwilling to involve the brigade in what might develop into a long, drawn-out fight, refused but offered instead to give Dietl the 163d Infantry Division, which was still attached to the Finnish Army, and to take over the Ukhta sector after a German corps arrived to relieve III Corps. The offer did not promise any immediate help, but Dietl decided to accept, since, in the long run, he would gain a division

---

[21]*AOK Lappland, Ia Nr. 1750/42, Zusammenfassender Bericht ueber die Abwehrkaempfe der Armee Lappland vom 24.4–23.5.42,* AOK 20 27252/7 file.

[22]*Gen. Kdo. Geb.-Korps Norwegen, Ia Nr. 965/42, Bericht ueber die Abwehrkaempfe des Gebirgskorps gegen die russische Umfassungoperation vom 27.4.–16.5.42,* AOK 20 27252/6 file.

INFANTRY TAKE COVER IN THE III CORPS SECTOR

and be freed of responsibility for the Ukhta sector.[23]

In the first week of May, seeking a showdown, *Twenty-sixth Army* put in two new units, *186th Rifle Division* and *80th Rifle Brigade,* against the III Corps left flank. Dietl brought two more battalions from XXXVI Mountain Corps, and III Corps brought one from Ukhta. By also taking 2 battalions out of his right flank, Siilasvuo managed to oppose the 2 Soviet divisions and 2 brigades with 9 battalions. Whether they would be enough was highly questionable from the first, and on 3 May when the *8th Ski Brigade* and a regiment of the *186th Rifle Division* swept wide to

the west and south to cut the III Corps supply road west of Kestenga, Siilasvuo wanted to evacuate Kestenga and withdraw to a line in the narrows between Pya Lake and Top Lake. Dietl, believing a retreat would entail too great a loss of men and supplies, ordered Siilasvuo to hold even if he should be cut off.

The Fade-out

On the 5th, the ski brigade and the rifle regiment came within two miles of the road west of Kestenga and had advance parties out almost to the road, but in the swamps northwest of the town the main bodies lost momentum. In another two days, the Germans and Finns were able to encircle the two Soviet units and virtually wipe them out.

[23]*AOK Lappland, Ia Kriegstagebuch, Band I, Nr. 2,* 1 and 4 May 42, AOK 20 27252/1 file.

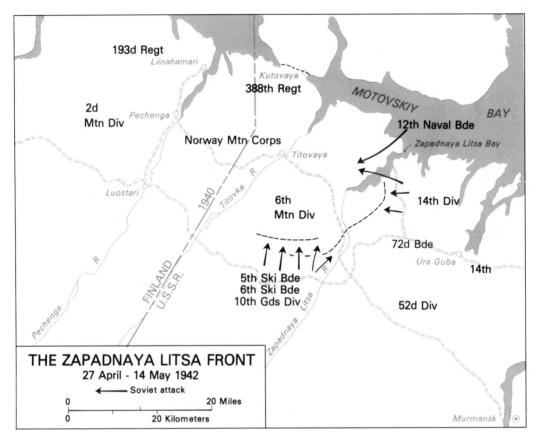

MAP 18

The *8th Ski Brigade,* according to prisoners' accounts, was reduced to between three and four hundred men, approximtely a tenth of its original strength.

Elsewhere, too, *Twenty-sixth Army'*s drive was coming apart, and on the 6th, Dietl and Siilasvuo concluded that the crisis had passed. The defense had been successful, largely because of a failure by *Twenty-sixth Army* to employ its vastly superior numbers effectively. It had dissipated its strength in uncoordinated attacks by single divisions, with the result that *186th Rifle Division* and

23d Guards Division were reduced to between 30 and 40 percent of their original strengths. The *80th Rifle Brigade* fared almost as badly, and the *8th Ski Brigade* was nearly destroyed. At the end, the Soviet *politruks* were often no longer able to drive their men into battle. On the 7th, certain that *Twenty-sixth Army* could not launch another thrust without fresh units, Dietl decided to counterattack.[24]

------

[24]*AOK Lappland, Ia Nr. 1750/42, Zusammenfassender Bericht ueber die Abwehrkaempfe der Armee Lappland vom 24.4.–23.5.42,* AOK 20 27252/7 file.

The fighting on the Zapadnaya Litsa front never reached a crisis like that in the III Corps sector, but the Germans, Hitler in particular, believed the situation there to be the more serious because of the supposed danger of a United States–British landing on the Arctic coast. Since late December 1941, when a British cruiser and destroyer force staged a raid on the Lofoten Islands off northern Norway, Hitler had been expecting a British and American attempt to seize a foothold somewhere between Narvik and Pechenga, along the northern sea route.

On 9 May, Dietl and Schoerner decided to stake everything on a quick decision. They ordered 2d Mountain Division to the front and stripped the coastal defenses between Tana Fiord and Pechenga Bay. But before the last reserves were in the line, the battle shifted. On the 14th, *12th Naval Brigade,* its overwater supply line under constant dive-bomber harassment, gave up its beachhead on the Zapadnaya Litsa Bay. Thereafter *Fourteenth Army,* although it had brought in another division during the past week, also stopped the attack on the south flank. On the 15th, Mountain Corps Norway regained its original positions along the whole front.

North of Kestenga a thaw delayed the III Corps counterattack until 15 May. Meanwhile the Russians, characteristically, had thrown up elaborate field fortifications. When a flanking attack by three Finnish regiments became bogged down in impassible ground, the Germans had to resort to a succession of frontal assaults that finally broke the line on 21 May. With that, the Soviet resistance collapsed, and III Corps was almost back in its

GERMAN SKI PATROL, KESTENGA FRONT

original front when, on the 23d, contrary to his orders from Dietl, Siilasvuo stopped the advance.[25]

The last week and a half of the fighting north of Kestenga had seen a recurrence of constraint in the cooperation between the German and Finnish commands. Army of Lapland noted on 23 May, "In the course of the recent weeks the army has received the growing impression that the Commanding General, III Corps, either on his own initiative or on instructions from higher Finnish authorities, is avoiding all decisions that could involve Finnish troops in serious fighting."[26] The German liaison officer with III Corps reported that the German troops had

[25]*AOK Lappland, Ia Kriegstagebuch, Band I, Nr. 2,* 15–23 May 42, AOK 20 27252/1 file.
[26]*Ibid.,* 23 May 42.

made all the heavy attacks since 15 May, and Army of Lapland recorded that Siilasvuo had repeatedly issued orders on his own authority that he knew the army would not automatically approve, the last of those being the order to break off the operation.

Although III Corps had not regained the best defensive positions at several points, Dietl decided to let Siilasvuo's order stand, particularly since he saw a danger that otherwise the Finns would pull out entirely and leave the German troops stranded. On the 23d, he attempted to limit Siilasvuo's authority with regard to withdrawing troops from the line; but on the following day, disregarding that, Siilasvuo pulled all the Finnish troops out of the German sector of the front and demanded that within three days the Germans return all horses and wagons borrowed from the Finns. The last action would have left the German troops without supplies, and Dietl had to appeal to Siilasvuo in the name of "brotherhood-in-arms" not to leave the Germans in a hopeless position.[27]

Although the Finnish liaison officer with Army of Lapland assured him that the Finnish Army Command was not putting pressure on Siilasvuo to spare his Finnish troops or to get them out quickly, Dietl ordered the German units made independent of Finnish support as fast as possible and asked the OKW to speed up shipment of the 7th Mountain Division. The headquarters and two regiments of the latter, however, were by then tied down in the fighting on the Army Group North front. On 1 June, the XVIII Mountain Corps headquarters' staff arrived, and Dietl proposed having it take over the Kestenga sector at the middle of the month, but Siilasvuo refused to relinquish command there unless the majority of the Finnish troops were out by then. On the 18th Mannerheim finally agreed to an exchange at the end of the month, provided somewhat less than half of the Finnish troops were returned to him. On that basis, XVIII Mountain Corps took command at Kestenga on 3 July. One Finnish regiment remained in the corps area until mid-September, when it was relieved by the last elements of 7th Mountain Division.[28]

The battles east of Kestenga and on the Zapadnaya Litsa were defensive victories for the Germans and the Finns—but ones which could not be exploited, and so they brought small profit. The III Corps claimed to have counted 15,000 Soviet dead and maintained that Soviet losses behind the lines from artillery fire and aerial bombardment also were high. One of *Twenty-sixth Army*'s reinforcements, the *85th Independent Brigade,* for instance, was smashed by dive-bombers before it could get to the front. Mountain Corps Norway claimed 8,000 Soviet dead. The total German and Finnish casualties were 5,500 in the III Corps sector and 3,200 on the Zapadnaya Litsa.[29]

Neither of the major Soviet war histories says anything about the Kestenga offensive. With regard to the Zapadnaya Litsa operation, the *History of the Second World War* says only that it was "without results."[30] The *History of the Great Patriotic War* says the operation

---

[27]*Ibid.,* 23–25 May 42.

[28]Ziemke, *Northern Theater,* p. 228.
[29]*Ibid.*
[30]*IVMV,* vol. V, p. 141.

failed but "tied up enemy forces, disrupted his planned offensive [sic], and forced him to assume the defensive on the Murmansk axis." It adds, "For a long time, the situation on the northern sector of the Soviet-German front remained stable."[31]

The Arctic Convoys

The German Buildup

In mid-August 1941, the British had begun sending single merchant ships (and one small convoy) loaded with military equipment to Murmansk and Arkhangelsk. The first larger convoy, numbered PQ–1, sailed from Hvalfjord, Iceland, on 29 September. (Henceforth, until November 1942, convoys were given "PQ" numbers outbound and "QP" numbers homebound.)[32] The Germans, unwilling to divert effort from profitable targets elsewhere, did not respond until 20 December, when two aircraft attacked PQ–6.[33]

During the winter of 1941–1942, Hitler's preoccupation with possible British (and American) landings put the German Navy in position to do something about the Arctic convoys. In late December, Hitler told Keitel and Admiral Raeder, the commander in chief of the navy, "If the British go about things properly, they will attack northern Norway at several points. In an all-out offensive by their fleet and ground troops, they will try to displace us there, take Narvik, if possible, and

thus exert pressure on Sweden and Finland." He then gave Raeder an order to have "each and every vessel" of the navy stationed in Norway, including the battleships *Scharnhorst* and *Gneisenau* and the heavy cruiser *Prinz Eugen,* all three of which were docked at Brest and would have to break through the English Channel to get to Norway.[34]

The German Navy, taking advantage of the cover afforded by the long winter nights, began transferring its heavy ships to Norway in January 1942. The battleship *Tirpitz,* first to go, docked in Trondheim on the 16th. The *Tirpitz* was the navy's most formidable ship. With a displacement of 42,000 tons and eight fifteen-inch guns in its main batteries, it was a match for any vessel afloat. The navy had been planning to move the *Tirpitz* to Norway since November 1941, for the effect it would have of tying down heavy British ships. In that sense, the move was an immediate success. Churchill, in January 1942, believed that if the *Tirpitz* could be removed from the scene, the world naval situation would be changed and the Allies could regain naval supremacy in the Pacific.[35] In the second week of February, *Scharnhorst, Gneisenau,* and *Prinz Eugen* broke through the English Channel, reaching Germany on the 13th. The two battleships had been damaged by mines and had to be held in Germany for repairs. The *Prinz Eugen*(14,000 tons, eight-inch guns) proceeded to Norway together with the pocket battleship

[31]*IVOVSS,* vol. II, p. 468.

[32]See S. W. Roskill, *The War at Sea, 1939–1945* (London: Her Majesty's Stationery Office, 1954), vol. I, p. 492 and Samuel Eliot Morison, *The Battle of the Atlantic, September 1939–May 1943* (Boston: Little, Brown, 1947), p. 160.

[33]*IVMV,* vol. IV, p. 334.

[34]*Fuehrer Conferences on Matters Dealing With the German Navy, 1941* (Washington D.C.: Office of Naval Intelligence, 1947), vol. II, p. 94.

[35]*Ibid.,* p. 55; Winston S. Churchill, *The Hinge of Fate* (Boston: Houghton Mifflin, 1950), p. 112.

Scheer (11,000 tons, eleven-inch guns) and docked at Trondheim on 23 February, but *Prinz Eugen's* rudder was blown off by a torpedo while en route, and the ship had to return to Germany. By late February, the navy also had eight destroyers and twelve submarines based in Norway. In his "each and every vessel" order, Hitler had originally included the whole German submarine fleet, but he had later been impressed by reports of submarine successes off the U.S. coast and had decided to leave the main submarine force there.[36]

Meanwhile, the German Navy had recognized the target potential of the convoys, but, as of late February, it had only six submarines deployed against them. The other six were being kept on patrol off Norway, and the Naval Staff could not bring itself to allow the surface ships to burn precious fuel oil on what would be long, and perhaps fruitless, sorties. Convoy PQ–7, which made the voyage north in January 1942, lost one merchant ship out of eleven. The first convoy in which an American merchant ship made the run, PQ–8, had one ship damaged by a torpedo and a destroyer sunk. In February, three PQ convoys (9, 10, and 11) got through without being sighted.[37]

German Fifth Air Force, which was responsible for air operations in Norway and Finland, might also have operated against the convoys. It had 60 twin-engine bombers, 30 *Stukas*, 30 single-engine fighters, and 15 naval floatplane torpedo-bombers. However,

the Fifth Air Force commander, Generaloberst Hans-Juergen Stumpff, believed the darkness of the arctic winter made air operations against ships at sea unprofitable, and, from his headquarters in Kemi, Finland, he directed his main effort against the port of Murmansk and the railroad. For a time in early 1942, Stumpff employed geologists in an attempt to locate spots along the railroad where bombing might set off landslides and bury stretches of the track. The Germans had recently acquired some costly knowledge about arctic geology. In late September 1941, a Soviet bomber, striking at Army of Norway's only bridge across the Pechenga River, had dropped a load of bombs that missed the bridge but by their concussion had caved in both banks of the river, completely burying the bridge and damming the river. The site of the collapse was in an area in. which glacial drift (sand and gravel) had been laid down over a substratum of oceanic sediment. The latter, having never dried out, remained extremely unstable; and whenever it was cut, as by a river, it sustained its own weight and the drift overburden only in a highly precarious sort of equilibrium. Similar conditions were known to exist throughout northern Finland and the Kola Peninsula, but although they tried a number of times, the Germans did not succeed in exploiting these geologic factors in their attacks on the Murmansk Railroad.[38]

"Tirpitz" and PQ–12

By early March, the Naval Staff had

[36]*War Diary, German Naval Staff, Operations Division, Part A* (Washington: Office of Naval Intelligence, 1948), vol. 29, pp. 207, 217, 228.

[37]Roskill, *War at Sea*, vol. II, p. 119; Morison, *Battle of the Atlantic*, p. 160.

[38]British Air Ministry Pamphlet 248, p. 113. See Ziemke, *Northern Theater*, p. 236n.

GERMAN SUBMARINE ON THE WAIT IN THE ARCTIC

come to think that the mere presence of the *Tirpitz* at Trondheim would not fully achieve the desired effect of tying down enemy forces, and it therefore ordered the battleship to make a strike against the PQ–12 convoy, which was then at sea northeast of Iceland. The *Tirpitz* and five destroyers put out on 6 March. After failing to find the convoy in three days' cruising, they were ordered back to port on the 9th. The sortie had been a halfhearted enterprise from the start because the Naval Staff had qualms about risking a battleship in an action against merchant ships. Raeder concluded that anticonvoy operations were too dangerous for heavy ships without air cover, and he doubted whether they were justified in view of the ships' main task, defense against landings.[39] The *Tirpitz* operation did have one result: the steel allotment for building a German aircraft carrier, the *Graf Zeppelin,* was increased, but the carrier could not be completed before late 1943.

The *Tirpitz*'s abortive attempt on PQ–12 may, perhaps, have had one other result. On 14 March, Hitler issued the first order for intensive anticonvoy operations. Stating that the convoys could be used both to sustain Soviet resistance and as a device for a surprise landing on the Norwegian or Finnish coasts, he ordered the sea traffic on the northern route, "which so far has hardly been touched," to be interdicted. He was more than right on one

---

[39]*Naval War Diary,* vol. 31, pp. 20, 53, 56, 75, 81, 85.

score. By then, twelve PQ convoys had reached Soviet ports with a loss of only 1 ship out of 103 merchant vessels and 1 British destroyer.[40] Hitler's order directed the navy to increase its submarine commitment and the air force to strengthen its long-range reconnaissance, bomber, and torpedo-bomber forces. The air force, henceforth, was to keep Murmansk under constant bombardment, reconnoiter the sea area between Bear Island and the Murman Coast, and operate against convoys and enemy warships.[41]

When he received the Hitler order, Stumpff also suggested occupying Spitzbergen, which was being held by a small force of Norwegians. He pointed out that Fifth Air Force could use the airfield there to attack the convoys from two sides. Army of Norway believed a battalion would be enough to take and hold the island, but the OKW believed the occupation would tie up too much naval and air strength in the defense without offering sufficient compensatory advantages since, during most of the year, pack ice forced convoys to pass within 300 miles of the German air bases in Norway anyway. On 22 March, Hitler shelved Stumpff's proposal for the time being.[42]

In April, convoys PQ–13 and PQ–14 sailed, but bad weather and the spring thaw, which temporarily rendered the northern airfields unusable, kept nearly all of Fifth Air Force's planes grounded. The PQ–14 convoy ran into pack ice north of Iceland and sixteen of its twenty-four ships turned back. One of the eight that went on was sunk by a submarine. Convoy PQ–13, with nineteen ships, fared poorly and provided a preview of worse to come. After the convoy was scattered by a heavy storm on 24 April, German planes picked off two stragglers, and three German destroyers sank another—at an eventual cost of one of their own number. Submarines sank two more ships. The Germans also lost a submarine, and the British had a destroyer and a cruiser badly damaged, the latter by one of its own torpedoes. One of three Soviet destroyers that joined the escort off northern Norway was damaged. In gales and snow squalls, the action was haphazard on both sides. Neither the German ships nor planes could determine the size of the convoy or the makeup of the escort; consequently, the Naval Staff declined to risk its heavier ships.[43]

By late April, the buildup Hitler had ordered was taking effect. The heavy cruiser *Hipper,* sister ship to the *Prinz Eugen,* and the pocket battleship *Luetzow* had arrived in Norway. The navy also had 20 submarines stationed in Norway, 8 for defense and 12 for use against the convoys; and the *Luftwaffe* had brought in a dozen newly converted HE–111 torpedo-bombers. On 3 May, 9 of the torpedo-bombers, on their first mission, attacked PQ–15 and sank 3 ships.[44]

[40]David Irving, *The Destruction of Convoy PQ–17* (New York: Simon and Schuster, 1968), p. 2.

[41]*OKW, WFSt, Op. (M) Nr. 55493/42, 14.3.42,* OKW 119 file.

[42]*OKW, WFSt, Op. Nr. 55518/42, Vortragsnotiz, 13.3.42; OKW, WFSt, Op. (M) Nr. 55537/42, Betr.: Spitzbergen, 22.3.42,* OKW 119 file.

[43]Roskill, *War at Sea,* vol. II, pp. 124–27; Morison, *Battle of the Atlantic,* p. 166; *IVMV,* vol. IV, p. 335; *Naval War Diary,* vol. 32, pp. 13–18.

[44]Generalmajor a. D. Hans-Detlev Herhudt von Rohden, *Die Kampffuehrung der Luftflotte 5 in Norwegen, 1942,* von Rohden 4376–408 file. See also Roskill, *War at Sea,* vol. II, p. 129.

On 21 May PQ–16 sailed. It was the largest convoy yet, 35 merchant ships, and, with 4 cruisers and 3 destroyers (joined in the north by 3 Soviet destroyers), the most heavily protected. By then, the lengthening days were making submarine operations, except against single, unescorted ships, too dangerous, but for the bombers, the best season was just beginning. On 27 May, 100 twin-engine JU–88 bombers and 8 of the HE–111s attacked PQ–16 and sank 4 ships. The attack showed that high-level dive-bombing combined with torpedo-plane strikes from just above the waterline could dissipate and confuse a convoy's antiaircraft defense. In four days under almost around-the-clock attack, PQ–16 lost 8 ships and had several others so badly damaged that they reached port barely afloat.[45] The war in the Arctic had moved out to sea.

---

[45]Roskill, *War at Sea,* vol. II, pp. 130–32; Rohden, *Die Kampffuehrung,* Rohden 4376–408 file.

CHAPTER XII

Active Defense, Center and North

Stalin's Bid for the Initiative

Ordinarily, the coming of spring is welcome in the Soviet Union. It brings lengthening days, sunshine, and the promise of renewed life to a frozen land. But, in 1942, it also brought an uncertainty for the Soviet Command that has not been entirely resolved a generation later and may not ever be. In March, although the winter had not yet abated, the general offensive, despite strenuous efforts to keep it alive, was dying while the enemy still kept a hold on Leningrad and occupied the approaches to Moscow and the Caucasus. The Soviet General Staff, going by an intelligence report it received on 18 March, believed the German Eastern Front had received enough new divisions and replacements between January and March to be capable of shifting to the offensive any time after mid-April.[1]

The general offensive had imposed an unanticipated and, at times, nearly intolerable strain on the enemy, but it had also, in the end, disclosed that the Soviet leadership had not yet overcome some hazardous deficiencies in its conduct of operations. The *Stavka* had ordered attacks in too many directions at once, and the *front* and army commands had done the same. As a result,

the forces had been divided and redivided, and none of the final objectives had been achieved. Reserves had been wasted by being sent into battle piecemeal to such an extent that, on 16 March, the State Defense Committee undertook "to prohibit those practices categorically."[2]

The making of Soviet strategy in the spring of 1942 was in the hands of five men: Marshal Shaposhnikov, chief of the General Staff; his deputy, General Vasilevskiy; General Zhukov, the commander of *Western Theater;* Marshal Timoshenko, the commander of *Southwestern Theater;* and Stalin, the supreme commander of the Soviet Armed Forces, whose authority easily outweighed that of all the others together. In early March, they were agreed in believing, as the whole world did, that the Germans would make another strong bid to defeat the Soviet Union in the coming spring and summer. Consequently, they saw their task, as Vasilevskiy later put it, as being to "plan for the coming half year," or in other words, to find a way of frustrating the next German onslaught while getting their own forces into condition to strike back later.[3]

Stalin, Shaposhnikov, and Vasilevskiy believed they would not be able to

---

[1] *IVMV*, vol. V, p. 111.

[2] *Ibid.*, vol. IV, p. 327.
[3] Vasilevskiy, *Delo*, p. 203.

develop any more major offensives in the spring or early summer. They believed, also, that Soviet operations up to the beginning of summer would have to be restricted to an active defense that would "halt the enemy's blows, wear him down and weaken him" and prepare the way for "a large-scale offensive when adequate reserves were accumulated."[4] Zhukov concurred in the defensive strategy but wanted a buildup in early summer for an offensive to smash the Rzhev-Vyazma "bridgehead" west of Moscow.[5] Timoshenko also favored the defensive strategy in general except for his own command. He and General Leytenant I. Kh. Bagramyan, his chief of staff, and Nikita Khrushchev, his member of the Military Council (commissar), had planned an offensive for his command on a broad front that they proposed to start in May.[6]

In mid-March, the State Defense Committee established the national requirements for May through June as being to train reserves and accumulate guns, tanks, aircraft, and other war material for later offensive operations. The General Staff plan, drafted at the same time, envisioned a period of active defense through May during which reserves would be built up for "decisive operations" to follow.[7]

In a joint meeting at the end of March, the State Defense Committee and the *Stavka* undertook to settle on the "final variant" of the plan. Shaposhnikov presented the General Staff conception of an active defense coupled with a buildup of reserves, and Zhukov and Timoshenko again offered their proposals for offensives in the center and on the south flank. Timoshenko supported Zhukov, but Zhukov was opposed to any offensives other than his own, which put him actually in agreement with Shaposhnikov, since he did not expect to start the Rzhev-Vyazma operation before summer.[8]

The crucial question, however, was whether Stalin would accept as "active" a defense that did not include any offensives. Shaposhnikov and Zhukov had reason to believe he would not, and when Shaposhnikov and Zhukov attempted to explain the difficulties of organizing an offensive in the south, Stalin broke in, saying, "Are we supposed to sit in defense, idling away our time, and wait for the Germans to attack first? We must strike several preemptive blows over a wide front and probe the enemy's readiness."[9] Shaposhnikov and Zhukov had their answer. According to the *History of the Second World War*, "The meeting concluded with an order from the Supreme Commander to prepare and carry out in the near future offensives in the vicinity of Kharkov, on the Crimea, and in other areas."[10]

In the next several weeks, Stalin ordered or approved offensives along the whole front from the Barents Sea to the Black Sea. On the Crimea, the objective would be to clear the enemy from the peninsula. *Southwest Front* was to strike toward Kharkov from the northeast and the southeast. *Bryansk*

---

[4]*Ibid.*, vol. V, p. 113. See also *VOV*, p. 139.
[5]Zhukov, *Memoirs,* p. 365.
[6]Bagramyan, *Tak shli my k pobede,* pp. 48–54. See also *IVMV*, vol. V, p. 113 and Vasilevskiy, *Delo*, p. 212.
[7]*IVMV*, vol. V, p. 113.

[8]Zhukov, *Memoirs*, p. 366; *IVMV*, vol. V, p. 113.
[9]Zhukov, *Memoirs*, p. 366.
[10]*IVMV*, vol. V, p. 113.

Front was ordered to advance past Kursk and Lgov. Aiming ultimately for Smolensk, *West Front* and *Kalinin Front* were to top off the winter by smashing Army Group Center's Rzhev-Vyazma line. To assist in accomplishing this mission, General Belov's *I Guards Cavalry Corps* would hit the German railroads and bases between Smolensk and Vyazma. *Northwest Front* would eliminate the Demyansk pocket, and *Karelian Front* would attack on the Zapadnaya Litsa River, west of Kandalaksha, and at Kestenga. *Leningrad Front* had the self-proposed mission of breaking the Leningrad siege with its own forces and those of the former *Volkhov Front.*[11]

The offensives were to be conducted between April and June and were expected to give the operations in those months "an active character." In the same period, the Soviet forces, in general, would be "on the strategic defensive," reorganizing and reequipping units and assembling reserves.[12]

The active defense with the "preemptive blows," in effect extended the general offensive into the spring. In doing so, it repeated the error which, under more favorable conditions, had eventually crippled the general offensive during the winter. And it added a complication: as Vasilevskiy puts it, a requirement "to defend and attack simultaneously."[13] Zhukov maintains in his memoirs that he spoke against the preemptive blows, but Timoshenko seconded Stalin, and Shaposhnikov

"kept silent."[14] Vasilevskiy said after the war that people who did not know about the "difficult conditions" under which the General Staff worked during the war might justifiably find fault with the General Staff for not having demonstrated the "negative consequences" of the decision to Stalin.[15] The *Popular-Scientific Sketch* states, "It must be said that the leading members of the General Staff, the Chief of the General Staff, Marshal B. M. Shaposhnikov, and his deputy, General A. M. Vasilevskiy, as well as the member of the *Stavka*, G. K. Zhukov, in principle, adhered to the same opinion as the Supreme Commander, only with some reservations."[16]

Army Group Center's Second Front

At the End of Winter

As if it had settled through the melted snow, the Army Group Center line stabilized in April 1942 along the ragged leading edges of half-a-dozen once deadly, now stalled and blunted, Soviet thrusts. The winter had passed, too soon for the Russians, not soon enough for the Germans, but it had left behind many changes in the battlefield's configuration. The straight-line distance from the army group's northern boundary near Velikiye Luki to its southern boundary southwest of Orel was about 350 miles. The front in between, including most though not all of its convolutions, was more like 900 miles long. Its outstanding features were the 150-miles-deep and at least equally wide Toropets bulge on the

---

[11]*Ibid.*, p. 115; Meretskov, *Serving the People*, p. 207.
[12]*IVMV*, vol. V, p. 114.
[13]A. M. Vasilevskiy, "Nekotorye voprosy rukovodstva vooruzhennoy borboy letom 1942 goda," *Voyenno-istoricheskiy Zhurnal*, 8(1965), 10.

[14]Zhukov, *Memoirs*, p. 366f.
[15]Vasilevskiy, "Nekotorye voprosy," p. 10.
[16]*VOV*, p. 139.

north, a 75-by-125-mile salient on the south that had evolved from the old Sukhinichi bulge, and, between the two, a dogleg projection occupied by the Ninth, Fourth Panzer, and Fourth Armies. On the rim of the Toropets bulge, *Third Shock Army*'s troops were 285 miles west of Moscow and 50 miles west of the Army Group Center headquarters at Smolensk. At Gzhatsk, Fourth Panzer Army was within 90 miles of Moscow.

Rzhev, Vyazma, and Bryansk, commanding the immediate road and rail approaches to Moscow on the west, were in Army Group Center's hands and so kept alive a threat to the Soviet capital. Along a 250-mile line from Rzhev to south of Bryansk, however, the army group had acquired a second front that practically denied it territorial control east of Smolensk. From the army group boundary north to Bryansk and from there north to Roslavl and Kirov, partisans held sway in the broad spaces between the roads and railroads. Between the Smolensk-Vyazma railroad and the *Rollbahn* through Roslavl, Belov was the proconsul in a Soviet enclave dominated by his *I Guards Cavalry Corps*, parachute troops, partisans, and survivors of *Thirty-third Army.* A network of partisan bands provided almost continuous contact between Belov's territory and the Bryansk partisan concentration. North of the Smolensk-Vyazma railroad, *Thirty-ninth Army* and *XI Cavalry Corps* occupied a 30-by-40-mile pocket east of the Dukhovshchina-Belyy road. By the end of April, Fourth Panzer Army had tightened its front south of the *Rollbahn* and at Kirov enough to deny Belov and the Bryansk partisans unimpeded contact with Soviet territory, but *Thirty-*

ninth Army still had free access to the outside through an 18-mile-wide gap northeast of Belyy.

In late March, as a smaller alternative to BRUECKENSCHLAG, the Ostashkov operation, Ninth Army had proposed an attack west out of the Rzhev-Olenino area to Nelidovo. Taking Nelidovo would not have done much toward eliminating the Toropets bulge; but it would have deprived the Soviet forces in the bulge of a road and rail junction, could have been the first stage of a drive to Toropets, and would in particular have cut *Thirty-ninth Army*'s ground communications. By early April the Nelidovo attack, code-named Operation NORDPOL, had replaced BRUECKENSCHLAG, which by then had drifted beyond the range of feasibility. But NORDPOL, too, had troubles, first the thaw and then the abnormally heavy spring rains that extended the *rasputitsa* past its usual term. In the meantime, Fourth Army had prepared an operation, code-named HANNOVER, against the Belov forces. Although NORDPOL and HANNOVER hardly added up to a major offensive effort, they were together more than Army Group Center could afford in the spring of 1942.

The flow of reinforcements to the army group had stopped in March, and as soon as the *rasputitsa* had set in, Hitler had reversed the flow, using Army Group Center as a base from which to draw reinforcements for the south. In the first week of May, Headquarters, Fourth Panzer Army, departed, to be followed by five of the army group's twenty corps headquarters. From April to early June, Army Group Center had lost sixteen divisions, a good 20 percent of its overall strength, 30 percent of its panzer divisions. In the divisions that stayed, personnel and other shortages were not going to be filled until summer; consequently, regiments had to be reduced from three battalions to two, artillery batteries from four guns to three. Panzer and motorized divisions were such in name only. Most of the tanks and trucks that had survived the winter were awaiting repairs, and the shops could not keep more than 20 percent in running condition.

Army Group Center was to be a supernumerary in the 1942 campaign. Field Marshal Kluge, the army group's commander, told his generals on 18 April, "We must economize on the forces we have left."[17] By mid-May, Kluge became convinced that NORDPOL was too ambitious; and when Hitler, whose interest had drifted completely away from the area, did not object he canceled it and instructed Ninth Army to work on SEYDLITZ, a smaller operation against *Thirty-ninth Army* and *XI Cavalry Corps.* In the meantime, Fourth Army would go ahead with HANNOVER and when it was completed turn the troops over to Ninth Army for SEYDLITZ. HANNOVER and SEYDLITZ, being directed against conventional Soviet forces, could be expected to take reasonably predictable courses. Kluge knew from experience that operations against the partisans around Bryansk promised much less. The area was larger and the anticipated return for the effort certainly would be smaller. Since he also did not have any more troops to spare, Kluge gave Second Panzer Army one security division and

left the army to deal with the partisans in any way it could.

Hannover

Belov's territory stretched eighty miles from east to west and, at its widest, forty miles north and south, occupying almost the whole of the triangle formed by Smolensk, Vyazma, and Spas-Demensk. In April and early May, Belov was engaged in organizing the partisans, cavalry, and airborne troops to comply with orders coming to him from *West Front,* which was attempting to devise another thrust toward Vyazma as part of the active defense. In the less critical western two-thirds of the pocket, he set up two "partisan divisions." On the east, he had the cavalry, airborne troops, and more partisans. On 9 May, planes brought in a battalion of antitank guns and, with it, General Mayor V. S. Golushkevich, the deputy chief of staff of *West Front.* Golushkevich delivered a secret order for Belov to be ready to strike south, "not later than 5 June," to meet *Fiftieth Army,* which was being reinforced with tank corps and would be advancing north across the *Rollbahn.*[18] *(Map 19.)*

For HANNOVER, Fourth Army had a corps headquarters and three divisions from Third Panzer Army, which had taken over the Fourth Panzer Army sector, and a corps headquarters and three divisions of its own. These forces were plenty to handle Belov's cavalry and other regular troops, which were estimated at between ten and twenty thousand, but not enough to scour the entire 1,500-square-mile pocket. (Be-

[17]Hofmann, MS P–114b, vol. IV, p. 153.

[18]Belov, *"Pyatimesyachnaya borba,"* pp. 66–69.

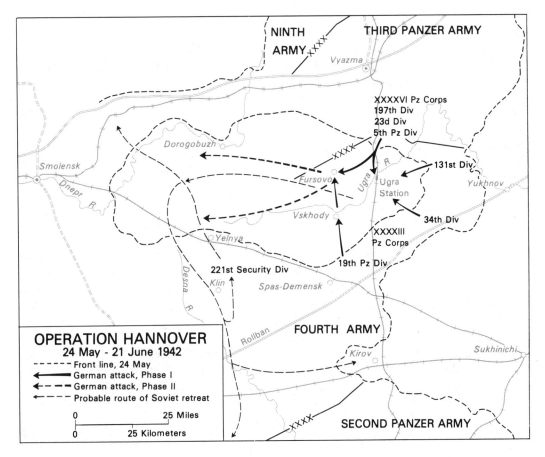

NINTH
ARMY XXXX

THIRD PANZER ARMY

Vyazma

XXXXVI Pz Corps
197th Div
23d Div
5th Pz Div

Dorogobuzh

131st Div

Smolensk

Dnepr R.

Fursovo

Ugra R.

Ugra
Station

Yukhnov

34th Div

Vskhody

XXXXIII
Pz Corps

19th Pz Div

Yelnya

Desna R.

221st Security Div

Klin

Spas-Demensk

OPERATION HANNOVER
24 May - 21 June 1942

- - - - - Front line, 24 May
◄━━━━ German attack, Phase I
◄ - ━ - German attack, Phase II
◄ - - - - Probable route of Soviet retreat

Rollban

FOURTH ARMY

Kirov

Sukhinichi

0   25 Miles
0   25 Kilometers

SECOND PANZER ARMY

MAP 19

lov's strength probably was close to twenty thousand, and he had a tank battalion with eighteen tanks.)[19] Furthermore, SEYDLITZ, although it had second priority in terms of time, was tactically more urgent than HANNOVER, since it was essential to the stability of the Rzhev salient. That, and Belov's presumed deployment, made a small, quick solution appear worthwhile. Radio intercepts and information from agents and prisoners placed his head-

quarters and the main body of his regular troops in the eastern end of the pocket, east of the Ugra River.[20] The estimate was wrong in what was going to be a significant respect: the elements of *IV Airborne Corps* and the *"Zhabo" Partisan Regiment* were east of the Ugra, but most of Belov's cavalry was west of it.[21]

The army group and Fourth Army settled on a plan to run Belov down in one fast swoop. Two divisions, striking

[19]See *ibid.*

[20]*AOK 4, Ia Kriegstagebuch Nr. 13,* 15–21 May 42, AOK 4 24336/1 file.
[21]Belov, *"Pyatimesyachnaya borba,"* p. 67.

south from Vyazma and one north from Spas-Demensk, would pinch off the eastern end of the pocket, trapping Belov east of the Ugra and the Vyazma-Kirov railroad. The other three would drive inward from a screening line around the tip of the pocket. Although it presented no exceptional tactical problems, HANNOVER, first set for 21 May, had to be postponed on several successive days because of prolonged heavy rains that turned the ground, still soft from the thaw, back to mud. As if the winter had not been enough, central Russia was experiencing a record wet spring.

While it was being planned, HAN-NOVER acquired one esoteric feature. Late in 1941, at Osintorf near Orsha, the *Abwehr* (the OKW intelligence organization) had begun training several hundred captured Soviet soldiers and officers as diversionists. The Germans had tried out somewhat similar groups earlier in the campaign, but those had been made up of emigres, members of minorities, or Russian-speaking Germans, and most had not lived in Russia recently or had lived on the fringes of Soviet life. The Osintorf trainees, except for their commander, an emigre, Colonel Konstantin Kromiadi, were all completely up-to-date, authentic products of the Soviet system, most particularly of the Soviet Army. In Soviet uniforms they could be expected to merge easily into Soviet formations, especially heterogeneous ones like Belov's. For HANNOVER, 350 of them were assigned to Fourth Army as the Experimental Organization Center.[22] Their

mission would be to disrupt the defense, if possible, by finding and killing Belov and his staff, or otherwise, by sneak attacks and by spreading false orders and information.

On 23 May cloudbursts inundated the area, but General Heinrici, commander of Fourth Army, afraid of losing the element of surprise by another delay, decided to let HANNOVER start the next morning. The Experimental Organization Center went into the pocket from the south that night. Fourth Army's troops moved out in the morning in pouring rain, in some places up to their waists in mud and water. The 19th Panzer Division, advancing from the south, nevertheless covered almost ten miles before 1200 when it arrived at the Ugra River near Vskhody—just in time to see the bridge there blow up, which was probably unnecessary effort by the Russians since the water was rising so fast that the bridge very likely would have been washed away anyhow. The division spent the rest of the day getting a bridgehead north of the river and building a pontoon bridge over the relentlessly rising water. Coming from the north, 197th Infantry Division took five hours to reach Ugra Station, where the railroad crossed the river. After ten more miles, the trap would be closed. From inside the pocket, what was taken to be Belov's radio was sending a constant stream of coded messages that seemed to give evidence of alarm, if not panic. Kluge congratulated the troops on their "fine successes," and Heinrici agreed that the performances were remarkable. He had not expected them to reach Vskhody and Ugra Station until the second day, because he had anticipated a more solid defense. However,

---

[22]Gerhard L. Weinberg, *The Partisan Movement in the Yelnya-Dorogobuzh Area of Smolensk Oblast* (Washington, D.C.: Air Research and Development Command, 1954), p. 99; Sven Steenburg, *Wlassow* (Cologne: Wissenschaft und Politik, 1968), pp. 60–66.

a disturbing thought occurred to him and Kluge both that the resistance so far had been more typical of partisans than of Soviet regular troops.[23]

The downpours continued through the night and the next day. Amazed, the Germans saw the Ugra, already a hundred yards wide, spawn a second channel twenty yards wide. For two days, tanks, trucks, infantry, and artillery came to a standstill in mud and water. The rain was so heavy that even the reliable little *Storch* reconnaissance planes could not fly. Fourth Army had no idea what the enemy forces were doing. Although Kluge could not imagine how the Russians might get across the swollen Ugra River, he knew they would have to try, and on the afternoon of the 25th he asked Heinrici to have his points bear ten miles west toward Fursovo, on the assumption that the Russians would have crossed the river by then. After another twenty-four hours passed without the encirclement being closed, Kluge and Heinrici agreed that if Belov had not already done so, he almost certainly would get away to the west, and HANNOVER would therefore have to go into a second phase.

The points met at Fursovo shortly before nightfall on the 27th. The mop-up, in the next five days, failed to bring either Belov or his main force to bay. Prisoners, deserters, and returned members of the Experimental Organization Center—of which about two-thirds came back—corroborated each others' statements that several Soviet staffs had been in the pocket, including Belov's and those of the *IV Airborne*

Corps and the *"Zhabo" Regiment.* For Fourth Army, the results were disappointing. About two thousand Russians were captured and another fifteen hundred killed, but Belov had obviously escaped with most of his troops.[24]

Prisoner interrogations indicated that Belov had had at least a day's warning about the attack through a deserter from the Experimental Organization Center. The Russians had known beforehand about the Experimental Organization Center, but they had not known where it would be operating. Consequently, according to the prisoners, just knowing the unit was in the area, had raised confusion and some panic. Members of the Experimental Organization Center reported having observed instances of Soviet units firing on each other.[25] Belov, in his account, states that on 23 May, the *8th Airborne Brigade* destroyed a group of "diversionists" whose mission had been to "wipe out" his staff and that he learned of the coming German attack from one of its survivors.[26]

Hannover II

At the conclusion of what the Germans were by then calling HANNOVER I, Belov still had 17,000 troops and his eighteen tanks, but he had been forced out of the eastern, tactically most valuable, third of the pocket. By his account, Belov had, meanwhile, concluded that the "hope" of meeting with *Fiftieth Army* was disappearing, and he, therefore, asked *West Front*, on 4 June, for permission to begin the march back

[23]*AOK 4, Ia Kriegstagebuch Nr. 13*, 24 May 42, AOK 4 24336/1 file.

[24]*Ibid.*, 27 May–2 Jun 42.
[25]*Ibid.*, 1 Jun 42.
[26]Belov, *"Pyatimesyachnaya borba,"* p. 70.

to the Soviet side of the front, which was granted because the tank corps and reserves for *Fiftieth Army* had, by then, been transferred to the Kharkov area.[27] This, Belov says, left him with three possible choices: to head west into Belorussia and convert to partisan operations, to go north toward *Kalinin Front*, or to go south toward the weak spot in the German line at Kirov. He rejected the first two, he maintains, because his force would sacrifice its "significance" as regular troops by becoming partisans and because he did not have the means to get his artillery and tanks across the Dnepr River, which he would have to do if he went north. His decision was to march west to the vicinity of Yelnya and then head south and east into the northern part of the Bryansk partisan area, from which he could make his exit near Kirov.[28]

HANNOVER II, of which Belov's account takes no specific notice, began on 3 June in more rain. Heinrici had turned his divisions on the near side of the Ugra pocket around to pursue Belov west between Yelnya and Dorogobuzh and to force him back against the Dnepr River. The better way would have been to cut straight through and head him off east of the river, but, in mud and water, the infantry could not move fast enough, and trucks, tanks, and artillery could not move at all. Without ever catching sight of Belov's main force, the Fourth Army troops reached Dorogobuzh and Yelnya after five days of slogging across an inundated landscape and skirmish-

ing with numerous small parties that appeared mostly to be partisans. Belov was then confined in a 30-by-30-mile pocket blocked on the north by the Dnepr, which was a torrent 200 yards wide, and on the south, between Yelnya and the Dnepr, by the 221st Security Division; but Heinrici and Kluge were beginning to doubt whether Belov was still around at all.[29]

On the morning of the 8th, German pilots over the pocket saw an astonishing scene: columns of Soviet cavalry, airborne troops, trucks, wagons, and tanks weaving in and out of clumps of woods, all heading south. Belov had, at last, come into the open and was obviously getting ready to break out. Kluge ordered a motorcycle battalion from the north to the south side of the pocket, and Heinrici took part of the 19th Panzer Division out of his front north of Yelnya to backstop the 221st Security Division. The reinforcements, however, came too late. During the night, the Russians overran a weak spot in the 221st Security Division's line and simply walked out. After daylight, the *Luftwaffe* reported about a thousand vehicles and some thousands of troops heading into deep forest around the headwaters of the Desna River south of Yelnya. When the motorcycle and panzer troops closed the gap later in the day, not much was left in the pocket.[30]

After passing Yelnya, Belov entered the area of the *"Lazo" Partisan Regiment* where ground troops could not readily pursue him, but, he says, German planes bombed his positions "all day" and came back at night to try to bomb

[27]According to Zhukov, Belov had been given orders in early May to begin bringing his troops out. See Zhukov, *Memoirs*, p. 357.

[28]Belov, *"Pyatimesyachnaya borba,"* p. 71f.

[29]*AOK 4, Ia Kriegstagebuch Nr. 13*, 3–7 Jun 42, AOK 4 24336/1 file.

[30]*Ibid.*, 8–9 Jun 42.

his supply planes.[31] In three days, Fourth Army built a screening line along the *Rollbahn,* which it now knew he would have to cross. In the meantime, Belov had halted in the woods near the village of Klin, halfway between Yelnya and the *Rollbahn,* to sort out his troops and receive air supply. After another two days, the Germans began to believe that he might have disappeared again. Monitors reported his radio operating near Klin, but deserters said he had been flown out, and his force was breaking up. Finally, just before 2400 on the night of 15 June, Belov reappeared, where he had been expected, on the *Rollbahn.*[32]

Belov and the German records give somewhat different versions of what happened that night (which Belov says was the night of the 16th) and afterward. In Belov's version, the breakout was to have been made in two echelons, with General Mayor V. K. Baranov, the commander of *1st Guards Cavalry Division* leading the first and Belov the second. When Baranov emerged from the woods a short distance north of the *Rollbahn,* Belov, who was several hundred yards behind, heard him shout, "Guards, advance! After me! Hurrah!" With more "Hurrahs," the cavalry charged and got across the road, but Belov soon learned that the infantry with the first echelon had not been able to do the same. Consequently, Belov says, he reassembled the *2d Guards Cavalry Division* and elements of *IV Airborne Corps* and *329th Rifle Division* and withdrew into the woods. The next day, he says, he came out of the woods about ten miles north of the *Rollbahn,* made a

wide sweep west and south, and crossed the road ten miles east of Roslavl.[33]

As the Germans saw it, there were three simultaneous attacks, one of which was led by a general on horseback whom they took to have been Belov. The first reports indicated that over three thousand Russians had broken out, but Heinrici could not quite bring himself to believe that so many men could have gone through three small gaps that were open less than an hour. Therefore, he concluded that, whether Belov had escaped or not, most of his men must still be north of the road. Patrols probing into the pocket during the day on the 16th found Russians still there, but they could not determine how many. Deserters said eight to ten thousand. Fourth Army thought six thousand was a more likely number.

During the afternoon of the 18th, a patrol found an order on a dead Soviet officer, which had been written that day and which bore Belov's signature. It gave detailed directions for a mass breakout across the *Rollbahn* and set the time for 2400 that day. The order could have been a deception, but one thing was certain: Belov would have to make his move soon. The noose was closing around him. Having nothing else at all to go by, Fourth Army hurriedly built three lines on the section of the *Rollbahn* the order specified—one on the road, two more farther back.

The Germans' earlier experience had shown that no single line was going to stop a charge by thousands of desperate men, and if the attack came at any other place it would very likely

[31]Belov, *"Pyatimesyachnaya borba,"* p. 72.
[32]*AOK 4, Ia Kriegstagebuch Nr. 13,* 10–16 Jun 42, AOK 4 24336/1 file.

[33]Belov, *"Pyatimesyachnaya borba,"* p. 73.

A CAMOUFLAGED TANK TRAP IN THE FOREST

succeed. But it did not. It began exactly on time, at 2400, straight into the muzzles of German artillery and machine guns. The fighting went on until after daylight. About fifteen hundred Russians got across the first line; five hundred got across the second; and a few across the third. The others were forced back into the pocket, and at 1200 the next day, believing Belov had made his final bid and lost, Heinrici gave the order to push into the pocket, which, by nightfall, had been reduced to an area one and one-half by three miles. Then the rain began again, and an infantry company left a gap in the line, and Belov marched out with what Fourth Army estimated to be between two and four thousand of his men. The Russians were on the move, and the Germans were tired. In the afternoon on the 21st, saying that they "should not march the men to death," Kluge told Fourth Army to stop HANNOVER II and give the troops a rest.[34]

Fourth Army's afteraction report on HANNOVER I and II claimed 11,000 Russians captured and 5,000 killed. How many of these were Belov's troops and how many partisans or civilians was uncertain. Until the end of the month, monitors traced a radio signal in the woods north of the *Rollbahn* that they believed to be Belov's.[35] Belov says he was brought out by plane to *Tenth Army* on the night of 23 June and that

---

[34]*AOK 4, Ia Kriegstagebuch Nr. 13*, 16–21 Jun 42, AOK 4 24336/1 file.
[35]*Ibid.*, 29 Jun–2 Jul 42.

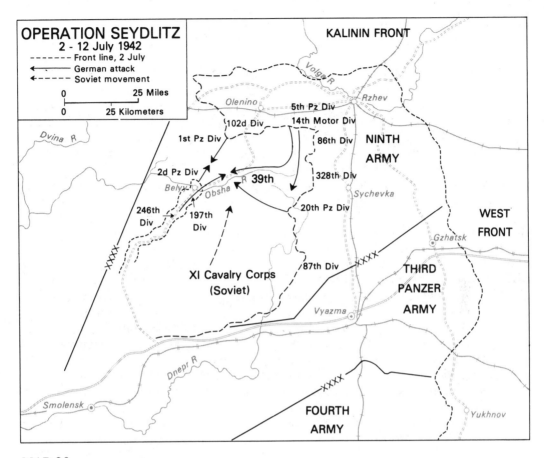

MAP 20

subsequently 10,000 of his troops crossed the front to the Soviet side near Kirov and that 3,000 more were evacuated by air.[36] The *History of the Great Patriotic War* states that "some" of Belov's troops crossed the lines at Kirov and northeast of Smolensk in July, while others stayed to fight as partisans.[37] Belov would command again, notably at Kursk and Berlin, and would be ranked as a hero in the Soviet Union for his raid behind the enemy front during the first winter of the war. Although the Germans did not often admire Soviet generalship, Halder was moved to remark, "The man did, after all, put seven German divisions on the jump."[38]

Seydlitz

Ninth Army's Operation SEYDLITZ had waited for the completion of HANNOVER to receive a corps headquarters, two divisions, and air sup-

[36]Belov, "Pyatimesyachnaya borba," p. 74f.
[37]*IVOVSS*, vol. II, p. 475.

[38]*Halder Diary*, vol. III, p. 458.

port. The delay afforded ample time for planning, and SEYDLITZ went through several revisions. In the final version, Kluge and General der Panzertruppen Heinrich-Gottfried von Vietinghoff, who was replacing Model as commander of Ninth Army while the latter was hospitalized recovering from a wound, settled on two thrusts, each by a panzer division backed by an infantry division, to close the Belyy gap. Single panzer divisions would make two other assaults from south of Olenino and east of Sychevka to split the *Thirty-ninth Army.* The second two depended on 5th Panzer Division, which was engaged in HANNOVER, and 20th Panzer Division, which was to be detached from Third Panzer Army. Four infantry divisions would hold the perimeter, and 14th Motorized Division would be the reserve. Eleven divisions was no small number, but although they were rested and recovered from the winter, they were all greatly understrength. Two hazards could not be mitigated by any amount of planning. One was the weather, which continued rainy through June. The second was the enemy's intention. Other than that *Thirty-ninth Army* and *XI Cavalry Corps* were somewhere in the forty-by-sixty-mile expanse of forest between Belyy and Sychevka nothing else was known about them. Like Belov's force, they had virtually disappeared with the winter's snow.

SEYDLITZ began in the early morning on 2 July, just after 2400, which at that time of the year was only about two hours before dawn. Kluge's command train was parked at Sychevka, and he and Vietinghoff were out behind 1st Panzer Division on the north side of the Belyy gap. The day brought two shocks: 1st Panzer Division made almost no headway, and what appeared to be several dozen Soviet tanks were reported heading toward the 2d Panzer Division flank northeast of Belyy. At the end of the day, both prongs of the attack were stopped, and the one on the south was having to brace for a counterattack. The next morning, after ground and air reconnaissance sighted over fifty Soviet tanks bearing toward Belyy, Kluge approved a change in the plan that would turn 5th Panzer Division west along the course of the Obsha River and bring it out northeast of Belyy behind the enemy tanks. But 5th Panzer Division was fighting through dense forest and was not yet on the Obsha, and at the day's end, SEYDLITZ was stalled everywhere. The Ninth Army journal entry for 3 July closed with, "Severe and fluctuating battles are to be expected in the coming days and weeks."[39] *(Map 20.)*

The morning of the 4th brought more discouragement: the 1st Panzer Division was at a standstill; enemy tanks were biting into 2d Panzer Division's flank from the east; and Vietinghoff had to put in 14th Motorized Division to help 5th Panzer Division ahead. During the day, though, the picture changed dramatically. The 20th Panzer Division began its push west of Sychevka and met astonishingly weak resistance. By nightfall, 1st Panzer Division had made a six-mile jump forward and 5th Panzer Division was turning into the Obsha Valley, leaving 14th Motorized Division to continue south. In another twenty-four hours, 1st Panzer Division had closed the

---

[39]*AOK 9, Ia Kriegstagebuch Nr. 6,* 3 Jul 42, AOK 9 31624/1 file.

BRINGING UP AN ANTITANK GUN IN THE BELYY GAP

Belyy gap, and 5th Panzer Division and 20th Panzer Division were driving east to split the pocket into three parts. The question still was: Where were *Thirty-ninth Army* and *XI Cavalry Corps*? The tank attack had made it seem that they were massed in the north, ready to break out, but by the fourth day, it looked as if they were going to play the same onerous, disappearing game Belov had.

The answer came in the morning on the 6th when Ninth Army's intelligence deciphered an intercepted radio message ordering all *Thirty-ninth Army* units to withdraw toward the northwest. By then, the clearings were filling with columns of Soviet troops. *Thirty-ninth Army* after all was going to attempt a breakout, but depending on how far

north and west they were, its elements would have to cross one, two, or three German lines. In the afternoon, 5th Panzer Division passed through the Obsha Valley and 197th Infantry Division pushing east met the 20th Panzer Division's point. At daylight the next morning, pilots flying over the southern loop of the pocket sighted a long column of cavalry, tanks, and infantry. The *XI Cavalry Corps* was now also out in the open and—to Ninth Army's gratified astonishment—marching north into 20th Panzer Division's arms.

The battle was over. The roads ahead and behind them blocked, the Soviet columns piled up on each other and became helplessly entangled. As the German divisions closed in, airplanes dropped a million leaflets telling the troops how to surrender. By the 10th most of the Russians appeared to be waiting to be rounded up, and on the 12th, Vietinghoff declared SEYDLITZ completed. On that day, the prisoner count stood at 25,000. In another twenty-four hours, it had risen to 37,000 men, 220 tanks, and 500 artillery pieces. The Ninth Army had figured the total *Thirty-ninth Army* and *XI Cavalry Corps* strength at about 50,000. No doubt, some thousands were still on the loose, but the army and the corps were destroyed. The Ninth Army chief of staff remarked, "This was a typical western European battle, no Belov performances, no hiding out in the woods."[40]

In August, the following Soviet proclamation was circulated by the partisans in the former SEYDLITZ area:

All members of the armed forces who escaped from the pocket . . . report to your regular units or join the partisan units! Those who remain in hiding . . . in order to save their skins, and those who do not join in the patriotic war to help destroy the German robbers, also those who desert to the fascist army and help carry on a robber war against the Soviet people, are traitors to the homeland and will be liquidated by us sooner or later. Death to the German occupiers! We are fighting for a just cause! In 1942, the enemy will be totally destroyed![41]

Vogelsang

Concurrently with HANNOVER II and SEYDLITZ, Second Panzer Army was running VOGELSANG ("bird song"), an operation, the first of many, against the

Bryansk partisans. In a 12,000-square-mile area, which was about the size of a small western European country (the Netherlands, for instance), the army had an ample selection of partisan centers to choose from. VOGELSANG was to be conducted in the V-shaped stretch of forest and swamp between the Desna and Bolva rivers due north of Bryansk, which on the northeast abutted the old Kirov gap and had during the winter been a highway for partisan traffic to and from the Soviet side of the front. The XXXXVII Panzer Corps, the tactical command, had the 707th Security Division and one of its own infantry divisions, the 339th, all told, about 6,000 men. *(Map 21.)*

The partisan strength was not known. Two regiments had been identified, one under a Lieutenant Colonel Orlov, the other, a Major Kaluga. Both had come through the front in the winter with several hundred Soviet officers and men to organize and command the partisans, who thereafter came under the control of the *Tenth Army* staff. Small industrial towns scattered along the rivers had provided a good recruiting base, and their nearness to the Kirov gap had made it possible for the partisans to be lavishly outfitted with automatic weapons, radios, mortars, antitank guns, and even some 76-mm. artillery pieces.

VOGELSANG began on 6 June along the west side of the Bolva River. In two days, 707th and 339th Divisions had strung skirmish lines around two five-by-ten-mile pockets west and north of Dyatkovo. The next and far more difficult step was to turn inward and flush out the partisans, and the Germans hoped to drive them into a space so small that they would have to stand and

[40]*Ibid.*, 3–13 Jul 42.
[41]*XXIII A.K., Ic, "Uebersetzung, Tagebuch der Kampfhandlungen der Partisanenabteilung des Oblt. Morogoff,"* 2 Aug 42, XXIII A.K. 76156 file.

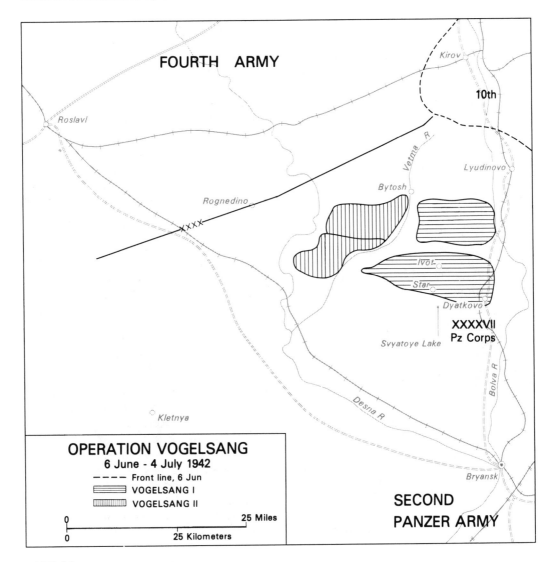

FOURTH ARMY

Kirov

10th

Roslavl

Vetma R.

Lyudinovo

Bytosh

Rognedino

XXXX

Ivot

Star

Dyatkovo

XXXXVII
Pz Corps

Svyatoye Lake

Bolva R.

Desna R.

Kletnya

OPERATION VOGELSANG
6 June - 4 July 1942
– – – – Front line, 6 Jun
VOGELSANG I
VOGELSANG II

0   25 Miles

0   25 Kilometers

Bryansk

**SECOND
PANZER ARMY**

MAP 21

fight. This meant beating through
mud, water, underbrush, and clouds of
mosquitoes in pursuit of an invisible
enemy who knew every trail and hiding
place, might strike at any moment
from the treetops or from concealed
bunkers, but who would almost never
come out into the open. The roads
were as dangerous as the deep woods
because of the "bell," an ambush laid in
a loop. At the open end, the partisans
would be far enough off to the sides to
be just able to see and fire on the road.
At the closed end, they would be near
enough to pin the enemy in the cross
fire.

On the other hand, VOGELSANG demonstrated that antipartisan warfare was a strain on the nerves more than anything. The casualties were usually not large, but the anxiety, effort, and misery were not balanced by any sense of satisfaction. The partisans were everywhere and nowhere.

Dyatkovo *rayon* was the stronghold of the *Orlov Regiment*. The regiment regarded itself as a unit of *Tenth Army* and was the command and control center for the area. It was the hard core, the model, and the symbol of a relentless Soviet presence imposed upon satellite local bands. Together, the regiment and bands pressed the population— men, women, and children—into service as laborers, supply carriers, informants, and auxiliary fighters. Snipers posted in treetops frequently were children. Under attack the objective was to save the organization.

In four days the two German divisions combed the north pocket, clashed several times with small partisan bands, were frequently under fire from the front and rear by an enemy they could not see, and came up empty-handed except for some hundreds of people who might have been partisans. The cleanup in the south pocket went the same way for a day and then was slowed by heavy fire from dugouts and bunkers. After working their way through a maze of defenses that they only managed to negotiate with help from a deserter, the Germans came upon the *Orlov Regiment's* base camp near Svyatoye Lake—it was empty. The partisans had gone out through a swamp over a path that the Germans were not able to follow. By then partisan activity had revived so strongly in the former north pocket that one battalion sent into the pocket to pursue a partisan band had to fight its way out of an encirclement.

On 22 June, XXXXVII Panzer Corps began VOGELSANG II in the woods, between the Vetma and Desna rivers, which were supposed to be the hideout of the *Kaluga Regiment* and the Rognedino *rayon* bands. The tactics were the same as before: form a pair of pockets and drive inward. The corps staff had, in the meantime, concluded that a halfway effective pacification could only be achieved by destroying all buildings and evacuating the inhabitants. Again, the partisans fought sporadically, never letting themselves be pinned in one place, and finally they slipped through the net. The *Kaluga Regiment's* base camp, if it was there, could not be found. When VOGELSANG ended, on 4 July, XXXXVII Panzer Corps reported 500 presumed partisans captured and 1,200 killed. Over 2,200 men aged sixteen to fifty had been taken into custody. The troops had picked up 8,500 women and children in the woods and evacuated 12,500 from villages. The 23,000 civilians were passed to the *Korueck*, who could not feed and house them and could only resettle them in some other partisan-infested area.[42]

Demyansk and the Volkhov Pocket

Offensive Against II Corps

To liquidate the Demyansk pocket was a logical objective of the Soviet spring offensive. As an exercise in the

---

[42]*Pz. AOK 2, Ia Kriegstagebuch Nr. 2, Teil III*, 5–30 Jun 42, Pz. AOK 2 28499/3 file; *Ibid., Teil IV*, 1–4 Jul 42; *339 Inf. Div., Ia Nr. 293/42, Bericht ueber Unternehmen Vogelsang*, 11.7.42, XXXXVII Pz. K. 28946/2 file.

active defense this action could have smashed a substantial enemy force and would have reduced German prospects for operating against the Soviet armies west of Ostashkov and, in the longer run, against Moscow. In April, the *Stavka* gave *Northwest Front* five rifle divisions and eight rifle and two tank brigades. General Kurochkin, the *front's* commander, distributed the reinforcements to *Eleventh Army* and *First Shock Army*, and, with these, he proposed to drive into the pocket from the northeast and southwest, isolate it completely, and destroy II Corps by grinding it to pieces against the stationary front on the east. The attacks began on 3 May and continued until the 20th, were resumed at the end of the month, and did not cease until late June.[43]

After having fought through the winter, in the cold, and on substandard rations, the German troops in the pocket were in poor condition. One of the divisions, the SS Totenkopf, which was probably no worse off than the rest, was down to a third of its normal strength, and of that, a third were troops who would ordinarily have been considered unfit for further service.[44] Nevertheless, II Corps survived, not with ease, but without ever being in doubt about the outcome. Tactically, *Northwest Front's* performance was stereotyped: Kurochkin struck repeatedly in the same places at two- or three-day intervals. After a time, II Corps was more mystified than alarmed by the Russians' persistence. The "bridge" to Sixteenth Army's main front stayed intact, protected by being mostly underwater during that wet spring. For the same reason, it was almost useless as a ground supply line, and the airlift had to be continued.[45]

Second Shock Army Goes Under

The failure at Demyansk was overshadowed by a concurrent Soviet disaster in the Volkhov pocket. Before he was relieved as commander of *Volkhov Front*, using a rifle division and other available reserves. General Meretskov had set up the *VI Guards Rifle Corps,* with which he intended to reinforce *Second Shock Army* after access to the pocket was restored. He did not, he says, know anything about Stalin's and Khozin's (commander, *Leningrad Front*) plans until 23 April, after he had been relieved, when he also learned that Khozin had agreed to let *VI Guards Rifle Corps* be transferred to *Northwest Front*. On the 24th, in Moscow, he told Stalin that, in its current state, *Second Shock Army* "could neither attack nor defend" and, unless it could be given the *VI Guards Rifle Corps*, it should be withdrawn from the pocket "at once." Stalin gave him a polite hearing, a noncommittal promise to consider his views, and sent him on his way to become Zhukov's deputy briefly and then commanding general of *Thirty-third Army.*[46]

For the Soviet leadership to contemplate resuming the offensive in the Volkhov pocket in the spring, with or without reinforcement, was futile. As a

[43]*IVOVSS*, vol. II, p. 474; *IVMV*, vol. V, p. 139.

[44]See Charles W. Sydnor, Jr., *Soldiers of Destruction* (Princeton: Princeton University Press, 1977), pp. 222–29.

[45]*H. Gr. Nord, Ia Kriegstagebuch, 1.–31.5.42*, 3–31 May 42, H. Gr. Nord 75128/10 file.

[46] Meretskov, *"Na volkhovskikh rubezhakh,"* p. 67; Meretskov, *Serving the People,* pp. 202–07.

MACHINE-GUN SQUAD AT THE VOLKHOV POCKET

result of the thaw and the wet weather, *Second Shock Army* was sitting in a vast quagmire and was wholly dependent on a single tenuous supply line that, besides being mostly underwater, was also under constant enemy fire. On the perimeter, the Germans had hemmed the pocket in tightly on all sides. Stalin and Khozin, in fact, were able to indulge in plans for an offensive only because the weather and the terrain had imposed a temporary standoff. By late April, Eighteenth Army had enough troops deployed to close the pocket and clean it out, but the army was having enormous trouble getting supplies to the troops where they were, and those would be doubled and redoubled by any movement. Local inhabitants said the ground dried out

somewhat in the middle of June, and the army expected to wait until then, proposing, in the meantime, to inch into the mouth of the pocket and bring the Erika and Dora Lanes under better surveillance.[47]

What happened on the Soviet side after the change in command is not clear. Khozin has stated that far from being in the "cheerful mood," which Meretskov attributes to him, he was nonplussed by his mission, concerned about *Second Shock Army*'s condition, and had taken a substantial part of the army out of the pocket by 4 May.[48] The

[47]*H. Gr. Nord, Ia Kriegstagebuch, 1.–31.5.42,* 11 May 42, H. Gr. Nord 75128/10 file.

[48]See Meretskov, *Serving the People,* p. 207 and M. S. Khozin, *"Ob odnoy maloissledovannoy operatsyy," Voyenno-istoricheskiy Zhurnal,* 2(1966), 35–46.

History of the Second World War, however, indicates that on 2 May, Khozin had submitted a proposal to execute the Leningrad relief.[49] The *History of the Great Patriotic War* states that the *Stavka* gave the order to withdraw *Second Shock Army* on 14 May, but "the *Leningrad Front* did not demonstrate sufficient operational capability in executing the order."[50] The *History of the Second World War* adds that, although the *Stavka* had given the order, *Second Shock Army* did not begin to withdraw until the 25th, "after the enemy had launched three simultaneous attacks against its weakened forces on 23 May."[51] Vasilevskiy, says the *Stavka* ordered Khozin to take *Second Shock Army* out of the pocket "fast," but, "most regrettably, the order was not executed."[52]

The Germans' observations tend, in small part, to vindicate Khozin. Eighteenth Army, which had an understandably close interest in what went on in the pocket, did not detect any outward movement in April or in the first three weeks of May. The traffic on the lanes appeared to be mostly in supplies, and very few troops went either into or out of the pocket. In mid-May, the number of deserters increased, which could be taken as a sign of disintegration. Some of them said that *Second Shock Army* was being evacuated, but probing attacks met sharp resistance all around the perimeter. The first outward movement, of about a thousand men, was seen on the 21st.

Another thousand went out on the 22d, and General Vlasov's radio closed down, a sign that he was shifting his *Twentieth Army* command post. General Kuechler, commander of Army Group North, then called General Lindemann, commander of Eighteenth Army, and told him it would be "awfully bad" to let the Russians escape. Lindemann said he was ready to stop them, but the ground was too wet.[53] On the 25th, after the Germans had seen another thousand men going out of the pocket during the previous two days, Lindemann asked General der Infanterie Siegfried Haenicke, the XXXVIII Corps commander, whether he could attack "in good conscience" on the 27th if he had air support. Haenicke said he could.[54] But it was raining as Lindemann and Haenicke talked, and a day later the ground was sodden and water was standing in every depression.

Finally, early on 30 May, XXXVIII Corps, on the south, and I Corps, on the north, pushed across the mouth of the pocket over still wet ground. During the day, XXXVIII Corps lost 30 percent of the troops it had committed, but the attacks continued through the night, and the two corps made contact near the Erika Lane at 0130 the next morning. By 1200 on the 31st, they had set up a front facing east, and in the afternoon, they turned west to lock in *Second Shock Army.*[55] While XXXVIII and I Corps braced for counterattacks, the units on the perimeter opened up with all their artillery and began to inch toward the pocket through mud and water.

The counterattacks did not start, though, until 4 June—and then they

---

[49]*IVMV,* vol. V, p. 139.

[50]*IVOVSS,* vol. II, p. 470.

[51]*IVMV,* vol. V, p. 140.

[52]Vasilevskiy, *Delo,* p. 185.

[53]*AOK 18, Ia Kriegstagebuch, 4c,* 22 May 42, AOK 18 22864/2 file.

[54]*Ibid.,* 25 May 42.

[55]*Ibid.,* 30 and 31 May 42.

GENERALS VLASOV AND LINDEMANN TALK AT EIGHTEENTH ARMY HEADQUARTERS

did so in a curious manner. The first Russian assault, during the day on the 4th, came from the west and could be beaten off easily because the troops were all drunk. The next came that night, from the east with tremendous artillery support, but the infantry troops, apparently green, stopped and fell back when they were hit by German fire. When nothing at all happened during the next two days, Kuechler and Lindemann talked about sending General Vlasov, the commander of *Twentieth Army,* a demand for surrender but decided to wait until his army had been pushed into tighter quarters.[56]

On 8 June, Stalin called Meretskov to Moscow and told him, "We made a great mistake in combining *Volkhov* and *Leningrad Fronts.* General Khozin sat and thought about the Volkhov direction, but the results were poor. He did not carry out a *Stavka* directive to evacuate *Second Shock Army.*" Saying that Meretskov knew *Volkhov Front* "very well," Stalin told him to go there, together with General Vasilevskiy, deputy chief of the General Staff, and get *Second Shock Army* out, "if necessary without heavy weapons and equipment."[57] By nightfall, Meretskov was back at his old headquarters, and Khozin, having been replaced at

---

[56]*H. Gr. Nord, Ia Kriegstagebuch, 1.–30.6.42,* 4–7 Jun 42, H. Gr. Nord 75128/11 file.

[57]Meretskov, *"Na volkhovskikh rubezhakh,"* p. 67.

Leningrad Front by General Leytenant L. A. Govorov, was on his way to take over *Thirty-third Army*.[58]

Beginning on the 10th, and for the next two weeks, Meretskov and Vasilevskiy engineered a succession of wild battles, carried on much of the time in pouring rain. On the 19th, they managed to open a corridor 150 yards wide that a dozen T–34 tanks held through the night only to be trapped themselves the next morning. The two had somewhat better luck on the 21st when *Fifty-ninth Army* opened a gap 500 yards wide. But XXXVIII Corps kept the whole stretch under constant artillery and small arms fire and did not believe any *Second Shock Army* troops could have gotten out.[59] Meretskov, who gives the dates for the opening of the gap as the 23d to the 25th, maintains that the Russians brought out wounded and some others.[60] At 2400 on the 22d, the Germans sealed the pocket for the last time.

By the next day, *Second Shock Army* was split into several pieces, crippled, and dying; and Kuechler decided not to bother with asking Vlasov to surrender. Some fifteen thousand of Vlasov's troops were piled up at the western ends of the Erika and Dora Lanes, and if they had made a concerted try, they might still have overrun the German lines holding them in, but they did not. Several hundred officers and *politruks* tried to break out on the 28th. The Germans stopped them and drove them back. The men were not

fighting any longer, and on that day the battle of the Volkhov pocket ended for Eighteenth Army with 33,000 prisoners counted and more coming in every hour.[61] Hitler promoted Kuechler to the rank of *Generalfeldmarschall*.

For the Soviet Union, the deepest psychological trauma was yet to come. On 12 July, a patrol combing the territory around the former pocket stopped to pick up two supposed partisans that a village elder had locked in a shed. The two turned out to be Vlasov and a woman companion who Vlasov said was an old family friend who had been his cook. Intelligent, ambitious, aware that he had no future in the Soviet Union, and impressed with consideration shown him first by Lindemann and later by German intelligence officers, Vlasov soon lent his name to anti-Soviet propaganda and eventually became titular commander of the Russian Army of Liberation, a scattering of collaborator units recruited from the prisoner-of-war camps. To the Germans, he was a sometimes useful figurehead, but he was too much a Russian nationalist for the Germans to give him any kind of free rein. The propaganda actions in which he participated, however, indicated that he had the potential to achieve a strong popular appeal in the occupied—and unoccupied—territories of the Soviet Union. To the Soviet regime, however, he became and has remained the archetype of a traitor. No Soviet account of the battle for the Volkhov pocket fails to implicate him in the disaster either as a weakling or a treacherous

---

[58]Meretskov, *Serving the People*, p. 215.

[59]*AOK 18, Ia Kriegstagebuch, 4c*, 19–23 Jun 42, AOK 18 22864/2 file.

[60]Meretskov, "*Na volkhovskikh rubezhakh*," p. 68f; Meretskov, *Serving the People*, p. 219.

[61]*H. Gr. Nord, Ia Kriegstagebuch, 1.–30.6.42*, 23–28 Jun 42, H. Gr. Nord 75128/11 file.

schemer. Vasilevskiy says, "The position of *Second Shock Army* was made even more complicated by the fact that its commander, Vlasov, turned out to be a foul traitor to his country, who voluntarily went over to the enemy side."[62]

---

[62]Vasilevskiy, *Delo,* p. 185.

CHAPTER XIII

Active Defense, South

Kerch Resolved

Competing Plans

In February of 1942, with the aid of an "ice bridge" over the Kerch Strait, *Crimean Front* had been raised to a strength of three armies. With these, General Kozlov, commander of *Transcaucasus Front,* resumed the offensive on 27 February. The *Sevastopol Defense Region,* its force increased by then to over eighty thousand men, joined in with a "demonstrative" attack by the *Independent Maritime Army* at the center of the fortress perimeter.[1] The collapse of a Rumanian division in the German line had allowed the Russians to drive a seven-mile-deep bulge into the northern half of the front on the Isthmus of Parpach before Kozlov stopped to regroup on 3 March. He made another start on the 13th, and thereafter, in waves that rose and receded every several days, he stayed on the attack into the second week of April, coming close at times but never succeeding in breaking out of the isthmus.[2]

As the key to the Black Sea and bridge to the Caucasus, the Crimea figured as heavily in the Soviet plans for the spring as it had in the winter offensive, and Kozlov had close to three hundred thousand troops, not an insignificant force. In March, Mekhlis, the chief army political commissar, joined *Crimean Front* as the *Stavka* representative, and on 21 April, the *Stavka* created the Headquarters, *North Caucasus Theater,* under Marshal Budenny. Budenny assumed overall command of *Crimean Front,* the *Sevastopol Defense Region,* and all naval and air forces in the Black Sea–Caucasus area. His mission was to coordinate these forces in the projected spring offensive, and Kozlov's and Mekhlis' mission was to liberate the Crimea.[3]

On 23 March, at about the same time as Stalin and the *Stavka* were laying out the Soviet spring offensive, Hitler conferred with his senior military advisers on the *Fuehrer* directive he was preparing for the coming summer's operations and ordered that the first preliminary operation should be the retaking of the Kerch Peninsula.[4] In fact, Hitler was merely underscoring decisions and actions already taken. In February, the OKH had earmarked the 22d Panzer Division and 28th Light Division, then being formed, for Eleventh Army, and the divisions had begun moving into the Crimea in the

---

[1]Vaneyev, *Geroicheskaya oborona*, pp. 208–11.
[2]Manstein, *Verlorene Siege,* pp. 250–53.

[3]*VOV,* p. 143f; *IVMV,* vol. V, p. 114.
[4]*Halder Diary,* vol. III, 23 Mar 42, p. 417.

middle of March.[5] Throughout the winter, the cleanup on the Crimea had had first priority because it would free a whole army and because the weather could be expected to improve there earlier than elsewhere. The only question—assuming that the front would hold, which had been far from certain in February and March—had been whether to start the effort with Kerch or Sevastopol. Manstein had preferred Kerch and Bock Sevastopol. Hitler had agreed with Manstein that to confront the enemy where he was strongest was better than to have him at one's back. On 31 March, Manstein issued the Eleventh Army preliminary directive for Operation TRAPPENJAGD ("bustard hunt"), the Kerch offensive.[6]

Manstein's major problem was one of strength. The most he could commit to TRAPPENJAGD were five infantry divisions and one panzer division, plus two Rumanian infantry divisions and one Rumanian cavalry division. That left three German infantry divisions, one Rumanian infantry division, and one Rumanian mountain division to contain Sevastopol. The Rumanians were mostly inexperienced troops, indifferently led, and, as past experience had shown, they could be more a danger than a help.

In the three Soviet armies on the Kerch Peninsula, *Forty-fourth, Forty-seventh,* and *Fifty-first,* the Germans counted 17 rifle divisions, 2 cavalry divisions, 3 rifle brigades, and 4 tank brigades.[7] The *Crimean Front* strength, as given by Vasilevskiy, was 21 rifle divisions. The *front,* according to Vasilevskiy's figures, also had superiorities over the Germans in artillery and mortars (3,577 to 2,472), tanks (347 to 180), and aircraft (400 to "up to" 400).[8] The *Sevastopol Defense Region* had 8 divisions and 3 brigades.[9]

Having more troops than they could conveniently deploy in the ten-mile-wide Isthmus of Parpach, the Soviet armies could stage a defense in depth that would potentially increase in strength farther east where the peninsula widened to fifteen and twenty miles and all of their troops could be brought into play. Over the fifty-mile distance to the city of Kerch, they could force the enemy to chew his way through four prepared lines: the front; the Parpach line proper, which since the February offensive had been seven miles behind the front in the north and a mile or two to the rear on the south; the Nasyr line, which ran parallel to the Parpach line five miles to the east; and the Sultanovka line, eighteen miles west of Kerch. The strongest were the Parpach and the Sultanovka. The Parpach line was fronted by an antitank ditch that had been dug in 1941 and deepened, broadened, and rimmed with concrete emplacements during the winter. The Sultanovka followed the remains of ancient fortifications spanning the peninsula that the Germans called the "Tatar Wall" and the Russians the "Turkish Wall." (*Map 22.*)

[5] *Bock Diary, Osten II,* 16 Mar 42. The 1942 "light" divisions, of which the 28th Light Division was one, were light infantry divisions. They were later renamed "Jaeger" divisions. See Manstein, *Verlorene Siege,* p. 253.

[6] Friedrich Wilhelm Hauck, MS P–114c, *Die Operationen der deutschen Heeresgruppen an der Ostfront 1941 bis 1945, Suedliches Gebiet, Teil II,* p. 42, CMH files; *O.B. der 11. Armee, Operationsabsichten, 31.3.42,* AOK 11 22279/23 file.

[7] *Der O.B. der 11. Armee, an Soldaten der Krim-Armee, 19.5.42,* AOK 11 28654/4 file.

[8] Vasilevskiy, *Delo,* p. 208.

[9] Vaneyev, *Geriocheskaya oborona,* p. 208.

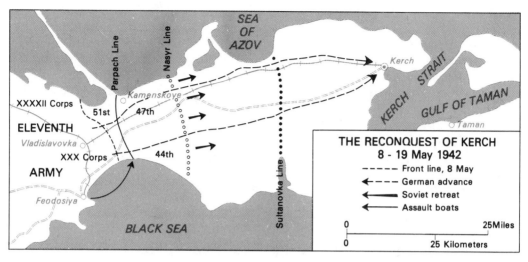

SEA OF AZOV

Parpach Line

Nasyr Line

Kerch

KERCH STRAIT

GULF OF TAMAN

XXXXII Corps

51st

47th

Kamenskoye

ELEVENTH

Vladislavovka

XXX Corps

44th

ARMY

Feodosiya

Sultanovka Line

Taman

BLACK SEA

**THE RECONQUEST OF KERCH
8 - 19 May 1942**

- - - - - Front line, 8 May

←- - - German advance

←— Soviet retreat

←— Assault boats

0   25 Miles

0   25 Kilometers

MAP 22

To accomplish anything at all, Manstein had to break the Parpach line and do so before Kozlov could bring his massive power to bear. On the narrow isthmus, hardly any deviation from an outright frontal attack was possible: Manstein saw just one. The Soviet Command was sensitive about its extended north flank, which could be the springboard into the Crimean mainland but which was also vulnerable. Manstein had inadvertently enhanced that concern on 20 March by putting 22d Panzer Division, which needed some seasoning, into an attack at the base of the bulge. A sudden rainstorm had deprived the division of its air support, and heavier Soviet armor had knocked out thirty-two of its tanks in the few hours before the affair was called off. During the following days, while Manstein and Bock were explaining the fiasco to Hitler, *Crimean Front* command had drawn its own conclusions and shifted more strength to the north flank. Manstein, therefore,

had judged his chances to be improved on the extreme south, where he would have to break the Parpach line right away and where the defense was less deep. Two or three miles would bring him through the line, and thereafter, a fast turn could make the north flank a deathtrap for the Russians.[10]

TRAPPENJAGD was a gamble. If he had his wits about him, Kozlov could quickly bring it to a calamitous finish. For Manstein everything had to work perfectly; even then, he could not expect to do more than unhinge the Parpach line. Manstein, who was not ordinarily one to underestimate himself or his troops, told Field Marshal Bock, the commander of Army Group South, and the OKH on 2 April that the discrepancy in the forces was too great.[11] The alternative was to wait

[10] *22. Pz. Div., Ia Nr. 227/42, Bericht ueber den Angriff auf Korpetsch am 20.3.42,* AOK 11 22279/23 file; *O.B. der 11. Armee, Operationsabsichten, 31.3.42,* AOK 11 22279/23 file.

[11] *Bock Diary, Osten II,* 2 Apr 42.

until after the middle of May when another division or two might become available for Eleventh Army. Bock wanted to go ahead in April and not give the Russians another month or more to do whatever they might have in mind.

Hitler was the one who supplied the final and, very likely, crucial ingredient. The winter had made him a devotee of air support, and on 13 April, he had told General Kuechler, the commander of Army Group North, that Toropets would not have been lost in January if the army group commands had understood the uses of air power. Three days later, when Manstein brought in the TRAPPENJAGD plan, he approved everything except the *Luftwaffe* dispositions, announcing that he would see to them in person.[12] He then ordered, over OKL protests, General Richthofen's VIII Air Corps, which was being transferred from Army Group Center to support Army Group South in the summer campaign, to set up first on the Crimea and support Eleventh Army. An air corps normally provided the tactical air support for an entire army group. TRAPPENJAGD had to wait while Richthofen brought in his squadrons of *Stuka* bombers and fighters and a whole flak division to protect their airfields, but it was, as Manstein said, going to have "concentrated air support the like of which has never existed."[13]

By the turn of the month, the *rasputitsa* had passed out of the Crimea. Under the influence of both the sea

and the mainland, the weather was changeable. Temperatures ranged from below freezing to the middle 70s, and strong winds blew clouds and showers across the peninsula. On the south coast the trees were in bloom, while upper slopes of mountains a few miles inland were still covered with snow. Bock was stirred by the contrast when he toured the Eleventh Army area at the end of April. The fronts were quiet, and the ground troops were ready on the isthmus, but VIII Air Corps was not yet fully settled. After a firsthand inspection, Bock was impressed by the "careful preparations" for the attack and uneasy about the "extraordinary risk" it would still entail.[14]

Manstein held his final briefing for the corps and division commanders on 2 May with Richthofen present. He described TRAPPENJAGD as a ground operation that had its main effort in the air, and he said the planes would have to "pull the infantry forward."[15] X-Day was set for 5 May but had to be put off until the 8th because Richthofen was not ready. By the first week in May, a complete surprise was out of the question. The Russians had already put up placards along the front reading, "Come on. We are waiting."[16]

How ready the Russians might be became an ominous imponderable as X-Day approached. Bock worried about how deep their defense was echeloned and considered giving up the turn to the north. Manstein believed he had to stay with the original plan.[17]

[12]*OKW, Stellv. WFSt, Kriegsgeschichtliche Abteilung Kriegstagebuch, 1.4.–30.6.42,* 16 Apr 42, I.M.T. 1807 file.
[13]*XXX A.K., Ia Kriegstagebuch, 1.–20.5.42,* 1 May 42, XXX A.K. 21753/1 file.
[14]*Bock Diary, Osten II,* 28 Apr 42.
[15]*XXX A.K., Ia Kriegstagebuch, 1.–20.5.42,* 2 May 42, XXX A.K. 21753/1 file.
[16]*Bock Diary, Osten II,* 5 May 42.
[17]*Ibid.*

GENERAL VON RICHTHOFEN (*second from right*) DISCUSSES AN AIR STRIKE WITH HIS STAFF

"The enemy," he said, "is certain that we are going to attack, but he does not know where or when."[18] In the confined space on the isthmus, that was a small consolation and would have been none at all without help from the other side, which Manstein, although he did not know it, was about to receive in generous measure.

The Soviet accounts agree that the attack was no surprise, even as to time. However, they give two versions of what was proposed to be done about it. Vasilevskiy says the *Stavka* gave Kozlov and Mekhlis a directive in the latter half of April in which it told them to discontinue preparations for the offensive and organize a "solid defense in depth" and to expect the German main effort to be against their left flank.[19] The *History of the Great Patriotic War* states that Kozlov and Mekhlis failed to organize a defense in depth.[20] The *History of the Second World War,* on the other hand, says that *Crimean Front* was ready to launch an attack of its own on the same day as the Germans but "failed to institute measures for an effective blow."[21] General Armii Sergei M. Shtemenko, who was at the time a colonel in the General Staff branch

---

[18]*AOK 11, Ia Aktennotiz fuer K.T.B. ueber Besprechung am 5.5.42,* AOK 11 28654/3 file.

[19]Vasilevskiy, *Delo,* pp. 208, 210.
[20]*IVOVSS,* vol. II, p. 405.
[21]*IVMV,* vol. V, p. 123.

responsible for the Caucasus and the Crimea, adds that *Crimean Front* was deployed for an offensive on the northern half of the line—exactly as Manstein had thought it would be.[22] All blame Kozlov and Mekhlis. Vasilevskiy says Kozlov, his chief of staff, his chief political officer, and Mekhlis were "manifest incompetents."[23]

Trappenjagd

At dark on the evening of 7 May, thirty German assault boats eased out of the mine-strewn Feodosiya harbor and steered northeast along the coast. At 2300, they stopped on the beach to take aboard a company of infantry, a heavy machine gun platoon, and an engineer platoon. Their mission was to land the troops just east of the Soviet antitank ditch at the same time the attack on the isthmus reached it, which was to be shortly after dawn. While the boats were loading in bright moonlight, a Soviet patrol vessel appeared offshore, cruising slowly, and they had to stay on the beach another hour and a half until it had passed out of sight and earshot. In the meantime, the temperature had dropped below freezing, and a strong wind had sprung up. To reach the landing point on time, the boats had to take a course that carried them out on the open sea. Designed for river crossings, they were propelled by outboard motors with straight shafts that gave them speed and maneuverability in quiet, shallow water. Against the wind and waves, two men operating each motor could barely

keep the boats headed in a straight line.[24]

During the night of the 7th, the 170th Infantry Division took position and completed the deployment for TRAPPENJAGD. The XXX Corps, under General der Artillerie Maximilian von Fretter-Pico, then had five of the six German divisions. To hold the northern half of the isthmus front, General Matenklott's XXXXII Corps had one German and three Rumanian divisions. Three divisions, 132d and 50th Infantry and 28th Light Divisions, would make the breakthrough. When they had crossed the antitank ditch and the engineers had built causeways for the tanks, 22d Panzer Division and 170th Infantry Divison would pass through and begin the turn north. Manstein had set up as his own reserve the so-called Grodeck Brigade consisting of a Rumanian motorized regiment and two German truck-mounted infantry battalions.

When the first gray streak of light appeared in the east, at about 0315, the infantry jumped off behind a rocket and artillery barrage. In one hour, Richthofen's *Stuka* and fighter squadrons, waiting on the airfields in the rear, would be hitting the Parpach line. At 0400, the assault boats were lying in wait off the beach, just out of sight of land, the lead boat's radio tuned for a signal from the shore. Forty minutes later it came. The 132d Infantry Division, hugging the coast, was almost up to the antitank ditch. The boats headed in. By then fighters were giving them cover overhead. A half mile out, they met artillery and small arms fire that

[22]S. M. Shtemenko, *The Soviet General Staff at War, 1941–1945* (Moscow: Progress Publishers, 1970), p. 53.
[23]Vasilevskiy, *Delo*, p. 209.

[24]*Sturmbootkommando 902, Angriff auf Parpatsch-Stellung, 9.5.42,* AOK 11 28654/3.

sank eleven boats, but only one man was killed and three wounded. At 0600, 132d Infantry Division crossed the antitank ditch. An hour later, its neighbor on the left, 28th Light Division, which originally had a longer way to come, was fighting in the ditch. The 50th Infantry Division had the most distance to cover and the most trouble. First, its rocket projectors failed to fire because their electric ignition system broke down; then it ran into a deep minefield and, behind that, a trench line with dug-in tanks.[25]

The early morning was hazy; the day sunny, bright, and warm. The VIII Air Corps had complete command in the sky, and a constant stream of its planes pounded the Soviet line. Behind 132d Infantry Division, which in midmorning was fighting its way through Soviet positions east of the antitank ditch, engineers leveled enough of the ditch with explosives to get two self-propelled assault gun batteries across. The worst possible mischance could still happen, though, if the Russians recovered their balance enough to bring the attack to a stop short of the breakthrough. In a few hours, they could muster a smothering numerical superiority. At 1200, Fretter-Pico began gathering whatever reserves he could for a late-afternoon push, but an hour later they were no longer needed. The enemy was retreating ahead of 28th Light Division and 132d Infantry Division "in droves." The divisions had advanced six miles by nightfall, and the air umbrella had expanded to reach east to Kerch. The VIII Air Corps had flown over two thousand sorties and shot down eighty Soviet planes.[26] Fretter-Pico ordered 22d Panzer Division to come forward during the night and asked Manstein for the Grodeck Brigade.[27]

In the morning, the infantry waited for an hour after dawn while the planes worked over the enemy line. The Soviet recovery overnight was less than expected, so little that in another hour or so, 132d Infantry Division appeared to have an open road to the east, maybe straight through to Kerch. Manstein wanted to stay with the planned turn to the north, but because the crossings on the antitank ditch were not wide enough or firm enough yet to take 22d Panzer Division's tanks, Fretter-Pico sent the lighter Grodeck Brigade across first. Before 1200, the brigade passed through 132d Infantry Division's line with orders to head east as far and as fast as it could. In the afternoon, 22d Panzer Division crossed the ditch and deployed alongside 28th Light Division. At 1600, with five hours of daylight left, it began to roll north. The Grodeck Brigade by then had passed the Nasyr line and was almost halfway to Kerch. If the tanks did nearly as well, they could close the pocket before dark, but the Crimea was about to live up to its reputation for changeable weather. In less than two hours, rain was pouring down on the peninsula, and everything was stopped.

Rain continued through the night and into the forenoon on the 10th, and 22d Panzer Division's tanks only began grinding slowly through the mud in

---

[25]XXX A.K., Ia Kriegstagebuch, 1.–20.5.42, 8 May 42, XXX A.K. 21753/1 file.

[26]Flivo AOK 11, Tagesabschlussmeldung VIII Flieger Korps, 9.5.42, AOK 11 28654/3 file.

[27]XXX A.K., Ia Kriegstagebuch, 1.1.–20.5.42, 8 May 42, XXX A.K. 21753/1 file.

AIMING A SIX-INCH ROCKET PROJECTOR

the afternoon. They had almost closed the pocket by dark, and by then, the Grodeck Brigade had crossed the Sultanovka line.[28] In the morning on the 10th, the *Stavka* had ordered *Crimean Front* to pull its armies back to the Turkish Wall (the Sultanovka line) and defend it, but, Vasilevskiy says, the *front* command delayed executing the order for forty-eight hours and then failed to organize the withdrawal properly.[29]

The *front* command may have been somewhat more effective than Vasilevskiy had credited it with having been. During the night on the 10th, Fretter-Pico learned that the Russians had been manning the Nasyr line, forward of the Sultanovka, on the 9th, and

the Grodeck Brigade had been lucky enough to hit a still unoccupied section on the extreme south. Consequently, he decided to send the 132d Infantry Division east the next morning along the route the brigade had taken and put the 170th Infantry Division in right behind it for a thrust to the northeast. The objectives would be to overrun the Nasyr and Sultanovka lines and get to Kerch and the coast on the Kerch Strait in time to prevent *Crimean Front* from organizing a beachhead defense or an evacuation.

During the morning on the 11th, 22d Panzer Division closed the pocket to the east of the Parpach line and together with 50th Infantry Division and 28th Light Division drew the ring tight. The three divisions then passed to XXXXII Corps for the mop-up, leaving XXX Corps to carry the drive east with two divisions and the Grodeck Brigade. Mud slowed all the movements and stopped the Grodeck Brigade, which was also running out of ammunition. At the day's end, the pocket was practically eliminated; 22d Panzer Division was turning east; 132d and 170th Infantry Divisions were halfway to the Sultanovka; and the Grodeck Brigade was standing off attacks on the other side of the wall with ammunition airdropped to it.

By the 12th, the Soviet commands had completely lost control of the battle. Their units, everywhere, were broken and jumbled. The 132d and 170th Infantry Divisions came within sight of the Sultanovka line during the day and crossed it early the next morning. When 22d Panzer Division passed through the infantry line several hours later, Fretter-Pico had three divisions bearing in on Kerch and the coast to

[28]*Ibid.*, 9 and 10 May 42.
[29]Vasilevskiy, *Delo*, p. 209.

the north and south. In the afternoon on the 14th, 170th Infantry Division pushed into the city, and 132d Infantry Division brought the port under fire from the south.

According to all previous experience, the battle should have ended on the 14th or, at the latest on the 15th when Kerch and the small peninsula northeast of the city fell. Eleventh Army's last concern had been that *Crimean Front* would stage a Dunkirk-type evacuation across the narrow strait. That did not happen, and for the next six days, disjointed small battles continued all the way back to the Parpach line. The first Germans on the heights overlooking the coast had seen Soviet troops boarding ships offshore, but afterward, very few ships had appeared. Later the talk among the prisoners was that those who had crossed to the mainland were being "called to account" and sometimes being fired upon. The prisoners claimed to have heard a Stalin order telling them not to expect to be evacuated because there were plenty of caves and gullies on the peninsula from which to carry on the resistance.[30]

Manstein, nevertheless, declared TRAPPENJAGD completed on the 19th. In the next several days, the prisoner count reached 170,000.[31] One Soviet account gives the number of *Crimean Front* troops lost in the battle as 176,000 and those evacuated as 120,000. Mekhlis lost his posts as deputy commissar for defense and as chief of the Army's

Main Political Directorate and was reduced to the rank of a corps commissar. Kozlov, his chief of staff, and his chief political officer and the commanders of *Forty-fourth* and *Forty-seventh Armies* were relieved of their posts and demoted.[32]

The Izyum Bulge

Prospects and Problems

In early March, the *Stavka* asked the command of *Southwestern Theater* to submit its strategic and operational estimates for the coming summer. On the 22d, Marshal Timoshenko, the theater's commander, sent in a proposal for a spring-summer offensive by *Bryansk, Southwest,* and *South Fronts*. It would aim to clear the line of the Dnepr River from Gomel south to Cherkassy and would conclude with a drive across the lower Dnepr to the line Cherkassy-Pervomaysk-Nikolayev. In the first phase, to be begun in late April or early May, *Southwest* and *South Fronts* would chop off the German-held north and south cornerposts of the Izyum bulge at Balakleya and Slavyansk, and *Southwest Front* would then advance north out of the western end of the bulge to take Kharkov.[33] Timoshenko asked for reinforcements amounting to 34 rifle divisions, 28 tank brigades, 24 artillery regiments, 756 aircraft, 200,000 bulk replacements, and "large quantities" of weapons, equipment, and motor vehicles.[34]

In the last week of March, Ti-

[30]*XXX A.K., Ia Kriegstagebuch, 1.1.–20.5.42*, 11–20 May 42, XXX A.K. 21753/1 file.
[31]*XXXXII A.K., Ia Kriegstagebuch Nr. 5*, 18 May 42, XXXXII A.K. 29071/1 file; *Der O.B. der 11. Armee, an Soldaten der Krim-Armee, 19.5.42*, AOK 11 28654/4 file; *Bock Diary, Osten II*, 24 May 42.

[32]*VOV*, p. 144; *IVOVSS*, vol. II, p. 406.
[33]Bagramyan, *Tak shli my k pobede*, p. 48; *IVMV*, vol. V, p. 126f; Vasilevskiy, *Delo*, p. 212; *IVOVSS*, vol. II, p. 411.
[34]Bagramyan, *Tak shli my k pobede*, p. 54.

moshenko, Khrushchev, his member of the Military Council, and General Bagramyan, his chief of staff, went to Moscow to defend the proposal before the *Stavka*. The discussions appear, from Bagramyan's account, actually to have been between the three of them and Stalin with Marshal Shaposhnikov, chief of the General Staff, and General Vasilevskiy, his deputy, present. Shaposhnikov had convinced Stalin beforehand that the offensive should not be attempted on the proposed scale, and in the first conference in the Kremlin, on the night of the 27th, Stalin said he only had a few dozen divisions in the whole reserve, not nearly enough to meet the requirements of the rest of the front and also give *Southwestern Theater* what it wanted.[35] Stalin then said that the offensive would have to be restricted to the Kharkov region.

In another night meeting on the 28th Stalin and Shaposhnikov reviewed the first plan for a Kharkov offensive and required that it be reworked to limit it exclusively to the Kharkov area and to reduce the number of units requested from the reserves.[36] What had been proposed was apparently an offensive by *Southwest* and *South Fronts* similar to the first phase of the original plan plus participation by *Bryansk Front*.

On the night of the 30th, Stalin accepted a proposal to develop an operation that could be executed with provision from the reserves of 10 rifle divisions, 26 tank brigades, 10 artillery regiments, and enough replacements to bring *Southwest* and *South Fronts* up to

80 percent of authorized strengths. The idea was to have *Southwest Front*, alone, take Kharkov and thereby set the stage for a subsequent thrust with *South Front* to Dnepropetrovsk.[37]

Timoshenko took command of *Southwest Front* in person on 8 April, and on the 10th, he turned in a plan for a two-pronged attack on Kharkov. One, the main drive, was to go out of the northwest corner of the Izyum bulge, the other out of the smaller Volchansk salient. The *Stavka* approved this proposal.[38] Shaposhnikov, Vasilevskiy says, pointed out the risks of launching an offensive out of a pocket like the Izyum bulge, but Timoshenko convinced Stalin that the operation would be a "complete success."[39] Moskalenko, who saw the decision from the point of view of an army commander *(Thirty-eighth)*, says the *Stavka* made a mistake in approving the plan, but it did so at the "insistence" of the theater command.[40]

The plan, as written on 10 April and issued in final form on the 28th, projected not only the liberation of Kharkov but an extensive encirclement that would trap most of German Sixth Army. The attack from the Volchansk salient would go due west and be spearheaded by *Twenty-eighth Army*, a new army with 4 rifle divisions from the *Stavka* reserves. It would be under Ryabyshev, an experienced general, who had successfully commanded *Fifty-seventh Army* during the winter offensive, and it would be supported on its flanks by elements of *Twenty-first* and

[35]Vasilevskiy, *Delo*, p. 212; Bagramyan, *Tak shli my k pobede*, p. 60.
[36]Bagramyan, *Tak shli my k pobede*, p. 62. See also *VOV (Kratkaya Istoriya)*, p. 161f.

[37]Bagramyan, *Tak shli my k pobede*, p. 66; *IVMV*, vol. V, p. 127.
[38]Bagramyan, *Tak shli my k pobede*, p. 212.
[39]Vasilevskiy, *Delo*, p. 213.
[40]Moskalenko, *Na yugo-zapadnom napravlenii*, p. 213.

TANKMEN FLUSH OUT SOVIET SOLDIERS AFTER THE BATTLE

Thirty-eighth Armies. The main thrust, out of the Izyum bulge, was assigned to *Sixth Army,* under General Leytenant A. M. Gorodnyanskov, and the *"Bobkin Group,"* under General Mayor L. V. Bobkin. The attack was to be made in two stages: the first, to break through the enemy's first and second defense lines and destroy his tactical reserves and the second, to smash the enemy's operational reserves and complete the encirclement. For the attack, *Sixth Army* and the *Bobkin Group,* between them, would have 10 rifle and 3 cavalry divisions, 11 tank brigades, and 2 motorized rifle brigades. To make the breakthrough on a fifteen-mile front, *Sixth Army* had 8 rifle divisions, 4 tank brigades, and 14 regiments of supporting artillery. The *Bobkin Group* was a newly formed mobile operational group composed of 2 rifle divisions, a cavalry corps, and a tank brigade. Its commander had successfully led a similar group in the *Thirty-eighth Army* area during the winter. Timoshenko had 560 tanks for the first stage and 269 more to be put in during the second. He held as the reserve of the *front* a cavalry corps, 2 rifle divisions, and an independent tank brigade, which, according to Moskalenko, had about a hundred tanks. He also had close at hand the *Ninth* and *Fifth-seventh Armies* of *South Front* and, potentially available, *South Front's* reserve of a tank corps and 7 rifle divisions.[41]

---

[41]*Ibid.,* pp. 182–84; Bagramyan, *Tak shli my k pobede,* pp. 69, 71–74, 84; *IVMV,* vol. V, p. 127.

In the meantime, Army Group South also had had its eyes on the Izyum bulge. A situation estimate Bock sent to the OKH on 10 March specified that the bulge would have to be wiped out as soon as the *rasputitsa* passed, because, otherwise, the Russians would use it as a springboard for an attack on Kharkov and because the army group could not keep on defending the extra length of front. Getting rid of the bulge was essential to the army group's summer operations. Bock asked for two fresh divisions for Seventeenth Army and two for Sixth Army.[42]

On 25 March, Army Group South had issued a directive for Operation FRIDERICUS. In concept, FRIDERICUS was simple enough, a matter of two thrusts, one from the north, the other from the south, meeting at Izyum. But the staff work had brought to light an irritating complication: owing to the lie of the front in relation to the Donets River, the best route for the thrust from the north was east of the Donets, straight along the Kharkov-Izyum road, which, however, would be wide open to attack on the east. Sixth Army, already having two exposed fronts, would be hard put to hold a third. To avoid this problem, the FRIDERICUS directive put the Sixth Army thrust west of the Donets, which would give it the protection of the river but which would also be awkward because of a double bend in the river. Because the river's protection would be greatest during the time of high water, the starting date was set for 22 April.[43]

Army Group South had given FRI-

DERICUS a name and an existence on paper. From there on, the operation acquired a life of its own. First off, it spawned a second version, FRIDERICUS II, after Hitler and Halder, chief of the General Staff, objected to the army group's choice and wanted the Sixth Army effort east of the Donets. Bock, in turn, complained that FRIDERICUS II was based on "all kinds of assumptions but not a single fact" and was convinced that the only practicable version was the army group's own, which became FRIDERICUS I.[44] When either could start depended on the weather and on the railroads that were already laboring at capacity under the weight of traffic for the coming summer campaign. The OKH released two new infantry divisions for FRIDERICUS in early April, but it could only deliver them by rail as far as Rovno and Grodno in Poland, and they had to make their way east another 500 miles by road. On 24 April, two days after the original starting date for the operation, Bock and Hitler were still debating the deployment.[45]

Finally, on 30 April, Bock issued a directive for FRIDERICUS II. It was "born in severe pain," he remarked, and "on the whole not pretty" but it was also unalterable because of the *Fuehrer's* insistence.[46] Setting the time for "probably" 18 May took another week.[47] While Army Group South's reinforcements came forward slowly, the rivers were subsiding, the roads were becom-

---

[42]*Bock Diary, Osten II,* 10 Mar 42.

[43]*Obkdo. d. H. Gr. Sued, Ia Nr. 585/42, Weisung Nr. 1 fuer den Angriff "Fridericus," 25.3.42,* Pz. AOK 1 25179/3 file.

[44]*Bock Diary, Osten II,* 31 Mar 42.

[45]*Ibid.,* 24 Apr 42.

[46]*Ibid.,* 30 Apr 42; *Obkdo. d. H. Gr. Sued, Ia Nr. 946/42, Weisung Nr. 2 fuer den Angriff "Fridericus," 30.4.42,* Pz. AOK 1 25179/3 file.

[47]*AOK 17, Ia Nr. 33/42, Befehl fuer Angriff "Fridericus," 8.5.42,* Pz. AOK 1 27179/3 file.

ing passible, and the Russians were stirring ominously in the northwest corner of the Izyum bulge and in the Volchansk salient. Hitler and Halder, who had done the same with earlier reports of similar Russian activity, dismissed the idea of an attack toward Kharkov, although, as the weather and condition of the ground improved, Halder did so "with less conviction than before."[48]

The Drive on Kharkov

On the morning of 12 May, Soviet *Sixth Army,* the *Bobkin Group,* and *Twenty-eighth Army* went over to the offensive, therewith opening what was going to be the Soviet battle of World War II that generated the most long-lasting controversy. While Stalin lived, it would be made to disappear from history. In the 1950s, it would be resurrected as a chief exhibit in the de-Stalinization campaign; and in the late 1960s, it would be turned against Stalin's critic and successor, Nikita Khrushchev. Consequently, as seen from the Soviet side, the battle appears in several versions, all, to some extent, tailored to purposes other than purely historical.

By both the Soviet and German accounts, the beginning was spectacular, in its impact, not a far second to the Moscow counterattack. The Soviet histories maintain that their initial advantage was not great. The *Short History* gives a 3:2 advantage in infantry and 2:1 in tanks at the points where the attacks were made. The *History of the Second World War* indicates an overall *Southwest Front* superiority of 1.51:1 in troops and 2:1 in tanks but says the

tanks were mostly light models.[49] The actual advantages could have been much greater, at least so it appeared to the Germans. Sixth Army reported being hit by twelve rifle divisions and 300 tanks in the first waves. Veteran troops, who had fought through the winter, were overawed by the masses of armor rolling in on them that morning.[50] Bock told Halder Sixth Army was fighting "for its life."[51]

Heaviest hit on the first day was Sixth Army's VIII Corps in the northwestern corner of the Izyum bulge. Against it, Soviet *Sixth Army* drove due north toward Kharkov, while the *Bobkin Group* pushed west and northwest to get the army elbow room on its left flank. *Twenty-eighth Army's* attack out of the Volchansk salient was less powerful but more dangerous because it had the shorter distance to go. *(Map 23.)* Before 1200, all three attacks had cracked the German lines, and by evening, *Twenty-eighth Army's* tanks were ranging to within eleven miles of Kharkov. After persuading Halder that these were not mere "cosmetic flaws," Bock released the 23d Panzer Division and 71st and 113th Infantry Divisions to General Paulus, the commander of Sixth Army. They were to have been Sixth Army's spearhead force for FRIDERICUS.[52]

In two days, the Soviet armies opened broad gaps south and northeast of Kharkov, and the *Bobkin Group* drove VIII Corps away from its contact with the Armeegruppe Kleist and back against the Berestovaya River. While

---

[48] *Bock Diary, Osten II,* 25 Apr and 5 May 42.

[49] *VOV (Kratkaya Istoriya),* p. 162; *IVMV,* vol. V, p. 128.

[50] *AOK 6, Ia Kriegstagebuch Nr. 11,* 12 May 42, AOK 6 22391/1 file.

[51] *Bock Diary, Osten II,* 12 May 42.

[52] *Ibid.,* 12 May 42.

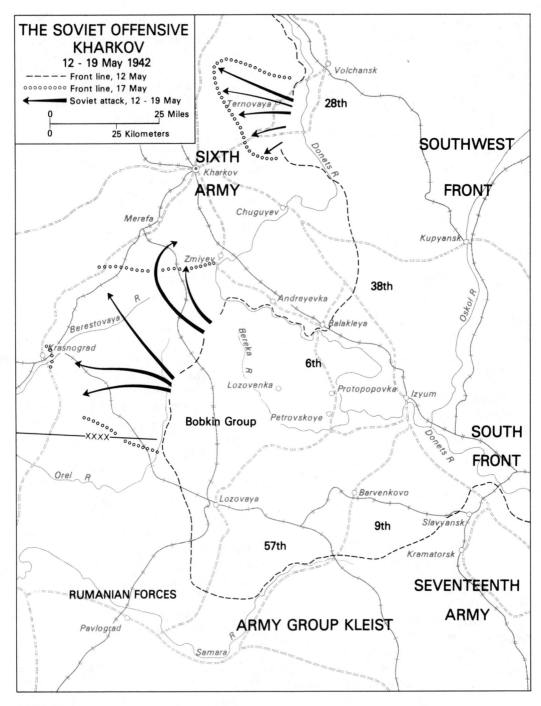

MAP 23

Paulus positioned the three divisions and elements of the 3d Panzer and 305th Infantry Divisions to parry the thrusts at Kharkov, Generaloberst Alexander Loehr, the *Luftwaffe* commander for the Army Group South zone, began shifting ground support units from Richthofen's VIII Air Corps north from the Crimea. The attack had come just at the time Soviet resistance was beginning to collapse on the Kerch Peninsula, and the VIII Air Corps units, added to those of IV Air Corps already operating around Kharkov and the Izyum bulge, would create in some days' time an extraordinarily powerful concentration of air support. By nightfall on the 13th, a ten-mile-wide gap had opened on the VIII Corps left flank southwest of Zmiyev. On its right flank, Soviet cavalry was probing westward toward Krasnograd through an even wider gap. The only obstacle in *Twenty-eighth Army*'s way on the Volchansk-Kharkov road was a party of Germans surrounded in the village of Ternovaya. On the 14th, it was time for Bock and his Soviet counterpart, Timoshenko, to make big decisions.

Timoshenko still had the tanks for the second stage. By the 14th, even though the breakthroughs had been achieved, Timoshenko did not put the armor in. The *History of the Second World War* says that the *front* and theater command did not take advantage of the favorable situation existing on 14 May and did not put in the mobile forces to complete the encirclement.[53] The *History of the Great Patriotic War* and the *Popular Scientific Sketch* maintain that Timoshenko was "misled" by mistaken intelligence reports of strong enemy armor being concentrated near Zmiyev and, therefore, delayed committing the tanks.[54] Bagramyan says that the "moment" had arrived, on the 14th, when *Twenty-eighth Army* should have committed its mobile groups, but the army staff's "poor organization" prevented that. He also says *Southwest Front* sent a report to the *Stavka* on the night of the 14th in which it described its successes but pointed out, as well, that two enemy panzer divisions still constituted "a serious impediment" to the advance on Kharkov.[55] The *Short History* implies that the *front* command could not make up its mind, waited for "a more favorable moment," and, so, missed the chance.[56] Moskalenko also maintains that the trouble was with the *front* command's indecision.[57]

Bock, of course, unaware of the help he was getting from the other side, had two choices on the 14th: he could act directly to save Sixth Army from an expensive trouncing, or he could try to accomplish the same effect and possibly more—while also risking two failures—by going ahead with FRIDERICUS. The circumstances were as peculiar as any in the war. No matter how successful the Kharkov battle was, it was going to be a dead end for the Russians. The Army Group South rear area, particularly the Kharkov region, was beginning to fill up with divisions for the summer offensive, more than enough to guarantee the strategic initiative. On the other hand, those divisions were under OKH control. Bock apparently did not even know where

[53]*IVMV*, vol. V, p. 129.

[54]*IVOVSS*, vol. II, p. 413; *VOV*, p. 140.
[55]Bagramyan, *Tak shli my k pobede*, pp. 95–97.
[56]*VOV (Kratkaya Istoriya)*, p. 162.
[57]Moskalenko, *Na yugo-zapadnom napravlenii*, p. 247.

T–34 TANK CREWS BRUSH UP ON TACTICS

all of them were or what their states of readiness were, and Hitler, who was having to painstakingly husband his manpower for the summer, was not disposed to release them. Consequently, the battle would have to be fought practically, if somewhat artificially, in the hand-to-mouth style of the winter.

From General Kleist, Bock learned that Seventeenth Army probably could carry out the southern half of FRIDERICUS. Doing so would narrow the mouth of the Izyum bulge to about twenty miles. But Kleist did not believe he could go any farther, and if his advance fell short, it would not have any effect at all. As an alternative, Kleist thought he could scrape together three or four divisions for a counterattack off the Armeegruppe left flank across the rear of the *Bobkin Group* and Soviet *Sixth Army*. Bock inclined toward the first possibility but felt compelled by prudence to recommend the second to Hitler. Having done this, he remarked to his chief of staff, "Now the Fuehrer will order the big solution [FRIDERICUS]. The laurels will go to the Supreme Command and we will have to be content with what is left." As expected, Hitler did promptly order the big solution, which Bock then said he could "approach cheerfully," particularly since Hitler had also undertaken to send out of the Crimea "every aircraft that can possibly be spared."[58]

_____

[58]*Bock Diary, Osten II,* 14 May 42.

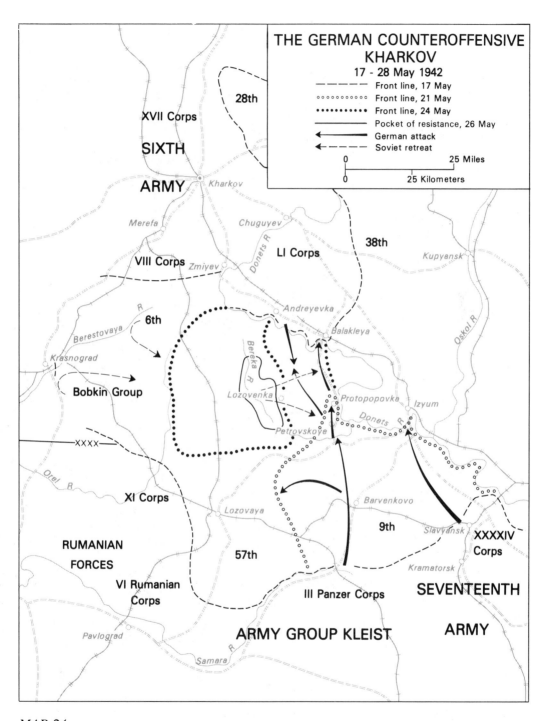

MAP 24

Fridericus

On the morning of the 17th, Timoshenko committed his second-stage forces, and Kleist began FRIDERICUS. Timoshenko was playing primarily his two biggest trumps, *XXI* and *XXIII Tank Corps,* which had been waiting behind *Sixth Army.* They were going in, however, after the first-stage attack had crested and was beginning to subside.[59] Nevertheless, during the day, in 90° F. heat, the Soviet tanks drove five miles deep into the loosely patched VIII Corps line south of Kharkov. *(Map 24.)*

FRIDERICUS was light on reserves but had powerful air support. The 22d Panzer Division, coming from the Crimea, probably would not arrive in time to count, but IV Air Corps, with the reinforcements from VIII Air Corps, had an imposing assemblage of fighter, *Stuka,* and bomber squadrons, all of which were able to take to the air when the day dawned bright and clear. The surprise was complete on the Soviet side and almost as great on the German—at how fast the Soviet *Ninth Army* collapsed. By sundown on that shimmeringly hot day, supported "most effectively by the *Luftwaffe,*" III Panzer Corps had gone fifteen miles to Barvenkovo, and the Seventeenth Army left flank divisions had covered sixteen or seventeen miles, more than two-thirds of the distance to Izyum.[60]

During the day, the commander of *South Front,* General Malinovskiy, lost contact with the *Ninth Army* headquarters and with reinforcements he was

trying to deploy south of Izyum. Bagramyan says that Malinovskiy had made two "errors" beforehand: he had put part of his reserves into the line on the south, and he and the army command had failed to set up a sufficiently solid defense.[61] According to the *Popular Scientific Sketch,* "The *Ninth Army* troops were not prepared to ward off the enemy blow."[62]

The 17th and the 18th were days of rising crisis for the Soviet Command— and of decisions made and not made that would remain in dispute decades later. The *History of the Great Patriotic War* passes over the events of the 17th in a single sentence confirming the German breakthrough. Bagramyan indicates that on that day, both the theater command and the *Stavka* believed *South Front's* right flank could be strengthened enough to master the crisis. Timoshenko, he says, ordered Gorodnyanskov to take out *XXIII Tank Corps* and get it to *Fifty-seventh Army* by the night of the 18th for a counterattack toward Barvenkovo, and the *Stavka* released two rifle divisions and two tank brigades from its reserves. The *Short History* maintains, however, that since the *Stavka* reserves could not have arrived in less than three days, Timoshenko should have stopped *Sixth Army* and shifted all of its offensive strength to the south. The acting chief of the General Staff, Vasilevskiy, the *Short History* says (as he does also), proposed doing that, but Stalin refused after the Military Council of the *Southwestern Theater* (Timoshenko, Khrushchev, and Bagramyan) told him it could continue the offensive and stop

[59]Moskalenko, *Na yugo-zapadnom napravlenii,* p. 201; *IVMV,* vol. V, p. 129.

[60]Pz. *AOK 1, Ia Kriegstagebuch Nr. 8,* 17 May 42, Pz. AOK 1 24906 file; *AOK 17, Ia Kriegstagebuch Nr. 3,* 17 May 42, AOK 17 24411/1 file.

[61]Bagramyan, *Tak shli my k pobede,* p. 106f.
[62]*VOV,* p. 141.

the German attack.[63] The *Popular Scientific Sketch* states, "The Supreme Commander let the Military Council of the *Southwest Front* [also Timoshenko, Khrushchev, and Bagramyan] persuade him that to continue the offensive was necessary and feasible and rejected the General Staff's arguments for breaking off the operation."[64]

On the 18th, lighter by a tank corps, Timoshenko's armor rolled against Sixth Army again. In places, the tanks broke through, but where they did, the Germans counterattacked, and at day's end, the front stood about where it had in the morning.[65] FRIDERICUS, meanwhile, almost became a rout. *South Front, Ninth Army,* and the latter's neighbor, *Fifty-seventh Army,* failed again to put together a cohesive defense. Against confused resistance, Seventeenth Army and III Panzer Corps fanned out and cleared the line of the Donets River north to Izyum and west to the mouth of the Bereka River.

The *History of the Great Patriotic War* and Bagramyan depict the 18th as the crucial day. The history states that Khrushchev, in his capacity as the member (political) of the Military Council of the theater and *front,* contacted Stalin and proposed to stop the offensive immediately and redeploy *Sixth Army*'s and the *Bobkin Group*'s forces to counter FRIDERICUS, but "the *Stavka* insisted on the execution of its previous orders."[66] Khrushchev told the Twentieth Party Congress, in Feb-

ruary 1956, that he had talked to Vasilevskiy and indirectly, through Malenkov, a member of the State Defense Committee, to Stalin by telephone. Vasilevskiy, in Khrushchev's version, refused to take up the matter of stopping the offensive with Stalin. Stalin would not talk on the telephone but had Malenkov give the answer, "Let everything remain as it is."[67]

Bagramyan says he had concluded, on the night of the 17th, that the offensive would have to be stopped and the mass of its forces shifted to the Barvenkovo area, but he had not succeeded in convincing Timoshenko of "the urgent necessity to take that cardinal decision." In fact, he says, on the morning of the 18th, Timoshenko told Stalin there was no need to take forces from *Sixth Army* or the *Bobkin Group* to beat off the German attack. Bagramyan, by his account, then initiated an appeal to Stalin through Khrushchev, but Stalin declined to reverse Timoshenko's decision.[68]

Vasilevskiy says he informed Stalin of the worsening situation in the Barvenkovo-Izyum area on the morning of the 18th. In writing his memoirs, Vasilevskiy remembered talking to Khrushchev by telephone, "either on the 18th or 19th," in approximately the sense Khrushchev described, except that he told Khrushchev he could not go to Stalin again with a proposal that contradicted what the military council of the theater was reporting.[69] According to the *Short History,* Vasilevskiy made another attempt to get Stalin to

[63]*IVOVSS*, vol. II, p. 413; Bagramyan, *Tak shli my k pobede*, p. 115; *VOV (Kratkaya Istoriya)*, p. 163. See also Vasilevskiy, *Delo*, p. 214.
[64]*VOV*, p. 141.
[65]*AOK 6, Ia Kriegstagebuch Nr. 11*, 18 May 42, AOK 6 22391/1 file.
[66]*IVOVSS*, vol. II, p. 414.
[67]*Congressional Record*, 4 Jun 1956.
[68]Bagramyan, *Tak shli my k pobede*, p. 116f.
[69]Vasilevskiy, *Delo*, p. 214.

PAK 40, 75-MM. ANTITANK GUN CREW ON THE WATCH

stop the offensive on the 18th and was turned down after Stalin again consulted Timoshenko.[70] To this Zhukov adds, "The version about the military council of the theater sending alarming reports to Stalin is not true. I maintain this because I was present in person when Stalin spoke over the telephone."[71]

No matter where the responsibility rested, with Stalin, with the military council of the theater, with Timoshenko, or with all three, *Southwest Front* had indeed been kept on the offensive south of Kharkov too long. Because it had, the trap that was about

to be sprung was going to be in good part one of the Russians' own making. Bock conferred with Kleist at the latter's headquarters in Stalino on the 18th. In the midst of an almost unbelievable success, the two were worried. When they reached Izyum and the mouth of the Bereka, which they were likely to do within hours, the FRIDERICUS forces would have gone as far north as Kleist had figured they could go; but so far, they had failed to accomplish their main mission, which was to draw *Southwest Front* away from Sixth Army. The Russians had not reacted at all. The next stage, as planned, would be to turn III Panzer Corps due west along the south side of the Bereka behind *Fifty-seventh Army*, but that hardly seemed likely to produce an

[70]*VOV (Kratkaya Istoriya)*, p. 164.
[71]Zhukov, *Memoirs*, p. 368.

effect that the more threatening north-ward thrust had failed to achieve. Before Bock departed, Kleist offered to try to have III Panzer Corps take a bridgehead north of the Bereka from which it could advance northwest in case the Russians, as it seemed they very likely would, proved insensitive to the push to the west.[72]

By comparison with the previous two days, the Armeegruppe Kleist almost stood still on the 19th. The III Panzer Corps was wheeling to the west. It did, though, send 14th Panzer Division over the Bereka to take Petrovskoye. The distance gained was only about five miles, but it deprived *Southwest Front* of a Donets crossing and narrowed the mouth of the Izyum bulge to fifteen miles. During the day, *Southwest Front* finally did begin to react. The pressure on VIII Corps, strong in the morning, became disjointed by midmorning. In the afternoon, air reconnaissance detected an increase in road traffic away from the VIII Corps front to the southeast, and at the end of the day, Sixth Army reported, "The enemy's offensive strength has cracked. The breakthrough to Kharkov is therewith prevented."[73]

In the evening on the 19th, an order went out to Soviet *Sixth Army* and the *Bobkin Group* to stop the offensive and redeploy to the southeast. The *History of the Great Patriotic War* implies that Timoshenko had to give the order on his own responsibility and only later received the *Stavka*'s approval.[74] The *History of the Second World War*, the *Short History*, and Vasilevskiy present the decision, made "at last," as having been entirely up to the theater command.[75] Bagramyan says, "the commanding general, *Southwestern Theater*, did not make the belated decision to stop the offensive until the latter half of the day on the 19th. . . ."[76]

Coming when it did, the most significant effect of Timoshenko's decision was probably to hasten the destruction of the Soviet forces in the Izyum bulge. Relieved of their concern over what might happen to Sixth Army, Hitler and Bock conferred by telephone on the night of the 19th and quickly agreed it would now be a good idea to try to accomplish the whole original FRIDERICUS by having the Armeegruppe Kleist go the rest of the way from Petrovskoye to the Sixth Army line at Balakleya. As soon as they had finished Bock called Kleist's chief of staff, gave him the gist of what he had talked about with Hitler, and said he wanted Protopopovka, the next Donets crossing north of Petrovskoye, taken "under all circumstances and as soon as in any way possible."[77]

The 14th Panzer Division took Protopopovka on the 20th, which reduced the mouth of the bulge between there and Balakleya to twelve miles. The bridgehead was then eight miles deep but only a mile or two across. The III Panzer Corps main force, still on the westward orientation, gained almost twelve miles, however, with disappointing results. The object was to smash *Fifty-seventh Army* in the western end of

[72]*Pz. AOK 1, Ia Kriegstagebuch Nr. 8*, 18 May 42, Pz. AOK 1 24906 file.

[73]*AOK 6, Ia Kriegstagebuch Nr. 11*, 19 May 42, AOK 6 22391 file.

[74]*IVOVSS*, vol, II, p. 414.

[75]*IVMV*, vol. V, p. 130; *VOV (Kratkaya Istoriya)*, p. 164; Vasilevskiy, *Delo*, p. 214.

[76]Bagramyan, *Tak shli my k pobede*, p. 119.

[77]*Bock Diary, Osten II*, 19 May 42.

the bulge, but the outer ring of front there was held by Rumanian divisions, and they showed little determination and less enthusiasm. One of the Rumanian division commanders had sent himself home on leave when he heard the attack was about to start. Having an alternative that he also preferred, Kleist began turning the 16th Panzer Division, 60th Motorized Division, and 1st Mountain Division around after dark and sending them into the Bereka bridgehead behind 14th Panzer Division. On Bock's urging, Paulus agreed to shift the 3d and 23d Panzer Divisions south from the Volchansk salient and thus partially to reconstitute his former FRIDERICUS force.[78] Bock observed, " . . . tonight, I have given orders aimed at completely sealing off the Izyum bulge. Now everything will turn out well after all!"[79]

On the 21st, 14th Panzer was the only division on the offensive. It jumped north four miles, reducing the distance to Balakleya to eight miles. The next day, 16th Panzer Division and 60th Motorized Division struck out northwestward from Petrovskoye, and 14th Panzer Division continued north. Well before dark, 14th Panzer had contact with Sixth Army at Balakleya. Early the next morning, 23d Panzer Division met 16th Panzer Division ten miles west of Balakleya. With that, 14th Panzer Division's narrow bridgehead was converted into a ten-mile-wide barrier across the mouth of the bulge.

On the west and south, the Soviet fronts were collapsing inward. In two more days, the *Sixth* and *Fifty-seventh*

Armies, the *Bobkin Group,* and the remnants of *Ninth Army* were piled against the III Panzer Corps line. An attempt at a breakout on the afternoon of the 25th carried almost to Petrovskoye. Another, the next morning, several miles to the north, came within four miles of succeeding. By afternoon on the 26th, all that was left was a ten-by-two-mile pocket in the Bereka Valley. From a hill south of Lozovenka, Bock could see over almost the whole of it. "An overpowering picture," he said, as shells exploded in the cloud of smoke hanging in the valley, and 23d Panzer Division and 1st Mountain Division troops, still on the attack, pushed past crowds of prisoners streaming out of the pocket.[80]

The battle ended in bright sunshine on the morning of the 28th. After they finished counting, which took some more days, Armeegruppe Kleist and Sixth Army found they had captured 240,000 prisoners, over 1,200 tanks, and 2,600 artillery pieces.[81] Seventeenth Army, which had taken over the front on the Donets, observed "with astonishment" that during the whole ten-day battle, virtually no relief had been attempted from the east.[82] According to Shtemenko, Stalin had told Timoshenko and Khrushchev, "Battles must be won not with numbers but by skill. If you do not learn to direct your troops better, all the armaments the country can produce will not be enough for you."[83]

[78]*Pz. AOK 1, Ia Kriegstagebuch Nr. 8*, 20 May 42, Pz. AOK 1 24906 file; *AOK 6, Ia Kriegstagebuch Nr. 11*, 20 May 42, AOK 6 22391 file.

[79]*Bock Diary, Osten II*, 20 May 42.

[80]*Ibid.*, 26 May 42; *Pz. AOK 1, Ia Vernichtungsschlacht im Donezbogen westl. Izyum*, Pz. AOK 1 75119/6 file.

[81]*Pz. AOK 1, Ia, Vernichtungsschlact im Donezbogen westl. Izyum*, Pz. AOK 1 75119/6 file; *AOK 6, Ia Sondermeldung*, 30.5.42, AOK 6 22391/7 file.

[82]*AOK 17, Ia Kriegstagebuch Nr. 3*, 28 May 42, AOK 17 24411/1 file.

[83]Shtemenko, *Soviet General Staff*, p. 56.

CHAPTER XIV

A Time for Decisions

Hitler's Strategy

A 1942 campaign—contingent on how much was accomplished before the current operations stopped for the winter—came within Hitler's range of concerns in November 1941. He gave General Halder, chief of the General Staff, an order of priorities on the 19th. First would come the Caucasus, in March and April; then Vologda and Gorkiy, at the end of May. Other, more distant, objectives would be set later and would depend on the capabilities of the railroads.[1] The directive of 8 December, terminating the 1941 offensive, would still give Army Group South the tentative mission of reaching the lower Don and Donets and would urge Army Group North "to clean up the situation" south of Lake Ladoga.[2] These plans, however, were only wisps, already being buried in the Russian snows. Nevertheless, until well into December, Hitler appears not to have been thinking of a break between the two years' operations, but instead of mere pauses in the action, more or less long depending on location and weather, after which the forces would continue in their previous deployments.

Hitler did not begin to take account of a strategic discontinuity in the operations until 23 December, when he talked to General Fromm, the chief of Army Armament and the Replacement Army. He told Fromm the army's aim would have to be "to clear the table" in the East during 1942. Fromm, in reply, told him the army would no longer be on a full war footing in 1942 and, apparently, recommended going over to the defensive for the whole year.[3]

A Question of Means

The Hitler-Fromm exchange brought out what would be Hitler's most pervasive strategic problem during 1942: how to bring his means into consonance with his objectives. Not new, it had been there all along, masked to a degree by the war's early and easy successes. In the past, though, while the margins of strength had often been less than they later appeared, he had always possessed some elasticity. The coming year was going to be different. The capacity to stretch would be gone. The knowledge of that also was not anything new. It accounted in major part for Hitler's—and Halder's—efforts in November and December to blanket as much as possible of the

---

[1] *Halder Diary*, vol. III, p. 295.
[2] *OKW, WFSt, Abt. L (I Op.) Nr. 442090/41, Weisung Nr. 39, 8.12.41*, German High Level Directives, CMH files.

[3] *Der Chef der Heeresruestung und Befehlshaber des Ersatzheeres, der Chef des Stabes, Tagebuch*, 23 Dec 41, CMH X-124 file.

unfinished business of the war in the Soviet Union into the 1941 campaign. Specifically, the problem involved two concerns: material and manpower.

When Hitler conferred with Fromm, on 23 December, the army was five months into a decline that was in part mandated. In Directive 32, of 11 June 1941, Hitler had laid down requirements for the period after the victory in the East. Since, as he saw it, no serious threat would exist any longer on the European mainland, he had announced that the army would be "substantially" reduced for the benefit of the air force and navy, the services that would henceforth carry the weight of the war against England.[4]

A month later, on 14 July, believing the victory to be almost at hand, he had issued an implementing directive. Under it, the main effort in armament was to be shifted immediately to the air force and navy. The only production increases for the army would be in tanks and heavy antitank weapons. How much the army was to be cut back would remain to be decided, but it would have to start, "at once," adjusting its replacement and procurement of "weapons, ammunition, and equipment," to reduced force levels. Orders for items for which more than a six months' supply stockpile existed were to be canceled.[5]

Fromm reminded Hitler that the army, expecting to disband about fifty divisions, had since curtailed all weapons' procurement other than tanks and

antitank guns. He added, too, that even with the new allotments of non-ferrous metals, granted just hours before their meeting, the army would be unable to complete more than 80 percent of its tank and antitank weapons programs.[6] Hitler indicated that he had already instructed Dr. Fritz Todt, the minister for Armament and Munitions, to restart ammunition production, and he told Fromm, "Air Force and Navy [production] are now stopped for the benefit of the Army."[7]

The stop was not quite as fast or as complete as Hitler's statement to Fromm seemed to imply, but he did issue a supplementary directive, "Armament 1942," on 10 January 1942. It upheld the air force and navy buildups, "in the long view," while specifying that the changed war situation "for the time being prohibits a decline in Army armament." The army was to be guaranteed a four months' stockpile of general supplies by 1 May 1942 and, in ammunition, one basic load plus six times the total August 1941 consumption in all categories. In armament, "preference" was to be given to the "elevated requirements of the Army."[8] The man to whom the job of executing the directive fell was Albert Speer, who replaced Todt on 8 February, the day the latter was killed in an airplane crash. Speer's appointment, as it turned out, was going to have several advantages: Speer very quickly displayed a high talent as a production organizer; he had Hitler's confidence;

[4]OKW, WFSt, Abt. L (I Op.) Nr. 448864/41, Weisung Nr. 32, 11.6.41, German High Level Directives, CMH files.
[5]OKW, WFSt, Abt. L (II Org.) Nr. 441219/41, Weisung Nr. 32b, 14.7.41, German High Level Directives, CMH files.

[6]Chef H. Ruest. und BdE, Stab OKH, Nr. 1441/41, Notizen ueber Vortrag beim Fuehrer am 23.12.41, 28.12.41, CMH X–124 file.
[7]Ibid.
[8]Willi A. Boelcke, Deutschlands Ruestung im Zweiten Weltkrieg (Frankfurt: Athenaion, 1969), pp. 61–64.

and he managed to acquire more authority than his predecessor had had.

Nevertheless, neither a directive nor the promise of its brilliant execution could circumvent the hard realities pressing in on all sides. The Germans had run the 1941 campaign on stockpiles of supplies accumulated beforehand. By November, they had almost exhausted these, and from then on, they had had to provide for their armies in the Soviet Union out of current production, which, even without the cutbacks made during the summer, would have been insufficient to keep them adequately supplied. Some kinds of artillery ammunition had been running short. Less than one in three of over two thousand tanks and self-propelled assault guns lost had been replaced.[9] Trucks and other motor vehicles had been worn out, destroyed, or broken down in such numbers and their production cut back so far that Halder had told the chiefs of staff at the Orsha Conference that same month that the infantry division would have to be completely demotorized.

In December and January, Hitler had counted on a several months' pause in the fighting, during which consumption would decline and production could catch up. What he was going to get was vast new wastage of all kinds of equipment during the winter and spring battles. The flow from the pipelines would have to be strong just to keep up, much less get ahead, and it would have to draw from a depleted reservoir. Electricity output in Germany was cut back more than 20 percent in January to conserve coal; even so, production of iron and steel in

tonnages declined in the first quarter of 1942. Nonferrous metals, particularly aluminum and copper, rationed since September 1941, could not be supplied to some high-priority industries in the allotted quantities.[10]

The most pervasive deficiency was in manpower. The factories needed men and so did the army, and after the campaign began in the Soviet Union, either one could only get more men at the other's expense. At least half of the July directive's purpose had been to get skilled workers out of uniform and back into the shops. A million and a half had been needed. As planned, the army reduction would have supplied a half million.[11] By January, that prospect had vanished completely. On the 5th, Fromm had told his senior generals in the Replacement Army, "We believed we would be able to put 500,000 men back into industry. Now we will have, instead, to take 600,000 men out."[12] For the most part, however, the loss to the labor force would not be translated into a net increase in fighting strength. The OKH was committed to supply 500,000 replacements for the Eastern Front by 1 April and expected to need 340,000 more by 1 June.[13] In the 14 July directive, Hitler had wanted to delay calling up the men born in 1922. That resolve had only lasted until October.[14] By February, virtually all of the 1922 class was at the front or would be there "before the 1942 [offensive] operations begin," and the OKH was

---

[9]Reinhardt, *Moskau*, p. 114.

[10]*Ibid.*, pp. 284–86.

[11]*Ibid.*, p. 39.

[12]*Der Chef der Heeresruestung und Befehlshaber des Ersatzheeres, der Chef des Stabes, Tagebuch,* 5 Jan 42, CMH X–124 file.

[13]*OKH, GenStdH, Org. Abt., Kriegstagebuch,* 1–5 Jan and 16–22 Feb 42, H 1/213 file.

[14]Reinhardt, *Moskau*, p. 40.

preparing to start taking in the 1923 class.[15]

An Offensive in the South

Hitler knew in November 1941 that, in all likelihood, he would be tied down in the Soviet Union during the coming year, and he knew that he would not have the resources to mount another general offensive like BARBAROSSA. Nonetheless, he at no time allowed those considerations or the mischances of the winter to sway him from an early turn to the attack with as much force as he could assemble. The directive of 8 December 1941 set as one of its three objectives "a basis for the resumption of larger offensive operations in 1942," with the other two being to hold the territory already taken and to rest and refit the armies in the East. The directive specified a drive into the Caucasus in the spring and a "clean-up" around Leningrad and south of Lake Ladoga "when reinforcements arrive."[16] On the 20th, when he was having to revise his instructions on resting and refitting, Hitler remarked that Italy, Hungary, and Rumania were going to be "induced" to furnish strong forces in 1942 and to have them ready to be brought east "before the snow melts."[17] Three days later, he ordered Fromm to set up half-a-dozen new divisions by spring for an offensive to Rostov and Maykop.[18] On 3 January, he told the

Japanese Ambassador, General Hirosi Oshima, that he did not contemplate any more offensives in the center of the German front in the Soviet Union but would concentrate on the south, the Caucasus, "as soon as the weather is better."[19] On the 18th, he gave Field Marshal Bock two missions for Army Group South: "to hold for the present and attack in the spring."[20] During the winter he often talked longingly about the campaigning season to come, and in March, making it clear that the main effort henceforth would be elsewhere, he began leaving Army Groups North and Center to shift for themselves.

Although Hitler was unswervingly determined to have an offensive on the south flank in 1942, the planning, particularly as compared to the elaborate work done on BARBAROSSA the year before, appears to have been almost desultory. OKH instructions, sent on 15 February, dealing with procedures to be followed during the rasputitsa, alluded "in very broad terms" to operations "contemplated" later in the spring.[21] On the 20th, Bock sent Hitler, "on Halder's suggestion," a memorandum on the probable situation in the spring and the conduct of an offensive. Eleven days later, Halder said Hitler had the memorandum but had not read it because he had "so little time for examining far-reaching operations."[22] Halder talked to his branch chiefs on 6 March about rebuilding the Eastern Front armies, particularly those that

[15]OKH, GenStdH, Org. Abt., Kriegstagebuch, 10–13 and 16–22 Feb 42, H 1/213 file.
[16]OKW, WFSt, Abt. L (I Op.) Nr. 442090/41, Weisung Nr. 39, 8.12.41, German High Level Directives, CMH files.
[17]Halder Dairy, vol. III, p. 361.
[18]Der Chef der Heeresruestung und Befehlshaber des Ersatzheeres, der Chef des Stabes, Tagebuch, 23 Dec 41, CMH X–124 file.
[19]Hans-Adolf Jacobsen, 1939–1945, Der Zweite Weltkrieg in Chronik und Dokumenten (Darmstadt: Wehr und Wissen Verlagsgesellschaft, 1961), p. 288.
[20]Bock Diary, Osten II, 18 Jan 42.
[21]Ibid., 15 Feb 42.
[22]Ibid., 20 Feb and 1 Mar 42.

would be on the offensive.[23] On the 15th, in his annual Memorial Day (*Heldengedenktag*) address in Berlin, Hitler, in effect, closed the books on the winter and promised to wreak unspecified destruction on "the Bolshevik colossus" in the coming summer.[24]

After mid-March, the pace of the planning did pick up. On the 18th, the OKH assigned a code name, SIEGFRIED, to the summer offensive. Halder and his staff went to work on the deployment, which they at first thought would take until August but later estimated could be mostly completed by the end of the first week in July with some elements left to come as late as August. Halder took the deployment plan to Hitler on the 28th, and in the subsequent discussion, Hitler gave him the objectives for the offensive and instructions for its execution.[25] The OKW Operations Staff, in its capacity as Hitler's personal staff, took the results and worked them into a draft directive, which Hitler signed on 5 April after "heavily revising" and adding "substantial new parts" to it. In the interim, he had also dropped the code name SIEGFRIED and substituted BLAU ("blue").[26]

The directive, *Weisung* 41, in somewhat ambivalent terms, gave two objectives for the summer: to destroy the Soviet Union's defensive strength "conclusively" and to deprive it of the resources necessary for its war economy "as far as possible." The "general intent" would be to bring about the fall of

Leningrad and to break into the Caucasus area. The main effort would be on the south flank where the aims would be to destroy the enemy forces forward of the Don River, take the Caucasus oil area, and gain possession of the Caucasus crossings. The action against Leningrad would be held in abeyance pending favorable circumstances or availability of forces.[27]

Although much of Directive 41 can be, and in some accounts virtually all of it has been, attributed directly to Hitler, the plan for executing the offensive appears to have been derived from the memorandum Bock had submitted in February. In it, he and the Army Group South staff had maintained that a drive into the Caucasus would first have to be covered on the north and east by advances that would extend the front east of Kursk ninety miles to Voronezh and thence southeast along the Don River to the vicinity of Stalingrad, a distance of close to three hundred miles at the latitude of Stalingrad. To go that far in one sweep on a front over three-hundred-and-fifty miles long would have required more strength than Bock could imagine having in the spring or summer of 1942. Consequently, he had projected a phased offensive. The first phase would carry east to the Don between Voronezh and Novaya Kalitva, providing cover on the north. (*Map 25.*) In the second phase, the armor used in the first would move southeast from Novaya Kalitva toward the lower Don while the army group's right flank drove east to Rostov and the Don. A third phase would then be required to

[23]*Halder Diary*, vol. III, p. 410.
[24]Domarus, *Hitler*, vol. II, p. 1850.
[25]*OKH, GenStdH, Op. Abt. Nr. 420110/42, 18.3.42*, H22 215 file; *Halder Diary*, vol. III, pp. 316, 417, 420–21.
[26]*OKW, Stellv. WFSt, Kriegsgeschichtliche Abteilung, Kriegstagebuch, 1.4.–30.6.42*, 2 and 5 Apr 42, I.M.T. 1807 file.

[27]*OKW, WFSt, Nr. 55616/42, Weisung 41, 5.4.42*, German High Level Directives, CMH files.

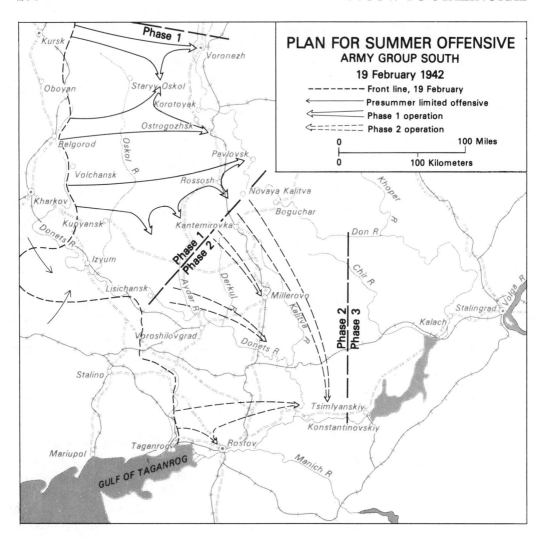

MAP 25

take possession of the Don bend and the narrows between the Don and the Volga west of Stalingrad. Bock had believed he would need eighty-five divisions at the start, thirty-nine more than he had had in February 1942. Because he could not see where the divisions would come from or, considering the condition of the railroads, how they would get deployed in time,

he had described the memorandum as a "theoretical inquiry into the operational possibilities."[28]

Directive 41 took the device of the phased offensive from the Bock memorandum, keeping the progression from north to south but altering the

[28]*Der Oberbefehlshaber der H. Gr. Sued, Ia Nr. 276/42, Betr: Fortfuehrung der Operation im Sommer 1942, 19.2.42,* MS P–114c, pt. III, CMH files.

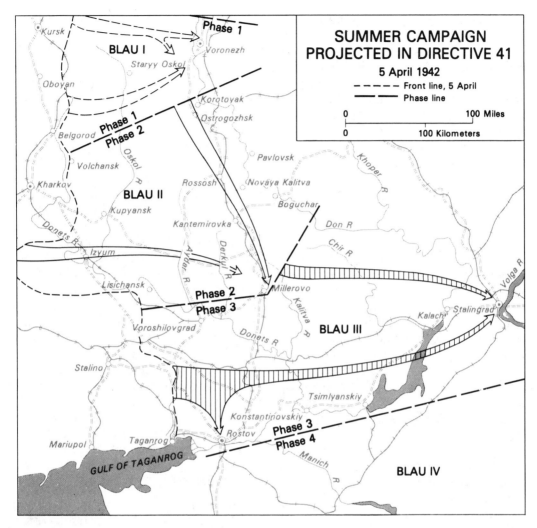

MAP 26

distribution. The first two phases, subsequently known as BLAU I and BLAU
II, by carrying the advance between
the Donets and Don to the vicinity of
Millerovo, only slightly enlarged on the
first phase proposed in the memorandum. BLAU III, on the other hand,
omitted the third phase proposed in
the memorandum by merging it with
the second phase to complete the drive

to Stalingrad. A "BLAU IV," the advance
into the Caucasus, was implicit in the
directive but not described. *(Map 26.)*

The rearrangement of the phases,
far from being merely cosmetic or a
matter of tactical taste, was for several
reasons the actual heart of the plan.
For one, it would let BLAU be run on a
feasible schedule. The deployment, as
Bock had pointed out in the memoran-

dum, was going to be difficult and slow, and it would be most difficult and slowest on the south. In their compressed form, however, BLAU I could be completed and BLAU II be started and brought well along while troops and material for BLAU III were still being deployed. Secondly, BLAU was going to depend heavily on young, inexperienced, hastily trained troops. A small BLAU I and an only somewhat larger BLAU II would give opportunities to build experience and confidence, particularly confidence. As Hitler put it, "The operation must start with success: young troops cannot be exposed to setbacks. Setbacks must not occur."[29]

Finally, the object of the summer campaign would be not just to advance but to destroy the Soviet forces while doing so. Hitler believed this had to be done by small, tight encirclements. The sweeping maneuvers of the previous summer, he maintained, had let too many of the enemy get away. The BLAU operations, he said, were designed so that "in each one of these attacks the ground and air forces can achieve the highest degree of concentration at the decisive points."[30]

Obliquely, Directive 41 also addressed the question of forces raised in the Bock memorandum. In a postscript to the operational plan, it assigned the long stationary front that would develop on the Don below Voronezh to the allies—Hungarians on the north, Italians in the center, and Rumanians on the southeast. The deployment was significant because the Hun-

garians and Rumanians, who would rather have fought each other than the Russians, could not be stationed in adjacent sectors. All three would have to be backstopped by German divisions, but many fewer of those would be needed than if they had to man the whole line alone. Hitler, who had not particularly welcomed allied participation in the 1941 campaign, had let Field Marshal Keitel, chief of the OKW, do the recruiting during the winter. Hungary, jealous at earlier German favoritism toward Rumania, had been the slowest to "volunteer." Italy had been the most willing because the *Duce*, Benito Mussolini, had wanted since June 1941 to have his troops participate in the defeat of communism.[31] The allied troops were not trained or armed for fighting on the Eastern Front, and they were especially weak in armor and anti-tank weapons. Their sense of commitment and endurance also was doubtful, and Hitler's instructions were "to hold them to the cause" by showing them "fanatical loyalty" and by being "unstintingly generous" with praise.[32]

Hitler's Restless Spring

The coming of spring in Russia in 1942 gave Hitler time to turn to other affairs: relations with the allies, the defense of the Atlantic perimeter, and the home front. On 6 April, the Rumanian Chief of the General Staff, General Ilia Steflea, visited the *Wolfsschanze*, and in the last week of the month,

[29]*Halder Diary*, vol. III, p. 420.
[30]*OKW, WFSt, Nr. 55616/42, Weisung 41, 5.4.42*, German High Level Directives, CMH files.
[31]Walter Warlimont, *Im Hauptquartier der deutschen Wehrmacht, 1939–1945* (Frankfurt: Bernard & Graefe, 1962), p. 244; Walter Goerlitz, ed., *The Memoirs of Field-Marshal Keitel* (New York: Stein and Day, 1966), pp. 174–76.
[32]*OKW, Stellv. WFSt, Kriegsgeschichtliche Abteilung, Kriegstagebuch, 1.4–30.6.42*, 5 Jun 42, I.M.T. 1807 file.

HITLER'S "YOUNG" TROOPS ON THE MARCH

Mussolini came to Salzburg. In between, Hitler conferred decorations on the president of Finland, the king of Bulgaria, the "field marshal" of Croatia, and Admiral Miklos Horthy, the regent of Hungary.[33] Some weeks later, on 4 June, Hitler made a surprise trip by air to Finland to congratulate Marshal Mannerheim, commander in chief of the Finnish Army, on his seventy-fifth birthday.

Hitler had fretted endlessly throughout the winter about possible Anglo-American landings on the Atlantic frontier. That had been one of the reasons for sending General Falkenhorst, commander of the Army

of Norway, back to Norway. It had also motivated a train of orders on coastal defense and, in February, the dash through the English Channel by the warships *Scharnhorst, Gneisenau,* and *Prinz Eugen,* which were supposed to have gone on to Norwegian bases. Hitler had already sent the battleship *Tirpitz,* Germany's largest and one of the most powerful in the world, to Trondheim in January. In February, he had assigned Generalfeldmarschall Wilhelm List to inspect the defenses of Norway and northern Finland. Directive 40, of 23 March, dealt entirely with coastal defense, and a British raid on the naval base at St. Nazaire had prompted a shake-up of the commands in the West. Talking to Mussolini, on 30 April, Hitler dwelled at length on the

---

[33]Domarus, *Hitler,* vol. II, pp. 1860–62.

dangers of British landings in Norway or France and supposed Swedish and Vichy-French hostility.[34]

The winter was over but not forgotten, and Hitler decided to give an accounting to the German people on the afternoon of Sunday, 26 April. The forum he chose was the *Reichstag*, which having provided the stage for several authentic victory speeches, was now to furnish the window dressing for a somewhat spurious one. He had no conquests to claim. Instead, he undertook to elevate the winter campaign to a triumph over the elements, which he embellished with comparisons to Napoleon's experience in 1812. He said a battle had been fought during the winter that had raised problems "far exceeding what should or could be expected in normal wars," and he gave himself credit for having confronted, "with my own person, what destiny appeared to have in store for us."[35]

Goebbels, the German propaganda minister, rated the speech a resounding success.[36] Count Galeazzo Ciano, the Italian foreign minister, far less an admirer of Hitler than Goebbels was, found the tone "not very optimistic," and observed, " . . . there is not a hint of what all are waiting for—the ending of the war."[37] What struck Ciano particularly was that Hitler apparently took for granted a second winter of war in the Soviet Union, and he was sparing, for him almost diffident, in his predictions for the coming summer. In contrast, he talked at length about what he would do to be ready for the next winter "no matter where it finds us."[38] For the first time, Hitler was hedging on his own strategic initiative.

The speech also did not impress Ciano, "because by now all his speeches are more or less alike." Ciano noted that Hitler had asked for additional powers (which, of course, were granted) but dismissed that as merely a dramatic gesture since Hitler already possessed complete power.[39] What Ciano, and probably most other outsiders, did not catch was that Hitler's request was aimed at a group over which he did not yet have complete power, namely, the German generals. Although Hitler at one point spoke of his confidence in "my . . . Reichs Marshal, field marshals, admirals, colonel generals, and numerous other commanders at the fronts," in other passages, he barely took the trouble to conceal his displeasure with the generals. He shared the credit he gave himself for the winter campaign with the soldiers, noncommissioned officers, and officers "up to *those* generals who, recognizing the danger, risked their own lives to urge the soldier onward." Elsewhere, he remarked that he had been "compelled to intervene severely in a few individual cases where nerves gave way, discipline broke down, or insufficient sense of duty was displayed."[40] Talking to Speer, some weeks later, he said "almost all" of the generals had failed him during the winter.[41]

The request for more powers—which was, of course, granted—while

[34]*Diensttuender Adjutant (Schmundt), Bericht ueber Besprechung am 30.4.42*, CMH X–1010 file.

[35]Domarus, *Hitler*, vol. II, pp. 1867–71.

[36]Louis P. Lochner, ed., *The Goebbels Diaries* (Garden City: Doubleday & Co., 1948), pp. 191–93.

[37]Hugh Gibson, ed., *The Ciano Diaries* (Garden City: Doubleday & Co., 1946) p. 476.

[38]Domarus, *Hitler*, vol. II, p. 1873.

[39]Gibson, *Ciano Diaries*, p. 476.

[40]Domarus, *Hitler*, vol. II, pp. 1872–73.

[41]Boelcke, *Ruestung*, p. 127.

ostensibly motivated by a recent court decision on a civilian case, was put in terms that could not have been lost on the generals. Hitler asked for, " . . . an explicit confirmation that I have the legal right to hold everyone to the fulfillment of his duty and to reduce to the common ranks or remove from post and position, without regard for acquired rights or status, anyone whom I find not to have done his duty."[42] To Goebbels, Hitler remarked afterward that he was determined "to invoke sharper measures against certain types of swivel-chair generals."[43]

After the one-day *Reichstag* session, Hitler went south to meet Mussolini at Salzburg and spent several days at the *Berghof,* his Bavarian retreat, and returned to the *Wolfsschanze* on 3 May. He had intended to vacation longer at the *Berghof* but had cut his stay short because of snow, which he claimed he could not stand the sight of after the last winter. He was restless, and in May, he made several excursions to Berlin. On 1 June, he went to Bock's headquarters in Poltava to congratulate the army commanders on the Kharkov battle.[44] Three days later, he was in Finland on the birthday visit to Mannerheim. On the 8th, he went, aboard his private train, via Berlin to the *Berghof* to complete his interrupted vacation and did not return to the *Wolfsschanze* until the 24th.

German Strategic Estimates

Men, Firepower, and Mobility

While Hitler was occupied with plans for the summer and other activities,

the OKH was engaged in compiling a document that began as a precursor to Directive 41 and eventually became a subsidiary companion piece to it. On 19 March, the OKW had announced that it proposed to compile an estimate of the *Wehrmacht*'s strength for the spring of 1942 and asked the armed services to supply data.[45] The first army submission at the end of the month had been a gloomy recital. During the winter, the forces on the Eastern Front had lost nearly 7,000 artillery pieces ranging from 37-mm. antitank guns to 210-mm. howitzers. The new production, restarted in January, could not replace more than part of them. Of close to 75,000 motor transport vehicles lost, only 7,500 had been replaced; another 25,000 could be secured in Germany, but the absolute deficit would still be 42,500. More than 179,000 horses had died, and only 20,000 new animals had been secured. The 176 million gallons of motor fuel and 390,000 tons of ammunition consumed had cut deep into the stockpiles, which would therefore be proportionately smaller in 1942. The conclusion was, "The shortages cannot, for the time being, be covered by new production or by rebuilding. This will compel cutbacks and sharp emphasis on priorities in all areas."[46]

Five weeks later, the OKH refined its estimate to eliminate what it pronounced (internally) to be "nonsense" in an OKW draft summary and to take into account readiness for the require-

---

[42]Domarus, *Hitler,* vol. II, p. 1874.
[43]Lochner, *Goebbels Diaries,* p. 192.
[44]*Bock Diary, Osten II,* 1 Jun 42.

[45]*OKW, WFSt, Org. (I), Zusammenfassende Darstellung der Wehrkraft im Fruehjahr 1942, 19.3.42,* H 1 382 file.
[46]*OKH, GenStdH, Gen. Qu./Qu.3, Nr. 18270/42, Darstellung der Wehrkraft der Wehrmacht fuer 1942 durch OKW, 31.3.42,* H 1 382 file.

ments established by Directive 41.[47] The result was a mixed picture or as the OKH put it, a "review of efforts and accomplishments, taking into account also certain irremediable deficiencies." Of the latter, two were immediately acute: the inability of the industrial switchover to army production made in January to be effective before the start of the 1942 summer campaign and the pressures the winter had imposed on men, material, and time. They were affecting short-term readiness. Two other, the strain on raw materials and the mutually interacting civilian and military manpower shortages, affected the short- and long-term readiness. To relate the "accomplishments" and the deficiencies, the OKH expanded the estimate to include "striking power" *(Schlagkraft)* as well as conventional force strength.

Under the first category of the three considered—men, firepower, and mobility—the estimate gave the army's "strictly numerical" strength (in terms of divisions) as of 1 May 1942 as greater than that of June 1941 by 7 infantry and 3 panzer divisions with 4 more infantry divisions to come before late June 1942.[48] On the other hand, even though the Eastern Front had received 1.1 million replacements since 22 June 1941, it was short 625,000 men as of 1

May 1942. Army Group South had 50 percent of its original infantry strength; Army Groups Center and North each 35 percent. Army Group South could be fully replenished by the time the summer offensive began, but it would take until August to bring Center and North up to 55 percent of their original infantry strengths. Reserves in the form of new units could not be created. All of the men, weapons, and equipment becoming available in the summer, including the 1923 class of recruits, would have to be used to replace losses. The forces on the Eastern Front would have a solid core of veterans, but they would have to absorb large numbers of what formerly would have been regarded as underage and overage recruits, and owing to the losses during the winter, they would be short on experienced officers and noncommissioned officers.

As an "accomplishment" in sustaining firepower in spite of curtailed production, the army had sent to the Eastern Front 725,000 rifles, 27,000 machine guns, 2,700 antitank guns, and 559 pieces of light and 350 pieces of heavy field artillery. The weapons requirements for Army Group South would be "substantially" met by the time operations resumed. Army Groups Center and North would have enough infantry weapons to arm the troops they had, but their artillery batteries would have to be reduced from 4 to 3 guns and some of those would have to be old or captured pieces. All told, 3,300 tanks would be on hand in the East, 360 less than in June 1941, but heavier armament would make up the difference.[49] The most serious prob-

---

[47]The OKW draft has not been found. References to it are in *OKH, GenStdH, Org. Abt. Nr. 389/42, 10.5.42,* H 1 382 file.

[48]On 8 April 1941, Halder had proposed eliminating two divisions because they only existed on paper, and Hitler had refused. *OKW, KTB,* vol. II, pt. 2, p. 317. At the Orsha Conference in November 1941, the chief of the Organizational Branch, OKH, had talked about disbanding eleven divisions on the Eastern Front to bring the others up to strength. That also had not been done. *H. Gr. Sued, Der Chef des Generalstabes, Ia Nr. 21323/41, Vortragsnotiz, 17.11.41,* AOK 6 181117 file.

[49]The Mark III and IV tanks were being converted to mount long-barreled guns.

IMPROVISED MOBILITY: THE "MARDER" (MARTIN), *Captured Soviet 76.2-mm. Antitank Gun on an Obsolete Tank Chassis*

lem with firepower was likely to be ammunition. Output of artillery and some kinds of antitank ammunition would not get into full swing until the fall, and "strains" on the ammunition stocks could be expected by August.

Mobility was the least satisfactory category. Army Group South's armored and motorized units would attain about 80 percent of the mobility they had in 1941. The infantry, however, would have to make do with horses in place of trucks. Army Groups North and Center would not be capable of "larger operations" except along railroads. The 75,000-vehicle deficit in motor transport would not be covered by much more than half, and new production in the coming months would not

be enough to cover the expected summer's losses. Nearly a quarter million horses were being requisitioned in Germany and the occupied Soviet territory, but they would not be enough to compensate for the numbers lost and for those required to substitute for motor transport, and they would be lighter, less powerful animals than had been used in the past.

"A complete replenishment," the estimate concluded, "can only be achieved at Army Group South. And there the deficiencies in mobility and the wear of the winter campaign on men, horses, and vehicles raise a likelihood that the endurance will be less than it was in the summer of 1941. In all other theaters, the Army can meet its defensive obligations provided no presently unforeseeable events occur."[50]

The navy and air force estimates, as the OKW had probably desired, were cast in more general terms. The navy, which only had peripheral missions in the war in the East, balanced a "clear" German superiority in submarine warfare against an "oppressive" overall British and American naval superiority. The air force reported some decline in numbers of aircraft, compensated for by newer models, better armament, and more experienced crews.[51] In fact, the air strength in the East, 2,750 planes, would not be substantially less than it had been in June 1941 (2,770 planes), and a larger proportion (1,500) would be assigned to support Army Group South.[52]

On 20 June, eight days before the summer offensive began, Halder made his own capsule estimate. BLAU I was ready. The buildup of men and material for BLAU II was still underway but would be satisfactorily completed in time. It was too early to make a judgment on BLAU III. The Germans would have the initiative, and the morale and enthusiasm of the troops were "gratifying."[53]

Of Soviet Capabilities

At the Orsha Conference in November 1941, Halder told the chiefs of staff, "Although [we are] weak in the knees . . . , the enemy presently is worse off than we are; he is on the verge of collapse."[54] In the spring of 1942, Halder's aphorism acquired a renewed currency. Sober, even somber, as their view of their own condition was, the Germans felt compelled to believe that the Russians were worse off. Having endured the winter without breaking, the Germans felt that they had proved themselves superior to the enemy at his best. This appeared to reconfirm what they had, in fact, always believed, namely, that the strategic problem the Soviet Union posed for them was not qualitive but quantitative, a matter essentially of arithmetic. The winter had drastically altered the German numbers, but had it not done the same and more on the Soviet side?

Foreign Armies East, the OKH intelligence branch concerned with the Soviet Armed Forces, compiled a comprehensive estimate of Soviet strength in the coming summer as an annex to the first draft of Directive 41. It was a small masterpiece of staff intelligence work—logical, precise, and persuasive. It was also narrowly conceived and tied to its premises. The first and most crucial of the latter was that the Soviet Union used its manpower essentially the same way Germany did, which meant that the absolute ceiling on Soviet strength was roughly 18 million men. The losses in killed and captured between June 1941 and April 1942 (6.8 million) and in eligibles left behind in the occupied territories had brought the number down to 9.73 million, not far from a 50 percent reduction. The Soviet Armed Forces, as of 1 April, had 6.6 million men and were 20 percent below established strength. The dif-

---

[50]*OKH, Chef H. Ruest. u. BdE, AHA, Chef des Stabes Nr. 41/42, Wehrkraft der Wehrmacht im Fruehjahr 1942, 12.5.42,* H 1 382 file.

[51]*OKW, Wehrkraft der Wehrmacht im Fruehjahr 1942, 6.6.42,* in Jacobsen, *Chronik,* pp. 314–17.

[52]British Air Ministry Pamphlet 248, pp. 162, 178.

[53]*Halder Diary,* vol. III, p. 461.

[54]*H. Gr. Nord, Chef des Generalstabes, Ia Nr. 769/41, Niederschrift ueber die Besprechung beim Chef des Gen-StdH, 13.11.41,* AOK 18 35945/1 file.

ference between the potential and actual strengths, 3.13 million, Foreign Armies East figured, was the manpower reserve. After allowances were made for unreliables and physically unfit, it would yield 1.2 million men to cover the existing deficit and 1.12 million for new units. From the 1.12 million, the Soviet Army could form sixty rifle divisions, twelve tank brigades, and some lesser units. Soviet armament output, Foreign Armies East predicted, would stay as it appeared to be, adequate for current operations, with chronic shortages of hand weapons, and not sufficient to build reserves. Coke and steel shortages, however, could cause cutbacks. The sixty rifle divisions and twelve tank brigades, then, were the last real Soviet trump and, on the scale of past experience, not a hugely important one. The estimate concluded: "The enemy can no longer withstand losses such as he took in the battles from Bialystok to Vyazma-Bryansk [June to October 1941]. He also cannot for a second time throw reserves into the scales the way he did in the winter of 1941/42."[55] After another month of study, Foreign Armies East reported, "The figure '60' keeps recurring as the number of units in the Soviet operational reserve."[56] Hitler told the *Reichstag*, "The hour will come when the front frees itself from its torpor and then history will decide who won in this winter: the attacker who idiotically sacrificed his masses of men, or the defender who simply held his positions."[57]

Foreign Armies East had worked hard at counting Soviet divisions in the 1941 campaign and had compiled volumes of reports on those actually and supposedly destroyed. In November, Colonel Eberhard Kinzel, then the branch chief, had admitted that the count so far had been inconclusive, to say the least, and had said that counting divisions did not mean much insofar as the Soviet Union was concerned. It had had (by his estimate) 140 divisions in June 1941, had suffered gigantic losses during the summer, and had had 190 divisions standing in the line just before the battles of Bryansk and Vyazma in October. Nevertheless, he had maintained, the system had been improved and now reliably showed the total Soviet nominal strength to be 160 divisions and the actual effective strength to be the equivalent of 75 divisions and 40 tank brigades. By spring, he had predicted, the Soviet Union could have 150 divisions and 40 tank brigades at full strength and no more.[58] As of 20 June 1942, the Foreign Armies East count stood at 270 rifle divisions, 115 rifle brigades, 69 tank brigades, and 2 tank divisions. Nevertheless, five days later, Hitler speculated that BLAU would go faster and more easily than had been expected because the Russians, by his count, had already lost 80 divisions in the German preliminary offensives.[59]

[55]OKH, GenStdH, FHO, *Russischer Kraeftestand, 31.3.42*, H 3/113A file; *OKH, GenStdH, FHO, Auswerte-Gruppe, An Gr. II, 4.4.42* and *OKH, GenStdH, Fremde Heere Ost Nr. 803/42, an Op. Abt. 4.4.42*, H 3/198 file.

[56]OKH, GenStdH, Abt. Fremde Heere Ost, *Beurteilung der Gesamtfeindlage und ihre Entwicklungsmoeglichkeiten, 1.5.42*, H 3/198 file.

[57]Domarus, *Hitler*, vol. II, p. 1875.

[58]H. Gr. Nord, Chef des Generalstabes, *Ia Nr. 769/41, Niederschrift ueber Besprechung beim Chef des GenStdH, 13.11.41*, AOK 18 35945/1 file.

[59]Halder Diary, vol. III, p. 461; *OKW, WFSt, Kriegsgeschichtliche Abteilung, Kriegstagebuch, 1.4.–30.6.42*, 25 Jun 42, I.M.T. 1807 file.

The main German strategic interest had always been confined essentially to one question: Where would the Soviet forces have to stand and accept a fight to the finish? Most of the generals had thought that it would be in the Moscow region. Hitler had believed it would be in the south, the Ukraine and the Caucasus. In 1941, the Germans had tried both, had run out of time and had not proved—or disproved—the validity of either view. Late in the campaign, in November, the OKH contention, as put by Halder, still had been:

The oil region [of the Caucasus] is not essential to the Soviet conduct of the war, so his defense there will be passive, that is, to deny us the oil, not to preserve his own existence.

Moscow is the central point of all Russian life. It is also the western terminus of the land bridge between European and Asiatic Russia and has decisive operational import for Soviet offensive plans.[60]

Hitler, on the other hand, was more than ever certain, after the Moscow offensive failed, that he had been right all along. As the gist of a talk with Hitler in March 1942, Goebbels recorded:

The Fuehrer had a plan that was bound to lead to victory.

The Fuehrer had no intention whatever of going to Moscow. He wanted to cut off the Caucasus and thereby strike the Soviet system at its most vulnerable point. But Brauchitsch and his general staff knew better.[61]

Although the points of view about them apparently remained as far apart as ever, Moscow and the Caucasus did not reappear as rival objectives in 1942,

and the debate was not reopened. While the Moscow offensive still seemed headed toward a successful conclusion in late 1941, Hitler had designated the Caucasus as the next objective. From December on, the choice had been between the Caucasus and nothing, and the determinant had been the German, not the Soviet condition. General Fromm, for instance, who believed no major offensive should be attempted in 1942, had conceded that one in the south could be worthwhile for the sake of the oil but then doubted that the army would have enough strength to get to the oil fields.[62] By the spring of 1942, Army Group South was the only one of the three army groups anywhere near fit for an offensive, and a discussion of the strategic implications for the Soviet Union of an attack on Moscow would have been largely beside the point. Besides, Hitler was in no mood to listen. He was convinced, with some reason, that he had saved the army from a complete disaster in the previous winter by not paying attention to the generals.

Hitler gave his view of the Soviet strategic situation—in, no doubt, deliberately enhanced colors—to Mussolini on 30 April 1942. The "Bolshevik" industrial capacity had declined drastically. Outside help could only come through Murmansk, via Iran (in small quantity), or through Vladivostok that the Japanese had cut off. Therefore the "Bolsheviks" could not expect substantial material assistance from the outside. Food was already extremely

---

[60]H. Gr. Sued, Der Chef des Generalstabes, Ia Nr. 2123/41 Vortragsnotiz, 17.11.41, AOK 6 181117 file.
[61]Lochner, Goebbels Diaries, p. 136.

[62]Halder Diary, vol. III, p. 295; Chef H. Ruest. und BdE, Stab OKH, Nr. 1441/41, Notizen ueber Vortrag beim Fuehrer am 23.12.41, 28.12.41, CMH X–124 file.

short; cutbacks in the civilian rations would inevitably "radiate into the military sector"; and the Soviet Union would have to get along for another five months on the stocks it had. If Germany cut off the oil, then Soviet transport would also be paralyzed. The Soviet explosives and powder programs could not keep pace with the "highly developed German chemical industry." The Soviet losses in dead were "almost incalculable," and "the masses being thrown against us [now]" were "nowhere near" as effective as the Soviet troops had been in the 1941 campaign. He shied away, though, from predicting an outright victory, saying, "It can in no wise get worse [for Germany], only better. There can be no doubt that we will have classical successes in the forthcoming operations if we manage all of the time to concentrate our strength at the decisive points."[63]

As he had in 1940 and 1941, Hitler professed to see the Soviet Union as primarily a tool of British strategy. It was, he told Mussolini, England's "most valuable and most dangerous ally." It tied down German strength; if it defected, the British "could not do anything anymore"; and Stalin was blackmailing them by threatening a separate peace. However, unless they wanted to rid themselves of this onerous ally by conceding the German victory, the British would have to try to help him. Consequently, Germany would have to be on the alert for landings in Norway or France and be ready to occupy Vichy France.[64]

Soviet Strategy

The Soviet Condition

In mid-March 1942, Goebbels, as he did with nearly all of his best thoughts, confided to his diary, "Whether we shall succeed during the coming spring and summer in defeating the Bolsheviks—this no man can say. We know what we have and what we must risk, but we don't know what the Bolsheviks have and what they can risk."[65] There was—and is—the mystery. The Germans did not know then and the world does not know yet what the Soviet Union had and what it could risk. The Germans, it would appear from the result, must have been far off in their estimates. Soviet accounts, however, do not give sufficient information to support clear judgments about the extent of the German miscalculations.

The first five months of war had done enormous economic damage to the Soviet Union, particularly in the output of basic raw materials, and that would be felt more in 1942 than it had been in 1941. As the following table shows, output in most key categories during the first six months of 1942 would be less than half of that called for in the 1942 military-economic plan and substantially below 1941 levels.[66] The figures, of course, do not account for quantities in the production pipeline or stockpiles that may have existed.

On the other hand, unlike Hitler, Stalin had not hesitated to convert to a total war economy. By 1942, the metalworking industries (almost totally en-

---

[63]OKM, 1.SKL, Ia, Bericht ueber Besprechung am 30.4.42, CMH X–1010 file.
[64]Ibid.

[65]Lochner, Goebbels Diaries, p. 129.
[66]Based on Tyushkevich, Vooruzhennye sily, p. 269, and IVOVSS, vol. II, p. 491.

Category	1941 1st 6 mos.	2d 6 mos.	1942 Planned	1st 6 mos.
Electricity (bil., kwh.)	27.4	19.3	31.0	15.0
Coal (mil., tons)	91.9	59.5	96.9	35.7
Oil (mil., tons)	17.3	15.7	26.9	11.7
Pig Iron (mil., tons)	9.0	4.8	5.1	2.3
Steel (mil., tons)	11.4	6.5	9.4	4.0

gaged in war production) constituted 57 percent of all industry in the Soviet Union, up from 36 percent in 1940 when the emphasis on military production had already been heavy.[67] In comparison, only 43 percent of German industry was devoted to metalworking, with only 30 percent of that engaged in armaments production.[68] The allocations of iron and steel for ammunition, which had been 830,000 tons in 1940, were 1.8 million tons in 1942.[69] Output of artillery pieces went from about 30,000 in the last six months of 1941 to over 53,000 in the first half of 1942. In the same period, output of mortars more than trebled, and production of hand weapons and machine guns increased substantially; however, ammunition production went up less than 5 percent. Output of combat aircraft, 8,300, was about the same in the first six months of 1942 as in the last half of 1941, but it exceeded the German production, which was approximately 7,200.[70]

The most notable single production increase was in tanks, of which 11,200 were reportedly turned out in the first six months of 1942, more than twice the number for the last half of 1941 and close to 4 times the German output of approximately 3,000 tanks. The number of T–34s produced was apparently close to double the total 1941 output of 3,000. The achievement in tank production, however, great as it was, was less than it appeared to be because 60 percent of the output was in the light T–60 and T–70 types and mostly still T–60s.[71] The T–60, which had also made up more than half of the 1941 output, had "not demonstrated outstanding qualities in combat," but it was easier to manufacture and not dependent on the availability of diesel engines as the medium and heavy tanks were. The T–70, put into production in late 1941, was an upgraded T–60, with a three-man crew, weighing somewhat over nine tons, and carrying slightly more armor and a 45-mm. gun.[72] The alterations made the T–70 superior to the T–60 but left it inferior to the German Panzer IIIs and IVs.[73]

In the spring of 1942, the Soviet armored forces were undergoing their second major reorganization of the war. One defect observed during the general offensive had been a tendency by commands to break up the tank brigades and battalions and to commit their vehicles singly or in small batches in infantry support. A *Stavka* order of 22 January 1942 had required the bri-

[67] Voznesenskiy, *Economy of the USSR*, p. 43.
[68] Deutsches Institut fuer Wirtschaftsforschung, *Deutsche Industrie im Kriege*, p. 159.
[69] Voznesenskiy, *Economy of the USSR*, p. 43.
[70] *IVMV*, vol. IV, p. 158; Boelcke, *Ruestung*, p. 25.

[71] *IVMV*, vol. IV, p. 158; Boelcke, *Ruestung*, p. 24; Deborin and Telpukhovskiy, *Itogi i uroki*, p. 260.
[72] Tyushkevich, *Vooruzhennye sily*, p. 273.
[73] See Perrett, *Fighting Vehicles*, p. 20f and John Milsom, *Russian Tanks, 1900–1970* (London: Arms and Armour Press, 1970), pp. 92–94.

NEW T–34 TANKS MOVE UP TO THE FRONT

gades and battalions to be used only at full strength and with adequate infantry and air support, but that, to the extent that it was followed, had still not produced a capability to employ tanks in the mass. The units were too small. Consequently, in the spring, the armored forces began setting up tank corps consisting of 3 tank brigades (168 tanks), a motorized infantry brigade, a reconnaissance battalion, and artillery and rocket projectors. From May through August, 4 tank armies, *First, Third, Fourth,* and *Fifth,* were activated. Each of these was projected to have 2 tank corps, an independent tank brigade, infantry, and artillery.[74]

In spite of losses in the winter and heavier ones in the spring, the numerical strengths of the Soviet forces appear to have grown steadily throughout the first six months of 1942. The *History of the Second World War* gives the total armed forces strength "in action" in "early 1942" as 5.6 million men, of which approximately 4.9 million were in ground forces. The armies "in action" had 293 rifle divisions (at strengths between 5,000 and 9,000), 34 cavalry divisions, 121 rifle brigades, and 56 independent tank brigades.[75] At the beginning of the spring offensives, the ground forces had "over" 5.1 million men, "almost" 3,900 tanks, 44,900 artillery pieces and mortars, and the sup-

[74]*IVOVSS,* vol. II, p. 360; Tyushkevich, *Vooruzhennye sily,* p. 284; Krupchenko, *Tankovye voyska,* p. 55.

[75]*IVMV,* vol. V, p. 22.

port of 2,200 combat aircraft.[76] At the end of June, the ground forces "in action" had 5.5 million troops, over 6,000 tanks, 55,600 artillery pieces and mortars, and 2,600 combat aircraft in support. This amounted, with the brigades converted to an equivalent in divisions, to 410 divisions.[77] Elsewhere, the number of divisions, brigades, and independent regiments is given as 348 divisions, 239 brigades, and 329 regiments.[78] None of the above figures includes *Stavka* reserves, which the *History of the Second World War* gives as having been (in June) 10 field armies, 1 tank army, 3 air armies being formed, and "more than" 50 independent units.[79] Golubovich gives the reserves as 152 divisions, 107 brigades, and 225 independent regiments.[80]

Estimates of German Capabilities

In an order of 23 February 1942, the People's Commissariat of Defense initiated planning for the coming spring and summer with the admonition that it would be "inexcusably shortsighted" to be content with the winter's successes and assume from them that the German troops had been already beaten. The enemy had suffered defeats, but he was not defeated. He was still strong, and he would muster all of his forces to achieve successes.[81]

On 18 March, General Staff Intelligence submitted the following estimate:

... Preparation for a [German] spring offensive is confirmed by deployment of troops and material. In the period from 1 January to 10 March, as many as thirty-five divisions were brought in, and the field armies received a steady flow of replacements. Restoration of the railroad network in the occupied territories of the USSR is being worked on more intensively, and combat and transport aircraft are being supplied in greater numbers. ...

It cannot be ruled out that the decisive German offensive will be accompanied by a simultaneous Japanese attack on the USSR and that the Germans will, besides, put pressure on Turkey to permit transit of German troops to the Caucasus. ... The Germans cannot again attack on a broad front, because they cannot regroup their forces to accomplish that. They will concentrate all their efforts on preparing successive operations: first aiming at conquering the Caucasus and taking the Murmansk (Kirov) Railroad and subsequently at expanding the operations to take Moscow and Leningrad. In this manner the main strategic objectives could be attained: the USSR would be cut off from her allies; she would lose her oil; and even if she were not totally defeated, the country would be so weakened as to lose all significance. This is the main objective of the German leadership.

The main effort of the spring offensive will lie on the southern sector of the front, with a secondary attack on the north and a simultaneous feint in the center, towards Moscow.

Germany is preparing a decisive offensive on the Eastern Front, which will begin in the southern sector and expand to the north. For the spring offensive, Germany and her allies are bringing in as many as sixty-five divisions. ... The most likely time for the offensive will be mid-April or early May.[82]

On 23 March, the security organs of the State Defense Committee submitted a variant projection. The part of it

---

[76]*Ibid.*, p. 121. It appears likely that the Soviet figures on tanks for this stage of the war (perhaps also earlier) do not include the light tanks. See p. 300.

[77]*Ibid.*, p. 143.

[78]See Golubovich, "Sozdaniye," p. 17.

[79]*IVMV*, vol. V, p. 143.

[80]Golubovich, "Sozdaniye," p. 17.

[81]*IVMV*, vol. V, p. 30.

[82]*VOV*, p. 138f. See also *IVMV*, vol. V, p. 111f.

that has been made public read as follows:

The main blow will be in the southern sector via Rostov to Stalingrad and into the North Caucasus—and from there toward the Caspian Sea. In this fashion, the Germans hope to take possession of the Caucasus oil sources. If the operation succeeds, the Germans expect, on reaching the Volga at Stalingrad, to continue the offensive northward along the Volga. In this summer, they will not only want to get to the Volga and the Caspian Sea, but they will also undertake main operations against Moscow and Leningrad, because taking those places is a matter of prestige with the German Command.[83]

The *History of the Second World War* describes the two "prognoses" as having been "not without influence" on the decisions relating to the further conduct of the war.[84] However, their influence, apparently, was either small or virtually nonexistent. The *History of the Second World War*, Zhukov, and the *Popular Scientific Sketch* indicate that Stalin, whose opinion was the deciding one, believed the Germans had strength enough to conduct simultaneous offensives in the center and the south, and he gave particular importance to Moscow.[85] The *History of the Great Patriotic War* maintains that the *Stavka* recognized the possibility of a German offensive in the south but made "a strategic error" and assumed that the most probable German attack would not be toward Stalingrad and the Caucasus but toward Moscow and the central industrial region.[86] Vasilevskiy says that the enemy's strength on the

Moscow approaches ("more than seventy divisions") led the *Stavka* and the General Staff to conclude that his main attack would be in the center. "This opinion," Vasilevskiy adds, "I know very well to have been shared by the majority of the front commands."[87]

Soviet accounts have maintained that a crucial consideration for the Soviet Command, as it went into the second summer of the war, was a numerical inferiority in troop strength. The most frequently given figure, since it was first used by Platonov in 1958, has been 6.2 million German and allied troops at the outset of the 1942 summer campaign.[88] The *History of the Second World War* gives two figures: 5,655,000 German alone, as of 28 June 1942, and 6,198,000 German and allied, as of 1 May 1942. Of these, 5,388,000 were German.[89] The Germans' own count was 3.9 million men in the ground forces, distributed as follows: 2.6 million (allies not counted) on the Eastern Front proper, 212,000 in the occupied Soviet territory, 150,000 in Finland, and 1.3 million in the occupied territories outside the Soviet Union, in the Replacement Army in Germany, and in North Africa.[90]

---

[87]Vasilevskiy, *Delo*, p. 206.

[88]Platonov implied that the allied troops were not included in the 6.2 million. Platonov, *Vtoraya Mirovaya Voyna*, p. 286. The subsequent accounts give the figure as being inclusive. See *VOV (Kratkaya Istoriya)*, p. 157; Deborin and Telpukhovskiy, *Itogi i uroki*, p. 356; and Vasilevskiy, *Delo*, p. 207.

[89]The figures for the allies are as follows: Finnish, 300,000; Rumanian, 330,000; Hungarian, 70,000; Italian, 68,000; Slovakian, 28,000; and Spanish, 14,000. (Spain was not an ally but supplied a division of "volunteers.") *IVMV*, vol. V, pp. 121, 145.

[90]*OKW, KTB*, vol. II, p. 52.

---

[83]*IVMV*, vol. V, p. 112.

[84]*Ibid.*, p. 112.

[85]*Ibid.*, p. 113; Zhukov, *Memoirs*, p. 364; *VOV*, p. 139.

[86]*IVOVSS*, vol. II, p. 404.

A Second Front

In May 1941, Soviet Foreign Minister Molotov journeyed to the West, to London, to negotiate a treaty of alliance and to Washington to discuss a second lend-lease protocol. His most urgent task in both capitals was to secure a commitment from the Western Allies to open a second front in Europe in 1942. Prime Minister Churchill's response to the second front proposal was sympathetic but noncommittal.[91] President Roosevelt told Molotov that the U.S. government "hoped" and "expected" to open a second front in 1942.[92] On 11 June in Washington and 12 June in Moscow, the U.S. and Soviet governments released a joint communique, one sentence of which read, "In the course of the conversations full understanding was reached with regard to the urgent tasks of creating a Second Front in Europe in 1942."[93] Molotov had drafted the communique, and Roosevelt had approved it, although General George C. Marshall, the U.S. Army chief of staff, had objected that the statement was "too strong."[94] Marshall had told Roosevelt and Molotov earlier that the problem would be in getting the ships to transport U.S. troops and equipment to Europe.[95] On 10 June, in London, Churchill gave Molotov a statement which read, in part, "It is

impossible to say in advance whether the situation will be such as to make this operation [an invasion of Europe in 1942] feasible when the time comes. We can therefore give no promise in the matter. . . ."[96]

In the Soviet view, there could not have been any substantive reasons for the Western Allies' not opening a second front in 1942. In the Soviet view, also, a commitment was made during the May–June negotiations. The *History of the Great Patriotic War* maintains, ". . . the governments of the USA and England assured the Soviet delegation that a second front would be opened in 1942."[97] The *Short History* states, "The pertinent communique pointed out that complete agreement had been reached concerning [the second front's] opening in Europe in 1942."[98] The *History of the Second World War* and the *Popular Scientific Sketch* maintain that Washington and London were "forced to announce" the creation of a second front in 1942 by "progressive public opinion" and their obligations to the Soviet Union.[99]

That the second front did not materialize in 1942 was, in the Soviet view, the result of deliberate British-American policy decisions made "behind the back of the Soviet Union."[100] The *Short History* asserts, ". . . neither country, later events showed, had any intention of living up to its commitment."[101] The reason they did not, according to the *History of the Great Patriotic War* and the

---

[91]J. R. M. Butler, *Grand Strategy* (London: Her Majesty's Stationery Office, 1964), vol. III, pt. II, p. 594f.

[92]Maurice Matloff and Edwin M. Snell, *Strategic Planning for Coalition Warfare, 1941–1942* (Washington, D.C.: GPO, 1953), p. 231.

[93]*Ibid.*, p. 232; *IVMV*, vol. V, p. 73.

[94]Matloff and Snell, *Strategic Planning*, p. 232.

[95]Sherwood, *Roosevelt and Hopkins*, p. 563; *IVMV*, vol. V, p. 72.

[96]Butler, *Grand Strategy*, vol. III, pt. II, p. 597. See also *IVMV*, vol. V, p. 73.

[97]*IVOVSS*, vol. II, p. 400.

[98]*VOV (Kratkaya Istoriya)*, p. 152.

[99]*IVMV*, vol. V, p. 73; *VOV*, p. 480f.

[100]*VOV*, p. 481.

[101]*VOV (Kratkaya Istoriya)*, p. 152.

History of the Second World War, was because the "ruling circles" in Great Britain and the United States wanted to let Germany and the Soviet Union exhaust themselves "in heavy and bloody battles."[102]

In the Soviet accounts, the absence of the second front and the alleged duplicity of the Western Allies relative to it are depicted as having had critical bearing on Soviet strategic planning for the summer of 1942. The Soviet plans for spring and summer offensives, the *History of the Great Patriotic War* implies, were based on an assumption that they would coincide with "attacks by Anglo-American forces on Germany from the west" and that the plans might have been different if the Soviet Union had known "the real intentions of its allies."[103] Bagramyan has said Timoshenko and Khrushchev told him in March 1942, when *Southwestern Theater* began work on its plan, that there would be a second front created in the latter half of 1942, and it would "draw off part of the enemy's forces and his reserves."[104] The *History of the Second World War* contends that the Soviet government was left in uncertainty, until mid-August 1942, as to whether there would be a second front, while the Germans, all along, "counted on" one not existing, and they made their dispositions accordingly.[105] The *History of the Great Patriotic War* charges that the Germans knew there would not be a second front through "secret negotiations on a separate peace" conducted by "unofficial representatives of indus-trial and financial circles of the USA and England."[106]

A Strategic Defensive

As the Soviet spring offensives failed, one by one, the certainty that the initiative would change hands before summer became inescapable, and it became imperative for the Soviet Command to devise a defensive strategy. The problem, potentially deadly though it was, was less complicated than it had been the year before. The Germans' condition was known, and their options were limited. Time was on their side, but it was running out because they were going to have to restart from a dead stop. By mid-February, German Foreign Armies East had believed an offensive in the south could hardly be a surprise to the Russians. It observed that, according to agent reports, Marshal Timoshenko, the commander of *Southwestern Theater,* had talked as early as December about the Germans' being compelled to attack again in the south to get oil and that British newspaper reports from the Soviet Union had repeated the same theme several times since.[107] Estimates made in April and May by Foreign Armies East no longer questioned Soviet knowledge of the Germans' plans for the spring and addressed possible Soviet responses "to the expected German offensive."[108] The Soviet General Staff's and State Defense Committee's

[102]*IVMV,* vol. V, p. 71; *IVOVSS,* vol. II, p. 400.

[103]*IVOVSS,* vol. II, p. 401.

[104]Bagramyan, *Tak shli my k pobede,* p. 51.

[105]*IVMV,* vol. V, p. 111.

[106]*IVOVSS,* vol. II, p. 400.

[107]*OKH, GenStdH, Fremde Heere Ost, Nr. 61/42, Russischer Angriff im Fruehjahr 1942, 20.2.42,* H 3/2 file.

[108]*OKH, GenStdH, Fremde Heere Ost, Beurteilung der Feindlage, 10.4.42* and *OKH, GenStdH, Fremde Heere Ost, Beurteilung der Gesamtfeindlage, 1.5.42,* H 3/198 file.

estimates of German intentions cited above were singularly close to the mark, in fact almost prescient, considering that they were completed ten days to two weeks before Hitler put his own plans on paper. To them can be added, from the *Popular Scientific Sketch,* the general statement, "As the Supreme Command worked out the plans for further operations it had sufficient information concerning the intentions and measures of the enemy."[109]

The General Staff completed its calculations in mid-March, and the strategic plan for the spring and summer of 1942 was put into final form during the conference at the end of the month. Within that time, as has been seen, the General Staff's concept of an "active defense" against an expected German offensive gave way to Stalin's active defense, which aimed to forestall the German initiative entirely. This, while it did not invalidate the estimates of German intentions, made them largely irrelevant to the plan. In the stage of the active defense, May through June, the Soviet offensives would "improve the operative-strategic situation of the Soviet Armed Forces, uncover the enemy's intentions, deal his groupings a defeat, and by preemptive blows, frustrate the enemy's prospect of developing another large-scale offensive on the Soviet-German front." After the period of active defense, probably in July, the forces would develop "larger" offensives on a broad front "from the Baltic Sea to the Black Sea, with the aim of smashing the enemy's main groupings and bringing about the decisive turn of the war in favor of the Soviet Union

that had been initiated at Moscow in the winter 1941/42."[110] In the second stage, the main offensive effort would be in the south, but beyond that, the plan was not worked out because the details would depend on the results of the first stage.[111]

At what point the Soviet thinking turned from the active defense to what is called the "strategic defensive" is not entirely clear. The *History of the Second World War* indicates that defensive elements were included in the March plan, and the *fronts* operating in the western and southwestern "directions" were required to build up their defense lines and create reserves to be used either to support their own offensives or to counterattack "in the case of an unexpected enemy offensive."[112] On the other hand, the *History* implies that not until late June did the *Stavka* consider it necessary to observe Lenin's dictum that methods of warfare should change to accommodate changed circumstances. Then it decided to abandon its offensive plans and revert to the strategic defensive.[113] The *Popular Scientific Sketch* states:

By the end of June, the situation of the Soviet forces had worsened everywhere on the Soviet-German front. The spring operations of the year 1942, with which the Headquarters had wished to create conditions for development of a larger offensive in the summer, had been frustrated by the enemy. . . . The *Stavka* saw itself compelled to forego the offensive and resume the strategic defensive.[114]

---

[110]*IVMV,* vol. V, p. 117. See pp. 238–40.
[111]*Ibid.,* p. 114.
[112]*Ibid.,* p. 116.
[113]*Ibid.,* p. 142.
[114]*VOV,* p. 146.

---

[109]*VOV,* p. 139. See p. 302f.

By Vasilevskiy's account, the Soviet forces went over to the defensive in May, after Kharkov.[115] The timing of the Molotov mission appears also to have been the result of a change in Soviet thinking in the latter half of May. In March, Stalin had not believed the Soviet forces would be capable of "larger offensive operations" in the spring without a second front, but, by implication at least, he had thought they would have such a capability in the summer.[116] The British government had invited Molotov to come to London on 8 April, but the Soviet response had been slow, and for the more than five weeks before he arrived, the main Soviet concern had been with getting better territorial and political terms for itself in the alliance treaty. At the first meeting in London, on 21 May, at the height of the Kharkov battle, Molotov said he had come to discuss two matters: the treaty and a second front, and the latter was now the more important. In the subsequent sessions in London and Washington, he appeared to be talking in terms of two possibilities: a victory in 1942, with a second front that would draw at least forty German divisions off the Eastern Front, or a Soviet reversion to a defensive, the results of which could not be positively predicted.[117] The summer offensive had by then, most probably, become wholly contingent on the second front.

The *History of the Second World War* gives a picture of preparation by stages for the shift to the defensive. Beginning in March, the *fronts* and armies built up their lines to depths of six to seven miles. At the same time, and continuing into the summer, the theater commands and the *Stavka* saw to the construction of rear lines back to the Volga River, a distance of up to three hundred and fifty miles. This included renovating and improving works built in 1941, the Mozhaysk line, the Moscow and Oka River defenses, and lines on the Volga east of Moscow and on the Don, from Voronezh to Rostov. In May, work began on defenses for the Caucasus, between the Don and the Kuban, along the Terek River, and, among other places, around Voroshilovsk, Krasnodar, and Groznyy.[118] In May, "when the big battles in the south began," the *Stavka* "took measures" to strengthen the defenses of *Bryansk*, *Southwest*, and *South Fronts*.[119] In May and June, when, as the *History of the Second World War* puts it, "the *Wehrmacht* attacked only on the south" and not toward Moscow, the *Stavka* "made corrections" and began to prepare for a strategic defensive, which included building up the strength in the south.[120]

Although the *History of the Second World War* maintains that as part of the preparations for the strategic defensive, five of the ten reserve armies were redeployed from the center to the southwest (in early July, after BLAU began), Stalin, the *Stavka*, and the General Staff, apparently, at no time believed the German main attack would be aimed anywhere other than at Moscow. Vasilevskiy says they did not "exclude" an attack from the vicinity of Kursk to Voronezh but believed the

---

[115]Vasilevskiy, *Delo*, p. 218.
[116]*IVMV*, vol. V, p. 113.
[117]See Butler, *Grand Strategy*, vol. III, pt. II, pp. 592–96.

[118]*IVMV*, vol. V, p. 116.
[119]*Ibid.*, p. 146.
[120]*Ibid.*, p. 146f.

final objective would, nevertheless, be Moscow.[121] At the end of June, the main weight of the Soviet deployment was in the center. The former *Western Theater (Kalinin* and *West Fronts)* was somewhat stronger than the *Southwestern Theater (Bryansk, Southwest,* and *South Fronts)*. Expressed as percentages of total Soviet front line strength, relationships were as follows:

Command	Divisions	Artillery	Tanks	Aircraft
Western Theater ..	31.3	31.6	40.3	32.7
Southwestern Theater ..	28.3	29.6	38.3	29.2

These, however, did not comprise the whole difference. Of the reserve armies, six and the one tank army then operational were positioned to cover Moscow on the line Kalinin-Tula-Tambov-Borisoglebsk-Stalingrad, and four were ranged in a broad arc east of Moscow on the line Vologda-Gorkiy-Saratov.[122] Moreover, close to a third of

the former *Southwestern Theater* forces, almost all of *Bryansk Front,* were deployed on the north flank to defend the Tula approach to Moscow.

The implication to be drawn from the deployment is that a stronger concentration in the south would have produced a better result in the summer campaign. The *History of the Great Patriotic War* concludes:

The incorrect determination by the Soviet Supreme High Command of the direction of the enemy's attack in the first stage of the summer campaign led to decisions that were in strategic error. Instead of concentrating forces in the operations zone of the *Southwest* and *South Fronts* and establishing on the left flank a deeply echeloned defense that would have been insurmountable for the enemy, the *Stavka* continued to fortify the central sector of the front. . . .[123]

On the other hand, the course of the war in the coming months would show the "error" at least to be self-compensating and, perhaps, to have been a stroke of high good fortune.

---

[121]Vasilevskiy, *Delo,* p. 219.

[122]The *Western Theater* was terminated as a command on 5 May; the *North Caucasus Theater* on 19 May; and the *Southwestern Theater* on 21 June. *IVMV,* vol. V, p. 143.

---

[123]*IVOVSS,* vol. II, p. 404.

CHAPTER XV

Prelude to Summer

Preliminary Operations

Sevastopol Begun

Harko 306 was Eleventh Army's artillery command. A Harko (*Hoeheres Artillerie Kommando*) ordinarily controlled an army's heavy artillery, but in early April 1942, Harko 306 surveyed the Sevastopol perimeter not to emplace just heavy artillery—but the heaviest. At various places in Germany, guns, originally built to crack massive concrete and steel French and Belgian forts, were being dismantled to be shipped in pieces by train to the Crimea. The lightest were twelve 11-inch (280-mm.) coastal howitzers. The turret-mounted naval guns in several of the Soviet forts had calibers about an inch larger. Next heavier, and unmatched on the Soviet side, were a dozen 14-inch howitzers. But even those were dwarfed by GAMMA and KARL. Both were superheavy mortars. GAMMA, the "Big Bertha" of World War I, had a 17-inch (420-mm.) bore and fired a 1-ton shell. KARL had a 21-inch bore, and its shell weighed a ton and a half, four times more than the 14-inch howitzer's shells.[1] Harko 306 was to receive three KARL and six GAMMA weapons. Neither one was mobile, and KARL could only be assembled or disassembled with the aid of a 75-ton crane. But KARL, at 132 tons, was almost a light fieldpiece when compared to DORA, which weighed 1,345 tons and, to be dismantled and moved, needed a special sixty-car train. DORA had a 101-foot-long barrel, a 31½ inch bore (800-mm.), and fired a 7-ton shell to ranges up to thirty miles. In tests, it had demolished a concrete wall 24 feet thick and punched through 90 inches of steel with single shots. The most powerful artillery piece in the world, DORA was also highly visible, hence vulnerable, and had to have antiaircraft artillery and smoke generator detachments to protect it.[2]

At Cottbus, in Germany, Panzer Abteilung 300 was crating its equipment for a move to the Crimea. It operated demolition vehicles known as GOLIATH which, standing about 2 feet high and weighing less than half a ton, looked like a midget World War I rhomboid tank. It could be steered over distances up to a half mile by wires

---

[1]Rudolf Lusar, *German Secret Weapons of the Second World War* (New York: Philosophical Library, 1959), pp. 15–16. See also William G. Dooly, Jr., *Great Weapons of World War I* (New York: Walker and Co., 1969), pp. 53–55.

[2]Charles B. Burdick, "DORA, The Germans' Biggest Gun," *Military Review* 11(1961), 72–75; Lusar, *Secret Weapons*, p. 20; *Schw. Art. Abt. (mot.) 833, Ia Nr. 17/42, Einsatz Karl-Geraet, 11.4.42; LIV A.K., Ia Nr. 315/42, Vorbereitung des Angriffs auf Sevastopol, 10.4.42; AOK 11, Ia Nr. 1444/42, Einsatz Karl-Geraet, 10.4.42, AOK 11 28654/2* file.

attached to a control panel. The 150 pounds of superhigh explosive it carried made it most effective in confined spaces, but its blast could knock out a fully secured tank in the open at a radius of as much as 50 yards.[3]

In the winter, the OKH chief of artillery had looked at DORA and pronounced it to be "an extraordinary work of art but useless."[4] So also, in fact, were GAMMA, KARL, and GOLIATH. They were out of place in mobile war, throwbacks to Verdun and 1916—but then so was Sevastopol. As an objective in any strategic sense it was equally useless. Even General Manstein, the commander of Eleventh Army, whose own work of art the operation was, could not say it would accomplish more than the release of "three to four divisions" from what would otherwise be an extended siege.[5]

Hitler, who found it difficult to resist a challenge, especially one as visible as Sevastopol, also had doubts. In Directive 41 of 5 April 1942, he designated Sevastopol, the Kerch Peninsula, and the Izyum bulge as the targets for preliminary operations before the main summer campaign. When on 16 April he approved Eleventh Army's plan for the Kerch operation, he also reviewed one for Sevastopol, STOERFANG ("sturgeon catch"), but put off deciding when to execute it. By May, he had in mind starting the main offensive in mid-June, and on the 24th, he said BLAU I would have to start on 15 June even if it meant giving up on Sevastopol. A check by the OKW Operations Staff then indicated that STOERFANG probably would have to be abandoned because it could not begin enough ahead of BLAU I to be given full air support for more than three or four days.[6]

On the night of 26 May, Hitler's thinking took a new turn. The final reports of the Kharkov battle were coming in, and he believed the speed of the victory permitted "favorable inferences to be drawn with respect to the entire enemy situation."[7] Consequently, it was not necessary any longer, he said, to hold rigidly to the schedule set for BLAU. It could be postponed for a while. He thought it more important to strike fast and destroy more Soviet units while they were still under the shock of Kharkov. To do that he wanted two new operations: one northeast of Kharkov near Volchansk, the other east of the Donets River in the Izyum area.[8] The first became Operation WILHELM. The second, which had an antecedent in the original FRIDERICUS plans, was designated FRIDERICUS II. WILHELM and FRIDERICUS II and the postponement of BLAU also provided time for STOERFANG, which Manstein expected to have ready to start on 7 June.

The artillery, some six hundred pieces in all, including the heaviest, opened fire on the Sevastopol defenses on 2 June. The VIII Air Corps joined in. DORA and KARL concentrated on the forts north of Severnaya Bay and claimed hits on ones the Germans called Maxim Gorkiy I, Malakov, and

[3]AOK 11, Ia Nr. 1843/42, Einsatz von ferngelenkten Sprengstofftraegern, 23.5.42, AOK 11 28654/4 file.
[4]Halder Diary, vol. III, p. 333.
[5]Manstein, Verlorene Siege, p. 262.
[6]OKW, Stellv. WFSt, Kriegsgeschichtliche Abteilung, Kriegstagebuch, 1.4.–30.6.42, 2 and 5 Apr 42, 24 May 42, I.M.T. 1807 file.
[7]Ibid., 26 May 42.
[8]Ibid.

GERMAN 150-MM. K–18 GUNS OPEN FIRE

White Cliffs (apparently ones with the Soviet designations Pillbox 2, 37, and 38).[9] The infantry, meanwhile, were still being redeployed from the eastern end of the peninsula.

The defenders were ready, as ready as they could be. Admiral Oktyabrskiy's *Sevastopol Defense Region* had worked through the winter to bring in men and supplies, and Oktyabrskiy had been told, on 19 May, to make his final preparations. On that day also, *Crimean Front* had gone out of existence, and the *North Caucasus Theater* had become *North Caucasus Front*. Still under Marshal Budenny, it had the missions of holding Sevastopol and preventing a German crossing from Kerch to the Taman Peninsula.[10] General Petrov's *Independent Maritime Army* had eight full strength divisions and several brigades and separate regiments. The defenders also had about six hundred artillery pieces, although none were equal to the heaviest the Germans had; and their strength is given as having been 188,000 men (and some women), 106,000 of them in "line units."[11]

Manstein moved into his forward command post on the night of 6 June. It was situated in a sheltering valley directly behind the front, about midway on the perimeter. From a nearby height, he could look out over the

---

[9]See Vaneyev, *Geroicheskaya oborona*, p. 112.

[10]*IVMV*, vol. V, p. 132.

[11]*IVOVSS*, vol. II, p. 407. See also *IVMV*, vol. V, p. 132; *VOV (Kratkaya Istoriya)*, p. 160; and Vaneyev, *Geroicheskaya oborona*, pp. 249–57.

whole Sevastopol fortress. The distances were not great, at most, sixteen miles east to west, fourteen miles north to south. The LIV Corps stood on the north with four divisions and a reinforced regiment. The XXX Corps was on the south, with three divisions, and Rumanian Mountain Corps occupied the center with two divisions. The artillery was almost all on the north, not by choice but because the roads in the center and south were hopelessly inadequate for moving guns and ammunition. The north also afforded the only viable line of attack. The center crossed the western rim of the Yaila Mountains, a jumble of ridges covered with scrub forest. The south, almost equally rugged, offered one attraction, steep-sided valleys covering a road that ran from the coast near Balaklava northwestward to Sevastopol, but the ground was studded with obstacles, and the fields of fire for artillery were restricted. There the GOLIATHS would have to be tried as substitutes for artillery. An attack in the center promised nothing; from the south, not much more; but if ones were not made, the defense could concentrate entirely on the north, where the approach was only somewhat less forbidding. Everywhere away from the coast, the daytime temperatures in June regularly rose above 100° F.[12]

The infantry attack began on the north, in the LIV Corps sector, at dawn on 7 June. The XXX Corps, which had not fully redeployed its units from Kerch, would have to wait another four days. Rumanian Mountain Corps' mission was to tie down the defense in the center. Having had the winter and spring to get ready, the defenders were prepared, even having swastika flags that they intended to lay out to confuse the German aircraft. *(Map 27.)*

In the late afternoon on the 7th, after LIV Corps reported having not yet found a single weak spot, Hitler sent word through Army Group South that the operation would either have to make headway fast or be stopped and converted again into a siege. Hitler was seeing WILHELM and FRIDERICUS II as a pair of quick, cheap victories, and he now tied STOERFANG to them. He wanted to start WILHELM on 7 June, FRIDERICUS II on the 12th, and have both of them and STOERFANG completed in time to begin BLAU I on the 20th.[13]

Wilhelm, Fridericus II, and Stoerfang

While STOERFANG had about it the aspect of head-on encounter of the World War I style, WILHELM and FRIDERICUS II depended on maneuver to an extent that made them almost reminiscent of the eighteenth century. A matched set of elegant double envelopments, they were designed to achieve tactical effects beneficial to BLAU, cut into the Soviet defensive strength, and accomplish a psychological mission Hitler had set for the preliminary operations in Directive 41, namely, to restore the German troops' confidence and "hammer into the enemy" a sense of inferiority.[14]

---

[12]Manstein, *Verlorene Siege*, pp. 263–72.

[13]*AOK 11, Ia Kriegstagebuch Nr. 12*, 7 Jun 42, AOK 11 28654/1 file; OKW, *Stellv. WFSt, Kriegsgeschichtliche Abteilung, Kriegstagebuch, 1.4.–30.6.42*, 1 Jun 42, I.M. T. 1807 file.

[14]*OKW, WFSt, Nr. 55616/42, Weisung Nr. 41, 5.4.42*, German High Level Directives, CMH files.

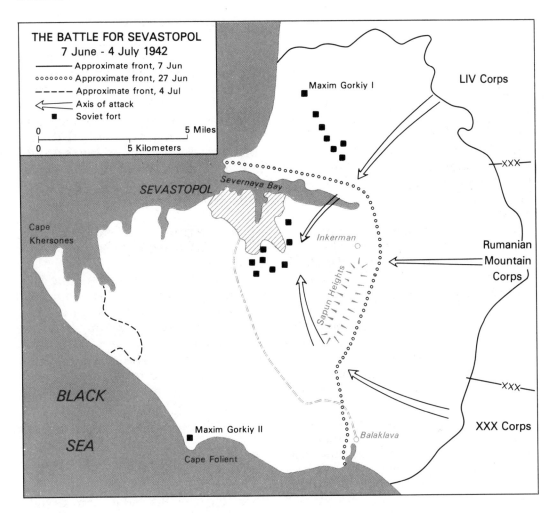

MAP 27

WILHELM would trap the Soviet *Twenty-eighth Army* in what was left of the Volchansk salient and provide cover on the south for Sixth Army's main thrust in BLAU I, which was to carry northeastward from the vicinity of Belgorod. The objectives of FRI-DERICUS II were to encircle the Soviet *Ninth* and *Thirty-eighth Armies* north and east of Izyum and bring the First Panzer Army front east thirty miles into

starting position for BLAU II, on the Oskol River below Kupyansk. The key to both operations was III Panzer Corps. The attack in May across the mouth of the Izyum bulge had brought it north into the Sixth Army sector. For WILHELM, it was attached to Sixth Army and was to strike northeastward along the Burluk River to form the southern arm of the envelopment. For FRI-DERICUS II, it would revert to First

Panzer Army, make a 90° turn, and bear east and south, past Kupyansk, to complete the second encirclement from the north and bring itself into position for BLAU II.[15]

On the Soviet side, Marshal Timoshenko, commander of *Southwestern Theater* and *Southwest Front,* and Khrushchev and General Bagramyan, both members of his staff, knew they were headed for more trouble, but not how much or what to do about it. On 29 May, they sent an appraisal to the *Stavka* predicting renewed German attacks in "five to ten days." However, Timoshenko and his two staffs, both theater and *front,* believed, as the *Stavka* and the General Staff apparently also did, that the big German drive on Moscow was also about to begin and regarded whatever might happen in the south as secondary.[16] Nevertheless, Timoshenko knew he would need reinforcements, and not wanting at that point to face Stalin himself, he persuaded Khrushchev and Bagramyan to go and ask for them. They found Stalin less reproachful than they had expected. Bagramyan says one of Stalin's outstanding characteristics as a wartime leader was his "iron self-control." And they were given reinforcements, but not on a lavish scale—7 rifle divisions, 2 tank corps, and 4 tank brigades.[17]

In WILHELM, speed was the first essential, as it was also for FRIDERICUS II. The envelopments would be shallow,

not exceptionally difficult to evade, and wet weather in May had kept the roads muddy. The first week of June was dry and sunny, with temperatures in the 80s until the 6th when an overcast sky dropped the temperature twenty degrees and brought intermittent rainsqualls. Because of the rain, III Panzer Corps reported that its tanks would have hard going on level ground and might get stuck on inclines, and IV Air Corps' landing strips became too soggy to let loaded *Stukas* and bombers take off. Sixth Army, which had been ready to start WILHELM on the 7th, ordered a day's delay.[18]

While Sixth Army waited one day and then another for the ground to dry enough to let WILHELM begin, Eleventh Army clawed its way into the Sevastopol north front at a disconcertingly slow pace. The heavy artillery scored hits on the forts, but it was all but useless against the hundreds of natural and man-made caves that gave the defenders cover and interlocking fields of fire in seemingly endless combinations. The infantry had to deal with these, 645 of them in the first five days, and at a high price, 10,300 casualties. On the 8th, Manstein already wanted to bring the 46th Infantry Division in from Kerch, which Hitler would not allow, although he added that he wanted STOERFANG to continue as long as it had a "chance" to succeed. The chance did not appear to be much of one, especially after XXX Corps began its attack on the 11th and, as Field Marshal Bock, the commander of Army Group South, observed, accomplished "nothing at all." On the 12th,

---

[15]*AOK 6, Ia Nr. 1999/42, Armeebefehl Nr. 47, 30.5.42,* AOK 6 22391/7 file; *Armeegruppe von Kleist, Ia Nr. 43/42, 1. Weisung fuer FRIDERICUS 2., 15.6.42,* Pz. AOK 1 25179/4 file.

[16]*IVMV,* vol. V, p. 138. See also Moskalenko, *Na yugo-zapadnom napravlenii,* p. 221.

[17]Bagramyan, *Tak shli my k pobede,* p. 131.

[18]*AOK 6, Fuehrungsabteilung Kriegstagebuch Nr. 12,* 6 Jun 42, AOK 6 22855/1 file.

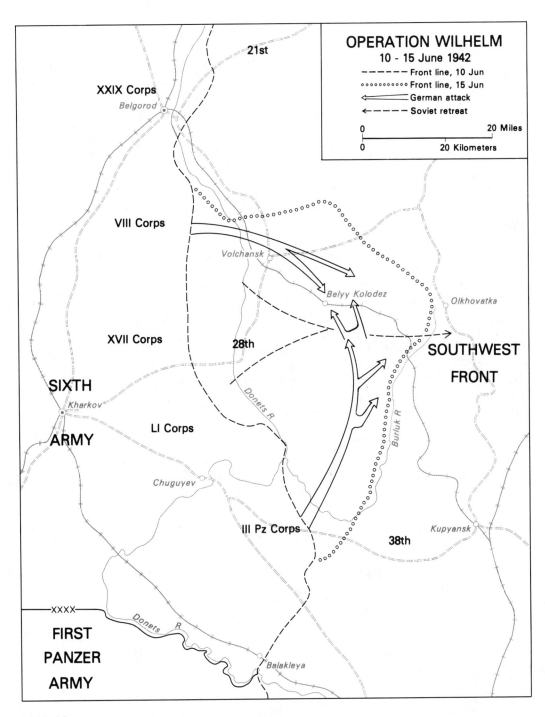

MAP 28

Bock demanded a situation estimate, and Manstein answered that he believed he could complete the operation if he had three more infantry regiments. Bock passed the estimate to the OKH, adding that one thing was certain: without the reinforcements Manstein wanted, STOERFANG was a hopeless case.[19]

In the meantime, WILHELM had started on 10 June, and for Bock, the first day's results had been "gratifying."[20] In spite of occasional rain, III Panzer Corps crossed the Burluk River, after capturing two bridges, and began the advance upstream. The VIII Corps did even better north of Volchansk. It took three bridges on the Donets and was passing Volchansk on the northeast by late afternoon.[21] (Map 28.)

During the night on the 10th, Bock had gone by train from Poltava to Kharkov to be with III Panzer Corps the next day. He arrived at the front in the early afternoon, just in time to witness a downpour that in less than an hour engulfed the tanks in mud.[22] The VIII Corps, mostly infantry, kept moving in the rain and reached Belyy Kolodez, ten miles southeast of Volchansk, in the late afternoon. The tanks were supposed to have been there to meet it, but they were thirty miles away on the Burluk River.[23]

When Bock had arrived back at Sixth Army headquarters after dark, he had learned what General Paulus, the commander of Sixth Army, had known for several hours, namely, that *Twenty-eighth Army* had abandoned its front west of the Donets and was marching east. Throughout the day on the 12th, III Panzer Corps, under orders from both Bock and Paulus to forget about everything else and close the encirclement, ground its way north, while Soviet columns headed southeast past Belyy Kolodez and out of the pocket. At the last, before it made the contact in the midmorning on the 13th, III Panzer Corps had to fight through several lines of Soviet tanks dug-in to hold open the pincers' jaws. Thereafter, the mopping-up went quickly, bringing in 24,800 prisoners.[24]

While WILHELM was not quite living up to its expectations, STOERFANG was looking more and more like a throwback to World War I. The LIV Corps took the fort known as Maxim Gorkiy I, with its heavy naval guns and underground galleries, on the 13th. One of the armored turrets had been shattered beforehand by fire either from KARL or DORA. There were, though, a dozen similar forts north of Severnaya Bay and hundreds of smaller emplacements. Army Group South gave Manstein one fresh infantry regiment, let him exchange two worn-out regiments from LIV Corps for 46th Infantry Division regiments, and prepared to send him three more regiments.[25]

But Bock was getting impatient. He had counted on having the air units

[19]*AOK 11, Ia Kriegstagebuch Nr. 12,* 8–12 Jun 42, AOK 11 28654/1 file; *Bock Diary, Osten II,* 11–12 Jun 42.

[20]*Bock Diary, Osten II,* 10 Jun 42.

[21]*AOK 6, Fuehrungsabteilung Kriegstagebuch Nr. 12,* 10 Jun 42, AOK 6 22855/1 file.

[22]*Bock Diary, Osten II,* 11 Jun 42.

[23]*AOK 6, Fuehrungsabteilung Kriegstagebuch Nr. 12,* 11 Jun 42, AOK 6 22855/1 file.

[24]*Ibid.,* 12–15 Jun 42; *Bock Diary, Osten II,* 11–12 Jun 42.

[25]*AOK 11, Ia Kriegstagebuch Nr. 12,* 12–15 Jun 42, AOK 11 28654/1 file.

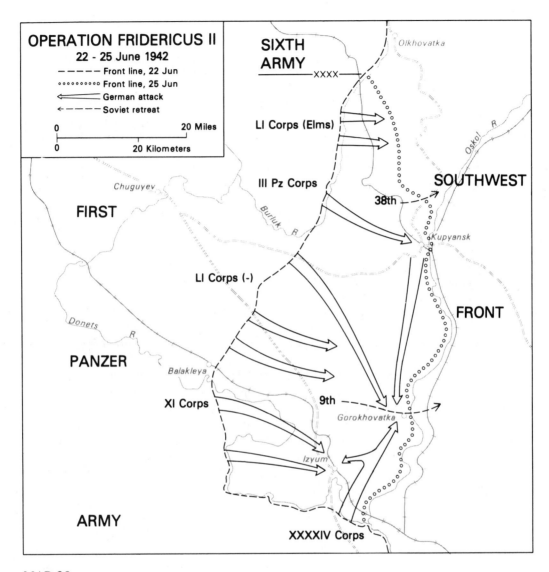

OPERATION FRIDERICUS II
22 - 25 June 1942
- – – – – Front line, 22 Jun
- ∘∘∘∘∘∘∘∘∘ Front line, 25 Jun
- ⟵——— German attack
- ⟵– – – Soviet retreat

0   20 Miles
0   20 Kilometers

MAP 29

from Sevastopol in time to start BLAU on the 20th, and he observed that it did not make sense to keep the troops for the main operation standing by their loaded vehicles with no place to go. On the 13th, he considered going ahead with BLAU I and leaving the planes on the Crimea. That idea evaporated the next day when he noted with no pleasure at all, "FRIDERICUS II has surfaced again."[26] Apparently he had thought FRIDERICUS II would be forgotten. Hitler, who was vacationing in Bavaria, had not shown any recent interest in

---

[26] *Bock Diary, Osten II*, 12–14 Jun 42.

it—or in BLAU either for that matter—
and the OKH had seemed to sym-
pathize with Bock's concern about
time. Late on the night of the 14th, the
OKH relayed an order from Hitler to
execute FRIDERICUS II and begin BLAU I
"as soon as the *Luftwaffe* can be spared
from FRIDERICUS." The earliest first day
for BLAU I would be the 23d.[27] Meanwhile, STOERFANG would continue.

After having had an impression the
day before that the Soviet infantry was
weakening, LIV Corps made a big
sweep on the 17th, taking six forts—
Bastion, Malakov, Cheka, G.P.U. Siberia, and Volga—and driving a wedge
through almost to the north shore of
Severnaya Bay. On the 18th, while LIV
Corps engaged North Fort and batteries at the mouth of the bay, XXX
Corps pushed two spearheads through
to the Sapun Heights. Next they would
have to clear the approaches to the bay
and the heights. Then they would face
the inner defenses.[28] Manstein asked
for time to regroup the infantry and
reposition the artillery, time which
Bock remarked would "also benefit the
enemy."[29]

FRIDERICUS II was scheduled to begin
the 17th, but because of daily rainstorms was not ready until the 20th,
and did not actually begin until the
morning of the 22d. The III Panzer
Corps again was the main force. Its
mission was to strike east from the
vicinity of Chuguyev to Kupyansk and
turn south along the Oskol River. On
the south, XXXXIV Corps was to cross
the Donets between Izyum and the
mouth of the Oskol and head north.

In rain, III Panzer Corps went halfway
to Kupyansk on the first day and began turning three divisions south, with
22d Panzer Division in the lead. The
XXXXIV Corps took a bridgehead on
the Donets. The next morning, everywhere between Kupyansk and Izyum,
the Soviet units were on the march
toward the Oskol. Overrunning some
of these, 16th Panzer Division was into
the northwestern quarter of Kupyansk
by nightfall. In the late afternoon on
the 24th, 22d Panzer Division, going
south, met the 101st Light Division,
coming north, at Gorokhovatka on the
Oskol northeast of Izyum, and FRI-
DERICUS II was completed. In two more
days, the pockets were mopped up and
First Panzer Army's tally of prisoners
reached 22,800.[30] *(Map 29.)*

Bock congratulated First Panzer
Army, saying, "The First Panzer Army
can look on its latest victory with justi-
fiable pride." Kleist added his own
thanks "to the officers and the troops,
including our young comrades from
the Labor Service."[31] At the higher
command levels, though, the reactions
to FRIDERICUS II and WILHELM were
mixed. As battles went, they had been
easy, but they had also brought in comparatively few prisoners. Talking to
General Halder, chief of the General
Staff, Bock speculated that the Russians were waiting for the Americans to
intervene and had decided, until then,
to avoid exposing themselves to big

[27]*Ibid.*, 14 Jun 42.
[28]*AOK 11, Ia Kriegstagebuch Nr. 12*, 16–18 Jun 42,
AOK 11 28654/1 file.
[29]*Bock Diary, Osten II*, 18 Jun 42.

[30]*Pz. AOK 1, Ia Nr. 43/42, 1. Weisung fuer Fridericus 2.*,
15.6.42, Pz. AOK 1 25179/4 file; *Pz. AOK 1, Ia
Kriegstagebuch Nr. 8*, 22–26 Jun 42, Pz. AOK 1 24906
file; *Pz. AOK 1, Mit Kleist in den Kaukasus*, Pz. AOK 1
85602 file.
[31]*Pz. AOK 1, Ia Kriegstagebuch Nr. 8*, 27 Jun 42, Pz.
AOK 1 24906 file.

defeats.[32] One Sixth Army staff paper stated, "The Soviet capacity for resistance has declined markedly in comparison with the previous year. The infantry, in particular, lacks spirit."[33] Another, also from Sixth Army, added, however, "The objective of enemy operations in 1942 will be to slow the German advance to the Don and the turn toward the Caucasus.... [The Soviet Armies] will evade envelopments and attempt to build new fronts...."[34]

Stoerfang Completed

By the time WILHELM and FRIDERICUS II were finished, STOERFANG had gone too far to be stopped without looking like a defeat but not far enough to bring an end in sight. The LIV Corps cleared the north shore of Severnaya Bay on the 23d, and thereby unhinged the outer defenses in the center and the south as well. But XXX Corps and Rumanian Mountain Corps needed another four days to bring themselves face to face with the line of the Sapun Heights. When they had, Eleventh Army confronted the inner Sevastopol perimeter. To breach it from the north meant crossing the bay, which acted as a half-mile-wide moat that could be raked by artillery and small arms fire from the steep south shore. From Inkerman, at the head of the bay, the Sapun Heights ran almost due south, forming a right angle with the bay. A continuous escarpment broken only by one road, the heights had lost none of

their natural defensive potential since the British and French had used them in the Crimean War to hold off a Russian relief army while besieging Sevastopol on the other side. Behind them, still lay at least one other line, more forts, and the city itself.

On the 22d, the day after Tobruk had surrendered in North Africa, Manstein had asked Halder to try to persuade the OKW to have the British garrison commander flown to the Crimea so that he could be dropped by parachute into Sevastopol as evidence of the surrender. Because Tobruk had become a symbol of resistance by withstanding a siege in 1941, Manstein had said he anticipated "a strong demoralizing effect."[35] It was an idea that ignored practicality, and the Geneva Convention as well, and no more was heard of it or, for several days following, of anything better. On the 24th, Eleventh Army designated U-day as the day on which LIV and XXX Corps would simultaneously attack the inner defenses, but it did not say when U-day would be or where or how the attacks would be made.

Finally, on the 26th, Manstein decided to gamble on surprise and strike straight across the bay. After dark on the 28th, engineers eased a hundred assault boats down the rock bank into the water. At 0100 on the 29th, the boats pushed off, carrying troops from the 22d and the 24th Infantry Divisions. Artillery was ranged and ready along the entire length of the shore but under orders not to open fire until the enemy did. The first wave was across and landed east of the city before the

[32]*Bock Diary, Osten II*, 24 Jun 42.

[33]*AOK 6, Ic/AO, Beurteilung der Feindlage am 24.6.42*, AOK 6 30155/5 file.

[34]*AOK 6, Ia, Beurteilung der Feindlage am 24.6.42*, AOK 6 30155/52 file.

[35]*AOK 11, Ia Kriegstagebuch Nr. 12*, 22 Jun 42, AOK 11 28654/1 file.

Soviet Rear Guards Engage an Enemy Armored Car

defense reacted. From then on artillery spotters on the north shore and in the beachhead brought down fire wherever Soviet guns showed themselves. The XXX Corps' artillery opened fire on the Sapun Heights just as the assault boats were landing, and its infantry moved out a half-hour later. By early afternoon, LIV Corps had a solid beachhead and XXX Corps a foothold on the heights. Manstein, expecting still to have to besiege the city, ordered both corps to carry the attack west past Sevastopol to Cape Khersones.

On the 30th, LIV Corps took Fort Malakov, a refurbished relic of the Crimean War, on the city line; XXX Corps cleared the Sapun Heights and broke into Balaklava, the defensive anchor on the south coast; and VIII Air Corps

and the artillery mounted a day-long bombardment designed to paralyze the resistance, particularly inside Sevastopol.[36]

Meanwhile, the garrison had run out of reserves and was using its last ammunition, rations, and water. (Surface warships and submarines had brought in another 25,000 men and 15,000 tons of supplies during June.) Early on the 30th, Oktyabrskiy asked Marshal Budenny, commander of the *North Caucasus Front,* to cancel a planned diversionary landing at Kerch and ordered him to organize an evacuation. The *Stavka*'s approval came during the night, and Oktyabrskiy departed by air

---

[36]*Ibid.,* 24–30 Jun 42.

to take charge of the evacuation at Novorossiysk, leaving Petrov in command at Sevastopol.[37]

During the night on the 30th, the garrison troops began withdrawing to Cape Khersones and other likely evacuation points. Over the next four days, while some rear-guard actions went on and a few bypassed forts held out, several hundred officers and other priority personnel of the *Black Sea Fleet, Sevastopol Defense Region,* and *Independent Coastal Army* were evacuated by air.[38] The last of the forts to fall (on 4 July) was one the Germans called Maxim Gorkiy II, on Cape Folient. It was the strongest and most modern of the whole Sevastopol complex, and select *Independent Coastal Army* personnel, including women, defended it, apparently expecting to be evacuated by sea. The ships did not come, however, and those of the defenders who refused to surrender were buried alive by the Eleventh Army engineers as they demolished the fort and its underground galleries.[39]

The battle ended on 4 July. Eleventh Army counted "over 90,000" prisoners.[40] According to the *History of the Second World War,* the cost to the Eleventh Army was "approximately 150,000" casualties (a figure which seems high).[41]

On 5 July, Manstein staged a victory celebration for the corps, division, and regimental commanders and bearers of the Knight's Cross of the Iron Cross

and the German Cross in Gold. He had received his promotion to field marshal three days earlier. For the Eleventh Army officers and troops, Hitler authorized the *Krim Schild* ("Crimea Shield"), a bronze patch with an outline of the Crimea and the numerals "1941" and "1942" in low relief, to be worn on the left sleeve below the shoulder. It was one of only four similar devices awarded, the other being for Narvik (1940), Kholm, and Demyansk, all of which were victories by narrow margins. On the Soviet side, the medal "For Defense of Sevastopol" was instituted, and 39,000 were awarded. On 8 May 1965, the Presidium of the Supreme Soviet awarded to the city of Sevastopol the Order of Lenin and the Gold Star medal.[42]

Deployment for Blau

Bock's Plan

Bock's entry in his diary for 29 April reads, "In the evening, on the insistence of the OKH, the first draft of our directive for the [summer] offensive was hastily thrown together."[43] Taken by surprise and not having had time to do terrain studies or solicit proposals from the armies, Bock and his staff had done the draft entirely as a desk exercise. Contrary to past practice, there also had been practically no consultation between the army group and the OKH. Hitler had been in Berlin and at the *Berghof* and had been tending to diplomatic affairs. Bock had been on leave for twelve days, and Halder had gone to Berlin for a week beginning on the 27th to audit lectures

[37]*VOV (Kratkaya Istoriya)*, p. 160; *IVMV*, vol. V, p. 135; Vaneyev, *Geroicheskaya oborona*, p. 313f.
[38]*IVOVSS*, vol. II, p. 410. See also Vaneyev, *Geroicheskaya oborona*, pp. 312–20.
[39]*AOK 11, Ia Kriegstagebuch Nr. 12*, 4 Jul 42, AOK 11 28654/1 file.
[40]Manstein, *Verlorene Siege*, p. 282.
[41]*IVMV*, vol. V, p. 137.
[42]*Ibid.*
[43]*Bock Diary, Osten II*, 29 Apr 42.

at the War Academy and, among other things, to have his teeth fixed. Although Directive 41 had been dated 5 April, it had not reached Army Group South until after the 10th, while Bock was on leave, and he had not seen it until the 23d.[44]

Aside from the contents of Directive 41, about all Bock knew was that divisions were beginning to move into his area, that he would receive an additional panzer army headquarters, and that at some point in BLAU, Army Group South would be divided in two. He did not know how many divisions were to come, nor, probably, did anybody else. General Hoth, the commander of Seventeenth Army, had been told just before he went on leave that when he returned, in May, he would take command of Headquarters, Fourth Panzer Army, which was being transferred from Army Group Center. On 14 April, Hitler had ordered the OKH Organization Branch to set up a new army group headquarters that would come under Field Marshal List, who had commanded the 1941 campaign in the Balkans and had been there since as the Southeastern Theater commander. Bock had been informed that List's headquarters would come into BLAU sometime after the operation started and would have primary responsibility for the advance into the Caucasus. What Bock did not know—and he would, doubtless, not have been flattered if he had—was that several days before he gave the order to create the new army group, Hitler had said that he wanted only the *best*

commanders used in the all important drive into the Caucasus.[45]

Army Group South's Directive 1, written on the night of 29 April, was, consequently, not much more than a detailed expansion of Directive 41. The three phases of BLAU, as given in Directive 41, were the framework. The one new element was the introduction of a second army group headquarters. Bock and his staff assumed that they would retain exclusive command until BLAU II was completed. Thereafter, they projected, Headquarters, Army Group South, would become Headquarters, Army Group B, and List and his staff would take over the south flank as Headquarters, Army Group A. From then on, Army Group B's mission would be to hold a line from Kursk to Voronezh and along the Don River to the vicinity of Stalingrad. Army Group A would take the main responsibility for BLAU III, the drive to Stalingrad, and would be solely responsible for planning and executing the advance into the Caucasus (BLAU IV).

For BLAU I, Army Group South had on the left Second Army, Fourth Panzer Army, and Hungarian Second Army—temporarily combined under General Weichs, the commanding general, Second Army, as Armeegruppe Weichs—and on the right Sixth Army. Fourth Panzer was to make the main thrust east of Kursk to Voronezh. Second Army would cover Fourth Panzer Army on the left and build a front from the Army Group Center boundary to the Don north of Voronezh. Sixth Army, at Belgorod, eighty miles

[44]*Halder Diary,* vol. III, p. 435; *Bock Diary, Osten II,* 10–22 Apr 42.

[45]*OKH, GenStdH, Org. Abt., Kriegstagebuch, Band III,* 14 Apr 42, H 1/213 file; *OKW, WFSt, Kriegsgeschichtliche Abteilung, Kriegstagebuch, 1.4.–30.6.42,* 11 Apr 42, I.M.T. 1807 file.

FIELD MARSHAL VON BOCK *(seated in car)*

south of Kursk, would put its mobile divisions under Headquarters, XXXX Panzer Corps for a secondary thrust to Voronezh. Just short of the halfway point, Fourth Panzer Army and XXXX Panzer Corps would each divert one panzer division off their inner flanks toward Staryy Oskol to create a pocket that would be tightened and cleaned out by Hungarian Second Army and some of the Sixth Army's infantry. After taking Voronezh, Fourth Panzer Army would make a fast right turn, pick up XXXX Panzer Corps, and drop south forty miles along the Don to Korotoyak where it would be in position for BLAU II. Hungarian Second Army and elements of Sixth Army would mop up the BLAU I area, while the Sixth Army main body also turned

south and ranged itself on Fourth Panzer Army's right. If the offensive were to begin approximately on 15 June, Army Group South expected to finish the first phase during the second week of July.

In BLAU II, First Panzer Army would strike east of Kharkov along the north side of the Donets, and Fourth Panzer Army would continue south along the Don. Their points would meet midway between the rivers, north of Millerovo. On the way and in conjunction with Sixth Army, they would divert forces to divide the large pocket being formed between them into two or three smaller ones. Italian Eighth Army, on First Panzer Army's right, would make a short drive south of the Donets to Voroshilovgrad. BLAU II would be completed in the second week of August and end on a line from Boguchar on the Don to the confluence of the Derkul and the Donets, its center approximately 180 miles due west of Stalingrad. Just before BLAU II began, Headquarters, Army Group A, would take command of Italian Eighth Army, Seventeenth Army, and Eleventh Army, which by then was expected to have come out of the Crimea to take over the front on the Mius River west of Rostov.

Before BLAU III began, Army Group A would take control of First Panzer Army and Fourth Panzer Army. It would then use Eleventh and Seventeenth Armies to take Rostov and occupy the eastern Donets Basin and the two panzer armies to clear the lower Don and develop the main thrust to Stalingrad. Army Group South, by then Army Group B, would participate in BLAU III with Sixth Army, which would advance east along the right bank of the Don. When BLAU III was completed, Army Group B would have Second Army, the allied armies, and Sixth Army dug-in on a front from the Army Group Center boundary to Voronezh to Stalingrad and from then on would cover the rear of Army Group A as its armies headed south across the lower Don toward the Caucasus.[46]

The Buildup

In the first week of May, General Greiffenberg, who had been Bock's chief of staff at Army Group Center and would be List's, began assembling the Army Group A staff in *Zeppelin,* the OKH compound at Zossen south of Berlin. Two weeks later, he took a forward echelon to the Army Group South headquarters in Poltava and from there dispatched an advance party to Stalino, which would be the Army Group A headquarters. Until it took control in the front, the staff would go under the cover name "Coastal Staff Azov." To preserve security, Hitler's orders were that no new unit symbols, flags, or other identifying markings were to be introduced in the Army Group South area until BLAU began, and the other staffs coming in were also assigned cover names. Fourth Panzer Army became "Superior Special Purpose Staff 8." Six corps headquarters were designated fortress staffs. Division headquarters became "sector staffs."[47]

Between March and late June, new arrivals from the west and from Army Group Center brought the Army Group South strength to 65 divisions, of these 45 were infantry, 5 light infantry, 4 motorized infantry, and 11 panzer divisions. Twenty-five allied divisions brought the grand total to 90. This was 5 more than Bock had estimated he would need in the February proposal, but the allied divisions, being smaller and more lightly armed, even leaving aside any questions about their performance, could not be rated as equivalent to more than half their number of German divisions. The German troops probably numbered close to a million men. The allies added another 300,000. The panzer divisions had spaces for 1,900 tanks, but hardly any

[46]*Obkdo. der H. Gr. Sued, Ia Nr. 820/42, Weisung Nr. 1 fuer den Ostfeldzug 1942, 30.4.42,* Pz. AOK 1 25179/7 file.

[47]*Obkdo. d. H. Gr. Sued, Ia Nr. 1131/42, Tarnung fuer Operation Blau, 12.5.42,* H. Gr. Don 55479/2.

had their full allotments. Since they were being refitted in or near the front and some were in action until late June, it was impossible to tell how many tanks they had in operating condition at any one time.[48] However, increasing numbers of tanks were carrying long-barreled 50-mm. (on Panzer IIIs) and 75-mm. guns (on Panzer IVs) that tests showed were capable of knocking out Soviet T–34s from all angles, though in the case of the Panzer IIIs, only at ranges less than 400 yards.[49] A tank designed to be superior to any of the Soviet models, the Panzer VI "Tiger" that mounted an 88-mm. gun, had been expected to be ready in time for BLAU, but its debut had to be postponed in May and again in June because of mechanical troubles.[50] On the other hand, the output of 75-mm. heavy antitank guns had been unexpectedly high, and Hitler ordered them to be used to the maximum, especially on the static front Second Army would be building west of Voronezh.[51] The hitch was that until ammunition production picked up in the summer, there would be only 70 to 150 75-mm. rounds per gun, including those mounted on the Panzer IVs, and only 30 to 50 rounds would be of the most effective armor-piercing types. Consequently, the gun and tank crews would have to be very sparing with the

75-mm. ammunition. Second Army instructed its antitank units to use the 75s only for head-on shots. If the Soviet tanks exposed their less heavily armored sides or rears, they were to be left to the 50-mm. pieces.

Soviet Deployment

The principal Soviet commands in the BLAU area were *Bryansk Front* (General Golikov), *Southwest Front* (Timoshenko), *South Front* (General Malinovskiy), and *North Caucasus Front* (Budenny). For the first three, Headquarters, *Southwestern Theater,* had apparently ceased being a fully effective command before it was abolished in June, and Timoshenko and his staff had been engaged mostly in the command of *Southwest Front* during May and June. Stalin had told Timoshenko and Bagramyan at the end of March that *Bryansk Front* would not be part of the theater much longer, and thereafter, it had been, as a practical matter, under *Stavka* control.[52] The four *fronts* together had a total of seventeen field armies. *Southwest, South,* and *Bryansk Fronts* had five a piece, and *North Caucasus* two. Each had one air army attached. *Bryansk Front* had the *Fifth Tank Army* in its reserve and gave up one army, *Sixty-first,* to *West Front* on 29 June.

In the first week of June, before WILHELM and FRIDERICUS II, Army Group South calculated that it would have to contend with 91 Soviet rifle divisions, 32 rifle brigades, 20 cavalry divisions, and 44 tank brigades.[53]

[48]*OKH, Org. Abt., (I) Nr. 854/42, Gliederung und Kampfkraft der Verbaende und Truppen der H. Gr. Sued, 27.5.42,* H 1/382 file; *Schematische Kriegsgliederung der H. Gr. Sued, Stand: 24.6.42, In Hauck, Die Operationen der deutschen Heeresgruppen an der Ostfront, Suedliches Gebiet, Teil III,* MS P–114c.
[49]*Pz. AOK 1, Ia Kriegstagebuch Nr. 8,* 17 Apr 42, Pz. AOK 1 24906 file.
[50]*OKH, GenStdH, Org. Abt., Kriegstagebuch, Band III,* 1–6 Jun 42, H 1/213.
[51]*Ibid.,* 5 May 42; *AOK 2, Ia Nr. 658/42, 17.6.42,* AOK 2 29585/9 file.

[52]Bagramyan, *Tak shli my k pobede,* p. 62.
[53]*H. Gr. Sued, Ic/AO, Vermutete Feindkraefte vor Heeresgruppe Sued, Stand 4.6.42,* 5 Jun 42, H. Gr. Sued 75124/1 file.

These were the estimated combined totals for *Bryansk, Southwest,* and *South Fronts.* For them, as of 1 July, the *History of the Second World War* gives 81 rifle divisions, 38 rifle brigades, 12 cavalry divisions, and 62 tank brigades with totals of 1.7 million troops and 2,300 tanks.[54] Army Group South intelligence estimated another 36 rifle divisions, 16 rifle brigades, 7 cavalry divisions, and 10 tank brigades were deployed in the Caucasus. Grechko gives the strength in the Caucasus in June as 17 rifle divisions, 3 rifle brigades, 3 cavalry divisions, and 3 tank brigades. As is usual, the Soviet figures apparently do not include the available *Stavka* reserves. Four reserve armies were stationed behind the Don River, to the rear of *Bryansk* and *Southwest Fronts*—at Stalingrad, Tambov, Novokhopersk, and Novosnninskiy—and two were farther back, at Saratov and Stalingrad.[55]

In the view of Stalin, the *Stavka,* and the General Staff, *Bryansk Front* was strategically the most critical front of the four. Its right flank, north and east of Orel, covered the Tula approach to Moscow, and its left flank straddled the Kursk-Voronezh axis. General Armii M. I. Kazakov, who was at the time Golikov's chief of staff, has said, as has

Vasilevskiy, that two possible German thrusts were considered, one from Orel via Mtsensk toward Tula and one from Shchigry (northeast of Kursk) toward Voronezh, and the first was considered the most likely.[56]

On 23 April, the *Stavka* ordered Golikov to prepare a drive on Orel to run concurrently with Timoshenko's Kharkov offensive. Golikov could not get ready on time, and after the German counterattack began, all of his air support had to be diverted to *Southwest Front.*[57] For the operation, Golikov had been given 5 tank and 2 cavalry corps, 4 rifle divisions, and 4 tank brigades.[58] Those stayed with the *front,* and in June, Golikov was getting ready to counterattack in either of the two anticipated directions of German attack. His reserves, on 28 June, consisted of 2 cavalry corps, 4 rifle divisions, 6 tank corps (including 2 in *Fifth Tank Army* and 2 being transferred from the north flank of *Southwest Front*), and 4 tank brigades, a total of 1,640 tanks. Of these, 191 were KVs, 650 were T–34s, and 799 were older models and T–60s. One problem Golikov had, according to Kazakov, was that the General Staff had activated the tank armies and corps without giving guidance to their commands or the *front* and army commands as to how they were to be employed.[59]

[54]*IVMV*, vol. V, p. 144. Using the figures given in Tyushkevich, *Vooruzhennye sily* (p. 284), the average strength of a tank brigade would be 56 tanks, or a total of 3,472 for 62 brigades. Elsewhere, the actual strengths of tank corps at *Bryansk Front* in June 1942 are given as 24 KVs, 88 T–34s, and 68 T–60s, for a total of 180; a brigade strength of approximately 60; and a total for 62 brigades of 3,720. From this, it appears that the 2,300 figure excludes all T–60 tanks. See M. Kazakov, "Na voronezhskom napravlenii letom 1942 goda," *Voyenno-istoricheskiy Zhurnal*, 10 (1964), 28n.
[55]Grechko, *Gody voyny*, p. 182; *IVMV*, vol. V, map 9.

[56]Kazakov, "Voronezhskom napravlenii," p. 30. See also Vasilevskiy, *Delo*, p. 219. See p. 307f.
[57]Kazakov, "Voronezhskom napravlenii," p. 29f.
[58]Vasilevskiy, *Delo*, p. 219. Kazakov gives the reinforcements received from the *Stavka* reserves in April and early May as 4 tank corps, 7 rifle divisions, 11 rifle brigades, 4 tank brigades, and "a significant number of artillery regiments." Kazakov, "Voronezhskom napravlenii," p. 28n.
[59]Kazakov, "Voronezhskom napravlenii," pp. 30–32.

NEW 75-MM. SELF-PROPELLED ASSAULT GUN AT PRACTICE

On the Eve

Army Group South's Readiness

Concurrently with the OKW's broader analyses of *Wehrmacht* strength, the OKH Organization Branch made a study of Army Group South's readiness for the summer offensive in terms of its basic units, the divisions. The study disclosed, in the first place, that whereas formerly all divisions of one type, say infantry, could be assumed to be nearly identical in quality, that was no longer true. The divisions for BLAU would fall from the outset into three categories. In the first were fifteen infantry and six panzer and motorized divisions which were either new or fully rebuilt behind the front. They would be at full allotted strength and would have had time to let their experienced troops rest and to break in the replacements. The second category, consisting of seventeen infantry and ten panzer and motorized divisions, would be the same as the first, but the divisions would be rebuilt in the front, and there would be no time to rest. In the third category were seventeen infantry divisions, a good quarter of the total number, that would neither be rested nor fully rebuilt. They would be at "approximately" full strength in personnel and material, but they would be short on officers and noncommissioned officers, and they would have to depend on the output of the repair shops for equipment.

In all three categories, some corners had been cut. The infantry divisions' supply trains would be horse-drawn, and every division would have to take about a thousand of the so-called young troops, eighteen- and nineteen-year olds who had no more than eight weeks' training. In the panzer divisions, the rifle battalions would be reduced from five to four companies. The panzer and motorized divisions would also have fewer tracked personnel-carrying vehicles. They would reach about 80 percent of full mobility, but about 20 percent of that would have to be attained by using trucks and, in consequence, would entail some loss of cross-country capability. Since there was nothing in reserve, all equipment would have to come from current output, which meant that the schedules for rebuilding could not be accelerated, and unanticipated losses in preliminary operations could not be replaced.[60]

Army Group South looked at the same divisions in terms of probable performance and concluded:

Owing to diverse composition, partial lack of battle experience and gaps in their outfitting, the units available for the summer operation in 1942 will not have the combat effectiveness that could be taken for granted at the beginning of the campaign in the East. The mobile units, too, will not have the flexibility, the endurance, or the penetrating power they had a year ago. The commands will have to be aware of this, and in assigning missions and setting objectives, they will have to take into account the composition and battle-worthiness of the individual divisions. The attack elements will have to be put together with painstaking care.[61]

The question was how serious the flaws would be. Army Group South saw reason for concern. Others, closer to the front, were downright worried, as the following letter from General Paulus, commander of the Sixth Army, to his corps commanders indicates:

Recently numbers of reports have come to my attention and that of the higher leadership in which division commanders have described the condition of their divisions with extreme pessimism. This I cannot tolerate.

The personnel and material deficiencies afflicting the divisions are well known to the higher leadership. Nevertheless, the higher leadership is determined to carry out its intentions in the eastern theater of war to the full. Therefore it is up to us to get the most out of the troops in their present condition.

I request that you exert influence on the division commanders in this sense.[62]

Operation Kreml

After Kharkov, the strategic initiative reverted to the Germans; any doubts about that fact that might have lingered on either side no longer existed. Welcome as this was to Hitler for its effects on his own troops' and the enemy's morale, by presumably putting the Soviet south flank on the defensive alert it could also impair BLAU's chances for a smooth start. Surprise was going to be less easy to achieve—and more essential. On the one hand, Hitler had seen to it, in person, that the deployment for BLAU was carried out in great-

---

[60]OKH, Org. Abt., (I) Nr. 854/42, Gliederung und Kampfkraft der Verbaende und Truppen der H. Gr. Sued, 27.5.42, H 1/382 file. See pp. 293–96.

[61]H. Gr. Sued, Ia Nr. 820/42, Anlage 2, Richtlinien fuer die Kampffuehrung, 30.4.42, Pz. AOK 1 25179/7 file.

[62]Der O.B. der 6. Armee, Ia Nr. 55/42, an die Herren Kommandierenden Generale, 4.7.42, AOK 6 39342/7 file.

est secrecy. All new headquarters and units were billeted well away from the front, in scattered locations, and disguised as elements of the permanent rear echelon. At the height of the Kharkov battle, to prevent giving their presence away, Hitler had refused to put in any of the new troops. On the other hand, the new troops were still untested, and the losses and wear and tear on men and equipment in the veteran units that had fought at Kharkov were not going to be made good in time for BLAU. The objective was still to destroy the Soviet main forces, but having them on the alert and on the scene at the start would be very inconvenient.

All in all, it was worthwhile to do whatever could be done to divert Soviet attention away from the south flank. The mission fell to Army Group Center, which was low on muscle, but—because of its proximity to Moscow—high in potential for attracting Soviet notice. On 29 May, Headquarters, Army Group Center, issued a top secret directive. The first sentence read, "The OKH has ordered the earliest possible resumption of the attack on Moscow." All subsequent correspondence regarding the operation was to go forward under the code name KREML ("Kremlin").[63]

KREML was a paper operation, an out-and-out deception, but it had the substance to make it a masterpiece of this somewhat speculative form of military art. In the first place, it coincided with Soviet thinking—which, of course,

the Germans did not know. In the second, its premise—to simulate a repeat of the late 1941 drive on Moscow—was solid; in fact, it made better strategic sense than did that of BLAU. The front, though badly eroded, was close to where it had been in mid-November 1941, and Second and Third Panzer Armies, which had been the spearheads then, were in relatively the same positions southwest and northwest of Moscow that they had held when the fall rains stopped and the advance resumed. The army group directive, which assigned the two panzer armies the identical missions they had received in the previous fall, could have been taken for the real thing even by German officers who were not told otherwise, and most were not.

In the first week of June, the army group distributed sealed batches of Moscow-area maps down to the regimental level with instructions not to open them until 10 June. On that day, army, corps, and division staffs began holding planning conferences on KREML with a target readiness date of about 1 August. Security was tight, and only the chiefs of staff and branch chiefs knew they were working on a sham. At the same time, the air force increased its reconnaissance flights over and around Moscow; prisoner-of-war interrogators were given lists of questions to ask about the city's defenses; and intelligence groups sent out swarms of agents toward Moscow, Tula, and Kalinin.[64] Since very few agents sent across the lines in the past had been heard from again, it could be assumed that Soviet counterintelli-

---

[63]H. Gr. Mitte, Ia Nr. 4350/42, Befehl fuer den Angriff auf Moskau, 29.5.42, AOK 4 24336/25 file. On Operation KREML see also Earl F. Ziemke, "Operation KREML: Deception, Strategy, and the Fortunes of War," Parameters, vol. IX, 1 (1978), 72–82.

[64]H. Gr. Mitte, Ia Nr. 4570/42, "Kreml," 3.6.42, AOK 4 34226/25 file.

gence did its work thoroughly. That the prisoner-of-war compounds were loaded with Soviet agents and that almost every civilian in the occupied territory was at least an indirect informant for Soviet agents or partisans also could be taken for granted. The barest trickle of information would suffice.

The Soviet postwar accounts have little to say about KREML. The *History of the Second World War,* however, mentions it twice, once in conjunction with an actual order alerting Army Group Center to the possibility of a radical Soviet weakening in the center after BLAU began. The *History* describes the operation as comprising a "varied complex of desinformation [*sic*]" designed to mislead the Soviet Command and says, "However, Operation KREML did not achieve its aim."[65] In the *Popular Scientific Sketch,* where KREML is associated with the Soviet strategic planning in March 1942, it is said to have been an "attempt" to disguise the direction of the main attack and "arouse an impression" of a strong offensive in the Moscow direction. "But," the account continues, "the Fascists miscalculated. The plans of the enemy were uncovered in good time."[66]

Timing and Trouble

As the deployment entered its final stage, the timetable for BLAU was coming into question from the two almost diametrically opposed points of view. Hitler saw WILHELM and FRIDERICUS II as having demonstrated that "the Soviet ability to resist has become substantially weaker in comparison with the previous year." He believed the phases

of BLAU would be executed "more easily and faster than had been assumed," and he talked about taking some divisions out of BLAU II and transferring them to Army Group Center, where they could be used to acquire jump-off positions for a later attack toward Moscow.[67] Army Group South also believed BLAU would go faster than had been anticipated, but added, "The experiences in FRIDERICUS II and WILHELM have demonstrated that the enemy no longer holds on stubbornly and lets himself be encircled, hence, large-scale withdrawal of his forces must be taken into account." The army group considered merging BLAU I and BLAU II, which would give the Russians less chance to escape but would also force First Panzer Army back into action before it had time to rest and refit.[68]

More immediately in doubt was the starting date for BLAU. After having talked about 15 June, Hitler had put WILHELM and FRIDERICUS II into the schedule and then had gone to the *Berghof* for a vacation. By the 20th, waiting for the rain to let up enough for FRIDERICUS II to begin, Bock was worried that in the midst of the prolonged delay something untoward—a Soviet spoiling attack, for instance—might occur. He did not know it yet, but something already had happened.

Contrary to standing orders reinforced by the extraordinary security measures Hitler had demanded for BLAU, a 23d Panzer Division staff officer, Major Joachim Reichel, had, on

---

[65]*IVMV,* vol. V, pp. 121, 243.
[66]*VOV,* p. 138.

[67]*OKW, WFSt, Kriegsgeschichtliche Abteilung, Kriegstagebuch, 1.4.–30.6.42,* 25 Jun 42, I.M.T. 1807 file.
[68]*Obkdo. d. H. Gr. Sued, General der Pioniere, Taetigkeitsbericht, 29.6.42,* H. Gr. Sued 34303 file.

the 19th, carried plans for BLAU I with him on a flight in a light airplane. The plane had strayed across the front and had landed two and a half miles in on the Soviet side. A German patrol found it some hours later, intact except for a bullet hole in the gas tank. Reichel, the pilot, and the papers had disappeared without a trace. Two days later another patrol found two bodies but no sign of the papers.

Bock's first reaction, when a report reached him late on the 20th, was that it was high time to start BLAU before the Russians could exploit the information they might have acquired. The OKH apparently agreed and told him to arrange for the offensive to start, if ordered, on the 26th.[69] For the deployment, the 22d became X-day minus four, but the final decision to start depended on Hitler, and he was still in Bavaria.

When Hitler returned to the *Wolfsschanze* on the afternoon of the 24th, BLAU appeared for a time almost about to slip out of sight. Bock was summoned to report in person on the Reichel incident, and Halder grumbled about "a great agitation conducted against the General Staff" in the OKW over the affair.[70] Field Marshal Keitel, chief of the OKW, "visibly nervous," met Bock on his arrival the next day and "depicting the situation in black on black," told him that Hitler was convinced the generals were not obeying orders, was determined to make examples of some of them, and had directed that Bock be told not to try to persuade him otherwise. Hitler, however, appeared more depressed than angry and interjected only a few questions as Bock told him the army group's investigation had not revealed any disobedience other than by the dead Major Reichel. If he or any of the senior generals suspected anything of the sort, Bock added, they would "intervene mercilessly." Hitler appeared to be reassured, and the rest of the interview, Bock observed appreciatively, was "very friendly."[71]

By the time Bock arrived back in Poltava, BLAU I was on twelve to thirty-six hours' standby. The code word *Dinkelsbuehl* would be the signal to start the next morning. *Aachen* would postpone the decision until the following afternoon. Heavy rain was falling all along the front, and the code word on the 26th was *Aachen*. The next afternoon, after consulting Weichs, who thought he could start, and Paulus, who thought he could not because of continuing rain, Bock sent out *Dinkelsbuehl* to Armeegruppe Weichs and *Aachen* to Sixth Army.[72]

BLAU was getting under way at last— but not smoothly. An hour after the code words were sent, Keitel told Bock by telegram to relieve the commanding general and chief of staff of XXXX Panzer Corps and the 23d Panzer Division commander. Almost simultaneously, a plane carrying their replacements landed at Poltava. Dismayed at having to make command changes in crucial units at the last minute, Bock called Halder and General Schmundt, Hitler's chief adjutant, who told him that Hitler had been reading the file on the Reichel affair and had

[69]*Bock Diary, Osten II*, 18–22 Jun 42. See also Walter Goerlitz, *Paulus and Stalingrad* (New York: Citadel, 1963), pp. 183–89.
[70]*Halder Diary*, vol. III, p. 464.

[71]*Bock Diary, Osten II*, 25 Jun 42.
[72]*AOK 6, Ia Kriegstagebuch Nr. 12*, 23–27 Jun 42, AOK 6 22855/1 file.

concluded that an attempt was being made to shift the blame to a subordinate. (One report raised the possibility of bringing charges against a clerk in the 23d Panzer Division.) Later, Hitler listened while Bock explained that the charges against the clerk had been dropped several days before, but when Bock asked whether he still wanted the officers relieved, Hitler answered curtly, "Yes."

On the 28th, the code word for Sixth Army was *Aachen* for one more day, and Paulus began talking about recommending a court-martial for himself over the Reichel affair. Bock told him, "That is out of the question. It is time now to point your nose forward and follow it."[73]

Soviet Readiness

By mid-June, Golikov had stationed his reserves to meet the anticipated German attacks. *Fifth Tank Army* and *VIII Cavalry Corps* were at Chern, on the Orel-Tula road, and *VII Cavalry Corps* and two tank brigades were somewhat farther north. On his left flank, facing Kursk, he had the *I, XVI,* and *IV Tank Corps.* By then, also, air reconnaissance had begun sighting heavy enemy traffic in the Kursk-Shchigry area, but these reports were regarded as less significant than one from General Staff intelligence on the 18th concerning ten German infantry and four panzer divisions supposedly massed near Yukhnov, off *Bryansk Front's* north flank.[74]

On 20 June, Timoshenko talked to Stalin by telephone. He had the papers Reichel had been carrying. He told Sta-

lin there had been three men [*sic*] in the plane, the pilot and two officers. The pilot and one officer had burned to death in the crash. The other officer, a major, had survived the crash but had been killed when he refused to surrender. To Timoshenko's report on the contents of the documents, Stalin replied, "First, keep it secret that you have intercepted the directives. Second, it is possible that what has been intercepted is only part of the enemy's plan. It is possible that analogous plans exist for other fronts."[75]

Golikov had received copies of the documents from Timoshenko on the 19th. On the 22d, Golikov reported the presence of "six or seven" panzer and motorized divisions in the Kursk-Shchigry area. Two days later, air reconnaissance observed enemy columns going south out of the vicinity of Orel toward Kursk. Bombers and *Shturmovik* dive-bombers went out to attack them.[76]

On the 26th, Golikov was summoned to Moscow, where Stalin told him he did not believe the BLAU plan was "plausible" and that it was a "big trumped-up piece of work by the intelligence people." It was necessary, Stalin said, to beat the enemy to the punch and deal him a blow, and he ordered Golikov to be ready to attack toward Orel by 5 July.

Golikov and his staff finished drafting the plan for an Orel operation in the early morning hours, "between two and three o'clock," on 28 June. They expected to start work on the "details" during the day.[77]

[73] *Bock Diary, Osten II,* 27–28 Jun 42.

[74] Kazakov, "*Na Voronezhskom napravlenii,*" pp. 30, 32.

[75] A. M. Samsonov, *Stalingradskaya bitva* (Moscow: Izdatelstvo "Nauka," 1968), p. 72f.

[76] Kazakov, "*Na voronezhskom napravlenii,*" p. 33.

[77] *Ibid.*

CHAPTER XVI

Operation BLAU

"The Enemy Is Defeated"

Breakthrough

At daylight on 28 June, General Weichs, the commander of Second Army, ascended a low hill slightly east of Shchigry. From the top, he saw, on either side, lines of artillery and rocket launcher emplacements still partly obscured by the morning haze. Looking ahead through field glasses, he could make out Fourth Panzer Army's tanks standing in attack formations with their motors off. The troops were nearly as immobile as their vehicles and weapons. For the moment, everything that needed to be done had been done. Then, timed to a second, the artillery opened fire with a shattering crash and salvos from the rocket launchers screamed away trailing plumes of white flame behind them. The preliminary barrage lasted only half-an-hour, which was long enough, though, to give Weichs a clue as to how the battle would go. The Soviet artillery's response was slow and ragged; the enemy might have been taken by surprise after all. When the guns paused to lay their fire deeper, the armor rolled forward, and in the few minutes it took for the new ranges to be set, the second wave of tanks began to file between the artillery positions.[1]

The morning was cloudy and warm, promising rain. Soon most of the action was not visible from where Weichs stood. The offensive swept east without a hitch, and the armor disappeared into the distance. Fourth Panzer Army's spearhead, XXXXVIII Panzer Corps, had gone ten miles to the Tim River by 1200. There it captured and crossed an undamaged railroad bridge. That afternoon it moved another ten miles to and across the Kshen River. *(Map 30.)* Passing the Kshen put it on the so-called land bridge to Voronezh, a five- to ten-mile-wide divide between the basins of the Oskol and the Sosna rivers. Russian resistance was spotty—determined in some places, feeble in others. One thing was certain: the enemy had not pulled out beforehand. Battlefield evidence, prisoners, dead, abandoned command posts, and so forth, showed that all the units previously identified were still there fighting, at least they were trying to. Before dark, XXXXVIII Panzer Corps covered another ten miles, the last of these in heavy rain. By then its neighbor on the left, XXIV Panzer Corps, had drawn up to the Kshen.[2] For Sixth Army the code word again was *Aachen*, which meant another twenty-four-hour postponement. The rain in the Sixth Army sector

---

[1]Maximilian Freiherr von Weichs, *Tagesnotizen, Band 6, Teil I*, p. 1, CMH X-1026 file.

[2]AOK 2, Ia Kriegstagebuch, Teil VI, 28 Jun 42, AOK 2 23617/2 file.

PANZER III TANKS ON THE ATTACK

had almost stopped during the day, but the roads were still impassable.

At General Golikov's *Bryansk Front,* *Thirteenth* and *Fortieth Armies* were hard-hit, but his reserve tank corps and brigades were intact. The *IV* and *XXIV Tank Corps* were on the way from *Southwest Front,* and the *Stavka* was sending in the *XVII Tank Corps* from its reserve, which would bring the total complement of tank corps to seven. During the day, the front's air support was increased by four regiments of fighters and three of *Shturmovik* dive-bombers. At the day's end, Golikov gave *Fortieth Army* two tank brigades and ordered the *I* and *XVI Tank Corps* to the Kshen River. The trouble was, Kazakov says, that the *front* did not know how capable of "decisive action" the tank corps

were, and there was not enough fuel for the fighters and *Shturmoviks.*[3]

The rain lasted until 1200 the next day. In the mud, XXXXVIII Panzer Corps made just enough headway to confirm its breakthrough onto the land bridge. The XXIV Panzer Corps worked on bridgeheads across the Kshen. On Fourth Panzer Army's right, Hungarian Second Army could not get past the Tim River. It was being held up less by the rain or by the enemy than by its command's inability to stage a coordinated attack. Sixth Army canvassed its corps in the afternoon; all of them reported their roads passable; and Field Marshal Bock, the commander of Army Group South,

---

[3] Kazakov, *"Na voronezhskom napravlenii,"* p. 34.

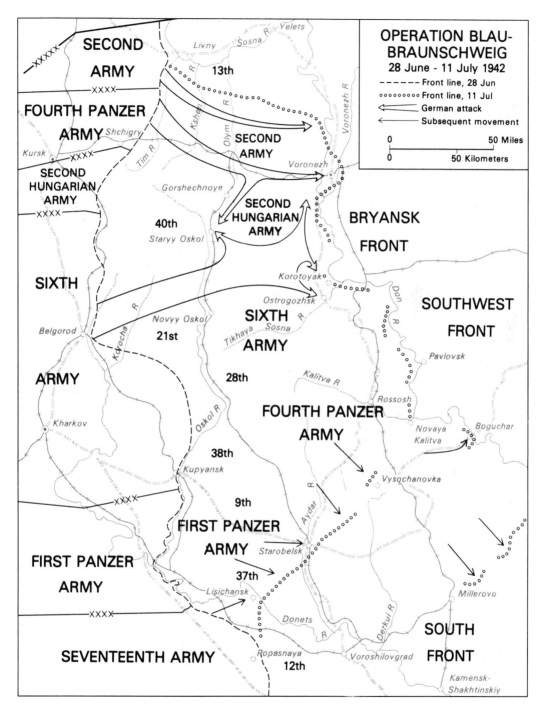

OPERATION BLAU-
BRAUNSCHWEIG
28 June - 11 July 1942

- - - - - Front line, 28 Jun
∘∘∘∘∘∘∘ Front line, 11 Jul
⟵ German attack
⟵ Subsequent movement

0   50 Miles
0   50 Kilometers

SECOND ARMY

FOURTH PANZER ARMY

Shchigry

Kursk

SECOND HUNGARIAN ARMY

SIXTH

ARMY

Kharkov

FIRST PANZER ARMY

SEVENTEENTH ARMY

Livny   *Sosna R.*   *Yelets*

13th

Kshen R.   *Olym R.*   *Voronezh R.*

SECOND ARMY

Voronezh

SECOND HUNGARIAN ARMY

BRYANSK

FRONT

Gorshechnoye

40th
Staryy Oskol

Korotoyak

Ostrogozhsk

Tim R.

Kvocha R.

SIXTH

ARMY

Novyy Oskol

21st

Belgorod

28th

Tikhaya Sosna R.

Don R.

SOUTHWEST

FRONT

Pavlovsk

Kalitva R.

Rossosh

FOURTH PANZER

ARMY

Novaya Kalitva

Boguchar

Oskol R.

38th

Kupyansk

9th

Vysochanovka

FIRST PANZER

ARMY

Starobelsk

37th

FIRST PANZER

ARMY

Lisichansk

Aydar R.

Millerovo

Donets R.

Derkul R.

Ropasnaya

12th

Voroshilovgrad

SOUTH

FRONT

Kamensk-Shakhtinskiy

MAP 30

then issued the code word *Dinkelsbuehl* for Sixth Army, effective at daybreak on the 30th.[4]

While Fourth Panzer Army was held up again by rain on the 30th, Sixth Army behaved like a panzer army and made a clean, twenty-mile-deep breakthrough to the Korocha River.[5] The code name BLAU, which had been compromised by the Reichel affair, went out of official existence on the 30th and was replaced by BRAUNSCHWEIG for the whole offensive. BLAU II became CLAUSEWITZ and BLAU III, DAMPFHAMMER ("steam hammer"). None of the three was going to be much used, however. Plans previously made were about to be overrun by events.

On the 30th, Golikov had a blunt wedge driven into his line. It was bisected by the Kursk-Voronezh railroad. The *I* and *XVI Tank Corps* were on the north side, but the main weight of the German armor, XXIV and XXXXVIII Panzer Corps, was ranged on the railroad and south of it. The position of the panzer corps and Sixth Army's developing breakthrough on the south presaged an encirclement that would engulf *Fortieth Army's* left flank. Talking to Stalin late in the day, Golikov reported that *IV* and *XXIV Tank Corps* were moving "extremely slowly," and the *front* did not have any regular contact with them. The *XVII Tank Corps*, he added, was coming west from Voronezh but running out of diesel oil because the corps staff had not organized its fuel supply properly. Golikov believed it would be best to take *Fortieth Army's* left flank back and out of the way

of the developing encirclement. But Stalin insisted on a counterattack by *IV, XXIV,* and *XVII Tank Corps* near Gorshechnoye, to stop the German armor south of the railroad and to drive it back. General Leytenant Ya. N. Fedorenko, the army's chief of tanks, had arrived at the *front* during the day to organize the counterattack. Finally, Stalin admonished Golikov to "keep well in mind" that he had "more than a thousand tanks and the enemy not more than five hundred," that he had over five hundred tanks in the area of the proposed counterattack "and the enemy three hundred to three hundred and fifty at the most," and that "everything now depends on your ability to deploy and lead these forces."[6] During the night, elements of *IV Tank Corps* engaged the enemy near Gorshechnoye, and *XVII Tank Corps* "maneuvered" in the area south of the railroad without getting into the fighting. All of the *XXIV Tank Corps* was miles away, at Novyy Oskol.[7]

In the morning, on 1 July, Bock went to the Fourth Panzer Army command post, where he and General Hoth, the army commander, agreed the army would have to head straight for Voronezh, "without looking to either side." Because the roads were clogged with supply columns bogged down in the mud, Bock could not get close to the front.[8] It was, to say the least, not good weather for tanks, and during the day, the Grossdeutschland Division's infantry took the lead at XXXXVIII Panzer Corps and passed the headwaters of the Olym River, forty miles

---

[4] *AOK 6, Ia Kriegstagebuch Nr. 12,* 29 Jun 42, AOK 6 2394811 file.

[5] *Ibid.,* 30 Jun 42.

[6] Kazakov, *"Na voronezhskom napravlenii,"* pp. 34–36; *IVMV,* vol. V, p. 150.

[7] Kazakov, *"Na voronezhskom napravlenii,"* p. 36.

[8] *Bock Diary, Osten II,* 1 Jul 42.

west of Voronezh. Meanwhile, the 16th Motorized Infantry Division, operating on the XXXXVIII Panzer Corps right flank, had come abreast and, in the afternoon, turned south toward Staryy Oskol.[9]

By late afternoon, Sixth Army had smashed the whole right half of *Southwest Front* west of the Oskol River and had a bridgehead across the river. Early in the day, however, the *Stavka* had realized that the counterattack by the tank corps was not likely to accomplish anything and had given *Fortieth* and *Twenty-first Armies* permission to take their forces out of the pocket.[10] In the afternoon, the Soviet units west of the Oskol were going back so fast that Bock did not think enough of them could be trapped by closing the pocket at Staryy Oskol to make it worthwhile to turn Sixth Army north, and he talked to Hitler about letting the army go northeast, instead, "to cut off what is still to be cut off" by trapping the Russians between the flanks of Sixth Army and Fourth Panzer Army somewhere farther east.[11] General Paulus, the commander of Sixth Army, believing the Russians were in full retreat and would not let themselves be caught anywhere west of the Don, wanted to head due east.[12]

On 2 July, Kazakov says, "The road to Voronezh was, in effect, open to the enemy."[13] To close it on the Don, the *Stavka*, during the day, shifted two armies, *Sixth* and *Sixtieth,* out of its reserve, while at the same time ordering another reserve army, *Sixty-third,* up to the river behind *Southwest Front. Fifth Tank Army,* which had been under *Stavka* control, was released and ordered to assemble near Yelets. Golikov, leaving his headquarters in Yelets under General Leytenant N. Ye. Chibisov, his deputy, went to Voronezh to take command of *Sixth, Sixtieth,* and *Fortieth Armies.*[14] He would not have much time. Vasilevskiy says, "By the end of the day on 2 July, conditions had drastically deteriorated in the Voronezh direction."[15]

Hitler at Poltava

At 0700 on the 3d, Hitler's Condor transport, carrying him, General Halder (chief of the General Staff), Field Marshal Keitel (chief of the OKW), General Schmundt (Hitler's chief adjutant), and others of his retinue landed at Poltava. The plane had taken off from Rastenburg at 0400, an unusual hour for Hitler to be abroad, particularly on a mission that later appeared to have had no discernible purpose.

All Hitler did of any substance was to put Bock "at liberty" to refrain from taking Voronezh if doing so would involve "too heavy fighting." Months afterward, Keitel told Bock that this had been the reason for the trip.[16] However, Halder had given Bock the same instruction about Voronezh by telephone the night before.[17]

---

[9]*AOK 2, Ia Kriegstagebuch, Teil VI,* 1 Jul 42, AOK 2 23617/2 file.

[10]*AOK 6, Ia Kriegstagebuch Nr. 12,* 1 Jul 42, AOK 6 2394811 file; Kazakov, *"Na voronezhskom napravlenii,"* p. 37.

[11]*Bock Diary, Osten II,* 1 Jul 42.

[12]*AOK 6, Ia Kriegstagebuch Nr. 12,* 1 Jul 42, AOK 6 22855/1 file.

[13]Kazakov, *"Na voronezhskom napravlenii,"* p. 38.

[14]*IVMV,* vol. V, p. 151; Vasilevskiy, *Delo,* p. 220; Kazakov, *"Na voronezhskom napravlenii,"* p. 39.

[15]Vasilevskiy, *Delo,* p. 220.

[16]*Bock Diary, Osten II,* 21 Mar 43.

[17]*Ibid.,* 2 Jul 42.

SELF-PROPELLED ASSAULT GUN AND MOUNTED TROOPS CROSSING THE OSKOL RIVER

During the meeting, Halder revived a proposal that had been made before, namely, to give Field Marshal List's Army Group A command of First Panzer Army for BLAU II/CLAUSEWITZ. Bock, as he had before, objected because he believed it would do nothing but complicate the lines of command. Hitler said nothing; nevertheless, Halder's proposal may well have been the original reason for the flight to Poltava. On the 2d, the OKH had instructed Coastal Staff Azov (Army Group A) to prepare to take command of the panzer army on 5 July or any time thereafter.[18] Perhaps Hitler had expected a more complaisant reaction

from Bock, and when none was forthcoming, his nerve failed. He could at times be quite diffident about taking up unpleasant matters with the older senior generals.

To Bock, who one may suspect was not an exceptionally acute judge of the *Fuehrer's* moods, Hitler seemed in high good humor. Apparently having in mind the recent relief of Lieutenant General Neil M. Ritchie as commanding general, British Eighth Army, in North Africa, Hitler joked about what he saw as a peculiarly British tendency "to saw off every general for whom things do not go exactly right."[19] At 0900 he reboarded his aircraft, and by 1200 he was back at the *Wolfsschanze.*

[18]*H. Gr. A, Ia Kriegstagebuch, Band I, Teil I,* 2 Jul 42, H. Gr. A 75126/1 file.

[19]*Bock Diary, Osten II,* 3 Jul 42.

The day was gratifying for Bock. He could assume he had the *Fuehrer's* full confidence, and the reports from the front registered nothing but successes. In only occasional light rain, XXXXVIII Panzer Corps was making its final push to the Don, with just a few miles left to go. The pocket west of the Oskol was almost closed at Staryy Oskol. Sixth Army was pursuing an enemy who was not making even a pretense of coherent resistance. After the day's reports were in, Bock sent a teletyped message to Weichs and Paulus. The opening sentence read, "The enemy opposite Sixth Army and Fourth Panzer Army is defeated." For Paulus, he included an order to turn XXXX Panzer Corps east to cover Fourth Panzer Army's right flank. It would then drive to Korotoyak on the Don and Ostrogozhsk on the Tikhaya Sosna River. Paulus, Bock added, was to swing the infantry on XXXX Panzer Corps' right flank east and southeast to clear the line of the Tikhaya Sosna upstream from Ostrogozhsk.[20] In the morning, on learning that Paulus had all of XXXX Panzer Corps headed due east, Bock ordered him to divert 23d Panzer Division to the northeast toward Hoth's flank.[21]

"Stampede to Voronezh"

The offensive was rolling at full speed on the ninth day, 5 July. The XXXXVIII Panzer Corps had three solid bridgeheads across the Don in the morning, one reaching to within two miles of Voronezh. The XXXX Panzer Corps was bearing in on Ostrogozhsk and approaching Korotoyak. Bock, seeing himself as master of the battlefield, issued Directive 2 for Operation BRAUNSCHWEIG. In part it read:

The enemy has not succeeded in organizing a new defense anywhere. Wherever he was attacked his resistance collapsed quickly and he fled. It has been impossible to discern any purpose or plan in his retreats. At no point thus far in the campaign in the East have such strong evidences of disintegration been observed on the enemy side.[22]

Specifically, the object was "to exploit the present condition of the Soviet Army for the furtherance of our operations and not to permit the defeated enemy to come to rest." Sixth Army was to "stay on the enemy's heels," and Armeegruppe Weichs was to release Fourth Panzer Army "at the earliest possible time" and put it at the disposal of the army group.[23]

While Bock was preparing to continue what he considered to be his display of virtuosity, his performance was being judged differently in the OKH and at *Fuehrer* Headquarters. Hitler and Halder believed that turning 23d Panzer Division north was a waste of time and effort. Both thought Bock and Hoth were launched on a mindless "stampede" toward Voronezh. Hitler, moreover, querulously asked Halder to find out why XXXX Panzer Corps had not yet reached the Don. Bock's high-handed reply that much of the reason why was the firing of the two best generals in the corps because of the Reichel affair probably did not

---

[20]*H. Gr. Sued, Ia Nr. 1934/42, an AOK 6, und A. Gr. Weichs, 3.7.42, AOK 6 30155/39 file.*
[21]*AOK 6, Ia Kriegstagebuch, Nr. 12, 4 Jul 42, AOK 6 22855/1 file.*

[22]*H. Gr. Sued, Ia Nr. 1950/42, Weisung Nr. 2 zur Operation "Braunschweig," 5.7.42, AOK 6 30155/39 file.*
[23]*Ibid.; H. Gr. Sued, Ia Nr. 1956/42, 5.7.42, AOK 6 30155/39 file.*

improve the atmosphere at the upper levels.[24]

During the evening, the OKH liaison officer with Fourth Panzer Army raised another doubt. (Liaison officers were attached to every army headquarters, and they reported independently to Hitler via the OKH.) The officer, a general staff major, radioed, *"Coup de main* at Voronezh has failed. 24th Panzer Division opposed by strong enemy south of the city. Grossdeutschland also strongly opposed in its bridgehead. Concerted attack being planned for tomorrow." The reality was not quite so dramatic. On the outskirts of Voronezh, the 24th Panzer Division's lead elements had encountered Soviet troops and workers' militia with mortars but no artillery and only a few tanks. Grossdeutschland Division was having to beat down some resistance to expand its bridgehead.[25] At *Fuehrer* Headquarters, however, the liaison officer's message raised a vision of street-fighting and a debilitating battle for the city, and Hitler thereupon forbade using the "fast" divisions, Grossdeutschland or 24th Panzer, and instructed Bock and Hoth to leave Voronezh to less valuable divisions.[26]

One more day brought BLAU I/ BRAUNSCHWEIG to a superficially glorious and profoundly anticlimactic conclusion. Voronezh was taken on the 6th with hardly a shot having to be fired. The 24th Panzer Division patrols ranged through the streets in the morning without seeing an enemy. A motorcycle battalion from the 3d Infantry Division did the same in the afternoon. In acrimonious telephone calls to Halder, Bock asked permission to occupy the city, which Hitler granted late in the day.

By then the Germans had had another, greater surprise: *Southwest Front* was retreating all along the Sixth Army front on the Tikhaya Sosna River even though the army was stopped on most of its line west of Ostrogozhsk. No one knew for certain what this highly untypical Soviet behavior meant, but if the Russians were in full retreat, it was time to be heading south. That, however, was to have been Fourth Panzer Army's job, and Hoth's panzer divisions and the Grossdeutschland Division were still at Voronezh and north of it. Paulus only had one panzer division and one motorized infantry division.

The victory was turning sour, and the whole offensive was on the verge of being thrown into disarray. While Bock and Halder exchanged "enervating" telephone calls, Hitler talked about every hour being important, and Keitel showered "ill-judged" pronouncements on all. Halder longed for "time to contemplate quietly and then give clear orders." He also believed he knew the cause of the problem—Bock's generalship: Bock, Halder concluded, had let himself be taken in tow by Hoth and had piled too much of his armor into the north flank.[27]

A Strategic Retreat

The Soviet Dilemma

While the Germans were finding their success awkward, the Soviet forces were running more deeply into

---

[24] *Halder Diary,* vol. III, p. 473; *Bock Diary, Osten II,* 5 Jul 42.

[25] *AOK 2, Ia Kriegstagebuch, Teil VI,* 5 Jul 42, AOK 2 23617/2 file.

[26] *Bock Diary, Osten II,* 5 Jul 42.

[27] *Halder Diary,* vol. III, p. 475.

PANZER III TANK IN VORONEZH

genuine trouble. On 2 July, the best initial move seemed to be to bring *Bryansk Front's* still powerful armor into play against the enemy spearhead aimed for Voronezh. To do that, the *front* was able to gather, under Headquarters, *Fifth Tank Army,* five tank corps (the army's two plus *I* and *XVI* and *VII Tank Corps* from the *Stavka* reserves) and eight rifle divisions. This brought together about six hundred tanks, at least twice the number of Hoth's two panzer corps. But Golikov's departure to Voronezh and, apparently, a drop in confidence in him and his staff in Moscow created a hiatus in command. Kazakov says the General Staff and the *Stavka* took over on the night of 3 July and issued orders directly to *Fifth Tank Army.* The next day,

Kazakov adds, General Vasilevskiy, who had become chief of the General Staff, came in person, explained the mission to the army staff "in very cautious terms," and departed again (on the 5th) before the counterattack began.[28] Vasilevskiy maintains that he and the *Stavka* had to intervene because *Bryansk Front* was not giving any orders. According to Kazakov, only Golikov could make decisions concerning the counterattack, and he was away at Voronezh.[29]

The 4th through the 6th of July were days of high crisis in the Soviet Command, which, no doubt, accounts for

---

[28] Kazakov, *"Na voronezhskom napravlenii,"* p. 39.
[29] Vasilevskiy, *Delo,* p. 220; Kazakov, *"Na voronezhskom napravlenii,"* p. 39.

Vasilevskiy's abrupt coming and going at *Bryansk Front*. The Soviet literature is more than usually sparing in its treatment of the decisions taken at this stage. Nevertheless, it leaves a clear impression that Stalin, the *Stavka,* and the General Staff saw themselves as having to deal with a dangerous tactical surprise that confirmed their previous strategic estimates, specifically, that the march on Moscow had begun. In one version of his memoirs, Vasilevskiy said that the *Stavka,* in considering Voronezh as a possible German objective, "believed the subsequent development of the offensive would not be to the south, as actually occurred, but to the north, in a deep encirclement of Moscow from the southeast."[30] Consequently, the primary Soviet strategic concern was directed to the area north and northeast of the line Kursk-Voronezh. (Although the prospect of a successful deception had appeared vastly diminished after the Reichel affair, Operation KREML, had continued and the OKW had announced, on 1 July, that an offensive had begun "in the southern and central sectors" of the Eastern Front.[31] (The *History of the Second World War* describes both as having been important in the German scheme but does not attribute any significance to them from the Soviet standpoint.)[32]

Against a drive on Moscow, the Soviet Command, apparently, saw itself as having two strong trumps still to play: the Orel offensive and the *Fifth Tank Army*'s counterattack. These could change the picture swiftly and mightily. They would, in fact, do that, but not in the way expected.

General Zhukov, whose *West Front* initially had a share in the Orel operation, had taken it over entirely after *Bryansk Front* was hit. On 5 July, three of his armies, *Tenth, Sixteenth,* and *Sixty-first,* hurled a massive attack against the Second Panzer Army line from north of Orel to Kirov. Second Panzer Army, which had not anticipated such earnest evidence of its status as a threat to Moscow, was shaken but, with much luck, managed to bring the attack to a standstill within a day and, thereby, to give the impression of much more strength than it actually had.[33]

Owing to the mix-up at the higher levels, responsibility for planning and executing *Fifth Tank Army*'s counterattack fell almost entirely to the army commander, General Lizyukov, and his staff. Lizyukov had been one of the first officers to win the decoration Hero of the Soviet Union in the war, and he was, Vasilevskiy says, "a very energetic and determined" commander, but neither he nor his staff were experienced in leading large armored forces.[34] In Kazakov's account, Lizyukov coordinated his tanks, artillery, and *Shturmovik* air support "weakly" and gave his corps commanders their instructions in superficial map briefings that they, in turn, repeated to their subordinate comman-

---

[30]A. M. Vasilevskiy, "*Delo vsey zhizni,*" *Novy Mir,* 5 (1975), 251. While the excerpts printed in *Novy Mir* are otherwise identical with the book, this passage does not appear in the book (See *Delo,* p. 219).

[31]*OKW, KTB,* vol. II, p. 73.

[32]See *IVMV,* vol. V, p. 243.

[33]*Pz. AOK 2, Ia Kriegstagebuch Nr. 2, Teil IV,* 5–7 Jul 42, Pz. AOK 2 28499/4 file; Zhukov, *Memoirs,* p. 375. See also *IVMV,* vol. V, p. 243, which implies that the purpose of the offensive was to draw away German reserves, and Bagramyan, *Tak shli my k pobede,* p. 141, who says the purpose was to prevent the enemy from using Army Group Center as a reservoir of reinforcements for the offensive in the south.

[34]Vasilevskiy, *Delo,* p. 221.

ders.[35] By the time the tank army went into action on the 6th, it was already too late to save Voronezh. Moreover, Lizyukov and his corps commanders, unable to manage a quick thrust, reverted to tactics of attrition that were highly inconvenient to the enemy but more costly to themselves. During the day, 9th Panzer Division smashed two of the tank army's brigades in a single encounter.[36]

On the 6th, the Soviet Command faced a dilemma. The prospects of halting a thrust toward Moscow in the first stage were evaporating. In fact, the attempts seem to have disclosed greater enemy strength than had been anticipated. On the other hand, the actual situation was worse on the south flank than in the center. *Southwest Front* was dislodged, floating loose between the Donets and the Don, and being shoved into and behind the flank of its neighbor, *South Front*. Under these two pressures, the *Stavka,* for the first time in the war, ordered a strategic retreat. Unlike the previous year, when armies and *fronts* had been riveted in place regardless of the consequences, the whole south flank was allowed to pick up and pull out to the east.

The *History of the Second World War* gives the date of the decision as 6 July and says the retreat started on the night of the 7th. German Sixth Army, however, observed a general withdrawal in full swing during the day on the 6th, which leaves open the possibilities that the decision was made earlier or that it was not as deliberate as the Soviet accounts present it. A captured officer from *Southwest Front's* *Twenty-first Army* had told his interrogators on the 2d that by then control had slipped entirely from the army's command.[37]

The actual order must be pieced together from a half-dozen sentences in three sources. The *History of the Second World War,* while it is specific as to time, merely says that the *Stavka* undertook to "extricate" *Southwest* and *South Fronts* "from the enemy's blows."[38] The *History of the Great Patriotic War* states that *Southwest Front* and the right flank of *South Front* were ordered to withdraw to the line of Novaya Kalitva (on the Don)–Popasnaya (on the Donets), a distance of roughly 60 miles (100 kilometers), and dig in there.[39] The *Popular Scientific Sketch* states, ". . . Supreme Headquarters ordered *Southwest* and *South Fronts* to retreat to the Don. . . ."[40]

The decision to retreat did not apply in the Voronezh area or anywhere to the west and north. Golikov had orders to clear the enemy off the entire east side of the Don "at all costs" and to establish a solid defense on the river "in the whole sector."[41] On the 7th, Golikov's three armies became *Voronezh Front,* and General Rokossovskiy, who had been one of Zhukov's best army commanders during the winter, was appointed to command *Bryansk Front.* Golikov had with him as *Stavka* representatives, General Vatutin, the deputy chief of the General Staff, and Army Commissar Second Rank P. C. Stepanov, the chief air force commissar. General Vatutin was designated to take

[35]Kazakov, "Na voronezhskom napravlenii," p. 40.
[36]*Bock Diary, Osten II,* 6 Jul 42.

[37]*IVMV,* vol. V, p. 152; *AOK 6, Ia Kriegstagebuch Nr. 12,* 2 and 6 Jul 42, AOK 6 22855/1 file.
[38]*IVMV,* vol. V, p. 152.
[39]*IVOVSS,* vol. II, p. 421.
[40]*VOV,* p. 148f.
[41]*IVMV,* vol. V, p. 152.

over the *front* command and would do so in a week.[42] Zhukov's Orel offensive ran for five days and then stopped as abruptly as it had begun. Lizyukov was killed on 24 July while fighting to beat off German efforts to improve their line that apparently the Russians had taken as having had farther reaching objectives.[43]

"Blau II Is Dead"

That the Soviet Command might go over to a flexible defense was not exactly a surprise to the Germans. They had talked about it as a possibility since WILHELM and FRIDERICUS II and during BLAU I, which, for all its apparent success, produced a disappointing bag of 70,000 prisoners. Bock had told Hitler on 3 July that the Russians were "gradually getting smart" and had learned to evade encirclements.[44] Nevertheless, the entire BLAU concept had assumed a repeat of the Russians' 1941 performance. BLAU's small, tight, deliberate envelopments were fine against an enemy who stayed put, but one inclined to disappear over the far horizon required different handling not easily administered by demotorized infantry and rebuilt armor.

This was the Germans' problem, but to deal with it, they had to believe it really existed, and on that they could not make up their minds.[45] Halder could not see *Southwest* and *South Fronts'* abandoning defenses they had worked

on for half a year without a fight. Hitler, going by foreign news reports, was "inclined" to think the Russians might be attempting an "elastic" defense, but apparently saw no profound implications in that.[46] Bock came closest to the point in a teletyped message he sent to Halder on the afternoon of the 8th. In it he said BLAU II was "dead"; if the armies maneuvered as they were required to under existing plans, they would "most likely strike into thin air"; therefore, the OKH needed "to consider" what the objectives ought to be and, in particular where the armored forces should go.[47]

Bock would have to wait for his answer. The Soviet retreat, whatever else it might yet do, had at its outset created a monumental distraction. In the week after 6 July, almost the whole German command effort was absorbed by the accelerating pace of the offensive. To switch the main effort from north to south, Bock ordered Headquarters, Fourth Panzer Army, XXXXVIII Panzer Corps with 24th Panzer Division and Grossdeutschland, and XXIV Panzer Corps with 3d and 16th Motorized Infantry Divisions away from Voronezh. On reaching the vicinity of Rossosh–Novaya Kalitva, Hoth was also to pick up and take command of VIII Corps and XXXX Panzer Corps on Sixth Army's left flank. The latter two corps were already in motion south, toward the headwaters of the Derkul and Kalitva rivers. The others

---

[42]*Ibid.*, p. 152; Vasilevskiy, *Delo*, p. 223.

[43]*Pz. AOK 2, Ia Kriegstagebuch Nr. 2, Teil IV,* 10 Jul 42, Pz. AOK 28499/4 file; Vasilevskiy, *Delo*, p. 222; Rokossovskiy, *Soldier's Duty,* pp. 120–22.

[44]*Bock Diary, Osten II,* 3 Jul 42.

[45]The first documented evidence of the retreat Army Group South had was an order of the day signed by Timoshenko, captured on 12 July, that

instructed commanders to evade encirclements and not to make it a point of honor to hold their positions at all costs. (Apparently, some Soviet commanders also did not comprehend what was going on.) *H. Gr. A, Ia Nr. 317/42, an Pz. AOK 1,* 12 Jul 42, Pz. AOK 1 24906/1 file.

[46]*Halder Diary,* vol. III, p. 475.

[47]*Bock Diary, Osten II,* 8 Jul 42.

AN INFANTRY DIVISION HEADS EAST AT THE PACE OF ITS HORSES

would first have to cross 110 miles of previously occupied territory on their own tracks and wheels. On the 6th, the OKH had transferred First Panzer Army, which was in the midst of refitting its panzer divisions, to the Coastal Staff Azov. To List it had given orders to have First Panzer Army ready to start on the 12th. These had been canceled within hours, and List then had been told to get First Panzer started on the 9th, at which time the Coastal Staff would become Army Group A.[48] Bock, who had not been consulted, had observed wryly that the battle was now "sliced in two."[49]

By the 9th, when the second phase went into full swing, the offensive was a good two weeks ahead of its projected schedule and nearly as much behind in terms of current readiness. The 23d Panzer Division, after having run out of motor fuel two or three times, was just catching up to Sixth Army; 24th Panzer Division and the Grossdeutschland Division were stopped halfway between Voronezh and Novaya Kalitva, waiting to be refueled; and the 3d and 16th Motorized Infantry Divisions could not depart from Voronezh until infantry divisions arrived to relieve them. First Panzer Army had to lead off with its infantry. The panzer divisions were still in bivouac areas thirty or forty miles behind the front. Hitler, moreover, had begun to worry about a

[48] H. Gr. A, Ia Kriegstagebuch, Band I, Teil I, 6 Jul 42, H. Gr. A 75126/1 file.
[49] Bock Diary, Osten II, 5 Jul 42.

British landing in the West and was holding back Army Group A's best equipped motorized division, the SS Leibstandarte "Adolf Hitler," for transfer to the Channel coast.

Strike at Millerovo

Meanwhile, BLAU II was all but dead, and it had no successor. First Panzer Army put its right flank in motion on the morning of the 9th with instructions to strike across the Donets at Lisichansk, then veer sharply north, crossing the Aydar River at Starobelsk, and meet Fourth Panzer Army at Vysochanovka. The assumption was that Sixth Army would tie the enemy down north and west of Vysochanovka and so set the scene for an envelopment from the south.[50] First Panzer Army, if it held to the assigned course, would likely run into Sixth Army's left flank about the time it reached Starobelsk.

During the day on the 9th, it became apparent that while First Panzer Army would probably be across the Donets in another twenty-four hours, Sixth Army, with nothing ahead of it but long columns of Soviet troops heading east, would by then have passed the line of the Aydar from Starobelsk north, and XXXX Panzer Corps would be well south of Vysochanovka. Obviously there was no point in having First Panzer Army continue past Lisichansk on its assigned course, and in the early morning hours on the 10th, the OKH issued a new directive which, in its general concept, reverted to the BLAU II plan. First Panzer Army was to

head due east past Lisichansk toward Millerovo. Fourth Panzer was to aim its right flank at Millerovo, its left at Meshkovskaya between the Don and upper Chir, and to take a bridgehead on the Don at Boguchar as a springboard for a subsequent thrust left of the Don toward Stalingrad.[51]

On the morning of the 11th, Hoth had command of XXXX Panzer Corps and VIII Corps, which were heading south and east, but XXXXVIII Panzer Corps and XXIV Panzer Corps were strung out behind. The Grossdeutschland Division and 24th Panzer Division were stalled, as they had been for two days, in the valley of the Tikhaya Sosna waiting to be refueled, and the two motorized divisions were still at Voronezh, where Soviet counterattacks and the inexperience of the infantry, mostly "young" troops sent to relieve them, slowed their disengagement. During the day, the 29th Motorized Infantry Division passed through Boguchar, and the OKH dropped the idea of taking a bridgehead after the division reported the bridge there over the Don destroyed. The offensive was now moving over open steppe in searing heat and choking clouds of fine dust. First Panzer Army reached the Aydar River during the day, and Seventeenth Army reported the enemy pulling away from its north flank.

After 2400, fresh OKH orders came in over the teletype machines at Army Groups A and B. First Panzer Army was to aim its left flank at Millerovo, its right toward the Donets crossing at Kamensk-Shakhtinskiy. Bock was to put all the forces he "could lay hands on" into a drive via Millerovo (which

[50]*H. Gr. A, Ia Kriegstagebuch, Band I, Teil I,* 7 Jul 42, H. Gr. A 75126/1 file; *Pz. AOK 1, Ia Kriegstagebuch Nr. 8,* 7 Jul 42, Pz. AOK 1 24906/16 file.

[51]*Ibid.,* 10 Jul 42.

Fourth Panzer Army's advance elements reached during the day) to Kamensk-Shakhtinskiy and finally to the confluence of the Donets and the Don. He was to use any remaining strength to provide flank cover on the east and to "create conditions for an advance to Stalingrad." To Bock's protests that this was going to create a useless pileup of First and Fourth Panzer Armies' armor around Millerovo and scatter his other panzer divisions "to the winds," the OKH replied that his mission was now in the south. Halder further admonished General Greiffenberg, Bock's chief of staff, by telegram "to avoid any unnecessary commitment of mobile forces toward the east." Fourth Panzer Army, he added, had to be ready "at any time" to turn southwest and strike behind the Soviet forces holding north of Rostov.[52]

From "a variety of reports," the OKH believed the Russians were going to make a stand on the line Millerovo–Kamensk-Shakhtinskiy–Rostov.[53] Bock knew differently, and after grumbling about it to himself for a day, he could not resist telling Halder so in a telegram on the morning of the 13th. The enemy ahead of Fourth and First Panzer Armies, he said, was retreating to the east, southeast, and south, particularly the south. An operation centered on and past Millerovo would to some extent plow into the midst of the Soviet columns but would not accomplish a substantial encirclement. The place for Fourth Panzer Army's right flank to go was to Morozovsk, seventy-five miles east of Kamensk-Shakhtinskiy. There it might still catch some of the enemy, and from there it could turn either southwest or east as conditions required.[54]

Bock Goes Home

By then, the same or similar conclusions were beginning to come to mind at *Fuehrer* Headquarters—with consequences for Bock that he had not anticipated. Hitler opened the afternoon situation conference with "expressions of utmost indignation" over the delays in getting 23d and 24th Panzer Divisions and the Grossdeutschland Division headed south. He also suddenly recalled that back in May, Bock had originated the "unfortunate proposal" to oppose the Soviet attack south of Kharkov frontally instead of pinching off the gap at Izyum.[55] In an hour, a message was on the wire transferring Fourth Panzer Army to Army Group A and telling Bock to turn over the Army Group B command to Weichs.

Over the telephone, Keitel "advised" Bock to report himself sick and added that Army Group B was now "practically shut down" anyway. To Bock's question why he was being dismissed just when he "presumed" he had produced a great success, Keitel said it was because the mobile divisions were too slow coming away from Voronezh, and their fuel supplies were "not in order." When Bock protested that his dispositions around Voronezh had been "clear as the sun" and pointed out that the OKH, not the army group, was responsible for the motor fuel supplies, Keitel urged him not to "make a racket right now." Things were not irreparable, he

---

[52]*Bock Diary, Osten II*, 12 Jul 42.
[53]*Halder Diary*, vol. III, p. 478.
[54]*Bock Diary, Osten II*, 13 Jul 42.
[55]*Halder Diary*, vol. III, p. 480. See p. 275f.

said, and there would be time later to straighten them out. For the moment, though, he hurriedly added, any kind of discussion with the *Fuehrer* was out of the question.[56]

Later it would appear that the most consequential charge to be raised against Bock was that he had involved too much armor on the advance of Voronezh and thereby delayed the turn south. At the time, however, even Halder, who was the first to raise it, saw it as, at most, a tactical blemish, not as a major failing. As of 13 July, Hitler, in particular, with his armies seemingly on the edge of their greatest victory, had no compelling reason to resurrect the irritations of the past two weeks unless he was responding to some far more deep-seated impulse. One possibility is that he had become uneasy as he saw the enemy repeatedly slip from his grasp. The haul of prisoners, 88,000 thus far, was relatively low, and the unexpected Soviet retreat had unhinged his plans, but his subsequent actions indicate that his premonitions, if any, could not have been very strong. The 13th was for him a day of minor misgivings and great opportunity. In getting rid of Bock, he was not disposing of a failed general but of a rival in credit for the victory.

Weichs caught a glimpse of that the first time he went to *Fuehrer* Headquarters as commanding general, Army Group B. Talking to Schmundt, he suggested that Hitler be persuaded to take notice of Bock's accomplishments in some form "for the sake of public opinion and troop morale." Schmundt replied that Hitler would never do any such thing because he had developed "a distinct antipathy for Bock." On the same occasion, in talking to the *Reich* press chief, Weichs learned that Hitler would not allow the General Staff to be mentioned in newspaper articles about himself because he believed it detracted from his image and his military reputation.[57]

On 15 July, Bock relinquished his command and, having been told his presence at *Fuehrer* Headquarters would not be welcomed, went to Berlin. He would divide his time between there and his estate in East Prussia for the rest of the war, brooding about his downfall, searching for the reason, and more than half hoping the cloud would one day lift and the *Fuehrer* would find employment for him again.

[56] *Bock Diary, Osten II,* 13 Jul 42.

[57] Maximilian von Weichs, *Nachlass des Generalfeldmarschalls Freiherr von Weichs, Band 6,* 15 Jul 42, CMH X–1026 file.

CHAPTER XVII

Hitler's Grand Design

"A Certain Crisis"

BLAU II/CLAUSEWITZ, such as it had been, came to an end between 13 and 15 July under clouds and in oppressive heat broken by intermittent rainstorms that settled the dust over the moving columns but turned the ground beneath them to mud. Within a 25-mile radius of Millerovo, First and Fourth Panzer Armies' tanks hit line after line of Soviet columns headed east. In the melee, some were dispersed and some smashed. Others slipped through or veered south away from the onslaught. During the day on the 15th, First Panzer's 14th Panzer Division and Fourth Panzer's 3d Panzer Division met south of Millerovo thereby technically completing the encirclement, but they did not form a pocket. With gaps in all directions, the armies were slicing through, not enveloping, the enemy. *(Map 31.)* Fourth Panzer Army reported 21,000 prisoners taken, First Panzer did not stop to count. It certainly took as many, and it may have taken two or three times as many; nevertheless, the greater part of the potential catch escaped. The most remarkable capture was twenty-two trainloads of American and British lend-lease tanks and supplies taken on the railroad between Millerovo and Kamensk-Shakhtinskiy.[1]

Tactically, what Field Marshal Bock had predicted was happening; Army Group A was developing a knot of mostly superfluous armored muscle around Millerovo and on a line to the south. Shoulder to shoulder, First and Fourth Panzer Armies were punching into thin air. *Twenty-fourth Army, South Front*'s reserve army, made a feeble and short-lived attempt to stand at Millerovo on the 13th. *Southwest Front,* which had its headquarters east of the Don, had lost control of its armies. They were turned over to *South Front,* but after the Germans reached Millerovo it had troubles enough of its own and did not succeed in establishing contact with any of them except *Ninth Army.*[2] One thing the German armies did have was command of the field, and that at a low price. After better than two weeks in action, General Hoth, the commander of Fourth Panzer Army, rated the condition of his motorized and panzer divisions and the Grossdeutschland Division as very good. Their main deficiencies were mechanical breakdowns and fuel shortages. General Kleist put First Panzer Army, after six days, at 30 percent of its optimum efficiency, but it had started at below 40 percent because most of its troop and equipment replace-

---

[1] *H. Gr. A, Ia Kriegstagebuch, Band I, Teil I,* 17 Jul 42, H. Gr. A 75126/1 file; *Pz. AOK 1, Ia Kriegstagebuch Nr. 8,* 17 Jul 42, Pz. AOK 1 24906 file.

[2] *IVOVSS,* vol. II, p. 421.

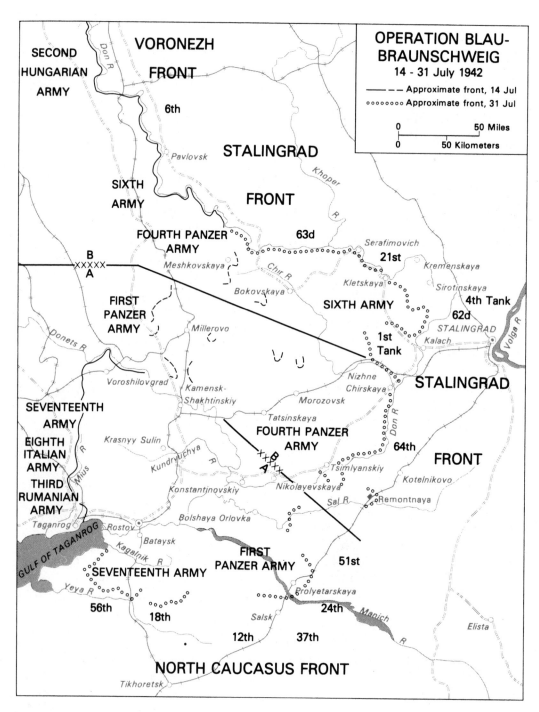

OPERATION BLAU-
BRAUNSCHWEIG
14 - 31 July 1942

– – Approximate front, 14 Jul
ooooooo Approximate front, 31 Jul

0   50 Miles
0   50 Kilometers

SECOND
HUNGARIAN
ARMY

VORONEZH
FRONT

6th

STALINGRAD

FRONT

Don R

Pavlovsk

Khoper R

SIXTH
ARMY

FOURTH PANZER
ARMY

63d

Serafimovich

21st

Kremenskaya

Meshkovskaya

Chir R

Kletskaya

Sirotinskaya

B
XXXXX
A

FIRST
PANZER
ARMY

Bokovskaya

SIXTH ARMY

4th Tank

62d

Donets R

Millerovo

1st
Tank

Kalach

STALINGRAD

Volga R

Voroshilovgrad

Kamensk-
Shakhtinskiy

Morozovsk

Nizhne
Chirskaya

Don R

STALINGRAD

SEVENTEENTH
ARMY

Krasnyy Sulin

Tatsinskaya

FOURTH PANZER
ARMY

64th

FRONT

EIGHTH
ITALIAN
ARMY

Kundryuchya R

XXX
B
A

Tsimlyanskiy

Kotelnikovo

THIRD
RUMANIAN
ARMY

Mius R

Konstantinovskiy

Nikolayevskaya

Sal R

Remontnaya

Taganrog

Rostov

Bolshaya Orlovka

Bataysk

FIRST
PANZER ARMY

51st

GULF OF TAGANROG

Kagalnik R

Manich R

Elista

Yeya R

SEVENTEENTH ARMY

Prolyetarskaya

56th

18th

Salsk

24th

12th

37th

NORTH CAUCASUS FRONT

Tikhoretsk

MAP 31

ments were still en route from Germany.[3]

New Missions

Late in the night on 13 July, Army Groups A and B received orders "for continuing operations on the lower Don." The objective would be to prevent *South Front* and whatever was left of *Southwest Front* from escaping by closing the line of the Don down to Rostov. BLAU II had died, and BLAU III was forgotten. The orders did not mention Stalingrad, the original BLAU III objective. The whole offensive was to be reoriented to the south and somewhat to the west to accomplish one grand encirclement inside the great bend of the Don. Field Marshal Keitel, chief of the OKW, had not exaggerated when he had told Bock that Army Group B was being shut down. Sixth Army's missions would be to establish a front on the Don from northeast of Meshkovskaya to Pavlovsk and to turn over all units not needed to do this to Fourth Panzer Army. First Panzer Army was to turn south, cross the Donets at Kamensk-Shakhtinskiy, and bear in on Rostov from the northeast. Fourth Panzer Army, running parallel to First Panzer east of the Donets, would keep its main weight on its right flank, but (as Bock had proposed) would let its left sweep east to Morozovsk. From the line between Kamensk-Shakhtinskiy and Morozovsk, it would drop south to the Don, take bridgeheads at Konstantinovskiy and Tsimlyanskiy, and pre-

pare to run along the south bank of the Don westward toward Rostov.[4]

A day later, Hitler shifted the *Fuehrer* Headquarters from East Prussia to Vinnitsa in the western Ukraine. This *Fuehrer* compound at Vinnitsa, code-named *Werwolf*, in contrast to the fortress-like *Wolfsschanze*, consisted, except for two concrete bunkers, of prefabricated wooden buildings erected in a patch of pine forest half-a-dozen miles outside the town. General Halder, chief of the General Staff, and the OKH occupied quarters in Vinnitsa. The move appeared to lend emphasis to a statement in the orders of the 13th in which Hitler assigned control of the offensive to Headquarters, Army Group A "subject to my directives." Actually, he could have exercised just as close supervision from Rastenburg as from Vinnitsa. The *Werwolf*, however, did not place him symbolically on the battlefield and, as he liked to claim, at the head of his troops, which possibly enhanced his psychological leverage and undoubtedly would give him a personal claim to the victory when it came.

Coincident with the move to the *Werwolf* Hitler released a strategic directive written four days earlier, Directive 43 for Operation BLUECHER. It gave Eleventh Army the mission of crossing the Kerch Strait to the Taman Peninsula, from which it was to take the Soviet naval bases at Anapa and Novorossiysk and to strike along the northern fringe of the Caucasus to Maykop. General Manstein, the army's commander, was

---

[3]*H. Gr. A, Ia Kriegstagebuch, Band I, Teil I,*16 Jul 42, H. Gr. A 75126/1 file.

[4]*OKH, GenStdH, Op. Abt. (I) Nr. 420538/42,* H 22/215 file; *H. Gr. B, Ia Nr. 2043/42, Weisung fuer die Fortfuehrung der Operation an den unteren Don, 13.7.42,* AOK 6 30155/39 file.

GERMAN TANKS ROVE OVER THE STEPPE IN SEARCH OF TARGETS

to be prepared to execute BLUECHER in early August. [5]

Stalingrad Front

For the *Stavka,* the German entry into the great bend of the Don opened the contest for Stalingrad regardless of what Hitler's intentions for the moment might be. The *Popular Scientific Sketch* says, "Already in mid-July 1942, the Soviet leadership had discerned the enemy's aim to advance to the Volga in the Stalingrad area to occupy this important strategic point and at the same time, seize the country's largest industrial region. On 14 July, a state of war

was declared in the Stalingrad area."[6]

Whether the Soviet leadership had altered its fundamental assessment of German strategy, however, remains in doubt. Stalin's official biography published in 1949, undoubtedly written with his approval and possibly with his help, maintains, "Comrade Stalin promptly divined the plan of the German command. He saw that the idea was to create an impression that the seizure of the oil regions of Groznyy and Baku was the major and not the subsidiary objective of the German summer offensive. He pointed out that, in reality, the main objective was to envelop Moscow from the east." Consequently, the biography con-

---

[5]*OKW, WFSt, Op. Nr. 551208/42, Weisung Nr. 43, 11.7.42* and *OKW, WFSt, Op. Nr. 002353/42, 13.7.42,* German High Level Directives, CMH files.

[6]*VOV,* p. 149.

tinues, he anchored the defense on Stalingrad.[7] It appears that again, as he had earlier in the month, Stalin drew the best possible conclusion for the long-term from a mistaken premise.

On 12 July, the *Stavka* created the *Stalingrad Front,* using Marshal Timoshenko's Headquarters, *Southwest Front,* and three reserve armies, *Sixty-second, Sixty-third,* and *Sixty-fourth,* plus what was left of the former *Southwest Front's Twenty-first Army.* Timoshenko's mission was to defend the left bank of the Don from Pavlovsk to Kletskaya and, from Kletskaya south, to hold a line inside the Don bend to the point at which the river turned west forty miles east of Tsimlyanskiy. *North Caucasus Front's Fifty-first Army* was stationed on the river's left bank between *Stalingrad Front's* flank and the Sea of Azov.[8]

The armies were far from being in full-fighting trim. General Leytenant V. I. Chuikov, acting commanding general of the *Sixty-fourth Army,* stopped at Headquarters, *Twenty-first Army* on the 15th and observed that although it was supposedly defending the Don between Kletskaya and Serafimovich it was "living on wheels," that is, operating out of trucks and vehicles as if to be ready to pick up and move at any moment. A day later, his own army, which was assigned to the southern half of the front inside the Don bend, was only beginning to detrain between the Volga and the Don. Another week would pass before all of it arrived. His neighbor on the north, *Sixty-second Army,* was in position and, in accordance with orders

from the *front,* had a picket line on the Chir River, but it was keeping its headquarters well behind the Don, fifty miles from the troops.[9]

Stalingrad Bypassed

For the moment, *Stalingrad Front* had almost as little bearing on the Germans' real concerns as *Voronezh Front* had had a week before. Hitler's attention and the efforts of his generals were directed elsewhere.

South of the Donets, opposite Seventeenth Army's center and right flank, *South Front* held tight to its original positions until the 15th, when it began to pull away from Voroshilovgrad to the southeast. Seventeenth Army was ready to attack, but the day before, Field Marshal List, the commander of Army Group A, had told General Ruoff, the army's commander, to wait until the pocket was closed on the east between the lower Donets and Rostov. By 1200 on the 16th, *South Front's* right flank was clearly in full retreat, and List, after giving Ruoff permission to let infantry follow, scheduled the general attack for the morning of the 18th. Ruoff believed that even though the Russians appeared to be standing firm on the southern half of the front in their heavily fortified line on the Mius River, he was not going to catch many of them if he waited another day and a half. The infantry advancing along the south bank of the Donets was hardly seeing a trace of the enemy. When it took Voroshilovgrad on the 17th the city was empty.[10]

[7]G. F. Aleksandrov, et al., *Iosif Vissarionovich Stalin, Kratkaya biografiya* (Moscow: Izdatelstvo Politicheskoy Literatury, 1949), p. 197.

[8]A. M. Borodin, ed., *Bitva za Stalingrad* (Volgograd: Nizhniye-Volzhskoye Knizhnoye Izdatelstvo, 1969), p. 17; *IVOVSS,* vol. II, p. 426.

[9]Vasili I. Chuikov, *The Battle for Stalingrad* (New York: Holt, Rinehart and Winston, 1964), pp. 15–17.

[10]*AOK 17, Ia Kriegstagebuch Nr. 3,* 14–17 Jul 42, AOK 17 24411/1 file; *H. Gr. A, Ia Kriegstagebuch, Band I, Teil I,* 14–16 Jul 42, H. Gr. A 75126/1 file.

In the Don bend, all the *Sixty-second* and *Sixty-fourth Armies* were to see for some days after the 15th were stragglers, not just single soldiers but frequently whole staffs—thirsty, dirty, and demoralized—coming out of the west over the steppe.[11] The Germans were not all that far away, forty to fifty miles, but Sixth Army had slowed down, and General Paulus, the commander of Sixth Army, was dutifully turning his attention north toward the Don. And Fourth Panzer Army was running due south, parallel to the Soviet line that was forming off its left flank. By 1200 on the 16th, Fourth Panzer Army's tanks were in Tatsinskaya and Morozovsk, and before nightfall, Hoth had a spearhead standing at Tsimlyanskiy on the Don. By then, First Panzer Army was across the Donets and headed toward Rostov. During the day on the 17th, advance detachments of two of Paulus' divisions after meeting only light resistance entered Bokovskaya on the upper Chir River.[12] The appearance of the Germans on the Chir on 17 July is taken in the Soviet literature as the beginning of the defensive battle for Stalingrad.[13]

An encirclement was forming on the lower Don, but an eighty-mile stretch of the river from the confluence of the Donets to the Gulf of Taganrog was still open, and to reach the crossings, particularly at Rostov, the Russians in the pocket had shorter distances to go than did the Germans. Hitler was determined not to let the quarry escape although there was reason to suspect it had in part already done so. On the night of the 17th, disregarding Halder's protest that all he would accomplish would be to create a useless pileup of armor, Hitler set all of List's armies on the shortest courses to Rostov. He instructed List to stop Fourth Panzer Army at Tsimlyanskiy and Konstantinovskiy and to turn it west along the north bank of the Don. Ruoff was to shift Seventeenth Army's attack, which had not yet started, fifty miles south, from the upper Mius to the coast just north of Taganrog. When List and Ruoff both objected that while the distance to Rostov was somewhat shorter, the regrouping would waste three or four days, Colonel Heusinger, the OKH operations chief, said he shared their opinion, but the *Fuehrer* had given the order "and it is not to be supposed that he will alter his decision."[14]

Hitler included in the night's dispatches, also, an order to Army Group B. Sixth Army's mission would remain as it had been, to cover the flank on the Don, but it would be expanded. The two divisions whose advance detachments had reached Bokovskaya during the day would press on to the east, "advance detachments ahead!," occupy the whole northeastern quarter of the Don bend, and "by gaining ground in the direction of Stalingrad make it difficult for the enemy to build a defense west of the Volga."[15]

[11]Chuikov, *Stalingrad*, p. 18f.

[12]*AOK 6, Ia Kriegstagebuch Nr. 12*, 15 and 16 Jul 42, AOK 6 22855/1 file; *H. Gr. A, Ia Kriegstagebuch, Band I, Teil I*, 15 and 16 Jul 42, H. Gr. A 75126/1 file; *AOK 6, Ia Kriegstagebuch Nr. 12*, 17 Jul 42, AOK 6 22855/1 file.

[13]*VOV*, p. 151; *IVMV*, vol. V, p. 159.

[14]*OKH, GenStdH, Op. Abt. (IS/A) Nr. 420504/42, an H. Gr. A*, 17.7.42, H 22/215 file; *Halder Diary*, vol. III, p. 485n; *H. Gr. A, Ia Kriegstagebuch, Band I, Teil I*, 17 Jul 42, H. Gr. A 75126/1 file.

[15]*OKH, GenStdH, Op. Abt. (IS/B) Nr. 420505/42, an H. Gr. A*, 17.7.42, H 22/215 file; *AOK 6, Ia Kriegstagebuch Nr. 12*, 17 Jul 42, AOK 6 22855/1 file.

Encirclement at Rostov

While the orders were being written in Vinnitsa, it was raining in the great bend of the Don, not just in local showers but as a continuous downpour that had begun in the early afternoon. The rain lasted through the night and the entire next day. No motor vehicles moved. The panzer divisions were "paralyzed." Seventeenth Army's redeployment could not begin, and Sixth Army's drift along the Don came to a standstill. The only significant change reported came from the Grossdeutschland Division that reached the lower Donets with its infantry and put some troops across. Hitler's mood matched the weather. Halder and Heusinger were on the phone to all the armies repeatedly during the day on the 19th voicing the *Fuehrer*'s impatience.[16]

In between times, they transmitted notices of impending changes in the army group's directives to List and General Weichs, the Army Group B commander, and their chiefs of staff. To Halder's professional relief—intermingled with personal annoyance at having had his advice to the same effect coldly ignored two days earlier— Hitler had decided to hedge on the Rostov encirclement.[17] Hoth was to send four of Fourth Panzer Army's panzer and motorized divisions, including Grossdeutschland, toward Rostov along the north bank of the Don; but another four were to cross the river at Tsimlyanskiy and other places downstream to the mouth of the Donets "as fast and in as much strength as road conditions and fuel supplies in

any way permit." Those four would strike east twenty-five miles to cut the Salsk-Stalingrad railroad and to take possession of the Sal River valley between Bolshaya Orlovka and Remontnaya. There they would position themselves "to proceed either southwest or west with the object of destroying forces the enemy has withdrawn south of the river."[18]

The greater change was in Army Group B's and Sixth Army's mission. Paulus was to leave light security on the Don and "take possession of Stalingrad by a daring high-speed assault." He would get as reinforcements from Fourth Panzer Army, the LI Corps with three infantry divisions, and XIV Panzer Corps with two motorized divisions and one panzer division.[19] The LI Corps was northeast of Morozovsk and XIV Panzer Corps north of Millerovo. Their transfers were accomplished by shifting the Army Group B boundary south to the line Millerovo-Morozovsk and switching their heading from south to east.

The stage was set on the 20th for the last act around Rostov. Seventeenth Army finished regrouping north of Taganrog, and First Panzer Army's point, slowed a little by Soviet rear guards, crossed the Kundryuchya River forty-five miles north of the city. When Seventeenth Army jumped off the next morning against what had been the strongest sector of the whole Soviet south flank, the Russians were gone. They had pulled out during the night. After picking their way through minefields, Ruoff's lead divisions had

---

[16]*H. Gr. A, Ia Kriegstagebuch, Band I, Teil I,* 18 and 19 Jul 42, H. Gr. A 75126/1 file.

[17]*Ibid.,* 19 Jul 42; *Halder Diary,* vol. III, p. 486.

[18]*OKH, GenStdH, Op. Abt. (I) Nr. 420508/42, an H. Gr. A und H. Gr. B,* 19.7.42, H 22/215 file.

[19]*Ibid.; AOK 6, Ia Kriegstagebuch Nr. 12,* 19 and 20 Jul 42, AOK 6 22855/1 file.

GENERAL HOTH *(center)* GIVES AN ORDER AT THE DON CROSSING

covered thirty miles to the western arc of the Rostov defenses, which had been considered exceptionally strong, by 1200 on the 22d and had broken through before dark. First Panzer and Seventeenth Armies both drove into the city on the 23d and secured it during the day after sporadic house-to-house fighting. In less than another twenty-four hours, Seventeenth Army, which had brought bridging equipment in its train, had parts of three divisions across the Don; and on the 25th, it had a five-mile-deep bridgehead on the south bank reaching past Bataysk.[20]

The Rostov pocket had never developed. At the last, nobody expected it to. First Panzer Army's tally showed 83,000 prisoners taken in the whole 200-mile drive, not anywhere near enough to have cut decisively into the Soviet Union's supply of manpower. Several months later a First Panzer Army souvenir history featured the Don bridgehead as the big achievement of the campaign thus far.[21] Halder's expectation of a traffic jam at Rostov, however, was amply fulfilled. On the 25th, twenty divisions were standing within a fifty-mile radius of the city, most with nothing useful to do.

Fourth Panzer Army took bridge-

---

[20]*H. Gr. A, Ia Kriegstagebuch, Band I, Teil I,* 20–25 Jul 42, H. Gr. A 75126/1 file.

[21]*Pz. AOK 1, Abt. Ia/Ic, Abschlussmeldung der 1. Pz-Armee, 31.7.42,* Pz. AOK 1 24906/19 file; *Mit Kleist in den Kaukasus,* Pz. AOK 1 85602 file.

heads at Tsimlyanskiy, Nikolayevskaya, and Konstantinovskiy on the 21st and a day later had one at the mouth of the Sal River, taken by the Grossdeutschland Division. The two at Nikolayevskaya and Konstantinovskiy were joined on the 23d and expanded south twenty miles to Bolshaya Orlovka on the Sal, but Hoth was still short of being ready to make a long sweep to the west and south. Losing two corps headquarters and six divisions had weakened his flank on the east, and on the 22d, Hitler had also transferred Headquarters, XXIV Panzer Corps and the 24th Panzer Division to Sixth Army.[22] The Germans were beginning to feel the effects of operating simultaneously in two directions.

On the Road to Stalingrad

Sixth Army, after a ten-day hiatus, had the strength to come back into the offensive in earnest. Its opposition in the Don bend was still weak, but it was increasing. *Sixty-second Army* had 6 rifle divisions, a tank brigade, and 6 independent tank battalions on its half of the line, and *Sixty-fourth Army* had 2 rifle divisions and a tank brigade. Between the Volga and the Don, *Fifty-seventh Army* was being reformed as the *front* reserve and the Headquarters, *Thirty-eighth* and *Twenty-eighth Armies*, together with those of their troops that had survived, were being used as cadres for building the *First* and *Fourth Tank Armies*. East of the Don, virtually the whole able-bodied population of Stalingrad was at work simultaneously building four concentric defense lines around the city. The *Stavka* had given

Eighth Air Army, which was supporting *Stalingrad Front*, 10 air regiments with 200 planes. On the 23d, General Leytenant V. N. Gordov, who had been commanding general, *Twenty-first Army* and had nominally commanded *Sixty-fourth Army* for a few days, replaced Timoshenko as commander of *Stalingrad Front*.[23] On that same day, Paulus submitted his plan to take the city. He proposed to sweep to the Don on both sides of Kalach, take bridgeheads on the run, and then drive a wedge of armor flanked by infantry across the remaining thirty miles.[24]

Sixth Army had been running into and over *Sixty-second* and *Sixty-fourth Armies'* outposts since the 17th without knowing it. On the 23d, it did notice a change when it hit their main line east of the Chir. The VIII Corps, on the north, encountered several Soviet rifle divisions in the morning, and those delayed its march east four or five hours. The XIV Panzer Corps, bearing in toward Kalach, reported 200 enemy tanks in its path and knocked out 40 during the day. (If the German tally after this date of the numbers of Soviet tanks was anywhere near accurate, more tank units must have been in the field than are given in the Soviet accounts.) On the 24th, VIII Corps cleared the northern quarter of the Don bend except for a Soviet bridgehead at Serafimovich and another around Kremenskaya and Sirotinskaya. To the south, as the daily report put it, Sixth Army "consolidated," because XIV Panzer Corps ran out of motor fuel and the infantry could not

---

[22]*H. Gr. A, Ia Kriegstagebuch, Band I, Teil I,* 21–25 Jul 42, H. Gr. A 75126/1 file.

[23]*IVOVSS,* vol. II, pp. 426–28; *IVMV,* vol. V, p. 157; *VOV (Kratkaya Istoriya),* pp. 168–70.

[24]*AOK 6, Ia Kriegstagebuch Nr. 13,* 23 Jul 42, AOK 6 23948/11 file.

make headway against stiffening resistance north and east of Kalach. The next day, while XIV Panzer Corps was still waiting to refuel, 60 Soviet tanks cut the road behind it, and 3d and 60th Motorized Divisions, the ones closest to Kalach, became entangled with 200 Soviet tanks. The army chief of staff told the army group operations chief, "For the moment a certain crisis has developed." At the day's end, XIV Panzer, LI, and XXIV Panzer Corps were ranged shoulder to shoulder on the Stalingrad axis, but the Russians were still holding a forty-mile-wide and twenty-mile-deep bridgehead from Kalach to Nizhne Chirskaya.[25]

Directive 45 —Order No. 227

Hitler Divides His Forces

The battle for the line of the Don was joined everywhere downstream from Serafimovich on 25 July. Under the original BLAU concept, which had partially reemerged in the orders given during the previous week, the next stage would have been to establish a secure north flank anchored on the Volga at Stalingrad. During the day on the 25th, Directive 45 reached Army Groups A and B. It was entitled "for the continuation of Operation BRAUN-SCHWEIG [BLAU]." However, the opening sentences indicated that the primary objective, the "conclusive destruction of the Soviet defensive strength," was already accomplished. The sentences read: "In a little more than three weeks the deep objectives I set for the south flank of the Eastern Front have in substance been reached. Only weak enemy forces have suc-

ceeded in escaping encirclement and reaching the south bank of the Don." The intent of the directive was not to continue BRAUNSCHWEIG but to complete it, in one swoop, by conducting what was left of BLAU II (Stalingrad) simultaneously with BLAU IV (the Caucasus and the Caspian oil fields).

What had been BLAU IV was for the first time spelled out, and it was assigned to Army Group A as Operation EDELWEISS. It was to be carried out in three stages. In the first, "the enemy forces that have escaped across the Don" would be "encircled and destroyed south and southeast of Rostov." The envelopment would be formed by Seventeenth Army's infantry on the west and First and Fourth Panzer Armies' armor on the east, and the ring would be closed ninety miles south of Rostov, near Tikhoretsk. Army Group A would concentrate in the second stage on clearing the Black Sea coast to eliminate the Soviet Navy, while at the same time employing "all the excess mountain and Jaeger divisions" to take the high ground around Maykop and Armavir and close the passes in the western Caucasus. In the third stage, a mobile force would head south and east to close the Ossetian and Grusinian Military Roads (across the Caucasus), take Groznyy, and strike along the Caspian coast to Baku. All three appeared to be so well within Army Group A's capabilities that the Grossdeutschland Division could be taken out and shipped to the Western Theater and Operation BLUECHER, the crossing from the Crimea to the Taman Peninsula, could be reduced to a much smaller BLUECHER II. Consequently, five of Eleventh Army's seven German divisions were to be shifted to Army

---

[25]*Ibid.*, 23–25 Jul 42.

SOVIET ANTITANK GUN CREW COMES UNDER FIRE

Group North for an attack on Leningrad.

Under the code name FISCHREIHER ("heron"), Army Group B would retain the two missions it already had, namely, to defend the line of the Don and to take Stalingrad. After it had possession of Stalingrad and had set up a solid front between the Don and the Volga, it would dispatch a mobile force downstream along the Volga to take Astrakhan. The *Luftwaffe* would assist FISCHREIHER by "timely destruction of Stalingrad."[26]

In Directive 45, Hitler committed the cardinal tactical sin of splitting his forces and sending them off in two directions at right angles to each other. Henceforth they would be conducting separate campaigns, each having to be sustained independently without either being fully independent. The effects were already beginning to be felt by both. The railroad between Millerovo and Kamensk-Shakhtinskiy was the only one taken reasonably intact, and the forces were having to share the motor transport out of the Kamensk-Shakhtinskiy railhead. Whatever one received, no matter how inadequate it might have been, was always somewhat at the other's expense.[27]

Sixth Army felt the pinch first. Short on motor fuel and ammunition for two days and not likely to get a full re-

[26]OKW, WFSt, Op. Nr. 551288/42, Weisung Nr. 45 fuer die Fortsetzung der Operation "Braunschweig," 23.7.42, German High Level Directives, CMH files.

[27]Pz. AOK 1, O. Qu., Qu. 1 Nr. 647/42, Beurteilung der Versorgungslage, 29.7.42, Pz. AOK 1 24906/53.

plenishment for at least the next several, Paulus had to pull his spearhead around Kalach back on the 26th. Half of his daily supply tonnage was going to Army Group A that had divisions closer to the railhead and higher priority under Directive 45. By the 28th, Sixth Army was almost on the defensive, and XIV Panzer Corps was down to 100 rounds of artillery ammunition per battery and half of a normal load per tank.[28] At the *Werwolf,* Sixth Army's fuel trouble put Hitler into a state of "great agitation," and Halder confided to his diary that this was "intolerable grumbling" over mistakes the *Fuehrer* had provoked by his own previous orders.[29]

Army Group A's armies were no better supplied, particularly with motor fuel and ammunition, than Sixth Army was. They had panzer and motorized divisions standing all around Rostov and along the lower Don with nearly empty tanks. They had covered much more distance faster than had been anticipated in calculating the supply schedule, and First Panzer Army had had to relinquish 750 tons of transport to help get Sixth Army moving after the 19th.[30] One complication Army Group A did not have to be concerned with was enemy resistance. Except at Fourth Panzer Army's bridgeheads, most notable the one at Tsimlyanskiy, the Russians were not showing any sign of even attempting to make a stand.

List's problems were to get his divisions sorted out and refueled—and then to determine where they should go. The OKH told him on the 27th not to let Seventeenth Army, which being mostly infantry was in the best condition to advance, go too fast south of Rostov because that might push the enemy east before First and Fourth Panzer Armies could make the sweep to Tikhoretsk and complete the encirclement specified in Directive 45. But List did not believe there was going to be an encirclement, especially not after Ruoff told him that the Russians were already in full retreat ahead of Seventeenth Army without having been pushed. Later in the day, List met with Kleist and Hoth at Kleist's headquarters in Krasnyy Sulin, north of Rostov. The three agreed that the Russians were not going to let themselves be encircled and, therefore, First and Fourth Panzer Armies ought not to bear southwest toward Tikhoretsk but due south and southeast. List, however, regarded himself as bound by Directive 45.[31]

On the 28th, Seventeenth Army reached and crossed the Kagalnik River, twenty miles south of Rostov, and First Panzer Army took a bridgehead on the Manich. The Manich, though, was going to be troublesome. It was a river emptying into the lower Don that had been converted into a canal by damming and some canalization. The dams, which had sizable lakes behind them, were upstream from First Panzer Army's crossing point. The Russians had opened the dams; the river was flooding; and, except for some infantry and engineers in the

---

[28]*AOK 6, Ia Kriegstagebuch Nr. 13,* 26–28 Jul 42, AOK 6 23948/11 file.

[29]*Halder Diary,* vol. III, p. 493.

[30]*Pz. AOK 1, O. Qu. Kriegstagebuch, 1.4.–31.10.42,* 25 Jul 42, Pz. AOK 1 24906/52 file.

[31]*H. Gr. A, Ia Kriegstagebuch, Band I, Teil I,* 27 Jul 42, H. Gr. A 75126/1 file; *Pz. AOK 1, Ia Kriegstagebuch Nr. 8,* 27 Jul 42, Pz. AOK 1 24906 file.

bridgehead, all of First Panzer Army was on the north side.

"Not a Step Back!"

While Army Group A's situation on 28 July was not entirely satisfactory, and Sixth Army's was less so, the condition of their opponents was worse. The Soviet armies did not have a trace of a genuine front anywhere south of the Don bend. A. A. Grechko—then a major general and commander of the *Twelfth Army* and after the war, a Soviet marshal, defense minister, and historian of the Caucasus campaign—has written, "By the end of the day of 28 July there were huge gaps between the armies. The defensive front was cracked."[32] The strategic retreat was in danger of becoming a rout.

On 28 July, Stalin, as people's commissar of defense, signed Order No. 227. Under its familiar name, *"Ni shagu nazad!"* ("Not a step back!"), it is regarded in the Soviet literature as a successful impetus to the Soviet Army's will to fight. In part, its most frequently quoted passages read:

Every commander, soldier, and political worker must understand that our resources are not unlimited. . . . After losing the Ukraine, Belorussia, the Baltic, the Don Basin, and other areas we now have a much smaller territory, fewer people and factories, less grain and metal. We have lost more than 70 million persons, over 800 million *pud* [14.5 million tons] of grain per year, and more than 10 million tons of metals per year. We no longer have superiority over the Germans either in manpower reserves or in grain stocks. To retreat farther is to cast oneself and the Homeland into ruin. Every clod of earth we give up strengthens the enemy and weakens our defense and our nation.

Not a step back! Such must be our highest purpose now.[33]

The *History of the Second World War* indicates that Order No. 227 was more than a patriotic appeal. "This order," it states, "contained the harsh truth about the dangerous situation on the Soviet-German front, condemned 'voices of retreat,' and pointed out the necessity to use all means to stop the advance of the fascist-German troops. It threatened all of those who showed themselves cowardly or unspirited in battle with the most severe punishments and projected practical measures to raise the fighting spirit of the soldiers and strengthen their discipline." The order, the history continues, " . . . was an extraordinary measure. The Central Committee of the Communist Party of the Soviet Union and the military leadership undertook this step in view of the difficult situation that had come to exist. They utilized the experiences of the party in the years of the Civil War and let themselves be guided by V. I. Lenin's advice that the party must resort to extraordinary measures when conditions demand it."[34]

The Soviet accounts do not give the whole *Ni shagu nazad!* order. A full text has survived in the German records, however. In it, the "harsh truth" includes the following:

The people of the nation, who have looked on the Red Army with love and respect, are disillusioned. They are losing faith in you. Many of them curse the Red Army because it is abandoning our people to the yoke of the German oppressors and itself fleeing to the east.

---

[32]Grechko, *Gody voyny,* p. 190.

[33]*IVOVSS*, vol. II, p. 430; *IVMV*, vol. V, p. 166.
[34]*Ibid.*, p. 165.

Another passage indicates that the order stemmed from Hitler's example of December 1941 as well as from Lenin's precept and the experience of the Civil War. It read:

The German troops were forced to retreat in the winter under the pressure of the Red Army. Their discipline was shattered. Then the Germans resorted to severe measures, and those have not shown bad results.

As is well known, those measures have had their effect, and the German troops now fight better than they did in the winter. The German troops now have good discipline even though they do not have before them the lofty mission of defending their homeland and have only the predatory objective of occupying enemy territory.

The "punishments and practical measures to raise the fighting spirit" were given as follows:

In each *front* area, from one to three punishment battalions of five hundred men each are to be created. Into them are to be placed all intermediate and senior commanders and political officers of comparable ranks who have shown themselves guilty of cowardice, of not preserving discipline, or of not maintaining resistance to the enemy. They will be committed in especially dangerous situations so that they may expiate their crimes against the homeland with their blood.

Corps and division commanders who allow troops to retreat without an order from the army commander are to be unconditionally removed. They will be turned over to the military councils of the *fronts* to be condemned by court martials.

In each army area, three to five well-armed blocking detachments of approximately two hundred men are to be created. They will be stationed directly behind unreliable divisions, and it will be their duty, in the event of panics or unauthorized retreats, to shoot spreaders of panic or cowards on the spot.

In each army area three to five punish-ment companies of one hundred fifty to two hundred men are to be created in which all enlisted men and junior officers are to be placed who are guilty of cowardice, not preserving discipline, or of failing to maintain resistance to the enemy. They will be committed in especially dangerous situations so that they may expiate their crimes against their homeland with their blood.[35]

The Missions Revised

Army Group A's biggest—and virtually only—troubles in the last three days of July were supplies and the Manich. The panzer divisions were having to be given motor fuel by airlifts to keep them from running dry. The flooded Manich was more than a mile wide, and water seeping outward was turning the ground on both sides to mud. The troops were having to manhandle and ferry their equipment across in intense summer heat. The Soviet resistance, though, if anything, was on the decline. First Panzer Army described the enemy ahead of it as being "in wild flight."[36] An intercepted Soviet radio message read, "We are going back. No reprisals (against the troops) work any more."[37] Seventeenth Army reached the Yeya River, forty miles south of Rostov; First Panzer Army had a spearhead fifty miles past the Manich and halfway to the Kuban River; and Fourth Panzer Army crossed the Salsk-Stalingrad railroad at Prolyetarskaya and Remontnaya. On the 29th, List asked the OKH to cancel

---

[35]*Pz. AOK 1, Ic Nr. 6329/42, Feindnachrichtenblatt Nr. 69, Anlage Nr. 6, 22.8.42, Pz. AOK 1 24906/29 file.*

[36]*Pz. AOK 1, Ia Kriegstagebuch Nr. 8,* 29 Jul 42, Pz. AOK 1 24906 file.

[37]*H. Gr. A, Ia Kriegstagebuch, Band I, Teil 1,* 30 Jul 42, H. Gr. A 75126/1 file.

the projected encirclement at Tikhoretsk because he was sure there would not be any Russians there.[38]

Sixth Army's fuel and ammunition drought continued as did the tempestuous Soviet counterattacks along the Kalach bridgehead, and Paulus was feeling pinched for infantry. Some help for the latter problem was on the way in the form of the Italian Eighth Army, which had earlier been attached to Seventeenth Army but had not been needed in the advance on Rostov. Eighth Army, with its six sonorously named divisions, Celere, Ravenna, Torino, Cosseria, Sforzesca, and Pasubio, was on the march via Millerovo to take over the Don front between Pavlovsk and the mouth of the Khoper River, which would let Paulus bring two of his infantry divisions east. In part, Sixth Army's continuing ammunition shortage was caused by the extraordinarily large numbers of Soviet tanks it was meeting in the Kalach bridgehead. The tally of XIV Panzer Corps alone ran to 482 tanks knocked out in the last eight days of the month, and the total Sixth Army claimed was well over 600.[39]

The Soviet accounts confirm that strong tank forces were in the Kalach bridgehead, but not as many tanks as Sixth Army claimed. General Mayor K. S. Moskalenko, who had taken command of *First Tank Army* three days before, began the counterattack on 25 July, with General Vasilevskiy present as *Stavka* representative. The army, Moskalenko says, had *XIII* and *XXVIII Tank Corps* (with just over three hundred tanks) and one rifle division. *Fourth Tank Army,* under General Mayor V. D. Kruchenkin, joined in on the 28th with one tank corps.[40]

Active as it was, the Soviet armor was apparently not giving fully satisfactory performance at this stage, and in early August, it became the subject of the following Stalin order:

Our armored forces and their units frequently suffer greater losses through mechanical breakdowns than they do in battle. For example, at Stalingrad Front in six days twelve of our tank brigades lost 326 out of their 400 tanks. Of those about 260 owed to mechanical problems. Many of the tanks were abandoned on the battlefield. Similar instances can be observed on other fronts.

Since such a high incidence of mechanical defects is implausible, the Supreme Headquarters sees in it covert sabotage and wrecking by certain elements in the tank crews who try to exploit small mechanical troubles to avoid battle.

Henceforth, every tank leaving the battlefield for alleged mechanical reasons was to be gone over by technicians, and if sabotage was suspected, the crews were to be put into tank punishment companies or "degraded to the infantry" and put into infantry punishment companies.[41]

The plans as outlined in Directive 45, which was just going on a week old, were coming unraveled at the end of the month. At the situation conference on the 20th, General Jodl, chief of the OKW Operations Staff, announced, "in portentious tones" according to

---

[38]*Ibid.*, 29 Jul 42.

[39]*AOK 6, Ia Kriegstagebuch Nr. 13,* 29 Jul–1 Aug 42, AOK 6 23948/11 file.

[40]Moskalenko, *Na yugo-zapodnom napravlenii,* pp. 263–80; *IVOVSS,* vol. II, p. 429.

[41]*Pz. AOK 1, Ic Nr. 6868/42, Feindnachrichtenblatt Nr. 70, Anlage Nr. 6, Befehl Nr. 156595 vom 10.8.42, 22.9.42,* Pz. AOK 1 24906/29 file.

ABANDONED T–34 TANK PROVIDES COVER FOR A GERMAN OBSERVER

Halder, that the fate of the Caucasus would be decided at Stalingrad, and therefore some of Army Group A's strength would have to be shifted to Sixth Army. On the whole, though, Halder was gratified at this thought's having finally arisen in "the brilliant society of the OKW." On the other hand, General Jodl still wanted to have First Panzer Army turn west and make the Tikhoretsk encirclement, which Halder thought was "vapid nonsense." "The enemy," he maintained, "is running as fast as he can run and will be on the north slope of the Caucasus ahead of our mobile units."[42] List, when Halder talked to him, of course, did not oppose abandoning the Tikhoretsk encirclement, but he did oppose giving up part of his strength to Sixth Army. It would be "a great gamble," he insisted, to send a "relatively weak force" deep into the Caucasus. In response, with less than faultless logic, Halder argued that it would at least mitigate the supply problems. Finally, Halder added that the Grossdeutschland Division, which List wanted to keep as a mobile reserve, would probably also have to go because Hitler had repeatedly said it would do him no good to win victories in the East if he lost the West.[43]

[42]*Halder Diary,* vol. III, p. 494.

[43]*H. Gr. A, Ia Kriegstagebuch, Band I, Teil I,* 30 Jul 42, H. Gr. A 75126/1 file.

During the day on the 31st, Hitler revised Directive 45. The cutting of the railroad between Stalingrad and the Caucasus, he said, had "torn to pieces" the enemy front south of the Don. Soviet forces would still make an effort to defend the Caucasus, but "no reinforcements worth mentioning" could get there from the interior of the Soviet Union. On the other hand, the enemy would throw "every bit of available strength" into the Stalingrad area to hold open his "vital artery," the Volga. Therefore, Headquarters, Fourth Panzer Army with XXXXVIII Panzer Corps, IV Corps, and Rumanian VI Corps would be transferred to Army Group B. The Grossdeutschland Division would be left with Army Group A approximately eight more days, two weeks at the most. Army Group B's mission was not changed. Army Group A's "next and most important assignment" would be to take possession of the Black Sea coast to eliminate the Soviet Navy and to open sea-lanes for its own supplies. The Tikhoretsk encirclement disappeared, but First Panzer Army, while sending detachments southeastward to Voroshilovsk and Petrovskoye, was still to bear mostly toward the southwest toward Maykop "to waylay the enemy retreating to the Caucasus." From Maykop, it would dispatch elements west to Tuapse on the Black Sea coast and south along the coast to Batumi.[44]

The revisions of the 31st completed the division of the offensive initiated in Directive 45. Fourth Panzer Army, which had provided a link between the two army groups, was split. Hoth would take his headquarters and three corps north toward Stalingrad. One of his former corps, XXXX Panzer, would go south with First Panzer Army. Army Group A had been weakened, and Army Group B had been strengthened, but Jodl was right when he said the fate of the Caucasus would be decided at Stalingrad. What remained to be seen was whether Army Group B's gain (four German and four Rumanian Divisions) would be enough to ensure the outcome.

---

[44]OKH, GenStdH, Op. Abt. (I) Nr. 420573/42, an H. Gr. A und H. Gr. B, 31.7.42, H 22/216 file.

CHAPTER XVIII

Operation EDELWEISS

The Kuban and the Caucasus

"Sunflower" would have been a more appropriate code name than EDEL- WEISS, if such had been desired. The region Army Group A had entered into south of the Don was one of sun- flowers, grain, and oil—but also of desert, mountains, few railroads, and hardly any roads worthy of the name. Between the Kuban River and the Don and from the Black Sea coast inland to the headwaters of the Kuban the land was as productive as any in Europe. At first glance, the agricultural specialists attached to the army group estimated the crops standing in the fields would be enough to feed the troops and the population and leave a substantial sur- plus for export to Germany. Not easily impressed by Soviet farming methods, they were awed by the model state farm "Gigant," located near Salsk, which had three-quarters of a million acres and its own laboratories, shops, and process- ing plants.[1] From the upper reaches of the Kuban and east of Salsk to the Caspian shore, however, the land shaded off rapidly into desert where survival, even for a modern army, could depend on widely scattered wells and water holes. Much of the territory, particularly in the east and south of the Kuban and in the mountains was in-

habited by non-Slavic peoples, the Kal- myks, Adygei, Cherkess, Kabardins, Chechens, Ingush, Karachai, Balkars, and Ossetians. They were fiercely inde- pendent Moslem tribes who had not been brought into the Russian empire until the nineteenth century, had been restive under the tsars, and for re- ligious and other reasons had no taste at all for the Soviet regime.[2]

The oil, which Army Group A hoped would sustain its own operations and from which Hitler expected to fuel the entire *Wehrmacht,* was produced in fields situated at and to the southwest of Maykop, around Groznyy, and near Baku on the Caspian coast. These were the summer's ultimate strategic objec- tives because of their value to the Ger- man war effort and the presumed effect of their loss on the Soviet ability to resist. Although after the march to the Don they appeared to be easily within grasp, the actual distances the Germans would have to go to reach them were enormous. In straight lines, not taking into account mountains, rivers, deserts, road conditions, or tac- tically required twists and turns, May- kop was 180 miles from Rostov; Groznyy was 400; and Baku 700. The last was somewhat more than the whole distance of the advance across the So- viet Union to Rostov.

---

[1] *Pz. AOK 1, Ia Kriegstagebuch Nr. 8, 5 Aug 42,* Pz. AOK 1 24906 file.

[2] See R. Conquest, *The Soviet Deportation of Na- tionalities* (London: Macmillan & Co., 1960), pp. 1–41.

SOVIET MACHINE GUNNERS DUG-IN OUTSIDE NOVOROSSIYSK

North Caucasus Front

The greatest advantage Army Group A had at the beginning of August was that the Soviet grip on this vast area, for the moment, was weak. The armies defending it were, in the most part, shattered remnants of past defeats. On 28 July, the *Stavka* had merged what was left of *South Front* into the *North Caucasus Front* under Marshal Budenny. He then had the *Twenty-fourth, Ninth, Thirty-seventh, Fifty-sixth, Twelfth, Eighteenth, Fifty-first,* and *Forty-seventh Armies* and one independent infantry corps and a cavalry corps. Six of the eight armies had made the retreat to the Don, and two, *Ninth* and *Twenty-fourth,* were so far gone that they had to be sent to the rear to be rebuilt. Two,

Forty-seventh and *Fifty-first Armies,* had been resurrected after the defeat on the Kerch Peninsula in May.

Having better than 250 miles on an almost quarter-circle arc to cover, Budenny had been compelled to divide his forces into a *Maritime Operational Group* under General Cherevichenko and a *Don Operational Group* under General Malinovskiy. The *Maritime Group,* with *Eighteenth, Fifty-sixth,* and *Forty-seventh Armies* and the two separate corps, was considerably the stronger, and its mission was to cover Krasnodar and the Black Sea naval bases at Novorossiysk and Tuapse. The Don Group had *Fifty-first, Thirty-seventh,* and *Twelfth Armies* and theoretical responsibility for the whole sweep of territory east of Krasnodar. By 31 July, *Fifty-first*

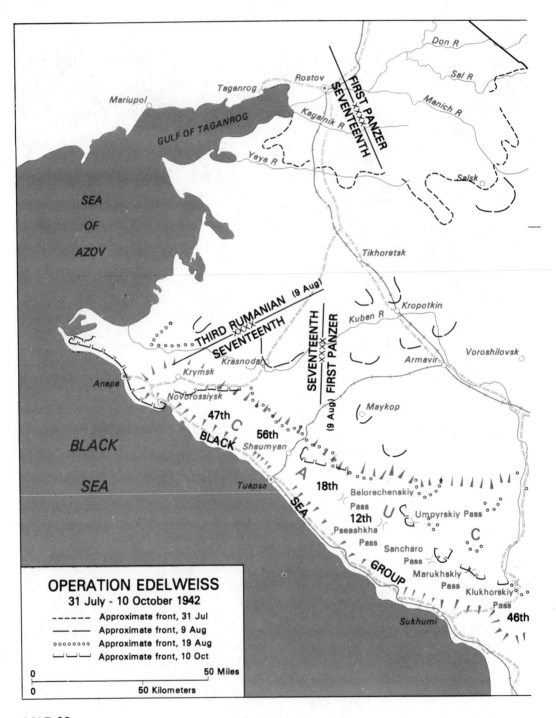

Don R

Sal R

Manich R

Mariupol

Taganrog

Rostov

FIRST PANZER
XXXX
SEVENTEENTH

Kagalnik R

GULF OF TAGANROG

Yeya R

Salsk

SEA

OF

AZOV

Tikhoretsk

Kropotkin

Kuban R

THIRD RUMANIAN (9 Aug)
XXXX
SEVENTEENTH

SEVENTEENTH
XXXX
FIRST PANZER
(9 Aug)

Voroshilovsk

Armavir

Krasnodar

Krymsk

Anapa

Maykop

Novorossiysk

47th   C

BLACK   BLACK

56th

Shaumyan

A

SEA

Tuapse

18th

U   Umpyrskiy Pass

Belorechenskiy
Pass

12th

Pseashkha
Pass

C

Sancharo
Pass

Marukhskiy
Pass

Klukhorskiy
Pass

GROUP

Sukhumi

46th

MAP 32

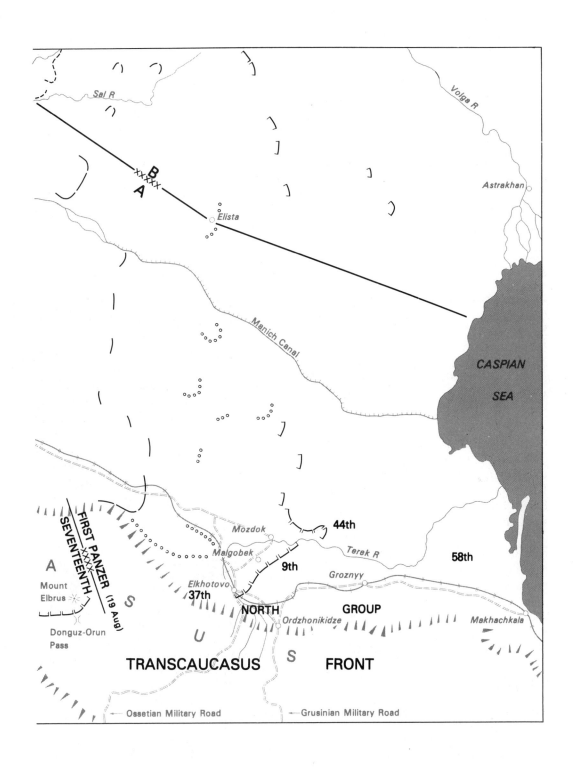

Sal R

Volga R

XXXX B
A XXXX

Astrakhan

Elista

Manich Canal

CASPIAN

SEA

44th

Mozdok

Terek R

58th

Malgobek

FIRST PANZER
SEVENTEENTH (19 Aug)

9th

Groznyy

A

Mount
Elbrus

S

Elkhotovo
37th

NORTH

Ordzhonikidze

GROUP

Makhachkala

U

Donguz-Orun
Pass

S

TRANSCAUCASUS

FRONT

←Ossetian Military Road   ←Grusinian Military Road

Army had been pushed away to the northeast, and it was then transferred to *Stalingrad Front.*[3]

Behind *North Caucasus Front*, General Tyulenev's *Transcaucasus Front* had *Forty-fifth* and *Forty-sixth Armies* and another of the Kerch armies, *Forty-fourth,* with which to hold the Black Sea coast from Tuapse to Batumi, the mountain passes, and the Turkish border and to defend the approaches to Baku on the Caspian. To do the latter, Tyulenev proposed to install *Forty-fourth Army* in a line on the Terek River and back it with a second line on the Sudak River.[4]

To the Caucasus

Even though Fourth Panzer Army broke contact and turned away toward Stalingrad, Army Group A only had one real problem in the first week of August, and that was to get enough gasoline and diesel oil to sustain the speed it was capable of achieving. On the 4th, General List, the commander of Army Group A, submitted a sweeping optimistic prediction: the enemy command most likely had in mind making a stand south of the Kuban River to protect Maykop and the naval bases, but the troops were "dispensing with any sort of unified command," and it could be assumed "that a fast thrust to the southeast with sufficient mobile forces will not encounter serious enemy resistance anywhere forward of Baku."[5] The succeeding days seemed to bear him out convincingly. Seventeenth Army, which had Rumanian Third Army coming along behind

it to guard the coast, reported the enemy retreating faster than before. First Panzer Army had a bridgehead on the Kuban; on the 5th it threw a bridge across the river and captured fifty-one loaded trains on the Kropotkin-Armavir railline south of the river. *(Map 32.)* The army group readied the Headquarters, XXXXIX Mountain Corps to take over the advance into the mountains south of Armavir. On the 6th, Seventeenth Army's infantry gained an astonishing thirty miles. In crossing the Kuban, First Panzer Army forced *Twelfth Army* westward into the area of the *Maritime Group,* thereby reducing Malinovskiy's *Don Group* to a single army, *Thirty-seventh.*[6]

In one respect, however, List's prediction was already beginning to break down. Off his left flank, on the Terek River, at the behest of the *Stavka, Transcaucasus Front* was building a *North Group,* under General Maslennikov, around *Forty-fourth Army* and Headquarters, *Ninth Army.* The *North Group* was not a force of much consequence for the moment, but seven divisions and four brigades were coming north from the Turkish border, and the *Stavka* was sending two guards rifle corps (seven brigades) and eleven separate rifle brigades by rail to Astrakhan and thence by sea to Makhachkala.[7] Army Group A's race to the sea would not be uncontested.

But what the Russians were doing on the Terek could not help them on the Kuban. First Panzer Army was across the river in strength and bearing west toward Maykop, guided night and day

[3]*IVMV,* vol. V, p. 209.
[4]Grechko, *Gody voyny,* p. 234.
[5]*H. Gr. A, Ia Kriegstagebuch, Band I, Teil II,* 4 Aug 42, H. Gr. A 75126/2 file.

[6]*Ibid.,* 4–6 Aug 42; Andrei Grechko, *Battle for the Caucasus* (Moscow: Progress Publishers, 1971), p. 67.
[7]Grechko, *Gody voyny,* p. 239.

by sheets of flame thousands of feet high: the oil refineries and tank farms were burning. The 9th was a day of almost nothing but good news for Army Group A. In hundred-degree heat and a swirling dust storm, Seventeenth Army took Krasnodar on the north bank of the Kuban while First Panzer Army passed through Maykop and into the oil fields, where it was disappointed to find the above ground equipment thoroughly wrecked but relieved to see that the wells were not on fire. Air reconnaissance reported heavy Soviet columns streaming south, and List concluded that the enemy had probably given up all thought of staging strong resistance anywhere north of the main Caucasus range. Seventeenth Army was encountering more of a fight on the Kuban than it had anywhere else on the 140-mile march from Rostov; nevertheless, the army group's most urgent problem had nothing in particular to do with the enemy but resulted from its orders under Directive 45. Almost the whole weight of First Panzer Army was being drawn to its right flank, and, as had happened at Rostov two weeks earlier, this development was creating a pileup of divisions around Maykop.[8]

This time, though, List and his staff, who earlier had let themselves be governed entirely by instructions from the OKH, had ready a plan of their own: one which would preserve the "intent" of Directive 45, stop the westward pull on First Panzer Army, under General Kleist, and make it possible to go after the opportunities beckoning in the east. It would also create another major

division in the offensive, but that appeared to be an acceptable price for the advantages gained. The plan was to reorganize and, by transferring LVII Panzer Corps and XXXXIV Corps, both of which were in the Maykop area, from First Panzer to Seventeenth Army, to make General Ruoff responsible for cleaning out the Black Sea coast and release Kleist to head east to Groznyy, Makhachkala, and Baku.

The mountains presented the one complication. The passes to the west of Mount Elbrus offered shortcuts, although somewhat arduous ones, to the coast between Tuapse and Sukhumi, and opening them would both assist and secure Seventeenth Army's advance. East of Elbrus, the Grusinian and Ossetian Military Roads gave potential access to the Transcaucasus, and First Panzer Army would have to control them before it could continue past Groznyy to Makhachkala and Baku. To make the march into the mountains, the army group had Headquarters, XXXXIX Mountain Corps, two German mountain divisions, and one Rumanian mountain division. List wanted to put the corps headquarters, one of the German divisions, and the Rumanian division west of Elbrus and leave the other German division for the military roads. The OKH approved the plan in general, but Hitler insisted on having both German mountain divisions west of Elbrus, which left First Panzer Army, as Kleist later put it, with "a single untried foreign division" to execute a very critical mission.[9]

The reorganization was to take effect

[8]*H. Gr. A, Ia Kriegstagebuch, Band I, Teil II*, 7–9 Aug 42, H. Gr. A 75126/2 file.

[9]*H. Gr. A, Ia Nr. 656/42, an Pz. AOK 1, 11.8.42*, Pz. AOK 1 24906/1 file; *H. Gr. A, Ia Kriegstagebuch, Band I, Teil II*, 9–12 Aug 42, H. Gr. A 75126/2 file.

as soon as First Panzer Army had full possession of the Maykop oil fields and Seventeenth Army had cleared the lower Kuban, which apparently would happen in a few days but turned out to take longer. Both armies found the going slower as they hit into the outlying mountains, which although they were not nearly as high as the main range, were steep and cut by heavily wooded gorges. South of Krasnodar and along the Kuban River east of the city, Seventeenth Army not only had to contend with mountainous terrain but, for the first time since it crossed the Don, met concerted Soviet resistance and had to go over to a methodical attack.

But the unexpected slowdown was accompanied by an unanticipated success. On the 12th, XXXXIX Mountain Corps plunged into the mountains south of Armavir and in four days was engaging Soviet rear guards at the important Klukhorskiy Pass, thirty miles west of Mount Elbrus, and was forming a party to climb Elbrus (18,481 feet) and plant a swastika flag at the summit (which was done on 21 August). If the mountain troops reached the coast near Sukhumi, they would undermine the entire Soviet defense north to Novorossiysk. To assist in exploiting that prospect, the army group dispatched two battalions of special high-mountain troops in motor buses from Stalino.[10]

The advance into the mountains was a tremendous shock for the Soviet Command. They had been presumed to be reasonably easy to defend. *Transcaucasus Front* had *Forty-sixth Army* to

man the passes and the military roads, and it had supposedly been at work fortifying them since June. According to all the postwar Soviet accounts the blame for the failure to make a better initial showing rested with *Transcaucasus Front*—for complacency—and on *Forty-sixth Army*—for general ineptitude in mountain warfare.

Another, and different, problem is seldom alluded to and then obliquely as follows:

The Fascist invaders placed great hopes in the instability of the Soviet rear area in the Caucasus. They estimated that as soon as the German forces broke through into the Caucasus, violence and uprisings would begin among its inhabitants. In order to facilitate this, Hitler's intelligence attempted to establish agent operations among the nationalistic elements in the Caucasus both prior to and during the offensive.[11]

There were, as far as the Germans knew, no actual uprisings, but many of the mountain peoples welcomed the invaders as liberators. No doubt, a good part of the German mountain troops' early success depended upon the availability of willing native guides. Some men from the region, who had been taken prisoner earlier in the war, were already enlisted in the German service, and the high-mountain battalions had with them platoons of Cherkess, Chechens, and Dagestani.[12]

The crisis in the Caucasus brought a sinister figure to *Transcaucasus Front*, People's Commissar of Internal Affairs, Lavrenti Beria, the head of the secret political police. Beria came as a

[10]*H. Gr. A, Ia Kriegstagebuch, Band I, Teil II*, 12–17 Aug 42, H. Gr. A 75126/2 file.

[11]*IVOVSS*, vol. II, p. 455.
[12]*Pz. AOK 1, Ia Kriegstagebuch Nr. 8*, 16 and 18 Aug 42, Pz. AOK 1 24906 file.

Stavka representative. For a time, he apparently tried to take personal command of the mountain defenses, but his primary job was to hold the population in line, which he and his NKVD troops, of whom many were stationed in the Caucasus border area, did thoroughly and ruthlessly.[13]

Tuapse and the Terek

The Tempo Slows

When Seventeenth Army reached Krymsk, halfway between the Kuban and Novorossiysk, on 17 August, List issued a directive putting the army group reorganization into effect the next day. Seventeenth Army then became responsible for all of the territory west of Mount Elbrus, and it acquired three interim missions. One was to complete the advance to Novorossiysk with its original forces; another to thrust along the road running southwest out of Maykop to Tuapse with the two corps taken over from First Panzer Army; and the third to push XXXXIX Mountain Corps through the passes and down the south slope of the mountains to Sukhumi. First Panzer Army, which had XXXX Panzer Corps approaching the Terek River and III Panzer Corps coming in from the northwest, had as its next missions to cross the Terek, take Ordzhonikidze and Groznyy, and open the Grusinian Military Road.[14]

None of the missions looked impossible or even very difficult. Seventeenth Army had twenty-five miles to go to

GERMAN 75-MM. ANTITANK GUN IN THE CAUCASUS FOOTHILLS

Novorossiysk and about the same to Tuapse. The approach to Sukhumi depended on which of a dozen passes was used. List and Ruoff preferred the Klukhorskiy Pass which was roughly fifty miles northeast of Sukhumi and necessitated a substantial bend to the east but offered a route that could be used by motor vehicles over most of its length while the others were only accessible to men and pack animals. First Panzer Army's point nearing the Terek was about sixty-five miles from Ordzhonikidze, ninety from Groznyy.

But the tempo was changing. By the 18th, the days of thirty-mile advances were already just a memory, and five miles a day or less was the rule. Thereafter, local gains of a mile or two began to be considered significant, particularly in the Seventeenth Army area.

---

[13]Erickson, *Road to Stalingrad*, p. 378; Seweryn Bialer, *Stalin and His Generals* (New York: Pegasus, 1969), p. 451.

[14]*H. Gr. A, Ia Kriegstagebuch, Band I, Teil II*, 17 Aug 42, H. Gr. A 75126/2 file.

GERMAN MOUNTAIN TROOPS IN THE SANCHARO PASS

The V Corps had been at Krymsk on the 17th and was still fighting there on the 20th. The LVII Panzer Corps and XXXIV Corps were completely tied down in seesaw battles in the mountains south and west of Maykop. The XXXXIX Mountain Corps was into the Sancharo Pass northeast of Sukhumi and through the Klukhorskiy, but the going was getting slower. First Panzer Army, constantly pinched for motor fuel, reached Mozdok on the north bank of the Terek on the 24th and then had to contemplate crossing the fast-flowing river that, being the last natural line forward of Groznyy and Makhachkala, was certain not to be given up without a fight.[15]

The Soviet forces, although they were to some extent still on the retreat everywhere, were beginning to benefit from being pushed into shorter lines, especially since these also traversed areas that were almost ideal for the defense. *North Caucasus Front* had *Forty-seventh* and *Fifty-sixth Armies* around Novorossiysk, *Twelfth* and *Eighteenth Armies* north and east of Tuapse. *Transcaucasus Front's North Group* had *Thirty-seventh, Ninth,* and *Forty-fourth Armies* in the line on the Terek and *Fifty-eighth Army* being raised at Makhachkala.[16]

Army Group A, on the other hand, was being relegated piecemeal to a supernumerary status. As General Halder, chief of the General Staff, put it,

---

[15]*Ibid.,* 17, 18, 20, 24 Aug 42.

[16]Grechko, *Gody voyny,* p. 245.

the "tempo" of the army group's operations was having to be permitted to decline to cope with demands in other sectors. The Grossdeutschland Division and the 22d Panzer Division left Army Group A in the second week of August, Grossdeutschland to go to the Western Theater via a detour to Army Group Center, 22d Panzer to go to Sixth Army. By the time they had departed, the army group was under notice to relinquish a *Flak* ("anti-aircraft") division and two rocket launcher regiments. The Italian Alpini Corps, with the mountain divisions Tridentina, Cuneense, and Julia, appeared briefly in the Army Group A area at midmonth and then was diverted to Italian Eighth Army without having gotten near the front. General Richthofen, who was commanding Fourth Air Force, the air support arm for Army Groups A and B, told List on the 20th he was having to switch all of the planes, "except for very small remnants," to the attack on Stalingrad. It was "regrettable," he said, but the order had come from Hitler. He thought the planes could be back in "six to ten days." Two days later, Hitler, who was worried about what he thought might be a strong Soviet concentration west of Astrakhan, ordered List to station the 16th Motorized Infantry Division at Elista on First Panzer Army's extreme left flank. To get fuel to move the division 150 miles from Voroshilovsk to Elista, General Kleist, the army's commander, had to drain the tanks of one panzer division.[17]

On the 24th, List went to Armavir to consult with Ruoff, Kleist's chief of staff

and the commander of XXXXIX Mountain Corps. Later he sent a summary to the OKH. In it he said the army group's operations had "lost their fluidity"; the fuel shortage and losses of troops and air support had given the enemy opportunity to dig in and bring up reserves. As a result, the "whole progress of the fighting" was being retarded, which in view of the long distances and advanced season was "a cause for serious thought."[18] The extent of the retardation became more apparent the next day when First Panzer Army had to give up its attempt to strike to Groznyy by way of Ordzhonikidze—because it did not have enough fuel for the tanks—and to begin regrouping for a frontal attack across the Terek via Mozdok.[19]

List, on the 26th, returned to the subjects he had raised with the OKH two days before. When it crossed the Kuban, he said, the army group had anticipated having Seventeenth Army in control of the Black Sea coast and First Panzer Army on the Caspian by the end of September; but, for the reasons given earlier, the operations so far had taken more than the time "justifiably allotted to them." Consequently, unless they could still reach the objectives, which would take substantial reinforcements and air support, they would soon have to be allowed to take up winter positions. "Unfortunately," he added, the time for doing that was almost at hand as far as XXXXIX Mountain Corps was concerned. There had already been several snowstorms at the higher elevations, and the deci-

[17]*H. Gr. A, Ia Kriegstagebuch, Band I, Teil II,* 13, 16, 20, 22 Aug 42, H. Gr. A 75126/2 file.

[18]*Ibid.,* 24 Aug 42.
[19]*Pz. AOK 1, Ia Kriegstagebuch Nr. 8,* 25 Aug 42, Pz. AOK 1 24906 file.

sion could not be put off past 15 September.[20]

List at the Werwolf

List's communications did have an effect but not the one he wanted. He did not get even a hint about reinforcements, and when his chief of staff tried to find out when the army group could expect to have air support again, he was told the planes would return "when Stalingrad is taken or given up as impossible."[21] In the situation conference on the 29th, though, Hitler made "very irritated remarks" about the conduct of operations at Army Group A and asked to have List report in person.[22] The trouble, he insisted, was not in the original plan but that List had not regrouped when he saw hitches developing.[23] Later Halder told List that Hitler had also raised several specific complaints. For one, he had heard through the air force that the terrain north of Novorossiysk was "comparable to the Grunewald [a parklike woods outside Berlin]" and therefore believed "a vigorous attack" ought to take it easily. He also thought XXXXIV Corps had failed to concentrate its forces sufficiently for the attack on Tuapse, and XXXXIX Mountain Corps ought not to have gone into the eastern mountain passes, the Sancharo and Klukhorskiy, but should have confined itself to those farther west.[24]

When List arrived at the Werwolf on the 31st, however, the reception was altogether different from what he had been led to expect. In the meantime, Seventeenth Army had made some progress toward Novorossiysk, and List had begun putting more weight on the approaches to Novorossiysk. Hitler's mood was so good that he invited List to lunch, and the atmosphere was so relaxed that later it was difficult to determine what, if anything, had been decided. Hitler told List he really did not have any objections to the way Army Group A had deployed its forces, although he would "rather have had the mountain corps somewhat closer to the Tuapse road."

Hitler apparently believed that List, who had come armed with aerial photographs from which to show why the mountain corps ought to be stopped, had undertaken to keep the corps going and to shift its main effort west. List, on the other hand, apparently believed Hitler had agreed to let the mountain corps' future operations be contingent on whether the army group could find an airfield from which its supplies could be flown in. Rechecking through the OKW did establish one solid result of the meeting: Hitler had authorized BLUECHER II, the amphibious attack across the Kerch Strait. It would eliminate a pocket of Soviet troops holding out against Rumanian Third Army on the Taman peninsula and would bring over a German infantry division and a Rumanian mountain division.[25]

BLUECHER II was executed on 2 September. Hitler had diverted enough

[20]*Der Oberbefehlshaber der H. Gr. A, Ia Nr. 174/42,* 26.8.42, Pz. AOK 1 24906/1 file.

[21]*H. Gr. A, Ia Kriegstagebuch, Band I, Teil II,* 28 Aug 42, H. Gr. A 75126/2 file.

[22]*Halder Diary,* vol. III, p. 513.

[23]Helmuth Greiner, *Die Oberste Wehrmachtfuehrung, 1939–1943* (Wiesbaden: Limes Verlag, 1951), p. 407.

[24]*H. Gr. A, Ia Kriegstagebuch, Band I, Teil II,* 29 Aug 42, H. Gr. A 75126/2 file.

[25]*Ibid.,* 31 Aug 42; *OKW, KTB,* vol. II, p. 662.

aircraft from Stalingrad to give support on the beach and to hold off the Soviet *Black Sea Fleet*. On the same day First Panzer Army established a bridgehead on the Terek at Mozdok, and on the 6th, Seventeenth Army broke into Novorossiysk, taking the center of the city and the naval base. List then wanted to concentrate on Tuapse and commit all of XXXXIX Mountain Corps there except for light security screens to be left in the passes, but Hitler demanded that advances be continued both toward Tuapse and through the western passes toward Sukhumi.[26]

Hitler Takes Command

On the 7th, General Jodl, chief of the OKW Operations Staff, who seldom left the *Fuehrer* Headquarters unless Hitler did, went to Army Group A's command post in Stalino on an urgent request from List. There, with General der Gebirgstruppe Rudolf Konrad, commanding general, XXXXIX Mountain Corps, present, List using aerial photographs and captured Soviet maps, showed him what continuing the mountain corps' operation as Hitler wished would entail: a long march over a single mountain trail, having to transport all supplies by pack animals of which the corps had 1,900 less than would be required, and exposure to attacks on both flanks. Jodl returned to the *Werwolf* carrying a "unanimous" recommendation against continuing the mountain corps' operations.[27]

Captain Helmut Greiner, keeper of the OKW War Diary, made the following entry in his notes for 8 September:

The Chief of the Armed Forces Operations Staff [Jodl], following his conference with the Commanding General, Army Group A, at the latter's headquarters on 7 September, has declared himself in agreement with Field Marshal List's contention that XXXXIX Mountain Corps, after leaving screening detachments in the passes, should be withdrawn to the north and recommitted in the Maykop area.

The Fuehrer is extremely put out at General Jodl's taking this position which is diametrically opposed to his own. He has demanded that all the records pertaining to Army Group A's conduct of operations since it crossed the Don River be brought to him.[28]

To List, Hitler "declined" to give any further orders, saying that if List was convinced he could not get the mountain corps through to the coast, then he should "leave it go."[29]

In the afternoon on the 9th, Keitel called on Halder, at Hitler's bidding, to tell him List ought to resign his command and to "infer" changes in other high posts, including Halder's and Jodl's.[30] Afterward, Keitel told Jodl's deputy, General der Infanterie Walter Warlimont, whose status also was in doubt, that he too expected to be relieved. The morning after he talked to Halder, Keitel had a "private interview" with List at the latter's headquarters, and List thereupon "withdrew from his command."[31]

As far as can be told from Greiner's

[26]Helmuth Greiner, *Greiner Diary Notes From 12 Aug 42 to 17 Mar 43*, 2–4 Sep 42, C–065a CMH file.

[27]*H. Gr. A, Ia Kriegstagebuch, Band I, Teil III*, 7 Sep 42, H. Gr. A 75126/3 file.

[28]*Greiner Diary Notes*, 8 Sep 42, C–065a CMH file.

[29]*Halder Diary*, vol. III, p. 519.

[30]*Ibid.; Greiner Diary Notes*, 9 Sep 42, C–065a CMH file.

[31]*H. Gr. A, Ia Kriegstagebuch, Band I, Teil III*, 10 Sep 42, H. Gr. A 75126/3 file.

notes or the Army Group A records, all of the fuss was raised over the deployment of one mountain corps. Warlimont recalled later that Hitler had also accused List of having consistently not followed orders and Jodl, who would have been responsible for detecting any such lapses, had maintained that List had scrupulously executed all of the orders given to him—hence, perhaps, the request for Army Group A's records. Jodl, according to Warlimont, believed—and regretted—that he put Hitler into the position of either doing what he did or taking the blame himself for the errors he imputed to List. Warlimont's own opinion, not made a matter of record until a number of years later, was that Hitler, knowing he was on the edge of a severe crisis in the war, resorted to a tactic he had used before and sacrificed his subordinates to protect himself.[32]

The atmosphere of the situation conference at the *Werwolf* on 11 September was, as Halder described it, "icy." Hitler, who otherwise did most of the talking, barely said a word. For the next two weeks, he transacted very little business through either the OKW or the OKH. He also did not name a successor to List. Instead, he ordered Ruoff and Kleist to submit to him, every other day, situation reports and maps detailed down to the battalions. Tactical proposals and requests were to be sent to him by telegraph through the OKH.[33] In effect, he assumed command of the armies himself and left Headquarters, Army Group A, to do the housekeeping.

"Stand to the Death"

The frustrations of fighting in the Caucasus had, meanwhile, also brought command changes on the Soviet side, though not nearly as radical ones. On 1 September, as the Germans were drawing up to Novorossiysk, the old cavalryman, Budenny, had been relieved as commanding general, *North Caucasus Front,* thereby ending for good his career as a field commander. At the same time *North Caucasus Front* went out of existence, and Budenny's replacement, General Cherevichenko, took over its staff and armies as commanding general of the *Black Sea Group, Transcaucasus Front.*[34]

For the first time in that summer, it began to look as if the game could go either way, but the stakes were still far from even. Hitler had come to the point of having to contemplate a major disappointment and possibly a massive failure. What confronted the Soviet Union, however, was no less than a national catastrophe. On 6 September, Moscow Radio broadcasted the following appeal from Stalin to the troops on the south flank:

The enemy is slowly advancing toward the ancient Russian river, the Volga, and the riches of the Caucasus. Our existence depends on the outcomes of the battles now being fought. Not a step back! Stand to the death! This is the summons of our country. The fate of the Fatherland, the future of our families, and the destinies of our children lie in our hands.[35]

Army Group B published the appeal to the troops of Sixth and Fourth Panzer Armies as evidence of Soviet despera-

[32]*OKW, KTB,* vol. II, pp. 697, 702.
[33]*H. Gr. A, Ia Kriegstagebuch, Band I, Teil III,* 12 Sep 42, H. Gr. A 75126/3 file.

[34]Grechko, *Battle for the Caucasus,* p. 125.
[35]*H. Gr. B, Ia Nr. 2965/42, Fernspruch vom 10.9.42,* Pz. AOK 4 28183/5 file.

tion, but Army Group A let it pass in silence, possibly because the interpretation of it by Kleist's and Ruoff's troops was somewhat uncertain. On the 11th, Seventeenth Army, indeed advancing slowly, came to a full stop at the wall of a cement factory on the southern outskirts of Novorossiysk. (And, in fact, the front would stay in that exact spot for just five days short of a year, that is, until the Germans withdrew from the Kuban entirely.)[36] In the morning on the 14th, *X Guards Rifle Corps* hit First Panzer Army's open left flank north of the Terek River and came close to cutting off the bridgehead at Mozdok.[37]

In Slow Motion

At midmonth, First Panzer Army and Seventeenth Army both needed either to complete their missions fast or to find tenable positions for the winter, and both were at a standstill. First Panzer was having to make its flank secure and clean out the Terek bend west of Mozdok to give itself a solid hold on the river before heading toward Ordzhonikidze and Groznyy. Hitler was sending the SS Viking Division from Seventeenth Army to give Kleist some additional weight when he started up again. Seventeenth Army was bringing two mountain regiments west out of the passes and preparing to direct its main effort to Tuapse, when and if it could get enough air support to make a start.

In a "special" report on the 16th, Kleist told Hitler, through the OKH, that "in the gigantic fields of sunflowers and corn and in the ravines and nooks and crannies of the mountains," the infantry he had would be "just barely enough" to keep on fighting until the SS Viking Division arrived. Two days later, however, LII Corps staged a tentative push against the west face of the Mozdok bridgehead and suddenly found itself plowing at a run through the lines of Soviet fortifications. The next eight days were almost like those of early August. Along the valleys and on the ridges inside the Terek bend, wherever the Germans turned the Russians gave way. On the 21st, Kleist made up his mind to commit the SS Viking Division as soon as it arrived and then strike south to Ordzhonikidze, with the 13th Panzer Division going along the west bank of the Terek through the Elkhotovo Gate and SS Viking Division and the 111th Infantry Division going to Malgobek and south along the northern extension of the Grusinian Military Road.

The SS Viking Division crossed the Terek after dark on the 25th and moved into the line north of Malgobek during the night. To the division commander, Kleist sent the message, "All eyes are on your division. The whole operation depends on its being unsparingly committed." The division went into action the next morning and in the course of a day and half got to within a mile of Malgobek, but it stalled there without getting onto the heights to the south from which it might have made a clean breakthrough. By then 13th Panzer Division was at Elkhotovo and also stopped. Kleist believed the Viking Division had the numbers and the weapons to have gone the thirty-five miles to Ordzhonikidze but lacked the internal cohesiveness. (The division had close to two thousand non-Ger-

---

[36]Grechko, *Battle for the Caucasus*, p. 129.
[37]*Ibid.*, p. 108; *H. Gr. A, Ia Kriegstagebuch, Band I, Teil III,* 11 Sep 42, H. Gr. A 75126/3 file.

SOVIET MORTAR SQUAD FIRING EAST OF TUAPSE

man troops, half Dutch and Belgian, the others, except for a few Swiss, Scandinavian.)

On 3 October, through the OKH, Kleist asked "to be informed when and in what strength the army can expect to get reinforcements to continue the advance to Makhachkala via Ordzhoni-kidze and Groznyy."[38] A week later, after repeated inconclusive statements from the OKH, Hitler answered that depending on developments at Sta-lingrad, the army would get either one or two mobile divisions later in the month. Until then its mission would be "to create the best possible conditions for an advance after the reinforcements arrive."[39]

While First Panzer Army was maneu-vering in the Terek bend, Seventeenth Army began its advance on Tuapse along the Maykop-Tuapse road on 23 September, with LVII Panzer Corps, and two days later with XXXIV Corps. The straight-line distance was about thirty miles. On the ground, across the western end of the main Caucasus range, it was somewhat more than that. Shaumyan, twenty miles from Tuapse, was the first objective. From there the march would be more downhill than up. The mountain regiments as the Di-

[38]Pz. AOK 1, Ia Kriegstagebuch Nr. 8, 16 Sep–3 Oct 42, Pz. AOK 1 24906 file.

[39]H. Gr. A, Ia Kriegstagebuch, Band I, Teil IV, 10 Oct 42, H. Gr. A 75126/4 file.

vision "Lanz," under Generalmajor Hubert Lanz, took the east flank where the distance was longer and the terrain the roughest.[40] Richthofen provided adequate, but not lavish, air support. Ruoff had insisted that he could not start without it.[41] The Soviet main force on the defense was *Eighteenth Army.*

The advance on Tuapse went slowly from the start. Without the benefit of enemy lapses such as had occurred in the Terek bridgehead, momentum was hard to generate and quickly lost. The Russians were dug in everywhere, and squad and platoon actions were the rule. The weather was nightmarish: late summer, with tropical downpours, in the valley and near winter on the mountains. On the sixth day, Ruoff reported that the experienced troops, having been on the march for more than two months, were either gone or worn out, and the replacements were undertrained and not sufficiently

hardened. "What is missing," he said, "is the old, battle-tested private first class whom nothing can shake."[42] After ten more days, the battle was rolling in on Shaumyan, and Ruoff thought the defense might be weakening, since there had not been any counterattacks in the past day or two even though Shaumyan was endangered.

On 10 October, at the same time that he told Kleist to wait for reinforcements, Hitler ordered Ruoff to "push ahead toward Tuapse forthwith" after taking Shaumyan.[43] On the 11th, the *Stavka* relieved Cherevichenko from command of the *Black Sea Group* and appointed General Petrov in his place. Ruoff said he proposed to do as Hitler had ordered, but he reminded the army group and the OKH that the Tuapse operation, so far, had cost him 10,000 casualties.[44]

---

[40]*Ibid.,* 23–25 Sep 42.
[41]*AOK 17, Ia Kriegstagebuch Nr. 4,* 18 Sep 42, AOK 17 25601 file.

[42]*Ibid.,* 28 Sep 42.
[43]*H. Gr. A, Ia Kriegstagebuch, Band I, Teil IV,* 9–10 Oct 42, H. Gr. A 75126/4 file.
[44]Grechko, *Battle for the Caucasus,* p. 156; *H. Gr. A, Ia Kriegstagebuch, Band I, Teil IV,* 12 Oct 42, H. Gr. A 75126/4 file.

CHAPTER XIX

From the Don to the Volga

No Enemy West of Stalingrad

Fourth Panzer Army turned northeast from Tsimlyanskiy and Remontnaya on 1 August. In another two days, after having captured several loaded Soviet troop trains near Kotelnikovo, the advance detachments of General Hoth's Fourth Panzer Army were on the Aksay River sixty miles southeast of Stalingrad. There they met *Stalingrad Front's South Group* that was being formed by General Chuikov, acting commander of *Sixty-fourth Army,* out of units from his army and some reserve divisions.[1] *(Map 33.)*

Sixth Army, under General Paulus, while waiting for its motor fuel and ammunition stocks to be replenished, was getting Headquarters, XI Corps, which had been held at Kamensk-Shakhtinskiy with two infantry divisions as the OKH reserve. On the 4th, when his mobile units had enough fuel to go about thirty miles, Paulus ordered the attack on the Kalach bridgehead to start on the 8th. The next day the OKH asked to have the attack start at least a day earlier because Hitler was worried that the Soviet troops would escape across the Don if Paulus waited longer.[2]

On the night of 1 August, General Eremenko was called to the Kremlin from the hospital where he had been since February when he had been wounded while commanding *Fourth Shock Army.* After ascertaining that he was ready to return to duty, Stalin told Eremenko that *Stalingrad Front* was being divided into two *fronts, Stalingrad* and *Southeast,* and he was the State Defense Committee's choice for command of one of them. In studying the situation in the Don-Volga area at the General Staff the next day, Eremenko learned that the boundary between the *fronts* was laid from Kalach to the line of the Tsaritsa River, which flowed east through Stalingrad at about the center of the city. That night, at the Kremlin, Eremenko suggested it might have been better to assign the entire city to one *front* or the other, but Stalin and General Vasilevskiy, chief of the General Staff, told him the attacks would be coming from the north and the south, and Eremenko sensed they were not disposed to reconsider the decision. During the interview, Stalin gave Eremenko command of *Southeast Front,* which would take over the sector from the Tsaritsa south.[3]

The realignment took effect on 5

---

[1]*Pz. AOK 4, Ia Kriegstagebuch Notizen Chef,* 1–4 Aug 42, Pz. AOK 28183/17 file; Chuikov, *Stalingrad,* pp. 44–50.

[2]*AOK 6, Ia Kriegstagebuch Nr. 13,* 2–5 Aug 42, AOK

6 2394811 file; *H. Gr. B, Ia Nr. 2383/42, an AOK 6,* 5.8.42, AOK 6 30155/39 file.

[3]Eremenko, *Pomni voyny,* pp. 172–75.

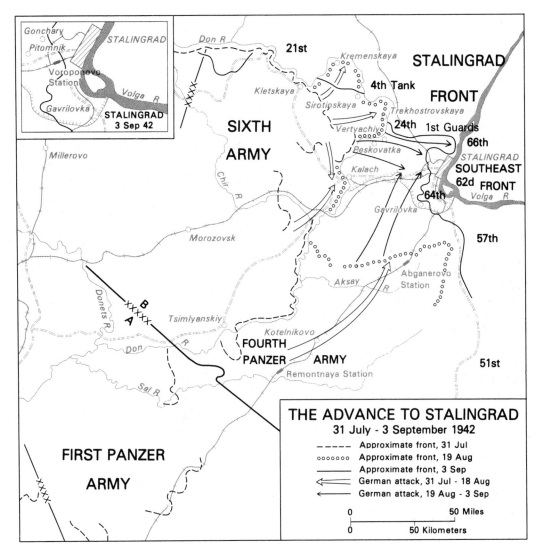

MAP 33

August. General Gordov kept *Sta-lingrad Front* and *Sixty-third, Twenty-first, Sixty-second,* and *Fourth Tank Armies.* Eremenko acquired *Sixty-fourth, Fifty-seventh,* and *Fifty-first Armies* plus *First Guards Army,* which was being brought out of the *Stavka* reserve. *First Tank Army* was disbanded. Its staff became the nucleus for the staff of *Southeast Front,* and what was left of its troops was incorporated into *Sixty-second Army.*[4] The headquarters of both *fronts* were situated in Stalingrad.

---

[4]*IVMV,* vol. V, p. 164; *IVOVSS,* vol. II, p. 431; Moskalenko, *Na Yugo-zapadnom napravlenii,* p. 288.

In the Don Bend

From the northeast and southwest, tight against the river, XIV and XXIV Panzer Corps struck into the Kalach bridgehead on the morning of 7 August. Their points had contact by late afternoon, and they had trapped the main body of *Sixty-second Army*. Together with the infantry of LI Corps, the two panzer corps cleaned out the pocket in four more days, eventually tallying nearly fifty thousand prisoners.[5]

At Kalach, Sixth Army was on the most direct route to Stalingrad, the one it had originally intended to take, but several considerations now spoke against using it. For one, the terrain between Kalach and Stalingrad was crisscrossed by *balkas*, deep gullies that often forced tanks into lengthy detours and could be used as trenches by the defense. Also, since Fourth Panzer Army was on the Aksay and had bridgeheads across it, the envelopment formed by a thrust due east from Kalach was likely to be shallow. Moreover, *Fourth Tank* and *Twenty-first Armies* were still holding a bridgehead line from Kletskaya to Peskovatka across the northeastern loop of the Don bend. To keep the Russians confined there, Paulus reckoned, would take more troops than would be needed to hold them on the river, and the terrain north of Peskovatka appeared to afford a somewhat better—and about five miles shorter—approach to Stalingrad. On the 11th, Paulus ordered

XIV and XXIV Panzer Corps to shift north, clean out the "northeast corner" of the Don bend, and get bridgeheads there for the advance to Stalingrad.[6]

The loss of the Kalach bridgehead brought the close-in defense of Stalingrad nearer to actuality on the Soviet side, and the *Stavka* was putting in more of its reserves, fifteen rifle divisions and three tank corps between 1 and 20 August. On the 9th, Vasilevskiy talked to Eremenko from Moscow and told him Stalin had decided to put *Stalingrad* and *Southeast Fronts* under Eremenko. He would have Gordov as his deputy for *Stalingrad Front* and General Golikov, the commander of *Tenth Army*, as deputy for *Southeast Front*, and General Moskalenko, who had been his deputy for the past several days, would take command of *First Guards Army*. NKVD Colonel A. A. Sarayev, who was bringing the 10th NKVD Division, would take command of the Stalingrad city defenses. While Eremenko's appointment ended the division of the city between two independent commands, it was, Eremenko has said, "an extremely heavy burden" to have to conduct operations through 2 deputies, 2 chiefs of staff, and 2 staffs.[7]

Eremenko took command on the 10th, with Khrushchev as his political officer for both *fronts*.[8] On the 12th, a high-ranking trio, consisting of Malenkov, secretary of the Central Committee of the Communist Party, as

---

[5]*AOK 6, Ia Kriegstagebuch Nr. 13*, 7–15 Aug 42, AOK 6 23948/11 file. In Moskalenko's account, Headquarters, *First Tank Army* turned over its troops to *Sixty-second Army* during the day on the 7th, after having received an order to do so the night before. Moskalenko, *Na Yugo-zapadnom napravlenii*, p. 288.

[6]*AOK 6, Ia Nr. 2948/42, Armeebefehl fuer die Gewinnung des Donbogens suedwestlich Ilowlinskaya, 11.8.42*, AOK 6 30155/42 file.

[7]Vasilevskiy, *Delo*, p. 234; Moskalenko, *Na Yugozapadnom napravlenii*, p. 292f; Eremenko, *Pomni voyny*, p. 187.

[8]Eremenko, *Pomni voyny*, p. 187. See also *IVOVSS*, vol. II, p. 432, which gives 13 August as the date of Eremenko's appointment.

representative of the State Defense Committee; Vasilevskiy as *Stavka* representative; and General Leytenant A. A. Novikov, commanding general, air force, as *Stavka* air representative, arrived in Stalingrad to assist and guide Eremenko.[9]

While Hoth, who in the meantime had moved his right flank up to Abganerovo Station on the railroad forty miles south of Stalingrad, waited, Paulus began the attack across the Kletskaya-Peskovatka line on the 15th. In two days, XIV and XXIV Panzer Corps cleared the entire loop of the Don, and VIII Corps took two small bridgeheads near Trekhostrovskaya. But complications had also begun to develop. The ground surrounding the bridgeheads proved to be marshy and not good for tanks, and Eremenko, on orders from the *Stavka,* was rushing *First Guards Army* to the Don. Moskalenko had the first of his five divisions across the river on the 16th, and by the 18th, he had reestablished a twenty-mile-long bridgehead from Kremenskaya to Sirotinskaya.[10]

This turn in events gave Paulus the choice of accepting a prolonged contest for the Don, which was undoubtedly just what the *Stavka* wanted, or making the drive to Stalingrad with his deep left flank exposed. He took the latter, expecting that an imminent threat to Stalingrad would be enough to divert Eremenko's attention from the bridgehead. The decision gave Paulus one almost instant advantage: on the morning of the 21st, LI Corps attacking east across the Don toward Ver-

tyachiy took the Russians completely by surprise and in a few hours carved out a three-by-five-mile bridgehead. By daylight the next morning, the engineers had thrown up two twenty-ton bridges and XIV Panzer Corps' tanks were rolling across.[11]

For three days past, Fourth Panzer Army had been cutting its way slowly through the Stalingrad outer defense ring north of Abganerovo Station. In a letter to Colonel Heusinger, chief of operations, OKH, on the 19th, Hoth told why:

Here on the border between steppe and desert the troops live and fight under unspeakably difficult conditions. In spite of shimmering heat that does not let up at night, in spite of indescribable dust and lack of rest at night owing to vermin and air raids, in spite of the absence of any kind of shade or ground cover, in spite of scarcity of water and poor health, they are doing their best to carry out their assigned missions.[12]

The Russians, of course, were no more comfortable. Eremenko says, "The days in Stalingrad were torrid and the nights were stifling."[13]

The Enemy Three Versts Away

The plan for the last act at Stalingrad had been ready for more than a week. The main effort would fall to Sixth Army. It would strike east past Vertyachiy to the Volga north of Stalingrad and from there send a force south to take the city. Between the rivers, Paulus would send a secondary force southeast to meet Fourth Panzer Army and

[9]*IVMV*, vol. V, p. 168.

[10]*IVOVSS*, vol. II, p. 432; Moskalenko, *Na Yugozapadnom napravlenii*, pp. 294–96.

[11]*AOK 6, Ia Kriegstagebuch Nr. 13*, 15–22 Aug 42, AOK 6 23948/11 file.

[12]*Der Oberbefehlshaber der 4. Panzerarmee, an General Heusinger, 19.8.42,* Pz. AOK 4 28183/5 file.

[13]Eremenko, *Pomni voyny*, p. 185.

SIXTH ARMY'S TANKS CROSSING THE DON AT VERTYACHIY

to envelop the Soviet forces standing east of the Don.[14] Somewhat ambivalently, the Sixth Army final order added:

The Russians will defend the Stalingrad area stubbornly.

In advancing across the Don to Stalingrad, the army will have to reckon with resistance at the front and heavy counterattacks on its north flank.

It is possible that the destructive blows of recent weeks have deprived the Russians of the strength for a decisive resistance.[15]

The XIV Panzer Corps pushed out of the Vertyachiy bridgehead on the morning of 23 August behind a curtain of bombs laid down by VIII Air Corps. During the day, the planes dropped 1,000 tons of bombs ahead of the panzer corps and on the northern quarter of Stalingrad. In a bit more than twelve hours, the tanks covered thirty-six miles and took a handhold on the Volga north of the city.[16] General Weichs, the commander of Army Group B, then ordered Paulus and Hoth to drive for a junction of their forces after which Sixth Army would take Stalingrad.

Hoth thereupon gathered all the strength he could and headed north, but Paulus had a long, exposed new front on his left flank to contend with.

[14]*AOK 6, Ia Kriegstagebuch Nr. 13*, 16 Aug 42, AOK 6 2394811 file.

[15]*AOK 6, Ia Nr. 3044/42, Armeebefehl fuer den Angriff auf Stalingrad, 19.8.42*, AOK 6 30155/42 file.

[16]Plocher, *German Air Force*, p. 231.

The XIV Panzer Corps had stretched itself very thin on the dash to the Volga. On the 26th, a counterattack carried away three miles of its front between the rivers. In the afternoon, General der Panzertruppen Gustav von Wietersheim, the corps commander, radioed, "It is not possible with present forces to stay on the Volga and hold open communications to the rear. . . . will have to pull back tonight. Request decision." Paulus replied, "Do not retreat," and stopped everything else while he put LI and VIII Corps to work at stretching their lines east to close up with XIV Panzer Corps. Since Fourth Panzer Army had not yet managed to break away on its front, the whole attack appeared to be about to stall.[17]

The German's sudden appearance on the Volga was a deep shock to the Soviet leadership. On 23 August, the city authorities began evacuating from Stalingrad civilians who were not workers in war industries, and two days later, the *Stavka* declared a state of siege. During the night on the 23d, the *Stavka* sent Eremenko the following order:

You have enough strength to annihilate the enemy. Combine the aviation of both *fronts* and use it to smash the enemy. Set up armored trains and station them on the Stalingrad belt railroad. Use smoke to deceive the enemy. Keep after the enemy not only in the daytime but also at night. Above all, do not give way to panic, do not let the enemy scare you, and keep faith in your own strength.[18]

On the 26th, Stalin named General Zhukov, the commander of *West Front,* deputy supreme commander. The next day he recalled Zhukov from *West Front,* where he had been directing an operation that had been considered as important as any on the south flank, and sent him to Stalingrad with instructions to assemble *First Guards, Twenty-fourth,* and *Sixty-sixth Armies* for a counterattack from the north to break Sixth Army away from the Volga.[19]

Zhukov arrived on the scene on the 29th, just in time to witness another blow. During the day, Fourth Panzer Army's XXXXVIII Panzer Corps reached the Karpovka River. The next morning it took a bridgehead at Gavrilovka, thirty miles southwest of Stalingrad. With that, *Sixty-second* and *Sixty-fourth Armies* were on the verge of being encircled and had to be withdrawn to the Stalingrad suburbs.[20]

In the afternoon on the 30th, at Sixth Army's command post, Weichs urged Paulus to strip his fronts east and west of the Don and put everything he could into getting a junction with Hoth. Afterward, Paulus told XIV Panzer Corps and LI Corps to be ready to strike south on short notice regardless of their other troubles. When Fourth Panzer Army made a clean break away from the Karpovka on the 31st, Weichs ordered Paulus and Hoth to seek a junction at Pitomnik due east of Stalingrad, smash the enemy west and south of there between them, and then turn east and drive into the center of the city along the Tsaritsa River.

Events at the turn of the month appeared to substantiate a report at-

[17]*Pz. AOK 4, Ia Kriegstagebuch Notizen Chef,* 23–26 Aug 42, Pz. AOK 4 28183/17 file; *AOK 6, Ia Kriegstagebuch Nr. 13,* 23–26 Aug 42, AOK 6 2394811 file.
[18]Vasilevskiy, *Delo,* p. 236.

[19]*IVMV,* vol. V, p. 175; Zhukov, *Memoirs,* p. 377.
[20]Vasilevskiy, *Delo,* p. 239; *IVOVSS,* vol. II, p. 438.

GERMAN MACHINE GUNNER LOOKS ACROSS
THE VOLGA NORTH OF STALINGRAD

tributed to General Richthofen, the commander of Fourth Air Force, that Stalingrad was virtually undefended. On the afternoon of 2 September, Fourth Panzer Army reported the territory ahead of it clear of enemy as far as Voroponovo Station six miles from the center of the city. Weichs thereupon told Hoth to turn east into Stalingrad without waiting for Sixth Army. On the 3d, VIII Air Corps, recently reinforced with practically all of IV Air Corps' planes from the Caucasus, staged a twenty-four-hour, round-the-clock raid on the city.[21] In the early morning hours, Sixth Army and Fourth Panzer Army had made contact at Gonchary, seven miles north-

west of Voroponovo. With that both armies were in position to head east, and at the *Werwolf* the word was, "There is no longer any enemy west of Stalingrad." Hitler issued orders to "eliminate the male inhabitants" and deport the women because the population, in his opinion, was strongly Communist and, hence, a danger.[22] During the day on the 4th, Paulus forwarded a plan to the OKH for going into winter quarters. It hardly seemed significant that *Sixty-second* and *Sixty-fourth Armies* had avoided an encirclement and fallen back into the city.

To the Soviet Command, as well, it looked like the end was in sight. On the 3d, Stalin cabled to Zhukov:

> The situation at Stalingrad has worsened. The enemy is within three versts [a mile and a half] of Stalingrad. Stalingrad could be taken today or tomorrow if the northern group of forces does not render immediate support.
> Order the troop commanders to the north and northwest of Stalingrad to attack the enemy immediately. . . .[23]

But Zhukov was not ready and had to wait another day and a half to bring up ammunition for his artillery.[24]

Confrontation

The City

Stalingrad was nothing special, a regional administrative center in the steppe with some war industry, a population just under half a million, and a hard climate both in summer and winter. (*Map 34.*) Strung out over some twelve

[21] *Greiner Diary Notes*, 28 Aug 42, C–065q CMH file; Plocher, *German Air Force*, p. 234.

[22] *Greiner Diary Notes*, 2 Sep 42, C–065q CMH file.
[23] *IVOVSS*, vol. II, p. 438.
[24] Zhukov, *Memoirs*, p. 379.

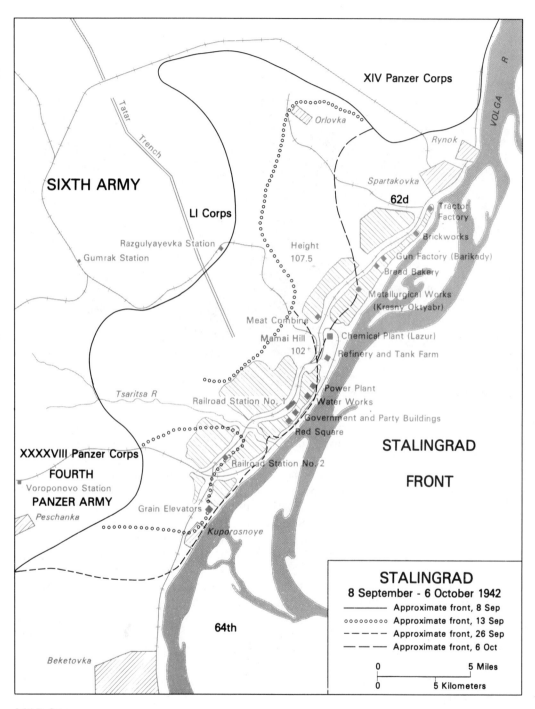

XIV Panzer Corps

Orlovka

Rynok

Spartakovka

SIXTH ARMY

62d

LI Corps

Tractor Factory

Razgulyayevka Station

Brickworks

Gumrak Station

Height 107.5

Gun Factory (Barikady)

Bread Bakery

Metallurgical Works (Krasny Oktyabr)

Meat Combine

Mamai Hill 102⁺

Chemical Plant (Lazur)

Refinery and Tank Farm

Tsaritsa R

Power Plant

Railroad Station No. 1

Water Works

Government and Party Buildings

Red Square

STALINGRAD

XXXXVIII Panzer Corps

FOURTH

Railroad Station No. 2

FRONT

Voroponovo Station

PANZER ARMY

Peschanka

Grain Elevators

Kuporosnoye

64th

Beketovka

VOLGA R

STALINGRAD

8 September - 6 October 1942

———————— Approximate front, 8 Sep

∘∘∘∘∘∘∘∘∘ Approximate front, 13 Sep

– – – – – Approximate front, 26 Sep

— — — — Approximate front, 6 Oct

0   5 Miles

0   5 Kilometers

MAP 34

GENERAL PAULUS *(right)* WATCHES THE ATTACK ON STALINGRAD. *Behind Him, the Commander of LI Corps, Seydlitz.*

miles along the Volga and flanked by suburbs extending several more miles to the north and south, it did not anywhere reach more than two-and-a-half miles inland. Its most prominent physical feature was the 300-foot-high Mamai Hill (shown on maps as Height 102), which was actually a *kurgan,* an ancient burial mound. The hill divided the city in two. On the south lay the old town, the prerevolutionary Tsaritsin. It, in turn, was bisected by the Tsaritsa River, to the south of which were railroad yards, light industry, grain elevators, and blocks of apartment buildings. North of the river were government buildings, clustered around the Red Square, the main railroad station, the waterworks and power plant, and more blocks of apartment build-

ings. The railroad ran north between Mamai Hill and an oil refinery and tank farm on the Volga. Ranged along the river north of Mamai Hill were the "Lazur" chemical plant, the Krasny Oktyabr metallurgical works, a bread bakery, the Barrikady gun factory, a brick works, a large tractor plant, and beyond it the suburbs of Spartakovka and Rynok. The plants and factories with their complexes of steel and masonry buildings were bordered on the west by workers' settlements made up mostly of small, tightly packed, unpainted, one-story, wooden houses, a type of structure also to be found in large numbers elsewhere in the city. Since, like other southern Russian rivers, the Volga's right bank is higher than the left, the Stalingrad river front was a line of cliffs that was in places as much as a thousand feet high.

Counterattacks

During the day on 4 September, Sixth Army's LI Corps took Gumrak Station, which put it in position to attack into Stalingrad between Mamai Hill and the Tsaritsa. Fourth Panzer Army was bearing in south of the Tsaritsa along the railroad east of Voroponovo and from the southwest by way of Peschanka. Paulus gave General Seydlitz, the LI Corps commander, another infantry division and told him to attack into Stalingrad the next day.[25]

At dawn on the 5th, Zhukov was at a *First Guards Army* observation post opposite the XIV Panzer Corps north front to watch the start of the counterattack. Moskalenko had made one start already on the 2d and then had stopped to wait for *Twenty-fourth* and *Sixty-sixth Armies* to get into position on his left and right. General Malinovskiy, who had taken over *Sixty-sixth Army* after his *front* was disbanded, had told Moskalenko on the night of the 4th that in the morning he would be starting the attack piecemeal because he still had divisions on the march. The same was as much or more the case with General Kozlov, who commanded *Twenty-fourth Army*.[26] Consequently, the counterattack hinged mainly on *First Shock Army*, which was the only one of the three that was fully deployed—and the only one to have seen previous action. *First Shock Army*, however, was not experienced enough to carry the

other two along. The artillery and rocket barrages began at 0600, and Zhukov saw that the density of fire was low. The fire the infantry met as it moved out showed him "that we were not to expect any deep penetration of our assault units."[27] *Sixty-sixth Army* joined in at 0900 and *Twenty-fourth Army* at 1300. By then, Moskalenko's divisions were stopped and being hit by counterattacks.[28]

Nevertheless, Stalin told Zhukov to try again the next day. The counterattack, he maintained, had already bought some time for Stalingrad.[29] Stalin was more right than he knew. At midday, Paulus had canceled the LI Corps attack into Stalingrad and had diverted all of Sixth Army's air support to the north front. The XIV Panzer Corps cleaned up half-a-dozen break-ins and had a tight front again before dark but, in doing so, had incurred "perceptible losses in men and material . . . and a heavy expenditure of ammunition."[30]

The second day was no better for Zhukov but was somewhat worse for XIV Panzer Corps, because ground fog prevented the planes from giving any help in the morning. In the afternoon Wietersheim called Paulus and told him his front was "strained to the limit." He had to have more infantry, he said, and constant air support, even if it meant putting off the attack into Stalingrad indefinitely, because that could only "be thought of" anyway after the north front was secure. Paulus

---

[25]*AOK 6, Ia Kriegstagebuch Nr. 13*, 4 Sep 42, AOK 6 23948/11 file; *Pz. AOK 4, Ia Kriegstagebuch Notizen Chef*, 4 Sep 42, Pz. AOK 4 28183/17 file.

[26]Moskalenko, *Na Yugo-zapadnom napravlenii*, p. 328.

[27]Zhukov, *Memoirs*, p. 379.

[28]Moskalenko, *Na Yugo-zapadnom napravlenii*, pp. 328–31.

[29]Zhukov, *Memoirs*, p. 380.

[30]*AOK 6, Ia Kriegstagebuch Nr. 13*, 5 Sep 42, AOK 6 2394811 file.

FOURTH PANZER ARMY'S INFANTRY ON THE
DEFENSIVE AT KUPOROSNOYE

replied that he knew Wietersheim's situation "clearly and exactly" but thought differently about how to handle it. "Stalingrad must fall," he said, "to free strength for the north front." The XIV Panzer Corps's mission, Paulus concluded, was to hold out until then.[31]

The LI Corps attacked at daylight on the 7th and in fourteen hours stretched its line east to Razgulyayevka Station, which put it five miles northeast of Mamai Hill. Seydlitz and his chief of staff went to the army command post the next morning with a proposal to drive into Stalingrad that day or the next, but Paulus now told them they could not. Paulus was not as sure about what to do next as he had

been when he talked to Wietersheim two days before, and he said LI Corps had to be kept loose for a while yet. Its next assignment, beginning on the 9th, would be to go northeast and to mop up behind XIV Panzer Corps to Orlovka. He added that for the time being Hoth would not be able to attack into the city either because he was having to turn south to take some of the strain off the infantry on his flank; so the advantage of a coordinated double thrust into the city would be lost anyway.

After a day's pause, the Soviet pressure on XIV Panzer Corps' north front resumed on the 9th as LI Corps began pushing northeast against an enemy who "tenaciously defended every single bunker." Late in the day, Seydlitz reported that the Soviet losses were high but "our own were not inconsequential."[32] Hoth's effort to free his flank had a notable success on the morning of the 10th when the 29th Motorized Division got a battalion through to the Volga at the southern Stalingrad suburb of Kuporosnoye. The battalion lost the half mile adjacent to the river again during the night when it was overrun by furious charges from the north and south, and wild melees continued there for four more days.[33]

The 10th was the darkest day yet for the defense. During the day, Fourth Panzer Army drove a wedge between *Sixty-second* and *Sixty-fourth Armies* isolating *Sixty-second Army* inside the city; and Stalin had to concur in Zhukov's assessment that on the north front, "further attacks with the same troops

[31]*Ibid.*, 6 Sep 42.

[32]*Ibid.*, 7–9 Sep 42.
[33]*I. R. 71 (mot.), Ia, Gefechtsbericht des III./71 vom 11.9.42, 20.9.42, Pz. AOK 4 28183/5* file.

and the same dispositions would be useless."[34] Moskalenko has pointed out that a tactical success had not been possible at any time because "the *front* command" underestimated the enemy's strength and because the enemy knew, after 5 September, that it only had to concentrate on one army, *First Guards.*[35] But the attacks had bought some time.

On the other hand, time was running out, and the battle was at the point of being carried into the streets of Stalingrad. On the 10th, Hoth told General der Panzertruppen Werner Kempf, the commanding general, XXXXVIII Panzer Corps, to start into the south quarter the next day and to take it "piece by piece."[36] In the morning on the 12th, Eremenko and Khrushchev briefed Chuikov, the newly appointed commanding general of *Sixty-second Army.* The previous commander, General Leytenant A. I. Lopatin, who had lost the greater part of the army in the Kalach bridgehead, "did not believe that his army could hold the city." Chuikov swore "to defend the city or die in the attempt."[37]

Chuikov Against Paulus

It was time also for LI Corps to be heading east again; only the corps became stuck outside of Orlovka all-day on the 11th and was fighting off counterattacks until 2400. Paulus told Seydlitz the next morning to turn the line around Orlovka over to XIV Panzer Corps and to get ready to strike "to the Volga" on the 13th.[38] Hoth was telling Weichs at the same time that the attack was "going to take a while" because the fighting was "more rigorous than any the troops have yet experienced in this war." Weichs and Hoth also talked about putting XXXXVIII Panzer Corps under Sixth Army in a day or two, which would give Paulus complete charge at Stalingrad and would let Hoth start thinking about the terminal phase of Operation FISCH-REIHER, the advance to Astrakhan.[39]

On the morning of the 13th, Chuikov was in the *Sixty-second Army* command post, a dugout on Mamai Hill, when LI Corps' artillery opened up from behind Razgulyayevka. In the wake of the barrage, the infantry came on from the northwest, its left flank aimed at Mamai Hill, its right following the Tatar Trench, another feature of ancient and indeterminate origin. By nightfall, the Germans were into a woods a mile west of the hill and at the terminus of the Tatar Trench, where the built-up area of the city began. Chuikov moved his command post south during the night to a bunker close to the Tsaritsa River that had earlier been the *Stalingrad Front* headquarters. It was secure enough with forty feet of compacted earth overhead, but it put Chuikov right between LI Corps and XXXXVIII Panzer Corps that were aiming for a meeting on the river.[40]

[34]Zhukov, *Memoirs,* p. 381.

[35]Moskalenko, *Na Yugo-zapadnom napravlenii,* p. 329.

[36]*Pz. AOK 4, Ia Kriegstagebuch Notizen Chef,* 10 Sep 42, Pz. AOK 4 28183/17 file.

[37]Chuikov, *Stalingrad,* p. 76.

[38]*AOK 6, Ia Kriegstagebuch Nr. 13,* 11 and 12 Sep 42, AOK 6 2394811 file.

[39]*Pz. AOK 4, Ia Fernsprechnotizen zum K.T.B. Nr. 5,* 12 Sep 42, Pz. AOK 4 28183/19 file; *Pz. AOK 4, Ia Kriegstagebuch Notizen Chef,* 12 Sep 42, Pz. AOK 4 2818317 file.

[40]*AOK 6, Ia Kriegstagebuch Nr. 13,* 13 Sep 42, AOK 6 2394811 file; Chuikov, *Stalingrad,* pp. 86–88; Samsonov, *Stalingradskaya bitva,* p. 190.

The 14th was another dark day for the defense. In the south quarter, XXXXVIII Panzer Corps reached the railroad station and forced a spearhead through to the Tsaritsa. North of the river, LI Corps rammed two divisions abreast into the center of the city, by 1200 had the main railroad station, and at 1500 reached the Volga at the waterworks. By dark, the corps held almost a mile of river bank, and antitank guns set up there had sunk two ferries and a steamer.[41]

When the report on the day's events reached Stalin, he was conferring with Zhukov and Vasilevskiy in the Kremlin on a matter that enormously enhanced the strategic value of holding any part of Stalingrad.[42] He instructed Vasilevskiy to have Eremenko send in the best division in the Stalingrad area, the *13th Guards Order of Lenin Rifle Division* under Hero of the Soviet Union, General Mayor A. I. Rodimtsev. Rodimtsev was at Chuikov's headquarters in the afternoon, and the 10,000-man division crossed the river during the night.[43]

Seydlitz's LI Corps began to experience on the 14th and 15th what XXXXVIII Corps already had for several days: street fighting in a city that was being contested block by block, building by building, even floor by floor. Nothing was conceded. Houses were fought over as if they were major fortresses. According to the *History of the Great Patriotic War,* the main railroad station changed hands five times on the morning of the 14th and another thirteen times in the next several days. Who held what at any particular time was almost impossible to tell. The LI Corps took Mamai Hill on the 15th. The next day, one of Rodimtsev's regiments stormed it, and some Soviet accounts maintain the regiment retook it and held it for at least another ten days.[44] The Sixth Army records, on the other hand, indicate that repeated Soviet attempts failed to dislodge the Germans from the hill after the 15th. Rodimtsev, however, did succeed in breaking the German hold on the Volga east of the railroad station. Realizing that he did not have a secure grip on any part of the city, Paulus, who on the 14th had wanted Seydlitz to turn north next, on the 15th ordered him first to join forces with XXXXVIII Panzer Corps, which was being attached to Sixth Army, and to clean out the central and south quarters.[45]

On the 17th, LI Corps and XXXXVIII Panzer Corps made contact with each other on the Tsaritsa, less than a mile upstream from Chuikov's headquarters bunker. Chuikov and his staff moved north to the vicinity of the Krasny Oktyabr works during the night. His own situation was precarious, but during the day, he had received good news: *Stalingrad* and *Southeast Fronts* were going over to the offensive, with the objective, no less, of pinching off the whole German Stalingrad force. *First Guards* and *Twenty-fourth Armies* would strike from the north and *Sixty-fourth Army* from the south. *First Guards Army* had been beefed up to a strength of

[41]*Pz. AOK 4, Ia Fernsprechnotizen zum K.T.B. Nr. 5,* 14 Sep 42, Pz. AOK 4 28183/19 file; *AOK 6, Ia Kriegstagebuch Nr. 13,* 14 Sep 42, AOK 6 2394811 file.
[42]See p. 442.
[43]Zhukov, *Memoirs,* p. 384; Chuikov, *Stalingrad,* p. 91; Samsonov, *Stalingradskaya bitva,* p. 193ff.

[44]*IVOVSS,* vol. II, pp. 441–42; Chuikov, *Stalingrad,* p. 97.
[45]*AOK 6, Ia Kriegstagebuch Nr. 13,* 14–22 Sep 42, AOK 6 2394811 file.

eight rifle divisions and three tank corps and had been shifted west, to the right of *Twenty-fourth Army*.[46]

The offensive began in the north, on both sides of Kotluban on the 18th and continued at intervals over the next four days, but it did not come near to making a breakthrough. Chuikov has said that the one effect his army noticed was that the German planes disappeared from overhead for five or six hours at a time while the attacks were going on.[47] Actually, although he may not have known it, Chuikov benefited more than that. The LI Corps advance in Stalingrad slowed almost to a stop on the 19th and 20th, and Paulus reported on the 20th, "The infantry strength of the army has been so weakened by our own and the Russian attacks of recent days that a supplement is needed to activate it."[48]

The "Main Effort" in Stalingrad

The "supplement," as Paulus saw it, could come from seven divisions he still had standing inside the Don bend upstream to the mouth of the Khoper River. Although he had not been able to eliminate the Soviet bridgeheads at Kremenskaya-Sirotinskaya or at Serafimovich and the Russians had in fact expanded them substantially, he regarded the sector as being "in little danger," and he had divisions to substitute for those that would be taken away. The Rumanian Third Army, eleven divisions all told, was coming in from Army Group A. It was not being brought north because of its prowess on the battlefield; in fact, the reason was just the opposite: Army Group A, in spite of its chronic shortage in strength, had wanted to get rid of the Rumanians since early August because they were unreliable on the defense, and their offensive plans paid more attention to fall-back positions than to objectives to be attained.[49]

Hitler had finally let Third Army be transferred, in early September, because he thought the fall of Stalingrad was imminent and he wanted to reward Rumanian Marshal Ion Antonescu, his ally strongest in divisions, by setting up a Rumanian army group under Antonescu. Hitler's assumption had been that Rumanian Fourth Army, part of which already was with Fourth Panzer Army, Rumanian Third Army, and Sixth Army would make up the army group and it would take over what would by then have become a stationary front.[50] Paulus' proposal of the 20th would bring the Rumanian Third Army into play earlier and in a more critical role than had been anticipated.

Apparently, an alternative also crossed Paulus' mind, namely, to go over to the defensive in Stalingrad. He had rejected that idea earlier when Wietersheim proposed it; and on the 16th, after one or two more exchanges of a similar nature, Wietersheim had been "called away to another assignment" and replaced at XIV Panzer Corps by Generalleutnant Hans Hube. He rejected it again on the 20th because "world-wide interest in the 'wall'

[46]Chuikov, *Stalingrad*, p. 102; Moskalenko, *Na Yugozapadnom napravlenii*, p. 336.

[47]Chuikov, *Stalingrad*, p. 113.

[48]*AOK 6, Ia Kriegstagebuch Nr. 13*, 20 Sep 42, AOK 6 2394811 file.

[49]*OKH, GenStdH, Op. Abt. (I) Nr. 420618/42, 18.8.42*, H 22/216 file.

[50]*OKH, GenStdH, Op. Abt. (I) Nr. 420662/42, Betr: "Stab Don," 3.9.42*, H 22/216 file.

of Stalingrad makes it essential that the army's main effort now be at Stalingrad." As a "supplement," Weichs let Paulus have the 100th Jaeger Division right away and agreed to consider releasing two more divisions.[51]

On the 22d, LI Corps pushed two spearheads through to the Volga east of the railroad station but had to withdraw them again after dark. During the night Soviet planes bombed Stalingrad, and heavy artillery fire from across the river kept activity down on the 23d while *Stalingrad Front*'s armies battered at the north front once more. The defense in the city's center, though, was breaking up on the 24th. The 71st Infantry Division took "half of what has been in enemy hands north of the Tsaritsa until now," and XXXXVIII Panzer Corps reached the Volga at the mouth of the Tsaritsa. In another day, 71st Infantry Division had taken the party and government buildings and pushed through to the mouth of the Tsaritsa on the north bank.

Paulus declared the center of the city secured on the afternoon on the 26th, after the docks, the last government buildings, and the big bunker in which Chuikov's headquarters had been were taken. "Since noon," he reported, "the German war flag has been flying over the party buildings." The resistance was actually far from over on either side of the Tsaritsa, but he had issued orders three days before to start the drive north on the 27th. In the meantime he had acquired one more division from the front on the Don.[52]

In troop strength, *Sixty-second Army*

was now more than keeping up. Within the next four or five days, it would have received, since mid-September, reinforcements amounting to 9 rifle divisions, 2 tank brigades, and 1 rifle brigade. And the front commands were being reorganized and tightened. General Rokossovskiy, who had proved himself during the summer at *Bryansk Front*, was being brought in to take over *Stalingrad Front*, which on 28 September was renamed *Don Front*. Eremenko relinquished his double command but kept *Southeast Front*, which, renamed, became *Stalingrad Front*.[53]

Sixth Army showed it was becoming accustomed to thinking in new orders of magnitude when it recorded the first day's accomplishments in the attack to the north. The objectives taken were "Height 107.5, the blocks of houses northwest of there, and the gully northwest of Krasny Oktyabr [the worker's settlement]." On the 28th, LI Corps took "about half" of the Barrikady settlement, "two-thirds" of a block of houses around the "Meat Combine" at the foot of Mamai Hill, and the "western part" of the Krasny Oktyabr works. The next day, while taking the blocks of houses west of the bread bakery that was situated between the Krasny Oktyabr and Barrikady plants, the corps lost the houses it had taken around the "Meat Combine" and lost and retook part of the Barrikady settlement. The 30th brought no change at LI Corps, but XIV Panzer Corps broke into Orlovka from the north.[54]

[51]*AOK 6, Ia Kriegstagebuch Nr. 13*, 20 and 21 Sep 42, AOK 6 2394811 file.
[52]*Ibid.*, 22–26 Sep 42.

[53]*IVOVSS*, vol. II, pp. 242–44; *IVMV*, vol. V, p. 187.
[54]*AOK 6, Ia Kriegstagebuch Nr. 13*, 27–30 Sep 42, AOK 6 2394811 file.

Deadlock

On 1 October, "in seesawing battle," Sixth Army held what it had so far taken and counted itself lucky to have done so. A day later, the war diary records, "The chief of staff informed the army group that in spite of the most intensive efforts by all forces, the low combat strengths of the infantry will prolong the taking of Stalingrad indefinitely if reinforcements cannot be supplied." Paulus told Weichs on the 3d, "At present even the breaking out of individual blocks of houses can only be accomplished after lengthy regroupings to bring together the few combat-worthy assault elements that can still be found." The next afternoon, following a visit to the front, the chief of staff reported, ". . . without reinforcements, the army is not going to take Stalingrad very soon. The danger exists that were the Russians to make fairly strong counterattacks our front might not hold, because there are no reserves behind it."[55]

Sixth Army's war diary entry for 6 October reads, "The army's attack into Stalingrad had to be temporarily suspended [today] because of the exceptionally low infantry combat strengths." In the divisions, the diary continues, average battalion strengths were down to 3 officers, 11 noncommissioned officers, and 62 men. The army could scrape together enough replacements from the supply service to make small advances, but, "The occupation of the entire city is not to be accomplished in such a fashion."[56]

---

[55]*Ibid.,* 1–4 Oct 42.
[56]*Ibid.,* 6 Oct 42.

CHAPTER XX

Summer on the Static Fronts

On the Moscow Axis

Believing that the enemy would, sooner or later, seek the decision there, the Soviet leadership did not in any wise regard the central sector as secondary in the summer of 1942. General Zhukov, who had been the chief troubleshooter the summer before, stayed in command of *West Front.* The *fronts* opposite Army Group Center—*Kalinin, West,* and the two right wing armies of *Bryansk Front*—had, all told, 140 divisions to the Germans' 70.[1] The *Stavka* held 4 field armies and the *Third* and *Fifth Tank Armies* as reserves in the Moscow area.[2]

The strategy of the active defense remained in effect on the Moscow axis. On 16 July, four days after the offensive north of Orel against Second Panzer Army was stopped, the *Stavka* instructed Zhukov and General Konev, the commander of *Kalinin Front,* to prepare an offensive in the Rzhev-Sychevka area. The objectives were to be to drive the enemy back to the Volga

and Vazuza rivers and take Rzhev and Zubtsov.[3]

When Operation SEYDLITZ ended, in the second week of July, Army Group Center, for its part, was ready to settle into a supernumerary role for the summer. HANNOVER and SEYDLITZ, by eliminating the most critical dangers to the army group's rear, had made it once more an almost credible threat to Moscow and, consequently, a bit more than a bystander in the war; but active campaigning would be out of the question at least until a partial rebuilding was accomplished in August. The armies had three operations in the paper stage of planning: DERFFLINGER, ORKAN ("tornado"), and WIRBELWIND ("whirlwind").[4]

DERFFLINGER, descended from the old BRUECKENSCHLAG, was to be a Ninth Army drive from the front north of Rzhev to Ostashkov. ORKAN and WIRBELWIND, as their code names suggest, were related. Both were to be conducted by Fourth and Second Panzer Armies against the Sukhinichi salient. In ORKAN, the two armies, striking from the north and the south, would eliminate the whole salient and carry the front out to Belev, Kaluga, and Yukhnov. WIRBELWIND, a considerably less ambitious alternative to ORKAN,

---

[1]*IVMV* (vol. V, p. 242) states that the German divisions, however, were "almost twice" the strength of Soviet divisions. Army Group Center's seventy divisions included two Hungarian divisions (used for rear area security) and five German security divisions. See *OKW, KTB,* vol. II, p. 1374.

[2]*IVMV,* vol. V, p. 243. The headquarters and staff of *Fifth Tank Army* reverted to the reserve in late July, and the army was rebuilt with results that will be observed later. See Rokossovskiy, *Soldier's Duty,* p. 122.

[3]*IVMV,* vol. V, p. 244.

[4]Georg von Derfflinger was a Prussian field marshal of the seventeenth century.

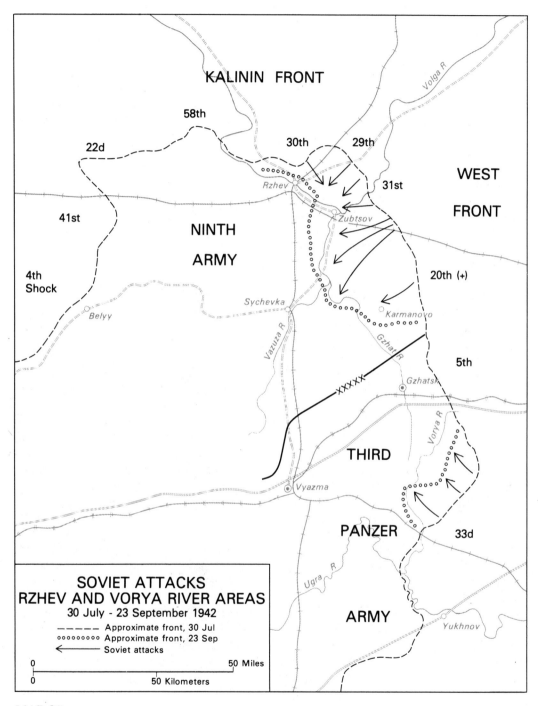

KALININ FRONT

58th

22d

30th   29th

WEST

31st   FRONT

Rzhev

41st

NINTH

Zubtsov

ARMY

20th (+)

4th
Shock

Sychevka

Karmanovo

Belyy

Vazuza R

5th

Gzhatsk R

Gzhatsk

XXXXX

THIRD

Vorya R

Vyazma

PANZER

33d

Ugra R

ARMY

Yukhnov

SOVIET ATTACKS
RZHEV AND VORYA RIVER AREAS
30 July - 23 September 1942

- - - - - Approximate front, 30 Jul
ooooooooo Approximate front, 23 Sep
←———— Soviet attacks

0   50 Miles
0   50 Kilometers

MAP 35

would only pinch off the western third of the salient and establish a line some miles east of Sukhinichi. Although ORKAN could have been substantially more effective than WIRBELWIND (by reopening the southwestern approaches to Moscow via Yukhnov and Kaluga), as of mid-July, barring a sudden Soviet collapse, there was almost no chance of its being attempted. Army Group Center was not likely to have enough troops or material to try anything that big. Whether DERFFLINGER could be executed was also doubtful. The buildup for it would have to come out of the forces used for WIRBELWIND, which had priority; therefore, DERFFLINGER could not start until September, which, at best, would put it uncomfortably late in the season.[5]

Rzhev-Sychevka

Konev was ready to start on 30 July. He had *Thirtieth* and *Twenty-ninth Armies* positioned north and northeast of Rzhev. Zhukov, who would carry the main effort and would coordinate the operations of both fronts after the offensive started, needed five more days. He had *Thirty-first* and *Twentieth Armies* in the line and 2 tank corps, 2 guards cavalry corps, and 5 cavalry divisions standing behind them. Each of the armies also had a mobile group of 3 tank brigades. *Thirty-first Army* was to sweep south of the Volga toward Zubtsov, where it would be able to threaten Rzhev from the southeast. *Twentieth Army* would bear southwest toward the

Vazuza River and Sychevka.[6] *(Map 35.)*

Ninth Army became aware of the buildups in the last week of the month. It identified several new divisions with *Thirtieth Army* and several more with *Thirty-first Army*. However, since *West Front* had already conducted several similar, seemingly vague, regroupments elsewhere, Ninth Army more than half suspected a deception, a Soviet counterpart to Operation KREML.[7]

At 0600 on 30 July, in pouring rain, after an hour-long artillery barrage accompanied by air strikes, *Thirtieth Army* hit Ninth Army's front on the Volga River bridgehead due north of Rzhev. By nightfall, it had broken open four miles of the line and had overrun artillery positions two miles in the rear. For the next four days, the Germans held tight to the cornerposts, the flanks of the breakthrough, and thereby prevented the attack from going deeper while they braced themselves also for the attack from the east, past Zubtsov toward Rzhev, that was now certain to come. The distances were short, on the north less than ten miles and on the east twenty-five miles, and the stakes were disproportionately high. If Rzhev fell, Army Group Center would lose the anchor of its north flank, every chance of closing the gap to Army Group North, and most, if not all, of its status as a threat to Moscow.

In the morning on 4 August, *Thirty-first Army* surged into and over the 161st Infantry Division on an eight-mile stretch east of Zubtsov. The breakthrough was complete almost at once.

[5]*AOK 9, Ia Kriegstagebuch Nr. 6,* 1–20 Jul 42, AOK 9 31624/1 file; *AOK 4, Ia Kriegstagebuch Nr. 13,* 1–31 Jul 42, AOK 4 24336/1 file; *Pz. AOK 2, Ia Kriegstagebuch Nr. 2, Teil IV,* 1–31 Jul 42, Pz. AOK 2 28499/4 file.

[6]*IVMV,* vol. V, p. 245.
[7]*OKH, GenStdH, Fremde Heere Ost, Kurze Beurteilungen der Feindlage,* 23–29 Jul 42, H 23/198 file; *AOK 9, Ia Kriegstagebuch Nr. 6,* 29 Jul 42, AOK 9 31624/1 file.

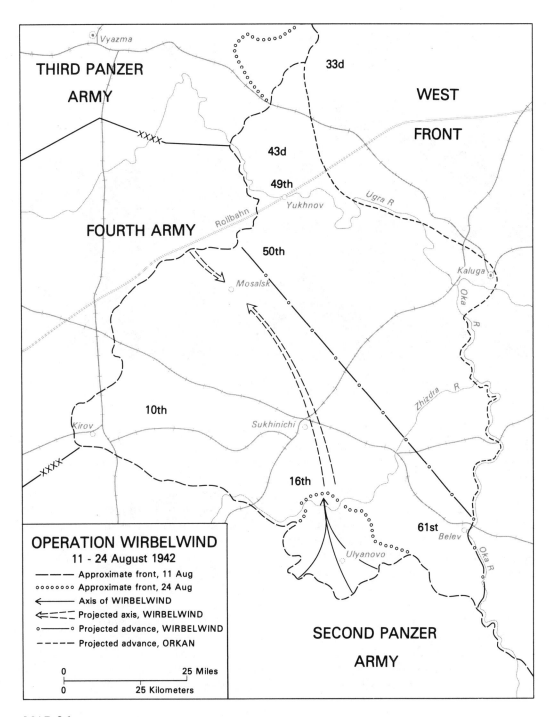

THIRD PANZER ARMY

WEST FRONT

Vyazma

33d

43d

49th

Rollbahn

Yukhnov

Ugra R

FOURTH ARMY

50th

Mosalsk

Kaluga

Oka R

10th

Kirov

Sukhinichi

Zhizdra R

16th

61st

Belev

Ulyanovo

Oka R

SECOND PANZER ARMY

OPERATION WIRBELWIND
11 - 24 August 1942

— — — Approximate front, 11 Aug
ooooooo Approximate front, 24 Aug
←——— Axis of WIRBELWIND
←≡≡≡ Projected axis, WIRBELWIND
o———o Projected advance, WIRBELWIND
— — — Projected advance, ORKAN

0   25 Miles
0   25 Kilometers

MAP 36

MACHINE-GUN NEST NORTH OF RZHEV

By dark, the only trace of the former front was occasional white flares that were sent up, here and there, over some bypassed strongpoint. During the day, Ninth Army had received two more shocks: the attack through the breech on the east was not only going toward Zubtsov but southwest toward Sychevka as well, and *Fourth Shock Army* appeared to be bestirring itself west of Belyy.[8]

It thereupon became clear to General Vietinghoff, the acting Ninth Army commander; to Field Marshal Kluge, the commander of Army Group Center, who returned from leave in Germany in the early afternoon on the 4th; and to Hitler that Ninth Army, which had no reserves of its own, could not hold Rzhev or the 175-mile northward loop of its front without early and substantial help. There was help to be had, and Hitler was more than usually quick to give it. It meant dismantling Fourth Army's force for WIRBELWIND, but Hitler did not at that point want to allow the Soviet Union a prestige victory at Rzhev. So, he released the 1st, 2d, and 5th Panzer Divisions and the 78th and 102d Infantry Divisions and instructed Kluge to see that the panzer divisions were only used in a concentrated counterattack from the south across the mouth of the *West Front's* breakthrough.[9]

---

[8]*AOK 9, Ia Kriegstagebuch Nr. 6,* 30 Jul–4 Aug 42, AOK 9 31624/1 file; *IVMV,* vol. V, p. 245.

[9]*AOK 9, Ia Kriegstagebuch Nr. 6,* 4 Aug 42, AOK 9 31624/1 file.

The front held north of Rzhev and at Zubtsov on the 5th and 6th, but it disintegrated on the southwest, leaving a broad road open to Sychevka. To take advantage of the latter development in particular, Zhukov revised his plan. On the 6th, he secured the *Stavka's* permission to stop *Twenty-ninth Army*, which had made no progress anyway, and to leave Rzhev to the *Thirtieth* and *Thirty-first Armies*. At the same time, he shifted the weight of the operation south, putting his spare armor and cavalry, *VI* and *VIII Tank Corps* and *II* and *VIII Guards Cavalry Corps*, in with *Twentieth Army*. Sychevka, which had originally not been one of them, now became the first of the objectives as *Twentieth Army's* mobile group, *VI* and *VIII Tank Corps*, and *II Guards Cavalry Corps* headed toward it.[10]

For Kluge and Vietinghoff, there was not time to assemble the panzer divisions for a counterattack. They had to be put in frontally along the Vazuza and Gzhat rivers, ten miles west of Sychevka. Talking to Hitler's adjutant, General Schmundt, on the night of the 6th, Vietinghoff said he might be able to counterattack if he could get one fully equipped panzer division (besides those coming, which were all under-strength), but the actual chance of his doing that was slight, and it disappeared entirely the next morning when *VIII Guards Cavalry Corps* struck south off the *Twentieth Army* flank.[11] The reinforcements were having to be thrown into the expanding battle as fast as they arrived, and they were being set upon just as fast by waves of Soviet infantry, tanks, and cavalry.

On the 7th, Ninth Army was on the defensive everywhere and on the verge of being overwhelmed. Once more, help was to be had. Three or four panzer divisions and a couple of infantry divisions could have been extracted from Second Panzer Army's force for WIRBELWIND. During the day, Kluge went to the *Wolfsschanze* to get a decision—and got one that was completely different from what he had wanted or expected. As Hitler saw it, the offensive on the south flank had reached its terminal stage, and Soviet diversionary attacks could be expected everywhere. These, such as the one against Ninth Army, he said, would have to be dealt with the way the Soviet winter offensive had been, by holding fast in spite of occasional breakthroughs. The correct way to proceed, he insisted, was to get WIRBELWIND going "immediately." After it was completed, the panzer divisions could be used to clean up at Ninth Army, and then Ninth Army could go on and finish off the summer with DERFFLINGER.[12] When Kluge returned to Smolensk, he brought General Model, who had been recalled from convalescent leave, with him to resume the Ninth Army command.

Wirbelwind

Since the starting date set in July for WIRBELWIND had been 7 August, Second Panzer Army was ready to begin almost "immediately." *(Map 36.)* Fourth Panzer Army's circumstances, on the other hand, had changed completely in the meantime, and its commander, General Heinrici, told Kluge he could

---

[10]*IVMV*, vol. V, pp. 245–47.
[11]*AOK 9, Ia Kriegstagebuch Nr. 6*, 6 Aug 42, AOK 9 31624/1 file; *IVMV*, vol. V, map 15.

[12]*Der O.B. der H. Gr. Mitte, Ia Nr. 6200/42, Der Fuehrer hat sich entschlossen, 8.8.42*, Pz. AOK 2 28499/42 file.

not do an operation that had been calculated to take seven or eight divisions
with only two, which were all he had
left. Hitler's order, however, included
Fourth Army, and Kluge, therefore, insisted on at least a token thrust ten
miles past its front to Mosalsk.[13] Nevertheless, that converted WIRBELWIND
into a one-armed envelopment and
lengthened the distance Second Panzer
Army would have to cover from about
forty to sixty-five miles. General
Schmidt, Second Panzer Army's commander, proposed to do it in two phases
with four panzer and three infantry divisions. In the first, the panzer divisions, starting in pairs from the east
and west sides of a twenty-mile-wide
dip in the front around Ulyanovo,
would traverse fifteen miles of heavily
wooded territory south of the Zhizdra
River, converging on the river fifteen
miles south-southeast of Sukhinichi. In
the second, over open ground north of
the river, they would sweep north fifty
miles to Mosalsk, passing Sukhinichi on
the way.[14]

Delayed two days by rain, WIRBEL-
WIND began on 11 August, in more
rain.[15] Coming from the east, 11th Panzer Division covered eight miles, about
half the distance to the Zhizdra, before
it was stopped just short of Ulyanovo.
The two panzer divisions on the west
gained about one mile. The day
brought two surprises: the Russians

had built fortifications at least all the
way back to the river, and they were
reacting with startling speed. In the
late afternoon, pilots flying support
missions reported columns of trucks
and tanks on all the roads leading in
from the north and east. The tank
corps that had been used in the Orel
offensive in July, and which Second
Panzer Army had thought were long
ago transferred out, had been refitting
east of Belev and north of the Zhizdra
and were being thrown into the battle.
In the trench lines laced through the
forest, the infantry, observing Stalin's
"no step back" order, frequently fought
to the last man. One panzer division
managed to claw its way to the Zhizdra
in another two days and to get a small
bridgehead on the 14th.[16]

Hitler could possibly have expected
WIRBELWIND to arouse enough concern
over Moscow to draw Soviet attention
away from the rest of the Army Group
Center front. That did not happen.
Zhukov, who had all of his original
force for the Rzhev-Sychevka operation committed by the 9th, also put the
right flank of *Fifth Army, Twentieth
Army*'s neighbor on the south, in motion east of Karmanovo. In four more
days, *Thirtieth Army*'s tanks were ranging into the municipal forest three
miles northeast of Rzhev. On the 13th,
in a surprise attack, *Thirty-third Army*
broke through Third Panzer Army's
right flank on the Vorya River. After
that, all of Kluge's armies except
Fourth Army were embroiled in desperate battles, and Fourth Army was in

[13]*AOK 4, Ia Kriegstagebuch Nr. 13*, 8 Aug 42, AOK 4
24336/1 file.

[14]*Pz. AOK 2, Ia Nr. 85/42, Befehl fuer die Operation
"Wirbelwind" 10.8.42*, Pz. AOK 2 28499/49 file.

[15]Rain affected all operations in the central sector
during the summer. The pattern was one of localized
sudden downpours and cloudbursts that rolled hap-
hazardly over the landscape leaving flooded roads
and mud behind them.

[16]*Pz. AOK 2, Ia Nr. 92/42, Beurteilung der Lage am
22.8.42*, Pz. AOK 2 28499/48 file; *Pz. AOK 2, Ia
Kriegstagebuch Nr. 2, Teil IV*, 11–14 Aug 42, Pz. AOK
28499/4 file.

some respects worse off than the others. It had to give an infantry division to Third Panzer Army on the 13th, after having sent a reinforced regiment to Ninth Army two days before. What was left of Fourth Army's force for WIRBELWIND had evaporated, and its divisions were holding from ten to fifteen miles of front apiece, hardly more than a picket line. The single bright spot in Army Group Center's picture was on Ninth Army's west front, where *Fourth Shock Army* had so far not managed to pull itself together enough to do anything consequential.[17]

Kluge spent the day on the 14th at Second Panzer Army, giving pep talks to the division commanders and privately concluding that the prospects for WIRBELWIND were too small to be worth the risks of losing Rzhev or having the enemy "chew in" deep into Third Panzer Army. Later he told General Halder, chief of the General Staff, the army group had no more reserves, and WIRBELWIND would have to be canceled to get some forces for Ninth and Third Panzer Armies. Halder, who, no doubt, knew what Hitler's reaction would be, "resisted" the thought of stopping WIRBELWIND but, at the late situation conference, persuaded Hitler to give Kluge another two divisions, 72d Infantry Division and the Grossdeutschland Division. The 72d Infantry Division, which had been scheduled to go to the Leningrad area with Eleventh Army, was just coming out of the Crimea. Grossdeutschland was at Rostov awaiting shipment to the West. Nei-

ther one could get to Smolensk in less than a week, and because of the railroads, both could not be there before the first week in September.[18] Kluge once more had reserves, but they were 700 miles away.

Crisis and Recovery

Two days later, Model presented Kluge with what amounted to an ultimatum. He told Kluge that Ninth Army was just about finished and had to have three more divisions. If those could not be given, he said, the army group would have to take responsibility for what happened next and "provide detailed instructions as to how the battle is to be continued."[19] Although neither could have imagined it at the time, Kluge and Model were at the psychological turning point for the summer's operations. Kluge needed to persuade Ninth Army to stay on its feet, and the army needed to believe it could. Kluge did that by offering the 72d Infantry Division and the "prospect" of another division, which Model assumed to be the Grossdeutschland Division. The Ninth Army war diary registered "new hope for the coming difficult days and weeks."[20] That hope would have to go a long way. The first trainload of 72d Infantry Division troops and equipment was due in Smolensk on the 17th, but it took upwards of thirty trains to move a division. Hitler, not Kluge, controlled the Grossdeutschland Division, and Hitler wanted it to be used in WIRBELWIND.[21]

---

[17]*IVMV*, vol. V, p. 247; *AOK 9, Ia Kriegstagebuch Nr. 6,* 13–14 Aug 42, AOK 9 31624/1 file; *AOK 4, Ia Kriegstagebuch Nr. 13,* 13–14 Aug 42, AOK 4 24336 file.

[18]Greiner, *Oberste Wehrmachtfuehrung,* p. 401; *AOK 4, Ia Kriegstagebuch Nr. 14,* 14 Aug 42, AOK 4 26937 file.
[19]*AOK 9, Ia Kriegstagebuch Nr. 6,* 16 Aug 42, AOK 9 31624/1 file.
[20]*Ibid.,* 16 Aug 42.
[21]Greiner, *Oberste Wehrmachtfuehrung,* p. 403.

QUADRUPLE ANTIAIRCRAFT GUNS GUARD A BRIDGE ON THE ZHIZDRA RIVER

By the third week of the month, Army Group Center was thoroughly ensnared in three World War I-style battles of materiel. Ninth Army had suffered over 20,000 casualties as of 17 August. Third Panzer Army was fighting in trenches on the Vorya River. At the bridgehead on the Zhizdra, Second Panzer Army's tanks were boxed in by minefields. Ninth Army's cornerposts were being shaved away east of Rzhev and around Karmanovo. On the 22d, Hitler finally gave up on WIRBELWIND. He wanted then to take out two panzer divisions and, with those plus the Grossdeutschland Division, try a new, smaller WIRBELWIND northeast of Kirov, but before he could get the divisions out, Second Panzer Army was hit by furious counterattacks that

forced it to evacuate the Zhizdra bridgehead on the 24th.[22]

According to the Soviet reckoning, the summer offensive against Army Group Center was "practically completed" by 23 August.[23] In terms of tactical accomplishment, it probably was over, particularly after Zhukov's departure, three days later, removed its chief architect. Between 24 and 30 August, Third Panzer Army eliminated a breakthrough across the Vorya, and thereafter its front held. By the end of the month, Second Panzer Army's front south of the Zhizdra was solid enough that Hitler could begin to

---

[22]*Pz. AOK 2, Ia Kriegstagebuch Nr. 2, Teil IV,* 22–24 Aug 42, Pz. AOK 28499/4 file.
[23]*IVMV,* vol. V, p. 248.

think about taking a panzer division out there. *Kalinin* and *West Fronts* were as close to Rzhev and Sychevka as they were going to get.

As a test of endurance, however, the offensive, particularly its main component, the Rzhev-Sychevka operation, was by no means ended. On 1 September, Kluge went once again to the *Fuehrer* Headquarters, this time to report what Model had told him the day before: Ninth Army was at the point of having its whole front collapse. Its casualties were up to 42,000 and rising at a rate close to 2,000 a day. Hitler refused to consider shortening the front, since doing so would involve losing Rzhev. He also refused to release the Grossdeutschland Division, which was assembling at Sychevka. Grossdeutschland, he said, was "a guards division" and as such should be used only for short periods in acute crises.[24] He would, he added, bring the 95th Infantry Division north from the Voronezh area in about two weeks and take 9th Panzer Division out at Second Panzer Army, but in the meantime, Ninth Army would have to get along as it was. "Someone," he concluded, "must collapse. It will not be us!"[25]

For a brief period, the enemy did seem to be weakening. Ninth Army registered three quiet days on 6, 7, and 8 September, the first such since 30 July. But the 9th was different. *Thirtieth Army* hit the Volga River bridgehead around Rzhev, and *Thirty-first Army* broke open six miles of front west of Zubtsov. *Thirty-first Army,* in particular, came on with such intensity that Model

suspected Zhukov was back in command. After much back and forth telephoning, Hitler, in the afternoon, allowed the Grossdeutschland Division to be deployed between Rzhev and Zubtsov. Finally, in the evening, he turned the division over to Model's command with strict instructions that it was only to be used offensively in a counterattack.

Thirty-first Army opened the next day at 0400 with an artillery barrage that, in fact, continued all day. Grossdeutschland began its counterattack an hour and a half later and ran head-on into Soviet infantry with strong air support coming the other way. Ninth Army from then on heard about nothing but successive calamities—a regimental commander wounded, the tank battalion commander wounded, tanks lost right and left. The division, brought up on the hit-and-run tactics of the blitzkrieg, appeared to be about to wreck itself trying to negotiate a few miles of woods and swamp. Twenty-four hours later, the division's affairs were in such confusion that Model put it temporarily under the commander of the neighboring 72d Infantry Division to find out, if possible, at least what had happened. Some hours later he knew: all but five of the division's forty tanks were out of commission; the troops were suffering more from confusion than from losses; and the counterattack was beyond salvation.

At the *Fuehrer* Headquarters on the 13th, Model persuaded Hitler to let him have the 95th Infantry and 9th Panzer Divisions for another try when they became available. It looked as if, in the meantime, the outcome at Rzhev would hang indefinitely, as Kluge put it, on a "knife edge," but the 15th was

---

[24]*General Halder's Daily Notes*, vol. II, 1 Sep 42, EAP 21–g–16/4/0 file.

[25]*AOK 9, Ia Kriegstagebuch Nr. 6*, 1 Sep 42, AOK 9 31624/1 file.

an astonishing and for Ninth Army a "beautiful" day. In the morning, *Thirty-first Army* pulled itself together to hit 72d Infantry Division with a tremendous rush of tanks and infantry. In the afternoon, one regiment, the 430th Infantry Regiment, stopped the Soviet main force, the *IV Tank Corps;* knocked out three dozen of its tanks; and reclosed the line. During three days of rain that followed, *Thirty-first, Thirtieth,* and again *Fourth Shock Armies* seemed to be getting poised for another onslaught, but when the rain stopped, only the *Thirty-first* went back on the attack, but not wholeheartedly. The artillery and air support subsided on the 22d, and two days later the infantry began breaking contact. Army Group Center had held its own through the summer—barely.[26]

Leningrad and Demyansk

Both sides' half-successes and near-failures of the past were tangibly evident on the fronts around the Oranienbaum pocket and Leningrad. As of July 1942, they had been stationary for almost ten months. The city was solidly in Soviet hands, and the landward approaches to it were equally under tight German control after the Volkhov pocket collapsed. The worst of the siege was over. Once navigation had resumed on Lake Ladoga in late May, boats and barges had been able to carry larger cargoes than could have been hauled across the ice in the winter. In June they had begun to evacuate women, children, old people, and some men with special skills on the return trips bringing out about a hundred thousand during the month. (Over two hundred thousand were evacuated in July and another hundred thousand in August leaving an almost exclusively male population of between seven and eight hundred thousand.)[27]

In June, a pipeline, laid in the lake, had gone into operation. It, henceforth, provided the troops in Leningrad and the Oranienbaum pocket with a secure motor fuel supply. Boats and barges would be able to bring in over a million tons of goods and military supplies and 290,000 military personnel during the summer. In late May, *Leningrad Front* had submitted a plan to lift the siege by breaking through the bottleneck east of the Neva River. The *Stavka* had approved the plan "in principle" but had postponed its execution because it could not then supply the required reinforcements. *Leningrad* and *Volkhov Fronts'* missions, as they entered the summer, were to improve the city's defenses and to stage limited offensives to weaken the enemy enough to prevent his mounting an assault on the city and to create the conditions for breaking the siege later.[28]

Army Group North's concerns were for the future more than for the present. Until frost again afforded ground conditions suitable for extensive operations, the bottleneck appeared to be securely in German hands. The bottleneck had survived the winter and would be more difficult to break in the summer; nevertheless, in so confined a space, the German defense could not

[26]*Ibid.*, 6–24 Sep 42.

[27]V. M. Kovalchuk, *Leningrad i bolshaya zemlya* (Leningrad: Izdatelstvo "Nauka," 1975), pp. 210, 262. *IVMV* (vol. V, p. 235) gives the total number of persons evacuated between 29 June 1941 and 1 April 1943 as 1.75 million.

[28]*IVMV*, vol. V, p. 235f.

afford any mistakes. Between the bottleneck and the Volkhov River, the Pogostye salient projected to within 10 miles of Lyuban. The Russians were not likely to use it in the summer because the ground was underwater for miles around on all sides, but when winter came, it would again threaten the rear of the Eighteenth Army front around Leningrad. East and west of the salient, two small German bridgeheads on the Volkhov, at Kirishi and Gurzino, served as very exposed, and expensive, "lightning rods" for the front on the river. Farther south the Soviet Volkhov bridgehead possessed the same potential for future use by the Russians as the Pogostye salient, and each enhanced the other. South of Lake Ilmen, Sixteenth Army's anchor, Staraya Russa, was just 2 miles inside the front and the corridor to the Demyansk pocket was no more than 3 to 5 miles wide over most of its 25-mile length. From the eastern tip of the pocket the mighty Toropets bulge reached west 125 miles before it dropped off into the Army Group Center zone north of Velikiye Luki. In the summer, particularly the wet summer of 1942, either side could profitably maintain only infantry outposts in the bulge's forests and swamps—and these were all Army Group North could afford.

Nordlicht and Other Operations

Like Army Group Center, Army Group North was assigned a secondary role for the summer, but with a difference: it had a prospective strategic mission. Under Directive 41 (of 5 April 1942), it was to finish off Leningrad, establish land contact with the Finnish

Army on the Isthmus of Karelia, and occupy Ingermanland (the area of the Oranienbaum pocket) "as soon as the [enemy] situation in the enveloped areas or the availability of otherwise sufficient forces permits."[29] Although its execution was deferred, in Hitler's thinking the mission was much more than one of opportunity. His concern went back to the fall of 1941 and particularly to the failure in December to get contact with the Finns on the Svir River after which Marshal Mannerheim, the Finnish Army's commander in chief, had made it clear that the Finnish forces would not take the offensive anywhere until they were at least relieved of the necessity for holding a front north of Leningrad. In the early winter, on Hitler's orders, Army Group North had devised a plan, code-named NORDLICHT ("aurora borealis"), to take Leningrad. Overwhelmed by its subsequent troubles, the army group had not taken the plan beyond the paper stage, but, for Hitler at least, it had continued to hold top priority as Directive 41 had demonstrated. One thing was certain: barring a near-total Soviet collapse, Leningrad, which during the winter had achieved heroic stature worldwide, was not going to come cheap. NORDLICHT, in the summer of 1942, was therefore going to be a major operation and would require substantially greater resources than Army Group North had or had any near prospect of getting. (Map 37.)

On 30 June, at the Wolfsschanze, General Kuechler, the commander of Army Group North, briefed Hitler on

---

[29]Der Fuehrer und Oberste Befehlshaber der Wehrmacht, OKW, WFSt Nr. 55616/42, Weisung 41, 5.4.42, German High Level Directives, CMH files.

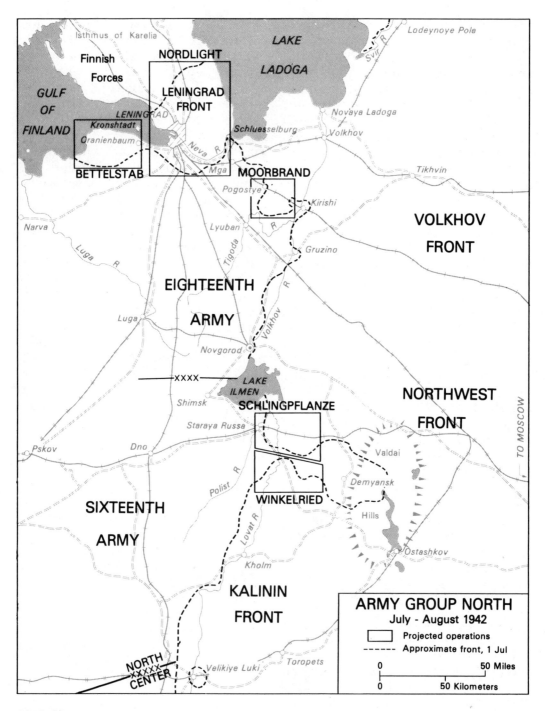

MAP 37

the operations aside from NORDLICHT that the army group might undertake after it had rested its units and received its scheduled troop and equipment replacements. He listed five possibilities: a joint attack with Army Group Center to Ostashkov (BRUECKENSCHLAG); expansion of the corridor to the Demyansk pocket; elimination of the Volkhov bridgehead and/or the Pogostye salient; and occupation of Ingermanland. He rated three of these— the Demyansk corridor, the Pogostye pocket, and the Ostashkov operation— as "urgent."[30]

Kuechler returned to his own headquarters on 1 July and put his staff to work on two operations, SCHLING-PFLANZE ("vine") and MOORBRAND ("moor fire"). SCHLINGPFLANZE, which was to widen the corridor to the Demyansk pocket on its north side, was to come first because II Corps in the pocket still could not get along without air supply. Aside from being exposed to enemy fire from two sides, the lanes the Germans had hacked through the corridor were underwater whenever it rained and muddy all the time. MOOR-BRAND would pinch off the Pogostye salient and so, Kuechler believed, "constrict" the Soviet options for deployment between the Volkhov River and Lake Ladoga. Hitler had liked the idea because, while the terrain generally was unsuitable for motor vehicles of any description, the German tanks might be able to run on the railroad embankment that conveniently crossed the base of the salient.[31]

On 2 July, the OKH let Army Group North know a special artillery reconnaissance group was being sent to check the ground between the Leningrad front and the Oranienbaum pocket for emplacement of very heavy artillery. Hitler was going to have DORA, which had finished its work at Sevastopol, transferred north for use against Kronshtadt, the Soviet naval fortress on Kotlin Island in the Gulf of Finland.[32] Kronshtadt, with a ring of forts on surrounding small islands and three miles of water separating it from the mainland, was a worthy companion piece to Sevastopol. In the next two weeks, Hitler added to DORA, the GAMMA and KARL batteries, the other siege artillery from Sevastopol, and four batteries ranging in caliber from 240- to 400-mm. that had not been at Sevastopol. All, including DORA, for which a five-mile railroad spur would have to be built, were to be emplaced by the last week in August. Because so much artillery would not achieve tactical profits worth the cost of the ammunition by shelling Kronshtadt alone, most of it was to be sited to fire on targets in the Oranienbaum pocket as well. Eighteenth Army then also began planning an infantry operation against the pocket under the code name BETTELSTAB ("beggar's staff").[33]

Before Eighteenth Army and Army Group North completed their first estimates for BETTELSTAB, Hitler's attention was turning toward Leningrad. In a teletyped message to the OKH Operations Branch on 18 July, he an-

---

[30]OKW, Stellv. WFSt, Kriegsgeschichtliche Abteilung, Kriegstagebuch, 1.4.–30.6.42, 30 June 42, I.M.T. 1807 file.

[31]H. Gr. Nord, Ia Kriegstagebuch, 1.–31.7.42, 1 Jul 42, H. Gr. Nord 75128/12 file.

[32]OKH, GenStdH, Op. Abt. (III) Nr. 429456/42, Zufuehrung des Dora-Geraets zu H. Gr. Nord, 2.7.42, H. Gr. Nord 75129/62 file.

[33]H. Gr. Nord, Ia Kriegstagebuch, 1.–31.7.42, 11–22 Jul 42, H. Gr. Nord 75128/12 file.

nounced that Operation BLUECHER, the attack across the Kerch Strait, would be canceled as soon as the Don was crossed and the break into the Caucasus region from the north was assured. The German divisions thereby released would be transferred out of Eleventh Army and sent north to take Leningrad. He made the decision final in Directive 45 of 23 July. Army Group North would get five divisions from Eleventh Army in addition to the heavy artillery already on the way and would be ready by early September to take Leningrad.[34] Two days before, in Directive 44, he had ordered Twentieth Mountain Army to get ready for a thrust together with the Finns to the Murmansk Railroad, on the assumption that "Leningrad will be taken at the latest in September and Finnish forces will be released (from the front on the Isthmus of Karelia)."[35] First given the code name FEUERZAUBER ("fire magic"), the operation against Leningrad was changed after a week to NORDLICHT for correspondence above the Eighteenth Army level and GEORG ("George") within the army.[36]

Hitler next instructed Kuechler to go through the docket of "local operations, SCHLINGPFLANZE, MOORBRAND, and BETTELSTAB, in "short order" and have them out of the way by the beginning of September.[37] The army group

knew from the outset, as Hitler in all likelihood also did, that anything of the sort was out of the question in the allotted time because troops, tanks, artillery, ammunition, and especially air support could not be mustered for more than one operation at a time. As it turned out, NORDLICHT in part afforded and in part compelled the solution. BETTELSTAB had from the first not raised real enthusiasm in the army group, and since it could probably be done more easily after NORDLICHT than before, it was postponed. On the other hand, the army group regarded SCHLINGPFLANZE and MOORBRAND as more vital to its survival in the approaching winter than NORDLICHT. But NORDLICHT was more important to Hitler and, presumably, to German grand strategy. When the early estimates showed that Eighteenth Army would in no way have enough strength to do MOORBRAND and NORDLICHT, even if one were done before the other, Kuechler "with a heavy heart" canceled MOORBRAND. Which left SCHLINGPFLANZE.[38]

SCHLINGPFLANZE, besides being the sole survivor of the so-called local operations, was also the only one of the three that was anywhere near ready to execute. Sixteenth Army, under General Busch, had positioned the troops for it in mid-July and had been set to start on the 19th when bad flying weather and Soviet attacks on the II Corps perimeter forced successive postponements. Later, a lingering spell of heavy rain flooded the entire area between the pocket and the main front.

[34]OKW, WFSt, Op. Nr. 551261/42, an GenStdH, Op. Abt. 18.7.42, H 22/215 file; OKW, WFSt, Op. Nr. 551288/42, Weisung Nr. 45, Fuer die Fortsetzung der Operation "Braunschweig," 23.7.42, German High Level Directives, CMH files.

[35]OKW, WFSt, Op. Nr. 551275/42, Weisung Nr. 44, 21.7.42, German High Level Directives, CMH files.

[36]OKH, GenStdH, Op. Abt. Nr. 420550/42, an H. Gr. Nord, 2.8.42, H. Gr. Nord 75129/55 file.

[37]OKH, GenStdH, Op. Abt. Nr. 420550/42, an H. Gr. Nord, 24.7.42, H. Gr. Nord 75129/55 file.

[38]H. Gr. Nord, Ia Kriegstagebuch, 1.–31.7.42, 24 Jul–3 Aug 42, H. Gr. Nord 75128/12 file.

At the turn of the month, Kuechler and Busch were waiting for three or four dry days but were almost at the point of starting SCHLINGPFLANZE regardless of the weather because II Corps was as badly off as it had been in the height of the winter. The corridor was underwater, and the airlift was only getting in 30 to 40 percent of the daily supply requirements. On 4 August, however, SCHLINGPFLANZE had another setback when all of the ground support and fighter aircraft assigned for it were flown out to help Ninth Army at Rzhev.[39]

At Fuehrer Headquarters

Four days later, Hitler summoned Kuechler to the *Werwolf* to review SCHLINGPFLANZE and NORDLICHT. He opened the conference with a surprise twist, something he liked to do to put the generals off balance and himself in control of the discussion. He told Kuechler that Army Group North would be getting the first of the new Tiger tanks and proposed putting some of them into the Kirishi bridgehead. A few of the Tigers, he implied, ought to be able to hold the bridgehead practically by themselves. When Kuechler pointed out that the army group had no means of getting the sixty-tonners across the Volkhov River, he suggested using them in SCHLINGPFLANZE, which Kuechler noncommittally agreed "would be easier to do than at Kirishi." Later, in private, Field Marshal Keitel, chief, OKW, told Kuechler that the Tigers were not yet off the assembly line, and he had better not count on having them in time for SCHLINGPFLANZE.

Turning to the agenda, Hitler told Kuechler the aircraft transferred out of his area would stay with Ninth Army until the crisis at Rzhev had been overcome and would then be used to support Second Panzer Army's Operation WIRBELWIND, which would mean SCHLINGPFLANZE could not start before 20 August. He asked Kuechler how much time he would need for SCHLINGPFLANZE. Kuechler said fourteen days. Hitler then asked when NORDLICHT, which would follow SCHLINGPFLANZE, would be completed, and Kuechler said at the end of October. Hitler said that was too late because NORDLICHT was itself not a terminal operation but a preliminary to the operation against the Murmansk Railroad that would have to be done before winter. He wondered, he added, why Army Group North was "insisting" on aiming SCHLINGPFLANZE north of the Demyansk corridor when the enemy was less strong on the south side. He remembered that there had been a supply road on the south during the winter. Such a road indeed had existed, Kuechler replied, but it had been made of logs, sawdust, and ice and had long since melted and floated away. The only actual road on either side of the corridor was the Staraya Russa–Demyansk road on the north, and, he pointed out, taking it was essential also to the defense of Staraya Russa.

After remarking that he would "feel better" about SCHLINGPFLANZE if the Tigers could be worked into it, Hitler turned to NORDLICHT. The object, he said, was to destroy Leningrad totally. General Jodl, chief, OKW Operations Staff, who was present, added that this was necessary because the Finns regarded the city "as a heavy burden on

---

[39]*Ibid.*, 30 Jul–4 Aug 42.

their future." The job, Hitler observed, could be compared to the one recently finished at Sevastopol, but it would not be nearly as difficult. For one thing, the area was smaller. For another, at Sevastopol the terrain was rugged and the fortifications exceedingly strong while Leningrad lay on flat land and was not nearly as well fortified. "The whole thing at Leningrad," he asserted, "must actually be done with simple mass of materiel." Jodl at one point asked whether it might not be well to put Field Marshal Manstein (Eleventh Army), the recent victor of Sevastopol, in command of the operation, but Hitler, Kuechler noted, "did not take that up."

When Kuechler countered that "in the last analysis" the operation would have to have adequate infantry, the conference reached what he and Hitler had both known all along was its real nub.[40] The army group had asked for 4 more divisions, 3 infantry and 1 panzer, before NORDLICHT started and either a constant flow of replacements or 2 to 3 more divisions to be supplied later.[41] Hitler maintained that the army group's estimates were too high. Anyway, he continued, he could not give what he did not have, and he had no more divisions. That was why he had provided the artillery—"in a mass greater than any since the Battle of Verdun in the World War"—a thousand pieces to the enemy's less than five hundred. The thing to do would be to drop hundreds of thousands of incendiary bombs. "If the city really burns, no defender will be able to hold out there."[42]

After returning to his own headquarters, Kuechler reexamined NORDLICHT. From Eighteenth Army's commander, General Lindemann, he learned that to get even two divisions out of its existing resources the army would have to give up the Kirishi and Gruzino bridgeheads, which would weaken its hold on the Volkhov line and the Pogostye salient. Lindemann also told him that the number of artillery pieces was not going to be 1,000 but exactly 598.[43] On the 14th, apparently for the first time, Kuechler went out to look at Leningrad. From the Alexander Tower, on the northern outskirts of Pushkin, the highest point on the front, he saw clumps and masses of concrete and stone factories and apartment buildings. "These," he concluded, "one can presume will only be in small measure vulnerable to fire."[44]

A Mission for Manstein

Meanwhile, SCHLINGPFLANZE was waiting on its air support. Finally, on the 16th, Colonel Heusinger, the OKH operations chief, told Kuechler's chief of staff not to expect the planes in less than another eight to ten days or more and to remember that Hitler was "hold-

[40]*H. Gr. Nord, Ia Kriegstagebuch, 1.–31.8.42,* 8 Aug 42, H. Gr. Nord 75128/13 file.
[41]*H. Gr. Nord, Ia Nr. 55/42, an OKH, GenStdH, Op. Abt.,* 26.7.42, H. Gr. Nord 75129/55 file.

[42]*H. Gr. Nord, Ia Kriegstagebuch, 1.–31.8.42,* 8 Aug 42, H. Gr. Nord 75128/13 file.
[43]*AOK 18, Ia Nr. 48/42, an H. Gr. Nord,* 9.8.42, H. Gr. Nord 75129/55 file. The figures on artillery vary. Kuechler later used the number 800. Apparently the numbers depended on how much of the front was being talked about: Leningrad only; Leningrad and the bottleneck; or Leningrad, the bottleneck, and the Oranienbaum pocket. Some of the heaviest pieces, DORA for instance, were considered not to have any worthwhile targets in Leningrad.
[44]*H. Gr. Nord, Ia Kriegstagebuch, 1.–31.8.42,* 14 Aug 42, H. Gr. Nord 75128/13 file.

ing onto NORDLICHT hard as iron." "We must now," Heusinger added, "make some very sober calculations." In the next day or two, he went on, Halder was going to propose evacuating the Demyansk pocket. If that failed, as it most likely would, Army Group North was going to have to do whatever it could "in the few good weeks left" to prevent an "untenable situation" when the fall rains and winter came. A day later, Kuechler canceled SCHLING-PFLANZE and substituted WINKELRIED, an operation to widen the Demyansk corridor on the south. On the 21st, Halder called, on Hitler's behalf, to ask Kuechler whether he could come to the *Fuehrer* Headquarters two days later to report on WINKELRIED and NORD-LICHT. He had also just heard, to his surprise he said, that Manstein would be put in command of NORDLICHT.

At the *Werwolf,* Hitler greeted Kuechler with the remark that "a stone" had fallen from his heart when he heard the army group was turning away from SCHLINGPFLANZE. He said he had "always regarded it as an extraordinarily difficult operation," and he added that Kuechler should be careful not to try to go too far south with WINKELRIED. Time was important. The Finnish Army's chief of staff and operations chief were coming the next day, and he wanted to give them a firm commitment on NORDLICHT, which he again characterized as an easy repeat of Sevastopol. When Kuechler brought out aerial photographs showing countless solid blocks of buildings still standing in Leningrad, Hitler admitted to being "impressed." But he had the answer: he was sending General Richthofen, commander of Fourth Air Force who was known as the master air

commander, to conduct the air support. That was why, he added, almost as an afterthought, he was giving Manstein command of NORDLICHT. Manstein and Richthofen had developed an "ideal collaboration" at Sevastopol.[45]

A day later, Hitler gave Manstein his mission, which he was to execute in any way he saw fit provided he accomplished two things: made contact with the Finns and "leveled Leningrad to the ground." As NORDLICHT commander, Manstein would be independent of Army Group North and would come directly under the OKH. Hitler also told Manstein he could expect some help from the Finns, and the next day Hitler secured a promise from the Finnish Chief of Staff, Jalka-vaenkenraali ("Lieutenant General") Erik Heinrichs, to have the Finnish Isthmus Front assist NORDLICHT with artillery and a feigned attack.[46] Manstein would have liked a great deal more help from the Finns, but Hitler had in fact gotten all that he could and possibly more than he had expected. Hitler knew from long experience that Mannerheim was exceedingly skittish about involving his forces in a direct attack on Leningrad.[47]

Meretskov at the Bottleneck

Seemingly, the Russians were going to allow Army Group North enough

---

[45]*Ibid.,* 18–23 Aug 42.

[46]Greiner, *Oberste Wehrmachtfuehrung,* p. 406; *Greiner Diary Notes,* 25 Aug 42, C–065q CMH file.

[47]Mannerheim maintained that he accepted command of the Finnish Army in 1941 on the condition that he never be required to lead an offensive against Leningrad because he did not want to lend credence to a long-standing Soviet claim that an independent Finland was a manifest threat to the second city of the Soviet Union. Mannerheim, *Erinnerungen,* p. 454.

time to itself to get NORDLICHT off the map tables and onto the ground. *Northwest* and *Volkhov Fronts* were busy through the summer gnawing at the Demyansk pocket and the Volkhov line, and Sixteenth and Eighteenth Armies were taking more casualties and heavier drains on their equipment and ammunition stocks than they could readily afford, but nothing big appeared to be in the making.

The appearance was deceptive. *Volkhov Front,* under General Meretskov, had been working in elaborate secrecy since early July on an offensive to break the Leningrad blockade at the bottleneck and, as the *History of the Second World War* puts it, "deal the enemy a preemptive blow in the Leningrad sector."[48] To do the job, Meretskov had *Eighth Army,* the *IV Guards Rifle Corps,* and *Second Shock Army,* which was in the process of being reconstituted. *Leningrad Front* had set up several divisions with artillery that would join in from the west as the *Neva Group.* By the last week in August, Meretskov had a 3:1 superiority in troops, 4:1 in tanks, and 2:1 in artillery and mortars; but, by his account, he did not know about the German buildup for NORDLICHT.[49]

Meretskov proposed to smash the whole 7-mile bottleneck front north of the Mga-Volkhov railroad, take the Sinyavino Heights, and finish at the Neva bend west of Mga near the Village of Otradnoye. *(Map 38.)* The distances were not great: 4 miles to the Sinyavino Heights; another 6 from there west to the Neva; and, at the base of the bottleneck, 15 miles from the front to Otradnoye. The terrain was another matter altogether. The entire area was a patchwork of woods, swamps, and peat bogs. Large stretches were underwater, and the water table was so close to the surface nearly everywhere that fortifications had to be built above ground, which complicated the defense but also made it impossible for an attacker to dig foxholes or trenches. The only really dry ground was on the Sinyavino Heights, which rose to a maximum of 150 feet and afforded unimpeded observation for miles in all directions. Meretskov expected his assets to be superiority in numbers and material, surprise, and speed; he hoped to have joined hands with *Leningrad Front* on the Neva in two or three days, before the Germans could bring in reinforcements. For a high-speed operation, however, the Soviet plans were cumbersome. *Volkhov Front's* force was split into three echelons, which would have to be committed separately; and the *Stavka,* remembering bad experiences it had with coordinated operations by the two *fronts* in the winter, ordered the *Neva Group* not to make its bid until after *Volkhov Front* had made a clear breakthrough.[50]

Full-fledged surprise was going to be all but impossible to attain, and this, although Meretskov does not mention it, was *Volkhov Front's* number one problem. The Germans had worked on their defenses in the bottleneck for almost a year, and they knew exactly what the consequences of a lapse could be. During the summer, Hitler had constantly kept an eye on the bottleneck as a likely spot for Stalin to try

---

[48]*IVMV,* vol. V, p. 238.

[49]Meretskov, *Serving the People,* pp. 224–26.

[50]*Ibid.,* pp. 224–31.

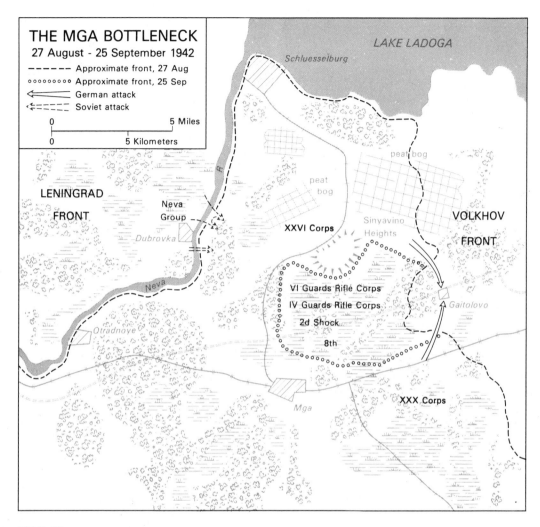

THE MGA BOTTLENECK
27 August - 25 September 1942

- - - - - Approximate front, 27 Aug
ooooooooo Approximate front, 25 Sep
←———— German attack
←===== Soviet attack

| 0 | | 5 Miles |
| 0 | | 5 Kilometers |

LAKE LADOGA

Schluesselburg

peat bog

LENINGRAD

peat bog

FRONT

Neva
Group

Dubrovka

Sinyavino
Heights

XXVI Corps

VOLKHOV

FRONT

Neva

VI Guards Rifle Corps

IV Guards Rifle Corps

Gaitolovo

2d Shock

Otradnoye

8th

Mga

XXX Corps

MAP 38

for a prestige victory to offset the defeats in the south. He told Kuechler in the conference on 23 August that the Russians would launch "rabid attacks ... above all against the Mga bottleneck" as soon as they caught wind of NORDLICHT. He advised Kuechler on that occasion to put the Tigers in behind the front. "Then," he said, "nothing can happen; they are unas-sailable and can smash any enemy tank attack."[51]

Nevertheless, Meretskov did achieve some surprise. From the second week of August on, the OKH and the army group became more and more convinced that an attack would take place

---

[51]*H. Gr. Nord, Ia Kriegstagebuch, 1.–31.8.42,* 23 Aug 42, H. Gr. Nord 75128/13 file.

at the bottleneck, and even though they exchanged information almost daily, they could not reach conclusions as to when it would come or how strong it would be. The pattern of the buildup was more vague—deliberately so according to Meretskov—than they were accustomed to seeing, and the Kirishi bridgehead and Pogostye actually appeared to be more likely places for something big to happen. On the 23d, XXVI Corps, which was holding the bottleneck with 227th Infantry Division north of the Mga-Volkhov railroad and 223d Infantry Division south of the railroad and which had 12th Panzer Division in reserve at Mga, asked for another infantry division to put into the bottleneck. Four days later, early on the morning of the 27th, the OKH alerted Kuechler to increasing signs of an attack at the bottleneck, and told him to move in the 170th Infantry Division, one of the Crimean divisions standing by for NORDLICHT. Kuechler confirmed that he would do so and added that he would also put in the Tigers, several of which were reportedly aboard a train near Pskov.[52]

While Kuechler and the OKH were thus engaged, Meretskov's first echelon, *Eighth Army*, was opening the offensive. Shortly before 1200 on the 27th, Lindemann reported attacks along the whole front north of the railroad. At one point twenty tanks had broken in, but no main effort could be detected. The situation was still much the same at nightfall, and XXVI Corps had not detected any units other than ones it had previously identified and had been ready to handle. Kuechler's main concern was for the NORDLICHT

timetable. He told Schmundt, "When the Russian attacks he keeps at it for weeks on end; consequently, substantial quantities of infantry and ammunition may become tied up in a direction that was not provided for in the army group's program."[53]

The next morning at 0900, Kuechler and Manstein had their first meeting, and Kuechler was pleased to hear that Manstein believed taking Leningrad would be every bit as hard a proposition as Army Group North had claimed it was. In his experience, Manstein said, he had not found the Russians susceptible to "terrorization" by bombing and shelling, and he thought it would be simpler just to seal the city off "and let the defenders and inhabitants starve."[54] While the field marshals were talking, XXVI Corps reported a break-in two-thirds of a mile deep on the bottleneck between the Sinyavino Heights and the railroad. A battalion commander had lost his nerve and ordered a retreat. When the rest of the day brought evidence of several previously unidentified Soviet divisions in and around the break-in area, Kuechler ordered the 5th Mountain Division and 28th Jaeger Division out of the NORDLICHT staging area to Mga. At the day's end, Hitler, who was "exceedingly agitated over the situation at XXVI Corps," diverted the 3d Mountain Division, which was at sea in the Baltic on the way from Norway to Finland, to Reval to be attached to Eighteenth Army.[55]

Eighth Army deepened the break-in to

---

[52]*Ibid.*, 23–27 Aug 42.

[53]*Ibid.*, 27 Aug 42.
[54]*Ibid.*, 28 Aug 42.
[55]*Ibid.*; *Greiner Diary Notes*, 28 Aug 42, C–065q CMH file.

A TIGER TANK WAITS FOR A TOW

three miles on the third day, almost to the Sinyavino Heights, and on the next, Kuechler committed the Tigers. He had four, but two broke down on the roads. Kuechler also went out to see for himself what was going on at XXVI Corps and reported to the OKH that he "had no particularly bad impression of the situation" but the fighting would "drag on for some time." On the 31st, Lindemann pronounced the crisis passed and the break-in contained.[56] At the same time on the other side of the front Meretskov was ordering in his second echelon, *IV Guards Rifle Corps*.[57]

Manstein at the Bottleneck

For the next several days, XXVI Corps felt the presence of *IV Guards Rifle Corps,* not in a heavy onslaught, but as a steady, stubborn infiltration through the woods and swamps south and west of the Sinyavino Heights. On 3 September, the *Neva Group* joined the battle briefly with attempts to cross the Neva in several places. These were beaten off so thoroughly by artillery and air strikes that the *Neva Group* lost most of its crossing equipment.[58] By the end of the day on the 4th, *IV Guards Rifle Corps*, in the woods southwest of the Sinyavino Heights, had deepened the penetration to almost

[56]*H. Gr. Nord, Ia Kriegstagebuch, 1.–31.8.42,* 29–31 Aug 42, H. Gr. Nord 75128/13 file.

[57]Meretskov, *Serving the People,* p. 234.

[58]*Ibid.,* p. 235.

five miles and was two-thirds of the way across the bottleneck. But XXVI Corps, troubled mostly by the terrain and thick forest growth that limited visibility to fifty feet or less, believed it had the push contained. Hitler, however, was "exasperated." Army Group North, he said, had four NORD-LICHT divisions tied up in the bottleneck and still was not able to bring the enemy to a stop, and that showed a lack of purposeful leadership.[59] By telephone, he told Manstein to take command in the bottleneck, where he said there had been "atrocious developments," and to "restore the situation offensively." Headquarters, Eleventh Army, was to come directly under the OKH, and Manstein was to "report immediately failures on the part of any commanders."[60]

The XXVI Corps had been right. The Soviet advance was stopped on 4 September, and Meretskov could not get it going again even though he put in his third echelon, *Second Shock Army,* on the 5th. On the 9th and 10th, XXVI Corps handily beat off attacks by the *Neva Group* from the west and *Second Shock Army* on the east.[61] Nevertheless, the Soviet offensive was having one very considerable success: it was badly scrambling the timetables for NORD-LICHT and WINKELRIED. NORDLICHT could not begin until the bottleneck was secure, and WINKELRIED had to wait until the air support could be

shifted from the bottleneck. Hitler had already put off the operation against the Murmansk Railroad until the winter. The latter decision removed one source of time pressure on NORD-LICHT and WINKELRIED but not another, namely, the approach of the fall rainy season.[62]

The last Soviet efforts to get the offensive going again gave Manstein what he thought might be an opportunity for a surprise, and on the 10th, he put the 24th and 170th Infantry Divisions and the 12th Panzer Division into a thrust northward from the southeastern corner of the breakthrough to close the gap behind the Russians. The infantry started at 0800 and were stopped almost at once by shattering artillery and mortar fire. In the afternoon, another try, this time also using the 12th Panzer Division, ended as quickly as the first when the infantry was once more pinned down by the enemy artillery and mortars, and the tanks ran into minefields. The next day, while the infantry was fighting off counterattacks, Manstein canceled the attack and ordered reconnaissance to locate the enemy strongpoints so that they could be picked off one by one. To Keitel, he said he was going to have to knock out the enemy artillery first and then go over to set-piece attacks from the north and the south.[63]

Manstein was ready to make another attempt on the 18th but then had to wait three more days because of rain and fog. The rain did not make much

---

[59]The divisions were 5th Mountain Division, 28th Jaeger Division, 170th Infantry Division, and 24th Infantry Division. The 24th Infantry Division went into the bottleneck on 4 September.

[60] *Greiner Diary Notes,* 4 Sep 42, C–065q CMH file; *AOK 11, Ia Kriegstagebuch Nr. 2,* 4 Sep 42, AOK 11 33167/1 file.

[61]Meretskov, *Serving the People,* p. 235; *AOK 11, Ia Kriegstagebuch Nr. 2,* 9–10 Sep 42, AOK 11 33167/1 file.

[62]*H. Gr. Nord, Ia Kriegstagebuch, 1.–30.9.42,* 1 Sep 42, H. Gr. Nord 75128/14 file.

[63]*AOK 11, Ia Kriegstagebuch Nr. 2,* 10–11 Sep 42, AOK 11 33167/1 file.

difference to the infantry, because the ground was permanently sodden anyway, but the airplanes, which would be flying in close support, needed good visibility. In the meantime, artillery and *Stukas* had worked over the Soviet artillery emplacements. Manstein had four divisions at the ready: on the north, under XXVI Corps, the 121st Infantry Division and on the south, under XXX Corps, the 24th, 132d, and 170th Infantry Divisions. The objective for both thrusts was the village of Gaitolovo, which lay about midway in the mouth of the bulge astride the main—in fact the only—Soviet supply road. The start this time was good. The artillery and the *Stukas* had done their work well. By nightfall on the second day, 22 September, one regiment of the 132d Infantry Division was just two-thirds of a mile short of reaching Gaitolovo from the south. Having ample reason now to remember what had happened to *Second Shock Army* in the spring, the Russians fought furiously to hold Gaitolovo, but 121st Infantry Division was at the northern edge of the village on the 24th, and the two groups joined the next day. The bulge had become a pocket.[64]

Winkelried

While Manstein was engaged in the bottleneck, Kuechler raised the question with Halder of what to do about the Demyansk pocket. The season was getting late and soon would be too late even for WINKELRIED. With or without WINKELRIED, Kuechler maintained that the pocket would be horrendously difficult to hold through another winter.

Since the Ostashkov operation (to close the gap to Army Group Center) could certainly not be done in 1942, and he knew of no plan to do it in the coming year, he "suggested" it might be better to forget about WINKELRIED and evacuate the pocket. Halder replied that the pocket had to be held because it was "the sole solution" to the problem of the Toropets bulge and because, "The Fuehrer completely rejects the idea of evacuating II Corps."[65] Thereupon, Kuechler and Busch became desperate to get WINKELRIED going before the weather, which was beginning to turn, ruled it out altogether. Expecting Manstein's success at the bottleneck to release the air support, Kuechler, on the 24th, set WINKELRIED for either the 26th or 27th, depending on the weather and the speed with which the planes could be redeployed. When the OKH advised him, on the 26th, that the *Luftwaffe* high command had ordered half the planes to stay with Eleventh Army until the envelopment at Gaitolovo was "one hundred percent secure," Kuechler decided to go ahead with WINKELRIED the next day anyway.[66] *(Map 39.)*

After a whole summer's preparations, first for SCHLINGPFLANZE and then for WINKELRIED, Sixteenth Army hardly expected to achieve a surprise, but it did. The 5th Jaeger Division and 126th Infantry Division, striking out of the east face of the pocket, encircled the *1st Guards Rifle Division* east of the Lovat River in five days, thereby completing WINKELRIED-OST ("east"). Because the divisions did not have means

[64]*Ibid.*, 11–25 Sep 42.

[65]*H. Gr. Nord, Ia Kriegstagebuch, 1.–30.9.42,* 14 and 23 Sep 42, H. Gr. Nord 75128/14 file.
[66]*Ibid.*, 24–26 Sep 42.

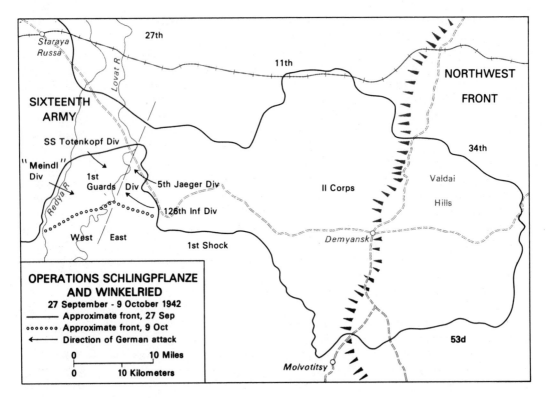

MAP 39

to cross the Lovat, 5th Jaeger Division then had to be drawn north and sluiced through the corridor to the west side of the river where it was joined by the SS Totenkopf Division, which after a winter and a summer in the pocket was reduced to 350 effectives, and the Air Force Field Division "Meindle," a half-dozen battalions of surplus *Luftwaffe* personnel being used as infantry. These began WINKELRIED-WEST on 7 October and completed it in three days.[67] The corridor then was ten miles wide at its narrowest point.

---

[67]*AOK 16, Ia Kriegstagebuch, Band II*, 27–30 Sep 42, AOK 16 36588/2 file; *AOK 16, Ia Kriegstagebuch, Band III*, 1–10 Oct 42, AOK 16 36588/3 file.

Mop-up at Gaitolovo

Meanwhile, Manstein had finished at the bottleneck, though not quite as quickly as he might have expected. For three days, beginning on 26 September, the *Neva Group* had made its strongest effort yet to cross the Neva and had taken three small bridgeheads opposite Dubrovka. The bridgeheads for a time raised a possibility of the German east front's breaking open just when the west front was closed, but after the *Neva Group* failed to expand them by the 29th, Manstein began mopping up the Gaitolovo pocket. The battle ended on 2 October. It had cost the *Volkhov* and *Leningrad Fronts* over twelve thousand men who were taken prisoner and an estimated three times as many wounded or killed, but it had also not come cheaply for the Germans who took over twenty-six thousand casualties. Several of the NORDLICHT divisions were "burned out," battle weary and weakened by losses. Manstein thought he could begin NORDLICHT in three weeks if he had to, but such an order was not likely to come.[68]

The Far North

Crosscurrents

In late April 1942, a day before the Soviet spring offensive against Army of Lapland began, General Dietl, the army's commander, had informed his superior headquarters, the OKW, that since the reinforcements allotted to him during the winter most likely would not all be delivered for another four or five months, he considered offensive operations by his army ruled out for the coming summer. A month later, in its directive on Army of Lapland operations in the summer, the OKW accepted his estimate and set only two specific tasks for his army: to reestablish a solid line east of Kestenga and then to transfer as many troops as could be spared from there to the Mountain Corps Norway. The Army of Lapland main effort, henceforth, would be in the Mountain Corps Norway sector, where the primary mission would be defense against possible United States–British invasion attempts. The OKW also stated that it considered the Rybachiy Peninsula

very important to the conduct of the war in the far north (because, in Soviet hands, it impeded access to Pechenga and was a lingering threat to the rear of the Litsa River line) and instructed Dietl to make preparations for taking the peninsula. Since the OKW could not foresee the time when the troop and supply situations would permit anything of that sort, however, the date was left open—possibly to be in the late summer of 1942 or the late winter of 1942–1943.[69]

The OKW's concern over Allied landings, which was, in fact, mostly Hitler's, was exaggerated but not an absolute delusion. Early in the year, to satisfy in some measure the Soviet call for a second front, the British had put forward a plan known as Project SLEDGEHAMMER in which they envisioned large-scale raids along the coast of Europe from northern Norway to the Bay of Biscay. In the spring, SLEDGEHAMMER had evolved into a proposed cross-Channel operation, and Prime Minister Churchill had presented Operation JUPITER as an alternative. In JUPITER, Churchill envisioned landings at Pechenga and at Banak, the latter in northern Norway, as means of operating in direct conjunction with the Russians and of eliminating German air and naval bases that endangered Allied convoys on the arctic route. JUPITER aroused little enthusiasm among Churchill's own military advisers and none at all on the part

---

[68]*AOK 11, Ia Kriegstagebuch Nr. 2*, 26 Sep–2 Oct 42, AOK 11 33167/1 file.

[69]*OKW, Stellv. WFSt, Kriegsgeschichtliche Abteilung, Kriegstagebuch, 1.4.-30.6.42*, 23 Apr and 16 May 42, I.M.T. 1807 file; *OKW, WFSt, Op. Nr. 55798/42, Weisung fuer die weitere Kampffuehrung des AOK Lappland, 16.5.42*, AOK 20 27253/6 file.

of the Americans, but Churchill kept it alive in the Allied high councils.[70]

When Hitler made his surprise birthday visit to Mannerheim on 4 June, which, incidentally, caused the Finns some anxiety and provoked a breach in consular relations between the United States and Finland, he conferred with Dietl, who told him that Army of Lapland would not have enough strength to take the Rybachiy Peninsula or to hold it if, by a stroke of luck, it were taken. Nevertheless, Hitler, unwilling to give up the effort, ordered Dietl to carry on the preparations and assured him that the weakness on the ground could be compensated for in the air. To General Stumpff, the Fifth Air Force commander, he then issued an order to ready the ground installations in northern Norway and Finland for "very strong forces."[71]

In June, it appeared that Army of Lapland's next mission would be to occupy the Rybachiy Peninsula, and the plans were then given the code name WIESENGRUND ("meadow land"). Since Mannerheim was about to take over the Ukhta sector, which would release 7th Mountain Division, the troop problem appeared to be solved. In the first week of July, however, the OKW informed Dietl that 7th Mountain Division could not be transferred to the Pechenga area because it was impossible to bring up enough supplies to maintain another full strength division there. The OKW proposed instead to send "in the long run" enough "static" troops (that is, without horses

or motor vehicles) to relieve 6th Mountain Division on the Litsa and to free it and 2d Mountain Division for WIESENGRUND. Dietl promptly protested that the Litsa line was no place for scantily equipped, third-rate troops, and WIESENGRUND was then shelved.[72]

After the Russians fell back from Kestenga, in late May, the front in Finland became quiet. In June, Army of Lapland set up five recently received fortress battalions on the coast, and during July and August it pushed work on coast artillery, emplacing twenty-one batteries in the zone between Tana Fiord and Pechenga Bay. In the late summer, Headquarters, 210th Infantry Division, was brought in to command the fortress battalions and the coast artillery. In the meantime, Army of Lapland had been redesignated Twentieth Mountain Army. In July, XVIII Mountain Corps had staged a small attack to recover a hill off its left flank that had been left in Soviet hands when General Siilasvuo, commander of III Corps, had stopped his unit's operations. Otherwise, throughout the summer, the Germans and Russians both contented themselves with harassment, which for the most part took the form of starting forest fires in each other's areas. White phosphorus shells easily ignited the evergreen trees, and the fires occasionally burned across minefields or threatened installations.[73]

The one summer's operation that came near having strategic significance was Operation KLABAUTERMANN

[70]Churchill, *Hinge of Fate*, pp. 256, 323, 350, 448, 477; Matloff and Snell, *Strategic Planning*, pp. 100, 189, 235, 244.

[71]*OKW, WFSt, Kriegsgeschichtliche Abteilung, Kriegstagebuch 1.4.–30.6.42*, 5 Jun 42, I.M.T. 1807 file.

[72]*(Geb.) AOK 20, Ia Nr. 1405/42, an Geb.-Korps Norwegen, 3.7.42*, AOK 20 27252/8 file.

[73]*AOK Lappland, Ia Kriegstagebuch Nr. 2*, AOK 20 27252/2 file; *(Geb.) AOK 20, Ia Kriegstagebuch, Band III*, 1 Sep 42, AOK 20 27252/3 file.

LOOKOUT NEAR KESTENGA

("hobgoblin"), which the German Navy and Air Force conducted from Finnish bases on the shore of Lake Ladoga. The idea of using small boats to interdict Soviet traffic on the lake had occurred to Hitler in the fall of 1941, too late to be put into effect. It was revived in the spring of 1942 when the Leningrad evacuation began. Hitler was concerned at the time that Leningrad would be completely evacuated; in which case, the northern flank would lose its importance to the Soviet Union and large numbers of troops could be shifted to the south to oppose Operation BLAU. Consequently, he had ordered the Soviet boat traffic on the lake to be "combated with all means."[74]

The German Navy brought German and Italian PT boats into action on the lake in early July. The *Luftwaffe* had its craft, Siebel-ferries, ready a month later. The Siebel-ferries were twin hulled, powered by airplane engines, and armed with antiaircraft guns. The invention of a *Luftwaffe* colonel, they had originally been built for the invasion of England. Both the navy and the air force claimed the overall command and so further impaired an operation that was already hampered by lack of air cover and the hazards of navigation on the lake that was studded with shoals and rocky outcroppings. Soviet

---

[74]*OKW, WFSt, Kriegsgeschichtliche Abteilung,*

Kriegstagebuch, 1.4.–30.6.42, 26 May 42, I.M.T. 1807 file.

accounts claim a victory for the Soviet Navy, which had its own armed vessels on the lake. The Germans regarded KLABAUTERMANN as an enterprise that was foundering under the weight of its technical and command problems long before it was abandoned, which was done on 6 November when the lake began to freeze.[75]

The Murmansk Railroad

Having a division to spare as a result of Operation WIESENGRUND's being canceled, Dietl returned to the idea of a double thrust to the Murmansk Railroad—by XXXVI Mountain Corps to Kandalaksha and by the Finnish Army to Belomorsk. In conferences, on 8 and 9 July, with General Erfurth, the OKW representative at Mannerheim's headquarters, and with Jodl, on the 13th, the project was further developed, and after Jodl carried it back to *Fuehrer* Headquarters, Hitler gave it his approval in Directive 44 of 21 July 1942. Twentieth Mountain Army was to prepare to take Kandalaksha in the fall and was assured that Leningrad would be taken in September at the latest to free the required Finnish forces and that 5th Mountain Division, which had been diverted to Army Group North in the winter and was still there, would be shipped to Finland by the end of September. To the Kandalaksha-Belomorsk operation, Hitler assigned the code name LACHSFANG ("salmon catch").[76]

No doubt, Hitler would have issued the directive for LACHSFANG soon, in any case, to cap off the victory he believed was developing in the south and to isolate the Soviet Union in its defeat. He knew the Americans and British were opening an alternative route to the Soviet Union through the Persian Gulf and Iran, but he expected to be able to close it as well and had Manstein in mind for the mission.[77]

The XXXVI Mountain Corps began its planning for LACHSFANG on 22 July. Success, it believed, hinged on two requirements, a fast breakthrough on the Verman River line and, subsequently, a quick thrust to Kandalaksha before the enemy could make another stand. The corps expected to have 80,000 troops, twice as many as it had employed in the summer of 1941; and Fifth Air Force agreed to provide 60 *Stukas,* 9 fighters, and 9 bombers, more planes than had been available for the whole Army of Norway operations in the previous summer. Time was a critical element. If necessary, operations could be continued until 1 December, but they would be impossible thereafter because of deep snow and extremely short periods of daylight. The late winter, mid-March to mid-April, would afford a second opportunity but a considerably less favorable one because the German troops were not trained for winter operations in the Arctic. The XXXVI Mountain Corps believed it would need four weeks for LACHSFANG and wanted to time the operation to end in mid-November, since by then the length of daylight would be less than seven hours, and in succeeding weeks,

---

[75]Ziemke, *Northern Theater,* p. 231; Kovalchuk, *Leningrad,* pp. 273–84.

[76]*OKW, WFSt, Op. Nr. 551275/42, Weisung Nr. 44, 21.7.42,* German High Level Directives, CMH files.

[77]*General Halder's Daily Notes,* vol. II, 19 Aug 42, EAP 21–g–16/4/0 file.

this amount would decrease by an hour a week.[78]

At Mannerheim's headquarters, Erfurth sounded out the Finnish reaction to LACHSFANG. In Directive 44, Hitler had described a companion Finnish thrust to Belomorsk as "desirable." Dietl and General Weisenberger, the commander of XXXVI Mountain Corps, regarded one as indispensable. Mannerheim's chief of staff, General Heinrichs, indicated that the Finnish attitude was "positive," but Leningrad would have to be taken first. The Finnish Command, he added, also regarded it "as necessary" that the left flank of Army Group North be advanced east to the middle Svir.[79] The Germans had expected the first condition but not the second. At the OKH they told Mannerheim's representative, Keneraaliluutnanti ("Major General") Paavo Talvela, that if the marshal insisted on the latter condition as a prerequisite, LACHSFANG would have to be dropped. This then became the subject of Heinrich's August visit to the *Werwolf*. In the talks there, Heinrichs exchanged a Finnish agreement to go ahead with LACHSFANG for a German promise to have Army Group North schedule an advance to the Svir River as its next assignment—after it had taken Leningrad. The Finns proposed to commit eight infantry divisions and an armored division in the Belomorsk operation. For them also, time was critical. Four of the divisions would have to come from the Isthmus Front north of

Leningrad, and because of poor roads, their redeployment could not be accomplished in less than three or four weeks after Leningrad fell.[80]

By itself LACHSFANG looked good; however, it depended on NORDLICHT, and NORDLICHT, as has been seen, was an uncertain enterprise. The German part of LACHSFANG also depended on XXXVI Mountain Corps' getting 5th Mountain Division, which would have had to leave Army Group North by 15 August to reach the front in Finland on time. But Kuechler insisted that Army Group North could not execute NORDLICHT and defend the rest of its front if it had to release the division, and Hitler, finally, on 15 August, decided to leave 5th Mountain Division with Army Group North and send 3d Mountain Division to Finland instead. When 3d Mountain Division had to be diverted to Army Group North during the battle for the bottleneck, Hitler drew the one conclusion left to him and, on 1 September, canceled LACHSFANG for 1942.[81]

The Arctic Convoys

Early in June, German agents in Iceland reported Convoy PQ-17 forming off the southwest coast of Iceland. Having that much lead time and twenty-four hours of daylight in the Arctic to assure good reconnaissance and air support, the German Navy

[78]XXXVI (Geb.) A.K., Fuehrungsabteilung, Kriegstagebuch und Anlagen zu "Lachsfang," 22 Jul 42, XXXVI A.K. 29155/1 file; XXXVI (Geb.) A.K., Qu., Unterlagen fuer "Lachsfang," 1.8.42, XXXVI A.K. 29155/2 file.
[79]Der Kdr. d. Verb. Stab Nord, Nr. 46/42, Kampffuehrung in Nordfinnland, 2.8.42, H 22/227 file.

[80]OKH, GenStdH, Op. Abt. IN, Operationen gegen die Murmanbahn, 5.8.42, H 22/227 file; Greiner Diary Notes, 25 Aug 42, C–065q CMH file; OKW, WFSt, Op. (H) Nr. 55139/42, Abschrift von Fernschreiben Gen. Erfurth, 10.8.42, OKW 119 file.
[81]H. Gr. Nord, Ia Kriegstagebuch, 1.–31.8.42, 10 Aug 42, H. Gr. Nord 75128/13 file; OKW, WFSt, Op. Nr. 002820/42, 15.8.42, German High Level Directives, CMH files; H. Gr. Nord, Ia Kriegstagebuch, 1.–30.9.42, 1 Sep 42, H. Gr. Nord 75128/14 file.

undertook another try at getting its heavy ships into action. *Luetzow, Scheer,* and six destroyers went to Alta Fiord, at the northernmost tip of Norway, and *Tirpitz, Hipper,* and six destroyers took up station in West Fiord, somewhat to the south on the Atlantic side of the peninsula. After PQ–17 left Iceland, on 27 June, the navy learned that, aside from cruisers and destroyers, the convoy also had a remote escort of two battleships and an aircraft carrier. (They were U.S.S. *Washington,* H.M.S. *Duke of York,* and the British carrier *Victorious*.) The Naval Staff then changed the deployment and ordered all the ships to Alta Fiord, where German air superiority would be sure to be sufficient to drive off the battleships and carrier.[82]

As PQ–17 approached the Spitzbergen–Bear Island passage, the time for the ships to set out had come, but the Naval Staff worried about the remote escort, and on 4 July, it concluded that a strike would be impossible. The next day, however, its confidence revived, when not only the battleships and the carrier but also the cruisers—there were seven in the escort—were sighted steering west.[83] They were under orders, of which the Germans, of course, were not aware, not to advance into the zone of German air dominance east of Bear Island.[84] Admiral Raeder, commander in chief of the German Navy, and the Naval Staff then decided to let the ships sail, but Hitler strongly enjoined Generaladmiral ("Admiral") Rolf Carls, the commanding admiral, North, not to let them engage the convoy unless the carrier could be located and eliminated first. At 1500 on the 5th, *Tirpitz, Scheer,* and eight destroyers put out from Alta Fiord. *Luetzow* and four destroyers stayed behind because they had damaged their bottoms on the trip from West Fiord.

Three hours after leaving Alta Fiord, Generaladmiral Otto Schniewind, in command aboard *Tirpitz,* knew his ships had been sighted when his radio monitors intercepted a message sent in the clear by a Soviet submarine.[85] An hour later, a British aircraft on patrol off North Cape reported a second sighting. Both messages were picked up in Berlin, where Raeder was torn for another hour between his desire to see the ships score a success against the convoy, which he knew by then was scattered and defenseless southeast of Spitzbergen, and his duty to respect Hitler's—not to mention his own—concern for their safety. (The British Naval Staff had ordered the convoy to scatter at the time the cruiser force turned back.) At 2100, Raeder ordered Schniewind, through Carls, to break off the mission and return to base. Having second thoughts later, Raeder concluded that to attack convoys was made excessively difficult by Hitler's insistence on avoiding risks to the big ships. PQ–17, he concluded, had offered an opportunity that had not occurred before and was not likely to

---

[82]*Naval War Diary,* vol. 35, pp. 36, 57. For U.S. and British dispositions with regard to PQ–17, see Morison, *Battle of the Atlantic,* p. 180f and Roskill, *War at Sea,* vol. II, p. 136.

[83]*Naval War Diary,* vol. 35, p. 70.

[84]Roskill, *War at Sea,* vol. II, p. 135. *IVMV* (vol. V, p. 261) maintains that the escort would have been adequate to assure safe passage for PQ–17, but the convoy was being used merely as bait to lure out the *Tirpitz,* and "the British Admiralty . . . regarded the security of the convoy as a secondary mission."

[85]*Naval War Diary,* vol. 35, pp. 70–72. See also *Fuehrer Conferences, 1942,* pp. 86, 91–93.

THE CRUISER *KOELN* ON STATION IN ALTA FIORD

come again; therefore, it was probable that the big ships would never be used against the convoys.[86]

But Fifth Air Force did not share the navy's doubts and troubles. It was in a position to hit PQ–17 with devastating power. By the time the convoy departed from Iceland, Stumpff had assembled, in the vicinity of North Cape, 103 twin-engine JU–88 bombers, 42 HE–111 torpedo-bombers, 15 floatplane torpedo-bombers, 30 *Stukas*, and 74 long-range reconnaissance planes, a total of 264 aircraft.[87] On 2 July, the reconnaissance planes deter-mined the position and course of PQ–17, and on the 4th the bombers and torpedo-planes began the attack, claiming four sinkings in the first strike. During the day, they saw the remote escort and the cruisers turn back; and they saw the destroyers in the escort go off as well. (The commander of the destroyers, expecting "to see the cruisers open fire and the enemy's masts appear on the horizon at any moment," had decided, without orders, to support the cruisers.)[88] Thereafter, PQ–17 was left only with what protection two submarines and a few trawlers could give it, and Fifth Air Force hunted down the merchant ships

[86]Roskill, *War at Sea*, vol. II, p. 139; Irving, *The Destruction of Convoy PQ-17*, pp. 163–66; *Naval War Diary*, vol. 35, p. 97.
[87]British Air Ministry Pamphlet 248, p. 114.

[88]Roskill, *War at Sea*, vol. II, p. 141; Morison, *Battle of the Atlantic*, p. 185.

almost at leisure. When it was over, the Germans believed they had sunk every last ship. In fact, eleven of thirty-six merchant ships in PQ–17 did reach Soviet ports, but three of those were almost to the point of sinking.[89]

The PQ–17 disaster led the British Admiralty to propose stopping the convoys until winter again brought the cover of darkness, but Stalin, who regarded any losses his allies might suffer in bringing aid to the Soviet Union as perfectly acceptable, protested violently.[90] As a compromise, after an interval of nearly two months, PQ–18 sailed in early September. The Germans were ready. Fifth Air Force had raised its HE–111 torpedo-bomber strength to ninety-two planes, and the navy had a dozen submarines stationed in northern Norway. Raeder and the Naval Staff struggled once more with their concerns about the surface ships and finally alerted *Tirpitz, Scheer, Hipper,* and the light cruiser *Koeln* for a sortie against either PQ–18 or QP–14, which was expected to be coming west at about the same time. The hitch again was an aircraft carrier in the escort, on this occasion, the U.S.-built, British-manned escort carrier *Avenger.* To get rid of the carrier, the navy organized seven submarines into a special group, *Traegertod* ("carrier's death"), and Fifth Air Force agreed to direct a strong part of its effort against the carrier.

On 13 September, as PQ–18 entered the Spitzbergen–Bear Island passage, a submarine fired two torpedoes at *Avenger* and missed. On the same day, Fifth Air Force began its attack with a strike by fifty-six bombers. The bombers could not approach the carrier that had its own aircraft defending it and that had the support of the antiaircraft cruiser *Scylla.* The German pilots also found it difficult to get at the merchant ships because they maintained a tight formation inside a screen of twelve destroyers. On the 14th, fifty-four bombers tried again, and from then on the attacks continued until the 19th. PQ–18 fared better than its predecessor but, nevertheless, lost thirteen out of forty ships. The price was also high for Fifth Air Force, which lost twenty bombers in the first two strikes. When the carrier continued on past Spitzbergen with PQ–18 and then picked up QP–14 on the return trip, the navy abandoned the sortie by the surface ships. In fact, it instructed the submarines as well to avoid QP–14 since experience with PQ–18 had shown that attacks on a convoy with surface and air protection were too risky.[91]

After PQ–18 put in at Arkhangelsk, thus mollifying Stalin for the time being, the convoys were again suspended. Shipping requirements for the North African invasion, which came in November, helped to justify the suspension, in Western Allied if not in Soviet eyes. The North African landings also had a significant impact on the anticonvoy forces. All of Fifth Air Force's HE–111 torpedo-bombers and most of its JU–88s had to be transferred to the Mediterranean, leaving

---

[89]Generalmajor a. D. Hans-Detlev Herhudt von Rohden, *Die Kampffuehrung der Luftflotte 5 in Norwegen, 1942,* Rohden 4376–4408 file; Roskill, *War at Sea,* vol. II, p. 143; Irving, *Convoy PQ–17,* p. 287.

[90]Churchill, *Hinge of Fate,* pp. 269–73. See also *IVMV,* vol. V, p. 262 and *IVOVSS,* vol. II, p. 468f.

[91]Roskill, *War at Sea,* vol. II, pp. 278–86; Morison, *Battle of the Atlantic,* pp. 360–65; British Air Ministry Pamphlet 248, p. 115; *Naval War Diary,* vol. 37, pp. 143, 153, 176, 212, 224.

only the floatplanes, some *Stukas,* and the long-range reconnaissance units in the north.[92] With the winter's darkness setting in and the conditions for air operations becoming poor, the immediate effect of the loss was not significant. What was important was that the German *Luftwaffe* would never again be able to muster similar strength in the Arctic.

[92]Roskill, *War at Sea,* vol. II, p. 288; *IVMV,* vol. V, p. 262; British Air Ministry Pamphlet 248, p. 115.

CHAPTER XXI

The Change of Seasons

Duty and Country

A New Spirit

The *"Ni shagu nazad!"* ("Not a step back!") order was meant to do more than bring a halt to a retreat that was threatening to get out of hand. Alexander Werth, who was the London *Sunday Times* correspondent in Moscow observed, ". . . something must have happened . . . in high Government, Military and Party quarters, for on the 30th [of July] the whole tone of the Press radically changed. No more lamentations and imprecations . . . but orders, harsh, strict, ruthless orders. Clearly what was aimed at above all was precise military results. . . ."[1] W. Averell Harriman, who was in Moscow two weeks later as President Roosevelt's special envoy, reported that he had found Stalin and everyone else he saw "exactly as determined as ever."[2] If, as Stalin most likely believed, the German's ultimate objective was neither Stalingrad nor the Caucasus but Moscow, then the nation and the armed forces were going to have to be readied by every means for the decisive battle.

As the *"Ni shagu nazad!"* order was being read to the troops, the massive apparatus of public communications was swinging into action to raise the will of the Russian nation, not just that of Stalin and the Communist party, behind it. A national, "patriotic" war had been proclaimed in 1941, but the government had preferred, particularly in the winter and spring of 1942, to emphasize the communist-fascist aspect of the conflict and the inevitable, and speedy, victory of communism. In his May Day order of the day, Stalin had called for a total German defeat during 1942.[3] The *Pravda* editorial marking the start of the second year of the war had stated that "all of Hitler's military as well as political plans have completely collapsed" and "all prerequisites have been created for defeat of the hateful enemy in 1942."[4]

After July, the war became a "patriotic" Russian war, and the word "Russian," hardly ever used before in context with the Soviet state, was given prominence in print and in military orders. Heroes of the "old army," from Alexander Nevskiy, who defeated the Teutonic Knights in 1242, to Alexey Brusilov, who, in 1916, staged the best conducted (and most costly) Russian

---

[1] Alexander Werth, *The Year of Stalingrad* (New York: Alfred A. Knopf, Inc., 1947), p. 164.

[2] W. Averell Harriman and Elie Abel, *Special Envoy to Churchill and Stalin, 1941–1946* (New York: Random House, 1975), p. 168.

[3] USSR Embassy, *Information Bulletin,* no. 53, 2 May 42.

[4] *Pravda,* 24 Jun 42.

THE "PATRIOTIC WAR": A TANK CREW AND THEIR TANK NAMED "KUTUZOV"

offensive of World War I, were publicized as examples for Soviet officers and troops. Newspapers printed accounts of Russian military achievements from the Middle Ages through World War I. In September, the prominent writer Sergey Sergeyev-Tsenskiy rushed into print several chapters of a novel entitled *The Brusilov Breakthrough* that portrayed the general as "a sagacious strategist and loyal patriot, trusting in the might of Russian arms and the adamant spirit of the Russian Army."[5] The Stalin Prize winner, Konstantin Simonov, staged a play, titled *The Russians*, in which one of the characters was a former Tsarist officer

who put on his old uniform to fight again when his town was besieged by the Nazi Germans.[6] Stalin's 6 September appeal to the troops concluded with the sentences, "The Russians have always defeated the Prussians. The military tradition of the Russian people lives on in the heroic deeds of Soviet fighting men."[7]

The duty of the patriot was also to hate the enemy. Mikhail Sholokhov, author of *And Quiet Flows the Don*, wrote "The Science of Hatred." In "Cherish Your Hatred for the Enemy," Alexey Tolstoy told the country, ". . . at this

[5]USSR Embassy, *Information Bulletin*, no. 116, 29 Sep 42.

[6]USSR Embassy, *Information Bulletin*, no. 112, 19 Sep 42.

[7]*H. Gr. B, Ia Nr. 2965/42, Fernspruch vom 10.9.42*, Pz. AOK 4 28183/5 file. See p. 378.

time our one overwhelming sentiment, our one passion must be hatred for the enemy. Man must rise from his bed filled with stubborn hatred, with the same hatred he must work and fight, and with hatred unsatisfied go to sleep."[8] Ilya Ehrenburg, who as columnist for the army newspaper *Red Star* would be in the vanguard of the "hate the enemy" campaign for the next two and one-half years, received the Stalin Prize for a novel, *The Fall of Paris,* in which he delivered two messages: that it was impossible to live under the Germans and that, in the words of one of the characters, "You won't get rid of them with tears. They're rats. You've got to kill them."[9]

Out of the public view and that of the outside world, the "patriotic war" and "hate the enemy" campaigns produced an offshoot: mistrust of the Western Allies, in particular Russia's old imperialist rival, Great Britain. In August, Prime Minister Churchill, who had gone to Moscow to persuade Stalin to give up the idea of a second front in 1942, proposed sending British and American air forces to help defend the Caucasus. Stalin had said that would be "a great help."[10] When Generalmayor P. I. Bodin, the chief of operations in the General Staff, went to the *Transcaucasus Front* in September he reportedly told General Tyulenev:

Are you aware that the Allies are trying to take advantage of our difficult position and obtain our consent to the despatch of British troops into Transcaucasia? That, of course, cannot be allowed. The State Defense Committee considers the defense of Transcaucasia a task of vital state importance and it is our duty to take all measures to repel the enemy's attack, wear them out and defeat them. Hitler's hopes and the desires of the Allies must be buried . . . .[11]

The loss for a second time of vast stretches of Soviet territory and the conversion to the patriotic war brought the partisan movement to the forefront of the war effort in the late summer. By the Central Staff's reckoning, membership in the movement reached 100,000 by September.[12] At the end of August, the most successful partisan commanders from Belorussia and the northern Ukraine had been brought to Moscow for a series of conferences with Stalin and members of the *Politburo.* These conferences had enhanced the status of the movement and had been, no doubt, also calculated to show that the Soviet authorities could reach at will into the territory behind the enemy's lines.[13] To cap the conferences, Stalin, on 5 September, issued an order "On the Tasks of the Partisan Movement" in which he called for a "broader and deeper" development of partisan warfare and expansion of the movement "to encompass the whole people."[14] The call for a partisan movement "of the whole people" was taken up in party resolutions and the press. Briefly, after 6 September, when Marshal Voroshilov was named its commander in chief, the partisan move-

[8]USSR Embassy, *Information Bulletin,* no. 91, 30 Jul 42.

[9]Ilya Ehrenburg, *The Fall of Paris* (London: Hutchinson & Co., 1942), p. 368.

[10]Churchill, *Hinge of Fate,* p. 483; Harriman and Abel, *Special Envoy,* p. 161.

[11]Shtemenko, *Soviet General Staff,* p. 62.

[12]*Bolshaya Sovetskaya Entsiklopediya,* 1978, vol. 19, p. 235.

[13]Vershigora, *Lyudi,* pp. 392–95.

[14]*IVMV,* vol. V, p. 288.

ment achieved the nominal status of a separate branch in the armed forces.[15]

A New Authority

During the revolution the word "officer" had been excised from the Soviet military vocabulary and "commander" substituted. Thereafter, through the first year of the war, rank and authority were counterbalanced by a concept of socialist equality and by political mistrust. After July 1942, "officer" became an acceptable equivalent for "commander." More importantly, the relationship of the military, particularly the officer corps, to the state was redefined. Professional competence was recognized, rewarded, and given fuller play, and the military leadership was released from overt political tutelage and surveillance.

By a decree of 29 July 1942, the Presidium of the Supreme Soviet authorized three medals for officers only, the Orders of Suvorov, Kutuzov, and Alexander Nevskiy.[16] The orders were to be awarded to "commanders for outstanding services in organizing and directing war operations."[17] In effect, they declared the Soviet officers to be heirs to the old Russian military tradition. For the moment, it was also significant that each of those for whom an order was named had been notably successful at getting his troops to stand against a superior enemy—Alexander Nevskiy at Lake Peipus (1242), Suvorov at Ismail (1791), and Kutuzov at Borodino (1812).

The Orders of Suvorov, Kutuzov, and Alexander Nevskiy would go mostly to commanders of larger units and to staff officers. The Order of Kutuzov, for instance, was to be awarded for "well worked-out and executed plans of operations by a *front*, an army, or a separate formation, as a result of which a serious defeat is inflicted on the enemy. . . ."[18] Recognition for junior officers and enlisted men had been provided for in May, in anticipation of a victorious 1942 campaign, with the official establishment of the designation "guards" and the founding of the Order of the Patriotic War. The latter was to be awarded for specific achievements: a certain number of planes shot down or tanks knocked out, a successful assault on an enemy blockhouse, a certain number of enemy firing points destroyed by a tank crew, and so forth.[19] In the summer, to stimulate professionalism in the ranks and "popularize the heroism of the Soviet soldier," the army began to award honorary titles, such as,

---

[15]In November 1942, because "the Soviet forces were about to go over from the strategic defensive to the strategic offensive," the post of commander in chief of the partisan movement was abolished, and the Central Staff was reincorporated into the Supreme Headquarters. *IVMV*, vol. V, p. 290.

[16]Tyushkevich, *Vooruzhennye sily*, p. 506. Alexander Suvorov (1729–1800) served the Empress Catherine II as a military reformer and as a field general who won every battle he fought. Mikhail Kutuzov (1745–1813) was the Russian commander in chief against Napoleon from 1812 until his death.

[17]USSR Embassy, *Information Bulletin*, no. 101, 22 Aug 42.

[18]*Ibid.*, no. 109, 12 Sep 42.

[19]*Ibid.*, no. 62, 23 May 42. Tyushkevich, *Vooruzhennye sily*, p. 506. The Soviet Armed Forces were on the way toward becoming probably the most decorated in World War II. By the war's end, 7 million medals, including 11,600 Hero of the Soviet Union awards, were given to individuals. Divisions and regiments received 10,900 unit citations, and the designation "guards" was given to 11 field armies, 6 tank armies, 80 corps of various kinds, and 200 divisions. Deborin and Telpukhovskiy, *Itogi i uroki*, p. 357f.

WOMAN SNIPER LIEUTENANT POSES WITH HER RIFLE AND MEDALS

"Sniper," "Expert Machine Gunner," and "Expert Artillerist."[20]

Indirectly but, nevertheless, emphatically, Stalin let it be known that henceforth, professionalism, initiative, and merit would take precedence in decisions on appointments to command. In the late summer, *Pravda,* which did not ordinarily carry such material, published a play by Alexander Korneichuk called *The Front.* Korneichuk later told British correspondent Werth that Stalin had personally given him the "general idea" for the plot.[21] In *The Front,* young army commander, Ognev, demonstrated mastery of the techniques of modern warfare. His opponents were the *front* commander, Gorlov, a fossilized relic of the civil war, and a *front* staff filled with Gorlov's "yes-men." At the end, Ognev was given command of the *front* with a speech that read:

Stalin says that talented young generals have got to be promoted more boldly to leading positions on a level with the veteran commanders and that the men to be promoted are those who are capable of waging war in the modern way, not in the old-fashioned way, men who are capable of learning from the experience of modern warfare. . . .[22]

S. M. Shtemenko says, "We, the youth of the General Staff . . . regarded *The*

[20]*IVMV,* vol. V, p. 307.
[21]Werth, *Russia at War,* p. 423n.

[22]Alexander Korneichuk, *The Front,* in *Four Soviet War Plays* (London: Hutchinson & Co., 1944), p. 57.

Front as an expression of the Party's policy, as its appeal for an improvement in standards of military skill and leadership."[23]

Rokossovskiy, himself one of the younger generals being advanced, saw another aspect of the new approach to command, which he describes in the following anecdote:

Shortly before the Voronezh operation I came again to Moscow to report to the Supreme Commander. When I had finished and was about to leave, Stalin said, "Don't go yet."
He phoned Poskryobyshev [Stalin's secretary] and asked him to call in a general just removed from the command of a *front*. The following dialogue took place:
"You say we have punished you wrongly?"
"Yes, because the GHQ [*Stavka*] representative kept getting in my way."
"How?"
"He interfered with my orders, held conferences when it was necessary to act, gave contradictory instructions . . . In general he tried to override the commander."
"So he got in your way. But you were in command of the *front*?"
"Yes."
"The Party and the Government entrusted the *front* to you. . . . Did you have a telephone?"
"Yes."
"Then why didn't you report that he was getting in your way?"
"I didn't dare complain about your representative."
"Well, that is what we have punished you for: not daring to pick up the receiver and phone up, as a result of which you failed to carry out the operation."
I walked out of the Supreme Commander's office with the thought that, as a new-fledged *front* commander, I had just been taught an object lesson.[24]

With less publicity but, probably, as much or more consequence and effect than most or all of the other adjustments to the military system, Stalin also brought visibly to the fore his two best generals, Zhukov and Vasilevskiy. General Zhukov's appointment, in August, as deputy supreme commander elevated his status in the chain of command and diminished—although only a certain degree—the distance between the supreme commander and the top military professional. General Vasilevskiy had less field command experience than did Zhukov, but he had seen more service at or near the top of the General Staff than any other officer except Marshal Shaposhnikov. Owing to Shaposhnikov's declining health, Vasilevskiy had been acting chief of the General Staff several times and had carried a good deal of the chief's work before his own appointment to the position in June 1942. Shaposhnikov had been known for his charm and excellence as a military theoretician but not for his ability to stand up to Stalin. Vasilevskiy, like Zhukov, was self-confident and willing to take the initiative. He had much of Shaposhnikov's charm, and "at the same time, he knew how to defend his own point of view in front of the Supreme Commander."[25]

After August 1942, Zhukov and Vasilevskiy, as a team, became Stalin's principal military advisers. Henceforth, at least until late in the war, he consulted both of them on strategic and operational decisions, whereas, formerly, *Stavka* decisions had often been made by him and whichever of the members he chose to draw upon—

---

[23]Shtemenko, *Soviet General Staff*, p. 66.
[24]Rokossovskiy, *Soldier's Duty*, p. 118.

[25]Shtemenko, *Soviet General Staff*, pp. 49, 126–28. See also *VOV*, p. 88.

which, in effect, meant by him alone. As a team, Zhukov and Vasilevskiy also became the premier *Stavka* field representatives. They were not, as they and others had been in the past, attached to *front* headquarters. Instead, they coordinated groups of *fronts*, and they bore the authority to issue orders and instructions to the field commanders. Zhukov apparently also acquired chain-of-command status that put him between the other officers and Stalin. General Moskalenko tells that when he was relieved of command of *First Guards Army* and summoned to the Kremlin in September 1942, it was Zhukov who talked to Stalin (while Moskalenko waited in an anteroom) and delivered the decision on Moskalenko's next appointment.[26]

Although they held their powers entirely at Stalin's pleasure, Zhukov's and Vasilevskiy's superior positions in the command structure were later—again to a certain degree—formalized. In December 1942, Vasilevskiy secured the appointment of General Antonov as his deputy, and thereafter, Antonov took over most of the chief of the General Staff's regular work. In May 1943, the State Defense Committee named Zhukov and Vasilevskiy, both by then marshals of the Soviet Union, to be first and second deputy commissars of defense.[27]

After 3 September 1942, when he sent the Zhukov-Vasilevskiy team to take charge at Stalingrad, Stalin, apparently, was also willing to go into what may be described as voluntary, partial military eclipse. The winter and

spring offensives had been his brainchildren. The counteroffensives in the coming fall and winter were going to be Zhukov's and Vasilevskiy's. Concerning the initial plan for an attack at Stalingrad, the *Short History* states: "This plan was set down on a map signed by General G. K. Zhukov, Deputy Supreme Commander in Chief, and General A. M. Vasilevskiy, Chief of the General Staff, and endorsed by J. V. Stalin, Supreme Commander in Chief." At the meeting of the State Defense Committee that gave final approval to the plan in November, the *Short History* says, "The Supreme Commander in Chief, who had devoted a great deal of time to the preparations for the operation, listened attentively to the arguments put forward by Zhukov and Vasilevskiy."[28]

In the Soviet view, then and now, the near-ultimate recognition was given to the military professionals on 9 October 1942, in a decree that abolished the political commissar system and established unitary command. The decree, issued by the Presidium of the Supreme Soviet, in its significant parts, read:

The system of war commissars which was established in the Red Army during the Civil War was based on mistrust of the military commands, which at that time still had in them specialists who were opposed to Soviet power.

In the years after the Civil War the process of reorienting and training the military commands was completed. As a result of the training and of the success in all areas of Soviet life, the situation of the military commands in the Red Army had changed fundamentally.

---

[26]*IVMV*, vol. V, p. 326; Moskalenko; *Na Yugozapadnom napravlenii*, pp. 348, 361–74.

[27]Shtemenko, *Soviet General Staff*, pp. 126–29; Tyushkevich, *Vooruzhennye sily*, p. 316.

[28]*VOV (Kratkaya Istoriya)*, p. 213. See also *IVMV*, vol. VI, p. 27 and Zhukov, *Memoirs*, pp. 380–88.

The present patriotic war against the German invaders has welded our commands together and produced a large corps of talented new commanders who have gathered experience and who will remain true to their honor as officers to the death.

Therefore, the Presidium of the Supreme Soviet directs:
1. The establishment of complete unity of command in the Red Army and the transfer of full responsibility to the commanders and chiefs of staff in all units of the Red Army.
2. The abolition of the war commissars . . . [in major units] and of *politruks* in lesser units.[29]

The decree did not attribute any deleterious effects to the commissar system; it only found the commissars no longer necessary. The commissars had been and continued to be portrayed as dedicated men, frequently of heroic stature. In *The Front*, for instance, it was the commissar, Gaidar, who, in the final scene, brought Gorlov to account and secured Ognev's promotion.

In fact, the abolition was not as complete as it appeared. A "considerable number" of commissars who had acquired on-the-job experience, as it were, were converted to line duty and given commands of their own, but that may have owed mostly to a shortage of officers.[30] As it had in 1940, the structure of the commissar system survived. The 9 October decree removed the commissar but restored the *zampolit*, the deputy commander for political affairs. Henceforth, a commander did have authority to make and carry out decisions at his own discretion, and the *zampolit*, in military matters, was under

his command, but the *zampolit* could report his judgments of the commander's performance through a separate channel.[31] In the higher commands, armies and *fronts* in particular, the deputies for political affairs continued (with the commanders and chiefs of staff) as members of the military councils. While they could no longer dispute or countermand the commanders' orders, they were still very often consequential and well-connected political figures whom the commanders could not lightly disregard. The abolition of the commissar system appears to have removed the stigma of potential unreliability from the officers and, in the longer run, to have created a kind of partnership between the political and the military leaders that both groups found useful, especially in promoting their careers.

Most particularly, the abolition of the commissar system in no wise signaled a decline of party influence or interest in the armed forces. While the total number of Communist party members in the Soviet Union as of 1 January 1943 was still down somewhat from 1 January 1941, 3.8 *vs.* 3.9 million (after a large drop, probably as a result of war losses, to 3 million on 1 January 1942), the number of party members on military assignments had risen between 1 January 1941 and 1 January 1943 from 654,000 to 1.9 million. A full third of that increase had come in 1942, most of it between May and December, and as of 1 January 1943, slightly more than 50 percent of the party membership was on military duty, as compared to

---

[29]*Pz. AOK 4, Ic Nr. 1811/42, Anlage 3, Erlass des Praesidiums des Obersten Sowjets der UdSSR, 10.9.42, 13.11.42,* Pz. AOK 4 29365/8 file.

[30]*IVOVSS*, vol. II, p. 489.

[31]Raymond L. Garthoff, *Soviet Military Doctrine* (Glencoe, Ill.: Free Press, 1953), p. 240.

16.5 percent in 1941.[32] Concurrently with the "patriotic war" campaign, the Army's Main Political Administration undertook, by means of a special council, to improve the political education of the troops, which was found "often to have had a formal, bureaucratic character" in the past.[33]

The Soviet Condition

The advances to Stalingrad and the Caucasus brought the Soviet territory under German occupation to 1 million square miles. This was less than an eighth of the total Soviet land area, but it was almost half of the European Soviet Union, and it was equal to a full third of the United States (Alaska and Hawaii excluded). In those 1 million square miles, 80 million people, almost 40 percent of the population, had lived, and this area contained 47 percent of the cultivated land—nearly all of the best land in the Soviet Union. From there also had come 71 percent of the pig iron, 58 percent of the steel, 63 percent of the coal, and 42 percent of the country's electrical energy.[34] However, as great as the damage was, if the Germans did not break out in some new direction and if Soviet confidence could be restored, the Soviet war potential was going to be substantially greater at the end of the 1942 summer than it had been at the same time in the previous year.

Although the retreat forced another wave of evacuations, war production was on the rise. Reportedly, the factories turned out 22,681 combat aircraft and 24,446 tanks in 1942, a good two-thirds more aircraft and better than three times as many tanks as in 1941. The German output was 15,456 aircraft and 5,958 tanks. In 1942, Soviet artillery output exceeded 33,000 pieces larger than 76-mm., more than twice as many as had been produced in 1941.[35]

As of November 1942, the Soviet forces in the field numbered 6.5 million men.[36] The German and allied troops in the four army groups on the main front totaled about 3.4 million, and the German and Finnish contingents in the far north would have brought the number to about 4 million. The Soviet figure, again, apparently does not include *Stavka* reserves, which are given as 162 divisions, 188 brigades, and 181 regiments at the start of the 1942–1943 winter campaign.[37]

During the summer, organizational improvements continued. Since late 1941, the armies had been using the mobile groups as partial substitutes for the disbanded corps. In the mobile groups, two or more divisions operated under the ad hoc command of one of their headquarters, which had to direct the group and its own troops as well and generally did not have the staff and the communications to do both. In 1942, twenty-eight rifle corps headquarters were formed, enough to take over the functions formerly assigned to the mobile groups. In the tank corps' structure, the motorized rifle brigades were not providing enough infantry support to make the corps equal

---

[32]Deborin and Telpukhovskiy, *Itogi i uroki*, p. 375; *IVMV*, vol. V, p. 313.

[33]*IVMV*, vol. V, p. 307.

[34]*Ibid.*, vol. VI, p. 14.

[35]*Ibid.*, vol. V, p. 48; Deborin and Telpukhovskiy, *Itogi i uroki*, p. 260; Boelcke, *Ruestung*, p. 24f.

[36]*IVMV*, vol. VI, p. 20.

[37]OKH, GenStdH, Fremde Heere Ost, Nr. 2669/42, *Gegenueberstellung der verbuendeten und der sowjetrussischen Kraefte, Stand 20.9.42*, H 22/235 file; Golubovich, "Sozdaniya strategicheskikh," p. 17.

matches for German panzer divisions; consequently, in September 1942, mechanized corps began to be created. These consisted of three mechanized brigades (a regiment of motorized infantry and a tank regiment in each) and one tank brigade, and they had 175 tanks, 7 more than the tank corps had. During the course of the year also, the "guards" designation had come to be regarded as more than a formal mark of distinction, and guards formations were given larger allotments of troops and weapons. The strength of a guards rifle division, for instance, was set at 10,670 men; that of an ordinary rifle division was 9,435. A guards rifle division was also allowed a third more automatic weapons and 4 more artillery pieces (9 batteries rather than 8) than a normal infantry division.[38] As had been the case with the shock armies, however, it appears that the guards designation was often given before the other requirements were met.

The most effective weapons were being brought into play in increased numbers. The T–34/76B, with a longer-barreled gun and an improved turret made its appearance in time for the Stalingrad fighting. The IL–2, *Shturmovik*, which had proved its worth as a dive-bomber in an antitank role, accounted for better than a third of the 1942 aircraft production (7,654 planes). Although Soviet designers had developed a number of good automatic weapons, particularly submachine guns, the Commissariat of Defense had somewhat neglected production of these before the war.[39] By mid-1942,

the troops were getting large numbers of what would become the infantry's most distinctive weapon, the drum-fed PPSh41 (Postolet-Pulemyot Shpagina) submachine gun. Designed by G. S. Shpagin, it has been described as "one of the most crudely made guns ever issued on a large scale."[40] Nevertheless, it was reliable and effective as well as cheap to manufacture, and simple to operate and maintain.[41]

Counteroffensive Plans

Operation Uranus

While Churchill and Harriman were in Moscow in August, Stalin told them about "a great counteroffensive in two directions" that he was going to launch "soon" to cut off the Germans. Harriman went back to Washington believing Stalingrad would be held, and in November he thought the offensive begun then around Stalingrad was the one "Stalin had promised . . . in August."[42] In the sense that the idea of a counteroffensive at Stalingrad had occured to Stalin in August—as it had also to Hitler—the November offensive may have been what Stalin had mentioned to Harriman, but the counteroffensive, as it was prepared and executed, was not born until a month after the Stalin-Churchill-Harriman meeting, and the idea, apparently, was not Stalin's but Zhukov's and Vasilevskiy's.[43]

[38]Tyushkevich, *Vooruzhennye sily*, pp. 284, 289, 317.
[39]Perrett, *Fighting Vehicles*, p. 35; Deborin and Telpukhovskiy, *Itogi i uroki*, p. 260. See *IVOVSS*, vol. I, pp. 415, 452.

[40]Ian V. Hogg and John Weeks, *Military Small Arms of the Twentieth Century* (New York: Hippocrene Books, 1977), p. 104.
[41]*IVOVSS*, vol. I, p. 452.
[42]Harriman and Abel, *Special Envoy*, pp. 162, 168, 174.
[43]See p. 456.

GENERAL N. F. VATUTIN,
COMMANDER OF SOUTHWEST FRONT

As Zhukov tells it, he, Vasilevskiy, and Stalin were discussing on 12 September how to break Sixth Army's hold on the Volga north of Stalingrad when it occurred to him and Vasilevskiy that they "would have to seek some other solution [than the shallow flank attacks then being tried]." Stalin's curiosity was aroused, and Zhukov and Vasilevskiy worked all the next day in the General Staff going over the possibilities. Late that night they returned to Stalin's office and proposed the following: "First, to continue wearing out the enemy with active defense; second, to begin preparation for a counteroffensive in order to deal the enemy a crushing blow at Stalingrad to reverse the strategic situation in the south in our favor." Then they went to Stalingrad, where the battle was in a critical phase, to study the conditions first hand, Zhukov to *Stalingrad Front* and Vasilevskiy to *Southeast Front.* Late in the month, on the 27th or the 28th, they returned to Moscow and presented their conception of the counteroffensive plotted on a map that both had signed and to which, after some discussion, Stalin added the word "Approved" and his signature.[44] The counteroffensive was code-named URANUS.

In October, while *Sixty-second Army* kept the battle alive in Stalingrad, Zhukov and Vasilevskiy worked out the specifics of URANUS and supervised a buildup on Sixth and Fourth Panzer Armies' flanks. A major requirement was to activate a new *front* headquarters, *Southwest Front,* in the zone of the main effort on the Don upstream from Kletskaya. *Southwest Front* would take over *Sixth, First Guards, Sixty-third,* and *Twenty-first Armies,* or better than half of Rokossovskiy's *Don Front,* and would also receive the *Fifth Tank Army.* Command of *Southwest Front* went to General N. F. Vatutin, who, at age forty-one, was apparently one of the younger generals being brought to the fore. His only previous field command in the war was *Voronezh Front,* for which he had nominated himself and to which, it is said, Stalin had appointed him on the spur of the moment.[45] The command of *Voronezh Front,* which General Golikov received as Vatutin's replacement, had not required a particularly high order of generalship, and Vatutin's selection for the crucial command in URANUS probably owed more to his

---

[44]Zhukov, *Memoirs,* pp. 382–87. See also Vasilevskiy, "Delo," p. 242; Samsonov, *Stalingradskaya bitva,* p. 347; and *IVMV,* vol. VI, p. 27.

[45]Vasilevskiy, "Delo," p. 223; *VOV,* p. 172.

earlier service as Vasilevskiy's deputy in the General Staff. While his age, in fact, may have counted after Budenny (fifty-nine) and Shaposhnikov (sixty) became inactive, the top Soviet generals were all relatively young men. Eremenko was fifty; Vasilevskiy and Timoshenko, forty-seven; Zhukov, forty-six; Rokossovskiy, forty-six; Meretskov, forty-five; Voronov, forty-three; Chuikov and Golikov, forty-two; and Grechko, thirty-nine.

The four field armies assigned to *Southwest Front* were reinforced with infantry and given mobile forces in the form of tank, mechanized, and cavalry corps. The same was also done opposite Fourth Panzer Army to *Stalingrad Front*'s *Sixty-fourth*, *Fifty-seventh*, and *Fifty-first Armies*. *Fifth Tank Army*, under General Leytenant P. L. Romanenko, consisted of 6 rifle divisions, 2 tank corps, a guards tank brigade, a cavalry corps, and artillery, antiaircraft, and mortar regiments.[46] It had been out of the front throughout the summer, being rebuilt and serving as a backstop against a German thrust toward Moscow via Orel and Sukhinichi.

The initial objectives of URANUS would be to tie down Sixth Army on the front between the Don and the Volga and, in Stalingrad, to smash the Rumanian armies on its left and right, and to thrust behind Sixth Army to cut its lines of communication across the Don. *Fifth Tank Army* was to be the spearhead on the north, where, after its rifle divisions, four in the first wave and two in the second, opened a gap in Rumanian Third Army's front, the two tank corps would break through aiming for Kalach on the Don due west of Stalingrad. Following behind the tank corps, the cavalry corps and three of *Sixty-third Army*'s rifle divisions would fan out on the right to cover the flank by establishing a line on the Chir River. Inside the arc of the tank army's advance, elements of *Twenty-first Army* and *Don Front*'s *Sixty-fifth Army* were to break through past Kletskaya and to encircle four German divisions Sixth Army had stationed west of the Don. They would get help from *Twenty-fourth Army* (also belonging to *Don Front*), which was to prevent the divisions from joining the Sixth Army main force by taking the Don crossings at Panshirskiy and Vertyachiy. To complete the encirclement, *Fifty-seventh* and *Fifty-first Armies* would cut through the Fourth Panzer–Rumanian Fourth Army line south of Stalingrad and would strike northwestward to meet *Fifth Tank Army* at Kalach.[47]

The whole plan hinged critically on keeping Sixth Army and Fourth Panzer Army locked in a contest for Stalingrad and on not allowing them to settle into a defensive deployment before URANUS was ready. Either of two eventualities would greatly becloud the prospects for URANUS. One could have arisen from the fortunes of war. If the Germans took Stalingrad, they could withdraw enough troops from the city to form a strong reserve. The other could bring about the same result even if the Germans only caught a scent of URANUS beforehand since they were tied down in Stalingrad by their own choice, not by necessity; consequently, the operation would need to achieve

---

[46][General Staff of the Red Army], *Sbornik materialov po izucheniyu opyta voyny, Nomer 6*, Apr–May 43.

[47]*Sbornik, Nomer 6*. See also *VOV*, p. 172; *IVMV*, vol. VI, p. 28; Vasilevskiy, *"Delo,"* p. 242f.

total surprise. To accomplish that goal, Zhukov and Vasilevskiy devised an elaborate *maskirovka* ("camouflage") for URANUS.[48] It consisted of three parts: concealment of the concept of the operation, the direction of the main effort, and the composition of the forces.[49]

To protect the concept of the operation, Zhukov and Vasilevskiy laid on a heavy blanket of security. They reduced the planning time allotted to the *fronts* and armies to an amount far below the previous norms. The *front* commanders were not told about the secret of URANUS until mid-October, and they were forbidden to initiate any planning of their own before the first week in November. To "disinform" the enemy, the *fronts* were ordered to go over to the defensive on 15 October, and from then on all visible effort was put into building defenses. The civilians were evacuated from villages within 25 kilometers of the front, and those were ringed with trenches—to give enemy air reconnaissance something to see. Orders pertaining to the defense were transmitted by telephone, a reliable and not too obvious way of getting them into enemy hands.[50]

Southwest Front made concealment of the direction of the main effort a particularly difficult and dangerous problem. No doubt, it would have been

better not to have installed another *front* headquarters at all, since these were difficult to conceal and always objects of intense enemy interest. But URANUS was too complicated an operation for two *fronts* to handle themselves at that stage. To limit potential damage to the *maskirovka*, Headquarters, *Southwest Front*, was not brought forward until 28 October.[51]

To prevent the enemy from determining the composition of the forces, the entire buildup, with the exception of *Fifth Tank Army*, was done with units of less than army size. The reserves, usually brought in close before an offensive, were held at Saratov on the Volga 200 miles upstream from Stalingrad. Reinforcements moved only at night, under strict radio silence. *Fifth Tank Army* made its 500-mile shift from the Orel-Sukhinichi area in three weeks of night marches, the last on the night of 9 November.[52]

At the last, the *maskirovka* itself had to be protected against two Soviet practices that could have brought it to grief: the *razvedka boyem* ("battle reconnaissance") and the artillery preparation. Soviet commands regarded the *razvedka boyem* as an indispensable preliminary to an offensive to feel out "objectives of attack, systems of fire, and the nature of the terrain."[53] Conducted, as it customarily was, repeatedly and over extended periods in as much as divisional strengths, it usually alerted the enemy well before an offensive began. Zhukov and Vasilevskiy could not convince the field commands

[48]*Maskirovka* is defined in the *Soviet Military Encyclopedia* as "a complex of measures directed toward deceiving the enemy. It includes camouflage by concealment and simulation, secrecy and security, feints and diversions, and disinformation" (deception).

[49]V. A. Matsulenko, "*Operativnaya maskirovka voysk v kontrnastuplenii pod Stalingradom*," *Voyenno-istoricheskiy Zhurnal*, 1(1974), p. 10.

[50]*Ibid.*, p. 11; *IVMV*, vol. VI, 35.

[51]*Sbornik, Nomer 6.*

[52]*Ibid.; IVMV*, vol. VI, p. 36; Matsulenko, "*Operativnaya maskirovka*," p. 13.

[53]A. Sinitskiy, "*Sposoby vedeniya voyskovoy razvedki*," *Voyenno-istoricheskiy Zhurnal*, 4(1976), 89–94.

to forego the *razvedka boyem*, but they undertook to reduce the risks it posed by requiring it to be conducted in strengths of no more than battalions and at the same time by all armies in the Stalingrad area. In the past, the commands had also engaged in artillery duels and staged lengthy fire preparations. For URANUS, the artillery preparation was limited to an hour and a half, and preliminary firing was prohibited.[54]

Mars and Uranus

All of the Soviet accounts depict URANUS as the main operation in the initial phase of the 1942–1943 winter offensive and most leave the reader to infer that it was the only one. There was, however, one other being prepared in October 1942—Operation MARS. The Soviet *History of the Second World War* gives it just two sentences in which its purpose is stated to have been "to destroy the enemy in the regions of Rzhev and Novo Sokolniki."[55] At Rzhev the objective apparently was to finish the work against Ninth Army started in the summer. Since Novo Sokolniki was already practically in the front on the western rim of the Toropets bulge and, by itself, a point of only modest tactical consequence, the aim there most likely was to strike deep to the southwest behind Army Group Center. Also, since the Rzhev area was well-known to Zhukov, and he had advocated concentration against Army Group Center, it can be assumed that he was as instrumental in devising MARS as he was in URANUS. After 16 November, he

left Vasilevskiy in charge at Stalingrad and went to *Kalinin* and *West Fronts* to take charge of the final preparations for MARS, which was scheduled to begin about a week after URANUS.[56]

MARS could, at the time, have been a great deal more important than can now be gathered from the few mentions of it given in the Soviet literature. It was laid in the area that, during 1941 and 1942, had consistently been regarded in Soviet thinking as the most important strategic direction, the one in which Soviet forces had already conducted a successful winter offensive and in which they could expect to be able to stage another on better terms than the first. URANUS, on the other hand, was a highly speculative venture. The *History of the Great Patriotic War* almost says as much in the following: "The *Stavka* . . . assumed that the enemy, in spite of his desperate efforts would not have achieved his goals, that his offensive would have failed but, yet, neither would he have succeeded in going on the defense along the entire Stalingrad sector nor changed the operational deployment of his forces. In Stalingrad itself, large enemy forces would still continue to carry on their hopeless attacks."[57] Even understated as they are, these were enormous assumptions. To expect that Sixth Army would not somehow manage to take Stalingrad sometime between the middle of September and the middle of November was a great deal. To anticipate the Germans'— with the memory of Moscow fresh in their minds—continuing a faltering offensive into the

---

[54]Matsulenko, *"Operativnaya maskirovka,"* pp. 11, 18.
[55]*IVMV*, vol. VI, p. 29.

[56]Zhukov, *Memoirs*, p. 407. See also Ziemke, *Stalingrad to Berlin*, p. 106.
[57]*IVOVSS*, vol. III, p. 19.

winter was even more. Furthermore, if the Germans did both, it then became necessary to assume that they would also not know how to extricate themselves from an encirclement.

URANUS was a gamble; the logical prospects for MARS were far better; and the deployment as of mid-November indicates strongly that the *Stavka* also took this view. On the 600 miles of front between Kholm and Bolkhov, that is, opposite Army Group Center, 1,890,000 troops, 24,682 artillery pieces and mortars, 3,375 tanks, and 1,170 aircraft were deployed. Opposite Army Group B, on slightly less than 500 miles of front from Novaya Kalitva to Astrakhan, 1,103,000 troops, 15,501 artillery pieces and mortars, 1,463 tanks, and 928 aircraft were deployed. The Kholm-Bolkhov sector, 17 percent of the total frontage between Lake Ladoga and the Caucasus, had 31.4 percent of the troops, 32 percent of the artillery and mortars, 45 percent of the tanks, and 38 percent of the aircraft. The Novaya Kalitva–Astrakhan sector, 14 percent of the total frontage, had 18.4 percent of the troops, 20.1 percent of the artillery and mortars, 19.9 percent of the tanks, and 30.6 percent of the aircraft.[58]

URANUS, if the doubts beclouding its prospects resolved themselves favorably, did have one significant advantage over MARS: the forces for URANUS would have a substantially larger numerical advantage over the enemy. The *History of the Second World War* maintains that the 1.1 million Soviet troops deployed in the Novaya Kalitva–Astrakhan sector were opposed by 1 million Germans and Rumanians;

hence the Soviet advantage was only 1.1:1.[59] The actual combined strength of Sixth Army, Fourth Panzer Army, and Rumanian Third Army, however, was very much less than a million men and in all probability just slightly more than a half million, which made the Soviet advantage 2:1. The ratio in the Army Group Center area was 1.9:1, using a German strength estimate of 1,011,500 for the army group in September 1942. While the ratios varied by only a tenth of a point, the difference in the composition of the forces they represented was considerable. The Army Group Center troops were all German. Of the total for the three armies in the URANUS area, close to 50 percent (245,000) were Rumanian troops.[60]

One Soviet account, by a notable authority, General Mayor V. A. Matsulenko, represents MARS as a deception incorporated into the URANUS *maskirovka*. Matsulenko states, "During the preparations for the counteroffensive at Stalingrad, the Supreme High Command had the forces of *Kalinin* and *West Fronts* display activity in the western direction against Army Group Center, creating the impression that the winter operations were being prepared precisely there and not in the southwest. This measure produced positive results."[61] In that mode, MARS would have repaid the Germans nicely for their own Operation KREML of the previous spring, but KREML was pure

[58]*IVMV*, vol. VI, table 4, p. 35.

[59]*Ibid.*, table 6, p. 45.
[60]Manfred Kehrig, *Stalingrad* (Stuttgart: Deutsche Verlags-Anstalt, 1974), app. 9, p. 667; *OKH, GenStdH, Fremde Heere Ost, Nr. 2669/42, Gegenueberstellung der verbuendeten und der sowjetrussischen Kraefte, Stand 20.9.42*, H 22/235 file.
[61]Matsulenko, *"Operativnaya maskirovka,"* p. 15.

sham and illusion, which MARS was not. More likely MARS figured in the URANUS plan not as a part of the *maskirovka* but as a potential means of keeping the battle for Stalingrad going until the time was ripe for URANUS. According to the *History of the Second World War,* MARS was ready as of 23 October, and the start order would have been given anytime thereafter if the Germans had begun taking troops from Army Group Center to reinforce the attack into Stalingrad. What the Soviet planners did was compromise MARS to preserve the essential condition for URANUS. However, it will be seen that in doing so they befuddled the enemy as much as if MARS had been a deception that in fact "produced positive results."[62]

"This Year's Campaign Has Been Concluded"

The Army in Decline

Musing unhappily on an old problem, General Halder, chief of the General Staff, in the first week of August observed, "According to our calculations of early May . . . we expected the enemy to be able to set up sixty new divisions by the fall muddy period." But he noted that sixty-nine new Soviet divisions had already been identified, and the fall rains were still a good two months away. "All told," he added, "we can, perhaps, anticipate seeing another thirty new divisions."[63] If the Soviet figures are correct, Halder erred substantially on the short side. Reportedly, in the period April to October 1942,

the *Stavka* had released from its reserves 189 rifle divisions, 78 rifle brigades, 30 tank and mechanized corps, and 159 tank brigades.[64] It was apparent that the Soviet manpower pool was a long way from running dry.

The same could scarcely be said for that of Germany. On 8 September, the Organizational Branch of the OKH announced, "All planning must take into account the unalterable fact that the predicted strength of the Army field forces as of 1 November 1942 will be 800,000, or 18 percent, below the established strength and that it is no longer possible to reduce those numbers. False impressions will result if units continue to be carried as before with this great loss of strength." The branch, thereupon, proposed reducing better than half the divisions on the Eastern Front from three regiments to two.[65] The two-regiment divisions would remove the fiction of a temporary understrength but would do so essentially by building it into the tables of organization.

After two summers and a winter in the Soviet Union, the German Army was having to consume its own inner substance. In Basic Order 1, the first of several issued in the fall of 1942, the OKH directed a 10 percent reduction in all staffs and the transfer of the personnel released to combat assignments. Additionally, all rear elements were to set up emergency detachments that could be sent to the front on short

[62]*IVMV,* vol. VI, p. 29.
[63]*Halder Diary,* vol. III, p. 497.

[64]Zemskov, *"Nekotoriye voprosy,"* p. 14; *IVMV,* vol. VI, table 4, p. 35; *OKH, GenStdH, (III) Nr. 420743/42,* H 22 file; *OKH, GenStdH, Op. Abt. (III), Pruef. Nr. 75940, Zahlenmaessige Uebersicht ueber die Verteilung der Divisionen, Stand 11.9.42,* H 22 file.
[65]*OKH, GenStdH, Org. Abt., Nr. 922/42, Organisatorische Planungen, 8.9.42,* H 22/235 file.

notice. Another basic order set a goal of 180,000 men to be secured from the rear echelons for front-line duty by replacing them with *Hilfswillige*, auxiliaries recruited among the Russian prisoners of war.[66] Another established "substitution of weapons for men" as a principle of command and specified that when new, improved weapons were issued the ones they replaced were to be left with the troops to augment their firepower.[67]

These were gestures, not answers. Since May, General der Infanterie Walter von Unruh, armed with the authority to order irrevocable transfers to the front, had been combing the rear areas as Hitler's personal representative. Unruh's visitations had aroused dismay verging on terror and had earned him the nickname General *Heldenklau* ("hero snatcher") but could not be shown to have added significant numbers to the combat strengths.[68] *Hilfswillige* were already being so widely used in noncombatant roles that there was no large block of troops left for them to replace. The substitution of weapons for men depended on having the weapons. The Panther tank, for instance, Germany's most promising new weapon, would for months yet be snarled in development and production difficulties.

The air force had a manpower surplus that Hitler, in September, agreed to tap, but at the insistence of Reichmarschall Goering, commander in chief of the air force, he decided not to use the men as army replacements but to form air force field divisions manned and officered exclusively by air force personnel. In September and October, he ordered that twenty such divisions be set up with a combined strength of about two hundred thousand men. From the army point of view, a more unsatisfactory arrangement would have been difficult to devise. The air force troops had no training in land warfare, and because Goering restricted the army's influence on them, by claiming that the "reactionary" spirit of the army would impair his troops' National Socialist indoctrination, they were not likely to be given enough training to make them anywhere near suitable for employment on the Eastern Front. Worse still, the army had to scrape together enough equipment to outfit the twenty divisions, and the diversion of vehicles alone forced postponement of plans to bring four or five panzer divisions to full strength.[69] Basic Order 3, which regulated the employment of the air force field divisions, required that they be given "only defensive missions on quiet fronts."[70]

Hitler added his own reinforcement to the basic order. It read:

The low combat strengths of the fighting troops are no longer tolerable.
The fighting troops have many personnel vacancies; those not directly engaged in combat almost none. That must cease!

[66]*OKH, GenStdH, Org. Abt. (III), Nr. 9900/42, Grundlegender Befehl Nr. 1, 8.10.42*, AOK 30155/57; *OKH, GenStdH, Org. Abt. Kriegstagebuch, Band IV*, 1–10 Oct 42, H 1/214 file.

[67]*OKH, GenStdH, Op. Abt. (III), Nr. 34149/42, Planung fuer Ausbau der Heerestruppen im Winter 1942/43, 3.9.42*, H 22/235 file; *H. Gr. Nord, Ia Kriegstagebuch, 1.–31.10.42*, 10 Oct 42, H. Gr. Nord 75128/15 file.

[68]*OKH, GenStdH, Org. Abt. Kriegstagebuch, Band IV*, 21–31 Aug 42, H 1/214 file.

[69]*Ibid.*, 1–10 Oct 42.

[70]*H. Gr. Nord, Ia Kriegstagebuch, 1.–31.10.42*, 15 Oct 42, H. Gr. Nord 75128/15 file.

I will—aside from measures to be taken outside the Army—also institute appropriate correctives within the Army. Those are to be carried out regardless of all opposition and appearances of impossibility. On this score every commander must display his competence as much as he does in troop leadership.

In every instance in which a troop unit experiences a setback, the next highest commander is to investigate whether the commander involved exhausted all of the possibilities to raise his combat strength provided for under my orders. In special cases, I reserve to myself the right to order an investigation.[71]

Overhaul at the Top

Hitler, as always, was inclined to transpose problems to which there were not pragmatic answers into questions of leadership and will. Apparently doing that also was uppermost in his mind on 24 September when he dismissed Halder as chief of the Army General Staff. In their last interview together he told Halder that it was now necessary to "educate" the General Staff in "fanatical faith in the Idea" and that he was determined to enforce his will "also" on the army. The new chief of the General Staff, General der Infanterie Kurt Zeitzler, initially at least, appeared to be well suited to Hitler's purpose. He was a competent but not supremely outstanding staff officer. As chief of staff, Army Group D, which was stationed in the Low Countries and along the Channel coast, his energy and a rotund figure had earned him the nickname General Fireball. His physical activity—plus a friendship with Hitler's adjutant, General Schmundt—had brought him atten-

tion at the *Fuehrer* Headquarters, and Hitler had remarked earlier that Holland would be a "tough nut" for the Allies because Zeitzler "buzzes back and forth there like a hornet and so prevents the troops from falling asleep from lack of contact with the enemy."[72]

Although Hitler, at the first, treated Zeitzler with "utmost friendliness," the change in chiefs of the General Staff did not signal a new approach to the conduct of the war such as the one Stalin was making.[73] Hitler valued Zeitzler for his energy. As a collaborator and adviser, he probably expected Zeitzler, who had been lofted from an army group staff on an inactive front to the highest command echelon, to be more complaisant and less independent-minded than Halder had been. The initial friendliness toward Zeitzler was also no mark of confidence in the generals. He had come to distrust them almost to a man, and after September 1942, he insisted on having a stenographer present to take down every conversation he had with them. At the same time, he gave up eating his meals with his inner military circle, which had been his practice since early in the war, and henceforth, ate alone or with the nonmilitary members of his staff.[74]

In the course of installing the new chief of the General Staff, Hitler also put himself in position to overhaul the whole officer corps, the General Staff and the general officer ranks in particular, by placing the *Heerespersonalamt* ("army officer personnel office") under Schmundt. To Schmundt he outlined a

---

[71]*Pz. AOK 1, Ia Kriegstagebuch Nr. 8,* 13 Oct 42, Pz. AOK 1 24906 file.

[72]Henry Picker, ed., *Hitlers Tischgespraeche* (Bonn: Athenaeum-Verlag, 1951), p. 166.
[73]*OKW, KTB,* vol. II, p. 795.
[74]*Ibid.,* p. 697.

policy of rapid promotion for younger, battle-tested, and presumably "educatable" officers. Zeitzler, forty-seven years old and a general officer for less than a year at the time of his appointment, was such an officer. Hitler also proposed to break the General Staff's hold on the higher commands by allowing line officers to qualify for the top posts and by requiring General Staff officers to show experience as troop commanders. Eventually he expected to abolish the General Staff's marks of distinction, the red trouser stripes and silver collar tabs.[75] Schmundt, who had built his career on subservience to Hitler, could be expected, without being told, to seek out and advance like-minded officers.

When he took up his post, Zeitzler made a contribution of his own to the shake-up of the command system. The army had long resented the influence of General Jodl's OKW Operations Staff on the drafting of strategic directives pertaining exclusively to the Eastern Front, which was an army theater. The resentment had increased after Hitler had become commander in chief, army, and had converted the Army General Staff into a second personal staff, and it had been sharpened by the freewheeling criticism Jodl and Field Marshal Keitel, chief, OKW, had indulged in from their technically loftier positions in the chain of command. Taking advantage of Jodl's having fallen into disfavor, Zeitzler demanded and secured the OKW's exclusion from the drafting of strategic directives that applied solely to the Eastern Front. Henceforth such directives were to be

issued as "operations orders" by the OKH. The orders, naturally, continued to be written, as the directives had been, entirely in accordance with Hitler's wishes.

Operations Order No. 1

A new course and style of command having been instituted, Operations Order No. 1, issued on 14 October, purported to do the same for strategy. Its first sentence read, "This year's summer and fall campaigns, excepting operations underway and several local offensives still contemplated, has been concluded." Army Group North, Army Group Center, and Army Group B were told to get ready for winter in the lines they held, and in this order and a supplement issued some days later, Hitler elevated to the level of doctrine the fanatical resistance formula he had employed during the 1941–1942 Soviet winter offensive. He ordered that the winter positions were to be held under all circumstances. There would be no evasive maneuvers or withdrawals. Breakthroughs were to be localized, and any intact part of the front was "absolutely" to be held. Troops cutoff and encircled were to defend themselves where they stood until they were relieved, and Hitler made every commander personally responsible to him for the "unconditional execution" of these orders.[76] The supplement extended the doctrine down to the lowest leadership level. "Every leader," it read, "down to squad leader must be convinced of his sacred duty to stand fast, come what may, even if the enemy

---

[75]*Taetigkeitsbericht des Chefs des Heerespersonalamts*, 1–5 Oct 42, H 4/12 file.

[76]*Der Fuehrer, OKH, GenStdH, Op. Abt. (I) Nr. 420817/42, Operationsbefehl Nr. 1, 14.10.42*, AOK 6 30155/49 file.

outflanks him on the right and left, even if his part of the line is cut off, encircled, overrun by tanks, enveloped in smoke or gassed." That was to be repeatedly "hammered into all officers and noncommissioned officers."[77]

The Exceptions

Operations Order No. 1, while ostensibly keeping the promise Hitler made in the spring to bring the summer campaign to a more timely close than had been done in the previous year, excepted, as stated, offensives in progress or still contemplated. Those in progress were at Stalingrad and toward Tuapse. Contemplated were NORDLICHT, against Leningrad, and TAUBENSCHLAG ("dovecote"), a recently conceived operation aimed at Toropets. First Panzer Army's march on Groznyy, in abeyance but not abandoned, fell into both categories. The exceptions left three of the four army groups with substantial offensive missions to be completed or undertaken. Both of Army Group A's armies were in fact exempted from Operations Order No. 1 and were instructed to await other orders.

Taubenschlag

By the time Operations Order No. 1 appeared, NORDLICHT, however, was hardly a viable enterprise. The state of Field Marshal Manstein's troops (Eleventh Army) after the fighting in the bottleneck and the lateness of the season spoke heavily against it. On 16 October, Hitler shelved NORDLICHT

and instructed Manstein to use the artillery to smash the Soviet defenses on the Leningrad perimeter and to inch his front forward.[78] While it would have been handy to have had Leningrad out of the way, another long-standing strategic liability of the north flank, the Toropets bulge, was becoming an even greater concern as winter approached. From it the Russians could strike in all directions: east into Ninth Army's flank, southeast behind Army Group Center, northwest behind Army Group North, north against Staraya Russa and the Demyansk pocket, or even if they were daring enough, due west to the Baltic coast. The German line on the western rim of the bulge was atrociously weak. All that was there on over a hundred miles of front was the Gruppe von der Chevallerie, a corps headquarters under Generalleutnant Kurt von der Chevallerie, with five infantry divisions.

On 14 October, maintaining that "the best defense is an attack of our own from the vicinities of Velikiye Luki and Kholm," Hitler ordered Sixteenth Army and the Gruppe von der Chevallerie to collaborate on Operation TAUBENSCHLAG that was to be aimed "in the general direction of Toropets."[79] A week and a half later while Manstein was at the *Werwolf* to receive his individually designed and handcrafted marshal's baton (the time for production of which caused the delay in his receiving it) and to discuss

---

[77]OKH, *Chef des Generalstabes des Heeres, Abt. L (I) Nr. 428858/42, I. Ergaenzung zum Operationsbefehl Nr. 1, 23.10.42,* AOK 6 30155/42 file.

[78]*AOK 11, Ia Kriegstagebuch Nr. 2,* 17 Oct 42, AOK 11 33167/1 file.

[79]*H. Gr. Nord, Ia Kriegstagebuch, 1.–31.10.42,* H. Gr. Nord 75128/15 file; *Gen. Kdo. LIX A.K., Ia Kriegstagebuch Nr. 4,* 14 Oct 42, LIX A.K. 30145/1 file.

the artillery deployment against Leningrad, Hitler, apparently on the spur of the moment, gave him command of TAUBENSCHLAG. At the end of the month, Manstein moved his headquarters to Vitebsk. By then, Hitler, in oral instructions to Manstein, had made TAUBENSCHLAG contingent on a Soviet attempt against Army Group Center. Manstein thereupon became custodian of a dormant front and a tentative operation until the afternoon of 20 November when he was called back from an inspection trip to be told he was appointed commanding general, Army Group Don, and with his headquarters would replace Headquarters, Army Group B in the Stalingrad sector. He and an advance party boarded a special express train the next day, and TAUBENSCHLAG, which would shortly be reduced to nothing by further transfers to the south, reverted to the Gruppe von der Chevallerie.[80]

Stalingrad

That Sixth Army's operations in Stalingrad would be exempted from Operations Order No. 1 went without saying. At the end of September, as he had in the years past, Hitler opened the drive for the Winter Relief with a speech in the Berlin *Sportpalast*. In it, he played on an old theme and ridiculed the publicity he had lately been receiving in the world news media. Pinpricks like the Dieppe raid in August, he complained, were touted as magnificent Allied victories while his own march from the Donets to the

Volga and the Caucasus was "nothing." "When we take Stalingrad," he went on, "and you can depend on it that we will, that also is [sic] nothing." Later he vowed a second time to take Stalingrad and assured the audience, "you can be certain no one will get us away from there."[81]

Tuapse

Like Sixth Army, Seventeenth Army was on the march and expected to continue. Tuapse, the prize, was coming into reach. A push in the mountains, begun on 14 October, carried to Shaumyan the next day and through the town the next. Soviet *Eighteenth Army* almost broke, even though it was getting a steady flow of reinforcements, and Grechko, who had become an artist of the stubborn defense at Novorossiysk, had to be brought in as the army's new commander.[82] Seventeenth Army reported on the 18th that the several days of easy going it had experienced had ended, and it was having to revert to dislodging the enemy piecemeal from positions he was again defending determinedly. A week of rain, flooding mountain rivers, and washed-out roads gave Grechko time enough to get his army in hand and to begin some counterattacks late in the month.[83] What these might have accomplished, however, would never be known because, after 4 November, three weeks of rain in the lower and snow in the higher elevations brought both sides to a full stop.

---

[80]*AOK 11, Ia Kriegstagebuch Nr. 2,* 26 Oct–21 Nov 42, AOK 11 33167/1 file.

[81]Domarus, *Hitler,* vol. II, p. 1914.
[82]Grechko, *Battle for the Caucasus,* p. 158.
[83]*H. Gr. A, Ia Kriegstagebuch, Band I, Teil IV,* 20–25 Oct 42, H. Gr. A 75126/4 file.

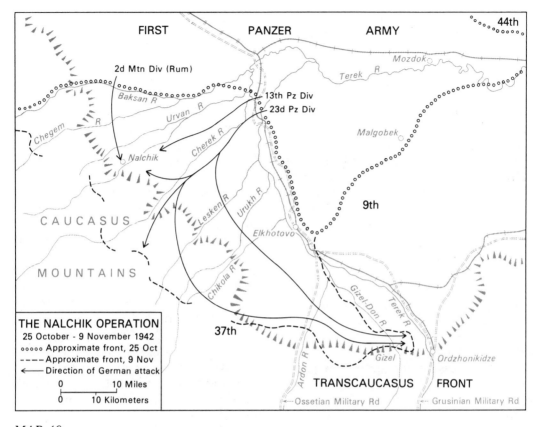

MAP 40

Nalchik

First Panzer Army, although it was at a standstill in mid-October, was exempted from Operations Order No. 1 because it still appeared to have some prospects if it could be given better reinforcements than those it had received recently. The SS Viking Division had been an "acute disappointment," and a newer arrival, the Special Purpose Corps "Felmy," showed signs of being more exotic than effective. It was an aggregation (in actual strength less than one full division) of Mohammedans, mostly recruited from prisoner-of-war camps, commanded by an air force general, General der Flieger Helmut Felmy. The Mohammedans were adequately anti-Soviet, but apparently many had not been told when they were recruited that they would also be expected to fight. Under orders to improve his positions pending arrival of reinforcements, General Kleist, commander of First Panzer Army, on 14 October, proposed to attack off his right flank to Nalchik, which would level his front somewhat and eliminate a threat to his rearward lines.[84] Hitler gave his approval two days later.

---

[84]*Ibid.*, 14 Oct 42.

Rumanian 2d Mountain Division began the Nalchik operation on the morning of the 25th with air support diverted from Seventeenth Army—which, no doubt, helped to slow the advance on Tuapse. The Rumanians were headed almost due south from the Baksan River. While the distance to Nalchik was only about ten miles, they had three swift mountain rivers to cross, the Baksan, Chegem, and Urvan. (Map 40.) Nevertheless, the day went exceedingly well. The division was across the Baksan in two hours and by nightfall had a spearhead on the Chegem three miles north of Nalchik. The 13th and 23d Panzer Divisions started west and southwest from the Terek the next morning. Running upstream in the valleys of the Cherek and Urvan rivers, they had easier going. For First Panzer Army, the operation was "progressing at a speed beyond all expectations." The Rumanians were in Nalchik on the afternoon of the second day, and the panzer divisions had closed the river crossings to the south and east trapping over seven thousand Soviet troops.[85] The attack had achieved a compound surprise: *Transcaucasus Front's North Group,* intent on an offensive of its own it was preparing against Mozdok, had neglected *Thirty-seventh Army* in the Nalchik area, and *Thirty-seventh Army* had lost control over its troops after its command post was bombed on the morning of the 25th.[86]

Turning east along the face of the mountains on the 27th and 28th, the two panzer divisions discovered that the Russians had not recovered

enough to make more than perfunctory stands on successive river lines, the Lesken, the Urukh, and the Chikola. Kleist then ordered them to keep going to the Ardon in the valley of which the Ossetian Military Road emerged from the mountains. When they reached the Ardon they would be a bare twenty miles from Ordzhonikidze, and on the 29th, seeing "a chance that will never come again," to take the city, Kleist told them to cross the Ardon and take Ordzhonikidze on the run.[87] In another two days, 13th Panzer Division was on the Ardon, and Kleist was beginning to talk about Ordzhonikidze as the "next," not the final objective. On 2 November, 13th Panzer Division took Gizel, five miles west of Ordzhonikidze, but by then the *North Group* had brought in a guards rifle corps, 2 tank brigades, and 5 anti-tank artillery regiments. In two more days, the tanks could not get past Gizel; on the 5th, the division was almost encircled by Soviet troops that had moved in behind it from the north and the south; and on the 9th, the Nalchik operation ended when 13th Panzer Division broke out of Gizel to the west.[88] By then, as in the Tuapse area, the weather was bringing both sides to a stop.

A Winter Offensive—Where?

Questionable as the other premises in Operations Order No. 1 were or would soon become, one was rock hard: there would be another Soviet winter offensive. No one in the German Command doubted it. On 28 Au-

[85]*Pz. AOK 1, Ia Kriegstagebuch Nr. 8,* 25–26 Oct 42, Pz. AOK 1 24906 file.
[86]Grechko, *Battle for the Caucasus,* pp. 169–73.
[87]*Pz. AOK 1, Ia Kriegstagebuch Nr. 8,* 27–29 Oct 42, Pz. AOK 1 24906 file.
[88]Grechko, *Battle for the Caucasus,* pp. 173–81.

gust, Foreign Armies East had submitted its forecast for the coming months and had concluded that the current Soviet objective was to preserve enough manpower and materiel to sustain a second winter offensive. Since the Soviet Command had very likely figured on losing the North Caucasus and Stalingrad, and possibly Moscow and Leningrad, and could have anticipated casualties on the scale of the 1941 summer campaign, the Foreign Armies East assumed that the final results for the Soviet Union would be better than had been expected, and the Soviet losses would be "[of a magnitude that would leave] combat-worthy forces available for the future."[89]

To identify the potential locales for a Soviet offensive was hardly a problem. The Army Group B and Army Group Center zones offered the best prospects and the greatest profitability. That the choice would be one of these could be assumed a priori. The trick was to know which one. At Army Group B, the extended front and relatively easy terrain invited a bid to recapture Stalingrad and raised the prospect of a thrust across the Don west of Stalingrad to Rostov, which, if successful, would collapse the greater part of the Army Group B front and would unhinge the entire Army Group A front. On the other hand, the Soviet Command would be under a heavy compulsion to liquidate the threat to Moscow posed by Army Group Center and would see the Toropets bulge and the Sukhinichi salient as natural springboards for converging attacks toward

Smolensk, which could not only drive the front away from Moscow but possibly destroy Ninth, Third Panzer, and Fourth Armies in the bargain. Foreign Armies East assumed that the Russians were not yet capable of directing or sustaining offensives toward remote objectives, for instance Rostov or the Baltic coast, and so to an extent would be governed by their tactical limitations. They would, therefore, stand to profit most reliably from an offensive against Army Group Center aimed at Smolensk.[90]

Six weeks later, on 12 October, Colonel Reinhard Gehlen, chief of the Foreign Armies East gave Zeitzler, for Hitler, a report "from a source described as generally reliable that allegedly has contacts reaching into the Russian leadership." The report in the main duplicated his branch's earlier estimate, and from this he said " . . . it can be assumed that the stated lines of thinking have at least been taken into consideration in the enemy's decision-making process."[91] In particular, Gehlen added, the idea of an operation in the Toropets bulge appeared to be attractive to the Russians.

By then the Germans were so much impressed with the Soviet activity around Toropets that Hitler would be issuing the first order for TAUBEN-SCHLAG in two days. They believed the Russians would be ready to start as soon as the fall rains ended, which would be in another two to three weeks.[92] Shortly before the middle of

[89]OKH, GenStdH, Fremde Heere Ost (I) Nr. 2492/42, Gedanken zur Weiterentwicklung der Feindlage im Herbst und Winter, 29.8.42, H 3/190 file.

[90]Ibid.
[91]Fremde Heere Ost, Chef, Nr. 2819/42, Vortragsnotiz, 12.10.42, H 3/1039 file.
[92]Gen. Kdo. LIX A.K., Ia Kriegstagebuch Nr. 4, 14 Oct 42, A.K. 30145/1 file.

the month, Foreign Armies East had also detected what seemed to be the beginnings of a Soviet buildup opposite Army Group B, but these did not appear to be on a scale that would indicate an offensive anytime soon. On the 15th, the branch concluded that the Russians would eventually attempt something against Army Group B, but the main significance of the activity at the army group for the present was that to make the forces available, the Russians would have to give up whatever thoughts they might have had of enlarging the forthcoming operation against Army Group Center.[93]

In the last two weeks of the month, the earlier impressions hardened. The Foreign Armies East reports indicated that the buildup against Army Group B was limited to the Serafimovich bridgehead in the Rumanian Third Army sector. On the 31st, the branch concluded that the activity in the bridgehead did not presage a major attack and would probably result in nothing more than a local effort of some kind. At the same time, in the Army Group Center zone, Ninth Army expected an offensive against it to begin any day, and as of 30 October, the army had anticipated at most no more than one more week's respite.[94]

Hitler appears to have rated at least the long-run potential for trouble in the Army Group B zone somewhat higher than his intelligence people did. As early as mid-August, he began to worry that Stalin might attempt, as he put it, the Russian "standard attack"— a thrust toward Rostov directed across the Don near Serafimovich—which the Bolsheviks had executed with devastating success in 1920 against the White Army of General Peter Wrangel.[95] On 26 October, he reiterated his concern and ordered in air force field divisions to stiffen the Italian, Hungarian, and Rumanian fronts on the Don.[96] Talking to Manstein the same day, he said he saw "an especial danger" in the front between Stalingrad and Voronezh.[97] On 2 November, when aerial photographs revealed that the Russians had thrown several new bridges across the Don to the Serafimovich bridgehead, he once more predicted a major thrust toward Rostov. Realizing the air force field divisions would count for little in a real crisis, he canceled the order concerning them and substituted a panzer division and two infantry divisions from the Western Theater.[98]

Hitler, however, did not see the "especial danger" as also an imminent one. He could not have expected the divisions he was sending, which were stationed on the Channel coast, to get to Army Group B before December. To Manstein, he said he anticipated an attack "in the course of the winter." On 31 October, he shifted his headquarters from the *Werwolf* back to the *Wolfsschanze*, where he stayed barely a week before going on to Bavaria to give a speech on the anniversary of the 1923 Beer Hall Putsch and to begin a two-week vacation at the *Berghof*. His arrival

---

[93]*OKH, GenStdH, Fremde Heere Ost, Kurze Beurteilung [en] der Feindlage vom 13.10, 15.10.42*, H 3/199 file.

[94]*Ibid.*, 26–28 Oct, 31 Oct 42; *AOK 9, Fuehrungsabteilung Kriegstagebuch, Berichtszeit 1.7.–31.10.42, Band II*, 30 Oct 42, AOK 9 31624/2 file.

[95] *Greiner Diary Notes*, 16 Aug 42, C–065q CMH file.

[96] *Ibid.*, 26 Oct 42.

[97] *AOK 11, Ia Kriegstagebuch Nr. 2*, 26 Oct 42, AOK 11 33167/1 file.

[98] *Greiner Diary Notes*, 4 Nov 42, C–065q CMH file.

in Munich on the morning of 8 November coincided with the Allied landings in North Africa, and the mood among his party comrades who had gathered that night to commemorate the Putsch was depressed. In his speech, for which he had no coherent theme, he virtually ignored North Africa and tried lamely to inflate the strategic significance of Stalingrad (as "a gigantic transshipment center") and to explain away his failure to finish the battle there. He was determined to avoid "another Verdun," he said, and therefore was employing "very small assault groups," and time was not important.[99] For the next ten days, Hitler, at the *Berghof,* and the OKW, which had hurriedly followed him and had set itself up in Berchtesgaden and Salzburg, were preoccupied with the North African events and their first response to them, an invasion of unoccupied France. Of the top leadership, only Zeitzler stayed behind in East Prussia.

In the meantime, Foreign Armies East was getting more clues on Soviet activity in the Army Group B area but not enough, in its opinion, to form a clear picture. As late as 6 November, the branch was certain the Soviet main offensive would be against Army Group Center and if there were to be one on the Don, it would come later.[100] By then, signs were being picked up of a buildup also south of Stalingrad against Fourth Panzer Army, and on the 8th, a division of *Fifth Tank Army* was identified opposite Rumanian Third Army. Two days later, another *Fifth Tank Army* division and the Headquarters, *Southwest Front,* were tentatively detected.[101] By the 12th, enough confirmation had come in to raise sharp ripples of concern in the staffs at Army Group B, Sixth Army, and Fourth Panzer Army. Foreign Armies East still regarded the situation as too obscure to warrant a definitive prediction but added that ". . . an attack in the near future against Rumanian Third Army with the objective of cutting the railroad to Stalingrad and thereby threatening the German forces farther east and compelling a withdrawal from Stalingrad must be taken into account."[102] For the next week, this remained the estimate from which the staffs worked. An attack was expected and soon. Because it would hit the Rumanians, it would be inconvenient and possibly more dangerous; but otherwise it was not expected to be different from the others that had gone before. Foreign Armies East could not find solid evidence of a major change in the Soviet deployment. The armies on the Don it had knowledge of were those that had been there since September. The *Fifth Tank Army* divisions it identified were all infantry. Not a single one of the army's armored elements could be located. Soviet radio traffic seemed clearly to indicate that *Fifth Tank Army* itself was still stationed in the Orel-Sukhinichi area and receiving reinforcements there.[103]

---

[99]Domarus, *Hitler,* vol. II, pp. 1932–38.
[100]OKH, GenStdH, Fremde Heere Ost (I), Beurteilung der Feindlage vor Heeresgruppe Mitte, 6.11.42, H 3/185 file.

[101]OKH, GenStdH, Fremde Heere Ost, Kurze Beurteilung[en] der Feindlage vom 4.11., 8.11., 10.11.42, H 3/199 file.
[102]Ibid., 12 Nov 42. See p. 467.
[103]Abt. Fremde Heere Ost, Vortragsnotiz, 21.11.42, H 3/1039 file.

CHAPTER XXII

Thrust and Counterthrust

The Battle on the Volga

The river was the prize, specifically the nine to ten miles of its right bank from the refinery southeast of Mamai Hill to Rynok. Stalingrad had ceased to exist, except as a wreck and a ruin. Those who inhabited the city now were fighting over a corpse, and they knew it. On the other hand, the area left to be contested became more precious as it became smaller and more murderously expensive either to keep or to acquire. By the terms that had made the city an objective in the first place, the issue at Stalingrad was settled: the Volga was closed and every inch of ground still in Soviet hands could be brought under German fire. Strict military logic no longer applied on either side, however, particularly not on the German. The battle had acquired a reason for existence of its own. No longer only the last phase of BLAU-CLAUSEWITZ, it was a drama being played for the world; and as such, Hitler would not consider it terminated until every shred of organized Soviet resistance was eliminated from the right bank of the Volga. By what amounted to mutual agreement, the summer campaign was being fought again in miniature on the river. For Stalin, each fraction of a mile that was held one more day partially redeemed the near collapse of July and August and brought Operation URANUS a small step closer to reality. For Hitler, to have denied the enemy the last fraction of a mile could have driven from mind the memory of the victory lost. The stakes, however, were not even. Stalin had little to lose and, possibly, much to gain. Hitler, if he wanted to possess the river bank, had to accept the suspension of the initiative and fight on his opponents' terms, not his. He did that on 6 October when he "reaffirmed the total occupation of Stalingrad as Army Group B's most important mission."[1]

Troops and Tactics

During the next week, Hitler and General Weichs, commander of Army Group B, worked with Sixth Army's commander, General Paulus, to get Sixth Army in trim for another push into the city. Hitler canceled Fourth Panzer Army's projected advance to Astrakhan and ordered its commander, General Hoth, to give the 14th Panzer Division, his last full-fledged armored division, to Sixth Army. Weichs and Hitler concurred in letting Paulus take another two infantry divisions, 79th and 305th, off his flank on the Don. Sixth Army had been engaged for a month on plans to advance its front northward somewhat, between the Volga and the Don, and to secure a

---

[1]*AOK 6, Ia Kriegstagebuch Nr. 14*, 6 Oct 42, AOK 6 33224/2 file.

better winter line. These now were dropped, and Weichs instructed Paulus to have the troops on the north front dig in for the winter where they stood.[2] Irked at having to wait for the divisions to be moved, Hitler ordered intensified bombing "to deprive the enemy of the opportunity to rebuild his defenses."[3] But the Russian defense was getting stronger. On 8 October, massed Soviet heavy artillery began firing into the city from east of the Volga.

On the 10th, Rumanian Third Army took over the Don front east of the Khoper River. The German strength was being drawn inward on Stalingrad as if by a powerful magnet. Fourth Panzer Army was also having to rely on the Rumanians to man most of its loose front on the chain of lakes south of Beketovka. Everyone, especially the Rumanians themselves, knew they were not trained, equipped, or motivated for fighting in the Soviet Union. Fourth Panzer Army had seen the Rumanians in action. On 28 September, several of their divisions on the army's right flank south of Beketovka had given way before a halfhearted Soviet attack and had fallen into a panic and retreat that took two days and a German panzer division to stop. Hoth had commented, "German commands which have Rumanian troops serving under them must reconcile themselves to the fact that moderately heavy fire, even without an enemy attack, will be enough to cause these troops to fall back and that the reports they submit concerning their own situation are worthless since they never

know where their units are and their estimates of enemy strength are vastly exaggerated."[4]

The 14th Panzer and 305th Infantry Divisions were ready at LI Corps on 13 October. The 79th Infantry Division was coming east but not yet in place, and Sixth Army was still awaiting the arrival of several ammunition trains. Nevertheless, although he might be pinched for ammunition in forty-eight hours if the trains did not get there in time, Paulus decided to resume the offensive the next day anyway.[5] To delay any longer had its danger as well. The weather was becoming unsettled, and although a spell of rain might not affect the fighting in the city too much, it could paralyze the army's supplies.

Lacking the strength to make a single sweep and having few other alternatives, Paulus proposed to take what was left of the city by pieces, working from north to south. In the first stage, XIV Panzer Corps would push through Rynok and Spartakovka to the mouth of the Gorodishche River, while LI Corps occupied the tractor factory and the brickworks and took a hold on the Volga south of the Gorodishche. The LI Corps would then turn south and take the gun factory, the bread bakery, the metallurgical works, and the chemical plant.[6] On the advance, engineers would take the lead and carve out corridors by leveling entire blocks of buildings with explosives; panzer grenadiers, as shock groups, would establish and maintain the for-

[2] *Ibid.*, 6–8 Oct 42.
[3] *Greiner Diary Notes*, 7 Oct 42, C–065q CMH file.

[4] *Pz. AOK 4, Ia Kriegstagebuch Nr. 5, Teil III*, 30 Sep 42, Pz. AOK 4 28183/1 file.
[5] *AOK 6, Ia Kriegstagebuch Nr. 14*, 13 Oct 42, AOK 6 33224/2 file.
[6] *AOK 6, Ia Nr. 3843/42*, 8.10.42, AOK 6 30155/43 file.

ward momentum; and infantry would do the clearing and mopping-up, the grueling job of stamping out the resistance yard by yard and man by man.

For the first, the formula was going to work. Describing the events of 14 October, General Chuikov, then commander of *Sixth-fourth Army*, has said, "Those of us who had already been through a great deal will remember this enemy attack all our lives."[7] Sixth Army would later remember the assault on the tractor factory as "the one really complete success in the battle for the northern part of Stalingrad."[8]

Stalingrad-North

Early in the morning on the 14th, Paulus set up his forward command post in Gorodishche, west of the tractor factory. The tanks and panzer grenadiers of the 14th Panzer Division had moved out at daylight in light rain. They were into the tractor factory by 1000. On their left, 305th Infantry Division pushed through the workers' settlement toward the Gorodishche River. North of the river, XIV Panzer Corps had begun clearing several hills west of Spartakovka, and in the afternoon, 14th Panzer Division's right flank reached the brickworks. The division kept going through the night, and by 0700 the next morning, it had one of its panzer grenadier regiments through to the Volga east of the tractor factory. With that, *Sixty-second Army's* bridgehead was cut in two. By dark, XIV Panzer Corps was at the western edge of Spartakovka; the tractor fac-

tory and brickworks were occupied; and 14th Panzer Division's line south of the brickworks was just 300 yards from Chuikov's command post that was dug into the cliff above the Volga east of the gun factory. *(Map 41.)*

The 14th Panzer and 305th Infantry Divisions turned south in the morning on the 16th. They had half of the gun factory by 1200. During the day, LI Corps and XIV Panzer Corps also made contact on the Gorodishche River west of Spartakovka and encircled parts of several Soviet divisions between there and Orlovka. When the gun factory and the blocks of houses to the west of it were taken on the 17th, it looked as if the battle could not last more than another two or three days. But Paulus decided to bring in the 79th Infantry Division anyway, "to be ready for all eventualities." The resistance had toughened in the last two days, particularly on the 17th, and numbers of fresh enemy battalions were being identified. At the same time Paulus' strength was fading again. His whole front was now within reach of the Soviet artillery across the river, and the nights were as wearing as the days because Soviet planes kept up a running bombardment from dark to daylight. The OKH liaison officer reported, "The Russians' air superiority over Stalingrad at night has assumed intolerable proportions. The troops cannot rest. Their endurance is strained to the limits. The losses in men and material are unbearable in the long run."[9]

One of Hitler's adjutants, a Major Engels, arrived at Sixth Army on the 17th "to gather personal impressions of

---

[7] Chuikov, *Stalingrad*, p. 180.
[8] *AOK 6, Ia Kriegstagebuch Nr. 14*, 3 Nov 42, AOK 6 33224/2 file.

[9] *Ibid.*, 15 Oct 42.

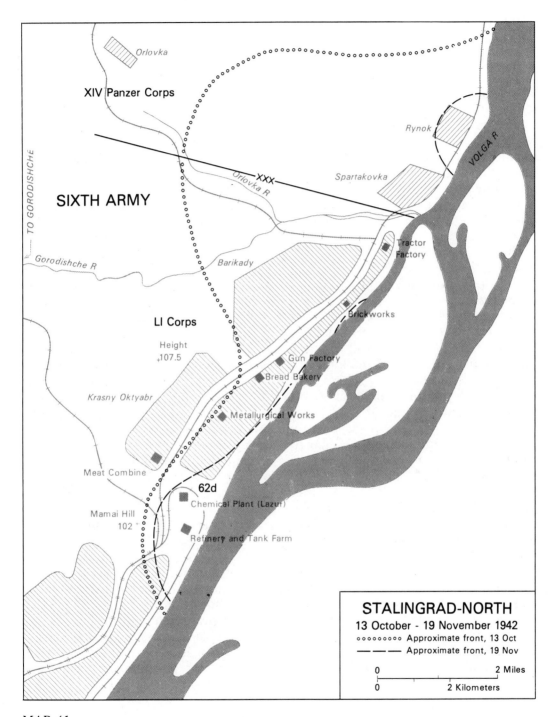

Orlovka

XIV Panzer Corps

TO GORODISHCHE

SIXTH ARMY

Gorodishche R

Barikady

LI Corps

Height
107.5

Krasny Oktyabr

Meat Combine

Mamai Hill
102

62d

Chemical Plant (Lazur)

Refinery and Tank Farm

Orlovka R

XXX

Spartakovka

Rynok

VOLGA R

Tractor
Factory

Brickworks

Gun Factory

Bread Bakery

Metallurgical Works

STALINGRAD-NORTH

13 October - 19 November 1942

ooooooooo Approximate front, 13 Oct

— — — Approximate front, 19 Nov

0   2 Miles

0   2 Kilometers

MAP 41

the battle for Stalingrad." Paulus and his chief of staff took him to an army observation post where he could see some of the fighting and then gave him a statistical rundown. Since 13 September, the army had lost 343 officers and nearly 13,000 enlisted men (killed, wounded, and missing), bringing its total losses since it crossed the Don on 21 August to 1,068 officers and 39,000 men. Enemy losses, judging from the numbers of prisoners taken—17,900 after 13 September and a total of 57,800 since 21 August—were much higher than Sixth Army's but not nearly as high as the Soviet losses had been in previous battles. The intensity of the fighting could be deduced from the ammunition consumed, which for the month of September amounted to 25 million rounds of rifle and machine gun ammunition, a half-million anti-tank rounds, and three-quarters of a million artillery rounds of all calibers.[10]

On the 18th, while the infantry worked on cleaning out pockets of resistance in the gun factory, LI Corps repositioned its artillery and rocket projectors to bring them to bear on the next objectives, the bread bakery and metallurgical works. Heavy rain had set in during the night, and by midday, the approaches to the Don bridges, over which all of the army's supplies had to come, were "passable only with difficulty." Paulus thought he might be able to resume the advance the next afternoon if the artillery and infantry were ready by then, if the roads did not get worse, and if the weather did not keep the airplanes grounded. But the roads did get worse as the rain, inter-

spersed with snow showers, continued for two more days, and pockets of Russians were still holed up in the gun factory shops on the 21st when the sky began to clear.

The LI Corps, under General Seydlitz, went back into motion on the 23d with 79th Infantry Division in the lead. It had half of the metallurgical works, the blocks of houses west of the bread bakery, and most of the bakery itself in its hands by afternoon and, at nightfall, had a spearhead on the Volga. The next day, XIV Panzer Corps, which had been diverted by Soviet attacks on its north front, took the western two-thirds of Spartakovka. But the momentum dropped off fast at both corps. The XIV Panzer Corps' troops had been in action without a break for ten days, and 79th Infantry Division, which had been at the Don bridgeheads for weeks before coming into Stalingrad, had, from the first, only been fresh by comparison with Seydlitz's other divisions. Infantry strength was being dissipated in a dozen or more small but costly actions around or inside shops and buildings in the metallurgical plant and against Soviet contingents dug-in along the river as far north as the brickworks. For a week after the 24th, LI Corps' effort was totally absorbed by day in fighting for what previously would have been considered miniscule objectives—shops number 1, 5, and 10 in the metallurgical plant and a furnace in the same plant—and by night in trying to disrupt boat traffic on the Volga that was bringing Chuikov replacements after dark for his losses in the daylight.[11]

[10]*Ibid.*, 17 Oct 42.

[11]*Ibid.*, 18–30 Oct 42.

ON THE ATTACK AT THE STALINGRAD GUN FACTORY

The Clock Runs Down

Paulus, Weichs, and their chiefs of staff met on 1 November to discuss the question "how the attack on Stalingrad can be nourished with new forces, since the strength of the 79th Infantry Division has so far declined that it can no longer be considered for larger missions."[12] Paulus thought of exchanging the 79th Infantry Division for the 60th Motorized Infantry Division, which was on the XIV Panzer Corps north front. Getting the one division into the line on the north, however, and the other out would take some time, and the 60th Motorized Infantry Division, which had not exactly been in a quiet

spot, would also need a few days rest. Weichs proposed possibly taking two regiments from the 29th Motorized Infantry Division, which was closer to and acting as the mobile reserve for both Fourth Panzer Army and Rumanian Third Army. General Richthofen, the commander of Fourth Air Force, had made an offer that was welcome on the one hand and troublesome on the other. He had said he would be willing to relinquish some of the air force's railroad haulage space to allow the army to ship in more artillery ammunition—because the fighting was getting to be at such close quarters that he believed "the *Luftwaffe* cannot be very effective any more."[13]

---

[12]*Ibid.*, 1 Nov 42.

[13]*Ibid.*

Two days later, Weichs' chief of staff, General Sodenstern, told General Schmidt, the Sixth Army chief of staff, that the OKH would not allow the two regiments to be detached from the 29th Motorized Infantry Division but had instructed Weichs to let Paulus have five pioneer (combat engineer) battalions from divisions in the line on the Don. The idea to use the engineers had come to Hitler, through air force channels, from the inveterate dabbler in the ground war, Richthofen, who had been impressed with the engineers' performance in the assault on the tractor factory.[14] Sodenstern said that the Army Group B staff believed getting the engineer battalions would not be "bad at all" for Sixth Army. Schmidt, however, replied that the engineers could "in no way be a substitute for infantry." They were specialists, he said, "particularly accomplished in cracking bunkers and other large objects," but what the army needed was the "strength" of infantry. The attack on the tractor factory, he pointed out, had succeeded because the army then had infantry to do the "permanent mopping up" behind the engineers and the panzer grenadiers.[15]

Chuikov, who had shifted his command post on the 17th, to the river bank east of the chemical plant, also had an interest, though of a different sort, in Sixth Army's problems. Watching the pressure on his front drop in the last days of the month, he knew his army would survive for at least one more round. On the other hand, his position was not all that good. As he has put it, he and his troops were sitting "dangling our legs in the Volga."[16] All *Sixty-second Army* held on the west bank were two small bridgeheads about a half-mile deep, the one taking in parts of Rynok and Spartakovka, the other around the chemical plant with a narrow, ragged tail reaching into the metallurgical plant and upstream along the river bank to the brickworks. Replacements continued to come across in as large numbers as the area could accommodate, and the artillery on the east bank had come prominently—perhaps decisively—into play. Sixth Army attributed the 79th Infantry Division's rapid decline primarily to the "effect of the enemy's massed artillery."[17]

But the predominant Soviet effort was being directed elsewhere. The buildup for URANUS was being brought to its conclusion. The Southeastern and Ryazan-Ural divisions of the railroad system, the ones serving the Stalingrad region, were running at ten times their normal capacities. Railroad workers were stationed along the track to supplement the mechanical signal systems and to make it possible to run trains at closer intervals, and cars were being heaved off the tracks at terminal points to avoid having to backhaul empties. From the railheads, 27,000 trucks and horse-drawn vehicles delivered cargo to the front. Troops moved only at night and bivouaced under cover during the daytime.[18] Between 1 and 19 November, vessels of the *Volga Flotilla* carried 160,000 troops, 430

[14]*Kehrig, Stalingrad*, p. 41.
[15]*AOK 6, Ia Kriegstagebuch Nr. 14*, 3 Nov 42, AOK 6 33224/2 file.

[16]Chuikov, *Stalingrad*, pp. 197–99.
[17]*AOK 6, Ia Kriegstagebuch Nr. 14*, 1 Nov 42, AOK 6 33224/2 file.
[18]*IVOVSS*, vol. III, pp. 20–22.

tanks, 600 artillery pieces, and 14,000 motor transport vehicles across the river to *Stalingrad Front*.[19]

Between 1 and 10 November, Generals Zhukov and Vasilevskiy, as *Stavka* representatives, conducted a round of conferences and inspections to make certain the plans were understood and preparations properly made.[20] These were things that could not yet be taken for granted in the Soviet Army, and they required a great deal of on-the-spot checking and coaching of the staffs. In his speech on 7 November commemorating the anniversary of the Bolshevik Revolution, Stalin dropped the "Not a step back!" appeal and, instead, struck a note of high confidence saying, "The enemy has already felt the force of the Red Army's blows at Rostov, at Moscow, at Tikhvin. The day is not far off when the enemy will feel the force of new blows by the Red Army. There will be a celebration in our street too!"[21] On 13 November, Zhukov and Vasilevskiy explained URANUS to the members of the *Politburo* and the *Stavka* and assured them that all commands, "from *front* to regiment," knew and understood the plan, the nature of the terrain, and the techniques of infantry, armor, artillery, and air coordination.[22] But Sixth Army was still on the offensive, and there would be another round in the contest for the city. Weichs told Paulus on 3 November, "The general situation requires that the battles around Stalingrad be ended soon." Sixth Army, he

added, would be getting the five pioneer battalions in the next week, and they should be combined with infantry under panzer grenadier regimental staffs. The next objective would be the chemical plant at Lazur.[23] Two days later, however, Sodenstern called Schmidt to tell him the army group had just received word that Hitler had "expressed the opinion" that the ground east of the gun factory and metallurgical plant ought to be taken first. The two chiefs of staff agreed— as later did General Zeitzler, chief of the General Staff—that doing so would consume too much strength and would most likely rule out a subsequent attack on the chemical plant. Nevertheless, the next day Paulus received the following by teletype from the army group:

The Fuehrer has ordered: Before resuming the attack to capture the Lazur Chemical Plant, the two sections of the city the enemy still holds east of the gun factory and east of the metallurgical plant are to be taken. Only after the bank of the Volga is entirely in our hands in those places is the assault on the chemical plant to be begun.[24]

On the 7th, the artillery began counterfire against the Soviet artillery across the river, and Paulus told Weichs he would start to move east of the gun factory on the 11th and at the metallurgical plant, "at the earliest on the 15th."[25]

While it waited, the army made some random observations that were not causes for high alarm but were not

[19]Matsulenko, *"Operativnaya maskirovka,"* p. 11.

[20]Zhukov, *Memoirs*, pp. 402–04; Vasilevskiy, *"Delo,"* p. 247.

[21]*IVMV*, vol. VI, p. 48.

[22]Vasilevskiy, *"Delo,"* p. 247f; Samsonov, *Stalingradskaya bitva*, pp. 350–52.

[23]*AOK 6, Ia Kriegstagebuch Nr. 14*, 3 Nov 42, AOK 6 33224/2 file.

[24]*Ibid.*, 6 Nov 42.

[25]*Ibid.*, 8–10 Nov 42.

RUBBLE PROVIDES COVER FOR SOVIET SOLDIERS

reassuring either. For one, in a short course the army was giving to qualify NCOs from other branches as infantry lieutenants, a number of the candidates declared they would rather not be infantry officers and asked to be returned to their original branches. Paulus ordered the men dropped from the course and sent to the infantry. For another, several days of below freezing temperatures signaled the end of the fall rains. On the 8th and in the days thereafter, reports on the Soviet buildup in the Don bridgeheads opposite Rumanian Third Army became more frequent. On the 10th, the army group transferred the Headquarters, XXXXVIII Panzer Corps, into the Rumanian Third Army area and alerted the 29th Motorized Infantry Division for a move in behind the Rumanians "on the shortest notice."[26]

On the other hand, owing to a quirk of nature, *Sixty-second Army* was confronted with the most immediately ominous new development. Unlike other Russians rivers, the Volga does not freeze quickly. It first forms slush, then ice floes that pile up along the banks, then a massive coat of drifting ice than can sink the strongest boat but is too treacherous to be crossed on foot by men or animals. Weeks, in some years, months, pass before the surface freezes solid, which could have meant an extended period of isolation for *Sixty-second Army* during the approach of winter in 1942.

---

[26]*Ibid.*

GERMAN FIELD ARTILLERY FIRES INTO STALINGRAD

The Last Round

Four hours before daylight on the 11th, in freezing weather, Seydlitz struck east of the gun factory. When Paulus arrived at his forward command post, just before 1000, word awaited him that the attack was moving—but slowly. By nightfall, one spearhead had reached the cliff overlooking the river and another was on the shore. Sixth Army reported to the OKH, "The attack east of the gun factory in Stalingrad achieved a partial success against a numerically strong enemy who defended himself bitterly." Paulus added that he would regroup the next day and resume the advance on the 13th.[27]

By the 12th, Paulus was having also to keep an eye on Rumanian Third Army. During the day, Weichs told him to squeeze 10,000 men out of his engineer and artillery units to man a support line behind the Rumanians. Meanwhile, Hoth was trying to interpret the meaning of heavy enemy movements opposite Fourth Panzer Army. One thing was certain, he remarked, the Russians were not going through all the trouble just to strengthen their defenses.[28]

East of the gun factory, on the 13th, LI Corps conducted what the army described as "successful shock troop actions," taking two blocks of houses and one large building called "the com-

---

[27]*Ibid.*, 11 Nov 42.

[28]*Pz. AOK 4, Ia Kriegstagebuch Nr. 5, Teil III,* 13 Nov 42, Pz. AOK 4 28183/1 file.

missar's house." On the Volga, ice was beginning to pile up along the bank. Two days later, after having regrouped once more, LI Corps launched more shock troop actions and "further narrowed the bridgehead east of the gun factory. During the night on the 15th, *Sixty-second Army* counterattacked along the whole line and was beaten off. Seydlitz's dispositions were unsettled enough, however, to rule out even shock troops actions for the next day. In the meantime, the drifting ice on the Volga had compacted into an almost solid cover extending as much as seventy-five yards out from the shore.

There could not be any more thought or talk of one last big push in Stalingrad. Artillery and troops were standing by to go out of—not into—the city to Rumanian Third Army and Fourth Panzer Army. On the morning of the 17th, a somewhat lame exchange took place between Hitler and Paulus. Hitler sent the following *Fuehrer* order:

I am aware of the difficulties of the fighting in Stalingrad and of the decline in combat strengths. But the drift ice on the Volga poses even greater difficulties for the Russians. If we exploit this time span, we will save ourselves much blood later.

I therefore expect that the leadership and the troops will once more, as they often have in the past, devote all their energy and spirit to at least getting through to the Volga at the gun factory and the metallurgical plant and taking these sections of the city.

Paulus replied:

I beg to report to the *Fuehrer* that the commanders in Stalingrad and I are acting entirely in the sense of this order to exploit the Russians' weakness occasioned during the past several days by the drift ice on the Volga. The *Fuehrer*'s order will give the troops a fresh impulse.

Hitler's expectation had become smaller, but Paulus' capabilities were smaller still.[29] The only progress of any kind on the 17th and 18th, and that not substantial, was on the north where XIV Panzer Corps had been chipping away at Spartakovka and Rynok for weeks. Paulus proposed, after more regrouping, to try a thrust to the Volga out of the northern part of the metallurgical plant on the 20th.

Sixth Army Encircled

Operation Uranus

During the night of 18 November, it snowed along the Don, so heavily that visibility at times fell to zero. The temperature was 20° F. At 0720 on the 19th, *Fifth Tank Army*'s artillery, in the Serafimovich bridgehead on the Don 110 miles northwest of Stalingrad, and *Twenty-first Army*'s artillery, on the Don west of Kletskaya, received the alert code word *Sirena* ("siren"). Ten minutes later, the command *ogon* ("fire") came through, and 3,500 guns and mortars opened up on Rumanian Third Army. At 0850, the first infantry echelon, *Fifth Tank Army*'s *14th* and *47th Guards Rifle Divisions* and *119th* and *124th Rifle Divisions*, went on the attack.[30] (Map 42.)

In Stalingrad and at Fourth Panzer Army, at daylight, the sky was overcast with low-hanging clouds and the temperature was just above freezing. At 1100, Sodenstern told Schmidt the offensive against Rumanian Third Army had begun. The Rumanians, he said, had reported several "weak" attacks earlier in the morning and a stronger

[29]*AOK 6, Ia Kriegstagebuch Nr. 14*, 17 Nov 42, AOK 6 33224/2 file.

[30]Samsonov, *Stalingradskaya bitva*, p. 375.

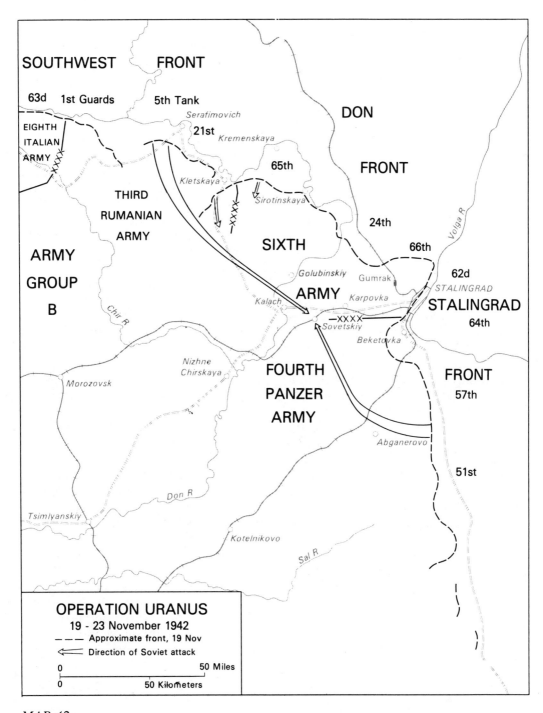

SOUTHWEST   FRONT

63d   1st Guards   5th Tank

Serafimovich

EIGHTH
ITALIAN   21st
ARMY   *Kremenskaya*

DON

THIRD
RUMANIAN   *Kletskaya*   65th
ARMY   *Sirotinskaya*

FRONT

Serafimovich

24th

Volga R

ARMY
GROUP
B

SIXTH

66th

62d

Golubinskiy   *Gumrak*   *STALINGRAD*

ARMY

STALINGRAD

Chir R

Kalach   *Karpovka*

Sovetskiy   64th

Beketovka

*Nizhne
Chirskaya*   FOURTH

Morozovsk   PANZER

FRONT

57th

ARMY

Abganerovo

Don R   51st

Tsimlyanskiy

Kotelnikovo

Sal R

OPERATION URANUS
19 - 23 November 1942
--- Approximate front, 19 Nov
⟵ Direction of Soviet attack

0 _____ 50 Miles
0 _____ 50 Kilometers

MAP 42

one at about 0900.[31] In the meantime, a momentary break in the clouds had given "a revealing insight into the enemy's movements" opposite Fourth Panzer Army. At an altitude of 300 feet, a scout plane had flown over a miles-long column of Soviet tanks headed west.[32] In Stalingrad, the first part of the day was somewhat better than usual: two more blocks of houses were taken east of the gun factory, and Paulus reported he would try to stay on the offensive there for another day.[33]

Fifth Tank and *Twenty-first Armies* had both cracked the Rumanian line by 1200, and between 1300 and 1400, *Fifth Tank Army's I* and *XXVI Tank Corps* began to move through. General Mayor I. M. Chistyakov committed *IV Tank Corps* and *III Guards Cavalry Corps* in the *Twenty-first Army* breakthrough an hour later. Rumanian Third Army had practically collapsed under the first assault, and the Soviet tanks, against which the Rumanians had no antitank weapons heavier than 47-mm., completed its demoralization. *Sixty-fifth Army,* under General Leytenant P. I. Batov, also had begun its attack in the morning, but it faced German divisions on the left flank of Sixth Army and made almost no progress except against a Rumanian cavalry division on its right flank and there advanced only about three miles as opposed to thirteen to fourteen miles gained by the other two armies.[34]

At 2200, the following message,

signed "Weichs," came off the teletype at Sixth Army: "The development of the situation at Rumanian Third Army compels radical measures to secure forces to protect the deep flank of Sixth Army. All offensive operations in Stalingrad are to be halted at once." Along with the message came an order to take three panzer divisions and an infantry division out of the city and to deploy them to meet the attack on the army's left flank.[35]

Stalingrad Front began the offensive on the 20th after General Eremenko had delayed the start for several hours because of fog. With ease, *Fifty-seventh Army,* under General Leytenant F. I. Tolbukhin, and *Fifty-first Army,* under General Leytenant N. I. Trufanov, broke through the Rumanian VI Corps front along the lake chain south of Beketovka.[36] Fourth Panzer Army recorded that the Rumanian corps disintegrated so rapidly that all measures to stop the fleeing troops became useless before they could be put into execution. At nightfall, the army concluded that by morning the Rumanian VI Corps would have no combat value worth mentioning. Hoth said the work of weeks had been "ruined in a day"; in many places, the Rumanians had offered no resistance at all—they had fallen victim to "an indescribable tank panic." He wanted to pull back Rumanian VII Corps, which was holding the army right flank south of VI Corps, but Weichs refused permission because he feared the Rumanians would not stop once they began to retreat.[37] (Head-

[31]*AOK 6, Ia Kriegstagebuch Nr. 14,* 19 Nov 42, AOK 6 33224/2 file.

[32]*Pz. AOK 4, Ia Kriegstagebuch Nr. 5, Teil III,* 13 Nov 42, Pz. AOK 4 28183/1 file.

[33]*AOK 6, Ia Kriegstagebuch Nr. 14,* 19 Nov 42, AOK 6 33224/2 file.

[34]*Sbornik, Nomer 6.* See also Samsonov, *Stalingradskaya bitva,* pp. 378–81.

[35]*AOK 6, Ia Kriegstagebuch Nr. 14,* 19 Nov 42, AOK 6 33224/2 file.

[36]*IVMV,* vol. VI, p. 56.

[37]*Pz. AOK 4, Ia Kriegstagebuch Nr. 5, Teil III,* 20 Nov 42, Pz. AOK 4 28183/1 file.

quarters, Rumanian Fourth Army, and VII Corps, with three divisions, had been brought in at the end of October.)

During the morning on the 20th, Headquarters, XIV Panzer Corps and the four divisions from Stalingrad shifted to the west side of the Don where, together with three divisions already on the scene, they prevented the *Twenty-first* and *Sixty-fifth Armies* from forming a secondary pocket west of the river. But, confronted by superior forces and unable to achieve full mobility because they were short on gasoline, they could not operate against the more important outer arm of the envelopment. The only obstacles in *Fifth Tank Army's* path were the XXXXVIII Panzer Corps and remnants of Rumanian Third Army. The Rumanians hardly counted any longer, although some, especially elements of one division under the Rumanian General Mihail Lascar, fought determinedly.[38]

Hitler at first pinned all his hopes on XXXXVIII Panzer Corps. It, however, could not establish contact between its two divisions and in the end, barely managed to escape to the west bank of the Chir River. (After XXXXVIII Panzer Corps got across the Chir, several days later, Hitler had its commanding general, Generalleutnant Ferdinand Heim, recalled to Germany, stripped of his rank, and jailed without trial.)[39] At most, all the Germans and Rumanians

accomplished was to set the *Fifth Tank Army* timetable back about twenty-four hours, and this was less their doing than a consequence of the tank army's allowing itself to be drawn into local engagements contrary to its original orders. After the delay, the army's two tank corps continued on toward Kalach and Chir Station while *VIII Cavalry Corps,* aided by several rifle divisions, cleared the line of the Chir, east of which the Germans and Rumanians had no hope of holding.[40]

Fourth Panzer Army was split in two by the end of the day. The bulk of its German contingent, IV Corps and the 29th Motorized Infantry Division, was trapped inside the pocket forming around Stalingrad. Outside the pocket, Hoth had left only the Headquarters, Rumanian Fourth Army, Rumanian VI and VII Corps, and the 16th Motorized Infantry Division. The latter, protecting the army's outer flank, was cut off at Khalkuta on the 20th and had to fight its way west to Jashkul. In such condition, Fourth Panzer Army could not stem the advance around Stalingrad, and it had no real prospect of preventing the Russians from advancing southwest along the left side of the Don.[41]

Although Hoth did not know it at the time, a command problem on the other side was doing more for him than anything he could have managed. After the breakthrough, *Fifty-seventh Army* had the relatively limited mission of turning in on the flank of Sixth Army while *Fifty-first Army* had the dual

---

[38]*AOK 6, Ia Kriegstagebuch Nr. 14,* 20 Nov 42, AOK 6 33224/2 file.

[39]Heim was released in August 1943, without having been tried. He was restored to rank a year later and appointed to command the Boulogne Fortress in France. Walter Goerlitz, *Der Zweite Weltkrieg, 1939–1945* (Stuttgart: Steingruben Verlag, 1951, 1952), vol. I, p. 398, vol. II., p. 363; Walter Goerlitz, *Paulus and Stalingrad* (New York: Citadel Press, 1963), p. 201n.

[40]*Sbornik, Nomer 6; AOK 6, Ia, Angaben ueber Vorgaenge seit dem 20.11.42,* AOK 6 75107/6 file.

[41]*Pz. AOK 4, Ia Kriegstagebuch Nr. 5, Teil III,* 20–21 Nov 42, Pz. AOK 4 28183/1 file.

mission of sending its mobile forces, *IV Mechanized Corps* and *IV Tank Corps,* in a wide sweep northwestward to complete the encirclement near Kalach and of simultaneously directing its infantry divisions southwestward toward Kotelnikovo to cover the left flank. Considering the shattered state of Fourth Panzer Army, *Fifty-first Army* should not have had trouble, but Trufanov and his staff had difficulty dealing with the complications of controling forces moving in divergent directions. As a result, the advances toward Kalach and Kotelnikovo were conducted more slowly and hesitantly than was necessary.[42] Toward Kotelnikovo, in particular, *Fifty-first Army* moved so cautiously as to make Hoth wonder. Nevertheless, Fourth Panzer Army was in near mortal danger. On the 22d, Hoth described Rumanian VI Corps as still presenting "a fantastic picture of fleeing remnants."[43]

Sixth Army Stays

An encirclement of a modern army is a cataclysmic event. On the map it often takes on a surgically precise appearance. On the battlefield it is a rending operation that leaves the victim to struggle in a state of shock with the least favorable of all military situations: his lines of communications are cut; his headquarters are often separated from troops; support elements are shattered; and his front is opened to attack from all directions. The moment the ring closes, every single individual is in the pocket. Escape is upper-most in the thoughts of commanders and men alike, but escape is no simple matter. With the enemy on all sides, with rivers to cross, turning around an army that numbers in the hundreds of thousands, with all of its men, weapons, vehicles, supplies, and equipment, and marching it ten, twenty, thirty, or more miles is cumbersome and perilous.

The first effect of an impending encirclement is to intensify vastly the normal confusion of battle because the attack is carried into the areas most difficult to defend and because, as the advance continues, the forces being encircled progressively lose the points of reference, the means and the ability to orient themselves for a coherent response. It was seventy miles from the Serafimovich bridgehead to the bridge at Kalach, a few miles more to Sixth Army's railhead at Chir Station. In between, in the angle of the Chir and the Don, lay army and corps staffs, ammunition and supply dumps, motor pools, hospitals, workshops—in short, the nerve center and practically the whole housekeeping establishment of the army. All of these merged into one southward rolling wave of men, horses, and trucks trying to escape the Soviet tanks. The Don was frozen and probably could have been crossed even by trucks, but few would retreat east as long as they had any other choice.[44]

In the *Fuehrer* Headquarters the events were not clear, but their probable consequences were obvious. Short of a miracle, Sixth Army would either have to be permitted to retreat out of Stalingrad, which from Hitler's point of

[42]*Sbornik, Nomer 6.*

[43]*Pz. AOK 4, Ia Kriegstagebuch Nr. 5, Teil III,* 22 Nov 42, Pz. AOK 4 28183/1 file.

[44]A graphic, semifictionalized account of the encirclement is given in Heinrich Gerlach, *Die Verratene Armee* (Munich: Nymphenburger, 1959).

view was unthinkable, or a relief would have to be organized. On 20 November, Hitler created a new army group, Army Group Don, which would be composed of Sixth Army, Rumanian Third Army, Fourth Panzer Army, and Rumanian Fourth Army, and he gave Field Marshal Manstein the command. Manstein would need about a week to transfer his headquarters.

Manstein's appointment completed the Stalingrad triumvirate of Hitler, Manstein, and Paulus. At Stalingrad, Hitler had publicly staked his personal prestige; no small matter for him. In Operations Order No. 1 of 14 October he had established the rigid defense, successful in the previous winter, as his answer to whatever the next winter might bring. Manstein had a reputation to uphold, and possibly enlarge, as an engineer of victories and as an inspired, even daring, commander and tactician. Had Hitler decided to appoint another commander in chief, army, Manstein would have been one of the likeliest candidates. In his own mind, Manstein seems to have begun to envision at least an appointment as chief of the General Staff, with enough added authority to make him Hitler's Ludendorff.[45] Paulus, in his first army command, had fought the campaign well thus far. Like Manstein's, his career was on the rise. Reportedly, Hitler planned to bring him to the *Fuehrer* Headquarters after Stalingrad to replace General Jodl, chief, OKW Opera-

tions Staff, who was in lingering disfavor.[46]

On the 21st, from the *Berghof* where he had been vacationing, Hitler ordered Sixth Army to stand where it was "regardless of the danger of a temporary encirclement."[47] On the same day, he told Manstein to expect reinforcements totaling 6 infantry divisions, 4 panzer divisions, an air force field division, and an antiaircraft artillery division, but of these, only 2 infantry divisions would be available immediately, the others were not to be expected until the first week of December.[48]

Hitler's order reached Paulus at Nizhne Chirskaya behind the Chir River and outside the developing encirclement, where Sixth Army's winter headquarters had been built. He had stayed in his forward command post at Golubinskiy, on the Don ten miles north of Kalach, until nearly 1200 on the 21st, when Soviet tanks heading toward Kalach came into sight on the steppe to the west.[49]

When Paulus left, the XIV Panzer Corps staff took over the Golubinskiy command post and from there, with parts of the 14th and 16th Panzer Divisions, tried to lure the Soviet spearheads into a stationary battle. Wherever they could, the Soviet tanks ignored the Germans and roared past them. The *IV Tank Corps* lost some speed; *I Tank Corps* let itself get tied up in a fight; but *XXVI Tank Corps* was not

[45]General der Infanterie Erich Ludendorff, although nominally subordinate to the head of state and commander in chief, Emperor William II, and to the chief of the General Staff, Generalfeldmarschall Otto von Hindenburg, had directed the entire German war effort during the last two years of World War I.

[46]*OKW, KTB,* vol. II, p. 12.
[47]*H. Gr. B, Ia, an AOK 6, Fuehrerentscheid, 21.11.42,* AOK 6 75107/6 file.
[48]*OKH, GenStdH, Op. Abt. (I S/B) Nr. 420947/42, an H. Gr. B, 22.11.42,* H. Gr. Don 39694/3b file.
[49]Heinz Schroeter, *Stalingrad* (New York: E. P. Dutton, 1958), p. 80; Kehrig, *Stalingrad,* p. 163.

affected at all. In a daring raid before dawn on the morning of the 22d, a battalion from *XXVI Tank Corps* captured the Don Bridge at Kalach and formed a hedgehog around it.[50]

That morning, Paulus flew into the pocket. From the Gumrak airfield, he informed Hitler by radio that the Russians had taken Kalach and that Sixth Army had been encircled.[51] In the strict sense, Paulus' report was not quite correct. The Germans in Kalach held out until the next day, and the southern arm of the encirclement was not completed. It was late on the 23d, that, after an exchange of green recognition flares, *IV Tanks Corps,* which had crossed the Don and covered another ten miles, met *IV Mechanized Corps* at Sovetskiy and closed the ring.[52]

In the message to Hitler, Paulus had also stated that he did not have any kind of a front on the south rim of the pocket, between Kalach and Karpovka; therefore, he would have to call XIV Panzer Corps back and use its divisions to close the gap. If enough supplies could be flown in and the gap could be closed—the latter being doubtful because of a shortage of motor fuel—he intended to form a perimeter around Stalingrad. If a front could not be built on the south, the only solution, as he saw it, was to evacuate Stalingrad, to give up the north front, pull the army together, and to break out to the southwest toward Fourth Panzer Army. He requested discretionary authority to

give such orders if they became necessary.[53]

Paulus waited in vain throughout the day on the 23d for a decision from Hitler, who was making his way back to the *Wolfsschanze* by rail and plane and, who at intervals, was admonishing Zeitzler by telephone not to make any decisions until he arrived.[54] Aware by nightfall that the Soviet ring had closed, Paulus radioed a second appeal to the OKH in which he stated that the gap in the front on the south would expose the army to destruction "in the very shortest time" if a breakout were not attempted. As the first step, he said, he would have to strip the northern front and deploy the troops south for the escape effort. He again asked for freedom of decision, buttressing his request with the statement that his five corps commanders concurred in his estimate.[55] In a separate message, Weichs seconded Paulus' request.

During the night, Seydlitz, having concluded that a breakout was inevitable and that Hitler would have to be presented a fait accompli, began pulling back several LI Corps divisions on the northeastern tip of the pocket. The next morning, Hitler demanded a full report on the LI Corps withdrawal and forbade any further actions contrary to Operations Order No. 1. Weichs attempted to gloss over the matter by explaining that the troops had been taken back to prepared positions to gain a division for other employment; but Hitler was not convinced and, suspecting Paulus, gave Seydlitz, of whose ac-

---

[50]Schroeter, *Stalingrad,* pp. 81, 83–85; Kehrig, *Stalingrad,* pp. 163–65, 170–72; Samsonov, *Stalingradskaya bitva,* pp. 382–84.
[51]*AOK 6, Ia, KR-Funkspruch an H. Gr. B, 22.11.42,* AOK 6 75107/3 file.
[52]*IVOVSS,* vol. III, p. 40.

[53]*AOK 6 Ia, KR-Funkspruch an H. Gr. B, 22.11.42,* AOK 6 75107/3 file.
[54]Kehrig, *Stalingrad,* p. 218.
[55]*Paulus, Funkspruch an OKH, Nachrichtlich H. Gr. B, 23.11.42,* AOK 6 75107/6 file.

T–34 Tanks Advancing at Speed

tion he apparently was not aware, command of the entire north front, making him personally responsible for holding that side of the pocket.[56]

Manstein and part of his staff arrived at Weich's headquarters on the morning of the 24th, where Weichs told him Sixth Army's position was untenable. After making his own calculations, however, Manstein sent the OKH a less pessimistic estimate than those of Paulus and Weichs. He agreed that a breakout was the safest course and that to hold out would be extremely dangerous, but he said he could not concur "at present" with Army Group B's stand in favor of a breakout. He said he believed a relief operation could start in early December if the promised reinforcements were supplied. At the same time, he warned that the breakout could still become necessary if a relief force could not be assembled.[57]

Whether Hitler would have been persuaded by the unanimous voices of Manstein, Weichs, and Paulus is doubtful. That he was not going to be influenced by the other two with Manstein dissenting was certain. In fact, Hitler had made what was going to be his final

[56]OKH, GenStdH, Op. Abt. (I S/B) Nr. 420964/42, an 6 Armee, H. Gr. B, H. Gr. Don, 24.11.42 and OKH, GenStdH, Op. Abt. (I S/B) Nr. 134/42, an H. Gr. B, AOK 6, 24.11.42, AOK 6 75107/6 file; H. Gr. B, Ia Nr. 4242/42, an H. Gr. Don, 24.11.42, H. Gr. Don 39694 file.

[57]Ob. Kdo. H. Gr. Don, Ia Nr. 4580/42, an OKH, Op. Abt., 24.11.42, H. Gr. Don 39694/3b file; Kehrig, Stalingrad, pp. 222–24.

decision on Sixth Army early on the
24th, without waiting for Manstein's
opinion. He instructed Paulus to draw
his northwest and southwest fronts inward slightly and then to hold the
pocket, and he promised to supply
Sixth Army by air. To Fourth Panzer
Army, he sent orders to stop the Russians north of Kotelnikovo and to get
ready to counterattack north to reestablish contact with Sixth Army. In
Hitler's mind, the correctness of the
decision was probably confirmed less
by Manstein's estimate than by an assurance from Reichsmarschall Goering, commander in chief, air force—
accepted over Zeitzler's strenuously expressed doubts—that the air force
would be able to fly 600 tons of supplies per day into the pocket.[58]

Two days later, Hitler put down his
thoughts on Stalingrad in a message to
Manstein. To evacuate the city, he said,
would mean giving up the "most substantial achievement" of the 1942 campaign; therefore, the city would have to
be held regardless of the cost, especially since to retake it in 1943 would
require even greater sacrifices. Fourth
Panzer Army would have to "extend a
hand" to Sixth Army from the Kotelnikovo area and would have to hold a
bridgehead around the confluence of
the Don and Chir rivers to facilitate a
secondary thrust toward Stalingrad
from the west. When contact with Sixth
Army was reestablished, supplies
would be moved in; the city would be
held; and Army Group Don could begin to prepare for an advance north to
clear out the area of the breakthrough
between the Don and the Chir.[59]

Hitler had made his decision and was
confident, but his confidence was not
shared at the front. On seeing the
order of 24 November, Seydlitz told
Paulus there could be no question of
holding; the army either had to breakout or succumb within a short time. He
believed supplies, which had already
been running short before the counteroffensive began, would decide the
issue. To found any hopes on air supply, he added, was to grasp at a straw
since only thirty JU–52s were at hand
(on 23 November), and even if hundreds more could be assembled, a feat
which was doubtful, the army's full
requirements could still not be met.
Paulus told Seydlitz to keep out of
affairs that were no concern of his but,
nevertheless, agreed with Seydlitz in
substance and, on the 26th, in a personal letter to Manstein, again asked
for authority to act at his own discretion, pointing out that the first three
days of air supply had brought only a
fraction of the promised 600 tons and
300 JU–52 flights per day.[60]

Manstein knew Hitler's thinking and
did not answer. After Army Group
Don was formally activated on the next
day, the 27th, Manstein learned more.
Zeitzler told him that he, too, would
not be given the authority to order a
breakout—which he had asked for in

[58]Kehrig, *Stalingrad*, p. 220; *OKH, GenStdH, an AOK 6, 24.11.42*, AOK 6 75107/3 file; *OKH, GenStdH, Op. Abt. (I S/B) Nr. 420961/42, an H. Gr. B*, H. Gr. Don 39694/3b file; *MS T–9, Der Feldzug in Russland ein operativer Ueberblick* (Generaloberst a.D. Gotthard Heinrici), ch. X, pp. 81–82.

[59]*OKH, GenStdH, Op. Abt. (I S/B) Nr. 420964/42, an Herrn Generalfeldmarschall von Manstein, 26.11.42*, H. Gr. Don 39694/3b file.
[60]*Der Kommandierende General des LI A.K., Nr. 603/42, an den Herrn Oberbefehlshaber der 6. Armee, 25.11.42*, AOK 6 75107/3 file; *O.B. der AOK 6, an Generalfeldmarschall von Manstein, 26.11.42*, AOK 6 75107/3 file.

the 24 November estimate. Later, Richthofen, who was running the airlift, told him the planes would not be able to deliver even 300 tons of supplies a day. In the meantime, that morning, Hitler had called on the troops in the pocket to stand fast and to convert the breakthrough into a Soviet defeat as they had the one at Kharkov in the spring.[61]

---

[61]Kehrig, *Stalingrad*, pp. 264, 279.

CHAPTER XXIII

Stalingrad, Finale

The Relief

Bad as the German situation was at Stalingrad, it could easily have been far worse. However, once *Southwest, Don,* and *Stalingrad Fronts* completed the encirclement, they devoted the greater part of their forces to fastening the grip on Sixth Army, and they virtually discontinued the offensive in the Chir River sector and against Fourth Panzer Army. By 28 November, they had concentrated 94 divisions and brigades against Sixth Army and had only 49 units opposing Fourth Panzer Army and Rumanian Third Army, no more than 20 of these actually in the line.[1]

On the Army Group Don front, XVII Corps held the line of the Chir in the north, and Rumanian Third Army held the rest south to the confluence of the Chir and Don. Actually, XVII Corps had most of the remaining Rumanian troops, and the only sizable German units in the line were two infantry divisions. Rumanian Third Army existed in name only; German staff officers manned its headquarters; and a scratch force of small German units held its front.[2] In the Fourth Panzer Army sector, the remnants of Fourth Panzer Army and Rumanian VI and VII Corps were redesignated Armeegruppe Hoth. Under General Hoth, Headquarters, Rumanian Fourth Army, took command of the two Rumanian corps. Hoth had reported that if the Russians made anything approaching a serious effort against his *Armeegruppe,* they could not help but have the "greatest" success. By 27 November, Kotelnikovo was within Soviet artillery range; but *Fifty-first Army* was advancing cautiously; and in the last four days of the month, the first transports of German troops for a relief operation began to arrive.[3]

Wintergewitter

Hitler had based his decision to keep Sixth Army at Stalingrad on two assumptions: that sufficient forces to conduct a successful relief operation could be assembled and that Sixth Army could be sustained as a viable fighting force by air supply until the relief was accomplished. The air supply problem appeared to be one of simple arithmetic—matching the number of planes to the required tonnages. Such was not the case, but even if it had been, the problem would still have been beyond solution. In late November 1942, the German Air Force was undergoing its greatest strain since the start of the war. At Stalingrad and in North Af-

---

[1] *Sbornik, Nomer 6.*

[2] *Der O.B. der H. Gr. B, Ia Nr. 4200/42, an den Fuehrer und Oberbefehlshaber des Heeres, 26.11.42,* H. Gr. Don 39694/3b file.

[3] *Pz. AOK 4, Ia Kriegstagebuch Nr. 5, Teil III, 24–30 Nov 42,* Pz. AOK 4 28183/1 file.

rica, it was fighting a two-front war in earnest. By the end of November, 400 combat aircraft had been transferred from the Eastern Front to North Africa, reducing the front's numerical strength by a sixth and its effective strength by nearly a third. Moreover, of 2,000 planes left on the Eastern Front, the OKW estimated that no more than 1,120 were operational on 29 November.[4]

General Richthofen, the commander of Fourth Air Force, reported on 25 November that he had 298 JU–52 transports; he needed 500 to supply Stalingrad. And he recommended that Sixth Army be allowed to break out, a suggestion that Hitler "rejected out of hand."[5] He then began to use HE–111 twin-engine bombers as transports, which reduced the number of aircraft available for combat missions without decisively improving the air supply. In any event, even those aircraft at hand could not be made fully effective because they had to operate across enemy-held territory, through contested airspace, in uncertain weather, and without adequate ground support (particularly on the Stalingrad end of the run). On 29 November, 38 JU–52s (maximum load 1 ton per plane) and 21 HE–111s (maximum load 1,000 pounds per plane) took off. Of these, 12 JU–52s and 13 HE–111s landed inside the pocket. The following day, 30 JU–52s and 36 HE–111s landed out of 39 and 38, respectively, committed.[6] At

that rate, Sixth Army would have to be saved soon.

On 1 December, Army Group Don began preparing the relief, under the code name WINTERGEWITTER ("winter storm"). The main effort went to Fourth Panzer Army's LVII Panzer Corps, which, with two fresh panzer divisions (6th and 23d) then on the way, would push northeastward from the vicinity of Kotelnikovo toward Stalingrad. Rumanian VI and VII Corps would cover its flanks. For a secondary effort toward Kalach, out of a small German bridgehead on the lower Chir, Fourth Panzer Army was given XXXXVIII Panzer Corps. Headquarters, XXXXVIII Panzer Corps, left its two original divisions, 22d Panzer Division and 1st Rumanian Armored Division, in the front on the Chir and assumed command in the bridgehead of three divisions coming in—the 11th Panzer Division, 336th Infantry Division, and 7th Air Force Field Division. General Paulus, the commander of Sixth Army, was to bring together all of his armor on the southwest rim of the pocket and to be ready to strike toward LVII Panzer Corps if ordered. He was also to be prepared to break out toward Kalach but was at the same time to hold his fronts on the north and in Stalingrad. Field Marshal Manstein, commander of Army Group Don, wanted to be ready to start the relief operation anytime after daybreak on 8 December.[7]

---

[4]British Air Ministry Pamphlet 248, p. 182; *Greiner Diary Notes*, 29 Nov 42, C–065q CMH file.

[5]*Greiner Diary Notes*, 25 Nov 42, C–065q CMH file.

[6]See Kehrig, *Stalingrad*, pp. 283–98. OKH, Gen-StdH, Gen. Qu., Abt. I, Qu. 1 Nr. I/8807/42, an H. Gr. Don, 26.11.42; H. Gr. Don, Einsatz Luftwaffe, 29.11.42

and *H. Gr. Don, Einsatz der Flugzeuge zur Versorgung der 6. Armee am 30.11.42*, H. Gr. Don 39694/3b file.

[7]*Ob. Kdo. der H. Gr. Don, Ia Nr. 0343/42, Weisung Nr. 1 fuer Operation "Wintergewitter,"* 1.12.42, H. Gr. Don 39694/3b file.

Doubts and Delays

The outlook for WINTERGEWITTER was not auspicious from the first and grew less promising with each passing day. Sixth Army shifted two motorized divisions and a panzer division to the southwest as ordered, but after 2 December, *Don* and *Stalingrad Fronts* hit the pocket hard for a week and tied the three divisions down in defensive fighting.[8] On 3 December, *Southwest Front* again became active along the Chir, in the Rumanian Third Army sector, forcing Manstein to commit the three divisions for XXXXVIII Panzer Corps there and, in effect, to drop the corps out of WINTERGEWITTER. Further, the two divisions for LVII Corps were slow in arriving, and the OKH instructed Manstein to use air force field divisions, of which he had two, for defensive missions only.

By 9 December, WINTERGEWITTER had dwindled to a two-division operation. Nevertheless, the next day, Manstein decided to go ahead, and he set the time for the morning of 12 December. Any more delay, he believed, could not be tolerated because supplies were running short and because Soviet armor had been detected moving in opposite Fourth Panzer Army. Sixth Army reported that an average of only seventy tons of supplies a day were being flown in, and rations, except for odds and ends, would run out by 19 December.[9]

Hitler was still confident. On 3 December, answering a gloomy Army Group Don report, he cautioned Manstein to bear in mind that Soviet divisions were always smaller and weaker than they at first appeared to be and that the Soviet commands were probably thrown off balance by their own success. A week later his confidence had grown, and concluding that the first phase of the Soviet winter offensive could be considered ended without having achieved a decisive success, he returned to the idea of retaking the line on the Don. By 10 December, he was at the point of planning to deploy the 7th and 17th Panzer Divisions on the Army Group Don left flank and to use them to spearhead an advance from the Chir to the Don. The next day he ordered Manstein to station 17th Panzer Division in the XVII Corps sector on the Chir, thereby, for the time being, ending the possibility of its being used in WINTERGEWITTER.[10]

Wintergewitter Runs Its Course

Jumping off on time on the morning of the 12th, LVII Panzer Corps made good, though not spectacular, progress. During the afternoon situation conference at *Fuehrer* Headquarters, General Zeitzler, the chief of the General Staff, tried to persuade Hitler to release the 17th Panzer Division for WINTERGEWITTER, but Hitler refused because a threat appeared to be developing on the Army Group Don left flank where it joined the right of Ital-

[8] *AOK 6, Ia, Notizen zur Beurteilung der Lage 6. Armee,* 7.12.42, H. Gr. Don 39694/4 file; Platonov, *Vtoraya Mirovaya Voyna,* p. 391.

[9] *Ob. Kdo. der H. Gr. Don, Ia Nr. 0356/42, an OKH, Chef GenStdH,* 10.12.42, H. Gr. Don 39694/4 file; *AOK 6, Ia Nr. 4727/42, an H. Gr. Don,* 11.12.42, H. Gr. Don 39694/4 file.

[10] *Anna 7851, Bezug: H. Gr. Don, Ia Nr. 0341/42,* H. Gr. Don 39694/3b file; *Greiner Diary Notes,* 10 Dec 42, C-065q CMH file; *OKH, GenStdH, Op. Abt. Nr. 1014/42, an H. Gr. Don,* 11.12.42, H. Gr. Don 39694/4 file.

SELF-PROPELLED ASSAULT GUNS ATTACK IN OPERATION WINTERGEWITTER

ian Eighth Army. In the conference, he restated his position on Stalingrad, saying, "I have reached one conclusion, Zeitzler. We cannot, under any circumstances, give that [pointing to Stalingrad] up. We will not retake it. We know what that means . . . if we give that up we sacrifice the whole sense of this campaign. To imagine that I will get there again next time is insanity."[11]

On the second day, LVII Panzer Corps reached the Aksay River and captured a bridge at Zalivskiy; but on the Chir and at the Don-Chir bridgehead, XXXXVIII Panzer Corps barely held its own against the *Fifth Tank* and *Fifth Shock Armies*, which were

trying to tighten the grip on Sixth Army by enlarging the buffer zone on the west.[12] *Fifth Shock Army* was newly formed out of two rifle divisions and a tank corps from the *Stavka* reserves.[13] Before 1200 Manstein told Hitler that the trouble on the Chir had eliminated every chance of XXXXVIII Panzer Corps' fleeing forces for a thrust out of the bridgehead and that without such help, LVII Panzer Corps could not get through to Sixth Army.

Manstein asked for 17th Panzer Division, to take over the attack from the

[11]*Stenogr. Dienst im F.H. Qu., Lagebesprechung vom 12.12.42*, CMH files.

[12][General Staff of the Red Army], *Sbornik materialov po izucheniiu opyta voyny, Nomer 8*, Aug–Oct 43; *Pz. AOK 4, Ia Kriegstagebuch Nr. 5, Teil III*, 13 Dec 42, Pz. AOK 4 28183/1 file.
[13]Vasilevskiy, *Delo*, p. 264f.

bridgehead, and for 16th Motorized Infantry Divison (then stationed at Elista, between the Army Group Don and Army Group A flanks) to reinforce LVII Panzer Corps. Hitler released the 17th Panzer Division but not the 16th Motorized Infantry Division. The decision about 17th Panzer Division was made easier by a growing impression in the OKH that the Russians were only simulating a buildup on the Army Group Don left flank.[14]

For another four days, WINTERGEWITTER went ahead without gathering enough momentum to ensure an early success. On the 14th, however, the part of the Don-Chir bridgehead east of the Don had to be evacuated. The attack out of the bridgehead would have been abandoned in any case, since 17th Panzer Division was having to be sent to LVII Panzer Corps. On the 17th and 18th, LVII Panzer Corps, increased to three divisions by 17th Panzer Division, became tied down in fighting around Kumskiy, halfway between the Askay and Mishkova rivers.

On the 19th, LVII Panzer Corps shook itself loose and drove to the Mishkova, thirty-five miles from the pocket. Manstein, however, told Hitler that LVII Panzer Corps, because of its own losses and stiffening enemy resistance, probably could not get through to Sixth Army and certainly could not open a permanent corridor to the pocket. He had, he added, sent his intelligence officer into the pocket, and he had reported that Sixth Army only had rations for another three days.

Consequently, Manstein said, he believed the only answer was to order Sixth Army to break out, gradually pulling back its fronts on the north and in Stalingrad as it pushed toward LVII Panzer Corps on the south. That, he maintained, would at least save most of the troops and whatever equipment could still be hauled.[15]

To Paulus, Manstein sent notice to get ready for Operation DONNERSCHLAG ("thunderbolt"), which would be the breakout. The army's mission, Manstein said, would have to include an initial push to the Mishkova. There, after contact with LVII Corps was made, truck convoys, which were bringing up 3,000 tons of supplies behind the corps, would be sluiced through to the pocket. Subsequently, Sixth Army, taking along what equipment it could, would evacuate the pocket and withdraw southwestward. Paulus was to get ready but was not to start until ordered.[16]

Hitler, encouraged by LVII Panzer Corps' getting to the Mishkova, refused to approve DONNERSCHLAG. Instead, he ordered the SS Viking Division transferred from Army Group A to Fourth Panzer Army. Sixth Army, he insisted, was to stay put until firm contact was established with LVII Corps and a complete, orderly withdrawal could be undertaken. In the meantime, enough supplies were to be flown in, particularly of motor fuel, to give the army thirty miles' mobility. (Hitler had heard

---

[14]O.B. der H. Gr. Don, Ia Nr. 259/42, an Chef des Generalstabes, OKH, 13.12.42, H. Gr. Don 39694/4 file; Greiner Diary Notes, 13 Dec 42, C–065q CMH file.

[15]O.B. der H. Gr. Don, Ia Nr. 0368/42, an Chef des Generalstabes des Heeres zur sofortigen Vorlage beim Fuehrer, 19.12.42, H. Gr. Don 39694/5 file. See also Kehrig, Stalingrad, pp. 390–93.
[16]Ob. Kdo. H. Gr. Don, Ia Nr. 0369/42, an 6. Armee, 19.12.42, H. Gr. Don 39694/5 file.

that the army had only enough fuel to go eighteen miles.)[17]

On the 21st, after LVII Panzer Corps had failed to get beyond the Mishkova in two more days of fighting, Generalmajor Friedrich Schulz, Manstein's chief of staff, conferred with General Schmidt, Paulus' chief of staff, by means of a newly installed high-frequency telecommunications system. Schulz asked whether Sixth Army could execute DONNERSCHLAG. The operation had not been approved, he added, but Manstein wanted to be ready to go ahead as soon as possible because of the unlikelihood of LVII Panzer Corps' getting any closer to the pocket. Schmidt replied that the army could start on 24 December, but he did not believe it could continue to hold the pocket for any length of time thereafter if the first losses were heavy. If Stalingrad were to be held, he said, it would be better to fly in supplies and replacements, in which case the army could defend itself indefinitely. In the case of DONNERSCHLAG, he and Paulus thought the chances for success would be better if the evacuation followed immediately upon the breakout, but they regarded evacuation, under any circumstances, as an act of desperation to be avoided until it became absolutely necessary.[18] The conference ended on that indeterminate note.

Manstein transmitted the results of the exchange to the OKH. He could give no assurance, he added, that if Sixth Army held out, contact with LVII Panzer Corps could be reestablished,

since further substantial gains by the panzer corps were not to be expected.[19] In effect WINTERGEWITTER had failed, and both Manstein and Paulus had sidestepped the responsibility for DONNERSCHLAG, which neither could legally order without Hitler's approval. Later in the day, on the 21st, Hitler talked at length with the chiefs of the Army and Air Force General Staffs, but to those present, "the Fuehrer seemed no longer capable of making a decision."[20]

Sixth Army Isolated

After it turned over the Stalingrad sector to Army Group Don, Army Group B had just one function—to protect the rear of its neighbors to the south, Army Groups Don and A. On the critical 200-mile stretch of the Don from Voronezh downstream to Veshenskaya, that function fell to the Hungarian Second Army and Italian Eighth Army. How well they might be expected to perform under attack was predictable because the Rumanians had been considered the best of the German allies.

A glance at the map *(Map 44)* reveals how vulnerable Army Groups Don and A were and how much their existences depended on the few raillines that reached into the steppe east of the Dnepr, the Donets, and the Don. The crucial points on these lines were the river crossings. Everything going east out of the Dnepr bend depended on the bridges at Dnepropetrovsk and

---

[17]*Greiner Diary Notes,* 19 Dec 42, C–065q CMH file.
[18]*FS-Gespraech Gen. Schmidt- Gen. Schulz, 21.12,42,* AOK 6 75107/2 file.

[19]*O.B. d. H. Gr. Don, Ia Nr. 0372/42, zu Fernspruch OKH, Op. Abt. Nr. 521021/42, 21.12.42,* H. Gr. Don 39694/5 file.
[20]*Greiner Diary Notes,* 21 Dec 42, C–065q CMH file.

Zaporozhye. The distance from Dnepropetrovsk to the Soviet line at Novaya Kalitva, in the center of the Italian Eighth Army sector, was 250 miles, while from Dnepropetrovsk to the Army Group Don front on the Chir River was 330 miles; to the left flank of Army Group A, 580 miles. But the Russians did not need to strike as far west as Dnepropetrovsk. On the left flank of Army Group Don they were within 80 miles of three Donets crossings: Voroshilovgrad, Kamensk-Shakhtinskiy, and Belokalitvenskaya. A 150-mile march from the left flank of Army Group Don would take them all the way to Rostov. Both Army Group A and Fourth Panzer Army were tied to the railroad through Rostov, and the Army Group A left flank was 350 miles and the Fourth Panzer Army right flank 220 miles from Rostov.

Saturn and Koltso

The anomalies of the German situation, of course, did not go unnoticed on the Soviet side, and on the night of 23 November, Stalin instructed General Vasilevskiy, chief of the General Staff, to work up a plan for an offensive by *Southwest Front*, under General Vatutin, and the *Voronezh Front*, left wing, under General Golikov, "in the general direction of Millerovo and Rostov."[21] Apparently Stalin also talked to General Moskalenko, commander of *First Guards Army*, that same night about something possibly even bigger, an offensive to liberate Kharkov and the Don Basin. In the last week of the month, Vasilevskiy and General Voronov, who would be coordinating

the operation as *Stavka* representatives, worked on the plan with the *front* commanders, Vatutin and Golikov. General Zhukov, first deputy commissar for defense, who had gone to *Kalinin* and *West Fronts* to take charge of MARS, nevertheless, stayed in close touch with Stalin and Vasilevskiy.[22]

On 2 December, Stalin and the *Stavka* approved the plan as Operation SATURN and set the readiness date as 10 December. The objectives were to encircle Italian Eighth Army and the Army Group Don elements inside the Don bend and, by taking Rostov and the line of the lower Don, to cut off Fourth Panzer Army and Army Group A. On the right, *Southwest Front*'s *First Guards* and *Third Guards Armies*, the latter to be formed by dividing *First Guards Army* and adding rifle divisions and a mechanized corps from the reserves, would break through the Italian Eighth Army's left flank near Boguchar, head almost due south to Millerovo, cross the Donets at Kamensk-Shakhtinskiy, and continue south to Rostov. On their right, *Voronezh Front*'s *Sixth Army* would provide flank cover and strike toward Voroshilovgrad. To form the second arm of the envelopment, *Fifth Tank Army* would break through across the Chir and run along the right side of the lower Don to Rostov.[23]

In Moscow, on 4 December, Stalin and Vasilevskiy decided also to finish off Sixth Army, and Stalin gave the op-

---

[21]Vasilevskiy, *"Delo,"* p. 252.

[22]Moskalenko, *Na Yugo-zapadnom napravlenii,* p. 357; Vasilevskiy, *"Delo,"* pp. 255–57; Zhukov, *Memoirs,* p. 412. See also Moskalenko, *Na Yugo-zapadnom napravlenii,* pp. 360–65.
[23]*VOV,* p. 178; Vasilevskiy, *"Delo,"* pp. 256f, 258; *IVMV,* vol. VI, p. 63 and map 2; *Sbornik, Nomer 8;* D. D. Lelyushenko, *Moskva-Stalingrad-Berlin-Praga* (Moscow: Izdatelstvo "Nauka," 1970), p. 134.

eration the code name KOLTSO ("ring"). The object would be to split the pocket on an east-west axis and then wipe out the two parts in succession. The main effort would be a thrust through the pocket from the west by *Don Front*, which would be given *Second Guards Army* from the *Stavka* reserves and would be ready to start by the 18th. In the same meeting, Stalin and Vasilevskiy decided to strengthen *Southwest Front*'s left flank for SATURN by putting in *Fifth Shock Army*. Zhukov indicated that he had devised the general scheme for KOLTSO and had proposed it to Stalin on 29 November.[24]

SATURN had not started, and KOLTSO was not ready when Manstein began WINTERGEWITTER. By Rokossovskiy's account, Vasilevskiy was at Headquarters, *Don Front*, on the morning of 12 December and, immediately after news of the German attack came in, telephoned Stalin to ask for and get *Second Guards Army* transferred to *Stalingrad Front*.[25] Vasilevskiy says he did not make the request until later in the day and did not get the *Stavka*'s decision until that night.[26] In any event, the loss of *Second Guards Army* put KOLTSO in abeyance.

On the night of the 13th, according to Vasilevskiy, the *Stavka* made "the very important decision" to reduce SATURN.[27] Zhukov says that he and Vasilevskiy and the General Staff had already decided for a "smaller SATURN" at the end of November, when he had also told Stalin to expect a German at-

tack toward the Stalingrad pocket from the Kotelnikovo area.[28] In any event, SATURN became MALYY SATURN ("small Saturn"). Instead of going south on the line Millerovo–Kamensk-Shakhtinskiy–Rostov, the right arm of the envelopment would bear southeast inside the Don bend; and the left arm, instead of going southwest, would go west. The two would meet near Tatsinskaya and Morozovsk.[29] The changes in direction reduced the projected depth of the advance by half.

The conversion to MALYY SATURN may also have, in part, been the result of a mood of caution induced by events elsewhere. *West Front* and *Kalinin Front* began MARS on the morning of 25 November. In its initial phase the offensive repeated the pattern at Stalingrad, with massive thrusts from the east and the west to pinch off the Rzhev salient. MARS, however, had to do with the battle-tested German Ninth Army. After *Twentieth Army*, carrying the main effort in the *West Front* sector on the east face of the salient, lost more than half its tanks by committing them piecemeal in trying to get a breakthrough, one panzer corps handled the defense there with ease.[30] *Kalinin Front*'s attacks on the west, south of Belyy and along the Luchesa River, went better and achieved depths of twenty and ten miles respectively; but a Ninth Army counterattack on 7 December turned the break-in south of Belyy into a pocket, in which the Germans eventually counted 15,000 Soviet

[24]Vasilevskiy, *"Delo,"* p. 264; *IVMV*, vol. VI, p. 64; Zhukov, *Memoirs*, p. 412.

[25]Rokossovskiy, *Soldier's Duty*, p. 152.

[26]Vasilevskiy, *"Delo,"* p. 270f.

[27]*Ibid.*, p. 272.

[28]Zhukov, *Memoirs*, p. 413.

[29]*Sbornik, Nomer 8;* Samsonov, *Stalingradskaya bitva*, pp. 470–72; Lelyushenko, *Moskva*, pp. 134–36.

[30][General Staff of the Red Army], *Sbornik materialov po izucheniiu opyta voyny, Nomer 9*, 1944.

A COLUMN OF T-34 TANKS IN OPERATION MALYY SATURN

dead and 5,000 prisoners. On 11 December, *West Front* launched a second attempt during the first two days of which Ninth Army counted 295 Soviet tanks knocked out. On the 13th and 14th, MARS slackened rapidly, leaving only the penetration along the Luchesa River to be fought over into the new year.[31]

Malyy Saturn Begins

On 16 December, *Sixth Army*, under General Leytenant F. M. Kharitonov, and *First Guards Army*, under General Kuznetsov, broke into the Italian Eighth Army's line on the Don east of Novaya Kalitva. The next day, *Third Guards Army*, under General Leytenant D. D. Lelyushenko, joined them to extend the push downstream along the river.[32] By the third day, all three armies had broken through, and on the 20th, the Celere and Sforzesca Divisions on the Italian Eighth Army right flank collapsed, carrying with them two Rumanian divisions on the left flank of Army Group Don. In four days, *Southwest Front* had ripped open a 100-mile-wide hole.[33] *(Map 43.)*

For the Germans, the problem now

[31]*AOK 9, Fuehrungsabteilung, Kriegstagebuch, Band 3,* 1–16 Dec 42, AOK 9 31624/3 file.

[32]Samsonov, *Stalingradskaya bitva,* p. 472. See also Lelyushenko, *Moskva,* p. 139.

[33]*Kriegstagebuch des deutschen Generals beim ital. AOK 8 v. 11.7.42–31.1.43,* 15–20 Dec 42, AOK 8 36188/1 file; *H. Gr. Don, Ia, Lage H. Gr. Don, 19–21.1.43,* H. Gr. Don 39694/16 file.

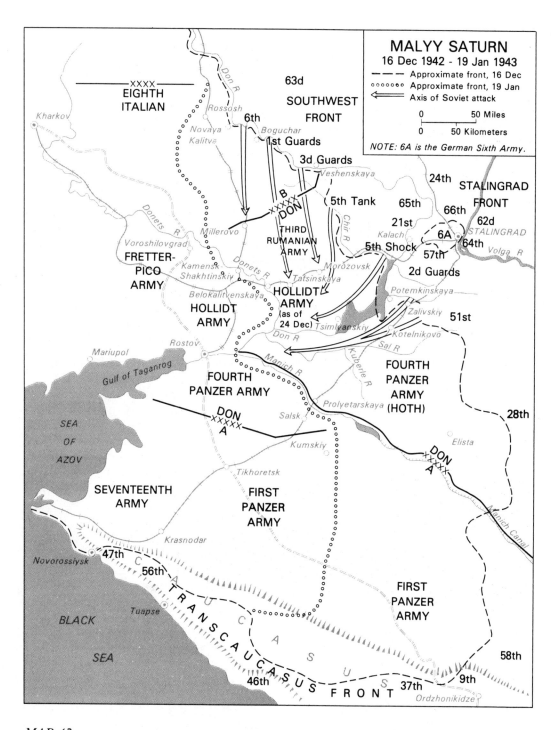

MALYY SATURN
16 Dec 1942 - 19 Jan 1943

- – – Approximate front, 16 Dec
- ooooooo Approximate front, 19 Jan
- ⟵ Axis of Soviet attack

0   50 Miles
0   50 Kilometers

NOTE: 6A is the German Sixth Army.

EIGHTH
ITALIAN

Kharkov

Don R

Rossosh

Novaya
Kalitva

63d

SOUTHWEST
FRONT

6th

Boguchar

1st Guards

3d Guards

Veshenskaya

24th

STALINGRAD
FRONT

Donets R

B
XXXX
DON

5th Tank

65th

66th

21st

62d
STALINGRAD

Chir R

Millerovo

THIRD
RUMANIAN
ARMY

Kalach

6A

64th

Volga R

FRETTER-
PICO
ARMY

Voroshilovgrad

Donets R

5th Shock

57th

Kamensk
Shakhtinskiy

Morozovsk

2d Guards

Belokalitvenskaya

HOLLIDT
ARMY
(as of
24 Dec)

Tatsinskaya

Potemkinskaya

HOLLIDT
ARMY

Zalivskiy

51st

Tsimlyanskiy

Don R

Kötelnikovo

Mariupol

Rostov

Manich R

Sal R

Kuberle R

FOURTH
PANZER
ARMY (HOTH)

Gulf of Taganrog

FOURTH
PANZER ARMY

Salsk

Prolyetarskaya

DON
XXXXX
A

SEA
OF
AZOV

Kumskiy

DON
XXXX
A

Elista

28th

SEVENTEENTH
ARMY

Tikhoretsk

FIRST
PANZER
ARMY

Manich Canal

Krasnodar

Novorossiysk

47th

C

56th

A

U

C

A

S

U

FIRST
PANZER
ARMY

BLACK

Tuapse

T
R
A
N
S
C
A
U
C
A
S
U
S

58th

SEA

46th

FRONT

37th

9th

Ordzhonikidze

MAP 43

was somehow to screen the deep northern flank of Army Group Don. *Fifth Tank Army* had not managed to get its share of MALYY SATURN going, but a single envelopment could be just as bad as a double one. The OKH transferred a corps headquarters, commanded by General Fretter-Pico, from Army Group North to take over the Army Group B right flank as Armeeabteilung Fretter-Pico. It gave the *Armeeabteilung* one fresh infantry division, the headquarters and elements of 3d Mountain Division, and remnants of a weak German corps that had been stationed as a backstop behind the Italians. With them, Fretter-Pico was to protect the Donets bridges at Voroshilovgrad and Kamensk-Shakhtinskiy (which were open, even though the Russians were, for the moment, not aiming toward them) and somehow stretch a line east of the Donets to tie in with Army Group Don.

On the 23d, Manstein told Hitler that he would have to take at least one division, perhaps two, away for LVII Panzer Corps to cover Army Group Don's left flank. Doing so, he added, would mean giving up the idea of relieving Sixth Army anytime soon and would necessitate long-term air supply for the army. Paulus needed 550 tons a day, but Richthofen believed 200 tons were the most that could be delivered. If, as it appeared, air supply could not be guaranteed, Manstein saw a breakout as the only solution despite the risk. The appearance of Soviet reinforcements (*Second Guards Army*) along the Mishkova, he pointed out, meant that the Russians would soon be going over to the offensive there also, which would be extremely dangerous since Fourth Panzer Army was having to rely on Rumanian troops to cover its flanks.[34]

Hitler's decision, which was, in fact, no decision at all, came early the next morning. He authorized Manstein to transfer "elements" of LVII Panzer Corps to the army group left flank to protect the air bases at Morozovsk and Tatsinskaya, which were essential for Sixth Army's air supply. But LVII Panzer Corps was to stay on the Mishkova until the advance to Stalingrad could be resumed. As if it would make all the difference, he informed Manstein that one battalion of Tiger tanks being sent to the army group by railroad would cross into Russia near Brest Litovsk during the day.[35]

Sixth Army's Last Chance

A month is a long time to an encircled army. Its moral and physical sustenance reduced, it begins to wither. Most dramatically and dismayingly affected are the men themselves. In 1941 the Germans had noticed, and then forgotten, that large numbers of Russians captured in the great encirclements died suddenly without detectable symptoms. In December 1942, the same sort of deaths began to be reported in the Stalingrad pocket. A pathologist flown in to perform autopsies in secret discovered that undernourishment, exhaustion, and exposure had caused the complete loss of fatty tissue, changes in the internal organs and bone marrow, and, as the apparent direct cause of these deaths, a

[34]*O.B. d. H. Gr. Don, Ia Nr. 0374/42, an Chef des GenStdH, 22.12.42,* H. Gr. Don 39694/5 file.

[35]*OKH, GenStdH, Op. Abt. (I S/B) Nr. 421026/42, an Generalfeldmarschall von Manstein, 23.12.42,* H. Gr. Don 39694/5 file.

shrinking of the heart except for the right ventricle, which was greatly enlarged. Such heart damage, in normal medical practice, had been regarded as a condition that chiefly affected the aged; among the soldiers at Stalingrad, as the days passed, it was observed to be common in both the dead and the living.[36] In the Stalingrad pocket death was no novelty. Sixth Army had lost 28,000 men between 22 November and 23 December.

On 18 December, the army reported a ration strength of 246,000, including 13,000 Rumanians, 19,300 Russian auxiliaries, and 6,000 wounded; but these numbers were far from representing its effective combat strength.[37] Already in mid-October, the army had reported that it was reduced to a frontline infantry strength of 66,500. By 21 December, it had only 25,000 infantry.[38] Service troops were converted to infantry, but experience showed that even under the exceptional conditions of an encirclement, such conversions were not easy to accomplish or especially worthwhile in terms of combat effectiveness.

At the end of the first month, the hard winter had not yet set in. The temperature lingered close to freezing—some days above, some below. Cold days were likely to be clear with only occasional snow or wind. Warmer days brought clouds, fog, light rain, snow, and, always when there were two or three such days in succession, mud.

Not as extreme as it might have been, the weather, nevertheless, was not easily borne by soldiers who were inadequately sheltered and clothed and were living on slender rations of bread, soup, and occasional horse meat.[39] The instability of the weather also affected the airlift. In the early winter, continental and maritime air masses met over the region of the lower Don and Volga, producing not only frequent and rapid changes in the weather but great variations within relatively short distances. Consequently, when the skies over the air bases at Tatsinskaya and Morozovsk were clear, the Stalingrad pocket was sometimes buried in fog.

The relief attempt had failed. That another could be made or that Sixth Army could survive until then was becoming more doubtful every day. On the afternoon of 23 December, Manstein called for a conference via teletype with Paulus. He asked Paulus to consider whether, if no other course remained open, the breakout (which by then was assumed automatically to include the evacuation) could be executed provided limited quantities of motor fuel and rations could be flown in during the next few days. Paulus replied that the breakout had become more difficult because the Russians had strengthened their line, but if an attempt were to be made, it was better done right away than later. Then he asked, "Do you empower me to begin the preparations? Once begun, they cannot be reversed."

Manstein replied, "That authority I cannot give today. I am hoping for a decision tomorrow. The essential point

---

[36]Hans Dibold, *Arzt in Stalingrad* (Salzburg: O. Mueller, 1949), p. 18.

[37] The figures are from Helmut Arntz, "Die Wende des Krieges in Stalingrad," a manuscript apparently written late in the war from official German records.

[38]Schroeter, *Stalingrad*, p. 208; Kehrig, *Stalingrad*, p. 407.

[39]Hauck, MS P–114c, vol. IV, table Xa.

is do you consider the army capable of forcing its way through to Hoth if supplies for a longer period cannot be assured?" Paulus answered, "In that case, there is nothing else to be done." He added that he thought the army would need at least six days to get ready and 300,000 more gallons of motor fuel plus 500 tons of rations before it could attempt to break out.[40]

Within the hour, Manstein dispatched a situation estimate to Hitler in which he outlined three possibilities: (1) leave Sixth Army where it was and assure a daily air supply of a minimum of 500 tons; (2) order Paulus to break out, taking the risk that the army might not get through; (3) transfer the 16th Motorized Infantry Division and two panzer divisions from First Panzer Army immediately to enable Fourth Panzer Army to resume the advance toward Stalingrad.[41] Again, Hitler could not make up his mind and countered with a series of questions. Was a breakout actually possible, and would it succeed? When could it start? How long could Paulus stay in the pocket, given the current level of supplies or, perhaps, "somewhat" increased air supply? When could the relief operation be resumed if Manstein were given both the SS Viking Division and 7th Panzer Division? Did Manstein think the Russians would soon be stopped by their own fuel and supply shortages? Would Manstein "welcome" being given command of Army Group A as well as Don?[42]

Manstein answered that the breakout could begin, as reported, in six days. Nobody could predict whether it would succeed or not, and the only way to secure a moderate degree of assurance of its success would be to transfer two more panzer divisions from First Panzer Army. The SS Viking Division and 7th Panzer Division would be needed on the army group left flank when they arrived. There were no reasons to think the Russians were going to run out of supplies. As far as Manstein's also taking command of Army Group A was concerned, nobody would "welcome" it in the existing circumstances, but it was unavoidable. Even so, it appeared that for Sixth Army, and possibly Army Groups Don and A as well, all subsequent decisions would come too late. Manstein concluded, "I ask that it be considered how the battle would develop if we commanded on the other side."[43]

Operations Order No. 2

On 24 December, *First Guards Army* pushed a spearhead through to Tatsinskaya, and *Third Guards Army* came within artillery range of Morozovsk. That same day, *Second Guards Army*, General Malinovskiy commanding, forced LVII Panzer Corps back to the Aksay River.[44] To hold the air-supply base for Sixth Army at Morozovsk and recapture the one at Tatsinskaya, Manstein had to take the 11th Panzer Division from Fourth Panzer Army. Out of the staff of XVII Corps, he created the

[40]*FS-Gespraech, Gen. Feldmarschall von Manstein an Gen. Obst. Paulus, 23.12.42,* AOK 6 75107/5 file.

[41]*Manstein, an Chef Gen. Stab, Antwort auf heutige Anfrage, 23.12.42,* H. Gr. Don 39694/5 file.

[42]*OKH, GenStdH, Op. Abt. Nr. 421030/42, an H. Gr. Don, 24.12.42,* H. Gr. Don 39694/5 file.

[43]*O.B. d. H. Gr. Don, Ia Nr. 0376/42, an Chef des GenStdH, 24.12.42,* H. Gr. Don 39694/6 file.

[44]*VOV,* pp. 183–87. See also Samsonov, *Stalingradskaya bitva,* pp. 478–80 and Lelyushenko, *Moskva,* p. 147.

Headquarters, Armeeabteilung Hollidt, under General der Infanterie Karl Hollidt, the XVII Corps commander, and gave it command of the whole north front. Manstein sent the Headquarters, Rumanian Third Army, behind the Donets to collect Rumanian stragglers and to start building defenses downstream from Kamensk-Shakhtinskiy.[45]

To get a respite at Tatsinskaya and Morozovsk, Manstein had been forced to reduce Fourth Panzer Army's effective strength by a third; nevertheless, Hitler still hoped to bring in the SS Viking Division and 7th Panzer Division in time to restart the advance toward Stalingrad. Manstein's situation report of 25 December demonstrated how slight that hope actually was. In a few days, he said, *Fifty-first* and *Second Guards Armies* would attempt to encircle Fourth Panzer Army on the Aksay River. Nothing could be expected of the Rumanian VI and VII Corps, and the two divisions of LVII Panzer Corps could muster no more than nineteen tanks between them. If Sixth Army were not to be abandoned entirely at Stalingrad, a panzer corps (two divisions) and an infantry division would have to be shifted from Army Group A to Fourth Panzer Army, and at least one infantry division would have to be added on the Army Group Don left flank.[46]

The next two days proved that Manstein was by no means painting too dark a picture. On the 26th, Paulus reported that casualties, cold (the temperature that day was −15° F.), and hunger had so sapped his army's strength that it could not execute the breakout and evacuation unless a supply corridor to the pocket were opened first. The next day, Rumanian VII Corps, on LVII Panzer Corps' east flank, collapsed and fell into a disorganized retreat. After that, the best Hoth, commander of Fourth Panzer Army, thought he could do was to take LVII Panzer Corps back to Kotelnikovo and, maybe, make another temporary stand there.[47]

Hitler, however, was still looking for a cheap way out, and on the 27th, he ordered Army Groups Don and A to hold where they were while Army Group B, to protect the rear of Don, retook the line of the Rossosh-Millerovo railroad. Army Group A, he told Manstein, could not spare any divisions, and Army Group Don would have to make do with the SS Viking and 7th Panzer Divisions and the battalion of Tiger tanks.[48] Manstein protested that Fourth Panzer Army's two panzer divisions and the 16th Motorized Infantry Division faced a total of forty-three enemy units (divisions, brigades, and tank, cavalry, and mechanized corps) while First Panzer Army, in a well-constructed line, was opposed by only an equal number of enemy units, and Seventeenth Army had to deal with no more than twenty-four Soviet

[45]*H. Gr. Don, Ia, Lage H. Gr. Don 22–27.12.42*, H. Gr. Don 39694/16 file.

[46]*OKH, GenStdH, Op. Abt. 421030/42, an H. Gr. Don, 24.12.42*, H. Gr. Don 39694/6 file; *O.B. d. H. Gr. Don, Ia Nr. 378/42, an Chef d. GenStdH, 25.12.42*, H. Gr. Don 39694/6 file.

[47]*AOK 6, Ia Nr. 6010/42; an O.B. H. Gr. Don, 26.12.42*, H. Gr. Don 39694/6 file; *Pz. AOK 4, Ia Kriegstagebuch Nr. 5, Teil III*, 27 Dec 42, Pz. AOK 4 28183/1 file.

[48]*OKH, GenStdH, Op. Abt. (I S/B) Nr. 421033/42 an den O.B. d. H. Gr. Don, 27.12.42* and *OKH, GenStdH, Op. Abt. Nr. 321034/42, Weisung fuer die weitere Kampffuehrung, 27.12.42*, H. Gr. Don 39694/6 file.

units. He was convinced, he wrote, that events would compel a shift of forces from A to Don. The sooner the decision was made, the less costly it would be in the long run.[49]

Hitler countered with Operations Order No. 2. Under it, Army Group A, holding its line on the Black Sea coast and in the Caucasus, was to swing its left flank back by stages to Salsk, where it would be able to take over its own flank defense. Fourth Panzer Army, if forced, could fall back to the line Tsimlyanskiy-Salsk. To coordinate these movements, Manstein would assume command at a time to be decided by himself. Hitler ignored an earlier contention of Manstein's that his taking control of Army Group A would be worthwhile only if it included his having full operational freedom.[50]

The last days of the year brought another crisis. On the afternoon of 28 December, Hoth had to rescue LVII Panzer Corps by allowing it to withdraw past Kotelnikovo to the Sal River. That opened up the left bank of the Don to Rostov and exposed the deep right flank of Armeeabteilung Hollidt, and the next day, the Russians pushed out of a small bridgehead they held near Potemkinskaya. Hollidt then had to shift the 11th Panzer Division to Tsimlyanskiy, seventy miles downstream on the Don, to block their advance toward Rostov. Hitler, in consequence, ordered the 7th Panzer Division to be held at Rostov for a

possible last-ditch defense of the city.[51]

On the 28th, Manstein had told Hitler that Fourth Panzer Army was no longer capable of holding a broad front south of the Don and that the Armeeabteilung Hollidt line could be penetrated from the north or south at anytime. He said he intended to turn Fourth Panzer Army east south of the Sal River to protect the rear of Army Group A, taking the chance that the Russians might cut through to Rostov between the Sal and Don. Armeeabteilung Hollidt would have to be pulled back, possibly to a line slightly forward of the Donets, more likely to the river itself.[52]

Sixth Army Destroyed

On New Year's Eve, Manstein told Paulus that Army Group Don's primary objective was to liberate Sixth Army, but the army would have to hold out in the pocket a while longer. Hitler, he said, had ordered Reichsmarschall Goering, commander in chief, air force, to raise the air supply to at least 300 tons a day.[53] Whether he knew it or not, Manstein had said farewell to Sixth Army. Army Group Don would henceforth be fighting for its own life.

To the Manich and the Donets

When they reached the general line Millerovo-Tatsinskaya-Morozovsk on

[49]O.B. d. H. Gr. Don, Ia Nr. 0384/42, an Chef des GenStdH, 27.12.42, H. Gr. Don 39694/6 file.

[50]OKH, GenStdH, Op. Abt. Nr. 421042/42, Operationsbefehl Nr. 2, 28.12.42, H. Gr. Don 39694/6 file; O.B. d. H. Gr. Don, Ia Nr. 0376/42, an Chef des Generalstabes zu Fernspruch vom 24.12.42, H. Gr. Don 39694/6 file.

[51]Pz. AOK 4, Ia Kriegstagebuch Nr. 5, Teil III, 28–31 Dec 42, Pz. AOK 4 28183/1 file; H. Gr. Don, Lage H. Gr. Don, 28–31.12.42, H. Gr. Don 39694/16 file; OKH, GenStdH, Op. Abt. (I S/B) Nr. 1959/42, Einzelanordnungen des Fuehrers Nr. 79, 30.12.42, H. Gr. Don 36964/6 file.

[52]O.B. d. H. Gr. Don, Ia Nr. 0394/42, an OKH, Chef des Generalstabes, 31.12.42, H. Gr. Don 39694/6 file.

[53]O.B. d. H. Gr. Don, Ia Nr. 0396/42, an AOK 6, 31.12.42, H. Gr. Don 39694/6 file.

24 December, *Sixth, First Guards,* and *Third Guards Armies* had essentially completed their share of MALYY SATURN, and *Second Guards* and *Fifty-first Armies* on taking Kotelnikovo, which they did on the morning of 29 December, had wiped out the last of WINTERGEWITTER. By then, Zhukov was back in Moscow working with Stalin on plans for a general offensive similar to the one in the previous winter.[54] The orders for the first phase in the south went out on the night of 31 December. In what Vasilevskiy refers to as Operation DON, *Stalingrad Front* (renamed *South Front* as of 1 January) was required to leave behind its three armies on the Stalingrad pocket and strike toward Salsk and along the south side of the Don toward Rostov with *Second Guards, Fifty-first,* and *Twenty-eighth Armies* (the latter being brought in from the east into the area north of Elista). *Fifth Shock Army,* which would be attached to *South Front,* would run along the north side of the Don toward Rostov. *Southwest Front* would take Morozovsk and Tatsinskaya and veer its armies west to and across the Donets to execute what Zhukov refers to as "Bigger Saturn." On 29 December, Zhukov had also instructed *Transcaucasus Front* to prepare to strike out of the area between Novorossiysk and Tuapse to Krasnodar, Tikhoretsk, and Rostov.[55] If all of the operations worked, the Soviet forces would have cleared the Donets Basin west to the line of Slavyansk-Mariupol and encircled Fourth Panzer, Seventeenth, and First Panzer Armies.

For his part, Hitler ignored Manstein's report of 28 December and, on New Year's Day, announced in a supplement to Operations Order No. 2 that he was going to send the Grossdeutschland Division in addition to the SS divisions Adolf Hitler and Das Reich and the 7th SS Division to relieve Stalingrad. Army Groups B and Don were to hang on to the most favorable positions for the jump-off. All the provisions of Operations Order No. 2, in which he had directed Hollidt not to withdraw any farther than to the line Morozovsk-Tsimlyanskiy were to remain in effect.[56]

Even Hitler did not expect the divisions for the relief to be deployed before mid-February. To imagine that fate and the Russians would allow the Germans that much time was pure self-deception. However, although what might come next, as Manstein had said, could easily be imagined, very little had been done by the turn of the year to improve the German position. The withdrawals Hitler had approved were piecemeal, and he still talked in terms of "definitive" lines and was beginning to lose himself in nebulous plans for a counteroffensive. The decision to bend back the left flank of Army Group A was a significant step, but after Hitler had issued the order for it he showed no desire to see it executed quickly and, on the contrary, seemed to welcome delays.

On 2 January, in a dispatch to Zeitzler, Manstein pointed out that although it could have been seen as soon as Sixth Army was encircled that the

[54]*VOV,* p. 186f. See *IVMV,* vol. VI, p. 91 and map 5.
[55]Vasilevskiy, *"Delo,"* p. 287; *IVMV,* vol. VI, pp. 72, 92 and maps 5 and 7; Zhukov, *Memoirs,* p. 418; Grechko, *Gody voyny,* p. 405.

[56]*OKH, GenStdH, Op. Abt. (I S/B) Nr. 421052/42, Ergaenzung zum Operationsbefehl Nr. 2, 1.1.43,* H. Gr. Don 39694/6 file.

Russians were developing a major offensive on the south flank of the Eastern Front and might strike in the rear of Army Group A, the OKH (Hitler) had done nothing until the last few days about evacuating the wounded and the heavy equipment from the Caucasus. The consequences of that neglect would be either to slow Army Group A's movements or to force a sacrifice of large quantities of equipment. Because the OKH was controlling all the substantial shifts of Army Group A's forces, Manstein added, no purpose would be served by his taking over Army Group A. Since the OKH had also ordered the divisions intended for Fourth Panzer Army—the 7th and 11th Panzer Divisions—sent elsewhere, all he could do to protect Army Group A was to order Hoth to hold out as long as he could keep his flanks free. Army Group A would have to speed up its withdrawal and take a hand in defending its rear by transferring a corps to Salsk.[57] Unlike some that had gone before, this communication did have at least one effect: Hitler did not again mention Manstein's taking command of Army Group A.

In the first week of the new year, as *First* and *Third Guards* and *Fifth Tank Armies* bore in on it from the north and east, the Armeeabteilung Hollidt began a hectic ninety-mile retreat to the Donets. On 3 January, the Armeeabteilung Fretter-Pico warned that the 304th Infantry Division, which had been deployed to keep touch with Hollidt's left flank, could not be depended upon. It lacked training and combat

experience and could panic easily.[58] Since it was then known that Vatutin had massed two tank corps east of the Fretter-Pico–Hollidt boundary for a probable attack toward the Donets crossing at Belokalitvenskaya, Hitler had to release the 4th Panzer Division on 4 January to prevent a breakthrough. On the 5th, having retreated forty miles in six days, Hollidt gave up Morozovsk, the air base closest to Stalingrad. The next day, Hitler tried to call a halt "for the sake of morale and to conserve the strength of the troops"; but with the Russians probing across the Don in the south and threatening to advance down the Donets from the north, Hollidt had no chance to stay in any line east of the Donets for more than a few days.[59]

On the other side of the Don, Fourth Panzer Army ranged its two panzer divisions and the SS Viking Division along the Kuberle River, which flowed into the Sal from the south. In the gap between the Don and the Sal, the *III Guards Tank Corps* pushed downstream along the south bank of the Don and, at the end of the first week in January, sent reconnaissance patrols to within twenty miles of Rostov. Hitler urged Manstein to commit the Tiger tanks, which he predicted would be able to destroy the whole tank corps; but when the Tigers went into action, which was the first combat experience for their crews, they failed to live up to Hitler's notice. They claimed to have knocked out eighteen enemy tanks, but of the twenty Tigers in the battalion, half

[57]*O.B. der H. Gr. Don, Ia Nr. 0399/42, an Chef des Generalstabes des Heeres, 2.1.43,* H. Gr. Don 39694/6 file.

[58]*A. Abt. Fretter-Pico, Ia Kriegstagebuch, 18.12.42– 2.2.43,* 3 Jan 43, A. Abt. Fretter-Pico 31783/1 file.

[59]*OKH, GenStdH, Op. Abt. Nr. 171/43, an H. Gr. Don, 6.1.43,* H. Gr. Don 39694/7 file.

SOVIET INFANTRY ON THE MARCH TOWARD THE DONETS RIVER

were damaged. Hoth reported that the crews needed more training and experience.[60]

When a mechanized corps and a guards rifle corps began making their way around Fourth Panzer Army's north flank, Hitler, on 6 January, had to let Manstein take the 16th Motorized Infantry Division away from Elista. Manstein warned that the division could do no more than stabilize the Fourth Panzer Army line temporarily, and protesting that everything was expected of Army Group Don while nothing was possible for Army Group

A, he again asked for a corps from Army Group A.[61]

In the second week of January, even though new trouble was developing in the north against Hungarian Second Army, the fronts of the two southern army groups began to assume some coherence.[62] Armeeabteilung Hollidt, shifting its panzer divisions back and forth to counter threats from the north and the south, continued its march to the Donets, and Hitler allowed Fourth Panzer Army to swing back to a line facing north along the Manich Canal.[63]

[60]OKH, GenStdH, Op. Abt. Nr. 233/43, an O.B. der H. Gr. Don, 6.1.43 and Pz. AOK 4, Ia, Erfolgsmeldung Tiger-Panzer, 7.1.43, H. Gr. Don 39694/7 file.

[61]OKH, GenStdH, Op. Abt. Nr. 249/43, an H. Gr. Don, 6.1.43, H. Gr. Don 39694/7 file; O.B. der H. Gr. Don, Ia Nr. 0402/43, an Chef GenStdH, 7.1.43, H. Gr. Don 39694/7 file.

[62]See Ziemke, Stalingrad to Berlin, pp. 81–84.

[63]OKH, GenStdH, Op. Abt. (I S/B) Nr. 430028/43, H. Gr. Don 39694/7 file.

First Panzer Army, though slowed by its heavy equipment and by what Manstein, at least, considered exaggerated worries about what the Russians might do, gradually narrowed the gap between the army groups.

By the end of the third week in the month, Armeeabteilung Fretter-Pico, after having extricated some fourteen thousand of its troops from an encirclement near Millerovo, was in a line behind the Donets. Armeeabteilung Hollidt likewise had gained the slight protection of the frozen river. On the Manich Canal, between the Don and Prolyetarskaya, Fourth Panzer Army had set up a strongpoint defense, and First Panzer Army had extended its left flank north to tie into Fourth Panzer Army east of Salsk.[64] At the closest point, Armeeabteilung Hollidt was 165 miles from the Stalingrad pocket, and Fourth Panzer Army was 190 miles from it, but by then for Sixth Army, the distances, no matter what they were, no longer made a difference.

The Stalingrad Ring

During the year-end planning for Operation DON and the enlarged SATURN, the *Stavka* also revived Operation KOLTSO for action against the Stalingrad pocket. After *Stalingrad Front* relinquished three of its armies for Operation DON on 1 January, General Rokossovskiy's *Don Front* controlled the entire perimeter of the pocket with seven armies, 281,000 troops.[65] General Voronov took over as *Stavka* representative with *Don Front*. Since Rokossovskiy would not have a fresh mobile force, such as *Second Guards Army* had been, the KOLTSO plan had to be revised. The initial objective was still to split the pocket on a west-east line, but it would be done by stages instead of in a single sweep and would be directed more against the weaker western and southern faces of the pocket. In the first stage, *Sixty-fifth Army* would carry the main effort with a thrust from the northwest to the southeast toward Karpovskaya Station. In the second stage, *Twenty-first Army* would take over and lead a drive to Voroponovo Station, and in the third, five armies would storm in from the northwest, west, and southwest aiming to split what was left of the pocket by making contact in Stalingrad with *Sixty-second Army*.[66] KOLTSO, originally scheduled to begin on 6 January and to take seven days, was postponed to the 10th. In the meantime, Rokossovskiy sent Paulus a surrender ultimatum, which was rejected.[67]

By the beginning of the year, Sixth Army at Stalingrad was dying a lingering death from starvation and exhaustion. Between 1 and 23 December,

[64]A. Abt. Fretter-Pico, Ia Kriegstagebuch, 18.12.42–2.2.43, 14–18 Jan 43, A. Abt. Fretter-Pico 31783/1 file; H. Gr. Don, Ia, Lage H. Gr. Don, 15.–19.1.43, H. Gr. Don 39694/7 file.

[65]Sbornik, Nomer 6; IVMV, vol. VI, p. 76 gives the Don Front strength as 212,000 and Sixth Army's as 250,000. IVMV gives the weapons' strengths as 6,860 (Soviet)

and 4,130 (German) artillery pieces, 257 (Soviet) and 300 (German) tanks, and 300 (Soviet) and 100 (German) combat aircraft. Sbornik Nomer 6 gives them as 6,200 (Soviet) and 3,770 (German) artillery pieces, 1,800 (Soviet) and 250 (German) tanks, 13,700 (Soviet) and 7,300 (German) machine guns, and 18,000 (Soviet) and 9,400 (German) motor vehicles. The Sbornik adds that the figures on German equipment probably include pieces knocked out or otherwise rendered unusable before the final battle began. Sixth Army reported a strength of about one hundred tanks as of early December.

[66]IVMV, vol. VI, p. 75.

[67]Sbornik, Nomer 6; IVMV, vol. VI, pp. 75–77; Rokossovskiy, Soldier's Duty, pp. 157–65.

supplies airlifted in had averaged 90 tons a day and on only one day, 7 December, did they reach the army's daily minimum requirement of 300 tons. In the first three weeks of January, the average was 120 tons a day, but that was still far short.[68]

Nevertheless, Sixth Army was not yet totally at the Russians' mercy. All of *Don Front's* armies had been in constant action a long time, and losses, the weather, hunger, and fatigue had also taken their toll of them. In fact, Sixth Army had some advantages. One was that the pocket encompassed nearly all of the built-up areas in and around Stalingrad; consequently, the German troops had some shelter and could obtain wood for fuel from demolished buildings, while the Russians had none. The Germans also had the advantage of field fortifications they had built during the siege and, particularly, of the Soviet defense lines constructed in the summer. Between the lines, the terrain was generally flat and treeless but cut by deep *balkas* ("gullies"), which favored the defense.

On the morning of 10 January, Rokossovskiy was with General Batov, commander of *Sixty-fifth Army*, at the latter's command post when *Sixty-fifth, Twenty-first,* and *Twenty-fourth Armies* began KOLTSO against the western "nose" of the pocket.[69] The first day brought gains of two or three miles, which was disappointing for Rokossovskiy but dismaying for Paulus. In the night, Paulus reported that after the day's fighting there was no longer any prospect of holding out until mid-February; relief would have to come much sooner; the promised quantity of supplies would have to be delivered; and replacement battalions would have to be flown in at once.[70]

The Germans managed to prevent an outright breakthrough in the next two days by maneuvering back nineteen miles to the line of the Rossoshka River. *(Map 44.)* When they reached the Rossoshka on the night of the 12th, the Soviet armies, which had kept the offensive going night and day, completed the first stage of KOLTSO, but they faced, next, on the river, what had been the original outer ring of the Stalingrad defenses. On the 13th and 14th, Rokossovskiy regrouped to shift the main effort to *Twenty-first Army,* which would be heading due west toward Voroponovo Station while *Sixty-fifth Army* aimed past Pitomnik.[71]

After *Sixty-fifth* and *Twenty-first Armies,* joined on the north by *Twenty-fourth Army* and on the south by *Fifty-seventh* and *Sixty-fourth Armies,* cracked the Rossoshka line on 15 January and after repeated pleas from Paulus, Hitler appointed Generalfeldmarschall Erhard Milch to direct the air supply for Sixth Army. In the appointment, Hitler gave Milch authority to issue orders to all branches of the *Wehrmacht* and, for the first time, established a command powerful enough to override all other claims on planes, fuel, and ground crews and to organize the air supply on the scale which had been promised for Stalingrad.[72] Daylight

---

[68]*Tageseinsatz der Luftflotte 4, 1.–23.12.42,* H. Gr. Don 30694/3b–5 file.

[69]Rokossovskiy, *Soldier's Duty,* p. 166.

[70]*AOK , Ia, an H. Gr. Don O.B., 10.1.43,* H. Gr. Don 39694/7 file.

[71]Kehrig, *Stalingrad,* pp. 506–11; *IVMV,* vol. V, map 11; Rokossovskiy, *Soldier's Duty,* p. 167.

[72]*Der Fuehrer, OKW, WFSt Nr. 00284/43, 15.1.43,* H. Gr. Don 39694/8 file.

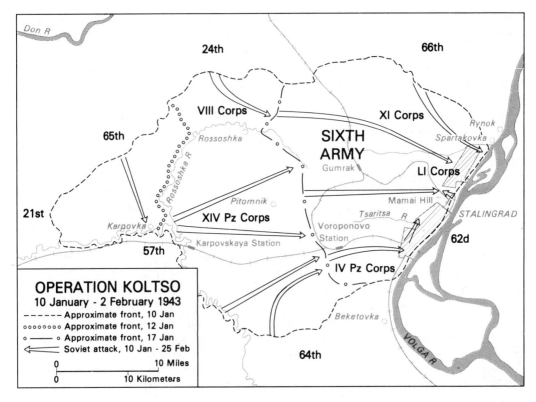

MAP 44

landings in the pocket were becoming exceedingly dangerous, and in another four days, *Southwest Front* would take the air base at Tatsinskaya, forcing the planes to shift to fields at Rostov and Novocherkassk, over two hundred miles from the pocket.

Early on the 16th, Sixth Army lost Pitomnik, the better of its two airfields in the pocket. Six of fourteen fighters based there took off under fire. Five attempted to land and crashed on the airstrip at Gumrak, which was still in Sixth Army's hands. The pilot of the sixth flew out to the west, thus ending the fighter defense over the pocket. On the 17th, Fourth Air Force for a time also suspended landings at Gumrak after a pilot mistakenly reported the troops were retreating past it.[73]

Don Front completed the second stages of KOLTSO on the 17th, reaching a line running from Voroponovo Station northwest to Rossoshka. The area of the pocket had been reduced by about two-thirds, but the seven days allotted to KOLTSO were used up. Sixth Army, moreover, had once more managed to hold its front together and was now, on the south, occupying the original main Stalingrad defense line. Something had gone wrong. *Sbornik Nomer 6* and Rokossovskiy put the

---

[73]Schroeter, *Stalingrad*, p. 166; *Fernspruch von Luftflotte 4, Ia, 17.1.43*, H. Gr. Don 39694/8 file.

blame on faulty intelligence. *Don Front,* they said, had gone into the offensive believing Paulus had eighty to eighty-five thousand troops, but it turned out he had closer to two hundred thousand.[74] For four days after the 17th, Rokossovskiy again regrouped. During the pause, Paulus reported, on the 20th, that the "fortress" could not hold out more than a few days longer. In some sectors, he said, the defenders had all been wiped out, and the enemy could march through the front "at will."[75]

The final stage of KOLTSO began on 22 January. *Fifty-seventh Army's* infantry, pressing in from the southwest on a three-mile-wide front along the railroad, broke through at Voroponovo Station and marched east into Stalingrad with battle flags flying. To close the gap this time was impossible. Ammunition had run out on that stretch of the front, and neither troops nor ammunition could be brought in from other sectors.

That night, Paulus radioed to Hitler via the OKH:

Rations exhausted. Over 12,000 unattended wounded in the pocket. What orders should I give to troops who have no more ammunition and are subjected to mass attacks supported by heavy artillery fire? The quickest decision is necessary since disintegration is already starting in some places. Confidence in the leadership still exists, however.[76]

Hitler answered:

Surrender is out of the question. The troops will defend themselves to the last. If possible, the size of the fortress is to be reduced so that it can be held by the troops still capable of fighting.

The courage and endurance of the fortress have made it possible to establish a new front and begin preparing a counteroperation. Thereby, Sixth Army has made an historic contribution to Germany's greatest struggle.[77]

As the front fell back from the west, the inner city, which after months of bombardment had the appearance of a landscape in *hell,* became a scene of fantastic horror. Sixth Army reported twenty thousand uncared-for wounded and an equal number of starving, freezing, and unarmed stragglers. Those who could took shelter in the basements of the ruins, where tons of rubble overhead provided protection against a constant rain of artillery shells. There, in darkness and cold, the sick, the mad, the dead, and the dying crowded together, those who could move daring not to for fear of losing their places.[78] Over the tallest of the ruins in the center of the city, Sixth Army ran out the *Reich* battle flag, "in order to fight the last battle under this symbol."[79]

On 26 January, *Sixty-second Army* took Mamai Hill, and tanks of *Twenty-first Army,* coming from the west, linked up there to split the pocket in two.[80] Thereafter, XI Corps formed a perimeter around the tractor works on the northern edge of the city while Sixth

[74]*IVMV*, vol. VI, p. 78; *Sbornik, Nomer 6;* Rokossovskiy, *Soldier's Duty,* p. 168.

[75]OKH, GenStdH, *Chef des GenStdH, Nr. 38/43, an O.B. d.,* H. Gr. Don 39694/8 file.

[76]*O.B. AOK 6, an Gen. Zeitzler zur Weitergabe an den Fuehrer und H. Gr. Don, 22.1.43,* H. Gr. Don 39694/9 file.

[77]*H. Gr. Don, Ia, Abschrift von Funkspruch an 6. Armee zur Vorlage an Herrn Generalfeldmarschall von Manstein, 22.1.43,* H. Gr. Don 39694/9 file.

[78]*H. Gr. Don, Ia, Tagesmeldung, 24.1.43,* H. Gr. Don 39694/9 file.

[79]*H. Gr. Don, Ia, Morgenmeldung, 25.1.43,* H. Gr. Don 39694/9 file.

[80]*IVMV*, vol. VI, p. 79; *VOV,* p. 189f.

SIXTH ARMY SURVIVORS MARCH OUT OF STALINGRAD UNDER GUARD

Army headquarters and LI and VIII Corps and XIV Panzer Corps dug in around and northwest of the main railroad station. The IV Panzer Corps, which had been holding the south front, was destroyed on that day by a Soviet push across the Tsaritsa River from the south. Sixth Army, by then, had asked the air force to drop only food: ammunition was not needed, there were too few guns.[81]

Sixth Army stopped issuing rations to the wounded on 28 January to preserve the strength of the fighting troops. That day the main theme of the midnight situation conference at the *Fuehrer* Headquarters was Hitler's desire to have "a" Sixth Army reconstituted quickly, using as many survivors of the original army as could be found.[82]

By 29 January, the south pocket was split, leaving Paulus, his staff, and a small assortment of troops in an enclave in the south and the remnants of LI and VIII Corps in the north. The XIV Panzer Corps ceased to exist on that day. During the night, ten small groups departed in a forlorn attempt to make their way out to the west across almost two hundred miles of enemy territory. By the next night, LI and

[81]*AOK 6, Ia, an H. Gr. Don ueber OKH, 26.1.43*, H. Gr. Don 39694/9 file; *AOK 6, Chef, an H. Gr. Don, 25.1.43*, H. Gr. Don 39694/9 file.

[82]*AOK 6, Ia, an H. Gr. Don ueber OKH, 28.1.43* and *AOK 6, Ia, an H. Gr. Don, 30.1.43*, H. Gr. Don 39694/10 file; Greiner, *Oberste Wehrmachtfuehrung*, p. 69.

VIII Corps had been pushed into a small area around a former Soviet Army engineer barracks, where they surrendered the following morning. Sixth Army headquarters was inside a 300-yard perimeter around the Red Square held by the survivors of the *194th Grenadier Regiment.*[83]

At 0615 on the morning of 31 January, the radio operator at Sixth Army headquarters in the basement of the *Univermag* ("department store") on Red Square sent the following message: "Russians are at the door. We are preparing to destroy [the radio equipment]." An hour later, the last transmission from Sixth Army came through: "We are destroying [the equipment]."[84] Paulus surrendered himself, his staff, and those troops with him but refused to give an order to XI Corps to do the same.[85] Promoted to field marshal just the day before, he became the first German officer of that rank ever to have been taken prisoner. Hitler, who had expected the promotion to lead Paulus to a different choice, declared, "Paulus did an about-face on the threshold of immortality."[86]

In the pocket around the tractor works, 33,000 men of XI Corps, under General der Infanterie Karl Strecker, fought on for another forty-eight hours. On 1 February, Hitler called on the corps to fight to the last man, saying, "Every day, ever hour that is won benefits the rest of the front de-

cisively."[87] At 0840 the next morning, Army Group Don received the last message from Strecker:

XI Corps, with its six divisions, has done its duty to the last.
Long live the Fuehrer!
Long live Germany!—Strecker[88]

In the Stalingrad pocket the Germans lost somewhat over two hundred thousand men. The exact total was apparently never determined. During the fighting, 30,000 wounded were flown out.[89] The Soviet accounts state that 147,000 German dead were counted on the battlefield and 91,000 Germans were taken prisoner, including 24 generals and 2,500 officers of lesser rank.[90] The Soviet Union has not released figures on its own losses in the Stalingrad battle. However, if the casualties given for two units, *III Cavalry* and *VIII Cavalry Corps*—36 percent and 45 percent, respectively, from 19 November to 2 December—are in any way representative, the Soviet losses must also have been substantial. An impression of the magnitude of Operation KOLTSO can be derived from *Don Front*'s ammunition expenditure between 10 January and 2 February 1943: 911,000 artillery rounds of calibers up to 152-mm., 990,000 mortar shells, and 24,000,000 machine gun and rifle rounds.[91]

As Hitler frequently stated, Sixth Army had performed a service at a critical time by tying down several hun-

[83]*AOK 6, Ia, an H. Gr. Don, 29.1.43* and *AOK 6, an H. Gr. Don, 30.1.43,* H. Gr. Don 36964/9 file.

[84]*AOK 6, Ia, an H. Gr. Don, 31.1.43, 0615* and *AOK 6, Ia, an H. Gr. Don, 31.1.43, 0714,* H. Gr. Don 39694/10 file.

[85]Rokossovskiy, *Soldier's Duty,* p. 171.

[86]Arntz, *"Die Wende des Krieges."*

[87]*OKH, GenStdH, Op. Abt. (I S/B) Nr. 1433/43, an Gen. Kdo. XI A.K., 1.2.43,* H. Gr. Don 39694/10 file.

[88]*XI A.K., an H. Gr. Don, Ia, 2.2.43, 0840,* H. Gr. Don 36964/10 file.

[89]Arntz, *"Die Wende des Krieges."*

[90]*IVOVSS,* vol. III, p. 62; *VOV,* p. 190; *VOV (Kratkaya Istoriya),* p. 223.

[91]*Sbornik, Nomer 9.*

dred thousand Soviet troops; on the other hand, it was a service performed for the wrong reasons. Hitler did not, in the first place, keep Sixth Army at Stalingrad for even so modestly valid a purpose. He was concerned entirely with preserving an appearance of success for a campaign he already knew had failed. At the last, having kept what was happening at Stalingrad from the German public until after KOLTSO began, he had nothing better in mind

than that he believed a fight to the last man would be less damaging to the national morale and his own image than a surrender.[92] Certainly one can imagine a less disastrous development of the battle on the southern flank of the Eastern Front for Germany if Sixth Army had been allowed to get its twenty divisions away from Stalingrad in time.

[92]See Domarus, *Hitler,* vol. II, p. 1973.

CHAPTER XXIV

Conclusion

"The Beginning of the Road"

Marshal Chuikov entitled his memoir of the Stalingrad battle *Nachalo puti (The Beginning of the Road)*. As of 19 November 1942, he said, " 'Not a step back!' now meant go forward . . . now meant we have to advance to the west."[1] The road would be long in distance and in time, to Berlin 1,500 miles and twenty-nine and a half months. Although it was new to Chuikov's *Sixty-second Army*, which later, rebuilt and renamed *Eighth Guards Army*, would be on it all the way to Berlin, the road, of course, was the same one on which German Sixth Army had begun its thousand-mile march from the Soviet border to Stalingrad seventeen months earlier.

On 25 January 1943, in the first congratulatory order of the day to be issued during the war, Stalin thanked the commands and troops of the southern *fronts* and gave them a new slogan: "Onward to defeat the German occupationists and to drive them out of our country!" His order of the day for 23 February 1943, which was the Red Army's twenty-fifth anniversary, asserted, "Three months ago Red Army troops began an offensive at the approaches to Stalingrad. Since then the

initiative has been in our hands. . . . The balance of forces on the Soviet-German front has changed."[2]

In his anniversary order of the day, Stalin also declared "the battle at the walls of Stalingrad" to have been "the greatest in the history of wars." Those who had participated in it were rewarded accordingly. A hundred and twelve officers and troops received the title and decoration Hero of the Soviet Union; 48 generals were awarded the Order of Suvorov or the Order of Kutuzov; 10,000 in all ranks received other decorations; and 700,000 were given the campaign medal "For the Defense of Stalingrad." Forty-four units were authorized to incorporate place-names associated with the battle into their designations; 55 received unit commendations; and 183 earned the title "guards."[3]

Charles E. Bohlen, the U.S. State Department's chief Soviet analyst, noted with some concern that Stalin omitted the Western Allies from the celebration. On 6 November 1942, in his annual speech on the eve of the anniversary of the 1917 revolution, Stalin had talked at length about the advantages a second front in Europe

---

[1]Chuikov, *The Battle for Stalingrad*, p. 218. Originally published as *Nachalo puti* (Moscow: Voyennoye Izdatelstvo, 1959).

[2]USSR Embassy, *Information Bulletin*, no. 10, 28 Jan 43, p. 1; *Ibid.*, no. 19, 25 Feb 43, p. 2.

[3]*IVMV*, vol. VI, p. 82; *VOV*, p. 190; USSR Embassy, *Information Bulletin*, no. 12, 28 Jan 42, p. 5.

would bring. In the 23 February 1943 order of the day, he merely remarked that in the absence of a second front, the Soviet Army had borne "the whole burden of the war" thus far, and he suggested that it alone would be capable of defeating Germany in the war. On 6 November, he had said, "We are not waging [the war] alone, but in conjunction with our allies." And he had proposed the slogan: "Hail the victory of the Anglo-Soviet-American fighting alliance!" He did not mention the alliance in the 23 February order of the day.[4]

The OKW's Armed Forces Report issued from the *Fuehrer* Headquarters on 3 February awkwardly attempted to transform a disaster into an epic. The opening sentences read: "The battle for Stalingrad has ended. True to its oath to the last breath, Sixth Army, under the exemplary leadership of Field Marshal Paulus, has succumbed to the overwhelming strength of the enemy and to unfavorable circumstances. The enemy's two demands for capitulation were proudly rejected. The last battle was fought under a swastika flag flying from the highest ruin in Stalingrad." Depicting the end as Hitler had wanted it to be but as the world, including most Germans, already knew it had not been, the report concluded, "Generals, officers, noncommissioned officers and men fought shoulder to shoulder to the last bullet. They died that Germany might live!"[5]

That the war in the East had changed course drastically was obvious

also to the Germans by January 1943, and Hitler and Propaganda Minister Goebbels were trying to convert the calamitous outcome of the 1942 campaign into a national commitment to total war. On 13 January 1943, Hitler issued a decree stating, "The total war confronts us with tasks ... that must unequivocally be mastered"; he named a three-man committee, consisting of Field Marshal Keitel, the chief, OKW; Martin Bormann, the chief of the Nazi Party Chancellory; and Hans Lammers, the chief of the Reichs Chancellory, to mobilize all military, party, and state agencies for the effort.[6] Speaking for Hitler on 30 January, the tenth anniversary of the Nazi seizure of power, Goebbels called "the gigantic winter battle in the East the beacon of total war for the German Nation." On 18 February, in an hour-long speech devoted solely to the total war theme, he declared Europe to be under an assault "out of the steppe" that only the German *Wehrmacht* and its allies could stop. The battle of Stalingrad, he said, had been "the great tocsin of German destiny," and the nation's watchword henceforth had to be "People arise—and storm break loose!"[7]

Germany was in fact far from being on a total war footing in early 1943. War production had been over 40 percent greater in 1942 than in 1941 (largely owing to Armament and Munitions Minister Speer's organizational improvements), and 1942 had been the first year in which consumer goods production had been cut significantly, but the assumption that the war would

---

[4]Dept. of State, *Foreign Relations, 1943*, vol. III, p. 506; USSR Embassy, *Information Bulletin*, no. 135, 1942, pp. 1–6; *Ibid.*, no. 19, 25 Feb 43, pp. 1–3.
[5]Domarus, *Hitler*, vol. II, p. 1985.

[6]Jacobsen, *Der zweite Weltkrieg*, pp. 373–75.
[7]Helmut Heiber, ed., *Goebbels-Reden* (Duesseldorf: Droste Verlag, 1972), pp. 165, 173–75, 208.

soon be over had governed economic planning until the end of the year. Consequently, although the output of consumer goods was 10 percent less in 1942 than in 1941 (but only 12 percent less than in the last prewar year, 1938), the tendency had been to preserve the consumer sector of the economy, and the numbers employed in such industries had held steady even though the war industry work force had declined almost 10 percent between 1939 and 1942.[8]

The declaration of total war terminated the phase in which the prospect of an early victory had governed policy; however, total war connoted a much more cogent and purposeful policy shift than actually occurred. After the 13 January decree was published, Hitler told the committee of three that what he really wanted them to do was to squeeze another 800,000 men out of the work force for military service, not to reorient the whole war effort. To the extent that it materialized at all thereafter, the total war program conformed to Hitler's request. On 27 January, the Office of the Generalplenipotentiary for Labor declared all men sixteen to sixty-five and all women seventeen to forty-five subject to a labor draft. After granting blanket exemptions in numerous categories, it registered 3.5 million persons and—over the next year and a half—put 700,000 of them to work. On 4 February, the Ministry of Economics ordered all non-war-related businesses to close and defined those as nightclubs, luxury bars and restaurants, jewelry stores, custom garment shops, and, among others, establishments trading in postage stamps.[9]

Paulus' surrender brought the road to a dead end for Germany's allies. By 31 January, the headquarters for the Rumanian, Italian, and Hungarian Armies were all out of the front and engaged in trying to reassemble what was left of their troops. (Hungarian Second Army had been smashed by a Soviet offensive begun on 12 January.) Marshal Mannerheim, commander in chief, Finnish Army, had asked Twentieth Mountain Army to release all the Finnish troops (five battalions) still attached to it.[10]

The governments of Finland, Hungary, and Rumania, whose countries lay athwart the Soviet road to the west and would be the first to experience the assault "out of the steppe," were looking to their own salvation, as was Italy's Mussolini, who was watching the British and Americans open another, and to him more dangerous, road in North Africa. Mussolini proposed making a separate peace with the Soviet Union. Rumanian Marshal Antonescu proposed doing the same, only with the Western Allies. In the early months of 1943, Finland, Hungary, and Rumania all began casting about for contacts and understandings with the Western Allies that might shelter them from the full consequences of a Soviet victory.[11]

---

[8]Deutsches Institut fuer Wirtschaftsforschung, *Deutsche Industrie im Kriege,* pp. 37, 46f, 49, 159, 178.

[9]*OKW, Stellvertretende Chef des Wehrmachtfuehrungsstabes, Kriegstagebuch vom 1.1.–31.3.43,* 16 and 22 Jan 43, I.M.T. Doc. 1786 PS; Jacobsen, *Der zweite Weltkrieg,* p. 378; Heiber, *Goebbels,* pp. 189, 199.

[10]Juergen Foerster, *Stalingrad, Risse im Buendniss, 1942–1943* (Freiburg: Verlag Rombach, 1975), pp. 46–66; (Geb.) AOK 20, Ia Nr. 133/43, an OKW, WFSt, 29.1.43, AOK 20 36560/2 file.

[11]Foerster, *Stalingrad,* p. 68; Paul Schmidt, *Statist auf diplomatischer Buehne, 1923–1945* (Bonn: Athenaeum Verlag, 1949), p. 555.

The Transitions

In the High Commands

From the outset of the war, Hitler and Stalin were the actual as well as titular supreme commanders of their respective armed forces. Both had sufficient power as heads of government in totalitarian states to conduct the war as they saw fit, and both made the 1942 campaign the definitive test of their generalship. How each construed the results of the campaign set the German and Soviet Commands on the courses they would follow to the war's end.

Until the late summer of 1942, Stalin maintained an appearance of collegial command vested in the *Stavka* and directed the war in person through the *Stavka* and its adjunct, the General Staff. At a higher level, he also controlled the whole war effort through the State Defense Committee, the GKO. In 1941, he could not have done differently without setting the state and the military systems that he had built around himself hopelessly adrift. He had preserved the systems, thereby probably also saving the nation; but his generalship after the Moscow counterattack had failed to capitalize decisively on that success and had paved the way for the second German summer offensive. Finally, with the *"Ni shagu nazad!"* ("Not a step back!") order of 28 July 1942, Stalin reached what could have been the last stop short of strategic bankruptcy: he had to demand that his forces sacrifice themselves to buy time for him. A month later he had to call on Zhukov and Vasilevskiy to augment his generalship.

The *History of the Second World War* states that by appointing a deputy supreme commander, Stalin "introduced a new element in the leadership at the strategic level" and that Zhukov and Vasilevskiy "were provided with plenipotentiary powers and possessed great authority in the fighting forces."[12] Specifically, Stalin had, in making Zhukov deputy supreme commander, for the first time installed a military professional in the direct chain of command above the operational level and had, by granting plenipotentiary powers to Zhukov and Vasilevskiy, created the nucleus of at least a provisional military high command.

The development of the high command continued through the rest of the year and into the early months of 1943. The planning and execution of the counteroffensive at Stalingrad brought the commanding general of the air force and the chiefs of artillery and armor, whose posts in the Defense Commissariat had until then been mostly administrative, into the line of command under Zhukov and Vasilevskiy. In December 1942, the artillery and armored and mechanized forces had acquired branch status (which the air force already had) and their chiefs had become commanding generals and deputy defense commissars. The mostly ad hoc command structure of late 1942 was formalized in May 1943 when Zhukov's and Vasilevskiy's appointments as first and second deputy defense commissars, respectively, put them at the heads of both the line and staff military chains of command.[13]

Stalin also gave the military professionals tangible evidence of his confidence and their worth to the extent

---

[12]*IVMV*, vol. V, 236.
[13]Zakharov, *50 let*, p. 333.

that they probably gained more in ranks and titles than they did in actual influence on the conduct of the war. On 18 January 1943, Zhukov became a marshal of the Soviet Union, the first general to be promoted to that rank in the war, and General Voronov became a marshal of artillery under a less than two-week-old Central Committee decree authorizing branch marshalships. Vasilevskiy advanced to *general armii* also on 18 January and to marshal of the Soviet Union a month later. The commanding general of the air force, Novikov, became a *general polkovnik* in January, a *general armii* in February, and received his star as marshal of aviation in March 1943. Three field commanding generals—Malinovskiy, Rokossovskiy, and Vatutin—moved through the ranks from *general leytenant* to *general armii* by April 1943. Stalin's generosity with promotions was lavish but measured. Fedorenko, the commanding general of armored and mechanized forces, had become a *general polkovnik* in January 1943, but apparently because the armored branch's performance had not yet equaled that of the artillery or the air force, Fedorenko was left to wait more than a year for his promotion to marshal of the armored forces. Stalin also made pointed distinctions between offensive and defensive success. Malinovskiy, whose army had smashed Operation WINTERGEWITTER, moved up two grades in rank and became a *front* commander in 1943 and a marshal in 1944. Chuikov, who had held the Stalingrad bridgehead through the siege, stayed an army commander and ended his service in the war as a *general polkovnik*. Rokossovskiy, who had wiped out the Stalingrad pocket, became a

marshal in 1944. General Eremenko, who had conducted the defense, was a *general armii* when the war ended. Eremenko and Chuikov eventually became marshals, but not until 1955, two years after Stalin died.[14]

The military's relationship to Stalin had changed. He had come as close to creating a high command and appointing a commander in chief as he ever would, and he had accepted the professionals' guidance. Vasilevskiy described the new relationship as it affected himself, Zhukov, and Stalin when he wrote, "The Stalingrad battle was an important turning point [in Stalin's development as a military leader]. J. V. Stalin began not only to understand military strategy well . . . but also found his way about well in the operational art. As a result, he exercised a strong influence on the working out of operations. . . ."[15] That Stalin had discovered an effective system of command, which was also satisfactory to himself, was evident in his own entry into the military as a marshal of the Soviet Union in March 1943. What is most remarkable, however, is that after late 1942, Stalin had managed successfully to foster and exploit military professionalism without relinquishing any of his authority over or within the armed forces. The army had performed as if it had a high command, but it did not. Orders continued to be issued in the name of the *Stavka*. Zhukov, as deputy supreme commander, and he and Vasilevskiy, as first and second deputy defense com-

---

[14]See the biographical entries in Ministerstvo Oborony SSSR, Institut Voyennoy Istorii, *Sovetskaya Voyennaya Entsiklopediya* (Moscow: Voyennoye Izdatelstvo, 1980) and in the registers of names in the appropriate volumes of *IVOVSS*.
[15]*IVMV*, vol. V, p. 326.

missars, wielded great authority when Stalin desired them to, but it was his authority not theirs. In terms of real power, the distance between Stalin and his deputies always was, when he wanted it to be, at least as great as that between a marshal and a private.

Like the Soviet, the German Command underwent a transition in 1942, in its instance completing the one begun in February 1938 when Hitler had made himself commander in chief of the armed forces. Although Hitler had progressively expanded his role in military affairs, especially during the early campaigns of the war, the Armed Forces High Command, the OKW, had not evolved into a true armed forces command, and during the 1941 campaign in the Soviet Union the service high commands had continued as semi-autonomous parts of the command structure represented in the high-level decision-making process by their commanders in chief. In BARBAROSSA and TAIFUN, the Army High Command, the OKH, had also figured as the designated high command for operations on the Eastern Front. However, following Field Marshal Brauchitsch's dismissal in December 1941, the OKH had ceased to be a high command in all but name, and Hitler had assumed direct personal control of the Eastern Front. Subsequently, the 1942 operations were planned and executed according to his specifications, and victory, nevertheless, eluded his grasp, bringing him at the end of August into about as close an encounter as Stalin's with strategic bankruptcy.

Stalin's response was rational and self-serving; Hitler's only self-serving. In September 1942, he further dismantled the command structure, leav-

ing himself alone atop the "heap of wreckage."[16] The clean sweep—of Keitel and Generals Jodl and Halder—that Hitler threatened did not materialize. Keitel and Jodl kept their posts in the OKW until the end of the war. But Hitler secured everything he wanted: an OKW and General Staff firmly brought into agreement with him and subservience to him and, through General Schmundt and the army officer personnel office, a direct hold on every officer from lieutenant to field marshal. On 30 September, just two weeks before he was going to have to issue Operations Order No. 1 putting the Eastern Front on notice to expect another bad winter, Hitler announced a victory, not over the enemy but over "an old world," that of military tradition. He told the German people they were about to see the Nazi social system take full effect. Birth, background, and schooling, he said, had ceased to be criteria for military preferment, which henceforth would go only "to the brave and loyal man, the determined fighter who is suited to be a leader of his people."[17] To Schmundt, he talked about advancing line officers to the top commands and abolishing the General Staff's distinctive red trouser stripes and silver collar tabs.[18] In short, Hitler placed the army under his tutelage.

But the winter was far worse than Hitler could have imagined it would be in September 1942, in fact, worse than he already thought it had been on the day Paulus surrendered in Stalingrad;

---

[16]Warlimont, *Im Hauptquartier*, p. 274.

[17]Domarus, *Hitler*, vol. II, p. 1922.

[18]*Taetigkeitsbericht des Chefs des Heerespersonalamts*, 1–5 Oct 42, H 4/12 file.

consequently, his relationship to the military came into question again. On 1 February 1943, Soviet forces began operations aimed toward Kursk, Kharkov, and the Dnepr River crossing at Dnepropetrovsk and Zaporozhye that could have engulfed not just armies but Army Groups Don and Center.[19] On the 6th, Hitler called Field Marshal Manstein, the Army Group Don commander, to the *Fuehrer* Headquarters and—although it was not evident at the time—laid the groundwork for a renewed partnership between himself and the military "old world" that would get him past the current crisis and sustain him through another twenty-six months of war.

Manstein came to the meeting as the representative of his world, that of the General Staff in the pre-Nazi tradition, and its leading candidate to be a chief of the General Staff with clear responsibility and genuine authority. Hitler had ignored the idea of a strong chief of the General Staff when it first arose in early 1942, and he dismissed it as impossible when Manstein proposed it on 6 February. But, although he tried for four hours, he could not do the same when Manstein confronted him with what he had come to regard as the General Staff's most pernicious principle, namely, that maneuver had to take precedence over position on the defensive as well as on the offensive. The events at Stalingrad had not shaken his conviction derived from the previous winter's experience that voluntary withdrawals always served the enemy better than they did oneself, but he

stopped short of putting his conviction to another test and authorized Manstein to take the Army Group Don front inside the bend of the Donets River back a hundred miles to the Mius River line.[20]

In the succeeding weeks, Manstein repaid Hitler's reluctant concession handsomely. On 20 February, he launched an operation that in the next twenty-six days demolished four Soviet armies and established a front on the Donets River north to Belgorod. (On the 20th, Soviet spearheads were seventy miles west of Kharkov, within artillery range of Dnepropetrovsk, and less than forty miles east of Manstein's headquarters at Zaporozhye.) In the second week of March, the recapture of Kharkov, an event that would attract worldwide attention, was taking shape, and on the 10th, Hitler went to Zaporozhye to add an Oak Leaf Cluster to Manstein's Knight's Cross of the Iron Cross and to greet and hear reports from all of the army and air corps commanders in the south. He was amiable, even jocular, and he found the generals' morale to be "fantastic." Three days later, he staged a similar scene at Army Group Center with Field Marshal Kluge and his generals, who were then completing a phased evacuation of the Rzhev salient that was releasing enough troops to block the Soviet advance past Kursk.[21]

Manstein stopped the offensive on 18 March at Belgorod, thirty miles north of Kharkov, which had fallen on

---

[19] The post-Stalingrad phase of the Soviet 1942–1943 winter offensive is treated in detail in ch. V of Ziemke, *Stalingrad to Berlin.*

[20] Manstein, *Verlorene Siege,* pp. 437–44.

[21] David Irving, *Hitler's War* (New York: Viking Press, 1977), pp. 497–99; Louis P. Lochner, ed., *The Goebbels Diaries* (Garden City, N.Y.: Doubleday & Co., 1948), p. 294.

the 14th. The full onset of the spring thaw forced him to make this decision, and he had to leave a deep bulge around Kursk, but Hitler could proclaim a victory in his annual Memorial Day address on the 21st (which he had postponed for a week in anticipation of such an announcement). From the Potsdam Armory, the shrine to Prussian and German feats of arms, he told the nation and the world that Europe had been saved, and preparations were under way to secure additional successes in the coming months and to assure the final victory. On 13 March, he had signed Operations Order No. 5 alerting Manstein and Kluge to be ready to seize the initiative again as soon as the spring muddy season ended.[22]

The field marshals and the rest of the "old world" military establishment would be ready with few exceptions in the spring of 1943 and for as long thereafter as Hitler wanted them. In a long talk with Goebbels on 9 March, the day before his visit to Manstein, Hitler had revealed how he meant to reciprocate. He said he did not trust a single one of the generals; they all tried to swindle him whenever they could; they did not even understand their own trade—war; the entire officer-training system had been wrong for generations. "Slowly but surely," he concluded, leadership selection for the armed forces would be changed; Schmundt would see to that.[23]

In Operations

The primary components of the blitzkrieg were the doctrine of combined arms, the deep operation, and the envelopment. The first two were late developments of World War I. The Germans and the Allies had used combined arms in 1918 to achieve deeper penetrations of the enemy front than they had previously managed at any time since 1914. During the interwar period, the deep operation (essentially as it had been conceived in the German General Staff's tactical instructions, "The Attack in Positional Warfare" of January 1918, a coordinated frontal thrust designed to break through multiple defense lines to depths of twenty-five or thirty miles in several weeks) was regarded as the most practicable means of averting another trench deadlock such as had occurred in World War I.[24] The envelopment dated back to 2 August of 216 B.C. when a Carthaginian force under Hannibal encircled and annihilated a much larger Roman force under the Consul Terentius Varro at Cannae. Hannibal's accomplishment had been long admired but seldom repeated. The pre-World War I Chief of the German General Staff, Generalfeldmarschall Alfred Graf von Schlieffen, analyzed the several dozen eighteenth and nineteenth century battles in which enveloping maneuvers had been employed and found only one fully successful encirclement—the Battle of Sedan in September 1870, which decided the Franco-Prussian

[22]Domarus, *Hitler*, vol. II, p. 1999; *OKH, GenStdH, Op. Abt. Nr. 430163/43, Operationsbefehl Nr. 5, 13.3.43,* CMH files.

[23] Jacobsen, *Der zweite Weltkrieg*, pp. 383–85.

[24]Erich Ludendorff, *Urkunden der Obersten Heeresleitung ueber ihre Taetigkeit 1916/18* (Berlin: E. S. Mittler u. Sohn, 1920), pp. 641–66; Hermann Foertsch, *Kriegskunst heute und morgen* (Berlin: Wilhelm Andermann, 1939), pp. 228–35.

War against France. [25] Schlieffen concluded, and military opinion generally concurred during and after World War I, that to attempt an encirclement, unless the opportunity for one arose by chance in the course of a battle, was an almost pure gamble because an envelopment, even by a numerically superior force, was difficult to complete and easy to evade. In Schlieffen's opinion, a complete battle of encirclement required a daring and imaginative Hannibal and a stubbornly inflexible Terentius Varro, "both cooperating for attainment of the great goal." [26]

In the German campaigns against Poland in September 1939 and France and the Low Countries in May and June 1940, strategic envelopments and combined arms deep operations conducted at high speed and to greater depths than had previously been thought possible produced the blitzkrieg. For the 1941 campaign against the Soviet Union, the envelopment was incorporated into the deep operation to form the *Zangenangriff* ("pincers movement"), the double envelopment repeatedly executed along the strategic lines of attack. The blitzkrieg attained the highest state of its operational development in the 1941 campaign in the East but did not achieve a decisive strategic result. On 6 July 1942, when the *Stavka* ordered the retreat in the southern sector, Stalin stopped playing

Terentius Varro to Hitler's Hannibal, and the encirclements accomplished thereafter were mostly of empty space.

In November 1942, the roles changed, and Hitler cooperated in German Sixth Army's encirclement and annihilation. Soviet histories rank the battle as "the Cannae of the twentieth century"; as "the first example in the history of war of such a powerful enemy grouping, equipped with the latest technology, being encircled and totally liquidated"; and as having "enriched the military art with a classical example of the modern offensive operation." [27] The envelopment is stated to have been the Soviet main form of maneuver in the operations conducted from late 1942 until the end of the war. [28]

In the months from November 1942 to February 1943, the envelopment was indeed the main form: the Soviet record shows ten major enveloping operations to have been initiated and to have been components of a second winter general offensive on the entire front from Leningrad south to the Taman Peninsula. Had they been completed by March 1943 as planned, the Soviet forces in the center and the south would have reached the Dnepr River seven months earlier and those in the north the Narva River–Lake Peipus line eleven months earlier than they actually did. However, only three of the operations were completed, the one at Stalingrad and two of lesser magnitude and effectiveness carried out against German Second Army and Hungarian

[25]Schlieffen himself designed the next envelopment to be attempted after Sedan. Executed after his death, it failed in September 1914. The battle of Tannenberg, the German victory on the Eastern Front in August 1914, produced the one successful encirclement in World War I.

[26]Alfred von Schlieffen, *Cannae* (Fort Leavenworth: The Command and General Staff School Press, 1931), pp. 297–306; Foertsch, *Kriegskunst*, p. 246.

[27]Bagramyan, *Istoriya voyn*, p. 205; *IVOVSS*, vol. III, p. 65; *VOV (Kratkaya Istoriya)*, p. 174.

[28]Platonov, *Vtoraya Mirovaya Voyna*, p. 867; *IVOVSS*, vol. VI, p. 235; Bagramyan, *Istoriya voyn*, p. 479.

Second Army in late January 1943. Of the others, MARS failed; SATURN was reduced to providing support on the approaches to the Stalingrad pocket; and two, on the Narva River–Lake Ilmen line and on the Taman Peninsula, did not materialize. The three directed toward Kursk, Kharkov, and the Dnepr bend regained substantial and important territory but also brought on a reverse that restored the initiative to the Germans in the spring of 1943.[29] The victory at Stalingrad, great as it was, was not economical in either time or effort. On the whole, in the 1942–1943 winter offensive, the Soviet commands did not demonstrate a capability to employ the envelopment as a consistently effective form of maneuver.

The *Stavka* did not include a single envelopment in its plans for the year 1943. The *Soviet Military Encyclopedia* lists nine encirclements completed between January 1944 and May 1945, but all of those, except possibly the last, resulted from opportunities that occurred in operations during which they had not been planned.[30] When Zhukov and Vasilevskiy proposed to open the 1943 summer offensive with envelopments, Stalin told them he had had enough of envelopments; they were a luxury; the mission was to drive the Germans off Soviet territory fast.[31] In his memoirs, General Shtemenko states that the General Staff, in which he was

the operations chief during the war, evaluated the envelopment in 1943 and concluded that "because of the time required, the complications of the maneuver, and other considerations, it was far from profitable to encircle every enemy grouping."[32]

In the summer of 1943, the Soviet forces abandoned the blitzkrieg tactics they had employed in the previous winter campaign and took up the "cleaving blow" (*rassekayushchiy udar*), a less sophisticated and inherently more ponderous mode of conducting operations but one vastly more reliable in the hands of Soviet commands and troops. The cleaving blow derived from a form of combined arms deep operation (based on the German General Staff's "The Attack in Positional Warfare" of 1918) developed in the Soviet Army in the early 1930s and emerged as the true main form of Soviet World War II operations in the 1943 summer offensive, the advance to the Dnepr River. In August, six *fronts* launched massive cleaving blows, frontal thrusts running parallel to each other.[33] The objectives were to overwhelm the enemy's defenses and to force him back on a broad front (over seven hundred miles broad in that instance).

The Decision

The eleven and one-half months from 5 December 1941 to 19 November 1942 were the time of decision on all fronts in World War II. On 5 December 1941, the Soviet forces counterattacked at Moscow. The Japanese

---

[29]*IVMV*, vol. VI, maps 2, 10, 11.

[30]The last, the encirclement of Army Group Center east of Prague, was completed on 11 May 1945, four days after the war against Germany had ended. *Voyennaya Entsiklopediya*, vol. VI, pp. 37, 494–96.

[31]G. K. Zhukov, *Vospominaniya i razmyshleniya* (Moscow: Izdatelstvo Agenstva Pechati Novosti, 1969), p. 518.

[32]S. M. Shtemenko, *Generalnyy stab v gody voyny* (Moscow: Voyennoye Izdatelstvo, 1981), vol. I, p. 236.

[33]On the operations and their form at this stage see Ziemke, *Stalingrad to Berlin*, ch. VIII.

attack on Pearl Harbor on 7 December and the German declaration of war four days later brought the United States into the war. During the summer of 1942, the Germans achieved their farthest advances in the Soviet Union and North Africa and the Japanese theirs in the Pacific. In November 1942, the British broke through at El Alamein on the 3d; American and British forces landed in Morocco and Algeria on the 8th; the Japanese Navy abandoned the fight for Guadalcanal at sea on the 15th; and the Soviet offensive began at Stalingrad on the 19th. After November 1942, the Axis was on the defensive and in recession on all fronts.

However, the Soviet victory at Stalingrad resulted from both sides' commitment of their main forces to a seventeen-month contest for the strategic initiative. By comparison, the Western Allies achieved their successes at Guadalcanal and in North Africa much more cheaply and easily. In the Soviet analysis, this disproportion in the scale of effort confirms the Eastern Front as the "main and decisive front" in the war and the decision there as having also "caused Germany and its allies to go over to the defensive in all of the World War II theaters." In the Soviet view, also, the Western Allies first roused themselves to genuine participation in the war "after it became apparent [in the winter of 1942–1943] that the Soviet Union was in the position to liberate the peoples of Europe from the fascist yoke by means of its own strength."[34]

But the Soviet Union did not liberate Europe by its own strength, and it remained a bystander to the Pacific war until Japan's defeat was assured. The Soviet Union did not single-handedly open the road to victory in World War II by the decision over Germany in the East. From December 1941 on, the United States carried the burden of a two-front war with Germany and Japan and assumed the tremendous task of building sufficient strength in ground, sea, and air forces to impose a second front on Germany. The roads that began at Stalingrad for the Soviet forces and in North Africa for those of the Western Allies converged in the heart of Germany. After the U.S. Navy had forced the Japanese Navy to withdraw from the waters around Guadalcanal, the "retreat of the Japanese armed forces would not end until Japan surrendered."[35]

The period of the decision over Germany as it is construed in this volume does not figure in the Soviet periodization of the Soviet-German war, the Great Patriotic War. It falls within two larger periods: that of the strategic defensive (22 June 1941 to 19 November 1942), in which the Moscow counteroffensive begun on 5 December 1941 produced a "radical change" (*povorot*) in the war, and that of the "radical turn" (*perelom*) (19 November 1942 to December 1943), which the encirclement at Stalingrad initiated. This treatment enables Soviet war history to do justice to the full unfolding of Soviet military power by bringing the battle of Kursk in July 1943 (a German offensive smashed at the start) and the summer offensive begun in August 1943 (proof that the Soviet forces did not

---

[34]*IVMV*, vol. VI, pp. 318, 504.

[35]Paul S. Dull, *A Battle History of the Imperial Japanese Navy (1941–1945)* (Annapolis: Naval Institute Press, 1978), p. 247.

need the help of "General Winter") into the period of the radical turn while also preserving the stature of the two great turning points, at Stalingrad and Moscow, without slighting either of them. On the other hand, non-Soviet war history is concerned with German failure as well as Soviet success and with the circumstances of and reasons for both. These concerns have determined the time span of this volume.

During the interval covered in this volume, the courses of the war and of world history turned. At Moscow, on 5 December 1941, the Soviet reserves and the weather transformed what would in any event have been a most unsatisfactory ending to the German 1941 campaign into a disaster. The United States' entry into the war made Germany's defeat inescapable if the German forces could not overcome the Soviet Union before the American power came into play, and that they could not have done after 5 December 1941. Germany could not have done more thereafter than to keep the strategic initiative out of Soviet hands, and it failed at that on 19 November 1942. The battles at Moscow and Stalingrad were indeed the radical *povorot* and the radical *perelom* of the war in the East. The first terminated Germany's bid for world power; the second put the Soviet Union on the road to a full share in the victory and to superpower status.

The governing factors in the Soviet decision over Germany were the Soviet manpower, industrial base, and territory. German strategies designed primarily to destroy Soviet manpower proved inadequate in 1941 and abortive in 1942. Despite the Germans' best efforts, the Soviet strength at the front grew from 2.9 million men in June

1941 to 4.2 million in December 1941 and then to 5.5 million in June 1942 and to 6.1 million in November 1942.[36] In March 1943, Hitler still rated the Soviet Union's running out of manpower "sooner or later" as his best strategic prospect in the war but conceded that he no longer counted on it.[37]

The Soviet industrial base figured in the December 1940 plan for Operation BARBAROSSA primarily as a German war aim. Had BARBAROSSA been terminated as planned on the Arkhangelsk–Volga River line, it would have brought the central (Moscow–Upper Volga) and southern (Donets Basin) industrial regions, which then accounted for over 80 percent of productive capacity, under German control. Hitler's decision in August 1941 to shift the main effort from the center to the south and thereby make the industrial base also a strategic objective closed down the southern region, which accounted for over half of Soviet output particularly of coal and steel, but in the subsequent course of events put Moscow and the central region out of German reach.[38] The drastic declines in Soviet coal (63 percent) and steel (58 percent) production in the last quarter of 1941 resulted from the disruption and partial loss of the southern industrial region. But the German reverse at Moscow in December 1941 left the Soviet Union in possession of the central region, and it and two other regions, the Urals and the western Siberian (Kuznets Basin),

---

[36]*IVMV*, vol. V, p. 143 and vol. VI, p. 35, table 4.

[37]Jacobsen, *Der zweite Weltkrieg*, p. 384.

[38]The estimates of the relative importance of the central and southern regions are based on Theodore Shabad, *Geography of the Soviet Union: A Regional Survey* (New York: Columbia University Press, 1951), pp. 79, 107.

sufficed to decide the contest for the industrial base in the Soviet favor.[39]

The German 1942 offensive totally crippled the southern industrial region and caused a drastic decline in oil output in the Caucasus. The following table shows that coal, steel, and oil production, in millions of tons, did not recover during the war:[40]

Commodity	1940	1941	1942	1943	1944	1945
Coal	165.9	151.4	75.5	93.1	121.5	149.3
Steel		18.3	17.9	8.1	8.5	10.9	12.3
Oil		31.1	33.0	22.0	18.0	18.3	19.4

German output, also in millions of tons, during roughly the same period was as follows:[41]

Commodity	1941	1942	1943	1944
Coal	246.0	258.0	269.0	281.0
Steel	31.8	32.1	34.6	35.2
Oil	4.8	5.6	6.6	—

Nevertheless, in 1942, Soviet output already had surpassed that of Germany in tanks and other armored vehicles (24,400 Soviet; 4,800 German), in aircraft (21,700 Soviet; 14,700 German), in infantry rifles and carbines (4 million Soviet; 1.4 million German), and in artillery (for which comparable figures are not available). Soviet accounts attribute this remarkable feat entirely to the Communist system's ability to overcome adverse circumstances, but it also appears likely that stocks of strategic materials, particularly steel and other metals, had been accumulated before

the war.[42] Certainly, the 3 million tons of lend-lease supplies delivered by 30 June 1943 and the Western Allies' commitment to provide much greater quantities thereafter (all told 17.5 million long tons, 16.4 million of them from the United States) helped the Soviet Union to devote its own resources to weapons and ammunition production.[43]

The vastness of its territory had been the most vexing strategic problem the Russian Empire presented to a would-be conqueror. In June 1811, a year before Napoleon I made his attempt, Tsar Alexander put it in classic form to General Armand de Caulaincourt, the French ambassador in St. Petersburg: "We have plenty space," Alexander said, " . . . which means that we need never accept a dictated peace, no matter what reverses we may suffer."[44] During the civil war of 1918–1921 and before that contest for the territory of the empire was resolved, Stalin propounded the principle of "the stability of the rear." In it he maintained that the Communist military success in the war then going on or in any other required possession of the Russian heartland, the broad belt of ethnic Russian territory lying roughly between Moscow and Leningrad in the west and reaching eastward into the Ural Mountains.[45]

---

[39]The decision could probably be attributed equally well to the five-year plans for industrialization, which during the 1930s had promoted industrial development in the eastern regions (for the purpose of putting the plants out of bombing range).
[40]*IVMV*, vol. XII, p. 161.
[41]Deutsches Institut fuer Wirtschaftsforschung, *Deutsche Industrie im Kriege*, p. 52.

[42]*IVMV*, vol. XII, pp. 161–68; Zakharov, *50 let*, p. 457f; Deutsches Institut fuer Wirtschaftsforschung, *Deutsche Industrie im Kriege*, pp. 71, 183.
[43]Jones, *Roads to Russia*, app. A, table 1.
[44]Armand de Caulaincourt, *Memoires du general de Caulaincourt* (Paris: Librierie Plon, 1933), vol. I, p. 292.
[45]Stalin defined the stable rear as being "of prime importance to the front, because it is from the rear, and the rear alone, that the front obtains not only all kinds of supplies, but also its manpower, sentiments, *(Continued)*

Alexander's principle of space (which, of course, was so generally accepted even in his time as to hardly need to be stated) and Stalin's of the stability of the rear dominated the strategies of both sides in the struggle for the decision. The Soviet leadership used space as a last resort, not as the weapon of choice Alexander had seemed to imply it was. It was ready on 22 June 1941 to fight a war of attrition but not one deep in its own territory; nevertheless, it did that—involuntarily in 1941 and deliberately from 6 July to 19 November 1942. On the other hand, it applied the principle of the stability of the rear, in the terms Stalin had stated it two decades earlier, as soon as the likely course of the war became apparent. From early July 1941 to 19 November 1942 (and for at least some weeks after), the Soviet main effort was always in the center, on the approaches to Moscow, the citadel of the heartland. The German blitzkrieg, the most effective form of the war of annihilation yet devised, had to come to grips with the Soviet main forces. It did not do that. Hitler had diverted the main effort from the center to the south in August 1941 and again in the summer of 1942, thereby, in the first instance, dissipating his best chance and, in the second, his last chance of annihilating the mass of the Soviet Army, which had been the stated primary objective in the original BARBAROSSA directive of December 1940 and all those issued thereafter. Whether the outcome could have been different if the diversions had not been made is now at best a moot question. However, their having been made could have had no other result than to substantiate a prediction Alexander had based on the principle of space, which was that under its conditions, the would-be conqueror was likely in the end to have to accept the terms of his intended victim.

(Continued)
and ideas." During World War II, he established the stability of the rear as the chief of several so-called permanent operating factors in war. Stalin, *Sochineniya,* vol. IV, pp. 284–88, 323–26; K. E. Voroshilov, *Stalin and the Armed Forces of the USSR* (Moscow: Foreign Languages Publishing House, 1951), pp. 107–23.

Appendix A

Table of Equivalent Ranks

German	*Soviet*	*U.S. Equivalent*
Reichsmarschall*	None	None
Generalfeldmarschall	Marshal Sovetskogo Soyuza	General of the Army
None	Glavnyi Marshal	None
None	Marshal	None
Generaloberst	General Armii	General
General der Infanterie, der Artillerie, der Flieger, and so forth	General Polkovnik	Lieutenant General
Generalleutnant	General Leytenant	Major General
Generalmajor	General Mayor	Brigadier General

---

*Created for Hermann Goering in July 1940 and held only by him.

Appendix B

Comparative Sizes of Major Commands, November 1941 to January 1943

German	*Soviet*

1. Army Groups
    On the Eastern Front 4 to 5 plus the Twentieth Mountain Army and the Finnish Army to September 1944
	1. *Fronts* (Soviet army groups)
	    10 to 12

2. Armies
    2 to 4 in an army group
	2. Armies
	    3 to 9 in a *front*. Probable average 5 to 7

3. Corps (including Panzer Corps)
    2 to 7 in an army
	3. Rifle Corps
	    Disbanded August 1941, reactivated late 1942 with 3 to 9 divisions

4. Divisions
    2 to 7 in a corps
	4. Divisions
	    2 to 3 in a corps

AUTHORIZED STRENGTHS, DIVISIONS		AUTHORIZED STRENGTHS, ARMORED CORPS AND DIVISIONS	
Panzer Division (103 to 125 tanks)	14,000 to 17,000	Tank Corps (189 tanks)	10,500
Motorized Division (48 tanks)	14,000	Mechanized Corps (186 tanks)	16,000
Infantry Division, 9 battalions	15,000	Rifle Division	9,375
Infantry Division, 6 battalions	12,700	Guards Rifle Division	10,585
Artillery Division (113 guns)	3,380	Artillery Division (210 guns)	6,550

Note on Sources

When the Center of Military History volumes on World War II in the Soviet Union were planned in the late 1950s, the German military records then in the custody of the National Archives were almost the only primary sources available. Although a vast quantity of Soviet literature having to do with the war has since been published, the accessible Soviet documentary evidence remains sparse. Consequently, the German records are still the source closest to the events. They are a vast collection even after having been selectively microfilmed under the auspices of the Committee for the Study of War Documents of the American Historical Association. Although the originals, from which this volume was written, have been returned to Germany, the documents cited can, for the most part, be located by unit or agency and folder number through the *Guides to German Records Microfilmed at Alexandria, Va.* (1974 to 1977) prepared and published by the National Archives and Records Administration, Washington, D.C. 20408–0001.

In the German military records, those of the Armed Forces High Command (OKW), Army High Command (OKH), and army field commands (army groups, armies, corps, and divisions) are the most useful. Relatively few German Air Force operational records survived the war. The best general summary of those that did is British Air Ministry Pamphlet 248, *The Rise and Fall of the German Air Force* (London: His Majesty's Stationery Office, 1948). Hermann Plocher, *The German Air Force Versus Russia, 1942*, USAF Historical Studies No. 154, published by the U.S. Air Force Historical Division, treats the 1942 operations in general from an air force point of view. The German Navy and the High Command of the Navy (OKM) were only peripherally involved in the war on the Eastern Front. The OKM, however, received and preserved a complete set of strategic directives, the *OKM, Weisungen OKW (Fuehrer), 1939–45,* which are cited in the text as German High Level Directives, CMH files, and have been published with a few variations and omissions as Walter Hubatsch, ed., *Hitler's Weisungen Fuer die Kriegsfuehrung 1939–1945* (Frankfurt: Bernard und Graefe, 1962).

Although the OKW occupied the next to highest place in the German chain of command and acted as Hitler's personal staff, its position with regard to the Eastern Front was somewhat anomalous because the East (Finland excepted) was designated as an OKH theater and because by 1941 rivalry between the OKW and the OKH had ripened into outright hostility. The conversion of the Army General Staff into a second personal staff after Hitler became commander in chief, army, in December 1941, added a complication. Nevertheless, until late September 1942 when it was bypassed almost completely, the OKW received detailed daily reports on the operations in the East, and the OKW Operations Staff had a significant hand in strategic decision making for the Eastern Front. A convenient compilation of OKW materials is Percy Ernst Schramm, gen. ed., *Kriegstagebuch des Oberkommandos der Wehrmacht (Wehrmachtfuehrungsstab)* (Frankfurt: Bernard & Graefe, 1961–1965). Volume I, 1940–1941 (Hans-Adolf Jacobsen, ed.), and Volume II, 1942 (Andreas Hillgruber, ed.), contain the so-called OKW War Diary for 1941 and 1942 with commentary by the former deputy chief of the OKW Operations Staff, General Walter Warlimont, and related documents. The most useful OKW document is the *OKW, WFST, Kriegsgeschichtlichen Abteilung, Kriegstagebuch,* the war diary fragment for the months April through June 1942 by Colonel Walter Scherff, Hitler's official war historian, that became International Military Tribunal Document 1809 PS. It is supplemented by Helmuth Greiner's *Aufzeichnungen ueber die Lagevortraege und Besprechungen im Fuehrerhauptquartier vom 12. August 1942 bis zum 17. Maerz 1943* (*Greiner Diary Notes,* Historical Division, United States Army, Europe, MS # C–065a). A description of the OKW role in the conduct of the war by an eyewitness who was also a professional historian is in Helmuth Greiner, *Die Oberste Wehrmachtfuehrung, 1939–1943* (Wiesbaden: Limes Verlag, 1951).

The OKH was the central staff for the conduct of the war against the Soviet Union, and after September 1942 the Eastern Front was its exclusive and sole responsibility. The OKH records that have survived, though substantial in bulk, are fragmentary. The

two most valuable are the *Halder Diary* and the *Lage Ost* situation maps. The *Halder Diary,* published as Franz Halder, *Kriegstagebuch* (Stuttgart: W. Kohlhammer, 1964), is the personal diary kept by the chief of the General Staff until September 1942. It is supplemented by *General Halder's Daily Notes* (Historical Division, United States Army, Europe, EAP 21–g–16/4/0 file). The *Lage Ost* maps, printed daily by the Operations Branch, OKH, at a scale of 1:1,000,000, are the source, with corrections and additions to the Soviet dispositions, for the maps that appear in this volume.

Among the OKH records, those of the most important branch, Operations, are the least complete, but, fortunately, Operations Branch documents and communications of other kinds frequently found their way into the files of other branches and of the field commands. The Organization Branch records still in existence give information concerning German strengths, losses, replacements, manpower resources, and changes in the army organizational structure. A branch war diary (*OKH, GenStdH, Org. Abt., Kriegstagebuch*) also exists for the months January through June 1942. The most nearly continuous of the OKH files are those of Foreign Armies East (*Fremde Heere Ost*), the Eastern Intelligence Branch. The branch turned out a vast number of intelligence estimates dealing with individual sectors and with the whole Eastern Front. It also issued frequent long- and short-range summaries and from time to time made comparisons of German and Soviet strengths. Enough of those have survived to form a complete intelligence picture for the Eastern Front as it appeared to the Germans. Unfortunately, the Eastern Intelligence Branch much of the time was more diligent than perspicacious. The most tantalizing of the OKH records is *Der Chef der Heeresruestung und Befehlshaber des Ersatzheeres, Der Chef des Stabes, Tagebuch*, the intermittent diary of the chief of staff to the powerful chief of Army Armament and the Replacement Army.

For the history of the war in the Soviet Union the army group records are prime sources. The army group headquarters were the direct link between the German High Command (Hitler and the OKH) and the front and were, within the limits Hitler imposed, themselves originating agencies for operational decisions. In accordance with German practice, the army group and other field commands each kept an Ia ("operations") war diary in which were recorded the incoming and outgoing orders, summaries of reports and conferences, situation estimates, the progress of operations, weather, temperature, and other items of operational or historical significance. The orders, reports, and other papers were filed separately in annexes *(Anlagen)* that were the central records of the field commands. At the army group level, the war diaries were generally kept with a conscious eye to history, sometimes by trained historians; and frequently the commanding generals and chiefs of staff confided matters to the diary that were not recorded elsewhere or transmitted outside the headquarters. The army group records also provide operational plans, after-action reports, transcripts of telephone and other conferences, message files, and files of *Chefsachen*—top secret doc-

uments that were not entered in the war diaries.

For the period this volume covers, the Ia war diaries of Army Group North and Army Group A are complete. The Army Group A *Anlagen* are missing; those for Army Group North are partial. Only the December 1941 segment of the Ia war diary and scattered *Anlagen* survive from Army Group Center, and from Army Group South (B), only a very few *Anlagen*. For the months January to July 1942, Generalfeldmarschall Fedor von Bock's *Kriegstagebuch, Osten* (the *Bock Diary*) is an adequate and in some respects superior substitute for the missing Army Group South Ia war diary. Wilhelm Ritter von Leeb's *Tagebuchaufzeichnungen und Lagebeurteilungen aus zwei Weltkriegen* (Stuttgart: Deutsche Verlags-Anstalt, 1976) supplements the Army Group North Ia war diary for the period to February 1942.

The army records, which are organized in the same manner as those of the army groups, provide tactical information and compensate in the main for the missing parts of the army group collections. While the army commands did not have as continuous access to the top or as broad a view as the army groups had, they were a great deal closer to the battlefield; consequently, the actual conduct of operations, even in the period of Hitler's ascendancy, was determined much of the time by the interaction of an army with the army group and the OKH (Hitler). The army records are sufficiently complete to give reasonable and, in the majority of cases, detailed coverage of all important operations.

Operations and aspects of command at various levels are dealt with from the points of view of participants in Walter Warlimont, *Inside Hitler's Headquarters* (New York: Praeger, 1961); Walter Goerlitz, ed., *The Memoirs of Field Marshal Keitel* (New York: Stein and Day, 1966); Erich von Manstein, *Lost Victories* (Chicago: Henry Regnery, 1958); Heinz Guderian, *Panzer Leader* (New York: Dutton, 1952); and a biography with papers, *Paulus in Stalingrad* (New York: The Citadel Press, 1963), by Walter Goerlitz. F. W. Mellenthin, *German Generals of World War II* (Norman, Okla.: University of Oklahoma Press, 1977) and Otto E. Moll, *Die deutschen Generalfeldmarschaelle, 1939–1945* (Rastatt/Baden: Erich Pabel, 1961) provide general biographical information and assessments.

Some aspects of the German conduct of the war in the Soviet Union that have been regarded as peripheral to this volume have been given extensive treatment elsewhere: occupation policy and practice in Alexander Dallin, *German Rule in Russia, 1941–1945* (New York: St. Martin's Press, 1957); the mass murder of Soviet Jews in Raul Hilberg, *The Destruction of the European Jews* (Chicago: Quadrangle Books, 1961); and the *Waffen SS* in George H. Stein, *The Waffen SS* (Ithaca, N.Y.: Cornell University Press, 1966); Charles W. Sydnor, Jr., *Soldiers of Destruction* (Princeton, N.J.: Princeton University Press, 1977); and James J. Weingartner, *Hitler's Guard* (Carbondale, Ill.: Southern Illinois University Press, 1974).

II

Except for scattered captured documents, interrogations, and analyses which filtered through the German wartime intelligence agencies, the only materials available for the study of the Soviet side of the war are those that have been processed by the Soviet publishing machinery. They are indispensable because there are virtually no others, but they pose problems, sometimes of credibility, more often of exegesis. The approved Soviet picture of the war is not false, but it is always controlled, often contrived, and, in spite of its earnestness and bulk, in some respects gives an impression of being historical trompe l'oeil. A comprehensive overview and an expert analysis of the Soviet World War II literature are available in Michael Parrish, *The USSR in World War II: An Annotated Bibliography of Books Published in the Soviet Union 1945-1975 With Addenda for the Years 1975-1980* (New York: Garland Publishing, 1981).

The Great Patriotic War is, next to the Bolshevik Revolution, the most important event in the history of the Soviet state. As such it has retained an immediacy for the Soviet government, military forces, and society that has long ago faded among the other participants in World War II. Consequently, in the Soviet official view, the war is not just history or nostalgia, it is a matter of present consequence with implications for the future. Marshal A. A. Grechko, in *The Armed Forces of the Soviet State* (Washington, D.C.: GPO, 1977; Moscow: Voyennoye Izdatelstvo, 1975), ranks the known lessons of the war and those still to be discovered equally with new technology and military theory as guidance for the Soviet armed forces in the 1970s and 1980s. The Soviet concern, therefore, goes beyond description and analysis and extends to protecting much that is considered still to be security information and to translating the war and its lessons into currently meaningful terms. As a result, the Soviet literature on the war has emerged incrementally, accumulating substance at times very slowly, at times in bursts, always stopping short of complete disclosure, always subject to revision in substance as well as in interpretation.

Although the Soviet Army's Directorate of Military History had been at work under Boris Shaposhnikov, the former chief of the Army General Staff, since late 1942, war history did not begin to appear in the Soviet Union in open form until more than a decade after the war ended. As long as Stalin lived, problems of security and credit (and blame) prevented release of anything beyond panegyrics to Stalin, blasts against former allies and enemies, and compilations of the wartime TASS communiques. One exception was the partisan aspect of the war, about which several substantial books appeared, notably P. Vershigora's *Lyudi s chistoi sovestyu* (Moscow: Sovetskiy Pisatel, 1951). Nikita Khrushchev launched the systematic Soviet study of World War II in his speech to the Twentieth Party Congress in 1956. He announced then that he had ordered a comprehensive history of the Great Patriotic War to be written, and during the hours-long speech he made a series of revelations about the conduct of the war that by themselves constituted a major act of revisionism.

While the big work was being written a number of single-volume histories were put into print to preview it and apparently to establish parameters of approach and treatment. The first of these was *Vazneyshye operatsiy Velikoy Otechestvennoy Voyny* (Moscow: Voyen-

noye Izdatelstvo, 1956) edited by Col. P. A. Zhilin. As a collection of battle studies rather than a continuous picture of military infallibility, this work dealt with the early defeats—as defensive successes. Stalin's name virtually disappeared, and the glory and credit were redistributed to the party, the army, and the Soviet people. Scattered mentions of mistakes and errors, none big enough or reaching high enough to roil the smooth surface, gave a touch of critical analysis. In 1958 General S. P. Platonov published a history of World War II, *Vtoraya Mirovaya Voyna* (Moscow: Voyennoye Izdatelstvo). The Platonov history carried somewhat further the trend toward limited objectivity Zhilin had begun and broached aspects of the Soviet conduct of the war that Zhilin's episodic approach had sidestepped. Both Zhilin and Platonov were associated with the Soviet Army Directorate of Military History, and Zhilin would later be its longtime chief. The *Vazneyshye operatsiy* and *Vtoraya Mirovaya Voyna* established standards for Soviet World War II historiography that have prevailed ever since. The deviations, though numerous, have never been in more than degree. Two other early works are K. S. Kolganov, *Razvitye Taktiku Sovetskoy Armii v Gody Velikoy Otechestvennoy Voyny 1941-45* (Moscow: Voyennoye Izdatelstvo, 1959) and B. S. Telpukhovskiy, *Velikaya Otechestvennaya Voyna Sovetskogo Soyuza 1941–45* (Moscow: Voyennoye Izdatelstvo, 1959).

Istoriya Velikoy Otechestvennoy Voyny Sovetskogo Soyuza 1941–45 [History of the Great Patriotic War] (Moscow: Voyennoye Izdatelstvo) began appearing in 1960 and was completed in six volumes in 1963. Prepared by the Institut of

Marxism-Leninism (Institut Marksizma-Leninizma), it covers in substantial detail the whole military, political, and economic history of the war in the Soviet Union, including its origins and its aftermath. The authorship is collective and includes prominently three of the writers mentioned above, Zhilin, Platonov, and Telpukhovskiy, among some dozens of others. Certain sections dealing with military operations appear to follow, in places almost word for word, the Platonov history. On the whole, the accounts of military operations carry forward the trends observed in the Zhilin and Platonov works without approaching full frankness or objectivity. Names, dates, units, tactical maneuvers, and operational plans are given more coherent treatment than in the earlier works. Soviet mistakes, defeats, and setbacks, with relatively few known exceptions, though not ignored, are often handled so obliquely as to escape all but the closest attention. Strengths, losses, production figures, and other statistics are given in detail for the German and other armies but not for the Soviet forces. For the first time Soviet strengths are occasionally given in concrete figures, but Soviet casualties and losses continue to be generally ignored, and Soviet statistics are most often presented as percentages and ratios derived from undisclosed bases. The volumes are heavily documented with sources published outside the Soviet Union but only with meaningless file-number references to Soviet documents. The process of high-level decision making is left nebulous except for frequent citations of presumably unanimous decisions and directives from the *Stavka*. Notable in the volumes is the all but total disappearance of Stalin and Marshal Zhukov and Khrushchev's elevation to a position of military prominence.

During the Khrushchev years the war history became or at least came to be regarded as a significant asset to the government, the party, and the armed forces and to many individuals in each. The credit Stalin had formerly monopolized could be redistributed and in the process increased not diminished. Even the mistakes, Khrushchev had demonstrated, could be interpreted to advantage. And the victory was there, indisputable, to be celebrated without end.

Particularly when it came to persons, however, past achievement had to be coordinated with current status; consequently, Khrushchev's enforced retirement in 1964 made the *History of the Great Patriotic War* politically obsolete a few months after its concluding volume was published. The *History* was not disavowed and has continued since as ostensibly the definitive work on the Great Patriotic War, but publication of book-length war history of any kind dropped markedly through the rest of the 1960s, apparently because a new orientation was being sought. In the interim, the organ of the Ministry of Defense, the *Voyenno-istoricheskiy Zhurnal (Military History Journal)*, became the forum for competing approaches and an outlet for persons and interests that had been slighted during the Khrushchev years. Articles from the journal form a substantial part of the source material for this volume.

The twenty-fifth anniversary of the victory brought a wave of war history publication in 1970. Most of the works were merely commemorative. One,

however, established a landmark: it was the second edition of the Institut Marksizma-Leninizma, *Velikaya Otechestvennaya Voyna Sovetskogo Soyuza, 1941–45 (Kratkaya Istoriya)* (Moscow: Voyennoye Izdatelstvo). The first edition of the *Kratkaya Istoriya (Short History),* printed in 1964, had been a one-volume summary of the six-volume history. In it already the larger work's frequent and often fulsome references to Khrushchev had disappeared, and Stalin had been partially rehabilitated as supreme commander in chief. The second edition, also later published in abridged form in English as the *Great Patriotic War of the Soviet Union, 1941–1945* (Moscow: Progress Publishers, 1974), was presented as a revision and expansion incorporating five years' progress in research and the results of recently published memoirs and monographs. It was in actuality a new work, more an interim substitute for the six-volume history than a short version of it. Like the Platonov volume in the late 1950s, it apparently also was designed to establish new standards for the future. Its chief attributes were factualness, meaningful use of statistics (by comparison with previous practice), determinedly evenhanded treatment of persons, and a heightened effect of objectivity in judgments on events.

Also in 1970, apparently as a companion piece to the *Kratkaya Istoriya,* P. A. Zhilin edited and the Izdatelstvo Politcheskoy Literatury (Moscow) published *Velikaya Otechestvennaya Voyna, Kratkiy nauchno-popularnyy ocherk (Great Patriotic War, Popular Scientific Sketch).* Since no Soviet work on the whole war, particularly one edited by the chief of the Military History Directorate, is meant to be merely a popularization, the *Popular Scientific Sketch* must be taken, along with the Platonov history, the *Kratkaya Istoriya,* and A. A. Grechko's *Gody voyny* (Moscow: Voyennoye Izdatelstvo, 1976), as a major part of Soviet war literature.

The Twenty-fourth Party Congress, held in early 1971, took note of recent Soviet achievements in military history and charged the historical profession with two tasks for the future: one was to delineate the Soviet collaboration with all "progressive" peoples in World War II; the other was to combat "falsifications" perpetrated in World War II history by bourgeois historians.[1] With that guidance and with the then Minister of Defense, Marshal A. A. Grechko, as chairman of the editorial commission, the historical organizations in the Ministry of Defense, the Institute of Marxism-Leninism, and the Academy of Sciences set about writing a comprehensive history of World War II in twelve volumes, the *Istoriya Vtoroi Mirovoi Voyny, 1939–1945* (Moscow: Voyennoye Izdatelstvo, 1973–1982). Aside from establishing an official Soviet version of the whole war, the *History of the Second World War* has provided a vehicle for rewriting the Great Patriotic War on a scale substantially the same as the six-volume history of the Khrushchev period. The approach parallels the *Kratkaya Istoriya* in treatment of information and persons. Notable are the reappearance of Stalin as the central figure, thoroughgoing discussions of strategic decision making, and lavish provision of statistics.

The *History of the Second World War* is

---

[1] "*XXIV S'ezd KPSS i vennoye-istoricheskiy nauka*," *Voyenno-istoricheskiy Zhurnal,* 5(1971), 1–13.

currently the most authoritative Soviet work on the war, and all others conform to it in fundamental matters of substance and interpretation (as they did previously to the *History of the Great Patriotic War*). It has brought Soviet historiography of the war to the state of being highly informative without being truly enlightening. On the latter score, it does somewhat less then the *Sbornik materialov po izucheniyu opyta voyny (Collection of Materials for the Study of the War Experience)* produced by the Directorate of Military History under the former chief of the General Staff, Shaposhnikov, between late 1942 and 1945 (for distribution only to division commanders and above).

The publication of the general histories in the 1960s and 70s was accompanied by a flood of memoirs of all descriptions. A generous sampling of the memoirs published in the early to mid-1960s is to be found—together with commentary and an extensive "selected" bibliography—in Seweryn Bialer's *Stalin and His Generals* (New York: Pegasus, 1969). Because of the roles of their authors in the war, the most significant memoirs are those of the Marshals G. K. Zhukov and A. M. Vasilevskiy, which were published as *The Memoirs of Marshal Zhukov* (New York: Delacorte Press, 1971) and *Delo vsey zhizni* (Moscow: Izdatelstvo Politicheskoy Literatury, 1976).

Vasili Chuikov's *The Battle for Stalingrad* (New York: Holt, Rinehart & Winston, 1964), published in Russian in 1959, has the distinction of being the first major war memoir, and it remains one of the best. The most prominent figure in many of the memoirs is Stalin, and some of the most revealing recollections of him are given in A. I.

Eremenko's *The Arduous Beginning* (Moscow: Progress Publishers, 1966) and *Pomni voyny* (Donetsk: Donbass, 1971). In two books, *The Soviet General Staff at War, 1941–45* (Moscow: Progress Publishers, 1970) and *The Last Six Months* (Garden City: Doubleday, 1977), S. M. Shtemenko has provided the closest, though still fragmentary, look into the workings of the Soviet General Staff. Nikita Khrushchev's *Khrushchev Remembers* (Boston: Little, Brown, 1970) offers sidelights on the war and the text of his speech to the Twentieth Party Congress. K. K. Rokossovskiy, in *A Soldier's Duty* (Moscow: Progress Publishers, 1970), and K. A. Meretskov, in *Serving the People* (Moscow: Progress Publishers, 1971), give army group commanders' views of the war. At the army level are I. Kh. Bagramyan's *Tak shli my k pobede* (Moscow: Voyennoye Izdatelstvo, 1977); D. D. Lelyushenko's *Moskva-Stalingrad-Berlin-Praga* (Moscow: Izdatelstvo "Nauka," 1970); and K. S. Moskalenko's *Na yugo-zapadnom napravlenii* (Moscow: Izdatelstvo "Nauka," 1969).

In the accounts of campaigns and battles, the line between history and reminiscence frequently is somewhat indistinct. Andrei Grechko's *Battle for the Caucasus* (Moscow: Progress Publishers, 1971) is a history written by a former minister of defense who had commanded armies in the Caucasus, where Leonid Brezhnev had also served—as a political officer. *Nachalnyy period voyny* (Moscow: Voyennoye Izdatelstvo, 1974) is a study of the prewar plans and the first phase of the war done under the supervision of S. P. Ivanov, commandant of the Voroshilov Academy of the General Staff. G. I.

Vaneyev, et al., *Geroicheskaya oborona Sevastopolya, 1941–1942* (Moscow: Voyennoye Izdatelstvo, 1969) is a collective work with participants in the Sevastopol siege among the authors. The most intensively researched works are A. M. Samsonov's *Stalingradskaya bitva* (Moscow: Izdatelstvo "Nauka," 1960, 1968); Dimitri Pavlov's *Leningrad 1941* (Chicago: University of Chicago Press, 1965); and V. M. Kovalchuk's *Leningrad i bolshaya zemlya* (Leningrad: Izdatelstvo "Nauka," 1975). Among the many works in which the contributors were also participants in the battle are *Bitva za Stalingrad* (Volgograd: Nizhniye-Volzhskoye Knizhnoye Izdatelstvo, 1969), edited by A. M. Borodin; *Stalingrad: yroki istorii* (Moscow: Izdatelstvo "Progress," 1976), edited by V. I. Chuikov; *Razgrom nemetsko-fashistikh voysk pod Moskvoy* (Moscow: Voyennoye Izdatelstvo, 1964), edited by V. D. Sokolovskiy; *Velikaya bitva pod Moskvoy* (Moscow: Voyennoye Izdatelstvo, 1961), edited by V. N. Yevstigneyev; and *Proval gitlerovskogo nastupleniya na Moskvu* and *50 let vooruzhennykh sil SSSR* (Moscow: Izdatelstvo "Nauka," 1966 and 1968, respectively), edited by M. B. Zakharov. Two works not of Soviet authorship but written from an intimate acquaintance with the events they describe are Harrison E. Salisbury's *The 900 Days* (New York: Harper & Row, 1969) and Alexander Wirth's, *The Year of Stalingrad* (New York: Alfred A. Knopf, Inc., 1947).

Background and miscellaneous information on a broad range of subjects having to do with the Soviet war experience are to be found in the following: G. A. Deborin and B. S. Telpukhovskiy, *Itogi i uroki velikoy otechestvennoy voyny* (Moscow: Izdatelstvo "Mysl," 1975), on the results and lessons of the Great Patriotic War; Embassy of the USSR, Washington, D.C., *Information Bulletin* (1942–1948); Ministerstvo Oborony, SSSR, *Istoriya voyn i voyennogo iskustva* (Moscow: Voyennoye Izdatelstvo, 1970), on the history of war and the art of war; Ministerstvo Oborony, SSSR, Institut Voyennoy Istorii, *Sovetskaya voyennaya entsiklopediya* (Moscow: Voyennoye Izdatelstvo, 1976–1980), a military encyclopedia; and S. A. Tyushkevich, et al., *Sovetskiye vooruzhennye sily* (Moscow: Voyennoye Izdatelstvo, 1978), on the organization and development of the Soviet armed forces. The *Information Bulletin* is the source for a number of the illustrations in this volume. *Itogi i uroki* also includes an essay on "bourgeois falsifiers" of World War II history, the present writer among them. The same subject is given book-length treatment in V. S. Makhalova and A. V. Beshensteva's *Voyna, istoriya, ideologiya* (Moscow: Izdatelstvo Politicheskoy Literatury, 1974).

Partisan and underground operations are treated separately in the general histories and have a literature of their own. The works cited here are a miniscule sample of the many that have been published. V. Ye. Bystrov, ed., *Geroi podpolya* (Moscow: Izdatelstvo Politicheskoy Literatury, 1970) and A. A. Kuznyaev, *Podpolnye partinynye organy kompartii belorussii v gody velikoy otechestvennoy voyny* (Minsk: Izdatelstvo "Belarus," 1975) deal with the underground. In addition to Vershigora's *Lyudi s chistoi sovestyu*, already mentioned, representative works on partisan warfare are L. Tsanava's *Vsenarodnaya partizanskaya voyna v Belorussii protiv fashistskikh zakhvachnikov* (Minsk:

Gosizdat, 1949–1951) and A. I. Zalesskiy's *Geroicheskiy podvig millionov v tylu vraga* (Minsk: Izdatelstvo "Belarus," 1970). The more analytical accounts are those in the Soviet general war histories and in studies of partisan warfare done outside the Soviet Union. The most comprehensive of the latter are the monograph series published as War Documentation Project, *Project "Alexander" Studies* (Washington, D.C.: Air Research and Development Command, 1953–55). Others are *The Soviet Partisans in World War II* (Madison: University of Wisconsin Press, 1964), edited by John A. Armstrong, which presents some of the War Documentation Project monographs in condensed form with an introduction and extensive bibliography; Erich Hesse's *Der sowjetrussische Partisanenkrieg, 1941 bis 1944* (Goettingen: Musterschmidt, 1969); and Edgar M. Howell's *The Soviet Partisan Movement, 1941–1944* (Washington, D.C.: GPO, 1956).

III

To provide the Army with a comprehensive record of the German military experience in World War II, the Foreign Military Studies Program of the Historical Division, United States Army, Europe, produced, by the time it was terminated in 1961, some 2,400 manuscripts. The authors were, for the most part, former high-ranking German officers. At first they wrote mainly from memory about events in which they had played key roles. Beginning in 1948 more comprehensive projects were initiated. These were assigned to teams that then made use of records in the custody of the United States Army, records secured through private sources, interviews, and the members' own experience. Overall supervision and direction of the projects was in the hands of a Control Group, headed throughout its existence by Generaloberst a.D. Franz Halder. In 1954 the Historical Division, United States Army, Europe, published a complete list of the manuscripts, then completed or projected, in the *Guide to Foreign Military Studies 1945–54*. A full set of the manuscripts is on deposit in the Center of Military History, Department of the Army, Washington, D.C. A second set has been furnished to the historical office of the German *Bundeswehr*. That part of the war in the Soviet Union with which this volume is concerned is covered by the series at the strategic level by MS # T–9, Generaloberst a.D. Gotthard Heinrici, *Der Feldzug in Russland ein operativer Ueberblick;* and at the operational level by MS # P–114a, Generalleutnant a.D. Friedrich Sixt, *Der Feldzug gegen die Sowjet-Union im Nordabschnitt der Ostfront* and by MS # P–114c, General der Artillerie a.D. Friedrich Wilhelm Hauck, *Die Operationen der deutschen Heeresgruppen an der Ostfront 1941 bis 1945 suedliches Gebiet.*

The Center of Military History, Department of the Army, has projected in its Army Historical Series a three-volume history of the German-Soviet conflict. The present volume is the second, and the third is Earl F. Ziemke, *Stalingrad to Berlin: The German Defeat in the East* (Washington, D.C.: GPO, 1968). Additionally, the Center of Military History has published Department of the Army Pamphlet 20–261a, George Blau, *The German Campaign in Russia— Planning and Operations, 1940–1942* (Washington, D.C.: GPO, 1955) and

Earl F. Ziemke, *The German Northern Theater of Operations, 1940–1945* (Washington, D.C.: GPO, 1959).

The Historical Office of the German *Bundeswher* has published Manfred Kehrig's *Stalingrad* (Stuttgart: Deutsche Verlags-Anstalt, 1974) and Klaus Reinhardt's *Die Wende vor Moskau* (Stuttgart: Deutsche Verlags-Anstalt, 1972), and is engaged in publishing a ten-volume official history, *Das Deutsche Reich und der Zweite Weltkrieg* (Stuttgart: Deutsche Verlags-Anstalt, 1979–   ). The Academy of Sciences, Central Institute for History, of the German Democratic Republic is publishing a projected eight-volume history, *Deutschland im zweiten Weltkrieg* (Berlin: Akademie-Verlag, 1974–   ).

IV

The body of general literature dealing with the German-Soviet conflict is large and growing. Comprehensive bibliographies, periodically brought up-to-date, are to be found in the *Revue d'Histoire de la Deuxieme Guerre Mondiale* and the *Buecherschau der Weltkriegsbuecherei*. Both list books and articles in all languages and carry bibliographic articles and reviews of significant works.

Two comprehensive studies in English are John Erickson's *The Road to Stalingrad* (London: Weidenfeld and Nicholson, 1975) and Albert Seaton's *The Russo-German War 1941–1945* (New York: Praeger, 1971). A noteworthy account in German is Kurt von Tippelskirch's *Geschichte des Zweiten Weltkrieges* (Bonn: Athenaeum-Verlag, 1956). The author was both a trained historian and a corps and army commander on the Eastern Front. Brief authoritative accounts of the whole war are to be found in Vincent J. Esposito's *A Concise History of World War II* (New York: Praeger, 1964); Martha Byrd Hoyle's *A World in Flames* (New York: Atheneum, 1970); and Hans-Adolf Jacobsen's *1939–1945, Der Zweite Weltkrieg in Chronik und Dokumenten* (Darmstadt: Wehr und Wissen Verlagsgesellschaft, 1961).

The German-Soviet conflict has been set in the contexts of politics and grand strategy in a variety of works. The Soviet Union's relations with its Western Allies are treated in, among others, Winston S. Churchill's *The Hinge of Fate* (Boston: Houghton Mifflin, 1950); Herbert Feis' *Churchill, Roosevelt, Stalin* (Princeton: Princeton University Press, 1957); J. M. A. Gwyer's *Grand Strategy* (London: Her Majesty's Stationery Office, 1964), vol. III, pt. I; Maurice Matloff and Edwin M. Snell's *Strategic Planning for Coalition Warfare, 1941–1942* (Washington, D.C.: GPO 1953); Robert E. Sherwood's *Roosevelt and Hopkins* (New York: Harper, 1950); and Llewellyn Woodward's *British Foreign Policy in the Second World War* (London: Her Majesty's Stationery Office, 1962). *Hitler, Reden und Proclamationen, 1932–1945* (Munich: Sueddeutscher Verlag, 1965), edited by Max Domarus, is a mine of information on Hitler's war leadership including relations with his allies, as is also, in a more limited fashion, *Goebbels-Reden* (Duesseldorf: Droste Verlag, 1972), edited by Helmut Heiber. Other works dealing with the German coalition are Wipert von Bluecher's *Gesandter zwischen Diktatur und Democratie* (Wiesbaden: Limes Verlag, 1951); Galeazzo Ciano's *The Ciano Diaries 1939–1943* (Garden City: Doubleday, 1946); Waldemar Erfurth's *Der*

Finnische Krieg, 1941–1944 (Wiesbaden: Limes Verlag, 1977); Mario D. Fenyo's *Hitler, Horthy, and Hungary* (New Haven: Yale University Press, 1972); Juergen Foerster's *Stalingrad, Risse im Buendniss, 1942–1943* (Freiburg: Verlag Rombach, 1975); and Paul Schmidt's *Statist auf diplomatischer Buehne, 1923–1945* (Bonn: Athenaeum-Verlag, 1949).

Albert Speer, in *Inside the Third Reich* (New York: Macmillan, 1970), and Nikolai Voznesenskiy, in *The Economy of the USSR During World War II* (Washington, D.C.: Public Affairs Press, 1948), describe their countries' war economies from the points of view of the men who ran them. Two other significant works on German war production are Willi A. Boelcke, *Deutschlands Ruestung im Zweiten Weltkrieg* (Frankfurt: Athenaion, 1969) and Deutsches Institut fuer Wirtschaftsforschung, *Die Deutsche Industrie im Kriege, 1939–1945* (Berlin: Duncker & Humboldt, 1954). The Soviet war economy is covered in the general histories.

Allied aid shipments to the Soviet Union through the Arctic ports and the Persian Gulf are treated in David Irving, *The Destruction of Convoy PQ–17* (New York: Simon and Schuster, 1968); Robert H. Jones, *The Roads to Russia: United States Lend-Lease to the Soviet Union* (Norman, Okla.: University of Oklahoma Press, 1969); Richard M. Leighton and Robert W. Coakley, *Global Logistics and Strategy, 1940–1943* (Washington, D.C.: GPO, 1955); Samuel Eliot Morison, *Battle of the Atlantic, September 1939–May 1943* (Boston: Little, Brown, 1947); T. Vail Motter, *The Persian Corridor and Aid to Russia* (Washington, D.C.: GPO, 1952); and S. W. Roskill, *The War at Sea, 1939–1945* (London: Her Majesty's Stationery Office, 1954).

Information on weapons, fighting vehicles, and aircraft is available in John Batchelor and Ian Hogg, *Artillery* (New York: Charles Scribner's Sons, 1972); Peter Chamberlain and Hilary L. Doyle, *Encyclopedia of German Tanks* (New York: Arco, 1978); Ian V. Hogg and John Weeks, *Military Small Arms of the Twentieth Century* (New York: Hippocrene Books, 1977); John Kirk and Robert Young, Jr., *Great Weapons of World War II* (New York: Bonanza Books, 1961); I. E. Krupchenko et al., *Sovetskiye tankovye voyska* (Moscow: Voyennoye Izdatelstvo, 1973); Rudolf Lusar, *German Secret Weapons of the Second World War* (New York: Philosophical Library, 1959); John Milsom, *Russian Tanks, 1900–1970* (London: Arms and Armour Press, 1970); Ian Parsons, ed., *The Encyclopedia of Air Warfare* (London: Salamander Books, 1974); B. Perrett, *Fighting Vehicles of the Red Army* (London: Ian Allen, 1969); and Christopher Shepherd, *German Aircraft of World War II* (London: Sidgwick & Jackson, 1975).

Glossary

Active defense
: A Soviet theory of defense conducted by generally offensive means, espoused particularly by Stalin.

Armeeabteilung
: A German command intermediate between a corps and an army, usually under an enlarged corps headquarters.

Armeegruppe
: A German command arrangement in which one army headquarters was subordinated to another.

Army group
: *Heeresgruppe* (Ger.), *front* (Russ.)—a headquarters established to command two or more armies.

Balka
: Deep gullies in the steppe regions of the Soviet Union.

Berghof
: Hitler's Bavarian retreat.

Commissar
: A cabinet minister in the Soviet government. In the Soviet Armed Forces, prior to October 1942, a political officer assigned to each military headquarters with the power to countermand orders given by the commander.

DORA
: German 800-mm. gun.

front
: A Soviet army group.

Fuehrer
: Hitler's title as German chief of state.

GAMMA
: German 420-mm. gun.

Gestapo
: *Geheime Staatspolizei,* the German Secret State Police.

Guards
: An honorific designation given to elite units and to Soviet units that had distinguished themselves in combat.

Hero of the Soviet Union
: Title given for acts of exceptional bravery or exceptional performance in command. The award consisted of the Order of Lenin, the highest decoration for valor, a certificate signed by the chairman of the Presidium of the Supreme Soviet, and the Gold Star Medal, which was awarded only to Heroes of the Soviet Union and Heroes of Socialist Labor.

Hiwi, Hilfswillige	Russian auxiliaries, mostly prisoners of war, who served with German units on the Eastern Front in various noncombatant capacities.
Jaeger	Term used to designate German light infantry.
JU–52	The German *Junkers* 52 trimotor transport plane.
KARL	German 540-mm. siege mortar.
Knight's Cross of the Iron Cross	The highest class of the Iron Cross and the most prized of the German World War II military decorations.
Komsomol	*Kommunisticheskiy Soyuz Molodyezhi,* the (Soviet) Communist Youth League for adolescents and young adults aged 14 to 28 years.
NKVD	*Nadrodnyy Komissariat Venutrennikh Del* (People's Commissariat of Internal Affairs), the Soviet internal security and secret political police ministry.
OKH	*Oberkommando des Heeres,* the German Army High Command.
OKL	*Oberkommando der Luftwaffe,* the German Air Force High Command.
OKM	*Oberkommando der Kriegsmarine,* the German Navy High Command.
OKW	*Oberkommando der Wehrmacht,* the German Armed Forces High Command.
Panje	German World War I army slang for Poles and Russians. Used in World War II to describe the Soviet peasant wagons.
Panther	A German tank, designated Panzer V. It mounted a long-barreled 75-mm. gun, and in its sloping armor and low silhouette was patterned after the Soviet T–34. It was not in quantity production until early 1943.
Panzer III	A German prewar-model tank, mounting in its latest version (1942) a long-barreled 50-mm. antitank gun.
Panzer IV	The latest of the prewar German tanks, and mounting in its latest version (1942) a long-barreled, high-velocity 75-mm. gun, which supplanted a short, 75-mm., low-velocity gun.
Panzergrenadier	Armored infantry.
Politruk	*Polit rukovoditel,* a low-echelon political officer.
rasputitsa	Literally, time without roads. The fall and spring muddy periods in the Soviet Union.

RSFSR	Russian Soviet Federated Socialist Republic, the largest of the Soviet republics, comprising 75 percent of the USSR's total land area and 55 percent of its population.
Rollbahn	A highway.
SS	*Schutzstaffel,* elite guard of the Nazi Party.
Self-propelled assault gun	A lightly armored, tracked vehicle mounting a relatively heavy gun and intended to be used as close-support artillery.
Shock army	An army (Soviet) reinforced to lead break-through operations.
Shturmovik	Soviet *Ilyushin* Il–2 ground attack bomber.
Stavka	*Stavka Verkhovnogo Glavnokommandovaniya* (Staff of the Supreme High Command), under Stalin, the top-level Soviet military executive committee. Decisions made in the name of the *Stavka* appear frequently to have been made by Stalin alone.
Stuka	*Sturtzkampfflugzeug* (dive-bomber). Although all German bombers in operational use during World War II were built to have a dive-bombing capability, the *"Stuka"* as such was the *Junkers* JU–87.
T–34	The tank that was the mainstay of the Soviet armored forces throughout World War II. It mounted (1942) a short-barreled 76.2-mm. gun. Sloping armor on the turret and glacis plate gave it particularly good protection against antitank fire.
Tiger	A German tank, designated Panzer VI, mounting an 88-mm. gun. At 57 tons, the heaviest tank on the Eastern Front in 1942 where it appeared first (in small numbers in the late summer).
Totenkopf	Death's head. The emblem of the SS concentration camp guards.
Waffen-SS	The combat units of the SS.
Wehrmacht	The German Armed Forces.
Werwolf	Hitler's headquarters at Vinnitsa in the Ukraine.
Winter War	The Soviet-Finnish war of 1939–1940.
Wolfsschanze	Hitler's headquarters in East Prussia.

Code Names

German

BARBAROSSA	The 1941 offensive in the Soviet Union.
BETTELSTAB ("Beggar's Staff")	Proposed operation against the Oranienbaum pocket, summer 1942.
BLAU ("Blue")	The 1942 summer offensive in the Soviet Union, with phases I, II, and III.
BLUECHER	Attack across Kerch Strait, August 1942.
BRAUNSCHWEIG ("Brunswick")	BLAU renamed, 30 June 1942.
BRUECKENSCHLAG ("Bridging")	Projected offensive to close the Toropets bulge, spring 1942.
CHRISTOPHORUS	Program to secure vehicles from the civilian sector for Army Group Center, January 1942.
CLAUSEWITZ	BLAU II.
DAMPFHAMMER ("Steam Hammer")	BLAU III.
DERFFLINGER	Projected Ninth Army drive from Rzhev to Ostashkov, summer 1942.
DONNERSCHLAG ("Thunderbolt")	Projected Sixth Army breakout from Stalingrad, December 1942.
EDELWEISS	Advance into the Caucasus, July–November 1942.
ELEFANT	Program to secure trucks from the civilian sector, January 1942.
FEUERZAUBER ("Fire Magic")	Original code name for NORDLICHT.
FISCHREIHER ("Heron")	Army Group B final attack to Stalingrad, July–November 1942.
FRIDERICUS	Operation against the Izyum bulge, May 1942.
GEORGE	Eighteenth Army share of NORDLICHT.
GOETZ VON BERLICHINGEN	Air operation against Soviet naval forces at Leningrad, April 1942.
HANNOVER	Operation against the Soviet-held pocket west of Vyazma, May–June 1942.
KLABAUTERMANN ("Hobgoblin")	Boat operation against Soviet traffic on Lake Ladoga, July 1942.
KOENIGSBERG position	German rear line west of Moscow, winter 1942.

KREML ("Kremlin")   German deceptive operation, May–July 1942.

LACHSFANG ("Salmon Catch")   Proposed German-Finnish drive to Kandalak-
                                 sha and Belomorsk, summer 1942.

MOORBRAND ("Swamp Fire")   Operation to pinch off the Pogostye salient,
                                 summer 1942.

NORDLICHT ("Aurora   Projected operation to take Leningrad, fall
   Borealis")   1942.
NORDPOL ("North Pole")   Projected attack into the Toropets bulge, March
                                 1942.

ORKAN ("Tornado")   Proposed operation to eliminate the Sukhinichi
                                 salient, summer 1942.

RAUBTIER ("Beast of Prey")   Operation against the Volkhov pocket, March
                                 1942.

RHEINGOLD   Program to create six new divisions with called-
                                 up deferred men, January 1942.

SCHLINGPFLANZE ("Vine")   Operation to widen the corridor to the Dem-
                                 yansk pocket, October 1942.
SEYDLITZ   Operation west of Sychevka, July 1942.
STOERFANG ("Sturgeon   Operation against Sevastopol, June 1942.
   Catch")

TAIFUN ("Typhoon")   Drive on Moscow, October–December 1941.
TAUBENSCHLAG ("Dovecote")   Projected attack on Toropets, October 1942.
TRAPENJAGD ("Bustard   Operation on the Kerch Peninsula, May 1942.
   Hunt")

VOGELSANG ("Bird Song")   Antipartisan operation in the Bryansk Forest,
                                 June 1942.

WALKUERE ("Valkyrie")   Program to set up four new divisions, January
                                 1942.
WIESENGRUND ("Meadow   Army of Lapland project to occupy the
   Land")   Rybatchiy Peninsula, June 1942.
WILHELM   Operation against the Volchansk salient, June
                                 1942.
WINKELRIED   Substitute for SCHLINGPFLANZE, executed Oc-
                                 tober 1942.
WINTERGEWITTER ("Winter   Operation to relieve Sixth Army at Stalingrad,
   Storm")   December 1942.
WIRBELWIND ("Whirlwind")   Operation to pinch off part of the Sukhinichi
                                 salient, August 1942.

Soviet

KOLTSO ("Ring")

Final attack on Sixth Army at Stalingrad, January 1943.

MALYY SATURN ("Little Saturn")

Reduced version of SATURN and the one actually executed.

MARS

Offensive against the Ninth Army Rzhev salient, fall and winter 1942.

SATURN

Projected offensive west of Stalingrad aimed at Rostov, November 1942.

URANUS

Counteroffensive at Stalingrad, November 1942.

Index

Divisions, Soviet—Continued
13th Guards Order of Lenin Rifle: 394
14th Guards Rifle: 468
14th Rifle: 228
18th Rifle: 170
23d Guards: 228, 230
47th Guards Rifle: 468
80th Cavalry: 189
119th Rifle: 468
124th Rifle: 468
186th Rifle: 229–30
258th Infantry: 63
327th Rifle: 188–89
329th Rifle: 247
345th Rifle: 108
Dnepr bend: 32
Dnepr River: 5, 21, 28–29, 33–34, 103, 141, 156–59, 170, 176, 202, 246, 269, 483, 509, 511–12
Dnepr-Dvina line: 21, 23, 28–30, 32, 61, 140, 202
Dnepropetrovsk: 91, 139, 141, 156–58, 160, 270, 483–84, 509
Dno: 140, 147, 153
DON Operation: 493, 496
Don River: 44, 54, 65, 95, 283, 287, 289–90, 307, 319, 322–24, 326, 337, 339, 343, 346–47, 349–61, 363, 365, 366–67, 372, 377, 382, 396, 412, 442–43, 455–57, 458–59, 462, 468, 471–74, 476, 478, 480, 482–84, 486, 489, 492–94, 496
Don River bend: 288, 352–61, 384–87, 395–96, 485
Donets Basin: 16, 33, 39, 41, 69, 105, 135, 141, 324, 493, 515
Donets River: 105, 137, 139, 141, 156–58, 272, 279, 281–83, 289, 310, 316, 318, 323–24, 343, 346–47, 349, 353–55, 452, 483–84, 488, 491–96, 509
DONNERSCHLAG: 482–83
Donskoi, Dimitry: 41
DORA: 309–10, 316, 411
Dora Lane: 191–93, 197, 256, 259
Dorogobuzh: 246
Double envelopment: 132, 312, 511. *See also* Encirclement operations, German; Encirclement operations, Soviet.
Dovator, General Mayor L. M.: 88, 92–93
Dubna: 94
Dubrovka: 422
Duke of York, H.M.S.: 428
Dukovshchina: 171, 241
Dutch troops: 381
Dvina River: 21, 23, 27–30, 32, 61, 140, 170, 202
Dyatkovo: 252, 254

East Prussia: 5, 8, 55, 80, 348, 351
Economy, German wartime: 15, 299, 504–05
Economy, Soviet wartime: 135, 299, 440
Eden, Anthony: 135
Ehrenburg, Ilya: 434
EDELWEISS: 358, 366–81
El Alamein: 513
Elbrus, Mount: 371–72

Electricity: 135, 285, 440
ELEPHANT: 120, 177
Elista: 375, 482, 493, 495
Elkhotovo: 379
Encirclement operations, German: 14, 27–28, 30, 33–34, 37, 39–40, 52, 182–83, 290, 314, 316, 336, 344, 349, 354, 358, 387, 488, 511
Encirclement operations, Soviet: 71, 120–22, 125, 129, 139–40, 153–55, 170–71, 270, 275, 443, 472, 474, 478, 485, 488, 493, 496, 511–13
Engels, Major: 460
English Channel: 233, 291, 346, 423, 449, 456
Envelopment. *See* Double envelopment; Encirclement operations, German; Encirclement operations, Soviet.
Eremenko, Marshal Sovetskogo Soyuza A. I.: 18, 443
and *Bryansk Front*: 33–34, 36–37, 148, 150
and Soviet offensive, January 1942: 148–49, 169, 171
and Stalingrad: 382–85, 387, 393–94, 396, 470, 507
Erfurth, General der Infanterie Waldemar: 225–26, 426–27
Erika Lane: 191–92, 194, 196–97, 256–57, 259
Estonia: 32
Experimental Organization Center: 244–45

Falkenhorst, Generaloberst Nikolaus: 220–22, 225, 291
Fedorenko, General Leytenant Ya. N.: 336, 507
Fedorovka: 62, 66
Fegelein, Brigadefuehrer Otto Hermann: 131
Felmy, General der Flieger Helmut: 453
Feodosiya: 105, 107–17, 141, 266
Finland: 4, 8–10, 14–16, 28, 39–40, 54, 135, 220, 303, 418, 424, 426–27, 505. *See also* Winter War, 1939–1940.
Finland, Gulf of: 139, 143, 189–91, 411
Finnish Army: 4–5, 7, 10, 32, 35, 37, 40, 44, 46, 81, 134, 192–93, 195, 220–33, 291, 409, 412–13, 415, 426–27, 440, 505. *See also* Army, Finnish 11th; Corps, Finnish III; Divisions, Finnish.
FISCHREIHER: 359, 393
Folient, Cape: 321
Foreign Armies, East: 296–97, 305, 455–57
Foreign Ministry, German: 222
Fortifications: 21, 316, 321
Fortresses: 42, 105–08, 154–55, 324, 411
Forts, Soviet: 310, 316, 318, 320–21
France: 15, 177, 292, 299, 457, 511
Fretter-Pico, General der Artillerie Maximilian von: 267–68, 488
FRIDERICUS: 272–73, 275–82, 310, 312–14, 317–19, 325, 330, 344
Frolov, General Leytenant V. A.: 35, 226–27
Fromm, Generaloberst Friedrich: 84, 87
Fronts, Soviet: 8
Bryansk: 36–37, 148, 156, 217, 396, 398
and BLAU: 325–26, 332, 334, 341–42
composition of: 33–34, 49